Child Support Handbook

17th edition

Updated by Yvonne Snape and Martin Williams

Child Poverty Action Group

CPAG promotes action for the prevention and relief of poverty among children and families with children. To achieve this, CPAG aims to raise awareness of the causes, extent, nature and impact of poverty, and strategies for its eradication and prevention; bring about positive policy changes for families with children in poverty; and enable those eligible for income maintenance to have access to their full entitlement. If you are not already supporting us, please consider making a donation, or ask for details of our membership schemes, training courses and publications.

Published by Child Poverty Action Group
94 White Lion Street, London N1 9PF
Tel: 020 7837 7979
staff@cpag.org.uk
www.cpag.org.uk

A CIP record for this book is available from the British Library

ISBN: 978 1 906076 24 5

Child Povery Action Group is a charity registered in England and Wales (registration number 294841) and in Scotland (registration number SC039339), and is a company limited by guarantee, registered in England (registration number 1993854). VAT number: 690 808117

Cover design by Devious Designs
Typeset by David Lewis XML Associates Ltd
Printed in the UK by CPI William Clowes Beccles NR343 7TL
Cover photo by Joanne O'Brien/Photofusion

The authors

Yvonne Snape is an adviser for Gingerbread.

Martin Williams is a welfare rights worker at Child Poverty Action Group.

Acknowledgements

A huge debt is owed to Rachel Hadwen, author of the most recent editions of this book, as well as all the authors of previous editions: Alison Garnham, Emma Knights, Simon Cox, Jon Blackwell and Jacqui McDowell.

Thanks are also due to Alison Key for editing and managing the production of the book, Katherine Dawson for updating the index and Paula McDiarmid for proofreading the text.

Many thanks to Sarah Alcock for her support, and invaluable help in researching and writing this book.

The law described in this book was correct at 1 December 2009.

Contents

Terms used

'She' and 'he'

As the latest statistics from the Child Support Agency show 95 per cent of people with the care of a qualifying child are women, we use 'she' to describe the person with care and 'he' to describe the non-resident parent.

However, the law applies in the same way if the person with care is a man or the non-resident parent is a woman, or if both parents are men or both women.

We recognise that in a minority of cases the non-resident parent will be the mother and the parent with care the father and, in some cases, both will be of the same sex. However, for the sake of readability, we use 'she' for the person with care and 'he' for the non-resident parent.

'Second family'

We use the term 'second family' loosely to describe the situation where a parent of a qualifying child (in our examples, usually the non-resident parent) also has children who live with her/him. This could be a third or fourth family, or even a first family where, for example, a married man remains with his wife despite having a child with another woman. It may also apply where a parent is living with a same-sex partner who has responsibility for a child.

'Stepchild'

We use the term 'stepchild' to describe the child of a person's partner, whether or not they are a married couple or in a civil partnership.

Abbreviations

AA	attendance allowance
CA	carer's allowance
CAU	Central Appeals Unit
C-MEC	Child Maintenance and Enforcement Commission
CSA	Child Support Agency
CSAC	Child Support Agency Centre
CTB	council tax benefit
CTC	child tax credit
DCI	Departmental Central Index
DEO	deduction from earnings order
DLA	disability living allowance
DWP	Department for Work and Pensions
ECJ	European Court of Justice
ECHR	European Convention on Human Rights
ESA	employment and support allowance
EU	European Union
HB	housing benefit
IB	incapacity benefit
ICE	Independent Case Examiner
IMA	interim maintenance assessment
IS	income support
JSA	jobseeker's allowance
MAF	maintenance application form
MEF	maintenance enquiry form
NI	national insurance
PC	pension credit
RPC	regular payments condition
SDA	severe disablement allowance
WTC	working tax credit

Child support rates 2009/10

Note: many assessments in force during this year will have been calculated on the basis of earlier years' rates.

Dependent child's personal allowance
Under 19   £56.11*
* Pre-6 April 2004 claims with no child tax credit

Adult's personal allowance
Single   £64.30
Couple   £100.95*
* This is only used in the protected income calculation

Premiums
Family   £17.30*
Disabled child   £51.24*
Carer   £29.50
Disability (single)   £27.50
Severe disability (single)   £52.85
* Pre-6 April 2004 claims with no child tax credit

The following premiums are only used in the protected income calculation:
Disability (couple)   £39.15
Severe disability
  couple (if one qualifies)   £52.85
  couple (if both qualify)   £105.70
Pensioner/enhanced/higher pensioner
  single   £65.70
  couple   £97.50

Child benefit
Only or eldest child   £20.00
Other children   £13.20

Child support
Minimum payment of child maintenance ('old rules')   £6.50
Contribution towards child maintenance deducted from
  income support ('old rules')   £6.50

Minimum payment of child maintenance ('new rules')	£5.00
Benefit penalty	£24.20

Income tax (per year)

Personal allowance (under 65)	£6,475
Married couple's allowance (minimum)	£2,670
Blind person's allowance	£1,890

National insurance contributions

Lower earnings limit	£95.00
11% on earnings between £110 and 844	

Bands of taxable income

Basic rate – 20%	£0 – £37,400
Higher rate – 40%	over £37,400

Part 1

· ·

Introduction

Chapter 1

Introduction to child support

This chapter covers:
1. What is child support (below)
2. The Child Support Agency (p5)
3. Changes to child support from 2010 (p9)
3. Using this *Handbook* (p10)

1. What is child support

Child support is the name given to child maintenance paid by parents who do not live with their children, where the Government calculates and enforces liability for this maintenance. Child maintenance is intended to reflect the legal responsibility of parents to provide financial support for their children. Some people make voluntary arrangements to pay maintenance, others have arrangements made following a court order, and some people have maintenance (child support) calculated by the Child Support Agency (CSA). Some people may pay or receive child maintenance in more than one of these ways. This *Handbook* deals mainly with the rules of the child support scheme and the work of the CSA. It is intended to help parents who use the CSA and their advisers.

Since 1993 there has been a child support system administered by the CSA. This calculates the amount of child support people have to pay in different situations. The original complex formula for calculating child support (the 'old rules' formula) was replaced by a simpler calculation from 3 March 2003. This 'new rules' calculation mostly applies to applications made on or after this date (but see Chapter 7). An even simpler system of calculating child support, operated by a new body, the Child Maintenance and Enforcement Commission (C-MEC), is expected to be introduced in 2011 (see p9).

The main features of the existing child support scheme are:
- the CSA, which assesses and enforces child maintenance;
- the use of a standard mechanism to set the level of child maintenance;
- before 14 July 2008, special rules for parents claiming certain benefits if they did not live with the other parent of the child(ren) for whom they cared. These parents were treated as applying for child maintenance and may have faced a reduction in benefit if they did not co-operate.

Responsibility for child maintenance

It is a legal principle that both parents of a child have a duty to contribute to the maintenance of that child.[1] This liability is met when a parent who does not have the main care of a child makes payments of child maintenance assessed under the formula or calculation.[2]

This duty applies whether or not:

- the child is living with the other parent or with someone else who is not legally her/his parent (see below); *or*
- the child is living with a lone parent or with a couple; *or*
- the child's parents are on benefit.

Definitions

The following terms are used throughout this *Handbook*. For more detailed definitions, see Chapter 2.

A parent who does not live with her/his own child is a **'non-resident parent'**.

A child who does not live with both her/his parents is a **'qualifying child'**.

The person with whom the child is living and who provides her/him with day-to-day care is the **'person with care'**.

If a person with care is also a parent of the qualifying child, s/he is a **'parent with care'**.

A child living with the non-resident parent, for whom s/he or any new partner receives child benefit, is a **'relevant child'**.

'He' is used to refer to a non-resident parent, and 'she' to refer to a person or parent with care, although this will not always be the case.

Calculating maintenance: 'old rules' and 'new rules'

Whether a case comes under the 'old' or 'new' rules for calculating child support is important, not only because it dictates how much maintenance should be paid but also because there are some differences in how other aspects of child support apply – eg, enforcement. In addition, the legislative references are often different. The **'new rules'** are those that came into force on 3 March 2003 (not the proposed simplified system, planned to be introduced in 2011). The **'old rules'** are those introduced with the child support system when it started in 1993. Both sets of rules have been amended since they were introduced.

The 'old rules' use a complicated formula with several steps to work out how much maintenance should be paid (see Chapter 8). An application can be made for departure from the formula in certain circumstances (see Chapter 15). The 'new rules' use one of four rates of child support maintenance for each non-resident parent, based on his income (see Chapter 5). The calculation can be varied in certain circumstances (see Chapter 6).

Generally, if an application for child support is made on or after 3 March 2003, it is a 'new rules' case, and if the application was made before that date, it is an 'old rules' case. However, there are some exceptions to this, and some 'old rules' cases that are connected to a 'new rules' case may be converted to the new rules (see also Chapter 7). Apart from these cases, however, it is now unlikely that 'old rules' cases will convert to 'new rules', because the Government proposes that a third, and even more simple, calculation will be introduced in the future. No one will be able to apply under this new system, or be transferred to it, until 2011 at the earliest.[3] In the meantime, existing cases will continue to fall under either the 'old rules' or the 'new rules'.

The Child Maintenance and Enforcement Commission

C-MEC came into being on 24 July 2008. It took over responsibility for the child maintenance system, including the CSA, from the Department for Work and Pensions on 1 November 2008. C-MEC has a much wider remit than the CSA had and seeks to assist all separated families set up child maintenance arrangements, not just those who are clients of the CSA.

C-MEC has two delivery bodies: the CSA, which continues to administer the statutory schemes and the Child Maintenace Options service (see below). For this reason, this *Handbook* continues to use the term 'CSA' when referring to applications, calculations, decisions, and collection and enforcement procedures under the statutory schemes.

Child Maintenance Options

Child Maintenance Options was set up to offer impartial information and support to help both parents make informed choices about child maintenance arrangements. It aims to give unbiased information to any party involved in child maintenance arrangements. Child Maintenance Options is administered by C-MEC.

Child Maintenance Options can assist with:
- setting up a child support arrangement following separation;
- establishing child support arrangements for parents who are not in a relationship;
- switching from a private arrangment to a CSA calculation, or *vice versa*;
- situations in which an exisiting child support agreement has broken down or is not working how the parent would like.[4]

2. **The Child Support Agency**

The Child Support Agency (CSA) is responsible for calculating child maintenance payments and, in some cases, their collection and enforcement. This includes tracing non-resident parents and investigating parents' means. The Child Maintenance and Enforcement Commission (C-MEC) took over responsibility for the CSA on 1 November 2008. However, the CSA remains the delivery body continuing to administer the current statutory child maintenance schemes. This means that individuals continue to apply to the CSA if they cannot reach an agreement for maintenance themselves and wish to use the statutory collection scheme. Current users of the CSA will continue to deal with, and receive letters from, the CSA, not C-MEC.

The CSA works closely with Jobcentre Plus, which is responsible for identifying cases where a parent with care claims income support (IS) or income-based jobseeker's allowance (JSA). Jobcentre Plus staff will pass the parent with care's details to C-MEC's Child Maintenance Options service (see p40), which will contact her to discuss the different options for pursuing child maintenance.

The CSA has wide powers to gather information. These are covered in Chapter 4. If a parent is unhappy with a child support decision, there are procedures for challenging these (see Chapter 17), and for appealing most sorts of decisions (see Chapter 18).

Structure of the Child Support Agency

The CSA is divided into six regional business units. Apart from the one for the east of England, they are all based in the areas they serve (see Appendix 1). Each business unit has a Child Support Agency Centre (CSAC), which assesses child maintenance.

The CSA also has local offices around the country, called local service bases or field offices (some of these are based in Jobcentre Plus premises). These may be used to conduct face-to-face interviews with parents.

In February 2006, the Government announced a twin-track approach to reform of child maintenance. The first was an Operational Improvement Plan, which ran from 2006 to 2009 and attempted to stabilise the work of the CSA. This saw the CSA move towards the following structure:[5]

- new client teams supporting new applications;
- client service teams managing ongoing cases and processing changes of cirumstances;
- debt management teams taking action when a payment is missed;
- legal enforcement teams ensuring that payment is enforced.

There should also be specialist client teams for different areas of work, usually determined by the employment status of the non-resident parent (eg, teams dealing with benefit claimants, employed clients and self-employed clients).

The second task was to undertake a longer term re-design of the child maintenance system, which will see the introduction of a new, simplified, calculation in 2011.

Communicating with the Child Support Agency

The first port of call when contacting the CSA will usually be the CSAC which applies to the parent's area. You can write to or telephone the CSAC. It is advisable to keep copies of letters and make a note of the date, time and content of telephone calls. Telephone numbers and addresses are in Appendix 1.

Dates of postage

If you fall under the 'new rules' and the CSA posts a document to you, it will usually be treated as sent on the day of posting.[6] If you send a document to the CSA, it is treated as being sent on the day the CSA receives it.

If you fall under the 'old rules', documents are treated as being sent to you by the CSA on the second day after the day of posting (unless this day is a Sunday or bank holiday).[7] If more than one document is required to be sent and they are posted on different days, or they need to be sent to different people and this is done on different days, they are treated as having been posted on the latest of the dates concerned (and so sent on the second day after this).[8] If you send a document to the CSA, it is treated as being sent on the day the CSA receives it, but in some cases the CSA can treat documents as having been sent earlier if there was unavoidable delay.[9]

It is important to bear these rules in mind, especially where time limits are concerned.

Representatives

Anyone dealing with the CSA can appoint a representative to act on her/his behalf.[10] If the person is not legally qualified, authorisation for her/him to act needs to be confirmed in writing, although if the client is with the representative during a telephone call s/he can authorise the representative verbally for the duration of the call. An authorised or legally qualified representative can complete forms, receive documents and supply information. A person with care may also choose to have payments of child support made to a representative.

A representative who understands the law and/or is experienced in dealing with the CSA may find it easier to get a quick response and clearer information from the CSA. S/he can also help you to understand your rights and what options are open to you. For information about how to find independent advice, see Appendix 4.

Representatives with legal authority to act for a CSA client (eg, someone with power of attorney, a reciever, or a mental health appointee/Scottish mental health custodian) are able to act for the client in every respect, as if they were the client.[11]

The legal help scheme (advice and assistance scheme in Scotland) can cover child support cases. A client does not have to pay back any money out of sums recovered if the money is for maintenance.

What to expect when you contact the Child Support Agency

If you contact the CSA by telephone, you should be able to get through. The CSA's Business Plan states that it aims to answer telephone calls within one minute.[12] If you write to the CSA, it aims to reply to your letter, resolving the issue or agreeing what will happen next, within three weeks.[13] If you have difficulty in contacting the CSA or obtaining a response within a reasonable time, you should complain. For more information about standards of service and how to complain, see Chapter 20.

Face-to-face interviews

A CSA client can request a face-to-face interview with a CSA member of staff, or the CSA may decide that a face-to-face interview is needed to obtain information or resolve a parent's query. CSA guidance states that an interview should only be used where 'there is a clear business need or it is beneficial to the client'.[14] For example, you might request a face-to-face interview because of difficulties with written or telephone communication, or because English is not your first language.

In some cases, the CSA is required to hold a face-to-face interview – eg, where the results of a DNA test need to be communicated and it is important to check that the correct person has been tested.

If you are requesting a face-to-face interview, be aware that the guidance states the service should only be used if it is necessary, or the most effective way to make contact, or if all other ways of progressing the case have been tried.[15] However, if you feel that your request for a face-to-face interview has not been adequately considered, or you are not happy with the service, you should think about making a complaint (see Chapter 20).

If you are going to be interviewed, the CSA will contact you to arrange this. If you have any language or access needs, the face-to-face service should accommodate these. You may be interviewed at a Jobcentre Plus office or other approved venue, your place of work or, in certain circumstances, your home. A home visit will only be arranged where there is a clear business need (eg, you are housebound or the interview would otherwise involve unreasonable travelling time) and there is no threat to the safety of the face-to face officer. The interview will be recorded on the CSA database.[16]

Arrangements in Northern Ireland

The child support system is the same throughout the UK, but there is a separate Child Maintenance and Enforcement Division for Northern Ireland, which is part of the Department for Social Development (DSDNI). Its powers are the same as the CSA in England, Scotland and Wales. Before 1 April 2008 child support was dealt with by the Northern Ireland Child Support Agency. For the time being, cases will be dealt with in the same way as before this date. The changes that will take place in England, Scotland and Wales from 2010 (see p9) will also apply in Northern Ireland. See www.dsdni.gov.uk for updates.

The address of the Northern Ireland CSA is the same as the Eastern Business Unit that assesses cases for the eastern area of England. They are based at the same location, but they operate separately. Also part of DSDNI is the Social Security Agency, the Northern Ireland equivalent of Jobcentre Plus.

Where this *Handbook* is being used in Northern Ireland, references to the DWP should be read as references to DSDNI and references to Jobcentre Plus should be read as references to the Social Security Agency (see also p10). **Note:** some legislative references are different in Northern Ireland.

3. **Changes to child support from 2010**

After several years of problems with the child support system, particularly delays in assessments and difficulties in enforcing payment, the Government is bringing about the following changes to the child support system.

Timetable for change

From 2010:
The amount of the maintenance disregard for income support, income-based jobseeker's allowance and income-related employment and support allowance will be increased from April 2010, so that the whole amount of maintenance will be ignored for claimants of these benefits.

From 2011:
It is planned that a new scheme of calculating child maintenace will be introduced in 2011. All new claimants will have their claims calculated under these new rules. Existing Child Support Agency (CSA) claimants will be phased into this new scheme by 2014.[17]

The new calculation will be based on information from HM Revenue and Customs on the non-resident parent's gross income for the latest available tax year. The amount will be fixed for one year unless his income varies by 25 per cent.

As the new claculation will be based on gross income rather than net income, as currently used, the percentage amount that the non-resident parent will be expected to pay will change.

For a non-resident parent whose weekly income is less than £800, the rates will be:
- 12 per cent for one child;
- 19 per cent for two or more children.

If the non-resident parent's income is over £800 a week, the following rates will apply to the excess over £800:
- 9 per cent for one child;
- 12 per cent for two children;

- 15 per cent for three or more children.

2011-2014

Existing users of the CSA (both old and new rules) will be encouraged to choose between moving onto the new system or leaving the system altogther to set up a private arrangement.

This transfer process is proposed to start in 2011 and be completed by 2014. However, at the time of writing, there has been no information on how this transfer will take place in practice.[18]

4. **Using this** *Handbook*

This *Handbook* covers the child support scheme in England, Wales and Scotland as at 1 December 2009. Northern Ireland has a similar scheme, although some of its legislative references and guidance are different. Separate chapters detail how maintenance is worked out under the 'old' and 'new' rules. There are some references to earlier changes, but for full details of the scheme in previous years you should consult earlier editions. The other chapters cover general rules, such as how the Child Support Agency (CSA) obtains information or enforces payment, and how to challenge its decisions.

Structure of the book

Part 1 is an introduction to child support, the CSA and how to use this *Handbook*. **Part 2** explains the key principles and terms of the child support scheme, how applications are made (including for parents treated as applying) and how the CSA seeks information. Once all the information is available, the amount of maintenance can be worked out – **Part 3** does this under the 'new rules' and **Part 4** under the 'old rules'. The transitional rules on the conversion of existing cases to the new scheme are also covered in Part 3 (Chapter 8). **Part 5** covers CSA decisions, how to change, query or challenge them (by review and appeal), collection and enforcement of maintenance, and how to complain.

The **appendices** contain useful addresses, information about reference materials and an explanation of income support premiums. For child support rates, see pxii.

The best way to find the information you need is to use the index at the back of the book.

Footnotes

At the end of each chapter are the footnotes. These contain the legal authorities and other sources of information which support the text, and some further information. Parents and advisers can quote the reference to the CSA if the statement in the text is disputed. Appendix 6 explains the abbreviations used in the footnotes, with information on how to get hold of the sources.

Some footnotes refer to the online guidance material provided to CSA staff. These are only guidance and are *not* law. Different guidance applies to 'old rules' and 'new rules' cases. This *Handbook* also includes references to relevant caselaw.

Notes

1. **What is child support**
   1 s1(1) CSA 1991
   2 s1(2) and (3) CSA 1991
   3 Sch 5 CMOPA 2008, originally planned for 2010. Also see C-MEC Business Plan 2009/10
   4 *Child Maintenance: getting started*, Child Maintenance Options, May 2009

2. **The Child Support Agency**
   5 CSA Operational Improvement Plan 2006-2009
   6 Reg 2 CS(MCP) Regs
   7 Reg 1(6) CS(MAP) Regs
   8 Reg 1(8) CS(MAP) Regs
   9 Reg 1(7) CS(MAP) Regs
  10 Reg 22 CS(MCP) Regs; reg 53 CS(MAP) Regs; DMG paras 2023-24; PG, Client Communications
  11 CSA Business Plan 2008/09
  12 CSA Business Plan 2008/09
  13 CSA Business Plan 2008/09
  14 PG, Client Communications
  15 PG, Client Communications
  16 C-MEC Business Plan 2009/10

3. **Changes to child support from 2010**
  17 C-MEC Business Plan 2009/10
  18 CMOPA 2008 and C-MEC Business Plan 2009/10

Part 2

Using the Child Support Agency

Chapter 2

. . . .

Who is covered by the scheme

This chapter covers:
1. The duty to maintain (below)
2. Parent (below)
3. Qualifying child (p18)
4. Person with care (p20)
5. Non-resident parent (p21)
6. Relevant child (p23)
7. Welfare of the child (p24)
8. Family (p25)
9. Habitually resident in the UK (p26)
10. The role of the courts (p27)

1. The duty to maintain

Both parents of a 'qualifying child' (see p18) are responsible for maintaining her/him.[1]

The Child Support Agency (CSA) can only require a 'non-resident parent' (see p21) to pay child maintenance for a qualifying child. A 'parent with care' (see p20) cannot be required to pay child maintenance for the child for whom s/he is caring, unless s/he is treated as a non-resident parent because s/he provides care for less time than someone else or, in some cases, for the same amount of time (see Chapter 15).

The CSA can only make a calculation (or assessment in 'old rules' cases) if the person with care, non-resident parent and qualifying child meet the rules on habitual residence (see p26).

2. Parent

. . . .

The Human Fertilisation and Embryology Act

The Human Fertilisation and Embryology Act 2008, which came into force on 1 October 2009, amends the definition of 'parent' in the following ways.

In the case of assisted reproduction, in order for a man who has not provided the sperm to be treated as the father, at the time of implantation, the couple must each have consented to him being treated as the father and this consent is still in place.[2]

Female civil partners will be treated in the same way as married couples – ie, if one partner gives birth to a child conceived as a result of donor insemination (anywhere in the world), she is the mother of the child and her civil partner will automatically be the other parent, unless she did not consent to the mother's treatment.[3] If a couple are not civil partners and one has a child as a result of donor insemination in a UK-licensed clinic and at the time of the insemination or implantation resulting in conception there is in place a notice of consent to the other woman being treated as a parent, she will be a legal parent.[4]

There are new provisions extending the categories of couples who can apply for a parental order where a child has been conceived using the sperm or egg of at least one of the couple, but has been carried by a surrogate mother. The Act's provisions allow civil partners, unmarried opposite-sex couples and same-sex couples not in a civil partnership, but who are in an enduring family relationship, also to be able to apply.[5]

A '**parent**' is a person who is legally the mother or father of the child.[6] This includes:
- a biological parent (see below for human-assisted reproduction);
- a parent by adoption;[7]
- a parent under a parental order (used in surrogacy cases).[8]

If a child was conceived by artificial insemination or *in vitro* fertilisation:
- the mother is the woman who gave birth to the child (wherever in the world the insemination or fertilisation took place),[9] unless an adoption order or parental order is made;[10]
- the father is the man who provided the sperm (but there are exceptions depending on when the insemination or *in vitro* fertilisation took place);
- if the insemination was before 1 August 1991 *and* the child was born in England or Wales after 3 April 1988, the father is the man who provided the sperm, unless the mother is married, in which case the father is the husband, unless he did not consent to the insemination;[11]
- if the insemination or fertilisation was after 31 July 1991, the father is:[12]
  - the mother's husband, unless he did not consent to[13] or died before insemination;[14] *or*
  - if that was during licensed treatment services provided for the mother and a man, that man.[15] The man and woman must have received treatment services together.[16] This rule does not apply to a woman inseminated/ fertilised outside the UK.[17]

This means that if an unmarried woman self-inseminated without the involvement of licensed treatment services, the donor is the father.

If a person denies being the parent of a child, the Child Support Agency (CSA) must *assume* that the person is a parent of the child, unless the child has subsequently been adopted by someone else (see p18), if:[18]

- in England, Wales or Northern Ireland, a declaration of parentage or, in Scotland, a declarator of parentage, is in force about that person. This includes situations where the person with care or the CSA has applied to court for a declaration as to whether the person is a parent of the child;[19]
- in Scotland,[20] England and Wales,[21] the person is a man who:
  - was married to the mother at any time between the child's conception and birth; *or*
  - acknowledged his paternity *and* was acknowledged by the mother *and* was named as the father on the birth certificate issued in the UK;
- the person is a man who was found to be the father by a court in England or Wales in proceedings under certain legal provisions (see Appendix 3). The court decision usually states the legal provision under which it was made;[22]
- the person is a man who was found by a court in Northern Ireland to be a father in proceedings under similar legal provisions to those in Appendix 3;[23]
- the person is a man who was found by a court in Scotland to be the father in any action for affiliation or aliment;[24]
- the person is a man who refuses to take a DNA test, or where the results of the test show that he is the father (even if he refuses to accept it);[25]
- a parental order has been made in favour of that person following an application made within six months of a birth which is the result of a surrogacy arrangement;[26]
- certain types of fertility treatment have been carried out by a licensed clinic and the person is treated as a parent of the child under the Human Fertilisation and Embryology Act 1990.[27]

These rules apply even if paternity was not disputed in the proceedings.[28]

If none of the above applies, the CSA cannot make a calculation until parentage is admitted by a person or decided by a court.

Since the Civil Partnership Act 2004 came into force on 5 December 2005, for most child support purposes, civil partners (including those who have adopted a child) are treated in the same way as married partners.[29] Couples living with a same-sex partner but not in a civil partnership are treated in the same way as couples of the opposite sex who are not married. Before the Human Fertilisation and Embryology Act 2008 came into force, the rules about parentage and artificial insemination/*in vitro* fertilisation only applied to couples of the opposite sex.[30]

An **adoption order** means the child is, in law, the child of the adopter(s).[31] The liability of a biological parent to maintain her/his child ends on adoption and the parent(s) by adoption become the only people liable to maintain the child.

A person who has legal parental responsibility[32] is not necessarily a parent for child support purposes.[33] For example, a step-parent who has acquired parental responsibility (except one assumed to be a parent under the rules on p17) cannot be required to pay child support maintenance, but the courts could order maintenance (see p30).

A foster parent is not a parent for child support purposes because the child has been placed with her/him by a local authority (see p20).

Parentage disputes

If the parent with care does not name the other parent, or if the alleged non-resident parent denies parentage, the CSA investigates to identify the other parent and, if possible, show that he can be assumed to be a parent under the above rules (see pp58 and 62). If the alleged non-resident parent disputes that those rules apply (eg, he says the person named in a court order is someone else), he can appeal against the CSA decision. This appeal is dealt with by a magistrates'/sheriff's court rather than by the First-tier Tribunal (see also p62).[34]

However, if the alleged non-resident parent accepts that those rules apply, but disputes the correctness of the court order referred to by the CSA (ie, the court was wrong to name him as the father), he cannot dispute parentage through the CSA appeals system. Instead, he should consider applying to the court to set aside its order and/or making a late appeal against it.

If no one is assumed to be the other parent under those rules, the CSA usually tries to arrange voluntary DNA testing or applies to court for a declaration of paternity (see p66).

3. **Qualifying child**

Child support maintenance is only payable for a 'qualifying child'. A child is only a **'qualifying child'** if one or both of her/his parents are non-resident parents (see p21).[35] In addition, a child only counts as a qualifying child when working out maintenance if the parent with care has applied to the Child Support Agency (CSA) for maintenance for her/him.[36]

A **'child'** is defined as a person in respect of whom child benefit is payable.[37] In some circumstances, a young person is also a qualifying child for child maintenance purposes until s/he reaches 19 years of age.[38]

Therefore, a qualifying child is someone who is:

- under 16; *or*
- 16-19 years old and receiving full time, non-advanced education; *or*
- 16-18 years old, recently left education and who is registered for work or work based learning for young people.

Even if a person falls into one of these groups, s/he is *not* a child if s/he is, or has been, married or in a civil partnership. This applies even if the marriage or civil partnership has been annulled or was never valid – eg, s/he was under 16.[39]

Full-time, non-advanced education

A course is **non-advanced** if it is up to A-level or higher level Scottish Certificate of Education (this includes a Scottish certificate of sixth year studies and a national diploma or certificate from BTEC or ScotVEC). Courses of degree level and above (including DipHE, Higher National Diploma, or a Higher Diploma or certificate from BTEC or ScotVEC) count as advanced education.[40]

The child must attend a recognised educational establishment (such as a school or college) *or* the education must be recognised by the CSA.[41]

The CSA must treat a child as receiving **full-time** education if the child attends a course where the weekly contact time is more than 12 hours.[42] Contact time includes teaching, supervised study, exams and practical or project work which are parts of the course. It does not include meal times or unsupervised study, whether on or off school premises.

If a child is not attending such a course (eg, where contact is for less than 12 hours) the CSA must look at all the facts and decide if the education is full time.

After leaving school or college, a child still counts as being in full-time education until child benefit stops being paid. This is known as the 'terminal date'.[43] A school leaver still counts as a child for child support up to the Sunday following the child benefit stopping unless s/he is 19 before that date, in which case it is the Sunday following the Monday before the 19th birthday.[44]

If a child is under school-leaving age when s/he leaves school, s/he is treated as leaving school on the date s/he reaches that age. The upper limit of compulsory school age is, in England and Wales, the last Friday in June for a young person who will be 16 before the first day of the following September term. In Scotland, it is compulsory to be in education until 31 March if a young person's 16th birthday falls between 1 March and 30th September, or the first day of the Christmas holidays if the 16th birthday falls between 1 October and the following 28 February. If a child is entered for an external examination before s/he leaves school, the terminal date is the first one that follows the last exam.[45]

If a young person does any paid work of 24 hours or more a week before the terminal date, s/he no longer counts as a child unless the work is temporary and expected to end before the terminal date.[46]

Breaks in full-time education

Someone at school or college still counts as a child if there is a temporary break in full-time education.[47] It does not matter whether s/he is under or over 16 when education is interrupted.

Any break must be reasonable in the particular circumstances of the case. The break can be up to six months or, if it is due to physical or mental illness or disability of the child, longer. The break must not be (or likely to be) followed immediately by a period on work-based training for young people (Skillseekers in Scotland), or by education received because of the child's job.[48]

16/17-year-olds not in full-time education

A 16/17-year-old who is no longer at school or college full time still counts as a child for child support purposes if s/he is registered for work or work-based learning for young people, but has not actually started either.[49] This lasts for the child benefit 'extension period'.[50] S/he still counts as a child if s/he does paid work so long as it is *either* for less than 24 hours a week *or* is temporary and expected to end before the end of the extension period.[51]

A 16/17-year-old entitled to income support, income-based jobseeker's allowance or income-related employment and support allowance[52] in her/his own right does not count as a child in this situation.[53]

4. **Person with care**

A '**person with care**' is the person with whom the child has her/his home (see p21) and who usually provides day-to-day care (see below) for the child.[54] There may be more than one person with care of a particular child.[55]

A person with care is usually a parent of the child or another individual but could also be, for example, an organisation such as a children's home. However, a person with care *cannot* be a local authority, or someone looking after a child who has been placed with her by the local authority.[56] The only exception to this rule is if someone in England and Wales is the child's parent and the local authority has allowed a child it looks after to live with her/him.[57]

Day-to-day care

The Child Support Agency (CSA) normally looks at how many nights of care a person provides when deciding who is a person with care.[58] To count as providing day-to-day care, a parent must provide care of at least 104 nights per year on average.[59] The amount of care can be averaged over a different period if this will be more representative of actual arrangements. The CSA adds together the time a child spends with each parent and decides who is the principal provider of care. In some cases where care is shared equally, other factors may be taken into account to determine which parent is treated as a non-resident parent – eg, the parent who does not receive child benefit.[60]

A person who is responsible for a child's daily routine may be providing day-to-day care even if some things are done by another person – eg, a childminder. It may not be necessary for a person to be *with* the child for at least 104 nights a year if she is nevertheless the person responsible for overall care during that time.

Example

A mother on night shifts leaves her son in the care of grandparents for 22 nights a month. She decides what he will eat and when he will go to bed, and each morning she dresses him and takes him to school. Using the 104 nights average, she does not provide day-to-day care, but, using the ordinary meaning of those words, she is the principal provider of day-to-day care.

In two situations, the care actually being provided does not matter. Where a child is placed with her/his parent by a local authority in England and Wales, then even though the local authority is legally responsible, the parent is treated as providing day-to-day care.[61] Where a child is a boarding-school boarder or a hospital inpatient, the person who would otherwise provide day-to-day care is treated as providing day-to-day care.[62]

Where the CSA cannot identify one person with whom the child spends the most time, it may decide that the person receiving child benefit is the person with care.[63] The result can be that someone who would otherwise be a parent with care is treated as the non-resident parent (see below). On the other hand, in some cases, there may be no one providing day-to-day care and so no one who can be treated as a person with care.

Home

The person with care must have a home with the child. A home is the physical place where the child lives. It is different from a household (see p22). Where a child has her/his home is usually clear. A child may have more than one home, in which case the CSA decides which is the principal home.[64]

Parent with care

A 'parent with care' is a person with care who is also a parent (see p15) of a qualifying child (see p18).[65]

However, where there is a shared care situation, someone who might otherwise be a parent with care may be treated as a non-resident parent (see p100 in 'new rules' cases and p273 in 'old rules' cases).

5. **Non-resident parent**

A **'non-resident parent'** ('absent parent' is the terminology used in 'old rules' cases, but we use 'non-resident parent' throughout this *Handbook* for simplicity) is a parent (see p15) who is not living in the same household (see below) as his child, and the child has her/his home with a person with care[66] (see p20) – eg, where the parents of a child have separated. In cases where people share the care of a child, a person who would otherwise be a parent with care may be treated as a non-resident parent (see p100 in 'new rules' cases and p273 in 'old rules' cases).[67] If a parent thinks that a decision identifying him as a non-resident parent is wrong, he should seek advice. If the non-resident parent begins living in the same household as the parent with care, the calculation immediately ceases to have effect.

Both parents can be non-resident parents, in which case they can both be required to pay child maintenance (see p284).[68]

Household

'Household' is not defined in child support legislation. A household is something abstract, not something physical like a home (see p21). It is either a single person or a group of people held together by social ties.[69] In many cases, whether people are members of the same household is obvious. Where it is not obvious whether several people share a household, the Child Support Agency (CSA) will consider factors such as whether they have any alternative address, whether they share living areas, who pays bills and how household chores are divided.[70] No one factor on its own should be conclusive. There does not need to be any settled intention about future arrangements for a household to exist.[71]

The meaning of household has been considered in family law and social security cases as well as child support cases, and this caselaw may be used to help make child support decisions. For some of the social security caselaw, see CPAG's *Welfare Benefits and Tax Credits Handbook*.

Some guidelines from the caselaw are as follows.

- There can be two or more separate households in one house.[72] CSA staff are advised that 'household' and 'home' are different concepts and that a single home may contain a number of households.[73]
- One or more members of a household can be temporarily absent from the home without ending their membership of the household.[74]
- There does not need to be a relationship like marriage for people to share a household – eg, two sisters can form a household.[75]

Where there is a polygamous marriage there may be several partners in one household or several households.[76] The CSA will decide whether the qualifying child lives in a different household from at least one of the parents when establishing whether there is a non-resident parent.

A couple may become members of the same household even if they get back together briefly, assuming that they are hoping the relationship and, therefore, the domestic set-up will be indefinite.[77] In this case, a new household could be formed immediately, whether or not it then ceases to exist a few weeks or months later. A household can be formed as soon as people live together intending to form a household, and before they have arranged joint domestic and financial matters.

Advisers should be careful when arguing that a supposed non-resident parent shares a household with a parent with care on benefit. A decision by the CSA or First-tier Tribunal that the couple share a household for child support purposes is likely to mean that the couple share a household for benefit or tax credit purposes. For more information about cohabitation decisions in benefits and tax credits, see CPAG's *Welfare Benefits and Tax Credits Handbook*.

6. **Relevant child**

A '**relevant child**' is the term used by the Child Support Agency (CSA) in 'new rules' cases for a child other than the qualifying child for whom the non-resident parent or his partner receives child benefit.[78] This can include a child who does not live with the parent all the time – eg, because s/he is at boarding school or there is a shared care arrangement for her/him.

If this relevant child is cared for by a local authority either for part or all of the time, s/he will continue to count as a relevant child if the non-resident parent or his partner receives child benefit for her/him.[79]

The number of relevant child(ren) is important because it affects the calculation of child maintenance. In 'old rules' cases, the term is not used, but children who live with the non-resident parent may affect the maintenance assessment in different ways.

Relevant non-resident child

'**Relevant non-resident child**' is a term used by the CSA in 'new rules' cases to refer to a child of the non-resident parent for whom an application for child support cannot be made because the non-resident parent is liable to pay maintenance under a court order for her/him.[80] This is a child who would have been considered a qualifying child if an application for child support maintenance could be made for her/him. It could be a child who does not live with the non-resident parent, or a child whose care is shared between the non-resident parent and someone else in a situation where the child would be regarded as a qualifying child but for the court order. See p27 for more information about when a court order prevents an application for child support.

The number of relevant non-resident child(ren) also affects the calculation of child maintenance in 'new rules' cases. Although the term 'relevant non-resident child' is not used in 'old rules' cases, child maintenance paid under a court order may affect the calculation.

7. **Welfare of the child**

Whenever the Child Support Agency (CSA) makes a discretionary decision about a case, it must take into account the welfare of any child likely to be affected by the decision.[81] This also applies to discretionary decisions made by the First-tier Tribunal and Upper Tribunal.

Many child support decisions involve choosing between alternatives, such as whether a person is habitually resident or not, but these are not usually discretionary decisions. A person has discretion only if, once s/he has decided on the facts of a case and what the law requires, s/he still has a choice about what decision to make. An example of a discretionary decision in child support is how to collect or enforce maintenance, including whether to make a deduction from earnings order.

Only the welfare of a child has to be taken into account (see definition of a child on p18), not that of any adults involved. However, it is not just qualifying children or those named in the maintenance application who must be considered. The situation of any child likely to be affected by the decision must be looked at [82] – eg, a child of the non-resident parent's new family, known under the 'new rules' as a 'relevant child', or another child of the non-resident parent who does not live with him.

The welfare of children is 'a general principle' in child support law.[83] Considerable weight should be given to this.[84] However, because there is usually no discretion about whether to make a calculation (or 'old rules' assessment), or about the amount of maintenance due, there are only a limited number of cases in which the welfare of a child can make a difference. It is important to give the CSA full details at the earliest stage about the effect a discretionary decision may have on a child's welfare.

'**Welfare**' includes the child's physical, mental and social welfare. For example, if a deduction from earnings order (see p416) would prevent a non-resident parent from visiting a child, that child's emotional welfare may be affected. However, an order may mean the parent with care has more money coming in, which may improve the child's physical and social welfare.

Generally, the welfare of a child has to be balanced with the benefits of receiving maintenance for that child or other children. This is why it is usually only in certain situations that the welfare of a child will be deemed more important than the principle that parents should maintain their children. For example, if the non-resident parent has a child in his household who is disabled and who would be adversely affected if there were less money to spend on her/his living costs, or by the implications of enforcement action, this might mean that the welfare of the child meant certain enforcement action should not be taken. Guidance to decision makers states that in any discretionary decision, the child's best interests should always be considered.[85] However, decision makers are also reminded that, when deciding on enforcement action, the welfare of the child principle should not be applied so as to avoid full use of the CSA's powers of enforcement, unless it is genuinely appropriate,[86] and that generally, the principle should be considered along with the other principles of child support.[87]

Reasoning on the welfare of all children who could be affected has to be fully documented, and it may be useful to ask to see the welfare of the child considerations. If a decision has been made in ignorance of its effect on a child, the information should be supplied and the CSA be asked to reconsider. It may be possible for a decision which should involve the welfare of the child principle to be revised or superseded (see Chapter 17), or appealed (see Chapter 18). If the decision cannot be appealed – eg, if it is about enforcement, a CSA client should consider making a complaint or applying for a judicial review (see p352).

In addition to the general principle of the welfare of children expressed in child support law, the UK is also bound to comply with international obligations, including a commitment to the welfare of children under the United Nations Convention on the Rights of the Child. This means that in instances where more than one interpretation of the law is possible, the one chosen should be that which more closely complies with protecting the welfare of children.[88]

8. **Family**

'**Family**' is defined as a couple or a single person and any children in the same household for whom the single person or at least one member of the couple is responsible.[89]

A couple is:[90]

- a man and a woman who are married to each other and living in the same household;
- a man and woman who are living together as husband and wife but are not married to each other;
- a couple registered as civil partners who live in the same household;
- a same-sex couple living together as if they were civil partners.

The definition of family includes those living in polygamous marriages. For a discussion of when a couple are living together as husband and wife, or as civil partners, see CPAG's *Welfare Benefits and Tax Credits Handbook*. The children living with a couple or lone parent do not have to be biological or adopted children to count as family members, but foster children are not included. A person under 16 cannot be a member of a couple.[91]

Partners

A partner in the context of this *Handbook* means a married partner living with her/his spouse, a man or woman living with her/his civil partner, or someone living with a partner 'as husband and wife' or 'as if they were civil partners' (see above). Since December 2005, same-sex couples have been able to register as civil partners, and various aspects of the law have been changed to reflect this.[92] Child support legislation was amended with effect from 5 December 2005 to take account of these provisions.[93] From that date, civil partners who are parents (including those who have adopted a child) are treated, for most child support purposes, in the same way as married partners. Parents who are living with a same-sex partner but have not formed a civil partnership are treated in the same way as couples of the opposite sex who are living together but have not married. Before 5 December 2005, same-sex couples were *not* treated as partners. However, it has been decided that this treatment, which under the 'old rules' could have resulted in a non-resident parent in a same-sex partnership paying higher child support contributions than someone in an opposite sex partnership, did not constitute unlawful discrimination.[94]

9. Habitually resident in the UK

The Child Support Agency (CSA) cannot make a maintenance calculation unless the person with care, non-resident parent and qualifying child are all habitually resident in the UK.[95] The requirement for the person with care to be habitually resident does not apply if that 'person' is an organisation.[96]

The UK means England, Scotland, Wales and Northern Ireland (including coastal islands like the Isle of Wight). It does not include the Isle of Man or the Channel Islands.[97]

Habitual residence is covered fully in CPAG's *Welfare Benefits and Tax Credits Handbook*.

If a person is not habitually resident in the UK, see p31.

Meaning of habitual residence

A person is habitually resident if s/he is ordinarily resident and has been for an appreciable period of time.[98] For child support purposes, habitual residence is to be considered bearing in mind that the purpose of child support is the social need to require non-resident parents to contribute to the maintenance of their children.[99] Ordinary residence means 'residence for a settled purpose'.[100]

While each case is different and a decision has to take into account all of the person's circumstances and intentions, some of the most important factors to consider when deciding on habitual residence are:
- the person's normal centre of interest or connections to a particular place;
- the length, continuity and purpose of residence in the UK;
- the length and purpose of any absence from the UK; *and*
- the nature of the person's work.

If the non-resident parent is employed by the civil service, the armed forces, a UK-based company, a local authority or the NHS (including trusts) he will be deemed habitually resident.[101]

Although the cases do not directly concern the jurisdiction of the CSA, caselaw gives the following guidelines.

- A person can habitually reside in more than one country or in none.
- Habitual residence can continue during an absence from the UK.[102]
- A person cannot be habitually resident in the UK if s/he has never been here.
- A person who leaves the UK intending never to return to reside will stop being habitually resident in the UK on the day s/he leaves.[103]
- A person held in a country against her/his will may not be habitually resident there, even after long residence (but see below).[104]
- A person unlawfully in the UK may be habitually resident.[105]

A person returning to the UK after an absence may have remained habitually resident in the UK during her/his absence.[106] When deciding whether a person has ceased to be habitually resident in the UK for child support purposes, the emphasis should be on the nature and degree of past and continuing connections with the UK and intentions for the future.[107]

Children

For a child, habitual residence depends on where the parent or person with parental responsibility lives. If there are two such people who live apart, one parent should get the consent of the other parent to a change in the residence of the child, otherwise the child may be considered to have been abducted. If there is only one person with parental responsibility, the child's residence changes with that person's.[108]

If a child has been abducted, s/he is considered still to be resident with the person with whom s/he was lawfully living, unless that person later agrees to the move.[109] Agreement might be assumed if that person does not act.[110] However, if a child is of sufficient maturity, her/his views may prevail in a child abduction case.[111]

10. **The role of the courts**

You should seek legal advice about any court proceedings. The following is not intended to be a comprehensive guide to the law.

The courts cannot make or vary an order for periodic payments of child maintenance where the Child Support Agency (CSA) has jurisdiction to make a calculation.[112] The CSA has jurisdiction if the child is a qualifying child and all the relevant parties (child and parents) are habitually resident in the UK. This applies even if the CSA *would not* in fact make a maintenance calculation.[113]

However, courts have the power to make certain orders in relation to maintenance – eg, consent orders, orders in relation to special expenses or maintenance orders where the young person is no longer considered a child by the CSA. Courts can also vary orders, unless a maintenance calculation has been made or an application to the CSA is possible.[114]

The situation regarding 'consent orders' is complex. A **'consent order'** is an order made by the court with the written consent of both parties. It is legally binding and can be enforced like any other court order and cannot be changed by one party without the court's permission. Orders made before 3 March 2003 prevent an application to the CSA. Orders made on or after this date prevent an application for up to one year unless the parent with care applied for income support (IS) or income-based jobseeker's allowance (JSA) before July 2008. In these cases, the consent order would have been replaced by a CSA calculation.

Parents who want a consent order can agree with each other what should go in it, but should seek assistance from a family law solicitor to turn that agreement into a draft order to be submitted to the court. This is because a consent order needs to be made as part of a formal application to the court and must refer to the family law provisions under which it is made. The wording of the order is important – eg, a consent order containing an order to provide maintenance for the parent with care and undertakings to provide maintenance for the children may not prevent a calculation by the CSA.[115] However, in some circumstances it will be right to interpret both undertakings and orders as a whole without any distinction.[116]

From 3 March 2003 an application to the CSA, whether made by an adult or by a qualifying child in Scotland (see p36) cannot be accepted (ie, the CSA will refuse to make a calculation) if there is in force:[117]

- a written maintenance agreement made before 5 April 1993 (see p37);
- an order made before 3 March 2003; *or*
- an order made after 3 March 2003 that has been in force for less than a year.

The child support scheme does not change the court's powers in relation to other aspects of relationship breakdown – eg, contact and residence orders, maintenance for a spouse or civil partner, property division and related parentage disputes (for which see p18).

A CSA decision refusing to make a calculation can be appealed to the First-tier Tribunal (see Chapter 18). A court ruling that the court has no jurisdiction can be appealed or judicially reviewed (see p353).[118] No case should be outside the jurisdiction of both the CSA and the courts.

If a court order is cancelled because it was made by mistake when a CSA calculation was in force, any payments made under the order are treated as payments of child support maintenance.[119]

If a court order ceases to have effect because of a maintenance calculation (see p331), but the CSA revises the decision and decides no maintenance is payable as the previous decision was made in error, the court order revives and any child support maintenance already paid counts as paid under that order.[120]

The courts also deal with appeals about parentage (see p18).

If the Child Support Agency has jurisdiction

Until a calculation is made

Even where an application could be made to the CSA (but has not been), an agreement for periodical payments for a child (in Scotland, aliment) can be entered into.[121] However, any clause included which claims to prevent anyone from applying to the CSA is void.[122] Anyone who considers s/he would get a better deal from an agreement than under the maintenance calculation may wish to try to enter into one. If it is made into a consent order (registered agreement in Scotland) after 3 March 2003 it only stops a party to the agreement from voluntarily applying to the CSA for one year from the date it was made.[123]

The court can also use its powers to vary an existing agreement (whenever made) by *increasing* periodic child maintenance due under that agreement,[124] but not by *adding* a requirement to pay periodic child maintenance, unless the parties consent in writing.[125] A person who does not want to apply to the CSA, or who is waiting for a CSA decision, can go back to court to increase (or reduce) maintenance. This is especially important if it is unclear whether the CSA has jurisdiction (eg, the non-resident parent is no longer habitually resident in the UK), as it allows the level of child maintenance to be reconsidered quickly by the court and not left unchanged until any CSA decision is finally made.

Effect of a calculation on existing court orders and agreements

When a maintenance calculation is made, any existing court order or maintenance agreement either ceases to have effect or has effect in a modified form in relation to periodic payments.[126] The existence of a court order or agreement may mean that the amount of the calculation is 'phased in' (see p329). Before July 2008, if there was a pre-2003 court order, the CSA could make a maintenance calculation following an application from a parent with care on IS/income-based JSA or, if the order was made after 3 March 2003 and had been in force for more than one year, an application was made to the CSA. **Note:** since July 2008 parents with care on IS/income-based JSA are no longer treated as applying to the CSA.

These rules apply even to 'clean break' orders/agreements. There are conflicting court decisions on whether the child support scheme (or changes made to it) allows the court to re-open the capital/property part of such an order.[127] The arrangement may be self-adjusting to address the effect of any maintenance calculation which may be made. This could mean a legal charge on the transferred home so that the non-resident parent could recover any sums paid under the child support scheme from the transferred asset.[128] It could also mean an order that the non-resident parent top up any future calculation to a certain total amount of maintenance.[129]

If a child maintenance calculation is made for all of the children still covered by a court order, that order ceases to have effect on the effective date of the calculation – ie, two months and two days after an application to the CSA if the court order was made on or after 3 March 2003 and has been in force for at least a year (see p331).[130]

If the order includes provisions for additional maintenance, such as a child's education or training expenses or for a disabled child's special needs, only the elements for periodical maintenance for a qualifying child should cease to be in force. If the order is made solely for these additional expenses, it remains in force.[131] Parts of the order for matters other than periodic maintenance for the children named in the calculation (eg, other children or spousal maintenance) remain in force.[132]

In Scotland, if the CSA ceases to have power to make a calculation in respect of a child, the original order revives from the date it ceases to have that power.[133] The same is not explicitly stated for England and Wales, which means that the original order does not revive when CSA involvement ceases. However, it could be argued that it should apply since the court order has not been revoked but simply ceased to have effect for the duration of a maintenance calculation. If the original order does not revive, a new agreement or consent order will need to be negotiated. If this is no longer possible, a parent may have no other option than to use the CSA to calculate and enforce child maintenance.

Maintenance agreements are unenforceable from the effective date (see p341) of the calculation.[134] Again, this only affects the part of the agreement to pay periodic maintenance for the children named in the calculation. The agreement remains unenforceable until the CSA no longer has the power to make a calculation.[135] Any court order made after the agreement becomes unenforceable for children *not* covered by the CSA calculation can be backdated to the date of the calculation.

Notifications

As well as notifying the parties about the calculation (see p328), the CSA must notify the court in which the order was made or registered.[136] Similarly, where a court makes an order which affects, or is likely to affect, a maintenance calculation, the relevant officer of the court (see p54) must notify the CSA of this if s/he knows a calculation is in force.[137]

Additional maintenance

Even where the CSA has jurisdiction, the courts may still be able to make orders for children who are no longer qualifying children, and can still make orders for:[138]

- maintenance for stepchildren of the non-resident parent – ie, children who were accepted by him as members of his family when they used to live with him, but who are not qualifying children;[139]
- maintenance for expenses of a child's education or training for a trade, profession or vocation;[140]
- maintenance to meet expenses of a child's disability – a child counts as disabled if s/he is getting disability living allowance (DLA) or does not get DLA but is blind, deaf, without speech, or is substantially and permanently handicapped by illness, injury, mental disorder or congenital deformity.[141] The courts may even extend payments beyond the child's 19th birthday;[142]
- maintenance for a spouse or civil partner;
- maintenance from the person with care;[143] *and*
- child maintenance in excess of the maximum worked out under child support rules.[144]

The courts can backdate these maintenance orders to the effective date (see p341) of a maintenance calculation, if the application is made within six months of that date.[145] Backdating is at the court's discretion and can ensure that other maintenance is in step with child support.

The courts' power to make a lump-sum award for a child will not be used to provide regular support for the child, but only to meet a need for a particular item of capital expenditure – eg, acquiring a home.[146]

If the Child Support Agency has no jurisdiction

If the CSA does not have jurisdiction – eg, because one parent or the qualifying child is not habitually resident in the UK, the court may make and vary a maintenance order. In addition, where there is a pre-3 March 2003 court order for child maintenance, a post-3 March 2003 order which has been in effect for less than a year, or a pre-April 1993 agreement (see p37), the courts have the power to vary such orders and agreements.[147]

In the past, many courts used calculations under the 'old rules' CSA formula as a guide when setting levels of child maintenance. They may now decide to do so using the 'new rules' calculation, so parents seeking variation of an order or agreement can ask their solicitors to prepare a calculation. The calculation currently used for new CSA applications is likely to be seen as 'highly' persuasive but not legally binding on courts (as the 'old rules' formula was in the past).[148] This principle has been emphasised in relation to the 'new rules' scheme in Scotland.[149] The courts also have the power to enforce orders and agreements, including those made by courts in other countries.[150]

If an application to the CSA by an adult cannot be made because of a pre-April 1993 written maintenance agreement (see p37), the courts cannot make or revive an order, except with the parties' consent (see p27).[151]

Although the courts can revoke child maintenance orders, this is not usually done simply to allow an application to be made to the CSA.[152] If revocation is being considered, advice should be sought on the likely child maintenance calculation.

In England and Wales applications for maintenance are made to the family proceedings (magistrates') court, the county court or High Court. In Scotland they are made to the sheriff court or Court of Session.

If a maintenance calculation is cancelled because one of the parties moves abroad (see p335), an application for maintenance can be made to the court. If the application is made within six months of the end of the maintenance, the order can begin from that date.[153]

Notes

1. The duty to maintain
1 s1(1) CSA 1991

2. Parent
2 s41 The Human Fertilisation and Embryology Act 2008
3 s42 The Human Fertilisation and Embryology Act 2008
4 s43 The Human Fertilisation and Embryology Act 2008
5 s53 The Human Fertilisation and Embryology Act 2008
6 s54 CSA 1991
7 s39 AA 1976; s39A(S)A 1978; s26(2) CSA 1991 Case A
8 s30 HF&EA 1990; s26(2) CSA 1991 Case B
9 s27(3) HF&EA 1990
10 ss27(1) and 29(1) HF&EA 1990
11 s27 Family Law Reform Act 1987 came into force on 4 April 1988 (there was no equivalent provision for Scotland). The father of a child born before that date is always the man who provided the sperm; *Re M (Child Support Act: Parentage)* [1997] 2 3 FCR 383, [1997] 2 FLR 90, [1997] Fam Law 536. s49(4) HF&EA 1990 came into force throughout Great Britain on 1 August 1991. See also *J v C and E (a child)* [2008] EWCA Civ 551

12 s29(2) HF&EA 1990
13 s28(2) HF&EA 1990; *Re CH (Contact: Parentage)* [1996] 1 FCR 768, [1996] 1 FLR 569, [1996] Fam Law 274
14 s28(6) HF&EA 1990
15 s28(3) HF&EA 1990
16 See *Re D (a child appearing by her guardian ad litem)* [2005] UKHL 33
17 Because such a clinic would not have a UK licence: *U v W (A-G intervening)* [1997] 3 WLR 739, [1997] 2 CMLR 431, [1997] 2 FLR 282
18 s26 CSA 1991
19 Under s55A or 56 Family Law Act 1986, Art 32 Matrimonial & Family Proceedings (Northern Ireland) Order or s7 LR(PC)(S)A 1986
20 s26(2) CSA 1991 Case E and s5(1) LR(PC)(S)A 1986
21 s26(2) CSA 1991 Cases A1 and A2
22 s26(2) CSA 1991 Case F(a)(i) in 'relevant proceedings' under s12(5) Civil Evidence Act 1968 or affiliation proceedings
23 s26(2) CSA 1991 Case F(a)(i) in 'relevant proceedings' under s8(5) Civil Evidence Act 1968 (Northern Ireland) or affiliation proceedings
24 s26(2) CSA 1991 Case F(a)(ii) in affiliation proceedings
25 s26(2) CSA 1991 Case A3

26 s26(2) CSA 1991 Case B
27 s26(2) CSA 1991 Case B1
28 *R v Secretary of State for Social Security ex parte Shirley West*, CO/568/1998, 30 April 1999, unreported
29 CPA 2004; CP(PSS&CS)(CP)O; CPA 2004 (RACP)O
30 See also *J v C* [2006] EWCA Civ 551
31 **EW** s67 A&CA 2002
    S s40 A&C(S)A 2007
    Both s54 CSA 1991 'parent'
32 **EW** CA 1989
    S C(S)A 1995
33 **EW** s3(4) CA 1989
    S s3(3) C(S)A 1995
34 Arts 3 and 4 CSA(JC)O ('old rules') and Arts 3 and 4 CSA(JC)O 2002 ('new rules'); Art 3(1)(s) and (t) C(AP)O

3. **Qualifying child**
35 s3(1) CSA 1991
36 Sch 1 para 10C CSA 1991
37 s55(1) CSA 1991
38 Child Support (Miscellaneous Amendments) (No.2) Regulations 2009 No.2909
39 s55(2) CSA 1991
40 Sch 1 para 2 CS(MCP) Regs; CCS/12604/1996
41 s55(1)(b) CSA 1991
42 Sch 1 para 3 CS(MCP) Regs
43 See CPAG's *Welfare Benefits and Tax Credits Handbook* for more details.
44 Sch 1 para 5(1) CS(MCP) Regs
45 Sch 1 para 5(6) and (7) CS(MCP) Regs
46 Sch 1 para 5(5) CS(MCP) Regs
47 Sch 1 para 4(1) CS(MCP) Regs
48 Sch 1 para 4(2) CS(MCP) Regs
49 s55(1)(c) CSA 1991; Sch 1 para 1 CS(MCP) Regs
50 Reg 5 The Child Benefit (General) Regulations 2006 No.223
51 Sch 1 paras 1(1)(b) and 6 CS(MCP) Regs
52 Reg 1 The Child Support (Miscellaneous Amendments) Regulations 2009 No.396
53 Sch 1 para 1(3)(b) CS(MCP) Regs

4. **Person with care**
54 s3(3) CSA 1991
55 s3(5) CSA 1991
56 s3(3)(c) CSA 1991; reg 21 CS(MCP) Regs
57 Reg 21(1)(b) CS(MCP) Regs; s23(5) CA 1989
58 **Old rules** DMG para 2033
    New rules PG, Gathering Information and Evidence, Deciding Principal Provider of Day-to-Day Care

59 **Old rules** Reg 1(2) CS(MASC) Regs, 'day-to-day care'
    New rules Reg 1(2) CS(MCSC) Regs, 'day-to-day care'
60 Reg 8(2) MCSC Regs
61 Reg 13 CS(MCSC) Regs. This applies where a child is placed under s23(5) CA 1989
62 Reg 12 CS(MCSC) Regs
63 DMG para 2034
64 Reg 1(2) CS(MCSC) Regs, 'home'
65 s54 CSA 1991

5. **Non-resident parent**
66 s3 CSA 1991
67 Reg 8 CS(MCSC) Regs
68 s1(3) CSA 1991
69 *Santos v Santos* [1972] 2 WLR 889, [1972] All ER 246, CA
70 **Old rules** DMG paras 1566-73
    New rules PG, Gather Information and Evidence, Household
71 CCS/2318/1997
72 CSB/463/1986
73 **Old rules** DMG para 1569
    New rules PG, Gather Information and Evidence, Household
74 R(SB) 4/83
75 R(SB) 35/85
76 **Old rules** DMG para 1571
    New rules PG, Gather Information and Evidence, Household
77 CCS/2332/2006

6. **Relevant child**
78 Sch 1 para 10C CSA 1991
79 Reg 10 CS(MCSC) Regs
80 Reg 11 CS(MCSC) Regs

7. **Welfare of the child**
81 s2 CSA 1991
82 CCS/1037/1995
83 s2 CSA 1991
    Old rules DMG 2505
    New rules PG, Specialist Areas, Welfare of the Child
84 *R v Secretary of State for Social Security ex parte Biggin* [1995] 2 FCR 595, [1995] 1 FLR 851
85 **Old rules** DMG para 1151
    New rules PG, Specialist Areas, Welfare of the Child
86 **New rules** PG, Enforcement, Welfare of the Child
87 **Old rules** CSG para 151
88 *Smith v Secretary of State for Work and Pensions* [2006] UKHL 35

8. Family

89 Reg 1(2) CS(MCSC) Regs; the 'old rules' definition in Reg 1(2) CS(MASC) Regs is equivalent, but specifies children for whom the single person, or at least one member of the couple, has day-to day-care.

90 Reg 1(2) CS(MCSC) Regs

91 CFC/7/1992

92 CPA 2004

93 CPA 2004; CP(PSS&CS)(CP)O; CPA 2004 (RACP)O

94 *Secretary of State for Work and Pensions v M* [2006] UKHL 11

9. Habitually resident in the UK

95 s44(1) CSA 1991

96 s44(2) CSA 1991

97 Sch 1 Interpretation Act 1978

98 *Nessa v Chief Adjudication Officer* [1998] 2 All ER 728, [1998] 2 FCR 461, [1998] 1 FLR 879, [1998] Fam Law 329, CA applying *Re J (A Minor) (Abduction: Custody Rights)* [1990] 2 AC 562, [1990] 3 WLR 492, [1990] 2 All ER 961, [1991] FCR 129, [1990] 2 FLR 442, [1991] Fam Law 57, HL; *Cruse v Chittum* [1974] 2 All ER 940; *Brokelmann v Barr* [1971] 3 All ER 29; *Langford v Athanassoglou* [1948] 2 All ER 722

99 R(CS) 5/96; CCS/7207/1995

100 *Shah v Barnet LBC* [1983] 2 AC 309, [1983] 2 WLR 16, [1983] 1 All ER 226, HL

101 s44(2A) CSA 1991; reg 7A CS(MAJ) Regs

102 *Lewis v Lewis* [1956] 1 WLR 200, [1956] 1 All ER 375

103 *Re J (A Minor) (Abduction: Custody Rights)* [1990] 2 AC 562, [1990] 3 WLR 492, [1990] 2 All ER 961, [1991] FCR 129, [1990] 2 FLR 442, [1991] Fam Law 57, HL

104 *Shah v Barnet LBC* [1983] 2 AC 309, [1983] 2 WLR 16, [1983] 1 All ER 226, HL; *Re Mackenzie* [1940] 4 All ER 310

105 *Mark v Mark* [2005] UKHL 42, [2005] WLR 111

106 R(CS) 5/96

107 R(CS) 5/96

108 *Re J (A Minor) (Abduction: Custody Rights)* [1990] 2 AC 562, [1990] 3 WLR 492, [1990] 2 All ER 961, [1991] FCR 129, [1990] 2 FLR 442, [1991] Fam Law 57, HL

109 *Re M (Minors: Residence Order: Jurisdiction)* [1993] 1 FCR 718, [1993] 1 FLR 495, [1993] Fam Law 285, CA

110 *Re A (Minors: Abduction: Acquiescence)* [1992] 2 WLR 536, [1992] 1 All ER 929, [1992] 2 FCR 97, [1992] 2 FLR 14, [1992] Fam Law 381, CA

111 *Re M (A Minor) (Abduction: Child's Objections)* [1995] 1 FCR 170, [1994] 2 FLR 126, [1994] Fam Law 366, CA

10. The role of the courts

112 s8(1) and (3) CSA 1991. It has been decided that this lack of access to the courts is not inconsistent with art 6(1) European Convention on Human Rights – see *R v Secretary of State for Work and Pensions ex parte Kehoe* [2005] UKHL 48

113 s8(2) CSA 1991

114 s8(1) and (3A) CSA 1991

115 CCS/316/1998; CCS/8328/1995

116 CCS/316/1998

117 ss4(10) and 7(10) CSA 1991; reg 2 CS(APD) Regs

118 rs 8.1(2)-(6), 10.24 and 10.25 Family Proceedings Rules

119 Reg 8(2) CS(MAJ) Regs

120 Reg 8(1) CS(MAJ) Regs

121 s9(2) CSA 1991

122 s9(4) CSA 1991

123 ss4(10) and 7(10) CSA 1991; reg 2 CS(APD) Regs

124 s9(6) CSA 1991 (applies unless a calculation is made in an s6 case, when the agreement becomes unenforceable)

125 ss8(5) and 9(5) CSA 1991

126 s10(1) and (2) CSA 1991

127 *Crozier v Crozier* [1994] 1 FLR 126; *Mawson v Mawson* [1994] 2 FLR 985

128 *Smith v McInerney* [1994] 2 FLR 1077. However, an arrangement like this might be void under s9(4) CSA 1991 because it would 'restrict the right to apply for a maintenance assessment', though the commissioner in CCS/2318/1997 thought not.

129 See the arrangement in CCS/2318/1997

130 Reg 3(2) CS(MAJ) Regs

131 Reg 3(3) CS(MAJ) Regs

132 Reg 3(2) CS(MAJ) Regs

133 Reg 3(4) CS(MAJ) Regs

134 Reg 4 CS(MAJ) Regs

135 Reg 4(3) CS(MAJ) Regs

136 Reg 5(1) CS(MAJ) Regs

137 Reg 6 CS(MAJ) Regs

138 s8 CSA 1991

139 **EW** MCA 1973
S FL(S)A 1958

140 s8(7) CSA 1991

141 s8(8) and (9) CSA 1991

142 Sch 1 para 3(2)(b) CA 1989. In *C v F*
[1997] 3 FCR 405 the court held that
where s8(1) CSA 1991 applies, s8(8)
CSA 1991 limits this power to children
aged under 19. However, this seems to
be wrong because the fact that the CSA
1991 only applies to those aged under
19 can hardly prevent an order being
made under the CA 1989 for a person
aged over 19.
143 s8(10) CSA 1991
144 s8(6) CSA 1991
145 s29(7) MCA 1973; s5(7) DPMCA 1978;
Sch 1 para 3(7) CA 1989 as amended
by Sch 3 paras 3, 5, and 10 CSPSSA
2000 respectively
146 Sch 1 CA 1989; *Phillips v Pearce* [1996] 2
FLR 230
147 ss8(3A) and 9(6) CSA 1991; *McGilchrist v
McGilchrist* [1997] SCLR 800
148 *E v C* [1996] 1 FLR 472; *GW v RW* [2003]
EWHC 611 (Fam), [2003] 2FLR 108
149 *Sutherland v Sutherland* [2004] GWD 20-
436
150 MO(RE)A 1992
151 s8(3) and (3A) CSA 1991
152 s8(4) CSA 1991; *B v M (Child Support:
Revocation of Order)* [1994] 1 FLR 342,
[1994] 1 FCR 769, [1994] Fam Law 370
153 s29(7) MCA 1973; s5(7) DPMCA 1978;
Sch 1 para 3(7) CA 1989

Chapter 3

Applications

This chapter covers:
1. Who can apply to the Child Support Agency (below)
2. How to apply to the Child Support Agency (p39)
3. Withdrawing or cancelling an application (p42)
4. Multiple applications (p43)

1. Who can apply to the Child Support Agency

Any person with care (see p20) or non-resident parent (see p21) can apply to the Child Support Agency (CSA) for child maintenance, unless barred by an existing maintenance arrangement (see p37).[1] In Scotland, children who are aged 12 or over can apply to the CSA for child maintenance, provided no application has been made/treated as made by the person with care or the non-resident parent.[2]

If there is more than one person with care of a qualifying child and at least one, but not all, of them has parental responsibility for the child, only those persons with parental responsibility can apply for maintenance.[3] For example, if a child is cared for partly by her/his mother who has parental responsibility, and partly by her/his grandmother who does not have parental responsibility, only the mother can apply to the CSA. Parental responsibility has the same meaning as in other areas of law.[4] Parents who were married to each other when the child was born automatically have parental responsibility, which continues even if they divorce.[5] If the parents are not married, the mother can make a formal agreement giving the father parental responsibility.[6] In addition, in England and Wales, if a child's parent is married to (or in a civil partnership with) someone who is not the child's other parent (ie, a step-parent), the parent (or if both biological parents have parental responsibility, both parents) can make a parental responsibility agreement with the step-parent, giving her/him parental responsibility for the child.[7] The courts can also give parental responsibility to a person(s) (including a non-parent or step-parent) who apply/ies for it.[8] In England and Wales, if an unmarried father's name appears on a birth certificate on or after 1 December 2003, he has parental responsibility. In Scotland, this applies if an unmarried father jointly registers a birth on or after 4 May 2006. Unmarried fathers who signed a birth certificate before these dates cannot acquire parental responsibility without going through one of the other routes – ie, arranging a formal agreement with the mother or applying for a court order.

Written maintenance agreement

A written maintenance agreement for a child prevents an application being made for that child.[9]'**Maintenance agreement**' means a written agreement for making, or securing the making, of periodic payments of maintenance (or aliment in Scotland) to or for the benefit of a qualifying child.[10] An agreement only counts for this purpose if it:[11]

- was made before 5 April 1993. It does not need to have been actually in force before 5 April 1993, and it may have been varied after that date;
- is in writing. This can include an agreement made in correspondence headed 'without prejudice'.[12] While it need not be formal or prepared by lawyers, a spoken agreement is not enough, even if payments were made;[13]
- is an agreement. An offer that is never accepted in writing does not constitute a written agreement.[14] An undertaking made in court proceedings can be an agreement;[15]
- is made by the non-resident parent. The person with care does not have to be a party to the agreement. An agreement between the non-resident parent and the qualifying child does not count.[16] In practice, the agreement will usually be between the parents or their representatives;[17]
- is for periodic payments. An agreement to pay mortgage interest charges and fuel bills as they fall due can count, even though the amounts to be paid are not written down and are not paid at regular intervals;[18]
- is for the benefit of the child(ren). The child(ren) need not be named in the agreement and an agreement to pay the mortgage for the home where they live counts as for the benefit of those children;[19]
- is 'in force'. An agreement to pay only a nominal amount counts.[20] An agreed change to the arrangement may mean the original agreement is no longer in force.

Maintenance order

A maintenance order made by a court before 3 March 2003 prevents an application for the child(ren) concerned.[21] If the order was made after 3 March 2003 and has been in force for less than one year it also prevents an application.[22] A '**court order**' only counts for this purpose if it:

- requires the making, or securing the making, of periodic payments of maintenance (or aliment in Scotland) to or for the benefit of a qualifying child.[23] Orders for payment of the costs of education or training of the child, or because the child is disabled, or to 'top up' maintenance all count as maintenance orders.[24] Such top-up orders may be made in addition to any liability worked out by the CSA. For details of these, see p30. Because an order only prevents an *application* to the CSA, an order made *after* the application does not stop the CSA making a calculation ('old rules' assessment) or revising or enforcing an existing one. A court order directing capital payments (ie, not periodic payments) does not count as an order.[25] The wording of the order is important – eg, a consent order with provision for maintenance of the parent with care and undertakings to provide maintenance for the children may not prevent an application;[26]

- is in force. It may be arguable that an order is only 'in force' if it has a practical effect.[27] An order is in force where some undertakings or arrangements, such as for residence of the child, are still in effect, even though there is no further liability for maintenance payments[28] or the liability for child maintenance under the order has not yet begun.[29] If a court decides that it has no power to either vary or enforce an order, an application can be made to the CSA;[30]
- is made under one of certain legal provisions (see Appendix 3).[31] The order usually states the legal provision under which it was made.

Summary of who can apply to the Child Support Agency

Is there a pre-1993 written maintenance agreement? → Yes → There cannot be an application by a person with care or non-resident parent, or by a child in Scotland.

↓

No

↓

Is there a consent order or, in Scotland, a registered minute of agreement? → Yes →

↓

No

↓

Applications may be made to the CSA by a person with care or non-resident parent, and by a child in Scotland.*

* Alternatively, the parties may make an informal arrangement or draw up a written agreement that may be formalised into a consent order or, in Scotland, registered in the Court of Session.

A person who cannot apply to the CSA because of an agreement/order can:

- ask the court to vary or enforce the amount of maintenance under the order or agreement (see p29);
- where there is an agreement, agree with the other party to end the maintenance part of the agreement or possibly even unilaterally break the agreement so it is no longer in force;
- where there is an order, ask the court to revoke it so that a CSA application can be made (but see p31);

People with court orders or agreements can use the CSA's collection and enforcement service for amounts due under those orders/agreements, but this facility is currently only available where child support maintenance is also being collected (see p406).

2. **How to apply to the Child Support Agency**

Applications under the 'new rules' need not be in writing.[32] In some cases the Child Support Agency (CSA) may direct that the application must be in writing, in which case a form may be provided. Where the CSA issues a form or requests information, this must be provided within 14 days unless the CSA is satisfied that there was unavoidable delay.[33] Applications in 'old rules' cases had to be made on a maintenance application form.[34]

Making the application

In 'new rules' cases, applications may be made orally or in writing.[35] Where there is no assessment in force, a new application will always be treated under the 'new rules'. However, there may be some cases outstanding where an 'old rules' application has not yet been decided (see p45).

The wide provisions for 'new rules' applications mean they can be made over the phone, in person, or on an application form sent to the applicant, downloaded from the CSA website, or online via the CSA website. Note that downloaded forms must be printed, signed and returned by post to the Child Support Agency Centre (CSAC). Signing the form confirms that the information given is correct. This is important since there are penalties for knowingly providing false information (see p57).

If the form is completed over the phone, it will be sent to the applicant to be checked. The application forms used are slightly different depending on whether it is a person with care, child in Scotland or non-resident parent who is applying. There is no time limit to return the form – if it is not returned there is no effective application (see p41). If the non-resident parent wishes to apply at a point when the parent with care has already applied, he will be directed to complete a maintenance enquiry form rather than a maintenance application form.

If the CSA requests further information or reissues the application form, the information requested should be provided within 14 days.[36] If this does not occur and the CSA is not satisfied that there was unavoidable delay this may bring forward the date of an effective application (see p41) or where no information is received, cancel the application (see p42).

The application for child maintenance form

This form may be used to gather information to pursue maintenance. It includes sections on:[37]

- personal details – name, address, national insurance (NI) number, date of birth, phone numbers and the best time to phone, armed forces service number;
- child(ren) being applied for – name, date of birth, NI number if over 16, who gets child benefit for the child, maintenance arrangements, shared care arrangements (or local authority care);
- if the parent/person with care is applying, whether the non-resident parent knows s/he is being named as the parent;
- child's education (if between 16 and 19) – school/college, course, type of course, hours a week;
- local authority details (if the child is being cared for by it);
- non-resident parent details – name (other names), address or last known address and when lived there, NI number, date of birth, employment details, phone numbers, whether the parent is the father or mother of the child;
- if the parent/person with care is applying, whether the non-resident parent knows where the applicant lives;
- payment details – whether maintenance is to be collected by the CSA, preferred method and frequency of payment to the person with care, bank/building society details;
- representative details – name, address, phone numbers and the best time to phone. If the representative is not a solicitor, an attorney under a power of attorney, Scottish mental health custodian, mental health appointee or receiver, the applicant must sign the client authority declaration on the form;
- further information – a blank page to add other relevant information.

Any relevant court order or written maintenance agreement (original documents) and the representative's authority (eg, power of attorney document) should be sent with the form and will be returned.

Signing the form confirms that all the information given is correct and complete. This is important since there are penalties for knowingly providing false information (see p57).

The Child Maintenance Options service

From July 2008, the Child Maintenance and Enforcement Commission (C-MEC) has had a statutory duty to provide parents who live apart with information and guidance to help them make effective arrangements for child maintenance. This is now being provided by the Child Maintenance Options service. Services include a telephone helpline, giving information about different options to arrange child maintenance and encouraging parents to come to their own arrangements if they can. Child Maintenance Options also provides parents with information for other purposes, such as finances when a relationship ends.[38]

Applications with more than one non-resident parent

An applicant can choose from which non-resident parent she wishes to apply for child support maintenance. Thus, an application may be made for maintenance from some, but not all, non-resident parents.

When to apply

There are no time limits for making an application to the CSA. One can be made as soon as someone becomes a person with care or a non-resident parent, or at any later date. However, liability to pay child maintenance usually runs from the date the non-resident parent is notified and this cannot occur until an effective application (see below) is received by the CSA. Parents with care should be aware that the non-resident parent's liability will not start until after an application to the CSA is made, even if C-MEC has given them information about setting up voluntary arrangements. This means that delaying the application may delay the start of liability. There is no provision for applying in advance – eg, before the birth of a baby.

Refusal to accept an application

The CSA may decide not to accept an application – eg, because it believes an existing maintenance agreement prevents an application or because it does not have jurisdiction. If this happens, the would-be applicant should write to the CSA explaining why she believes she is entitled to apply and asking for a written CSA decision. If a written decision is issued, she can try to appeal this to the First-tier Tribunal (see Chapter 18). If this does not work or if the CSA refuses to respond in writing, a complaint (see p439) and/or judicial review (see p353) should be considered.

Effective applications

Only an effective application allows the CSA to make a maintenance calculation. An application is effective if it is made by phone or in writing according to the CSA's direction.[39] All applicants must provide information to enable the non-resident parent to be identified and traced, and the amount of child maintenance payable by him to be calculated and recovered (see Chapter 4).[40] If an applicant does not supply the information, the CSA may refuse to process the application (see p43).

The CSA may ask the applicant to provide further information or evidence to make an effective application; this may be done over the phone or in writing. The CSA may issue an application for child maintenance form to the applicant. If a form has been previously sent to the applicant, another may be issued. If the information or evidence is received within 14 days of the request, the application takes effect from the date the earlier application was treated as received by the CSA.[41]

Once an effective application has been made, any other relevant person (non-resident parent or person with care) is informed of the application either by phone or in writing.[42] The relevant person is asked to provide information to enable the maintenance calculation to be made. This can be done over the phone or the person may be asked to complete a form. This form is known as a child maintenance enquiry form. Non-resident parents are informed of the effective date of the calculation and rules on default maintenance decisions at the same time as they are informed of the application.[43] The CSA cannot refuse to deal with an effective application, even if it considers that processing it would be against the welfare of the children concerned.[44] If it refuses to accept an application, see p41.

For delays in dealing with applications, including where the non-resident parent is not co-operating, see p324.

Amending the application

An application can be amended at any time before a maintenance calculation is made, but not to take into account a change which occurs after the effective date (see p341).[45] For details of this and of changes after the effective date, see p325.

3. Withdrawing or cancelling an application

Request to cease acting by the applicant

An applicant may request that the Child Support Agency (CSA) ceases to act on her/his application for child maintenance.

The CSA cannot refuse this request.[46] The request can be made at any time, whether or not a calculation (or 'old rules' assessment) has been made. For more on cancelling calculations, see p334.

Requests to cease acting can be made by phone or in writing to the CSA office processing the application, or to the Child Support Agency Centre if it is not clear which office has responsibility.

An application is withdrawn or cancelled by the Child Support Agency

The CSA may withdraw or cancel an application before a calculation is made if:
- the applicant does not provide information; *or*
- the qualifying child dies.

An applicant does not provide information

An application can be withdrawn or cancelled by the CSA if insufficient co-operation is received from the person with care.[47] However, if the applicant is the non-resident parent and the person with care does not wish to co-operate but the non-resident parent does not wish to withdraw the application, it will not be cancelled. A maintenance calculation will be carried out, but no maintenance can be collected and passed on to the person with care.[48]

Cases can be cancelled only where no 'effective application' has been made (see p41). If there is an effective application, a decision must be made and notified, even if it is a decision not to make a calculation (see p326). If an effective application is cancelled against the wishes of the applicant, advice should be sought.

The qualifying child dies

If a qualifying child dies before a calculation has been made, the application is treated as if it had never been made with respect to that child.[49] If the child was the only child named in the application, any calculation ceases to have effect. Otherwise, any calculation is superseded because of a change of circumstances (see p359).

4. **Multiple applications**

If more than one application for child maintenance is made in respect of the same qualifying child, only one can go ahead.[50] Only an effective application (see p41) counts.[51] If a calculation has not yet been made, the applications are either treated as a single application or one is selected to be considered (see p44).[52] For applications made after a calculation has been made, see p45. For applications, some of which were made before 3 March 2003 (including where there is an existing 'old rules' assessment), see p45.

The decision on whose application goes ahead only determines which applicant has the power to withdraw an application or to request a cancellation of any resulting calculation. It does not affect the outcome of any calculation or have any effect on who is liable to pay any resulting child maintenance. Information included on any competing applications can be taken into account by the Child Support Agency (CSA).

If an application with priority is made by an applicant in Northern Ireland, the CSA there (see p323) deals with the application.[53]

Before a calculation has been made

The rules below apply unless a request is received to cease acting in relation to all but one of the applications.[54] See p45 if there is an existing application to which the 'old rules' apply.

Same person applies more than once

If a person applies and then applies again in the same circumstances before a calculation is made, both applications are treated as if they were the same application.[55]

If more than one application is made by the same child in Scotland and maintenance has not yet been calculated, it counts as a single application as long as it is made in respect of the same non-resident parent and person with care.[56]

More than one applicant

The CSA decides which application to deal with as follows.[57]

Applicant	Priority application
Only one person with care	
Person with care and non-resident parent.	Person with care.
Person with care or non-resident parent applies following an application by a child in Scotland.	Person with care/non-resident parent.
More than one qualifying child applies in relation to the same person with care and non-resident parent.	Elder or eldest child.
Both parents are non-resident parents and both apply.	Treated as a single application.
More than one person with care	
More than one person with care with parental responsibility (or, in Scotland, parental rights) applies, and one person is treated as a non-resident parent for calculation purposes (see p272).	Person with care not treated as a non-resident parent.
More than one person with care applies and none of the applicants has parental responsibility/rights, or all do and either none can be treated as a non-resident parent, or even after one of the applicants has been treated as a non-resident parent under the calculation, there is still more than one application.	The principal provider of day-to-day care (see p20) in the following order of priority: – the person who gets child benefit for the child(ren); – the person who, in the CSA's opinion, is the principal provider of day-to-day care.

If the applications are treated as a single one under these rules, that application covers all the children named in either, and the effective date (see p341) is set by the application which was made first.[58]

If more than one person with care applies and each application refers to different children, the CSA treats each application as covering all the children mentioned in all the applications.[59] If the same person with care does not provide the principal day-to-day care for all the qualifying children mentioned in the applications, then separate calculations are made in relation to each person with care.[60]

Once the calculation is in force

A calculation in force in respect of a person with care does not prevent the CSA making a new calculation because she becomes a parent with care. Once a calculation is in force, any subsequent application for maintenance made in the same circumstances in respect of the same person with care, non-resident parent and qualifying child(ren) will not be dealt with.[61] It may, however, be treated as a request for a supersession (see p359).

Applications for additional children

If there is an existing calculation and there is an application for an additional child(ren) of the same non-resident parent cared for by the same person with care, this is a relevant change of circumstances and a new calculation is made which supersedes the existing calculation.[62]

One application before 3 March 2003, and one on or after 3 March 2003

If no assessment is in force

If no assessment is in force, there are transitional provisions for determining how to proceed if there is an existing application under the 'old rules' and a further application is made under the 'new rules' in respect of the same person with care, non-resident parent or qualifying child.[63] These determine whether the applications are treated as a single application or only one is to proceed. The applications do not have to be received at exactly the same time. If one application is not determined by the time the other is received, the following rules apply.[64]

Applicant	*Priority application*
Person with care applies under the 'old rules' and then under the 'new rules'.	Treated as a single application.

Non-resident parent applies under the 'old rules' and 'new rules' in relation to the same qualifying child.	Treated as a single application.
Child in Scotland applies under the 'old rules' and then under the 'new rules'.	Treated as a single application.
Person with care applies under the 'old rules' or under the 'new rules' and the non-resident applies under either the 'old' or 'new' rules.	Person with care's application has priority.
Child in Scotland applies under the 'old rules' and a 'new rules' application is made by either the person with care or non-resident parent.	Person with care or non-resident parent's application has priority.
More than one child applies under either the 'old' or 'new' rules in relation to the same person with care and non-resident parent.	The application of the elder or eldest child has priority.
More than one person with care with parental responsibility applies, one under the 'old rules' the other under the 'new rules', and one person is treated as a non-resident parent for calculation/assessment purposes.	The application of the person with care not treated as a non-resident parent has priority.
More than one person with care applies (as above) but none has parental responsibility or they all do and either none can be treated as a non-resident parent or, even after one of the applicants has been treated as a non-resident parent for the calculation/assessment, there is still more than one application.	The application of the principal provider of day-to-day care in the following order of priority: the person who gets child benefit for the child(ren), otherwise the person who in the CSA's opinion is the principal provider of day-to-day care.

Whether the case is proceeded with as a 'new rules' or 'old rules' case then depends on the effective date of the application with priority or whether a maintenance assessment was previously in force in relation to the same person with care, qualifying child(ren) and non-resident parent. If an assessment was in force within the previous 13 weeks, the application is treated as an application for a maintenance assessment regardless of whether the effective date of the application is before or after 3 March 2003.[65]

A parent with care may cancel her application for a maintenance assessment and reapply after more than 13 weeks in order to have child support calculated under the 'new rules' instead. If, within 13 weeks of the cancellation of the 'old rules' assessment, the non-resident applies, his application will be dealt with under the 'old rules'. However, if the parent with care's 'new rules' application arrives before the non-resident parent's application has been assessed, the parent with care's application takes precedence under the above rules for multiple applications. The result will be to ignore the non-resident parent's application and treat the situation as a single 'new rules' application.

However, this is not a reason for the CSA to delay processing the non-resident parent's application under the 'old rules' before the parent with care's application is received. He may be entitled to compensation for the difference between his 'old rules' and 'new rules' liability (if the latter is more) for the period between the effective date of his application and the effective date of the parent with care's 'new rules' application.[66]

If a maintenance assessment is in force

If a maintenance assessment is already in force and an application is made or treated as made under the 'new rules' in relation to the same person with care, qualifying child(ren) and non-resident parent, the calculation application will not proceed.[67] It is only if the maintenance assessment has ceased, and a new application is made after at least 13 weeks, that it can be dealt with under the new rules (see Chapter 7).

If there is an existing assessment and there is an application for an additional child(ren) of the same non-resident parent cared for by the same person with care, this is a relevant change of circumstances and a new assessment is made under the 'old rules' which supersedes the existing assessment.[68] If a new application is made in relation to other people, it is likely to trigger conversion (see below).

New applications that trigger conversion of an existing case

Existing cases will continue to be dealt with under the 'old rules', unless there is a related decision that causes a conversion to the 'new rules'.[69] In many cases, this will be triggered by a new application from another person that involves either the non-resident parent or parent with care in the existing assessment. In addition, parents who form new partnerships with people on benefit or partners who each have maintenance but move onto benefit may be affected.

When an existing case converts to the 'new rules', transitional phasing may apply. For more information on when conversion is triggered, and on transitional phasing, see Chapter 7.

Notes

1. Who can apply to the Child Support Agency

1 ss4(1) and 6(1) CSA 1991
2 s7(1) CSA 1991
3 ss5(1) and 54 CSA 1991
4 As in the CA 1989 and the C(S)A 1995
5 s3(1) CA 1989; C(S)A 1995
6 s4(1)(b) CA 1989; C(S)A 1995
7 s4A CA 1989, as amended by s75 CPA 2004
8 ss4(1)(a), 4A(1)(b) and 5(6) CA 1989; C(S)A 1989
9 ss4(10)(a) and 7(10) CSA 1991
10 s9(1) CSA 1991
11 ss4(10)(a) and 7(10) CSA 1991
12 CCS/12767/1996
13 CCS/12797/1996
14 CCS/11052/1995
15 CCS/8328/1995
16 CCS/2908/1995
17 PG, Calculation and Decision Types, Written Maintenance Agreement
18 CCS/8328/1995
19 CCS/8328/1995
20 CCS/12849/1996
21 ss4(10)(a) and 7(10)(a) CSA 1991; reg 2 CS(APD) Regs
22 ss4(10)(aa) and 7(10)(b) CSA 1991; reg 2 CS(APD) Regs
23 s8(11) CSA 1991
24 Otherwise s8(6)-(8) CSA 1991 would be unnecessary
25 CCS/4741/1995, upheld by the Court of Appeal in *AMS v CSO* [1998] 1 FLR 955
26 CCS/316/1998
27 R(CS) 4/96. However, authorities differ as to whether changes in child(ren)'s residence (eg, from the parent with care to the non-resident parent) mean that an order ceases to have effect (CCS/ 3127/1995) or not (CCS/2567/1998). In the latter case, the commissioner suggested that it would instead be grounds to seek to vary the court order.
28 CCS/4741/1995
29 CCS/11364/1995
30 Reg 9 CS(MAJ) Regs
31 s8(11) CSA 1991; reg 2 CS(MAJ) Regs. Provisions repealed before 1 April 1980 are not listed.

2. How to apply to the Child Support Agency

32 Reg 3(1) CS(MCP) Regs
33 Regs 3 and 4 CS(MCP) Regs
34 Reg 2(1) CS(MAP) Regs
35 Reg 3(1) CS(MCP) Regs
36 Reg 3(4) and (5) CS(MCP) Regs
37 CSA maintenance application forms, CSF 001, CSF 003 and CSF 004
38 s1(5) CMOPA 2008
39 Reg 3(2) CS(MCP) Regs
40 ss4(4), 6(7) and 7(5) CSA 1991
41 Reg 3(4) CS(MCP) Regs
42 Reg 5(1) CS(MCP) Regs
43 Reg 3(2) CS(MCP) Regs
44 R(CS) 4/96; CCS/14/1994; CCS/17/ 1994 and CCS/16535/1996
45 Reg 3(6-7) CS(MCP) Regs

3. Withdrawing or cancelling an application

46 ss4(6) and 6(5) CSA 1991
47 PG, Gather Information and Evidence, Failure to Provide Requested Information
48 PG, Applications for Child Maintenance, PWC Does Not Wish to Co-operate
49 Reg 6 CS(MCP) Regs

4. Multiple applications

50 s5(2) CSA 1991
51 Sch 2 paras 1, 2 and 3 CS(MCP) Regs
52 s5(2) CSA 1991; reg 4 and Sch 2 CS(MCP) Regs
53 Sch 1 para 6 CS(NIRA) Regs
54 Reg 4(2) CS(MCP) Regs
55 Sch 2 para 1(1) CS(MCP) Regs
56 Sch 2 para 2 CS(MCP) Regs
57 Sch 2 para 3(1) CS(MCP) Regs
58 Reg 4(3) CS(MCP) Regs
59 Sch 2 para 3(12) CS(MCP) Regs
60 Sch 2 para 3(13) CS(MCP) Regs
61 Sch 2 para 4 CS(MCP) Regs
62 PG, Calculation and Decision Types, Relevant Change of Circumstances
63 Sch 3 CS(MCP) Regs

64 CCS/3868/2004
65 Reg 28(1) CS(TP) Regs
66 R(CS) 1/06
67 Sch 3 para 4 CS(MCP) Regs
68 Sch 2 para 6(1) CS(MAP) Regs
69 Reg 3 CSPSSA (Comm12)O; reg 15
    CS(TP) Regs

4

Chapter 4

Information

This chapter covers:
1. Information-seeking powers (below)
2. Contacting the non-resident parent (p58)
3. Parentage investigations (p62)
4. Further investigations (p71)
5. Duty to disclose changes (p74)
6. Disclosure of information by the Child Support Agency (p75)

1. Information-seeking powers

The Child Support Agency (CSA) has wide powers to obtain information from (among others) parents, employers, local authorities and HM Revenue and Customs.[1] The CSA can require information to be provided in order to make any child maintenance decision.[2]

In addition, the CSA can appoint inspectors who have extensive powers to obtain information (see p73). Staff at the regional Child Support Agency Centres (CSACs) (see p6) ask for information by telephone; those at local offices also conduct face-to-face enquiries.

Jobcentre Plus may also seek information under child support legislation – eg, when making decisions about deductions from benefits (see Chapter 19).

Although, legally, the powers to obtain information are now given to the Child Maintenance Enforcement Commision, it is the CSA that currently exercises them (see Chapter 1).

When the Child Support Agency can request information

All applicants are under a duty to provide information to identify and trace a non-resident parent, and calculate and collect maintenance.[3] The information may also be required to verify whether information already gathered is correct.[4]

In many cases, all the information needed will be collected by phone. Applications need not be in writing but, where this is requested, an application for child maintenance form is provided.

After an application has been made the non-resident parent will be contacted, usually by phone, to notify him of the application and gather information. In some cases, a face-to-face interview may be arranged or, if there is no phone number, a form called the 'child maintenance enquiry' is issued. The child maintenance enquiry form can be used to gather the information needed to calculate and collect maintenance (see p60). In 'old rules' cases, the original maintenance enquiry form issued sets the effective date of the maintenance assessment (see p341). A further form will not usually be issued, and as much additional information as possible will be collected by telephone.

Information can only be requested if it is necessary to:[5]

- decide whether there is a qualifying child, non-resident parent or person with care in relation to an application;
- decide whether the CSA has jurisdiction – ie, whether the qualifying child, non-resident parent, and person with care are all habitually resident in the UK (see p26);
- decide whether a written maintenance agreement made before 5 April 1993 or a court order made before 3 March 2003 is in force, or a court order made after 3 March 2003 has been in force for one year (see p37);
- decide which application has priority (see p43);
- decide, where there is more than one person with care, who has parental responsibility for a qualifying child (see p44);
- identify a non-resident parent (see p62);
- trace a non-resident parent (see p58);
- determine who is in receipt of child benefit either for a relevant child or qualifying child where a parent may be treated as a non-resident parent in shared care situations (see Chapter 14);
- calculate the amount of child maintenance;
- identify how much is payable under a court maintenance order;
- collect child support maintenance or maintenance under a court order from a non-resident parent;
- decide whether to enforce a CSA calculation or other maintenance through the courts (see p416);
- work out or collect interest on arrears (see p415);
- identify any proceedings for a court maintenance order;
- predict (from credit reference and other information) a non-resident parent's likelihood of compliance;
- verify whether information already gathered is correct.[6]

See p53 for who can be required to give information and p57 for the effects of failing to provide it.

Information the Child Support Agency can ask for

There are no specific restrictions on the kind of information the CSA can ask for, but the law is specific about the purpose for which the information must be needed (see p51). Issues on which the CSA can require information include:[7]

- the habitual residence of the person with care, the non-resident parent and any child covered by the application to determine jurisdiction (including if the individual works abroad);
- the name and address of the person with care and non-resident parent, their marital or civil partnership status, and the relationship of the person with care to any child covered by the application;
- the name, address and date of birth of any child covered by the application, the child's marital or civil partnership status and any education the child is undergoing;
- where there is more than one person with care:
  - who has parental responsibility (or parental rights in Scotland) for any qualifying child; *and*
  - how much time is spent by that child with each person with care;
- where parentage is disputed, whether someone can be assumed to be a parent (see p15) and if not, who is the parent of a child;
- the name and address of any current or recent employer of a non-resident parent and the gross earnings from any such employment;
- if the non-resident parent is self-employed, the address, trading name, gross receipts and expenses, any other outgoings of the trade or business and taxable profits;
- any other income of the non-resident parent;
- how much is paid or payable under a court maintenance order or maintenance agreement;
- details of anyone who lives in the same household as the non-resident parent, their relationship to him and to each other, and the date of birth of any child of those people;
- details and statements of any account in the name of the non-resident parent, including bank and building society accounts;
- whether a person counts as a qualifying child for the purposes of child support (see p18);
- information needed to decide whether a calculation should end (see p345).

In 'old rules' cases, additional information may be needed and can be required in order to work out maintenance liability, including, for example, housing costs, and the employment and income of other people who live with the non-resident parent or parent with care.[8]

Who has to give information to the Child Support Agency

Information can be required from the people listed on pp53–56. It can only be required from a person who has that information in her/his possession or can reasonably be expected to acquire it.[9] Information can also be given to the CSA when there is no obligation to provide it – eg, from a relative, neighbour, GP or landlord. However, any such voluntary disclosure of information made without the permission of the person(s) concerned could break professional codes of practice, civil contracts or the Data Protection Act 1984. Information supplied to the CSA can give rise to a libel action.[10] For information on disclosure by the CSA, see p75.

The relevant persons

The person with care, a non-resident parent (or a parent treated as non-resident for the purposes of the calculation) and in Scotland, a child applicant, must provide the information on p52 if requested.[11]

If information is not provided by a person with care or child applicant in Scotland, an application may be treated as withdrawn (see p42).

If a non-resident parent does not supply requested information, a default maintenance decision (or, in 'old rules' cases, an interim maintenance decision) may be made.

It is a criminal offence to fail to provide or knowingly provide false information. It is also an offence for a non-resident parent to fail to notify a change of address within seven days of that change.[12]

Someone who denies parentage of a child

Someone who denies parentage of a child named in a maintenance application can be required to give information *only* if it is needed:[13]
- to decide whether or not all the relevant persons are habitually resident in the UK and, therefore, whether the CSA has jurisdiction to make a calculation; *or*
- to identify a non-resident parent.

This means, for example, that if the CSA only wants to identify a person as the non-resident parent, employment details would not normally be necessary and so should not be requested until parentage is established.

Employers

The current or recent employer of the non-resident parent can be required to give information *only* if it is needed to:[14]
- identify a non-resident parent;
- trace a non-resident parent;
- calculate child maintenance;
- collect child support maintenance, interest or arrears of maintenance under a court order from the non-resident parent; *or*

- decide whether to pursue a garnishee or charging order (see Chapter 19).

An employer of an alleged parent can only be required to provide information to identify and trace that parent.[15]

The same rules apply where the employer is the Crown (eg, government departments).[16]

In 'old rules' cases, the parent with care's employer may also be required to provide information which is needed in order to make a maintenance assessment.[17]

Companies or partnerships

A company or partnership for whom a non-resident parent has had a contract for services may be required to provide information, but *only* if it is needed to:[18]
- trace a non-resident parent; *or*
- calculate child maintenance.

This means, for example, a self-employed IT consultant could be traced through companies for which he provides a service and his income investigated.

Accountants

The person who acts as the non-resident parent's accountant, or who has done so in the past, can be required to give information *only* where it is needed to:[19]
- trace a non-resident parent;
- calculate child maintenance;
- collect child support maintenance, interest or arrears, or maintenance under a court order from the non-resident parent; *or*
- decide whether to pursue a garnishee or charging order (see Chapter 19).

Court officials

The following court officials can be required to give information.[20] In **England and Wales:**
- the senior district judge of the High Court Family Division or, at a district registry, the district judge;
- the district judge of a county court, or the chief clerk or other officer who may be acting on her/his behalf;[21]
- the justice's chief executive for a magistrates' court.

In **Scotland:**
- the deputy principal clerk of the Court of Session;
- the sheriff clerk of a sheriff court.

Court officials can be required to give information *only* where there is, or has been, a court maintenance order, or an application for such an order has been made but not determined, and the information is needed to:[22]

- identify how much is payable under a court maintenance order;
- collect child support maintenance or maintenance under a court order;
- identify any proceedings about a court maintenance order;
- decide whether there is in force either a pre-April 1993 maintenance agreement (see p37) or a maintenance order made after 3 March 2003 which has been in force for a year; *or*
- decide, if there is more than one person with care, who has parental responsibility for the qualifying child.

Crown employees

Some Crown employees can be required to give information but *only* when it is needed to trace the non-resident parent.[23]

The Driver and Vehicle Licensing Agency

From 6 April 2008, in addition to requiring information needed to trace the non-resident parent, the CSA can request information from the Driver and Vehicle Licensing Agency needed to collect and enforce maintenance payments.[24]

Government benefit departments

Any Department for Work and Pensions agency may give information held for benefits purposes to the CSA.[25]

Local authorities

Local authorities may be required to give information but *only* if it is needed to:[26]
- decide whether there is a qualifying child, non-resident parent or person with care in relation to an application;
- identify a non-resident parent;
- trace a non-resident parent;
- calculate child maintenance;
- collect child support maintenance, interest or arrears or maintenance under a court order from the non-resident parent; *or*
- decide whether to pursue a garnishee or charging order (see Chapter 19).

This applies only to the local authority for the area where one or more of the following resides or used to reside:
- the person with care;
- the non-resident parent;
- the parent treated as non-resident;
- the alleged non-resident parent; *or*
- in Scotland, a child applicant.

This means the CSA may require a local authority to give information concerning housing benefit or council tax benefit – eg, the parent's bank account details if s/he pays by direct debit.[27]

HM Revenue and Customs

HM Revenue and Customs (the Revenue) can be required to disclose the current address or details of the current employer of a non-resident parent.[28] If the parent is self-employed, this also includes details of the taxable profits, gross receipts and expenses.[29] Any information disclosed must not go any further than authorised CSA staff, unless it is about civil or criminal proceedings under the Child Support Act 1991. However, where information is obtained under the Social Security Administration Act 1992, no such restriction applies. Information may also be obtained under the Tax Credits Act 2002.[30] It is unlawful for the Revenue to give the CSA any other information.[31]

In its 2006-2009 Operational Improvement Plan, the CSA stated that in the future it will work more closely with the Revenue to trace non-resident parents and make more use of information held by the Revenue to locate non-resident parents who owe maintenance.[32]

Credit reference agencies

The CSA can require information from credit reference agencies,[33] but only to enable:
- a non-resident parent to be identified or traced;
- an assessment of the non-resident parent's 'financial standing' to be made in order to predict his likely level of compliance;
- an amount of overpaid child maintenance to be recovered;
- from 6 April 2008, maintenance payments to be collected and enforced.[34]

Deposit takers

From 6 April 2008, the CSA can require 'deposit takers' (eg, a bank) to provide information needed to to trace the non-resident parent and to collect and enforce maintenance payments.[35]

Gas and electricity providers

Gas and electricity suppliers to the non-resident parent must disclose information if and when requested by the CSA.[36]

When information must be supplied

If information is requested to make an effective application from the person who has made it (eg, by the re-issue of a child maintenance application or maintenance administration form or request for further information) the information must be supplied in 14 days in order to ensure that the application is treated as made on the earliest date (ie, as if the initial application had been effective).[37] The CSA can allow information to be provided by a later date if it is satisfied that the delay was unavoidable.

No deadline is specified for providing information in other circumstances, only that it must be provided as soon as reasonably practicable in the circumstances.[38] It appears that in practice, the CSA allows seven days when making a calculation and one month for a revision/supersession.[39] The decision maker can allow longer if it is appropriate to do so. See p7 for when a document is treated as sent and received.

Failing to provide and providing false information

If a person fails to provide information there are a range of consequences s/he will face.
- The application may not be processed (see p42).
- If he is a non-resident parent, a default maintenance calculation may be made.
- A criminal fine of £1,000 may be imposed.[40]

A person charged with an offence of failing to provide information may be able to avoid conviction if there is a good reason why the information cannot be provided.[41] However, a non-resident parent who fails to return a child maintenance enquiry form or provide information may have both a default maintenance decision and a fine imposed. This also means that if a non-resident parent makes an application and the parent with care fails to provide information she can be fined, though this would be extremely rare.

If the person knowingly provides false information, or allows it to be provided, this is also a criminal offence.[42] The CSA can go to court and a fine of up to £1,000 can be imposed. This is paid to the court, not the CSA.

The CSA must notify the person that it is a criminal offence to refuse to supply, or knowingly supply false, information.[43] All forms and requests issued contain this notification to ensure the fine may be pursued.

If a parent fails to give information, the CSA may ask another person for that information – eg, a parent's employer or accountant. As they are required to give information, the criminal sanctions apply. This gives the CSA greater powers to investigate and pursue other sources of information. The CSA had been criticised in the past for failing to seek information from other sources when the parent did not return a form despite reminders,[44] but the legislation has now been amended to allow the CSA to obtain details of self-employed earnings from the Revenue (see p56).

Change of address

The non-resident parent has a duty to notify the CSA if and when he changes his address. This must be done within seven days of the change.[45]

Disputing the information required

If the CSA/Jobcentre Plus requires information:
- not relevant to the reason for the request;
- of a very different kind from the examples given in the regulations;
- from a person who cannot be required to give it; *or*

• despite having sufficient information to make a full calculation,

the request should be queried. If the CSA/Jobcentre Plus insists, a challenge should be considered (see p352).

If a person in this situation refuses to give information in order to avoid a penalty, s/he should explain that decision, preferably in writing. A complaint could also be made (see p439).

2. **Contacting the non-resident parent**

If the person with care has given the non-resident parent's telephone number and the non-resident parent is named on the birth certificate and is aware of the existence of the child, he is contacted by phone.[46] If the telephone number is not known, a child maintenance enquiry form may be issued (see p60). The date of contact is the date liability for child maintenance usually starts – this is known as the 'effective date' (see p341). In some cases there have been long delays in setting the effective date and the person with care could be owed compensation.[47]

Tracing the non-resident parent

The Child Support Agency (CSA) can use its information-seeking powers to identify and trace the non-resident parent. Only those people and agencies listed on pp53-56 can be required to provide information. CSA staff are advised to use the following sources of information when tracing a non-resident parent:[48]

• the applicant;
• another party;
• the telephone directory or directory enquiries;
• the Departmental Central Index (DCI) – this Department for Work and Pensions (DWP) computer network gives access to national insurance and DWP records;[49]
• the Common Enquiry Service – this gives access to other DWP computer systems, such as those for income support (IS) and jobseeker's allowance (JSA);[50]
• HM Revenue and Customs – for the address of a current employer (see p56);[51]
• the National Insurance Contributions Office, if the non-resident parent is employed or self-employed;[52]
• the army, navy, airforce or Ministry of Defence if the non-resident parent is serving in, or has recently been discharged from, the forces;[53]
• the Prisoner Location Service, Scottish Prison Service, Northern Ireland Prison Service;[54]
• employers, past and present.[55] If the employer does not supply the information, a warning will be given about the possibility of criminal charges, and if other

ways of obtaining the information have been exhausted, an inspector may be appointed;[56]

- local authorities – this method may only be used after attempts have been made to gather information from the non-resident parent;[57]
- DVLA/DVLNI – this method may only be used where all else has failed and there are special procedures for referring enquiries;[58]
- credit reference agencies (see p56);
- deposit takers (eg, a bank) (see p56);
- gas and electricity suppliers.

Finding a confident address

An address is usually considered confident if the information on the DCI matches exactly the non-resident parent's full name, date of birth and that address, and there is no information which suggests that the non-resident parent is not living there.[59] However, in terms of establishing an effective date for a maintenance calculation, an address does not have to be certain beyond all reasonable doubt (see p331). If the DCI gives the non-resident parent the same address as the person with care, this is not considered confident.

Information from the person with care

If the person with care has not given an address for the non-resident parent, she is contacted by telephone (or if this is not possible, by letter) and, if she does not know the address, she is asked to give any information that could help trace the non-resident parent. This could include:

- middle name(s) and any other names by which he may be known;
- other addresses at which he may have lived;
- his place of work and any previous employers;
- the name and address of his accountant;
- any benefit claims made; *and*
- if he has a car, the registration or make, model, colour and other details.

In addition, a face-to-face interview may be arranged. At this, the person with care may be asked to confirm a potential address or provide further information to allow a trace to be made. A parent may be asked to give a recent photograph of the non-resident parent where DNA testing may be involved. She is asked to bring any relevant documents, such as a marriage certificate or expired passport, and is warned that the CSA may contact friends and relatives with whom the non-resident parent may be living. The CSA must preserve confidentiality where this occurs and should not disclose the CSA's interest.

At the interview the person with care could be asked other detailed questions – eg, whether the non-resident parent ever lived with the person with care. Contact with these parents by the CSA is only likely where additional trace action is required – eg, to obtain details of the non-resident parent's car or where parentage is disputed.

Initial contact with the non-resident parent

Once an effective application (see p41) has been made, the CSA must give notice of that to any person(s) with care, the non-resident parent and any person treated as a non-resident parent, other than the applicant, as soon as reasonably practical.[60] The CSA may attempt to phone a non-resident parent to notify him of the application and gather information. If it is not possible to phone and the non-resident parent is aware of the child, a child maintenance enquiry form may be issued. If the parent is unaware of the child or not named on the birth certificate, the CSA will try to arrange a face-to-face interview.

There are special rules for young non-resident parents (see p62).

During the initial phone call, information will be checked to confirm the identity of the individual before proceeding.[61] The non-resident parent may be asked questions to confirm jurisdiction and whether he accepts parentage. He may also be asked to confirm any information needed to make a maintenance calculation.

The non-resident parent should be warned that a default maintenance decision may be issued if he fails to provide sufficient information to make a calculation. At various stages he will be given the opportunity to provide more information and be given a time limit of at least seven days in which to provide it.

The child maintenance enquiry form

The CSA intends that all, or most, of the information needed to work out maintenance will be provided or collected over the phone. This means a child maintenance enquiry form will only be issued when the non-resident parent requests it or if he has not co-operated. If the non-resident parent does not know he is an alleged non-resident parent, a face-to-face interview should be arranged.

In simple terms, a form cannot be issued unless:
- a 'confident' address for the non-resident parent is established (see p59);
- an alleged non-resident parent is aware that he is considered to be the father of the child;
- an alleged non-resident parent is at least 16 years old, or under 19 and still treated as a child (however, a statement of paternity is still sought in these cases – see p62).

When a child maintenance enquiry form is issued the parent is usually allowed seven to 14 days to return it, depending on what stage of the procedure has been reached. The CSA may only allow seven days or phone the parent after this period of time to check when the information will be returned.

Even where a form is issued the non-resident parent may instead choose to phone with the information.

Any notice sent to a non-resident parent must tell him the effective date (see p341) of any calculation to be made, and inform him about default maintenance decisions (see p326).[62]

The maintenance enquiry form asks for information on:

- personal details – name, address, other names used, phone number (work and mobile), national insurance number, date of birth, best contact times;
- whether he accepts paternity for all, or some, of the qualifying children named;
- any IS/income-based JSA, income-related employment and support allowance or pension credit being claimed by or for him;
- student details if appropriate – ie, college, course, qualification, full- or part-time status (evidence is requested);
- child(ren) who live with him – ie, date of birth, national insurance number (if appropriate), who gets child benefit for the child (evidence is requested);
- details of any shared care, average per week and any other special arrangements;
- employment details – title, employer (name, address and phone number), start and end dates (if appropriate);
- income details – frequency of pay, gross pay, bonus, expenses (pay slips are requested);
- self-assessment form or tax calculation notice if the parent is self-employed;
- tax credits in payment;
- other income – eg, pension;
- other payments made to a personal or private pension;
- collection details – when the CSA wants to collect, bank details such as account number and sort code. Direct debit is the preferred method but standing order, deductions from wages, transcash or bank giro credit are also available;
- representative details, name address, phone number and best contact times (signed authorisation is needed in certain circumstances).

The form may also ask for further information. The non-resident parent will have to sign a declaration and parents are informed that failure to provide the information requested or knowingly to provide false information is a criminal offence (see p57).

Information given can be amended at any time before a calculation is made, but not about changes after the effective date.[63] For changes after the effective date, supersession should be sought.

If the form is returned fully completed and no indication is made that paternity is denied, the CSA assumes that the alleged non-resident parent accepts paternity. If a parent disputes that he is non-resident and maintains that he has day-to-day care of the child (see p20), this is not a proper reason for refusing to return the form (this decision was made in reference to the 'old rules' maintenance enquiry form but would equally apply under the 'new rules').[64]

Young non-resident parents

It is understood that a face-to-face interview will be arranged with a young non-resident parent – ie, one under 16 years of age or between 16 and 19 but still treated as a child. He will be asked to confirm parentage, but no calculation can be made until he ceases to be treated as a child. An adult must be present at the interview.

If the non-resident parent is between 16 and 19 and no child benefit is being paid for him, a series of questions will be asked to establish if he is a child. He can be classed as a child if he is:

- in full-time non-advanced education;
- registered for work or work-based training for young people; *or*
- working temporarily for 24 hours or more a week, due to end before the terminal date for child benefit (see p18).

The young person is no longer treated as a child, if he is under 18 and:

- in employment after the terminal date;
- in work-based training (Skillseekers in Scotland); *or*
- on IS, income-based JSA or income-related ESA.

3. **Parentage investigations**

Where parentage is denied, a maintenance application cannot be decided unless the Child Support Agency (CSA) can assume parentage (see p15). In the vast majority of cases, it will be a non-resident father who is disputing paternity. Paternity is also investigated where there is some doubt about it (eg, more than one possible father is named).

Paternity investigations can take place before or after the calculation. For example, an alleged non-resident parent may deny paternity on the initial phone contact or on a child maintenance enquiry form (see p60). The dispute can be about one or all of the qualifying children. The CSA can proceed with the calculation, or collection in post-calculation cases, for those children for whom paternity is accepted or assumed while investigations are taking place for others. Once a calculation has been made, the person named as the non-resident parent of the child will have to pay maintenance until he provides conclusive evidence that he is not.[65]

In pre-calculation cases if a presumption of parentage cannot be made, the CSA cannot make a calculation until paternity has been resolved. For details of when paternity may be assumed see p15. The CSA will carry out investigations to determine if paternity may be assumed or established. This may involve interviewing both the non-resident parent and person with care; it may also include interviewing the other parent if s/he is not a person with care. The CSA may seek a DNA test or court action to establish paternity (though this is unlikely, given the presumptions and consequences of failure to take DNA tests). Court action may also be pursued by the person with care or alleged non-resident parent at any time.

In post-calculation cases the non-resident parent may dispute paternity and seek a revision. If the decision is not revised, the non-resident parent may have to apply to court for a declaration/declarator of parentage. A decision to refuse to revise can be appealed, but paternity can only ultimately be established by the court.

If the non-resident parent disputes parentage, he will be asked to provide evidence.[66] It is not sufficient in post-calculation cases simply to deny paternity; evidence must be given to raise doubt – eg, the parent with care was having another relationship when the child was conceived. In all cases, documentary evidence is preferred. If the evidence is a previous negative DNA test or declaration/declarator of parentage, this will be sufficient proof.[67] The calculation will be cancelled and any payments made refunded. The person with care may be re-interviewed to identify another alleged non-resident parent.

Where a doubt is raised, the parent with care will be contacted by phone or in a face-to-face interview for her comments on the non-resident parent's evidence. If the parent with care:

- accepts that there may be doubt about paternity, a DNA test may be offered;
- disputes the non-resident parent's evidence, the decision will not be revised. The non-resident parent will be advised to obtain a DNA test or declaration/declarator of non-parentage; the CSA will not offer a DNA test in this case.[68] He will also be informed of his right to appeal to a court.

Interviews where parentage is disputed

Interviews can be carried out by phone or in person. Where paternity is denied after initial contact or the issue of a child maintenance enquiry form, the parent with care may be interviewed in order to establish the case to be put to the alleged non-resident parent. In other cases, sufficient information may already be available to contact the non-resident parent. However, both parties are interviewed before offering DNA tests (see p69) and, even if the parent with care has already been interviewed or paternity is assumed, she may be re-interviewed to see how she responds to the alleged non-resident parent's version of events. If the parent with care has already filled in a paternity statement she will only be re-interviewed if the alleged non-resident parent introduces new evidence.

In the case of a face-to-face interview, if the interviewee does not want to come to the local office or another local Jobcentre Plus office if that is closer, s/he can be interviewed at home or at a friend's or relative's house.

It is understood that, if the parent with care or alleged non-resident parent is under 16 (or under 19 and treated as a child), her/his parent or guardian must consent to the case progressing. The young person must have a face-to-face interview in the presence of a parent or guardian. A calculation is not made for a non-resident parent under 16 (or 16–19 and treated as a child), but a paternity statement is required for future use – ie, action is suspended until the young person ceases to be a child and then a calculation may be made.[69] Additional information may be sought about an alleged non-resident parent aged between 16 and 19 to determine whether or not he should be treated as a child – eg, details of his current education/training and (in 'old rules' cases only) his marital/civil partnership status.[70]

It is not compulsory to attend any interview, but see p53 for who can be required to provide what information.

Interview with an alleged non-resident parent

When the non-resident parent is unaware of the qualifying child, a face-to-face interview may be arranged to notify him of the application (see p63).

When paternity is denied, the alleged non-resident parent will be asked if he has documentary or verbal evidence that he is not the parent. At the time of writing, confirmation of the CSA's current procedure was not available. However, it is understood that the alleged non-resident parent's evidence is recorded word for word on a paternity statement.[71] The alleged non-resident parent may ask for further time to obtain documentary evidence; seven days are usually allowed.

If documentary evidence cannot be supplied, the person with care may be interviewed to gather her evidence. If no evidence can be provided to assume paternity, the case may progress to DNA testing.

CSA guidance suggests that a non-resident parent should be asked:[72]

- whether he was in the country at any time between the date of conception and the child's birth;
- whether he had sex with the mother and, if so, over what period of time;
- where conception was assisted, was he in agreement with the treatment;
- how long the relationship lasted and whether he lived with the woman as husband and wife;
- whether or not he has had any contact with the child(ren);
- his reasons for thinking that he is not the father; *and*
- any other information which might support his view.

These questions are in guidance only, so others may also be asked. The non-resident parent need only answer such questions if he denies paternity and the information is needed to decide if he is the father.

The alleged non-resident parent is sent information about disputing parentage and the reduced-cost DNA test (see p66) before the interview. At the interview the possibility of DNA testing will be explained and the alleged non-resident parent's agreement sought.[73] The alleged non-resident parent will be told that he will be responsible for the costs of the tests for the parent with care and child(ren), as well as his own, if he is found to be the father. He will also be told that if he is found not to be the father, he will be able to re-claim from the CSA any costs he has incurred. If the alleged non-resident parent states that he cannot afford to pay for the test, the CSA will pay. However, the fee will have to be paid back if the test shows that he is the parent of the child.[74]

If the alleged non-resident parent accepts paternity, a child maintenance form is completed at the interview.

Interviewing officers should take notes and details of the interview recorded, including any statement made by the non-resident parent.

If the non-resident parent does not attend an interview, the interviewing officer attempts to arrange another and, if he does not attend the second one, the officer considers a home visit or court action at this point.[75]

Interview with a parent with care

If someone has been named as the parent of a qualifying child and denies it, the CSA contacts the parent with care to tell her of this and explain the procedures which follow. The interview can be conducted by phone or, if the parent does not want to be interviewed in this way, in the office or at her home.

The parent with care is asked if she has documentary evidence from which the CSA could assume parentage – eg, birth or marriage certificate.[76] She is also questioned about her relationship with the alleged non-resident parent at the time of conception to establish whether he could be the father.

If no evidence can be provided to assume paternity, the parent with care is asked if she is willing to take a DNA test (see p66).

The CSA will enquire about the alleged relationship and the circumstances of conception and birth. The parent with care is likely to be asked very personal questions. For example, the officer may ask about:[77]

- the place the child was born and whether the pregnancy was full term;
- whether the man is named as the child's father on the birth certificate;
- the man's reaction to the pregnancy;
- whether she and the alleged non-resident parent ever lived together and, if so, when and where;
- whether she considered them to be a couple at the time the child was conceived;
- whether the alleged non-resident parent has ever acknowledged the child;
- whether the alleged non-resident parent has ever paid any maintenance;
- whether there is, or has been, any contact with his family;
- whether she has any letters or cards acknowledging the child, or witnesses to her association with the alleged non-resident parent;
- whether the child's conception was assisted and, if so, whether the man was in agreement with the treatment and gave notice of this;
- whether she has any photographs of him; *and*
- whether she is willing to give evidence in court.

If a person considers the question(s) inappropriate, she should ask the interviewer the point of them. If the interviewer insists, the person with care could ask to end the interview to consider whether to give the information requested. She can ask the interviewer to write down the questions and the reason for them. If, at the interview or later, she refuses to answer any of the questions, she should indicate that she has given all the information that is necessary to trace and identify the father.

The parent with care may also be asked to make a parentage statement, which is recorded word for word.[78] The parent can refuse to sign this and the refusal will form part of the evidence, along with any reasons she gives. The parent may ask for a copy of the parentage statement or reasons for failing to sign the statement. This statement is added to the report of the interview and can be used in court proceedings (see p69).

Interviewing a person with care who is not the mother

If both parents are non-resident and an alleged non-resident parent continues to deny paternity after an interview, the person with care may be interviewed.[79] The questions depend on the person with care's relationship with the alleged parents – eg, a mother or sister is likely to know the length of the relationship between the parents. She is asked for the addresses of both parents, and any letters or cards from them. She is also asked why she is looking after the child(ren), whether there is any documentation regarding the care arrangements and whether she gives her consent for the child(ren) in her care to undergo a DNA test (see below) if she has parental responsibility. A statement is prepared if the case is to go to court.[80]

DNA testing

DNA testing involves taking a cell sample from the parent with care, alleged non-resident parent and qualifying child. The test establishes the genetic fingerprint of the individual and is virtually conclusive. The test is usually done by taking a cheek cell sample, which is gathered from the inside of the mouth using a swab. It is possible for blood to be taken for the DNA test instead, but all parties must use the same method. Where young children are involved, a cheek cell sample will usually be preferred. The use of cheek cell samples means that a fear of needles could not be used as a reason not to take the test.

DNA testing is used in cases where parentage cannot be presumed and the parties involved give consent. In cases where the CSA has applied to court for a declaration/declarator of parentage the court may order DNA testing.

The CSA has special arrangements with a private testing agency called Cellmark[81] and reduced testing rates may apply. There are special rules that apply where the alleged non-resident parent wishes to arrange his own test.

Consent

If there is a dispute about parentage, both the parent with care and the alleged non-resident parent are asked to agree to a DNA test. Written consent must be obtained before a test can be made.[82] If the qualifying child is under 16 the parent or guardian must give consent.

Refusal to take the test will have consequences.

- Before 14 July 2008, if a parent with care on income support or income-based jobseeker's allowance refused to take the test herself, a reduced benefit decision may have been made.[83]
- If the parent accepts DNA testing for herself, but refuses her consent for the child, a court can direct DNA testing if it is in the best interests of the child, but it cannot force the child to take the test.[84]
- An alleged non-resident parent may be assumed to be the parent (see p15).[85]
- If a non-resident parent already assumed to be the parent refuses to take a test, the CSA will not revise the calculation.
- If an applicant refuses consent for herself and/or a qualifying child, the case may be closed.
- There is no guidance on when a parent or guardian of a child applicant in Scotland refuses consent, but DWP policy indicates that action may be taken to get a declaration/declarator of parentage.

The reason for any refusal must be explored. The DNA test now usually involves taking a cheek cell sample. This means that objections on medical or religious grounds which applied to blood tests may no longer be viable. A blood test can be offered as an alternative to the mouth swab. In this case, all the other parties will be tested in the same way.

If the alleged non-resident parent agrees to the test, but fails to attend the appointment, parentage will be assumed unless there are good reasons – eg, he was in hospital, did not receive test notification or was ill.

Paying for the DNA test

The CSA offers discounted tests to alleged non-resident parents who are prepared to take it in advance. These are known as voluntary cases.[86] The cost varies depending on the number of people tested. In the latest edition of the CSA's leaflet on disputed parentage and DNA testing, the fee for testing three people in voluntary cases is £215.69.[87] The alleged non-resident parent must agree to the results being passed to the CSA.

In cases where the court directs the DNA test to be taken, the non-discounted fee is charged. Rates vary according to the number of people tested. In the latest edition of the disputed parentage leaflet, the non-discounted cost of a test for three people is £281.05.

If the alleged non-resident parent is found not to be the parent, a full refund of the cost of the test is made, as long as the parent with care confirms that the photograph of the person who attended for the test is the person she named as the father.[88]

If the alleged non-resident parent says he cannot afford to pay for the test in advance, the CSA may pay for the test initially if the alleged non-resident parent agrees to accept the results and to repay the fee should the test show that he is the father. If the alleged non-resident parent still refuses to take the DNA test, parentage may be assumed (see p15).

The CSA can recover the costs of the test from the alleged non-resident parent if the test does not exclude him from being the parent and:[89]

- he does not now deny that he is the parent; *or*
- a court has now made a declaration that he is a parent (in Scotland, a declarator of parentage).

Private testing

An alleged non-resident parent may arrange the test himself either through Cellmark or another firm. In the meantime, the CSA may still assume parentage if the CSA test has been refused.[90] In this case there would be no discount or CSA non-discounted rate offered. Prices vary depending on which firm is used but are likely to be at least £400. This fee may not be refunded if the test proves negative.

The test must be carried out by an approved agency and proper security measures must be in place, otherwise even where the test is negative the CSA and court may not accept the result.

Tests must involve the mother; a test with only the alleged non-resident parent and the qualifying child will not be accepted. The CSA will not provide the address of the parent with care to the alleged non-resident parent or the independent testing company. If the parent with care does not consent to a private test no action can be taken against her.

DNA test results

Once the DNA-testing company has received all the samples, the test usually takes 10 days. The results are sent by post to the parent with care, the alleged non-resident parent and the CSA. The results are confidential and will not be given over the phone.[91]

If the alleged non-resident parent is shown to be the parent, he will also be sent notification by the CSA. The CSA will also contact the non-resident parent to gather any additional information needed, or a child maintenance enquiry form may be issued. (If a form has been issued earlier, the date of liability for child maintenance is the date of the first contact – see p341.) If the alleged non-resident parent still does not accept paternity, he will have to take court proceedings to obtain a declaration/declarator of non-parentage. The CSA may make a calculation or refuse to revise because a positive DNA test is grounds to assume parentage.

If the DNA tests confirm that the person who took the test as the alleged non-resident parent is not the father, action is taken to confirm that the identity of the person tested was the alleged non-resident parent. If this is not the case, the CSA will pass the case to the fraud team if the alleged non-resident parent sent someone else, or pursue further tracing if the wrong person has been traced. If the identity is confirmed, the parent with care may be re-interviewed about any other possible non-resident parent.[92]

Preparation for court proceedings

When all possible action and investigations have been completed, a CSA supervisor decides whether to apply to court for a declaration of parentage (in Scotland, declarator of parentage).[93] CSA guidance indicates that court action should be rare, given the increased grounds on which to assume parentage. Examples of situations where court action may be possible include:[94]

- a DNA test is inconclusive;
- cases involving fertility treatment where the alleged non-resident parent denies he gave notice of consent to the treatment;
- in post-calculation cases where the parent with care disputes the non-resident parent's non-conclusive evidence. In this instance, the non-resident parent must apply to court (the CSA may not be involved in this action but may be informed of the outcome).

If the CSA intends to take court action, a file is compiled detailing, for example, official documents (such as marriage certificates), interviews, statements, phone calls, correspondence, investigations and other documentary evidence, including exhibits such as a birthday card from the alleged non-resident parent to the child.[95]

If the CSA decides not to take court action, the person with care may initiate proceedings.[96] The parent with care or non-resident parent may raise court proceedings at any time.

If a case is to go to court, a proceedings file is prepared by the CSA.[97] A copy of the child's full birth certificate is obtained from the Registrar if the parent with care cannot supply one.[98] If the parent with care has mentioned potential witnesses (see p66) – eg, to confirm that she and the alleged non-resident parent were in a relationship at the time of the conception, a record is made of the witnesses' names and addresses.[99] In Scotland, two written witness statements must be obtained to attest to the sexual nature of the relationship, otherwise the case cannot proceed to court.[100] In Scotland, such files are referred to the solicitors' office at the Scottish Office (Office of the Solicitors to the Advocate General for Scotland) and, in England and Wales, to the solicitors' branch of the Department for Work and Pensions (DWP) (SolB2).[101] In England and Wales, unless the solicitor advises that the case should not go ahead, the application proceeds for a declaration of parentage that may be heard under lay representation. This means that a local CSA officer (known as the court presenting officer) presents the case to court.[102] If the case is complex or contentious a solicitor will be present. In Scotland, the solicitor presents the case.[103] Slightly different arrangements may be needed if the alleged non-resident parent is in Northern Ireland, or the case has been referred from Northern Ireland.

The hearings

The CSA *or* the person with care can apply to court for a declaration/declarator of parentage. However, if the CSA is willing to do so, the person with care should normally not also apply, because she would probably have to pay her own legal costs (and those of the alleged non-resident parent) if she loses (see p71). If the CSA suspends the case (see p69), but the person with care wants to go to court herself, she should consider taking legal advice.

The hearing normally takes place in the alleged non-resident parent's area, unless the alleged non-resident parent knows the parent with care's address or both parties and the court agree to it being held in the person with care's area.[104]

The first court hearing is known as a directions hearing (a similar preliminary hearing is heard by the sheriff in Scotland). This is an informal hearing where the parties produce the documentary evidence and the clerk to the court arranges procedure, including directions for DNA tests.[105] There is no legal obligation for the alleged non-resident parent and parent with care to attend. However, in England and Wales, if the alleged non-resident parent does not attend, the court may adjourn the hearing and ask the CSA (or, if it is her application, the parent with care) to serve notice of the hearing on him in person.

Only the courts have the power to order blood tests (including DNA tests – see p66) in any civil proceedings in which paternity is an issue.[106] If convinced that blood testing would be against the child's interests, the court should not order it.[107] A court can direct that blood tests be used to ascertain whether or not a party is excluded from being a parent of the child, but cannot force anyone to give a blood sample. It can, however, overrule a child's lack of consent if it believes it is in the child's interests.[108] However, the court may draw its own adverse inferences if a person fails to comply, depending on all the circumstances of the case.[109] Courts can only order DNA or blood testing if a party applies for it and agrees to pay. However, if that party wins the case, the court will usually order the losing party to pay costs, which can include the costs of any test. In Scotland, if an alleged non-resident parent applies for a declarator of non-parentage or illegitimacy and the CSA does not defend the action, no expenses can be awarded against the CSA.[110]

In England and Wales, if DNA tests have been directed, a second informal hearing is arranged with the clerk once the result is obtained. If it is negative, the CSA withdraws the case.[111] If the result is positive, and the alleged non-resident parent admits he is the father, a full hearing before the magistrates takes place, if possible, on the same day. In other cases, notice of a full hearing at a magistrates'/

sheriff's court is sent to all parties. The magistrates (or sheriff) then considers whether to make a declaration/declarator of parentage on the available evidence.

Outcome of the court proceedings

The CSA prioritises cases where a declaration/declarator of parentage is issued and, if no calculation has been made, telephones the non-resident parent to gather the information needed to make a calculation.[112] If the court finds that the person is not the parent, the parent with care is approached to establish if a different alleged non-resident parent can be named.[113] Unless the parent can name an alternate alleged non-resident parent, the case may be closed.

The court can order any party to pay some, or all, of the legal costs of another party. Usually, the losing party is ordered to pay the other parties' costs. However, an order for costs cannot normally be made against a party who is legally aided. In addition to the costs of any test, the CSA usually asks the court to order the losing party to pay towards its own presentation costs – eg, solicitors' fees and witnesses' costs.

4. **Further investigations**

The Child Support Agency (CSA) may make further enquiries when considering an application, revision or supersession. In practice, the CSA normally makes no further investigation where:

- parentage is accepted; *and*
- information is provided to make a calculation; *and*
- any documents requested are provided – eg, copy of maintenance agreement, payslips or tax calculation notice.

Even where one parent challenges the details provided by the other, the CSA may be reluctant to make any further enquiries unless the parent can provide evidence to trigger a revision/supersession. Enquiries are normally made by telephone, if possible.

The need for evidence

Corroboration of evidence – other evidence to support what the CSA already has – is not requested unless the evidence the CSA has is self-contradictory, improbable, or contradicted by other evidence.[114] For example, if a self-employed parent says s/he has not worked for six months, this is normally accepted without any written evidence.

Evidence includes documentary, written and oral information.[115] CSA staff are advised to weigh carefully any direct, indirect or hearsay evidence. CSA guidance says that hearsay evidence (ie, evidence from one person of what another person has told her/him, or of what s/he has read) is of limited value – eg, a report from a parent with care that a non-resident parent's earnings have increased by £20 a week may be sufficient evidence to consider a supersession, but insufficient on which to base a new calculation.[116] (In other words, some more reliable evidence would be needed before deciding what level of earnings to include in any superseding decision.)

Verifying information

Verification of housing costs (in 'old rules' cases) and earnings is routinely sought by the CSA.[117] However, if every effort to obtain verification of earnings has failed, the amounts provided are accepted as long as they are reasonable. Verification of benefits, other income and costs (the latter where needed to make an 'old rules' assessment) is only sought where the amounts appear to be disproportionate or there is another reason to doubt them.

Verification for CSA purposes is defined in guidance as evidence corroborating information already held.[118] CSA staff can request evidence in the form of formal documents and signed statements but should, wherever possible, collect information by phone and then seek written confirmation if necessary.[119]

Verification of earnings from a non-resident parent's employer is only requested if the employee cannot provide it (see p53).[120] A parent and any employer who fails to provide information when requested may be liable for criminal sanctions (see p57).

Self-employed earnings are usually taken from the self-assessment return to HM Revenue and Customs (the Revenue), or from a tax calculation notice.[121] If not supplied, attempts will be made to obtain the information through phone calls, accountants, companies or partnerships with or for whom the parent works, a face-to-face interview, an inspector's visit, or a request to the Revenue for self-assessment details where all other means to obtain the information have failed.[122] Criminal sanctions may apply if those required to provide information have failed to do so (see p54).

When the Child Support Agency does not investigate

In some cases, the CSA fails to investigate to the satisfaction of one party. This situation does not usually arise until the calculation is made because the parent with care is only then notified of the non-resident parent's income (see p328). If, at any stage, a person believes that the CSA ought to make more enquiries, the CSA should be asked to do so. The most effective way is to phone the CSA explaining all the information the person has, asking what enquiries have already been made and suggesting further enquiries. Reference should be made to the CSA's power to require information (see p50) and use an inspector to conduct investigations (see p73). If the CSA refuses to say what steps have been taken or to make further enquiries, judicial review may be possible (see p353). The First-tier Tribunal can make enquiries as soon as an appeal is made (see p369). It has more powers than the CSA and it may be easier to persuade it to use them.

A person who is dissatisfied with CSA enquiries can also make her/his own enquiries and pass the information to the CSA – eg, a person with care applying for a court order for spousal or civil partner maintenance (see p30) may obtain information about the non-resident parent's income.

The inspectors

The CSA can appoint inspectors to obtain information required.[123] The inspectors are permanently appointed and are not tied to investigations on a specific case.[124] The inspector must have a certificate of appointment, which must be produced when entering premises.[125]

If an office in Great Britain needs to appoint an inspector in Northern Ireland, or the other way around, an inspector can be appointed in the other territory.[126]

Powers of inspectors

Inspectors have the power to enter premises (except those used only as a home),[127] to make enquiries and to inspect documents.[128] Premises can include vehicles, aircraft, moveable structures and offshore installations.[129] The power to enter premises does not include any power to enter by force. Premises include ones where:[130]
- the non-resident parent is, or has been, employed;
- the non-resident parent carries out, or has carried out, a trade;
- there is information held by someone whom the inspector has reasonable grounds for suspecting has information about the non-resident parent acquired in the course of her/his own trade, profession, vocation or business.

An inspector can question any person aged 18 or over found on the premises s/he has entered[131] and request all such information and documents s/he might reasonably require from:[132]
- an occupier of the premises;
- an employer or employee working there;
- anyone else whose work or business is based at those premises;
- an employee or agent of any of the above.

An inspector can enter Crown premises in order to obtain information as long as the Queen is not in residence. Crown employees or anyone carrying out Crown functions on the premises can be questioned and asked for information in the same way as anyone else.[133]

No person is required to give any evidence or answer any question that might incriminate her/him or her/his spouse or civil partner.[134] Deliberately delaying or obstructing an inspector carrying out her/his duties is an offence. Failing or refusing to answer a question or to provide evidence requested is also an offence, unless there is a good reason for not doing so.[135] The maximum fine is £1,000.[136]

A solicitor is entitled to claim privilege as regards information about a client's confidential affairs and can refuse to give information. Also, the CSA has given assurances that the powers of inspectors will not be used in relation to other representatives, except where information is required from an employer about an employee.

There are clear directions in CSA guidance regarding further investigations if fraud or misrepresentation is suspected.[137]

5. **Duty to disclose changes**

There is no general duty to volunteer information about any change of circumstances to the Child Support Agency (CSA), except if the non-resident parent changes his address.[138]

However, a person with care has a duty to tell the CSA if she believes that a calculation has ceased to have effect because:[139]

- the person with care, non-resident parent or qualifying child has died;
- the person with care, non-resident parent or qualifying child is no longer within CSA jurisdiction – ie, habitually resident in the UK or working for a relevant employer and treated as habitually resident (see p26);
- the non-resident parent is no longer a non-resident parent of the child or, if there is more than one, all the children named in the calculation – eg, because the child has been adopted;
- a child no longer counts as a child, or as a qualifying child (see p18); *or*
- she has stopped being a person with care in relation to the child or, if there is more than one, all the children named in the calculation.

The person with care is required to give the reasons for her belief in writing. She may be required to give further information for a decision to be made.

The person with care is not required to inform the CSA until the change has taken place. There is no duty to disclose information to the CSA except in the circumstances described above and where the CSA has the right to request the information – eg, a non-resident parent does not have to disclose a change of income. This is different from the position for social security claims, where there is a continuing duty to disclose any relevant change.

For the effect of not disclosing information, see p57.

6. Disclosure of information by the Child Support Agency

In the course of their investigations, Child Support Agency (CSA) staff collect information and evidence about people affected by maintenance applications. Some forms of disclosure are part of the CSA's duties, such as giving information to courts, the First-tier Tribunal, the Department for Work and Pensions (DWP) or local authorities. Each party to a maintenance calculation must be given details of how the calculation has been worked out (see p328). The CSA may disclose information given to it by one party to another party to explain:[140]

- why an application for child maintenance or for revision or supersession has been rejected; *or*
- why an application cannot proceed or why a calculation will not be made; *or*
- why a calculation is cancelled or ceases to have effect; *or*
- how a calculation has been worked out; *or*
- why a decision has been made not to arrange for, or to stop, collection of child maintenance; *or*
- why a particular method of enforcement has been used; *or*
- why a decision has been made not to use or to stop using a deduction from earnings order (see p416) or a liability order (see p416).

The parties to an assessment are the person with care, the non-resident parent and a child applicant in Scotland. If one of those people has died, a person appointed to represent that person or a personal representative handling a revision/supersession or appeal is also a party.[141] Any request for the above information must be made in writing to the CSA, giving reasons, but the CSA can provide the information without a request.[142]

The CSA must not disclose a person's address or other information which could reasonably be expected to lead to that person being located. This disclosure can only be made when the person concerned has given written permission. (This may not apply where a case is appealed – see p369.[143]) Also, the CSA must not disclose information which could reasonably be expected to lead to the identification of any person other than a person with care, non-resident parent, person treated as non-resident or qualifying child.[144]

The CSA can disclose any information it has to the First-tier Tribunal, court and, in 'new rules' cases, to anyone with a right of appeal, if it is for proceedings under the child support or benefits legislation.[145] In practice, in a child support appeal, CSA papers are included in the CSA submission sent to each party (see Chapter 18). The CSA can also disclose information to a court which has made, varied or revived a maintenance order or agreement if that information is required in relation to those proceedings or other matters arising from them.[146] The CSA can also disclose information it has to local authorities for their use in administering housing benefit or council tax benefit.[147] Otherwise, information cannot be given to third parties without the written permission of the person to whom it relates (see below). Any unauthorised disclosure of information is a criminal offence (see below).

Anyone wishing to see a copy of the information on her/him held electronically by the CSA can apply in writing. Under the Data Protection Act 1984 this information must be supplied within 40 days. If anyone has concerns about the collection, retention, accuracy or use of this information, the Data Protection Registrar can be contacted.

Disclosure to other government departments

The CSA can disclose information to government departments dealing with benefits, including the DWP agencies.[148] This includes information obtained by using CSA powers or disclosed to the CSA voluntarily.

As the DWP has close links with the Home Office, disclosure may create problems for people from abroad, in particular possible illegal entrants and those subject to the public funds requirement. If there are any doubts about whether information ought to be disclosed to the CSA, you should get advice first from a law centre or independent advice centre dealing with immigration problems (see Appendix 4). You cannot be prosecuted for refusing to give information unless it was requested by the CSA or an inspector (see p73).

CSA staff can exchange information with their counterparts in Northern Ireland and *vice versa*. Once disclosed, the information is subject to local rules about unauthorised disclosure.[149]

Unauthorised disclosure

Unauthorised disclosure of information is a criminal offence. This offence applies to anyone who is or has been a child support officer, a CSA employee, a civil servant carrying out a function under the Child Support Acts (eg, a Jobcentre Plus officer helping the CSA make enquiries), First-tier Tribunal staff, various ombudsmen and their staff, staff at the National Audit Office, those employed as a member of a Child Maintenance Enforcement Commission committee or sub-committee[150] and anyone who, whether or not a civil servant, is providing services to the DWP.[151] It does not apply to members of the First-tier and Upper Tribunals.

It is not an offence to disclose information if:[152]

- the CSA can do so under the disclosure regulations;
- the CSA has already done so under those regulations;
- it is in the form of a summary or statistics and it cannot be related to any particular person; *or*
- the person to whom the information relates gives consent or, if that person's affairs are being dealt with under a power of attorney, by a receiver under the

Mental Health Act, a mental health appointee or a Scottish mental health custodian, the attorney, receiver, custodian or appointee gives consent.

A person who has broken these rules would have a defence if s/he could prove that s/he believed s/he was making the disclosure under these rules, or believed that disclosure under these rules had already been made, and had no reason to think otherwise.[153]

On summary conviction (ie, where a case proceeds without a trial), the maximum prison sentence is six months and the maximum fine is £5,000. On conviction or indictment, the maximum prison sentence is two years.[154] No prosecutions have been brought.

Disclosure of information about spent convictions, other than as part of an official duty, is also a criminal offence.[155]

Notes

1. Information-seeking powers

1 s14 and Sch 2 CSA 1991
2 s12 CSPSSA 2000
3 ss4(4), 6(9) and 7(5) CSA 1991
4 Reg 3(1A) CS(IED) Regs
5 Reg 3(1) CS(IED) Regs ; reg 2 CS(MA) Regs 2006; reg 2 CS(MA) Regs 2008
6 Reg 3(1A) CS(IED) Regs
7 Reg 3(2) CS(IED) Regs
8 Reg 3(2) CS(IED) Regs before amendment by CS(IEDMAJ)(A) Regs
9 Reg 2(1) CS(IED) Regs
10 *Purdew v Seress-Smith* [1992] 23 September 1992 (QBD)
11 Regs 1(2) and 2(2)(a) CS(IED) Regs
12 Reg 9 The Child Support Information Regulations 2008 No.2551
13 Reg 2(2)(b) CS(IED) Regs
14 Reg 2(2)(c) CS(IED) Regs
15 Reg 2(2)(ba) CS(IED) Regs
16 Reg 2(2)(cc) and (cd) CS(IED) Regs
17 Reg 2(2) CS(IED) Regs before amendment by CS(IEDMAJ)(A) Regs
18 Reg 2(2)(g) CS(IED) Regs
19 Reg 2(2)(f) CS(IED) Regs
20 Reg 2(3) CS(IED) Regs
21 Order 1 r3 CCR 1981
22 Reg 2(2)(e) CS(IED) Regs
23 Reg 2(2)(h) CS(IED) Regs

24 Reg 2 CS(MA) Regs
25 See s3 SSA 1998
26 Regs 2(2)(d) and 3(1)(a) CS(IED) Regs
27 s122D SSAA 1992
28 Sch 2 para 1 CSA 1991
29 Reg 3(2)(h) CS(IED) Regs
30 Sch 5 TCA 2002
31 s6 and Sch 1 Taxes Management Act 1970; s182 Finance Act 1989
32 CSA Operational Improvement Plan 2006-2009
33 Reg 2(h) CS(MCP) Regs; credit reference agencies are as defined by s145(8) Consumer Credit Act 1974
34 Reg 2 CS(MA) Regs
35 Reg 2 CS(MA) Regs
36 Reg 4(j) and (k) The Child Support Information Regulations 2008 No.2551
37 Reg 3(4) CS(MCP) Regs
38 Reg 5(1) CS(IED) Regs
39 PG, Gather Information and Evidence, Evidence Timescales
40 s14A CSA 1991
41 s14A(4) CSA 1991
42 s14A CSA 1991
43 Reg 3A CS(IED) Regs

44 CCS/16535/1996 reported as R(CS) 2/98; CCS/12686/1996 reported as R(CS) 8/98

45 Reg 9 The Child Support Information Regulations 2008 No.2551

2. Contacting the non-resident parent

46 PG, Inform NRP of Application, Contacting the NRP for the First Time

47 CSA Operational Improvement Plan 2006-2009

48 PG, Specialist Areas, Basic Trace; Additional Trace

49 PG, Specialist Areas, DCI

50 PG, Specialist Areas, CES (Common Enquiry Screen)

51 PG, Specialist Areas, Inland Revenue

52 PG, Specialist Areas, NICO National Insurance Contributions Office

53 PG, Specialist Areas, Where the Employer is the Ministry of Defence

54 PG, Specialist Areas, Prison Service; Prison Addresses in Northern Ireland

55 PG, Specialist Areas, Employers

56 PG, Specialist Areas, Referring Case to Child Support Agency Inspector

57 PG, Specialist Areas, Local Authorities

58 PG, Specialist Areas, DVLA/DVLNI

59 PG, Specialist Areas, Fast Trace

60 Regs 1(2) and 5(1) CS(MCP) Regs

61 PG, Inform NRP of Application, Contacting NRP for First Time

62 Reg 5(2) CS(MCP) Regs

63 Reg 5(3) and (4) CS(MCP) Regs

64 R(CS) 8/98

3. Parentage investigations

65 *What Happens if Someone Denies They Are the Parent of a Child?* CSL304, October 2008

66 s26 CSA 1991

67 *What Happens if Someone Denies They Are the Parent of a Child?* CSL304, October 2008

68 s26 CSA 1991

69 PG, Inform NPR of Application, NRP Under 16; NRP Between 16 & 19 Years

70 PG, Inform NRP of Application, ANRP Child Details

71 PG, Specialist Areas, Gathering ANRP's Statement

72 PatG, Chapter 3, para 175(1)

73 PatG, Chapter 3, para 175(2)

74 *What Happens if Someone Denies They Are the Parent of a Child?* CSL304, October 2008

75 PatG, Chapter 4, para 162

76 PatG, Chapter 2, para 141

77 PatG, Chapter 2, para 141

78 PG, Specialist Areas, Parentage Statement

79 PatG, Appendix 4

80 PatG, Appendix 4

81 *What Happens if Someone Denies They Are the Parent of a Child?* CSL304, October 2008

82 PG, Specialist Areas, Consent for DNA Test

83 s46 CSA 1991

84 PG, Specialist Areas, PWC Refuses DNA Test for the QC

85 s26 CSA 1991, Case A3(b),

86 PG, Specialist Areas, DNA Test Referral

87 *What Happens if Someone Denies They Are the Parent of a Child?* CSL304, October 2008

88 *What Happens if Someone Denies They Are the Parent of a Child?* CSL304, October 2008

89 s27A CSA 1991

90 *What Happens if Someone Denies They Are the Parent of a Child?* CSL304, October 2008

91 *What Happens if Someone Denies They Are the Parent of a Child?* CSL304, October 2008

92 Paternity Guide, Chapter 6, para 210

93 s27 CSA 1991; PG, Specialist Areas, Court Action

94 PG, Specialist Areas, Court Action

95 PG, Specialist Areas, Gathering the Evidence for Court Proceedings

96 s27 CSA 1991

97 PG, Specialist Areas, Preparing the Case for Court Proceedings (separate guidance for England and Wales, and Scotland)

98 PG, Specialist Areas, Obtaining Birth Certificates

99 PG, Specialist Areas, Preparing the Case for Court Proceedings (England and Wales)

100 PG, Specialist Areas, Preparing the Case for Court Proceedings (Scotland)

101 PG, Specialist Areas, Authorising Court Proceedings (separate guidance for England and Wales, and for Scotland)

102 PG, Specialist Areas, Lay Representation (England and Wales)

103 PG, Specialist Areas, Authorising Court Proceedings (Scotland)

104 PG, Specialist Areas, Authorising Court Proceedings (separate guidance for England and Wales, and Scotland)

105 PG, Specialist Areas, Directions Hearing (England and Wales)

106 s20 FLRA 1969; *Re H (Paternity: Blood Test)* [1996] 2 FLR 65
107 *W v Official Solicitor* [1972] AC 24
108 s21 FLRA 1969
109 s23 FLRA 1969; *Re A (Paternity: Refusal of Blood Test)* [1994] 2 FLR 463
110 s28(2) CSA 1991; s7 LR(PC)(S)A 1986; r152 AS(CSA) (AOCSCR)
111 PG, Specialist Areas, Second Directions Hearing – DNA Cases Only (England and Wales)
112 PG, Specialist Areas, ANRP Declared to be the Parent
113 PatG, Chapter 17, para 121

4. Further investigations
114 PG, Gather Information and Evidence, Corroboration of Evidence; Self-contradictory Evidence; Uncorroborated Evidence
115 PG, Gather Information and Evidence, Types of Evidence
116 PG, Gather Information and Evidence, Hearsay Evidence
117 PG, Gather Information and Evidence, Verification Requirements; Evidence of Earnings and Income
118 PG, Gather Information and Evidence, Evidence and Verification
119 PG, Gather Information and Evidence, Collecting Evidence; Obtaining Further Evidence
120 PG, Gather Information and Evidence, Collecting Evidence
121 PG, Gather Information and Evidence, Treatment of Self-employed Earnings
122 PG, Gather Information and Evidence, Approaching Inland Revenue for Self-employed Income
123 s15(1) CSA 1991
124 PG, Gather Information and Evidence, Use of Inspectors
125 s15(8) CSA 1991
126 Sch 1 para 8 CS(NIRA) Regs
127 s14(4A) CSA 1991
128 s15(4) CSA 1991
129 s15(11) CSA 1991
130 s15(4A) CSA 1991
131 s15(5) CSA 1991
132 s15(6) CSA 1991
133 s57 CSA 1991; reg 7 CS(IED) Regs
134 s15(7) CSA 1991
135 s15(9) CSA 1991
136 s15(9) CSA 1991
137 PG, Specialist Areas, Criminal Compliance

5. Duty to disclose changes
138 Reg 9 The Child Support Information Regulations 2008 No.2551
139 Reg 6 CS(IED) Regs; ss44 and 55 and Sch 1 para 16 CSA 1991

6. Disclosure of information by the Child Support Agency
140 Reg 9A(1) CS(IED) Regs
141 Reg 9A(2) CS(IED) Regs
142 Reg 9A(3) CS(IED) Regs
143 r19(3) TP(FT) Rules
144 Reg 9A(4) CS(IED) Regs
145 Reg 8(1) and (2) CS(IED) Regs
146 Reg 8(3) CS(IED) Regs
147 s3 SSA 1998; PG, Gather Information and Evidence, Disclosure
148 s3 SSA 1998
149 Sch 1 para 7 CS(NIRA) Regs
150 Reg 14 CS(IED) Regs
151 s50 CSA 1991; reg 11 CS(IED) Regs
152 s50 CSA 1991
153 s50(3) CSA 1991
154 s50(4) CSA 1991
155 s9 Rehabilitation of Offenders Act 1974

Part 3

Amount of maintenance: 'new rules'

Chapter 5

The maintenance calculation ('new rules')

This chapter covers:
1. Maintenance calculation rates (below)
2. Net income (p90)
3. Shared care (p97)

1. Maintenance calculation rates

To carry out a child maintenance calculation the following information is needed:[1]
- the number of qualifying children;
- the number of relevant other children (see p23);
- the number of any relevant non-resident children (see p89);
- the number of persons with care;
- benefits (if any) received by the non-resident parent;
- whether the non-resident parent meets the conditions for the nil rate (see p85);
- the income of the non-resident parent (see p90);
- the number of nights (if any) that the non-resident parent has care of a qualifying child (see p101);
- the number of nights (if any) that a local authority has care of a qualifying child (see p103).

If a non-resident parent fails to provide sufficient information to calculate child support maintenance, a default maintenance decision may be made (see p326). A penalty for failing to provide information may also be imposed (see p57).

There are four rates of child support maintenance that can be applied:
- nil rate (see p85);
- flat rate (see p85);
- reduced rate (see p86);
- basic rate (see p88).

Child support maintenance will be calculated for each non-resident parent separately. This means a person with care may receive the flat rate of maintenance from one non-resident parent and an amount from the other non-resident parent worked out using the basic rate.

In all cases, the amount of child maintenance calculated is a weekly amount.[2] Rounding rules apply to the different rates as follows.[3]

- In basic rate and reduced rate cases, fractions of a pound are disregarded if less than half or rounded up to the next pound if a half or over.
- In all other cases, fractions of a penny are disregarded if less than a half or rounded up to the next penny if a half or over – ie, where there is apportionment or shared care.

There is a maximum amount of income which can be taken into account for maintenance purposes (see p97).

Future changes

In 2011 or later, a new child maintenance calculation will be introduced. The amount payable will be fixed for a year and based on the non-resident parent's yearly gross income (before tax and national insurance), using the latest available tax year information from HM Revenue and Customs. As the new calculation will be based on gross rather than net income, the percentage of income the non-resident parent will be expected to pay is lower. If the non-resident parent's income is below £800 a week, the rates will be:

– 12 per cent gross income for one child;

– 16 per cent for two children; *and*

– 19 per cent for three or more children.

If his income is over £800 a week, a different percentage will apply to the excess above £800:

– 9 per cent gross income for one child;

– 12 per cent for two children; *and*

– 15 per cent for three or more children.

Apportionment

If there is more than one person with care in relation to a non-resident parent the amount of maintenance due may be apportioned between them in relation to the number of qualifying children of each person with care.[4]

Where apportionment occurs and rounding provisions would result in the total amount of maintenance being different from the total amount before any apportionment, the maintenance due is adjusted.[5] This may mean that maintenance due to one of the persons with care has to be reduced by a penny, so that no one person with care is disadvantaged. This reduction will be reallocated between the persons with care from time to time.[6]

Apportionment occurs after the calculation of maintenance at the appropriate rate and before any decrease for shared care.[7]

In basic and reduced rate cases, where an adjustment is made which reduces the non-resident parent's liability to less than £5 (eg, because of shared care or a variation), the amount payable will be £5 apportioned between the people with care.[8]

If there is more than one person with care in relation to a qualifying child, the maintenance due for this child may be further apportioned between the persons with care, but only if a request to apportion maintenance has been agreed by the Child Support Agency (CSA) (see p87).

Nil rate

This applies if the non-resident parent is:[9]
- a student;
- a child;
- a prisoner;
- a 16/17-year-old and receiving income support (IS)/income-based jobseeker's allowance (JSA)/income-related employment and support allowance (ESA) (or his partner is);
- receiving an allowance for work-based training for young people or for Skillseekers training in Scotland. Work-based training includes schemes such as Entry to Employment and Modern Apprenticeships. Young people may receive an education maintenance allowance or a training allowance;
- resident in a care home or independent hospital, or is being provided with a care home service or/and independent healthcare service and who receives one of the prescribed benefits (as for the flat rate) or has the whole/part of the cost of his accommodation met by a local authority;
- a person with net income (including that from any of the prescribed benefits for the flat rate listed below), of less than £5 a week.

Example
Kerry is a parent with care of two children, Mia and Lewis. Her ex-partner, Craig, is in prison. In this case the nil rate applies. However, even though Craig is in prison, he is still sent a child maintenance enquiry form to complete. When he comes out of prison Kerry could ask for a supersession.

Flat rate

The flat rate of £5 applies where the non-resident parent does not qualify for the nil rate and:[10]
- his weekly income is £100 or less; *or*
- he receives one of the following:[11]

- bereavement allowance;
- retirement pension;
- incapacity benefit or contributory ESA;
- carer's allowance;
- maternity allowance;
- severe disablement allowance;
- industrial injuries benefit;
- widowed parent's allowance;
- widow's pension;
- contribution-based JSA;
- a training allowance (other than for work-based learning for young people or Skillseekers);
- war disablement pension;
- war widow's, war widower's or surviving civil partner's war pension;
- payments under the Armed Forces Compensation Scheme;
- a social security benefit paid by a country other than the UK;
- IS, income-related ESA or income-based JSA (or his partner does);[12]
- pension credit (PC).

The flat rate can be halved for couples where the non-resident parent's partner is also a non-resident parent with a maintenance application in force, and either he or his partner receives IS (or income-related ESA, income-based JSA or PC).[13] If the non-resident parent is in a polygamous relationship and there is more than one partner, if the non-resident parent or a partner receives IS, income-based JSA, income-related ESA or PC, the flat rate is apportioned between them.[14]

There are special rules about shared care in flat-rate cases (see p107).

Example

Craig has now come out of prison and gets income-based JSA. Kerry requests a supersession and Craig has £5 a week flat rate maintenance deducted from his benefit.

If Craig moved in with Josie and claimed income-based JSA as a couple, the flat rate of £5 would still apply and Kerry would receive £5 a week. However, if Josie were also a non-resident parent the flat rate would be halved. In this case, Kerry would receive £2.50 a week.

In the situation above, if Josie had two persons with care (Alison and Penny) each caring for one qualifying child, they would find their maintenance reduced as the flat rate applies at £2.50 and is then apportioned. Alison and Penny would each receive £1.25 each.

Reduced rate

This applies if neither the flat or nil rate applies and the non-resident parent has income of less than £200 but more than £100.[15] The flat rate of £5 is added to a percentage of the parent's income between £100 and £200.[16] This means that only the income above £100, but under £200, is used in the calculation – eg, if net income is £150 the percentage is applied to £50. The percentage depends on the number of qualifying children and the number of relevant children (ie, one for whom the non-resident parent or his partner receives child benefit[17]). Rounding is to the nearest pound.

Reduced rate percentages

Number of relevant other children	Number of qualifying children (including relevant non-resident children)		
	1	2	3 or more
0	25%	35%	45%
1	20.5%	29%	37.5%
2	19%	27%	35%
3 or more	17.5%	25%	32.5%

Step 1

Work out the net income over £100 but less than £200.

Step 2

Work out the relevant percentage depending on the number of relevant children and qualifying children. Apply this percentage to the income worked out at Step 1 and add this to £5, rounding to the nearest pound.

Step 3

If there is more than one person with care, apportion this amount between them depending on the number of qualifying children each cares for, rounded to the nearest penny. (If there is more than one person with care in relation to a qualifying child, maintenance may only be apportioned where a request to do so has been agreed by the CSA.)

Example

Simon is due to pay maintenance to Fiona for two qualifying children, John and Margaret. Simon lives with a new partner, Julie, and their baby, Paul. Simon's net income is £180 a week. The reduced rate of maintenance would apply.

Step 1   Net income = £180
             Income between £100 and £200 = £80

Step 2   Relevant percentage for one relevant child and two qualifying children is 29%
             £5 + (29% x £80) = £5 + £23.20 = £28.20 (rounded to £28)

Simon is due to pay £28 maintenance to Fiona.

If the situation were as above except that Margaret was cared for by Fiona and John stayed with his grandmother, there would still be two qualifying children but now there would be two persons with care. The maintenance calculated would need to be apportioned between them.

Step 3   Each person cares for one qualifying child, so the maintenance is divided by two.

£28 ÷ 2 = £14

Simon now pays Fiona £14 and the grandmother £14.

If the non-resident parent shares the care of any qualifying children, the reduced rate may be decreased further by applying the shared care rules (see p97).

Basic rate

The basic rate applies if none of the other rates (nil, flat or reduced) apply.[18] Thus, if the non-resident parent has net weekly income of £200 or more, maintenance will be calculated under the basic rate. The basic rate is a percentage of net income depending on the number of qualifying children. How much is paid will also depend on the number of relevant children. There may be other relevant non-resident children who are taken into account (see p89).

Basic rate percentages

Number of qualifying children (including relevant non-resident children)	Percentage of net income	Number of relevant children	Percentage by which net income is reduced
1	15%	1	15%
2	20%	2	20%
3 or more	25%	3 or more	25%

If the non-resident parent has one or more relevant children, his net income is reduced by an equivalent percentage (see p87) before the basic rate is calculated. Therefore, the basic rate may be worked out in two steps, depending on the circumstances.

Step 1

Work out the net income of the non-resident parent. Depending on the number of relevant children, reduce this by a percentage – ie, 15 per cent, 20 per cent or 25 per cent.

Step 2

Depending on the number of qualifying children, maintenance is a proportion of this remaining net income, rounded to the nearest pound.

Step 3

If there is more than one person with care, apportion this amount between them depending on the number of qualifying children each cares for, rounded to the nearest penny. (If there is more than one person with care in relation to a qualifying child, maintenance can only be apportioned where a request to do so has been agreed by the CSA.)

Example

Simon now has a net income of £240 a week. Paul is a relevant child, and John and Margaret are the qualifying children.

Step 1   Net income is £240. One relevant child means this is reduced by 15%.

15% x £240 = £36

£240 – £36 = £204

Step 2   There are two qualifying children, so maintenance is 20% of remaining net income.

20% x £204 = £40.80 (which is rounded to £41)

Simon, therefore, pays £41 in maintenance to Fiona.

If Margaret were cared for by Fiona and John stayed with his grandmother, this £41 would be split equally between Fiona and the grandmother.

Step 3   £41 is apportioned between two persons with care. Each would receive £20.50 in maintenance from Simon.

If the non-resident parent shares the care of any of the qualifying children, the maintenance calculated may be decreased further by applying the shared care rules (see p97).

Relevant non-resident children

A non-resident parent may have other children for whom child support maintenance cannot be applied because the non-resident parent is paying maintenance for them under a maintenance order (or in Scotland, registered maintenance agreement), the order of a court outside Great Britain, or under the legislation of a jurisdiction outside the UK.[19] The CSA calls these children relevant non-resident children, although they are treated like qualifying children in relation to the calculation.[20]

Where child support is payable at either the basic rate or the reduced rate, or is calculated at one of these rates after applying a variation (see Chapter 6) and would otherwise have been the flat or nil rate, the child is counted as a qualifying child.[21] The amount of maintenance calculated is then apportioned between the persons with care in relation to the number of qualifying children they care for, including any adjustment for shared care.[22] If the total amount payable by the non-resident parent would be less than £5, the non-resident parent will instead pay £5, apportioned between the persons with care as appropriate.[23]

No payment is actually made for the relevant non-resident child. There is also no adjustment of the notional amount worked out for the non-resident child because of the non-resident parent sharing care or the child being in local authority care for part of the time.[24]

Example

James lives with his new partner, Amanda, and her son, Liam. He has three other children. Two (Emma and Joshua) are cared for by Elizabeth; one (Rachel) is cared for by Hilary. James has court orders for child maintenance for Emma, Joshua and Rachel. Hilary cannot apply for child maintenance as the court order is in force (if it was made after 3 March 2003 she could apply for child maintenance had the order been in force for one year; otherwise the order must cease before she can apply). In this case:

Emma and Joshua are qualifying children.

Liam is a relevant child (even though he is not James's child, James's new partner, Amanda, gets child benefit for him).

Rachel is a relevant non-resident child.

If James had a net income of £275 a week his maintenance worked out using the basic rate would be as follows.

Step 1   £275 − (15% x £275) = £275 − £41.25 = £233.75

Step 2   25% x £233.75 = £58.44 (rounded to £58)

Step 3   Apportionment applies between Elizabeth and Hilary. Elizabeth receives two-thirds of the maintenance calculated – ie, £38.67 (when apportioning, rounding applies to the nearest penny).

Hilary receives her normal court order maintenance.

Note: if Hilary could apply for child maintenance, she would receive £19.33.

---

2. Net income

The non-resident parent's net weekly income includes earned income, self-employed earnings, tax credits and payments from a pension scheme, retirement annuity or other such scheme for provision of income in retirement,[25] less any relevant deductions. Only these forms of income will be included. All other income will be ignored.

Relevant week

The concept of the 'relevant week' is important in a child support calculation, particularly when calculating income.[26] The relevant week is:[27]

- on application by the non-resident parent, the seven days immediately before the application is made;
- on application in any other case, the seven days immediately before the date the non-resident parent was first given notice that an application for child support maintenance had been made, or treated as made;
- if the original decision is revised (or superseded because of ignorance, a mistake in material fact or error in law), the relevant week for the new decision is the same as the original decision;
- if the original decision is superseded because of a change in circumstances, the seven days immediately before the date on which the application to supersede was made;
- if the original decision is superseded by the Child Support Agency (CSA) on its own initiative (except for ignorance, a mistake in fact or error), the seven days immediately before the date of notification of that intention.[28]

In some cases, the CSA may make separate maintenance calculations for different periods in a particular case.[29] If this is because of changes of circumstances, the relevant week for each separate calculation made to take account of the changes is the seven days immediately before the date of notification of the change.[30]

Disregarded income

If a payment is made in a currency other than sterling, banking charges or commission for changing the payment into sterling are disregarded.[31] In addition, a payment made in a country outside the UK with a prohibition against transfer into the UK is ignored.[32]

Earnings from employment

Earnings means 'any remuneration or profit from employment' and, as well as wages, includes:[33]
- any payments for overtime;
- any profit-related pay;
- any bonus or commission;
- any royalty or fees;
- any holiday pay (except that payable more than four weeks after ending employment);
- any retaining fee;
- statutory sick pay, statutory maternity pay, statutory adoption pay and statutory paternity pay;
- pay in lieu of notice.

Earnings do not include:[34]
- payments of expenses 'wholly, exclusively and necessarily' incurred in carrying out the duties of the job. It may be possible to argue that such expenses can be

apportioned between private and work use if they are necessary to carrying out the duties of the job;[35]
- any tax-exempt allowance paid by an employer;
- any gratuities paid by customers (ie, tips);
- payment in kind;
- any advance earnings or loan made by the employer;
- payments made by an employer when the employee is on strike;
- payments for duties as an auxiliary coastguard, part-time firefighter, or within the lifeboat services, territorial army or reserve forces;
- payments made by a local authority to local councillors for performing their duties;
- payments made after employment ends which relate to a specific period of time, provided that a period of equal length has elapsed between the job ending and the effective date;
- earnings from a previous job if they are paid in the same week or period in which earnings from a second job are received.

Calculating normal weekly earnings

Averaged earnings are used in the child support calculation.[36] When calculating or estimating average earnings in the relevant week, the CSA considers the evidence of the person's earnings over any appropriate period, beginning not more than eight weeks before the relevant week and ending not later than the date of the calculation. The CSA may also consider cumulative earnings in the tax year in which the relevant week falls to the date of the calculation.

If the CSA believes that the amount of weekly earnings does not accurately reflect the person's normal amount of earnings, another period can be used, taking into account earnings received and those due to be received (from past, present or future employment) and the duration and pattern (or expected duration and pattern) of any employment.[37]

The CSA must be satisfied that the calculation of earnings in the relevant week produces a figure which is not normal,[38] and that the period chosen reflects the parent's usual pattern of work – eg, the amount of overtime worked or sick leave.[39] A future period can be used to take into account, for instance, earnings from a job which has not yet begun. The CSA must also consider the expected duration and pattern of any employment. A parent may want to suggest an alternative period to the CSA, giving reasons, as the CSA cannot be expected to consider this without substantial grounds and a prompt by one of the parents.[40] The CSA must use one continuous period.[41] If a bonus, commission or profit-related pay is paid during a year ending with the relevant week separately from earnings, or in relation to a longer period than other earnings, those payments are totalled over the year and divided by 52.[42]

The CSA has to take into account any change of circumstances it is aware of between the relevant week and the effective date (see p341).[43] However, it must first calculate earnings as above for the relevant week in order to determine whether there has been a material change of circumstances.[44] For changes after this date, see p325.

The calculation of earnings is one of the areas where errors are frequently made and, therefore, it should be checked carefully. The First-tier Tribunal must enquire into whether the process used to determine income was correctly carried out and whether the period used for the averaging of earnings gave an accurate picture.[45]

Calculating net earnings

Net earnings from employment are counted as net income in full. Net earnings mean gross earnings less:[46]

- income tax;
- Class 1 national insurance contributions;
- all of the contributions made to an occupational/personal pension scheme (unless the scheme is intended partly to pay off a mortgage on the parent's home, in which case 75 per cent of contributions).

Income tax will be the actual amount deducted, including any tax in relation to payments not included as earnings.[47]

Pension contributions are only deducted if they are made to HM Revenue and Customs (the Revenue)-approved schemes.

Earnings from self-employment

Income from self-employment is assessed on the basis of either:

- taxable profits from self-employment shown on a tax calculation notice issued by the Revenue; *or*
- in a small number of cases, the income from self-employment as calculated from gross receipts less relevant deductions.[48]

The non-resident parent must provide a tax calculation notice (or any revised notice) on demand.[49] The demand should explain the consequences of failing to provide the information. This may be an offence (see p57).

Earnings calculated using taxable profits less deductions

The net earnings taken into account will be the total taxable profit from self-employment less:[50]

- income tax (calculated using the personal allowances and tax rates applicable at the effective date[51]);
- national insurance (Class 2 and Class 4 contributions at the rates applicable at the effective date[52]);
- any personal pension premiums or retirement annuity contract premiums (but only 75 per cent of such premiums where the scheme is intended to pay off a mortgage).

Net weekly earnings can only be worked out as outlined above if they are for a period not more than 24 months before the relevant week.[53]

Earnings calculated using gross receipts less deductions

Earnings can be calculated by using gross receipts less deductions if:[54]
- the 24-month condition is not met (see above); *or*
- the CSA accepts it is not reasonably practicable for the non-resident parent to provide the forms submitted to, or issued or revised by, the Revenue.

It is relatively rare for a case to be assessed based on gross receipts rather than using figures submitted to the Revenue. The CSA will not consider revising or superseding a decision based simply on the fact that using the gross receipts method would produce a greater amount of maintenance due to the person with care than that calculated using the tax calculation notice. However, if a non-resident parent's earnings were assessed by the gross receipts method, but he now has self-assessment details or a tax calculation notice, the CSA may supersede the maintenance decision.

Net earnings are the gross receipts less:[55]
- income tax;
- national insurance;
- any premiums paid in respect of a pension or retirement annuity contract (or 75 per cent of such premiums if the scheme is intended to pay off a mortgage);
- any VAT paid in excess of VAT received in the same period as that over which the earnings are assessed; *and*
- any expenses which are reasonably incurred and which are wholly and exclusively for the business. If the CSA is not satisfied that the full expense was appropriate or necessary to the business, it will allow that part considered reasonable.[56] If an expense is part business and part private (eg, a car), the CSA decides on the breakdown between the two uses on the evidence available.[57]

Gross earnings include all of any board or lodgings payments if this is the self-employed earner's only or main source of income.[58]

Income tax and national insurance is calculated in the same way as for taxable profit.[59]

Business expenses include:[60]
- repayments of capital on loans used to replace or repair a business asset (but not for loans taken out for any other business purpose or if the costs are met by payments from an insurance policy);
- any income used to repair a business asset;
- any payment of interest on loans taken out for business purposes (this does not include loans taken out to acquire a share of a business, nor to pay business tax liabilities).[61]

Business expenses do *not* include capital expenditure, nor any expenses incurred in providing business entertainment.[62]

The net weekly income of the self-employed earner will be averaged over the 52 weeks up to and including the relevant week or, if the person has been self-employed for less than a year, over the period during which the person has been self-employed (including the relevant week).[63]

The self-employed person may be asked to provide other evidence of business receipts and expenses, such as business books, receipts of bills, bank statements, records of wages paid, Revenue forms and VAT bills.[64]

If the CSA believes that the above calculation would produce an amount which does not accurately represent the parent's true earnings, another period can be used.[65] This should not be used just because earnings fluctuate, receipts are irregular, trade is slow at times or work non-existent for a period, nor should a different period be used just because it is known that earnings will subsequently change.[66] In such cases, the CSA will take into account earnings received or due to be received, and the duration and pattern (or expected pattern) of any self-employment.[67]

Since most calculations will be based on the self-assessment form or tax calculation notice, this alternative method is only used if there has been a major change in trading which has resulted in higher or lower earnings, or if a person has been trading for less than a year.[68]

Challenging self-employed earnings

There have often been delays in the self-employed parent producing all the information necessary to work out the maintenance due. The CSA can impose penalties and a default maintenance decision (see p326) while waiting for the information. The person with care may want to request that this is done if there have been problems in the past. However, she cannot force the imposition of a penalty.

Some persons with care may allege that the self-employed non-resident parent, sometimes with the help of an accountant, is disguising his true income. If a person with care wants to challenge the earnings, once a calculation has been made she can seek a revision (see p354) and ask the CSA to use an inspector (see p73) to obtain more detailed information. In practice, if the non-resident parent's accounts have been accepted by the Revenue, it is very unlikely that the CSA would consider it worthwhile to undertake further investigations. However, recent caselaw states that the Revenue's declaration of income is not necessarily conclusive.[69] The CSA may also refuse to revise the calculation if the person with care cannot substantiate her allegations. This can be challenged if the belief is reasonably held as it is very difficult for one party to obtain definitive details of the other's income. The CSA is much better placed to obtain such details.

If the person with care takes the case to the First-tier Tribunal (see Chapter 18), she will see details of the income in the appeal papers and she may be able to argue that some of the expenses included are not reasonable or not wholly connected with the business. The First-tier Tribunal may adjourn the hearing for further information to be collected. Alternatively, it can estimate net earnings based on the available evidence, including oral evidence from the person with care.[70]

The person with care can apply for a variation from the calculation on the grounds that a person's lifestyle is inconsistent with his level of income or that assets which do not currently produce income are capable of doing so (see Chapter 6).

Tax credits

Working tax credit

Working tax credit (WTC) is counted as the income of the non-resident parent if it is solely based on his work and earnings.[71] If both members of a couple are working, WTC is treated as the income of the partner with the higher earnings over the period used for assessing earnings for tax credit purposes, or halved if their earnings are equal.[72] The earnings used for determining WTC are the ones used to determine who is treated as having WTC included in their income.[73] This means that should the earnings change later, the non-resident parent could be treated as having more income than he has. For example, if he is earning more than his partner when WTC is worked out, WTC counts in full as his income. If his partner's income later increases, but he does not notify the Revenue during the tax year and waits for an end of year adjustment, he will still have WTC counted as his income even though his partner currently earns more than he does. (It is not compulsory to report changes of income during the tax year.) The rate of WTC used is that payable at the effective date.[74]

Child tax credit

Child tax credit paid to the non-resident parent or his partner counts in full as income, at the rate payable at the effective date.[75]

Other income

Periodic or other payments from an occupational or personal pension, retirement annuity or other scheme to provide income in retirement count in full as income. Payments to compensate for the failure of pension schemes (Financial Assistance Scheme and Pensions Protection Fund payments) are treated in the same way. Income is calculated or estimated on a weekly basis by considering the 26-week period ending in the relevant week (see p209).[76] If the income has been received during each week of the period, the total received over the 26 weeks is divided by 26. In other cases, the total received is divided by the number of complete weeks for which the payment was received. However, the CSA can use a different period if the amount produced by the above calculation does not accurately reflect actual income.[77] Furthermore, a change occurring between the relevant week and the effective date (see p341) must be taken into account by the CSA if it is aware of the change, in the same way as for earnings (see p212).

Maximum amount of net weekly income

The maximum amount of net weekly income that can be included in the calculation of child maintenance is £2,000.[78] This includes all income, whether from earnings, tax credits, self-employment or pension and other payments. Even if a variation is being applied, the amount of net income cannot exceed this maximum figure.

In simple terms this means that the maximum amount of child maintenance that can ever be paid is £500 – ie, where the non-resident parent has three or more children and no other relevant children.

Maximum maintenance payable (using the basic rate)

Number of relevant children	1 qualifying child	2 qualifying children	3 or more qualifying children
0	£300	£400	£500
1	£255	£340	£425
2	£240	£320	£400
3 or more	£225	£300	£375

3. **Shared care**

Shared care is the term used to describe a situation where there is more than one person looking after a particular qualifying child and those people live in different households. If the people providing care live in the same household (see p22), this is not shared care.[79]

In real terms, a number of individuals may be involved in caring for a qualifying child – eg, parents, grandparents and babysitters. For the shared care rules to apply there must be either:

- a non-resident parent who shares care (ie, looks after the qualifying child at least 52 nights a year on average) (see p101);
- a person with care (ie, with day-to-day care of a qualifying child because she cares for the child at least 104 nights a year on average) who is treated as a non-resident parent (see p100); or
- a qualifying child cared for by a local authority for part of the time (see p285).

One, or all, of these situations may apply in any individual case.

The Child Support Agency (CSA) will make a decision on shared care by looking at all the evidence. As far as possible it will seek written evidence, although oral evidence will be accepted where the parents agree.[80] Normally this information is obtained on application (ie, from relevant forms or phone contact with the person with care and non-resident parent). The CSA calculates the amount of shared care by looking at regular weekly patterns, exceptional weeks and other occasional nights.[81] It is actual care provided which counts, whether or not it is authorised or agreed. This means that contact arrangements ordered by a court or agreed to in writing are only evidence and not decisive proof of the care situation.[82] If the evidence of the person with care and non-resident parent conflicts, the CSA will, if possible, make a decision on the balance of probability.[83] Further evidence may be required to resolve the issue.

A court should determine contact arrangements and the amount of shared care without regard to the effects on child support liability.[84] Therefore, neither parent can argue that a court should vary an order due to the amount of child support payable.

Parents should keep a note of the nights the child(ren) spends with them and, in case of dispute, be willing to supply further evidence – eg, a diary. The CSA (and any subsequent appeal at the First-tier Tribunal) must then determine the number of nights over the period spent in each person's care.[85]

What is day-to-day care

A person is treated as having day-to-day care of a child only if s/he cares for the child for at least 104 nights in the 12-month period ending with the relevant week.[86] See p209 for a definition of relevant week.

Another period ending with the relevant week may be used if that would be more representative of the current arrangement.[87] The number of nights of care in that period must be in the same ratio as 104 nights is to 12 months – ie, 52 nights in six months, 26 nights in three months, 13 nights in two months, nine nights in a month. It might be appropriate for the CSA to use a period other than 12 months because no pattern of care can be gathered from a 12-month period, or because there is an intended change. CSA guidance gives examples, including where the care arrangements have changed following a relationship breakdown or court ruling, or where the person now providing day-to-day care has been abroad, in prison, in hospital, away from home or otherwise unable to provide care.[88] If the arrangement has simply been renegotiated between the two parents, written acceptance of this should be provided so that the CSA knows that this is now the current arrangement and not a temporary change. A future period cannot be used, but if there is an intended change, a period before the relevant week may include a care distribution which is closer to the intended new arrangement, and the CSA can use this period rather than the 12 months.[89]

Example
The relevant week for Joan's maintenance application is 12.02.09 to 18.02.09. The effective date of Serge's maintenance liability is 26.03.09 (the effective date is later than

the relevant week because Joan was treated as applying and a court order is in force; this makes the effective date two days after the calculation is made). Serge is going to begin caring for Chloe (the qualifying child) two nights a week from 14.03.09. Joan confirms this change.

The CSA decides that looking at the care arrangements in the period ending with the relevant week would not give an accurate reflection of the current care arrangements, so an alternate period is used: 14.03.09 to 26.03.09 – ie, from the date of change to the effective date.

If a change occurs after the relevant week, the CSA should be informed as this may be grounds for supersession. If it refuses to use an alternative period, an appeal can be sought.

Example

A father who only looks after the children for six weeks in the school holidays would not be accepted as a person with care. However, he could request a supersession during the summer holidays on the grounds that he is now a parent with care and a shorter period should then be used to calculate who has day-to-day care to reflect the current arrangement. It is unlikely that this would be grounds for supersession if the six-week period had already been taken into account. However, if the arrangement for the holiday had not been known at the time, this may be successful. If day-to-day care were to be re-assessed over the summer holidays, the father would become the parent with care and the mother the non-resident parent. Indeed, the father may be able to apply for maintenance from the mother. (**Note:** the relevant week in this case is the seven days preceding the request for a supersession – see p358. The request, therefore, should not be made right at the beginning of the summer holiday.)

If it is held that a supersession cannot take place, the father remains the non-resident parent over the holiday when he has the children full time. He would be liable to continue paying the mother the full level of maintenance even for those weeks the children spent with him. The parents may be able to come to a voluntary arrangement to reflect the father's level of care over this time, but this may not be financially viable.

The parent does not have to provide continuous care throughout a period of 24 hours, but must provide care during the night.[90] If a child is a boarder at boarding school, a hospital inpatient, or temporarily in someone else's care, whoever would otherwise have day-to-day care is treated as providing care.[91] For example, if a babysitter or grandparent looks after the child one night a week, this would count as a night spent with the principal provider of day-to-day care. In the case of boarding school, the person who is treated as having day-to-day care for such periods need not be the person who pays the school fees.[92] However, a non-resident parent who pays school fees for a qualifying child may be able to apply for a variation (see p114).

Parent with care treated as non-resident

If there are two or more persons with care (of a child for whom an application has been made or treated as made) and at least one of them is a parent, special rules are applied.[93] In this case, a parent with care may be treated as a non-resident parent if s/he provides care:[94]

- to a lesser extent than the other parent or persons with care;
- to the same extent as the other parent but does not get child benefit; *or*
- to the same extent as the other parent and neither parent receives child benefit but the CSA decides she is not the principal provider of day-to-day care.

A lesser extent could be interpreted as meaning either for fewer *nights* a week on average or fewer *hours* a week on average. However, the CSA will normally consider the number of nights to be a determining factor.[95]

Example

Robert looks after Geraldine from Friday afternoon to Monday morning. Nikki looks after Geraldine from Monday afternoon to Friday morning. Each is a parent with care but Robert cares for Geraldine to a lesser extent so he is treated as the non-resident parent.

A year later, Robert has moved onto shift work. One week he has Geraldine four nights, the second week three nights. Nikki cares for Geraldine the rest of the time. They now share care equally but, as Nikki receives child benefit, Robert is still treated as the non-resident parent.

Note: as the right to receive child maintenance follows receipt of child benefit, this may lead to competing claims for child benefit. If more than one person who is entitled makes a claim for child benefit, an order of priority is used to decide who will receive it.[96] For example, the person with whom the child is living has priority over other claimants. If the priority rules do not decide the matter and the entitled claimants cannot come to an agreement, HM Revenue and Customs makes the decision. Priority can be conceded by a higher priority claimant to someone else, in writing. For more information on entitlement to child benefit and the priority rules, see CPAG's *Welfare Benefits and Tax Credits Handbook*.

In cases where a parent with care is treated as non-resident, a calculation is carried out to find out how much child maintenance s/he has to pay. This is worked out in the same way as for a non-resident parent who shares care.

If the situation includes a remaining parent with care who does not have to pay child maintenance, this assignment of non-resident parenthood can result in one parent paying child maintenance to another who has equal responsibility for the child. This can be particularly contentious where neither parent receives child benefit and the CSA has had to make a decision on the principal provider of day-to-day care.[97]

Who receives maintenance

If there are two or more people in different households who both have day-to-day care of a qualifying child, either can make an application for child maintenance as long as both or neither of them has parental responsibility.[98] If only one of them has parental responsibility, the person with parental responsibility must be the applicant. This means that if the person with parental responsibility decides not to apply, the other person with care could lose out on child maintenance, unless there is an application from the non-resident parent or a child in Scotland.

If both/all the persons with care make an application, only one will be accepted, depending on the order of priority (see p43). This may include a parent with care who is subsequently treated as a non-resident parent for the calculation.

If none of the persons with care is a parent who is treated as a non-resident parent, the person whose application is accepted will receive all the maintenance calculated.[99] The applicant or other person with care may request that the payment is apportioned between them.[100] In making the decision, the CSA considers all the circumstances of the case and representations from the persons with care.[101] If agreed, the maintenance payable will be apportioned in relation to the amount of care provided. See the example on p102.

If one of the persons with care is treated as a non-resident parent this split cannot take place. The entire amount of child maintenance from the actual non-resident parent is paid to the remaining person with care. In other words, a parent with care who shares care for the lesser amount of time can never receive child maintenance from a non-resident parent, irrespective of the amount being paid.

This may seem illogical, particularly where the application has been made by the parent with care or where, although applications have been made by both persons with care, the application from the parent with care has been given priority (see p43). A parent with care who applies to the CSA for maintenance from the non-resident parent but ends up being deemed non-resident and paying maintenance can request a withdrawal (see p334). However, she may find that the other person with care makes another new application (if that person has parental responsibility).

When a non-resident parent shares care

A non-resident parent shares care where he looks after a qualifying child at least one night a week on average.[102] The care must be provided overnight and the non-resident parent must stay at the same address as the child.[103] This means that the care could be provided away from the non-resident parent's normal home – eg, while on holiday or at other relatives' homes. It also includes the situation where the non-resident parent looks after the child overnight in the parent with care's home when the parent with care is away from home during the relevant nights.[104]

The number of nights is averaged over the 12 months ending with the relevant week.[105] A shorter period may be used – eg, because there is no pattern for the frequency or there is an intended change in frequency.[106] The number of nights of care in that period must be in the same ratio as 52 nights is to 12 months (52 weeks) – ie, 26 nights in six months (26 weeks), 13 nights in three months (13 weeks).[107]

Qualifying child is in hospital or at boarding school

If a qualifying child is in hospital or at boarding school, any night spent there will count as a night with the person who would normally provide care at that time.[108] This includes nights normally spent with the:

- non-resident parent;[109]
- person with care;
- local authority.[110]

These nights count in determining whether the non-resident parent or local authority shares care. They are also counted when establishing who is a person with care or which parent is to be treated as non-resident.

Example

A child who has been living with his mother during the week and spending Friday nights with his father goes to boarding school. The time as a boarder would continue to be treated as if he were living with his mother. Even if the care arrangement alters so that he spends alternate weekends with his father, the nights at school still count as spent with his mother.

If the parents agree, or the periods involved are infrequent, the case may be straightforward. However, if the normal arrangements break down, a normal pattern cannot be established or the parents disagree, the CSA must make a decision on shared care.

Example

Ella is a qualifying child cared for most of the time by her mother, Sarah, although her father, Stuart, looks after her on Wednesday and Saturday nights. Over the past year Ella has undergone treatment for cancer, which has resulted in her spending periods in hospital. Because of the periods in hospital Stuart has actually only looked after Ella for 42 nights in the year. On 16 of the remaining nights that Ella should have stayed with him she was in hospital. On the other nights that Ella should have stayed with Stuart she was unwell and wanted to stay with Sarah. The CSA would have to decide whether to consider Ella as staying with Stuart for 58 nights or accept that the intention was for her to stay with Stuart on 104 nights in the year.

If, having counted these nights, a person is not a:
- person with care;
- non-resident parent who shares care;
- local authority who has part-time care,

the night is treated as if the child is in the care of the principal provider of day-to-day care.[111] For example, if a babysitter looks after a child one night a week, then the child goes into hospital, the babysitter is not a person with care, non-resident parent or local authority. Therefore, that night is treated as one normally spent with the principal provider of day-to-day care.

Shared care and part-time local authority care

There are different rules depending on which calculation rate is applied.

The effect of shared care on the basic and reduced rate

A non-resident parent (or parent with care treated as non-resident) may share care in a number of situations – ie, be:
- caring for different qualifying children at different times; *or*
- caring for qualifying children with more than one person with care.

There may be any number of variations and permutations. Indeed, in any one family situation there may be a number of non-resident parents and children.

If a non-resident parent, or parent with care who is treated as a non-resident parent, shares care of a qualifying child for 52 or more nights a year, the amount of maintenance he is due to pay is reduced by a suitable fraction depending on the number of nights of shared care.[112] The amount depends on the relevant band.[113]

Number of nights	Fraction to subtract
52 to 103	One-seventh
104 to 155	Two-sevenths
156 to 174	Three-sevenths
175 or more	One-half

If the non-resident parent shares care of a qualifying child for a sufficient number of nights for the one-half fraction to apply, an additional £7 decrease in maintenance must also be applied.[114] The CSA refers to this situation as equal shared care, even though the amount of time spent with each may not be the same.[115] This extra allowance where there is equal shared care is known as **'abatement'**.[116] Abatement will be applied for each child for whom equal shared care applies.

If the decreases applied because of shared care result in the non-resident parent being liable to pay the person with care less than £5, the non-resident parent will instead pay the flat rate of £5.[117] This includes the situation where the total amount of maintenance due to all persons with care is decreased to less than £5, in which case the £5 is apportioned between the persons with care in relation to the number of qualifying children. For more details on situations involving more than one person with care, see p272.

When applying the decrease for shared care, the rounding provisions apply to the nearest penny.[118]

Example: shared care with one person with care
Alex shares care of Mark with the person with care, Diane. He looks after Mark on average two nights at the weekend and a couple of weeks in school holidays. Although Alex is a parent with care he is treated as a non-resident parent as he is not the principal provider of care. Alex's net income is £240.

Step 1   **Basic rate** 15% x £240 = £36
Step 2   **Apply decrease for shared care**
              Alex shares care in the 104 – 155 band (two-sevenths).
              £36 maintenance must be decreased by 2/7 – ie, £36 – £10.29 = £25.71
Alex pays Diane £25.71.

Alex increases the amount of time he shares care of Mark to three nights one week and four nights the next. In this case, Alex shares care for over 175 nights and the one-half fraction is applied. Alex's maintenance calculated under the basic rate remains £36.

Step 2   £36 decreased by 1/2 and a further £7 subtracted – ie, £18 – £7 = £11
Because of the increase in shared care, Alex pays £11 maintenance to Diane.

Alex's circumstances change and he now has income of £160.

Step 1   **Reduced rate** of maintenance £5 + (25% x £60) = £5 + £15 = £20
Step 2   **Apply decrease for shared care**
              The fraction to apply remains at one-half and there is an abatement of £7.
              (50% x £20) – £7 = £10 – £7 = £3
Step 3   **Maintenance due** is below £5 so Alex will pay £5 a week to Diane.

More than one qualifying child

If the person with care and non-resident parent have more than one qualifying child, the fractions that apply for shared care for each qualifying child are added together, then divided by the number of qualifying children.[119] This applies where care is shared for some, but not all, of the qualifying children or there are different shared care arrangements for each qualifying child.

Example: shared care where there is more than one qualifying child

Pat is the non-resident parent of Lea and Dylan. Both are cared for by their grandmother, Jean. Lea does not like staying with Pat and only does so occasionally. However, Dylan stays with him on Friday and Saturday nights. Both children stay with him for a few days at Christmas and during the school holidays. Pat has net income of £220.

Step 1   **Basic rate** for two children 20% x £220 = £44

Step 2   **Apply decrease for shared care**

      Lea does not stay with Pat sufficient days for it to count as shared care.

      Dylan is in the 104 – 155 band (two-sevenths).

      The fractions which apply are added together and divided by two, as there are two qualifying children for whom Jean cares.

      $(0 + 2/7) \div 2 = 2/14$

      Pat's maintenance is decreased by 2/14 (ie, £6.29)

Because of the shared care, Pat must pay £37.71 (£44 – £6.29) to Jean in maintenance.

Note: if Pat has costs for keeping in contact with Lea he may be able to apply for a variation (see Chapter 6).

Lea increases the amount of time she spends with her dad and now this counts as shared care.

Step 2   Lea is in the 52 – 103 band (one-seventh).

      Dylan is in the 104 – 155 band (two-sevenths).

      The fractions are added together and divided by two – ie, $3/7 \div 2 = 3/14$

      The maintenance due is, therefore, decreased by 3/14 because of shared care.

      Pat's maintenance is decreased by 3/14 (ie, £9.43)

Because of shared care, Pat must pay £34.57 (£44 – £9.43) to Jean in maintenance.

Dylan stays with his dad more often and increases the amount of care, so that:

Step 2   Lea is in the 52 – 103 band (one-seventh).

      Dylan is in the 175 or more band (one-half).

      The decrease will be $(1/7 + 1/2) \div 2 = 9/28$; $9/28 \times £44 = £14.14$

      £44 – £14.14 = £29.86. However, because care is shared equally for one qualifying child the abatement of £7 applies and maintenance due is decreased by a further £7.

Pat now pays Jean maintenance of £22.86 (£29.86 – £7).

More than one person with care

A non-resident parent may be due to pay maintenance to more than one person with care because there:

- are several qualifying children with different persons with care (known as multiple maintenance units);

- is more than one person with care in relation to a qualifying child(ren).

One or both of these situations may apply in any one case, and the non-resident parent may share care with only one or all of the persons with care. In these cases there may be apportioning and shared care adjustments made throughout the calculation.

Example: shared care in multiple maintenance units

Ivan is the non-resident parent for two children, Holly, whose parent with care is Ellen, and Jamie, whose parent with care is Laura. Ivan looks after Holly when Ellen is on night shifts, which is every other week apart from holidays, and takes her camping with him on the odd weekend. Jamie and Laura live further away so Ivan only sees Jamie for a long weekend once a month when he visits his parents and two weeks in the summer holidays. Ivan's net income is £230.

Step 1	**Basic rate** applies for two qualifying children, there are no relevant children and net income is £230.
	20% x £230 = £46
	There is apportionment between the persons with care. They each care for one qualifying child so halve the maintenance between them.
	To Ellen for Holly = £23
	To Laura for Jamie = £23
Step 2	**Apply decrease for shared care**
	Maintenance paid to Ellen for Holly
	Holly is in the 156 – 174 band (three-sevenths).
	3/7 x £23 = £9.86
	£23 – £9.86 = £13.14
	Maintenance paid to Laura for Jamie
	Jamie is in the 52 – 103 band (one-seventh).
	1/7 x £23 = £3.29
	£23 – £3.29 = £19.71
Step 3	**Total maintenance due** is £13.14 (to Ellen) + £19.71 (to Laura) = £32.85

The situation is as above but now Laura has a new job which means she is away from home on average two nights a week and the occasional weekend. Her sister (Alice) looks after Jamie and Laura asks the CSA to split the maintenance between her and Alice.

Step 1	**Basic rate** is £46.
	Apportion between the persons with care (there are two qualifying children but three persons with care – Ellen for Holly, and Laura and Alice for Jamie).
	To Ellen for Holly = £23
	Between Laura and Alice for Jamie = £23
	Alice looks after Jamie two nights a week on average (2/6 – ie, one-third).
	To Alice for Jamie = £7.67 (1/3 x £23)
	Laura looks after Jamie for the remaining four nights (4/6 – ie, two-thirds).

To Laura for Jamie = £15.33 (2/3 x £23)

Step 2 **Apply decrease for shared care.**
Maintenance paid to Ellen for Holly
Ivan's care for Holly is in the 156 – 174 band (three-sevenths).
3/7 x £23 = £9.86 (ie, £23 – £9.86 = £13.14)
Maintenance paid to Alice for Jamie
Ivan's care for Jamie is in the 52 – 103 band (one-seventh).
1/7 x £7.67 = £1.10; £7.67 – £1.10 = £6.57
Maintenance paid to Laura for Jamie
Ivan's care for Jamie is in the 52 – 103 band (one-seventh).
1/7 x £15.33 = £2.19; £15.33 – £2.19 = £13.14

Step 3 **Total maintenance due** is £13.14 (to Ellen) + £6.57 (to Alice) + £13.14 (to Laura) = £32.85

Overall, Ivan pays exactly the same amount of maintenance as before, but it is split between three people.

The effect of shared care on the flat rate

As with basic or reduced rate maintenance, the non-resident parent may share care with one or more persons with care. In these cases, it must be established whether the non-resident parent is liable for the flat rate because he has income of under £100. If the answer to this question is yes, there will be no adjustment of his maintenance liability regardless of how many nights of shared care there are. If the non-resident parent:

- is liable to pay the flat rate because he is in receipt of a relevant benefit (eg, incapacity benefit (IB) or maternity allowance – for full list, see p85) or he or his partner receives income support (IS), income-related employment and support allowance, pension credit or income-based jobseeker's allowance (including cases where a reduced flat rate of £2.50 applies); *and*
- cares for a qualifying child for at least 52 nights a year,

the amount of child maintenance due to the person with care of that qualifying child is nil.[120]

If there is more than one person with care, the flat rate is apportioned in relation to the number of qualifying children before any adjustment for shared care is made. This may mean that the non-resident parent's liability reduces to nil for one person with care because of shared care. However, he is still liable for the remaining amounts to the other person(s) with care, in which case he will pay an amount which is less than £5.

In simple terms the process is:
- **Step 1.** Check the reason why the flat rate applies.

- **Step 2.** Apportion the flat rate between the persons with care on the basis of the number of qualifying children. Where appropriate, apply any apportioning in relation to a qualifying child where there is more than one person with care.
- **Step 3.** Apply any reduction to nil because of shared care.

Note: apportioning and rounding may result in adjustments of a penny in some calculations done by the CSA – see p83.

Example

Alistair is the non-resident parent of Keith, who lives with his older brother Neil, and Katie who lives with her mum, Rachel. Alistair looks after Katie one or two nights a week but Keith and he do not get on. Both Neil and Rachel apply for maintenance. Alistair receives IB and IS.

Step 1   Alistair is due to pay maintenance at the flat rate of £5, as he receives IB and IS.
Step 2   Apportion the flat rate of £5 between the persons with care in relation to the
          qualifying children each cares for – ie, the amount is halved.
          To Neil for Keith = £2.50
          To Rachel for Katie = £2.50
Step 3   Alistair cares for Katie over 52 nights a year so the amount due reduces to nil.
          Alistair remains liable to pay £2.50 in maintenance to Neil for Keith.

The situation is as above but now Keith goes to stay with his grandfather two nights a week. Neil asks for maintenance to be split between them and the CSA agrees to do this.
Step 1   Remains the same.
Step 2   Rachel is due £2.50 but now the £2.50 for Keith is to be split between Neil and
          grandfather.
          Neil looks after Keith five nights out of seven, his granddad looks after him two
          out of seven, therefore:
          5/7 x £2.50 is due to Neil = £1.79
          2/7 x £2.50 is due to grandfather = £0.72
Step 3   The amount due to Rachel reduces to nil as Alistair cares for Katie over 52
          nights a year.
          Alistair remains liable to pay £1.79 to Neil and £0.72 to Keith's grandfather

In total, this would mean that Alistair is due to pay £2.51. This is more than the amount before apportioning because of the rounding provisions. Therefore, in this case, the maintenance will be adjusted by one penny to one of the persons with care. Neil has his adjusted to £1.78 for a period, after which the adjustment is made to grandfather's and he will receive £0.71 and Neil will receive £1.79.

The effect of care provided in part by the local authority

This section only applies if:

- the non-resident parent is liable to pay maintenance at the basic or reduced rate (including where a variation has been made which results in the non-resident parent paying maintenance at either of these rates);[121]*and*
- the qualifying child is cared for by the local authority at least one night a week on average but not more than five (see below).

Part-time local authority care does not affect how maintenance is worked out in flat-rate cases.

A local authority cannot be a person with care.[122] Therefore, if a child is in the care of the local authority for more than five nights a week, no child maintenance is payable by the non-resident parent because there is no person with care.

If the local authority cares for the child for 52 nights or more in the 12-month period ending with the relevant week, the maintenance to be paid by the non-resident parent will be decreased.[123] As in deciding day-to-day care, the CSA may use a period other than 12 months which it considers to be more representative of current arrangements. A future period may also be considered if the qualifying child is to go into local authority care on, or after, the effective date.[124] If an alternative period is used, the number of nights of care must be in the same ratio as 52 to 12 months.[125] (Nights spent in hospital or at boarding school which normally would have been spent in care are included – see p102.)

Local authority care only affects the calculation of maintenance when it applies to a qualifying child. If a relevant other child is in local authority care (whether full or part time), this will not affect how s/he is treated so long as the non-resident parent or his partner receives child benefit for her/him.

The decrease for part-time local authority care

If the local authority has part-time care of a qualifying child, the basic or reduced rate maintenance calculated from the non-resident parent is decreased in relation to the number of nights the qualifying child spends in local authority care.

This calculation may be carried out either on its own, where the non-resident parent does not share care, or alongside one carried out because the non-resident parent shares care (see p101).

The effect of part-time local authority care

Number of nights	Fraction to subtract
52 to 103	One-seventh
104 to 155	Two-sevenths
156 to 207	Three-sevenths
208 to 259	Four-sevenths
260 to 262	Five-sevenths

If the person with care and non-resident parent have more than one qualifying child, the fractions that apply for each qualifying child in local authority care are added together and divided by the number of qualifying children for whom maintenance is calculated.[126] This applies where the local authority cares for one or all qualifying children or there are different care arrangements for each qualifying child.

If the decrease because of part-time care by the local authority would reduce the amount of maintenance to less than £5 for the only or all persons with care, the amount due will be £5.

Example: local authority provides part-time care

Jake is the non-resident parent for Michael and Leanne. Michael has just been placed under local authority supervision, which means that over the next six months he is to spend four nights a week in a residential unit. The rest of the time he spends with his mum, Naomi. Jake has net income of £280 and currently pays maintenance of £56 (basic rate maintenance). This must be superseded because of local authority care. The CSA supersedes the decision, considering the ratio in the six-month period.

Step 1   **Work out amount of maintenance due**

        Basic rate 20% x £280 = £56

Step 2   **Work out the decrease because of part-time local authority care**

        Local authority care for Michael is in the 208 – 259 band (four-sevenths).

        The fractions which apply are added together and divided by the number of qualifying children – ie, $(0 + 4/7) \div 2 = 4/14$

        Jake's maintenance is decreased by 4/14 (ie, £16)

Jake now pays Naomi £40 (£56 – £16) in maintenance.

If Leanne were also in care for two nights a week:

Step 1   Same as above.

Step 2   Local authority care for Leanne is in the 104 –155 band (two-sevenths).

        Local authority care for Michael is in the 208 – 256 band (four-sevenths).

        The fractions are added together and divided by two:

        $(2/7 + 4/7) = 6/7 \div 2 = 6/14$

        Jake's maintenance decreases by 6/14 = £24

Jake now pays Naomi £32 (ie, £56 – £24) in maintenance.

The non-resident parent shares care and local authority has part-time care

If the non-resident parent shares care of a qualifying child and the local authority has part-time care of a qualifying child, in relation to the same person with care, the appropriate fractions are worked out under each provision and are added together.[127] The amount of maintenance due from the non-resident parent is then decreased by this fraction.

If this decrease would result in the non-resident parent being due to pay less than £5 to the only or all persons with care, he will pay £5.[128]

This calculation is carried out at Step 2.

Example: shared care and part-time local authority care

The situation is as in the first example above except that Leanne spends one night a week with Jake but Michael does not.

Step 2 Jake cares for Leanne in the 52–103 band (one-seventh).

The fractions which apply are added together and divided by the number of qualifying children:

$(0 + 1/7) \div 2 = 1/14$

Jake's maintenance because of shared care should be reduced by 1/14.

Because Michael is in local authority care the maintenance due should be reduced by 4/14. This is added to the amount because of shared care.

$1/14 + 4/14 = 5/14$

Jakes maintenance is reduced by £20 (5/14 x £56)

Jake now pays Naomi £36 (£56 – £20) in maintenance.

If Leanne is also in care two nights a week but still spends one night a week with Jake:

Step 2 Jake's maintenance because of shared care should reduce by 1/14 (as above).

Local authority care for Michael and Leanne should reduce maintenance by 6/14 (as in the second example above).

These fractions are added together:

$1/14 + 6/14 = 7/14 = 1/2$

Jake's maintenance is reduced by £28 (1/2 x £56)

Jake now pays Naomi £28 (ie, £56 – £28) in maintenance.

Notes

1. **Maintenance calculation rates**
   1 Sch 1 CSA 1991; reg 2(5) CS(MCSC) Regs
   2 Reg 2(1) CS(MCSC) Regs
   3 Reg 2(2) and (3) CS(MCSC) Regs
   4 Sch 1 Part 1 para 6 CSA 1991
   5 Reg 6 CS(MCSC) Regs
   6 Reg 6 CS(MCSC) Regs; PG Calculation and Decision Types, Apportionment
   7 Sch 1 Part 1 para 1(2) CSA 1991
   8 PG, Calculation and Decision Types, Apportionment
   9 Sch 1 Part 1 para 5 CSA 1991; reg 5 CS(MCSC) Regs
   10 Sch 1 Part 4 CSA 1991
   11 Reg 4 CS(MCSC) Regs
   12 Reg 4(1)(c) CS(MCSC) Regs
   13 Sch 1 Part 1 para 4(2) CSA 1991; reg 4(3)(a) CS(MCSC) Regs
   14 Reg 4(3)(b) CS(MCSC) Regs

15 Sch 1 Part 1 para 3 CSA 1991
16 Reg 3 CS(MCSC) Regs
17 Sch 1 Part 1 para 10C CSA 1991
18 Sch 1 Part 1(1) CSA 1991
19 Reg 11(1) CS(MCSC) Regs
20 PG, Gather Information and Evidence, Person is an NRP or NRP Partner in a Case
21 Reg 11(2) and (3) CS(MCSC) Regs
22 Reg 11(3) CS(MCSC) Regs
23 Reg 11(5) CS(MCSC) Regs
24 Reg 11(4) CS(MCSC) Regs

2. Net income
25 Sch 1 para 1 CS(MCSC) Regs
26 Sch 1 paras 3(1)(a) and 7(6) CS(MCSC) Regs
27 Reg 1(2) CS(MCSC) Regs
28 Reg 7C SS&CS(DA) Regs
29 Sch 1 Part II para 15 CSA 1991
30 Reg 1(2) CS(MCSC) Regs
31 Sch 1 para 2(a) CS(MCSC) Regs
32 Sch 1 para 2(b) CS(MCSC) Regs
33 Sch 1 para 4 (1) CS(MCSC) Regs
34 Sch 1 para 4(2) CS(MCSC) Regs
35 CCS/137/2007
36 Sch 1 para 6(1) CS(MCSC) Regs
37 Sch 1 Part II para 6(4) CS(MCSC) Regs
38 CCS/16/1994; CCS/11873/1996
39 CCS/6810/1995
40 CCS/511/1995
41 CCS/7312/1995; CCS/556/1995; CSCS/1/1996; CSCS/6/1996
42 Sch 1 Part II para 6(3) CS(MCSC) Regs
43 Reg 2(4) CS(MCSC) Regs
44 CCS/2750/1995
45 CCS/556/1995
46 Sch 1 Part II para 5 CS(MCSC) Regs
47 Sch 1 Part II para 5(2) CS(MCSC) Regs
48 Sch 1 Part III para 7(1) and (1A) CS(MCSC) Regs
49 Sch 1 Part III para 7(2) CS (MCSC) Regs
50 Sch 1 Part III para 7(3) CS(MCSC) Regs
51 Sch 1 Part III para 7(4) CS(MCSC) Regs
52 Sch 1 Part III para 7(5) CS(MCSC) Regs
53 Sch 1 Part III para 7(6) CS(MCSC) Regs
54 Sch 1 Part III para 8(1) CS(MCSC) Regs
55 Sch 1 Part III para 8(2) CS(MCSC) Regs
56 PG, Gather Information and Evidence, Reasonably Incurred Expenses
57 PG, Gather Information and Evidence, Wholly and Exclusively Defrayed Expense
58 Sch 1 Part III para 10 CS(MCSC) Regs
59 Sch 1 Part III para 8(4) CS(MCSC) Regs
60 Sch 1 Part III para 8(3)(a) CS(MCSC) Regs
61 CCS/15949/1996

62 Sch 1 Part III para 8(3)(b) CS(MCSC) Regs
63 Sch 1 Part III para 9(2) CS(MCSC) Regs
64 PG, Gather Information and Evidence, Business Receipts *and* Business Expenses
65 Sch 1 para 9(3) CS(MCSC) Regs
66 CCS/3182/1995; CCS/6145/1995
67 Sch 1 Part III para 9(3) CS(MCSC) Regs
68 PG, Gather Information and Evidence, Treatment of Self-employed Earnings
69 CCS/1263/2008
70 CCS/7966/1995
71 Sch 1 Part IV para 11(1) CS(MCSC) Regs
72 Sch 1 Part IV para 11(2) CS(MCSC) Regs
73 Sch 1 Part IV para 11(2A) CS(MCSC) Regs
74 Sch 1 Part IV para 11(1) CS(MCSC) Regs
75 Sch 1 Part IV para 13A CS(MCSC) Regs
76 Sch 1 Part V para 16 CS(MCSC) Regs
77 Sch 1 Part V para 16(2) CS(MCSC) Regs
78 Sch 1 para 10 CSA 1991

3. Shared care
79 Reg 8(1) CS(MCSC) Regs
80 PG, Gather Information and Evidence, PWC and NRP Provide Different Information
81 PG, Gather Information and Evidence, Calculate Shared Care
82 CCS/2885/2005
83 PG, Gather Information and Evidence, Contradictory Evidence
84 *Re B (A Child)* [2006] EWCA Civ 1574
85 CCS/11728/1996
86 Reg 1(2)(a) CS(MCSC) Regs
87 Reg 1(2)(b) CS(MCSC) Regs; CCS/6/1994
88 PG, Gather Information and Evidence, Alternative Period for Establishing Day-to-Day Care
89 Reg 7(4) CS(MCSC) Regs
90 Reg 1(2) CS(MCSC) Regs; CCS/449/1995
91 Reg 1(2)(b)(i) CS (MCSC) Regs
92 CCS/12686/1996
93 Reg 8 CS(MCSC) Regs
94 Reg 8(2) CS(MCSC) Regs
95 PG, Gather Information and Evidence, Deciding Principal Provider of Day-to-Day Care
96 s144(3) and Sch 10 SSCBA 1992
97 PG, Gather Information and Evidence, Deciding Who Should be Treated as the NRP
98 s5(1) CSA 1991
99 Reg 14(2)(a) CS(MCSC) Regs
100 Reg 14(2)(b) CS(MCSC) Regs
101 Reg 14(2)(c) CS(MCSC) Regs

102 Sch 1 Part 1 paras 7 and 8 CSA 1991
103 Reg 7(1) CS(MCSC) Regs
104 CCS/3056/2007
105 Reg 7(3) CS(MCSC) Regs
106 Reg 7(4) CS(MCSC) Regs
107 Reg 7(5) CS(MCSC) Regs
108 Reg 12 CS(MCSC) Regs
109 Reg 7(6) CS(MCSC) Regs
110 Reg 9(10) CS(MCSC) Regs
111 Reg 1(2)(b)(i) CS(MCSC) Regs
112 Sch 1 Part 1 para 7 CSA 1991
113 Sch 1 Part 1 para 7(4) CSA 1991
114 Sch 1 Part 1 para 7(6) CSA 1991
115 PG, Gather Information and Evidence,
    Equal Shared Care and Abatement
116 PG, Gather Information and Evidence,
    Equal Shared Care and Abatement
117 Sch 1 Part 1 para 7(7) CSA 1991
118 Reg 2(2) CS(MCSC) Regs
119 Sch 1 Part 1 para 7(5) CSA 1991
120 Sch 1 Part 1 para 8 CSA 1991
121 Reg 9(1) CS(MCSC) Regs
122 Reg 21(1)(a) CS(MCP) Regs
123 Reg 9(2) and (4) CS(MCSC) Regs
124 Reg 9(2)(c) CS(MCSC) Regs
125 Reg 9(5) CS(MCSC) Regs
126 Reg 9(7) CS(MCSC) Regs
127 Reg 9(8) CS(MCSC) Regs
128 Reg 9(9)(a) CS(MCSC) Regs

6

Chapter 6

Variations ('new rules')

This chapter covers:
1. Grounds for a variation (below)
2. Applying for a variation (p127)
3. Procedure (p128)
4. The decision (p134)

This information only applies to 'new rules' cases, including where a case has been converted to the new rules. There are additional provisions which must be read with this information in conversion cases where there is an existing departure direction or application for a departure (see Chapter 7).

An application for a variation to the maintenance calculation may be made before a calculation is made or once a maintenance calculation is in force.[1]

A variation to the calculation can only be made under a ground laid out in the legislation and only if it would be just and equitable to do so (see p133).

An application may be rejected in specific circumstances, either at preliminary consideration or at a later stage (see p129). In certain cases, the Child Support Agency may refer the application to the First-tier Tribunal for a determination (see p134).

If an application is successful, it may result in a maintenance calculation being made, or, where a calculation already exists, being revised or superseded with the variation incorporated (see p138).

There is no separate variation decision; the decision is whether to revise/supersede the maintenance calculation or to refuse to revise/supersede the maintenance calculation with or without a variation element. This means that any appeal is simply against the revised or superseded decision or against the refusal to revise/supersede.

1. Grounds for a variation

The grounds for a variation fall into three groups:[2]
- special expenses (see p115);
- property or capital transfers made before 5 April 1993 (see p120);
- additional cases (see p122).

Special expenses

Variation can be considered on special expenses grounds where there are:[3]
- costs of maintaining contact with the child(ren) for whom the calculation is, or will be, in force;
- costs of long-term illness or disability of a relevant child;
- prior debts, incurred before the couple separated;
- boarding school fees being paid for the child(ren) for whom the calculation is, or will be, in force;
- costs from paying a mortgage on the person with care's and child(ren)'s home.

Except for costs associated with an illness or disability of a relevant child, there is a threshold level, which must be exceeded.[4] If the net income of the non-resident parent is:
- £200 or more, the threshold is £15;
- below £200, the threshold is £10.

The threshold applies to one ground or, where there is more than one relevant ground, the sum of those costs. This also means that the first £10 or £15 of these special expenses are disregarded when calculating the variation and any subsequent adjustment to the calculation.[5] The disregard, like the threshold, does not apply to the costs associated with an illness or disability of a relevant child.

The Child Support Agency (CSA) can also substitute a lower amount for any special expenses costs that it thinks are unreasonably high or have been unreasonably incurred.[6] This may be below the threshold amount or nil. In the case of contact costs, any reduced amount must not be so low that it makes it impossible for contact to occur at the level of frequency stated in any court order, so long as those visits are taking place.[7]

Contact costs

The costs related to the non-resident parent's contact with the qualifying child can be included.[8] They can be for the non-resident parent or the child. The cost of a travelling companion can also be included – eg, because of disability, long-term illness or the young age of the child.

Costs of contact cannot include those that arise where the non-resident parent shares care of the child and that are already taken into account under the shared care provisions.[9] This means, for example, that the cost of travel to collect the child from an overnight stay which counts as a night of shared care cannot be grounds for a variation, as the non-resident parent already has that contact taken into account in his maintenance calculation.[10]

The costs of phone calls, day trips and upkeep of a car are not included.[11]

The following count as contact costs:[12]
- tickets for public transport;
- fuel for a private car;

- taxi fares, but only where the illness or disability of the non-resident parent or qualifying child makes it impractical to use another form of transport;
- car hire, where the cost of the journey would be less than by public transport or taxis, or a combination of both;
- accommodation costs for the parent or the child for overnight stays, where a return journey on the same day is impractical, or the pattern of care includes contact over two or more days;
- minor incidental costs, such as tolls or fees for roads/bridges. It may include parking fees and ticket reservation fees if it was necessary to incur these to maintain contact with the child.

The costs are based on an established pattern of visits, if one exists.[13] If there is no current established pattern, a previous one may be referred to if contact is to begin again, or an intended pattern, agreed between the non-resident parent and person with care, may be used. The pattern set out in a court order may also be used.

The costs are calculated as an average weekly amount. This will be based on a 12-month, or shorter, period which ends just before the first day of the maintenance period in which the variation would take effect.[14] In other cases, it can be based on anticipated costs. If it is based on a pattern which ends before the maintenance calculation, the CSA will consider the costs incurred between the effective date of the variation and the date on which it would cease (ie, the date on which the circumstances giving rise to the variation ended) and the date of the interim maintenance decision/maintenance calculation.[15]

When contact is set out in a court order, it may only specify an upper limit on visits. The CSA is advised to consider what is a reasonable balance between maintenance paid and visits made.[16] A non-resident parent who visits more often than the court order states may wish to change the order to reflect the true position.

To determine if the cost for fuel is reasonable the CSA will compare the amount claimed with an average figure.[17] The guidance uses petrol costs as at April 1999, resulting in suggested average petrol costs of 10.5p per mile. The CSA can adjust the figure to reflect changes in petrol prices. The figure is used only as a starting point for calculating whether the amount requested in the variation application is reasonable given the distance travelled.

If the non-resident parent returns from abroad and contact is only one reason for the trip, the CSA may limit costs to those of travel from his home in the UK. The CSA will only allow those costs that are a necessary and integral consequence of maintaining contact with the child.

Overnight costs only include reasonable accommodation costs where an overnight stay is necessary. They do not cover the cost of meals and sundries. The only exception is where breakfast is included as part of the accommodation cost – ie, its cost cannot be separately identified.[18]

Changes in contact may mean changes to the variation element. If contact stops, even through no fault of the non-resident parent, the calculation may be superseded to reflect this change (see p138).

Example

Bronwen has a net income of £428 and pays basic rate maintenance of £86 to Ivan for Ursula and Gretchen. She claims a special expenses cost for contact with her children, amounting to £450 over a six-month period since the girls attend boarding school. This includes travel from Northern Ireland by ferry, petrol and overnight stays in hotels, amounting to 18 nights over the six-month period.

The amounts included are deemed reasonable in the circumstances and the weekly amount is calculated:

£450 ÷ 26 = £17.30 a week on average.

This is above the threshold of £15. Therefore, a variation of £2.30 (£17.30 − £15) for contact costs may be considered.

The number of nights Bronwen sees the children is 18 (ie, less than 26 nights in six months), so the shared care rules would not result in a reduction of her maintenance.

Costs of a long-term illness or disability of a relevant child

In order to apply for a variaton, the costs of a child's long-term illness or disability may only relate to a relevant child – ie, a child for whom the non-resident parent or his new partner receives child benefit.

A long-term illness is one current at the date of the variation application or from the date the variation would take effect. It must be likely to last for a further 52 weeks or to be terminal.[19] The child is considered disabled if:[20]

- disability living allowance (DLA) is paid for her/him;
- s/he would receive DLA but for the fact s/he is in hospital; *or*
- s/he is blind or registered as blind.

Costs allowable are the reasonable additional costs of:[21]

- personal care, attendance and communication needs;
- mobility;
- domestic help;
- medical aids which cannot be provided under the NHS;[22]
- heating, clothing and laundry;
- food essential for a diet recommended by a medical practitioner;
- adaptations to the non-resident parent's home; *and*
- day care, respite care and rehabilitation.

Where an aid or appliance can be provided under the NHS (by health services or local authorities) a variation will normally not be agreed, even if the item is not available due to lack of funds at a particular time. However, a variation can be agreed where there is likely to be a serious delay in supplying an item which would prevent the child's condition from seriously deteriorating.[23] The decision maker will also consider the cost of the aid and whether it can be obtained at a cheaper price.

Any financial help towards these costs from any source, paid to the non-resident parent or a member of his household, is deducted.[24] This includes DLA but only where it relates to the expense claimed (eg, if costs for personal care are claimed, DLA care component could be deducted, but not the mobility component).[25] If DLA has been applied for but is not in payment it can be included if, when awarded, it will cover the date the variation starts. In other cases where no financial assistance is in payment, no amount will be offset against the costs.

Debts of the relationship

A non-resident parent may be repaying debts incurred *before* he became a non-resident parent (see p21) of the qualifying child (whether before or after April 1993). Repayment can count as special expenses, but only if the debt was incurred when the non-resident parent and person with care were a couple (see p25). The debts must have been taken out for the benefit of:[26]

- the non-resident parent and person with care, jointly;
- the person with care alone, if the non-resident parent is liable for the repayments;
- a person who is not a child but at the time the debt was incurred:
  - was a child;
  - lived with the non-resident parent and person with care; *and*
  - was the child of the non-resident parent, person with care or both of them;
- the qualifying child;
- any child other than the qualifying child who at the time the debt was incurred:
  - lived with the non-resident parent and person with care; *and*
  - is a child of the person with care.

Loans only count if they are from a qualifying lender, or from a current or former employer.[27] Qualifying lenders include banks, building societies or other registered lenders (eg, hire purchase).[28]

The following do *not* count as debts:

- debts incurred to buy something which the non-resident parent kept for his own use after the relationship ended;[29]
- a loan other than one obtained from a qualifying lender, or the non-resident parent's current or former employer;[30]
- a debt for which the applicant took responsibility under a financial settlement with the ex-partner or a court order;[31]

- a debt for which a variation has previously been agreed, but which has not been repaid in the period for which the variation has been applied to the calculation;[32]
- secured mortgage repayments, except for amounts incurred to buy or repair/improve (see p189)[33] the home of the person with care and qualifying child; *and*
- endowment/insurance premiums, except for mortgage/insurance incurred to buy or repair/improve (see p189) the home of the person with care and qualifying child.[34]

Payments or a debt taken out to pay off any negative equity on the former joint home do not count as debts, as the person with care no longer lives there.[35]

The following also do *not* count as debts:[36]

- debts of a business or trade;
- gambling debts;
- legal costs of the separation, divorce or dissolution of the civil partnership;
- credit card repayments;
- overdrafts, unless taken out for a specified amount repayable over a specified period;
- fines imposed on the applicant;
- any debt incurred to pay off one of these; *or*
- any other debt the CSA considers reasonable to exclude.

A debt incurred to pay a former debt which would have counted may be included. However, only that part which could have counted is included as special expenses.[37]

A variation is normally based on the original debt repayment period; any rescheduling of the debt is usually ignored.[38] However, if the applicant has been unemployed or ill and the creditors have agreed to extend the repayment period, the CSA can take the extended period into account. There is discretion on the length of time over which the debt may be taken as extended when setting the period for which the variation for prior debt applies to the calculation.

Boarding school fees

The maintenance element of boarding school fees incurred, or expected to be incurred, by the non-resident parent for the qualifying child may be considered.[39] Only term-time costs for non-advanced education at a recognised educational establishment can be included.[40]

If the maintenance element cannot be distinguished from other costs, the CSA can decide what to include, but this should not exceed 35 per cent of the total fees.[41]

If the non-resident parent receives financial help to pay the fees, or only pays part of the fees with someone else, a proportion of the costs are included. This is calculated in the same ratio as the maintenance element to overall fees.[42]

In all cases, a variation for boarding school fees should not reduce the amount of income to be considered for calculating maintenance by more than 50 per cent.[43]

. . . .

Example
Bronwen claims special expenses for her contribution to boarding school costs for Ursula and Gretchen. She pays the school £1,500 a term – ie, £4,500 a year. Ivan pays the rest of the fees – ie, £4,500 a year. Her net income is £428.
The fees for each child per term are £1,500 and the maintenance element is £500 a term.
Bronwen's contribution to maintenance is worked out as £250 a child each term – ie, £500. Over the three terms this amounts to £1,500, which is converted into a weekly figure (£1,500 ÷ 365 x 7 = £28.77). This is above the threshold of £15 so a variation for a contribution to boarding school fees of £13.77 may be considered. (If this were to be accepted, it would not reduce the net income by more than 50 per cent.)

. . . .

Payments for certain mortgages, loans or insurance policies

These cover payments made to a mortgage lender, insurer or person with care for a mortgage or loan where:[44]

- it was taken out to facilitate the purchase of, or repairs/improvements to, the property by someone other than the non-resident parent;
- the payments are not made because of a debt or other legal liability of the non-resident parent for the period in which the variation is applied;
- the property was the person with care's and non-resident parent's home when they were a couple, and it is still the home of the person with care and qualifying child; *and*
- the non-resident parent has no legal/financial rights in the property – eg, a charge or equitable interest.

Payments may also be considered for an insurance/endowment policy taken out to discharge a mortgage or loan as above, except where the non-resident parent is entitled to any part of the proceeds when the policy matures.[45]

Property/capital transfers

Variation is only possible where a pre-5 April 1993 court order or written agreement was in force between the non-resident parent and the person with care and/or the child(ren) in the child maintenance application.[46] The court order must have been to transfer property/capital in lieu of maintenance for the child either wholly or in part.[47] If the court order specifies that it is in lieu of spousal maintenance only, the variation will be disallowed.[48]

The court order must be made under one of the Acts listed in Appendix 3.[49]

The transfer must mean that the non-resident parent has transferred any beneficial interest in the property/capital to:[50]

- the person with care;
- the qualifying child; *or*
- trustees where the trust is set up solely, or as one of its objects, to provide maintenance for the qualifying child.

Where the transfer does not satisfy any of these conditions but the CSA is satisfied that some or all of the property subsequently transferred to the person with care, the transfer will be accepted.[51]

The CSA first works out the value of the transfer, ignoring any part which was not in lieu of child maintenance.[52] (Allowance is also made for any compensating transfer from the person with care to the non-resident parent.) Unless there is evidence to show otherwise, the CSA assumes that:[53]

- the property covered by the order/agreement was held in equal shares by the non-resident parent and person with care;
- if those parties had been married, half of the value of the transfer was for the person with care's benefit, and not for the child(ren);
- if those parties were *never* married, *none* of the value of the transfer was for the person with care's benefit.

The minimum value of the transfer must be £5,000.[54]

The equivalent weekly value is then worked out. The number of years of liability is deemed to begin on the date of the order/agreement and to end on the date it sets for maintenance to end (for the youngest child if there is more than one), or, if no date is given, when the youngest child reaches 18.[55] Using that figure and the interest rate at the date of the order/agreement, a multiplier is given by a table.[56] That gives an equivalent weekly value. If using that figure in the variation would lead to an amount of maintenance of less than the child maintenance payable under the order/agreement, a lower weekly value can be set.[57]

Example

Marcus and Helene divorced in 1992, when their youngest child, Robert, was one. Marcus transferred his share in the home to Helene, in lieu of maintenance for her and the children. Marcus applies for a variation on property transfer grounds.

The value of the house at that time was £46,000 but there was a mortgage of £14,000. The CSA considers that of the £16,000 transferred (£46,000 − £14,000 ÷ 2 as they each had equal shares) only £8,000 can be considered in lieu of child maintenance. This is above the threshold of £5,000.

The number of years of liability is worked out as 17 (ie, from the date of the order until Robert is 18). The interest rate for a judgment debt at the time of the order was 15 per cent. Based on the table of equivalent values this gives a multiplier of 0.00323.

The equivalent weekly value of the property transfer to be considered is £8,000 x 0.00323 = £25.84

Additional cases

There are additional cases in which a variation may be applied for by a person with care or child in Scotland. These are where the non-resident parent has:[58]
- assets over £65,000;
- a lifestyle which is inconsistent with his stated income;
- income which has not been taken into account in the calculation; *or*
- diverted income.

The effect of a variation on additional cases grounds will be to increase the net weekly income of the non-resident parent to be taken into account in the calculation.[59] The maximum net weekly income, after adding any amount for additional cases variation(s), cannot exceed the capped amount of £2,000.

If the non-resident parent is in receipt of a benefit that attracts the flat rate (other than income support (IS), income-based jobseeker's allowance (JSA), income-related employment and support allowance (ESA) or pension credit (PC)) even though he may not pay this because of shared care or because he qualifies for the nil rate (but not on income grounds), there are special rules regarding the maximum amount payable when a variation is agreed on additional cases grounds.[60] This is known as the 'better buy' provision (see p135).

Assets over £65,000

The CSA must be satisfied that the asset:[61]
- is under the non-resident parent's control, or is one in which he has a beneficial interest;
- has been transferred to trustees, but the non-resident parent is the beneficiary of the trust, and the transfer was made to reduce the amount of assets which could be considered under a variation application;
- is subject to a trust of which the non-resident parent is a beneficiary.

Assets include:[62]
- money – actual cash or deposits in banks, building society, Post Office accounts, premium bonds or savings certificates;
- legal estate, interest in, or rights over, land;
- stocks and shares;
- claims it would be reasonable to enforce;
- in Scotland, monies due or an obligation owed which it would be reasonable to enforce; *and*
- any of the above located outside Great Britain.

The CSA will not count assets if:[63]
- their total value is £65,000 or less after repaying any mortgage/charge on them. Any asset in respect of which income is taken into account following the application of the next type of variation described (income not taken into account – see p124) will be deducted from the non-resident parent's total assets before this test is applied;
- it is satisfied the non-resident parent is holding them for a reasonable purpose (eg, cash from the sale of a home that is intended to purchase a new home);
- they are compensation for personal injury;
- they are used for a trade or business (except property which produces rental income that produces a profit[64]). Shares are not used in the course of a business or trade if the trade or business is not that of the non-resident parent (eg, where he has invested in a company or even owns one, but it is not his trade/business);[65]
- the asset is the home of the non-resident parent or his child; *or*
- they are payments from certain trusts (eg, Macfarlane Trust or the variant CJD compensation trust), which would be ignored if the non-resident parent were on IS.[66]

If an asset is held in joint names, the CSA assumes that each person has equal shares, unless there is evidence to suggest otherwise.[67]

The weekly value of the assets is worked out by multiplying the value of the assets by the statutory rate of interest and dividing the resulting figure by 52.[68] The statutory rate of interest is that which applies on the effective date in the non-resident parent's country of habitual residence (ie, England, Wales, Scotland or Northern Ireland); this is currently 8 per cent.[69] If the non-resident parent works abroad for a UK-based employer the rate is based on the locality of the employer. The weekly value is added to other income, including benefits and bearing in mind the better buy rules for those on benefit (see p135).[70]

Example

Graham has a net income of £480 a week and pays maintenance to Andie of £96 a week. Andie applies for a variation on the grounds that Graham has substantial assets – ie, a holiday home in Spain and savings.

The property in Spain has a value of £52,000 and Graham has savings and investments of £17,000. The total value of his assets is £69,000, which is above the threshold of £65,000. A variation may be considered using a weekly value worked out as £106.15 (ie, £69,000 x 8% ÷ 52).

If Graham had owned the property in Spain jointly with his new partner, Nadia, the total value of his assets would have been £26,000 + £17,000 = £43,000, which is below the threshold.

Income not taken into account and diversion of income

Income not taken into account covers situations where the non-resident parent is on the nil rate (except where this is because income is below £5) or the flat rate because of receipt of a prescribed benefit (other than IS, income-based JSA, income-related ESA or PC), even though he may pay less because of shared care.[71] The CSA must be satisfied that the non-resident parent receives income which would be taken into account in the maintenance calculation if he were not due to pay the nil rate or the flat rate for these reasons.

A variation may also be agreed for income not taken into account if:[72]

- the non-resident parent has the ability to control the amount of income he receives from a company or business, including earnings from employment or self-employment or is able to control the amount that is taken into account as his net weekly income;[73] *and*
- the income from that company or business would not otherwise be taken into account in the maintenance calculation.

This variation could, for example, apply where income in the form of dividends is received by a company director.[74] However, it can also apply to other forms of income received from a company or business. Reimbursement to the non-resident parent of legitimate business expenses will be ignored. The additional income received from the company or business is added to the non-resident parent's net weekly income for the purposes of the maintenance calculation.

For a variation for income not taken into account to be made, the income not taken into account must be net weekly income of over £100. This can be from either of the situations described above or, if a variation is considered under both cases, income from both can be added together.[75]

When working out the earnings of students, the total income for the year, ending with the relevant week, is added together and divided by 52 to give a weekly amount. An alternative period may be used if the CSA considers it more representative.

The weekly value of any additional income is added to other income from benefits, bearing in mind that the better-buy provision (see p135) applies to those on benefit when calculating the maximum maintenance due.[76] Benefits include those prescribed for the flat rate (except IS/income-based JSA/income-related ESA/PC), less any disregards.[77]

Example

Joel is a mature student who works part time in a care home. He is on the nil rate for maintenance. Kaliani applies for a variation on income not taken into account grounds. Kaliani looks after one child, Selim.

Joel's student grant and loan do not count as income, so only his part-time earnings are considered. Over the year Joel's net earnings are £9,367.80, which is converted into a weekly amount (ie, £9,367.80 ÷ 52 = £180.15). As this is over £100 a variation may be considered using a weekly value figure of £180.15. Therefore, if the variation to the calculation is agreed, instead of paying nothing Joel will now be due to pay a reduced rate of £25 (£5 + (25% x £80.15) = £25.04 rounded to the nearest pound).

Diversion of income is considered where:[78]
- the non-resident parent has the ability to control the income he receives, including earnings from self-employment; *and*
- the CSA is satisfied that the non-resident parent has unreasonably reduced the amount of income he would have received (and which would have been taken into account in the maintenance calculation or under a variation for income from a company or business – see p124) by diverting it to someone else. The diversion does *not* have to have been arranged specifically to avoid child maintenance responsibilities.

Diversion of income may be made:
- to a third party, such as a new partner or close family member;
- to a business, such as where the non-resident parent takes a lower income, or to a pension scheme from which the non-resident parent will benefit later. It would, however, have to be reasonable to make a variation in such circumstances – eg, if the money is being used to develop the company, a variation should not be made;[79]
- towards other purposes, such as where the non-resident parent uses company assets for private use or business funds for day-to-day expenditure.

Example
Marcus runs his own import/export business, employing his new partner, Shamira, and his brother. Each has a company car, in his case a Jaguar. His brother is paid £600 a week and he and Shamira each receive £400. His ex-wife, Helene, gets basic rate maintenance of £80 for their two children. Helene applies for a variation because she thinks he is diverting income via the company, especially as Shamira does not seem to do any work.
Part of Marcus's day-to-day expenses are included in business expenses – eg, the car and business lunches. Shamira's salary could also be a token payment, as Marcus takes less from the business than he pays his brother. The CSA considers that, on balance, there could be diversion of income via the company and Shamira's wages. Given its contentious nature, the case is referred to an appeal tribunal.

The full amount of any diverted income will be added to net weekly income when working out maintenance.[80]

Lifestyle inconsistent with declared income

The person with care, or a qualifying child in Scotland, may apply for a variation on this ground if the CSA is satisfied that the income used (or which would have been used) in the calculation is substantially lower than that needed to support the non-resident parent's lifestyle.[81] This variation may be granted in cases where the flat rate applies because of benefit income, but not where the flat rate is payable because of receipt of IS, income-based JSA, income-related ESA or PC.

However, a variation will not be allowed where it is clear that the lifestyle is paid for by:[82]

- income which is, or would be, disregarded in the maintenance calculation;
- income which could be considered under the diversion of income ground;
- income which could be considered under a variation for income not taken into account from a company or business (see p124);
- assets, or income from assets; *or*
- a partner's income or assets, except if the non-resident parent is able to influence or control the amount of income, assets or income from the assets.

A variation cannot be granted where an inconsistent lifestyle is financed by borrowing, as this would not meet the requirement that the variation decision be just and equitable (see p133).[83]

In addition to these situations, if the calculation is not based on net weekly income a variation will not be allowed where the lifestyle is paid for from income of £100 or less, or which could be considered in the income not taken into account ground (see p124).[84]

The amount of income which will be taken into account will be the difference between the amount:[85]

- the non-resident parent needs to support his overall lifestyle; *and*
- taken into account (or which would have been taken into account) in the maintenance calculation.

This includes any income from benefits (ie, except for IS/income-based JSA/ income-related ESA/PC, benefits prescribed for the flat rate, less disregards), bearing in mind the better-buy rules for those on benefit (see p135).

CSA guidance indicates that this ground is most likely to be used in situations where the non-resident parent is self-employed or where it is suspected that he is working without fully declaring income for tax and national insurance purposes.[86] Before the non-resident parent is contacted, a fraud check will be made by the CSA in order not to jeapoardise any ongoing fraud investigation.

It would not be enough to show that the non-resident parent pursued one extravagant activity, as there may be good reasons for this. The non-resident parent must have an overall lifestyle that, in most respects, is inconsistent with his declared income – eg, a large, expensively furnished home, expensive car, frequent foreign holidays and expensive leisure activities would all be considered.

The use of declared capital to finance an otherwise inconsistent lifestyle, or a lifestyle supported by a partner's wealth or income, cannot lead to a successful variation.[87]

Example

Marcus lives with his new partner, Shamira, in a townhouse in central London. He runs his own import/export business. His ex-wife, Helene, gets basic rate maintenance of £80 for their two children. Helene applies for a variation because Marcus is able to afford to live in central London, drive a new Jaguar (changing cars every two or three years), he plays polo (keeping three ponies in stables), is a member of an exclusive golf club and he and Shamira frequently travel abroad.

Part of the expenses are included in business expenses – eg, the car and travel abroad on business trips, and the golf club membership is used for corporate entertaining. Shamira is also an employee of the company, meaning her income is under Marcus's control, though her wages are equivalent to those of other staff. The CSA considers that, on balance, his lifestyle does appear inconsistent with his income. However, it also considers that there could be a diversion of income. Given its contentious nature, the case is referred to the First-tier Tribunal.

Had the situation been reversed, with Shamira independently wealthy, owning the business and paying for the lifestyle, including paying Marcus's wages, the case may have been refused. Helene could appeal such a refusal, although it may be that a variation is not possible on this ground. The CSA would also have to consider whether there had been a diversion of income or assets which Marcus could control.

2. Applying for a variation

An application for a variation may be made before or after a maintenance calculation has been made.[88] Only a relevant person may apply – ie, a person with care, a non-resident parent or a qualifying child in Scotland. An authorised representative may also make an application. The Child Support Agency (CSA) also has the discretion to reinstate a previous variation without an application in certain prescribed circumstances (see p140).

The application for a variation may be made either orally or in writing.[89] This means an applicant may give details over the phone, although the CSA may ask for a written application – eg, because complicated special expenses are being asked for which could not be explained over the telephone. A form may be provided by the CSA, or the applicant can send the application in another written form which the CSA may accept as sufficient, depending on the circumstances.[90] Where a written application is required this should be provided within 14 days. If the time limit is exceeded without good cause, the effective date of the variation may be affected.

The application must state the grounds on which it is made.[91] If the application does not state the grounds, or at least give a reason, it will not be accepted as properly made.

Example

Joe applies for a variation because he believes his maintenance is too high. The CSA does not accept it as a properly made application.

Joe applies for a variation because he believes his maintenance is too high and he cannot afford it because of the high cost of pet food. The CSA accepts the application as properly made, but then rejects the application on preliminary consideration, as it is not on a regulated ground.

Joe applies for a variation because he believes his maintenance is too high because he cannot afford the kennel costs he incurs when he travels to see his children. The CSA accepts the application as properly made and it is given preliminary consideration. It rejects the application as kennel costs are not a recognised ground. However, had Joe referred to other contact costs (eg, tickets or fuel) his application would probably have proceeded.

If an application is made, but there is insufficient information to decide whether to progress it, the CSA may request further information.[92] The request may be made orally or in writing (including email).[93] The applicant is given one month from the date of notification in which to supply the information.[94] This time limit may be extended in special circumstances – eg, if the applicant is in hospital. If the information is not provided, the CSA may either reject the application or proceed with it at its discretion.[95]

An application for a variation may be amended or withdrawn at any time before a decision is made.[96] This may be done orally or in writing. No amendment can be made if the change relates to a period after the effective date of the application.[97]

3. **Procedure**

Once an application has been made the procedure is as follows:
- preliminary consideration of the application (see p129);
- unless rejected, other parties may be notified and asked to make representations ('contest') (see p130);
- an interim maintenance decision may be made (see p131);
- a regular payment condition may be imposed (see p132);
- the decision will be considered (see p133).

In addition, the case may be passed to the First-tier Tribunal after preliminary consideration for a determination (see p134).

The application will proceed for determination unless it has already failed.[98] It may fail (ie, the Child Support Agency (CSA) may refuse to consider it further before this point) because, for example:

- one of the grounds for rejection is established on preliminary consideration (see below);
- it is withdrawn; *or*
- the regular payment condition has not been met.

Two or more applications for a variation may be considered at the same time.[99] In addition, if appropriate, an application made on one ground may be treated as an application on a different ground.[100]

Preliminary consideration

Once an application is properly made there is a preliminary consideration of the case.[101] At this point, the CSA may reject the application and decide:

- to revise or supersede the maintenance calculation, or to refuse to revise or supersede;[102] *or*
- make the maintenance calculation, or make a default maintenance decision.[103]

Any decision carries the normal appeal rights.

Grounds for rejecting or refusing a variation

An application for a variation may be rejected because:[104]

- the requirements of the stated ground are not met;
- in special expenses cases, the threshold is not exceeded;
- in property/capital transfer cases, the £5,000 minimum value is not exceeded;
- in additional assets cases, their value does not exceed £65,000;
- in income not taken into account cases, this does not exceed £100;
- information requested by the CSA has not been provided within the one-month time limit;
- a default maintenance decision is in force;
- the application is made by the person with care or qualifying child on additional cases grounds and the capped amount of income is already applied, or the non-resident parent or his partner are in receipt of working tax credit;
- the application is made by the non-resident parent on special expenses grounds and after deducting these, net income exceeds the capped amount;
- the non-resident parent is on the flat rate as he or his partner is on income support (IS), income-based jobseeker's allowance (JSA), income-related employment and support allowance (ESA) or pension credit (PC) (including if the partner is also a non-resident parent), but is due to pay less than the flat rate or nil because of shared care or the transitional rules on conversion;

- the non-resident parent is due to pay the flat rate (or the lower prescribed amount) under the transitional rules on conversion, or a property or capital transfer reduces maintenance below the flat rate or because of part-time care by a local authority;
- the application is made by the non-resident parent; *and*
  - he is on the nil rate; *or*
  - he is on the flat rate because he receives a prescribed benefit (other than IS/income-based JSA/ESA/PC) or has income of £100 or less; *or*
  - he pays the flat rate of £5 (or less if apportioned) because of shared care, including care by a local authority.

In some cases, if a default maintenance decision applies, an application for a variation may contain sufficient information to revise the default decision and replace it with a maintenance calculation.

Contest

If the application has not been rejected on preliminary consideration the other relevant parties will usually be notified. However, in some situations where the CSA has discretion to reinstate a previous variation it does not need to notify or invite representations (see p140).

The notification may be done orally or in writing and must:[105]

- state the grounds on which the application has been made and provide any information or evidence the applicant has given to support it;
- invite parties to make representations about the circumstances within 14 days; *and*
- not contain information that should not be disclosed.

In practice, non-applicants are informed in writing and supplied with the evidence. Where the application has been via a phone call the evidence may be a transcript of the telephone conversation.

In some cases, the applicant may be late in supplying further evidence or information (ie, outside the one-month time limit) but the CSA may have decided to proceed with the application in the meantime and notify the other parties. This information may be passed to the other parties later and a further 14 days for representations allowed from the date of this later notification.[106] If the CSA is satisfied that it is reasonable, this time limit may be extended.[107]

The other parties may respond orally or in writing, although the CSA may require them to make a written submission. Where no contesting information is provided, the CSA may make a determination on the application as it stands.[108]

Any information which the other party provides, other than that which may not be disclosed (see p131), may be forwarded to the applicant if the CSA considers this reasonable.[109] This will only happen if the other party has contradicted the applicant's statement and the decision maker does not have sufficient evidence to decide the case, or s/he has provided supporting evidence to refute it.[110] The applicant will be given 14 days to comment on the evidence or information supplied by the other party.

Additional non-disclosure rules

There are additional rules on non-disclosure in variations cases. Supporting evidence or information from one party will not be notified to the other party if it contains:[111]

- details of an illness or disability of a relevant other child if the non-resident parent has requested that this is not disclosed and the CSA agrees;
- medical evidence which has not been disclosed to the applicant or a relevant person (person with care, non-resident parent or qualifying child in Scotland) which would be harmful to that individual;
- the address of a relevant person or qualifying child, or information which could lead to that individual or child being located, and there is a risk of harm or undue distress.

If an applicant requests that information is not disclosed, this will be discussed with her/him. It may be possible to make an amended application which does not include details s/he does not wish to be disclosed. If an applicant refuses to disclose information that is relevant for the other party to contest the application, the application can be rejected.[112] However, there may be a good reason for non-disclosure and each case should be considered on its own merits.

Contest not required

Representations from the other relevant parties are not required if:[113]

- the CSA is reinstating a variation at its own discretion (see p140);
- there is a property/capital transfer variation and a change of circumstances meant that the CSA no longer had jurisdiction, but a subsequent change means it does and an application for variation is made on a further application for a maintenance calculation;
- a variation is agreed and the non-resident parent has the maintenance calculation replaced by a default decision, but subsequently this is replaced with a maintenance calculation.

Interim maintenance decision

If an application for a variation is made before the maintenance calculation, an interim maintenance decision may be made.[114] This means an interim maintenance decision can be made if the first calculation has not been made or if the process is complete except for an outstanding variation application. The amount of the interim maintenance decision will be the maintenance calculated in the normal way, ignoring the variation. This is to allow the variation application to be considered. An interim maintenance decision may be replaced by a maintenance calculation, which is made whether or not a variation has been agreed. The effective date of the maintenance calculation will be the same as the interim maintenance decision.

The interim maintenance decision can be appealed in the normal way. However, when a maintenance calculation is made which replaces this, any appeal may lapse.[115] If the interim maintenance decision is superseded, the normal 5 per cent change in net income tolerance rule (see p360) does not apply.

Regular payment condition

A non-resident parent may have a regular payment condition imposed after the preliminary consideration.[116] It is intended that this will be used if a non-resident parent has:

- a poor payment record or arrears;
- failed to make payments while the variation application is being contested and considered; *or*
- special expenses which make it hard for him to meet the maintenance liability.

The amount due under a regular payment condition will be either the:[117]

- maintenance calculated, including that set under an interim maintenance decision; *or*
- amount of maintenance which would be due if the variation was agreed.

This means that if the CSA believes that the variation application will be successful, it may set a regular payment condition that adjusts the maintenance calculated to reflect the variation, reducing the financial burden on the parent. However, if it believes that the application will be unsuccessful and a regular payment condition is imposed, it will be set at the calculation rate.

A regular payment condition does not affect the amount of maintenance the non-resident parent is liable to pay.[118] Therefore, if the set amount is lower than the amount due there will be arrears if the variation application fails.

The condition is set independently of any other arrears arrangement the parent may have and ends either when the CSA makes a final decision on the maintenance calculation (whether or not the variation is agreed to), or when the application is withdrawn.[119]

When a regular payment condition is imposed, the non-resident parent, person with care and/or qualifying child applicant in Scotland will be sent written notification.[120] This will make it clear that if the condition is not met, the application may lapse.[121]

If a non-resident parent does not meet the regular payment condition within one month of this notification, the CSA will refuse to consider the application for a variation.[122] Written notification of this refusal will be sent to the non-resident parent, person with care and/or qualifying child applicant in Scotland.[123] A refusal to consider the application cannot be appealed.

Considering the decision

The CSA can exercise some discretion in variations to the maintenance calculation. In addition to the normal rules, the CSA must be satisfied that:[124]
- the grounds are met; *and*
- it is just and equitable to agree to the variation.

When considering the decision, the CSA must bear in mind the general principles that:[125]
- a parent is responsible for maintaining her/his children when s/he can afford to do so;
- a parent is responsible for maintaining all her/his children equally;
- the welfare of any child affected by an application for a variation must be taken into account.

A decision may be made to agree to the variation in full or to refuse it. This may result in a revision or supersession of the decision or replacement of the interim maintenance decision.[126] The revision/supersession decision is dealt with under the normal rules (see p138).

Just and equitable

Even though the grounds are met, a variation decision will only be agreed if it is just and equitable.[127] Certain factors must be taken into account when making the decision. These include:[128]
- whether agreeing to a variation would lead the non-resident parent or parent with care to give up employment;
- if the applicant is the non-resident parent, whether there is any liability to pay child maintenance under a court order or agreement prior to the effective date of the maintenance calculation; *or*
- if the non-resident parent has applied for a special expenses variation, whether he could make financial arrangements to cover those expenses or could pay for them from money currently spent on non-essentials.

This list is not exhaustive and other factors may be considered in deciding what is just and equitable.

The following must *not* be taken into account:[129]
- whether or not the child's conception was planned;
- who was responsible for the breakdown of the relationship between the non-resident parent and person with care;
- whether the non-resident parent or person with care is in a new relationship with someone who is not the qualifying child's parent;
- any contact arrangements;

- the income or assets of anyone other than the non-resident parent, and/or, if an application is made on the grounds of a lifestyle inconsistent with declared income, his partner;
- any failure of the non-resident parent to pay child maintenance under CSA arrangements, a court order or written agreement; *and*
- representations from individuals other than the person with care, non-resident parent or a qualifying child applicant in Scotland.

Referral to the First-tier Tribunal

Once the application has passed the preliminary consideration and contest stage, the case may be passed to the First-tier Tribunal for a determination on whether or not to agree to the variation.[130] This will normally only occur if a novel or particularly contentious issue is being considered.[131]

The decision maker should also consider whether only the First-tier Tribunal would be able to obtain the necessary evidence to determine the application, in which case the application should be referred.

The First-tier Tribunal will apply the same rules as a CSA decision maker and will determine that the variation should be either agreed or refused.[132] Its determination will be passed back to the CSA to make the decision. This decision by the CSA (ie, to revise/supersede, or refuse to revise/supersede, the maintenance calculation) may then be appealed in the normal way (see p142).

4. **The decision**

A variation is an element of the maintenance calculation. The Child Support Agency (CSA) may agree to, or refuse, the application for variation. In either case, it may result in a decision to:[133]

- revise or supersede the maintenance calculation/replace the interim maintenance decision, or refuse to revise or supersede;
- make a maintenance calculation (this may replace an interim maintenance decision) or default maintenance decision.

The CSA's internal guidance indicates when to refuse to revise or supersede – eg, refusing if an application does not meet one of the grounds, or fails at preliminary consideration or later.[134]

In some cases, a variation may be agreed which makes no difference to the amount of maintenance calculated. A revision or supersession will still be carried out, as each decision gives further appeal rights.

Once a variation is made it will continue to be considered each time there is a revision or supersession of the maintenance calculation, under the normal revision/supersession rules (see Chapter 17). Because of some changes in circumstances the variation may cease to have effect, in which case the calculation may be suspended or cancelled in order to remove the variation element. When there is a further change in circumstances the variation may be reinstated by the CSA without an application. In other cases, a new request for a variation may need to be made.

Following variation to the maintenance calculation, as with other maintenance calculation decisions, the amount of maintenance paid may be affected by the special rules on court order phasing (see p329) or conversions (see Chapter 7).

The effect of the variation

The effect of the variation should not reduce the total amount of maintenance to less than £5,[135] and the maximum amount of net income that can be taken into account is the capped amount of £2,000.[136] The following sections examine the effect of a variation on different grounds, including where there is more than one ground – eg, special expenses and additional cases. The CSA calls these 'concurrent variations'.

Additional cases

If a variation is made on additional cases grounds, the amount of any additional income is added to the net income of the non-resident parent.[137] Where this would result in a net income figure above the capped amount, the net income is restricted to the capped amount of £2,000.

> *Example*
> The case in the example on p125 is referred to the First-tier Tribunal. The First-tier Tribunal determines that there should be a variation for additional income, with a weekly value of £360 for both diversion of income and a lifestyle inconsistent with declared income. This is added to Marcus's net income, as used in the maintenance calculation, of £400. His net income is now £760. The amount he is now due to pay Helene is £152.

If the non-resident parent is in receipt of a benefit (other than income support (IS), income-based jobseeker's allowance (JSA), income-related employment and support allowance (ESA) or pension credit (PC)) that attracts the flat rate, even though he may not pay this because of shared care or because he qualifies for the nil rate (but not on income grounds) there are special rules regarding the maximum amount payable when a variation is agreed on additional cases grounds.[138] This is known as the 'better-buy' provision (see below).

Better-buy

The maximum amount of maintenance a non-resident parent on benefit (other than IS, income-based JSA, income-related ESA or PC) will have to pay after a variation on additional cases grounds is the lesser of:[139]

- the flat rate plus the amount calculated under the normal calculation rules on additional income (exclusive of the benefit income); *or*
- the amount calculated under the normal calculation rules on total income (including any benefit that attracts the flat rate liability, less disregards).

The amounts disregarded in benefit income are:[140]
- industrial injuries benefits – constant attendance and exceptionally severe disablement allowances;
- war disablement pension – constant attendance, exceptionally severe disablement, severe occupational and mobility supplement allowances;
- service pensions – the unemployability allowances.

Example
Adam gets retirement pension of £90.70 and is due to pay Carol the flat rate of £5 for one child. He has an occupational pension of £97.50 a week and a personal pension of £39 a week, providing a further £136.50 a week. Adam's total income is £227.20. Carol applies for a variation on income not taken into account grounds. As he has income over £100 the better buy calculation is carried out:
Flat rate (£5) + £5 + (25% x £36.50, rounded to the nearest pound = £9) = £19
Normal rules calculation on total income (£97.50 + £136.50 = £227.20)
Basic rate maintenance is 15% x £227.20 = £34.08 rounded to £34
Better-buy will mean a variation may be considered which would result in maintenance of £19 (ie, the lesser of the two amounts).

Special expenses

The total amount of any special expenses (less any threshold amounts) is deducted from the net weekly income of the non-resident parent and the calculation is carried out as normal using this amount.[141] Where there is more than one special expense included, the amounts are aggregated and only one threshold is applied (where applicable).[142]

If the net income is the capped amount, the effect of the variation is worked out by subtracting the special expenses from the actual net weekly income.[143] If this results in a figure above the capped amount of £2,000, the special expenses variation will be refused.

Example
Bronwen has a net income of £428 and pays basic rate maintenance of £86 to Ivan for Ursula and Gretchen. She claims special expenses costs for contact with her children, which amounts to £450 over a six-month period, and for the contribution to their boarding school fees of £1,500 a term.

Her special expenses are worked out as £17.30 for contact and £28.77 for boarding school costs, totalling £46.07. The threshold of £15 applies and £15 is deducted from the total, leaving £31.07.

This is deducted from her weekly net income (£428 – £31.07 = £396.93)

Her maintenance is now worked out in the usual way: 20% x £396.93 = £79.39 rounded to £79

Her variation for special expenses has reduced her maintenance from £86 a week to £79.

Property and capital transfers

The transfer is treated as an advance payment of maintenance.[144] Therefore, the equivalent weekly value is subtracted from the maintenance calculated to produce the amount due after a variation on property/capital transfer grounds.[145]

Example

Marcus has a property transfer variation agreed with a weekly value of £25.84. His net weekly income is £400 and under the maintenance calculation he is due to pay Helene maintenance of £80 a week for Robert and Heather. There is no reduction for shared care and so the weekly value of the property transfer is subtracted from the amount he is due to pay.

£80 – £25.84 = £54.16, the amount he must pay following the variation.

Concurrent variations

If there is more than one variation element (ie, special expenses, additional cases) to be applied, the calculation is carried out using the following steps.

Step 1

Work out the amounts of each element.

Step 2

Apply the additional cases element, capping the income at £2,000.

Step 3

Apply the special expenses element.

Step 4

Work out the maintenance due, applying any apportionment or reduction for shared care or part-time local authority care.

Step 5

Apply any property transfer element (only that which applies to the parent with care who benefited from the transfer).

Step 6

Check that the total amount of maintenance is not less than £5. If so, apportion this between the persons with care.

Example

The situation is as in the example on p121. In this instance, both the property transfer and the additional cases variation are applied to work out how much Marcus must pay Helene for Robert and Heather. His net income before variation is £400, as before.

Step 1   The additional cases variation is that £360 additional income should be included. The property transfer variation has a weekly value of £25.84.

Step 2   £360 + £400 = £760, which is below the capped amount.

Step 3   Does not apply.

Step 4   Basic maintenance due is 20% x £760 = £152

Step 5   Maintenance due is reduced by the property transfer (ie, £152 – £25.84 = £126.16)

Therefore, instead of receiving £80 from Marcus, Helene will now be due £126.16 a week.

Revisions and supersessions

A variation is not a separate decision to be challenged; it is a variation of the maintenance calculation. If a variation is agreed and applied to the calculation, this decision may be challenged by seeking a revision within one month. Any changes of circumstances, whether in relation to the variation or other factors, can result in a revision or supersession of the maintenance calculation under the normal rules, depending on the circumstances (see Chapter 17). This also applies to decisions referred by the CSA to the First-tier Tribunal for a decision – eg, contentious cases.[146]

The variation will be taken into account in any reconsideration. However, there may be changes of circumstances which mean that the variation ceases to have effect. In certain circumstances, a previous variation to the calculation may be reinstated, without an application, at the discretion of the CSA.

Date the variation takes effect

If the ground existed at the effective date of the maintenance calculation (ie, when the non-resident parent was notified of the application or the application was treated as made), the date the variation takes effect will be the effective date of the maintenance calculation if either:

- the application is made before the calculation is made;[147] or
- the application is made within one month of the maintenance calculation, or meets the other normal rules applying to revisions (eg, misrepresentation or failure to disclose information that meant the decision was to the person's advantage) or erroneous decisions.[148]

The exception to this rule is where the non-resident parent is applying for a variation on the grounds of prior debts or payments in respect of certain mortgages, loans or insurance policies, and payments towards these are treated as voluntary payments in the initial payment period.[149] In this case, the variation takes effect from the maintenance period following the date on which the non-resident parent was notified – ie, the start of the second week of liability.

If the ground did not apply at the effective date of the maintenance calculation the variation is effective from:

- the first day of the maintenance period in which the ground arose, where this is after the effective date but before the maintenance calculation is made;[150]
- the first day of the maintenance period in which the relevant person requested the variation.[151] However, if the CSA requests that the application is made in writing, and this is not supplied within 14 days, the date the request was made will be the date the application is received, unless the CSA accepts that the delay was unavoidable;[152]
- the first day of the maintenance period in which the ground will arise, where the application for variation is made in advance.[153]

A case may have a number of different grounds, agreed over time, and each may have different dates from which they take effect.

Example

Tara claims maintenance. The effective date is 26 August 2003. She is notified of her maintenance calculation on 19 September 2003. She takes advice and applies for a variation on the basis that an additional cases ground applied on 26 August 2003. She makes this application on 8 October 2003 (ie, within one month of her notification of the decision). The variation is agreed and the maintenance calculation is revised on 14 November 2003, with effect from 26 August 2003.

Juan takes advice and on 3 December 2003 applies for a variation on the grounds that he has been paying off the car which they bought before splitting up and which Tara needs, as she lives in a secluded cottage. He is also just about to start paying boarding school fees for their eldest child in late December. The variation is agreed and a revision is made on 3 January 2004 in which the elements for prior debts take effect from 2 December and the boarding school fees take effect from 16 December 2003.

However, even though the variation for prior debts only applies from December, Juan could ask that the amounts he paid toward the car before the calculation was made be considered as voluntary payments to offset initial arrears. Had Juan taken advice at the same time as Tara and applied for a variation at the same time as she did on the grounds of prior debts and that his repayments on the car were voluntary payments, then there could have been a further variation to the calculation, with the decision taking effect from 26 August 2003.

When a variation ceases to have effect

A variation will cease to have effect when the ground no longer applies or any other of the reasons for refusing a variation is met.[154] For example, a variation in favour of the person with care will always cease to have effect where the non-resident parent or his partner starts to receive working tax credit.[155] When a variation ceases a supersession is carried out, which takes effect from the first day in the maintenance period in which the change occurred.

Where there is a later change, unless the CSA has discretion to reinstate the variation, a further application may need to be made.

Situations where a further application for variation is required

Ground	When variation ceases	When a further application could be made following a later change
Additional cases	Net income before any variation is greater than £2,000. The non-resident parent or his partner receives working tax credit.	Net income before variation would be less than £2,000. Neither receives working tax credit.
Special expenses	Net income after any variation is greater than £2,000.	Net income after variation would be less than £2,000.

Discretion to reinstate a previous variation

In some cases, the CSA may revise or supersede a maintenance calculation to reinstate a variation that has previously been agreed. This discretion may be applied where there is:[156]

- a change of circumstances which means the non-resident parent's liability is reduced to nil or another rate where the variation cannot be taken into account; *then*
- a subsequent change of circumstances means his liability can now be adjusted to take the variation into account.

Examples of situations where this could apply could be where:

- the non-resident parent becomes a full-time student and so becomes liable for the nil rate, but subsequently returns to a basic or reduced rate;
- a variation is agreed and on a subsequent application for revision/supersession the non-resident parent fails to provide information. Therefore, the maintenance calculation is replaced by a default decision. Later on, the information required is provided and this default maintenance decision is

replaced with a maintenance calculation. The variation may then be reapplied without a fresh application.

Had the maintenance calculation ceased, this discretion would not apply. For example, if the parent had moved abroad and the CSA ceased to have jurisdiction, then s/he returns to the UK, a subsequent application would need to be made for a maintenance calculation, including an application for variation. However, in some circumstances the CSA may be able to reinstate the variation without contest (see p131).

In exercising the discretion to reinstate, the CSA must be satisfied that there has been no material change in circumstances which affects the earlier variation.[157] If this is satisfied, the previous variation can be reinstated without an application or any further contact with the relevant persons – ie, s/he is not invited to make representations. There is no obligation to investigate, so decisions are made based on the information available to the decision maker. There is no time limit on the period between the variation ceasing to apply and being reinstated, as long as the circumstances that gave rise to the variation remain unchanged. This is most easily satisfied in pre-1993 property/capital transfers.

Example

Joe applies for, and obtains, a variation from his basic rate maintenance on the grounds of contact costs with his children. He is later convicted of a criminal offence and sentenced to six months in prison. He becomes liable to pay the nil rate. On his release, three months later, he again becomes liable, this time at the reduced rate. The CSA is not satisfied that the circumstances relating to eligibility are still the same and does not reinstate the variation. Joe will need to make a new application for a variation on the grounds of contact costs.

Had the variation been granted on the grounds of a pre-1993 property/capital transfer, the CSA could probably have reinstated the variation without Joe having to make a further application, as there is no reason why this ground and its effect should be altered by his intervening imprisonment.

Revision and supersession of a previously agreed variation

If a variation has been agreed, it may be subsequently revised or superseded. When a request is received to revise or supersede such a decision, the CSA may notify the other relevant parties and invite them to make representations.[158] This need not be done if the CSA thinks it would not agree to vary the calculation or that a revision/supersession would not be to the advantage of the applicant.

If contest does take place, the usual procedure is followed (see p130).[159]

The CSA may decide to revise/supersede, or not to revise or supersede, the decision and notify the applicant and any relevant parties, as appropriate.

Appealing a decision

Decisions on the maintenance calculation in response to a variation application, or where a variation element is reinstated into a maintenance calculation, may be appealed under the normal procedure. As with other appeals, if, following the appeal application, there is a revision of the appealed decision that is to the advantage of the appellant, the appeal will lapse.[160] For further details on appeals, see Chapter 18.

Notes

1 s28A(1) CSA 1991 (note the modifications under the CS(V)(MSP) Regs only apply in cases where the application is made after a maintenance calculation is in force)

1. Grounds for a variation
2 Sch 4B CSA 1991 as substituted by s6 CSPSSA 2000
3 Sch 4A para 2(3) CSA 1991 as substituted by s6 CSPSSA 2000
4 Reg 15 CS(V) Regs
5 Reg 15(1) CS(V) Regs
6 Reg 15(2) CS(V) Regs
7 Reg 15(3) CS(V) Regs
8 Reg 10(1) CS(V) Regs
9 Reg 10(4) CS(V) Regs
10 CCS/821/06
11 PG, Specialist Areas, Unacceptable Expenses
12 Reg 10(1) CS(V) Regs
13 Reg 10(3)(a) CS(V) Regs
14 Reg 10(3)(b) CS(V) Regs
15 PG, Specialist Areas, Frequency of Visits
16 PG, Specialist Areas, Frequency of Visits
17 PG, Specialist Areas, Travel Costs
18 PG, Specialist Areas, Accommodation Costs
19 Reg 11(2)(c) CS(V) Regs
20 Reg 11(2)(a) CS(V) Regs
21 Reg 11(1) CS(V) Regs
22 Reg 11(2)(b) CS(V) Regs
23 PG, Specialist Areas, Illness or Disability of a Relevant Other Child
24 Reg 11(3) CS(V) Regs
25 PG, Specialist Areas, Illness or Disability of a Relevant Other Child
26 Reg 12(2) CS(V) Regs
27 Reg 12(3)(k) and (6)(a) CS(V) Regs
28 Reg 12(6)(a) CS(V) Regs (see also para 23 CCS.3674/07); s376(4) ICTA 1988; PG, Specialist Areas, Prior Debts
29 Reg 12(3)(a) CS(V) Regs; para 19, CCS/3674/07
30 Reg 12(3)(k) CS(V) Regs
31 Reg 12(4) CS(V) Regs
32 Reg 12(3)(l) CS(V) Regs
33 Reg 12(3)(h) CS(V) Regs
34 Reg 12(3)(i) CS(V) Regs
35 PG, Specialist Areas, Prior Debts
36 Reg 12(3)(b)-(g), (j) and (m) CS(V) Regs
37 Reg 12(5) CS(V) Regs
38 PG, Specialist Areas, Prior Debts
39 Reg 13(1) CS(V) Regs
40 Reg 13(5) CS(V) Regs
41 Reg 13(2) CS(V) Regs
42 Reg 13(3) CS(V) Regs
43 Reg 13(4) CS(V) Regs
44 Reg 14(2)(a) CS(V) Regs
45 Reg 14(2)(b) CS(V) Regs
46 Sch 4B para 3(1) CSA 1991; regs 16(1) and (2) and 17(4) CS(V) Regs
47 Sch 4B para 3(2) CSA 1991
48 PG, Specialist Areas, Property Capital Transfer - Overview
49 s8(11) CSA 1991; reg 16(1)(a) CS(V) Regs; PG, Specialist Areas, Property Capital Transfer - Overview
50 Reg 16(2) CS(V) Regs
51 Reg 16(3) CS(V) Regs

52 Sch 4B para 3 CSA 1991; reg 17(1) CS(V) Regs
53 Reg 17(2) CS(V) Regs
54 Reg 16(4) CS(V) Regs
55 Sch para 1(3)(b) CS(V) Regs
56 Sch para 2 CS(V) Regs
57 Sch para 3 CS(V) Regs
58 Sch 4B para 4 CSA 1991
59 Reg 25 CS(V) Regs
60 Reg 26 CS(V) Regs
61 Reg 18(1) CS(V) Regs
62 Reg 18(2) CS(V) Regs
63 Reg 18(3) CS(V) Regs
64 CCS/1263/2008
65 CCS/1026/2006
66 Reg 18(3)(f) CS(V) Regs
67 Reg 18(4) CS(V) Regs
68 Reg 18(5) CS(V) Regs
69 Reg 18(6) CS(V) Regs; PG, Specialist Areas, Assets
70 Regs 18(5) and 25 CS(V) Regs
71 Reg 19(1) CS(V) Regs
72 Reg 4 The Child Support (Miscellaneous and Consequential Amendments) Regulations 2009 No.736
73 Reg 19(4) CS(V) Regs
74 CCS/2979/2008
75 Reg 19(2) CS(V) Regs
76 Regs 19(5)(a) and 25 CS(V) Regs
77 Reg 26(3) CS(V) Regs
78 Reg 19(4) CS(V) Regs
79 PG, Specialist Areas, Diversion of Income
80 Regs 19(5)(b) and 25 CS(V) Regs
81 Reg 20(1) and (2) CS(V) Regs
82 Reg 20(3) and (4)(a) CS(V) Regs
83 CCS/2018/2005
84 Reg 20(4) CS(V) Regs
85 Reg 20(5) CS(V) Regs
86 PG, Specialist Areas, Lifestyle Inconsistent with Declared Income
87 PG, Specialist Areas, Lifestyle Inconsistent with Declared Income

2. Applying for a variation

88 s28A CSA 1991 (note the modifications under the CS(V)(MSP) Regs take effect where the application is made when the maintenance calculation is in force); s28G CSA 1991
89 s28A(4) CSA 1991 (note the modifications under the CS(V)(MSP) Regs take effect where the application is made when the maintenance calculation is in force)
90 Reg 4(1) CS(V) Regs
91 s28A(4)(b) CSA 1991
92 Reg 8(1) CS(V) Regs

93 PG, Specialist Areas, Insufficient Information Provided
94 Reg 8(1) CS(V) Regs
95 Regs 6(2)(c) and 8(2) CS(V) Regs
96 Reg 5(1) CS(V) Regs
97 Reg 5(2) CS(V) Regs

3. Procedure

98 s28D CSA 1991 (note the modifications under the CS(V)(MSP) Regs take effect where the application is made when the maintenance calculation is in force)
99 Sch 4B para 5(1) CSA 1991; reg 9(9) CS(V) Regs
100 Reg 9(8) CS(V) Regs
101 s28B(1) CSA 1991
102 Reg 6(1) CS(V) Regs
103 s28B CSA 1991 (note the modifications under the CS(V)(MSP) Regs take effect where the application is made when the maintenance calculation is in force); reg 7 CS(V) Regs
104 s28B CSA 1991(note the modifications under the CS(V)(MSP) Regs take effect where the application is made when the maintenance calculation is in force); regs 6 and 7 CS(V) Regs
105 Reg 9(1) CS(V) Regs
106 PG, Specialist Areas, Contest – New Information/Evidence Received
107 Reg 9(1) CS(V) Regs
108 Reg 9(5) CS(V) Regs
109 Reg 9(4) CS(V) Regs
110 Procedures Guide, Specialist Areas, Contest - Contradictory Evidence
111 Reg 9(2) CS(V) Regs
112 PG, Specialist Areas, Contest – Information for Non-disclosure
113 Reg 9(3) CS(V) Regs
114 s12 CSA 1991
115 s28F(5) CSA 1991 (note the modifications under the CS(V)(MSP) Regs take effect where the application is made when the maintenance calculation is in force)
116 s28C CSA 1991(note the modifications under the CS(V)(MSP) Regs take effect where the application is made when the maintenance calculation is in force)
117 s28C(2) CSA 1991(note the modifications under the CS(V)(MSP) Regs take effect where the application is made when the maintenance calculation is in force); reg 31(1) CS(V) Regs
118 PG, Specialist Areas, Regular Payments Condition

119 s28C(4) CSA 1991(note the modifications under the CS(V)(MSP) Regs take effect where the application is made when the maintenance calculation is in force)

120 s28C(3) CSA 1991(note the modifications under the CS(V)(MSP) Regs take effect where the application is made when the maintenance calculation is in force)

121 s28C(5) CSA 1991 (note the modifications under the CS(V)(MSP) Regs take effect where the application is made when the maintenance calculation is in force)

122 Reg 31(2) and (3) CS(V) Regs

123 s28C(7) CSA 1991(note the modifications under the CS(V)(MSP) Regs take effect where the application is made when the maintenance calculation is in force)

124 s28F(1) CSA 1991 (note the modifications under the CS(V)(MSP) Regs take effect where the application is made when the maintenance calculation is in force)

125 ss28E and 28F(2)(a) CSA 1991; PG, Specialist Areas, Discretion

126 ss28D(1) and 28F CSA 1991 (note the modifications on both sections under the CS(V)(MSP) Regs take effect where the application is made when the maintenance calculation is in force)

127 s28F(1) CSA 1991

128 Reg 21(1) CS(V) Regs

129 Reg 21(2) CS(V) Regs

130 s28D(1)(b) CSA 1991

131 PG, Specialist Areas, Role of Appeals Service

132 s28D(3) CSA 1991 (note the modifications under the CS(V)(MSP) Regs take effect where the application is made when the maintenance calculation is in force)

4. The decision

133 ss28B(2) and 28F(3) and (4) CSA 1991 (note the modifications to both sections under the CS(V)(MSP) Regs take effect where the application is made when the maintenance calculation is in force)

134 PG, Specialist Areas, Revising/Refusing to Revise a Maintenance Calculation to Take Account of a Variation Application; Superseding/Refusing to Supersede a Maintenance Calculation to Take Account of a Variation Application

135 Reg 27(5) CS(V) Regs

136 Reg 25 CS(V) Regs

137 Reg 25 CS(V) Regs

138 Reg 26 CS(V) Regs

139 Reg 26(1) CS(V) Regs

140 Reg 26(3) CS(V) Regs

141 Reg 23(1) CS(V) Regs

142 Reg 15(1) CS(V) Regs

143 Reg 23(2) CS(V) Regs

144 PG, Specialist Areas, Variation on the Grounds of a Property Transfer

145 Reg 24 CS(V) Regs

146 ss16(1A)(c) and 17(1)(d) CSA 1991

147 Reg 22 CS(V) Regs

148 s28G CSA 1991; reg 3A SSCS(DA) Regs

149 Reg 22(2) CS(V) Regs

150 Reg 22(1)(b) CS(V) Regs

151 s28G CSA 1991; regs 6A(6) and 7B(6) SS&CS(DA) Regs

152 Reg 4 CS(V) Regs; PG, Application Properly Made

153 Regs 6A(3) and 7B(5) SS&CS(DA) Regs

154 PG, Specialist Areas, Suspension of Variations

155 Reg 7(5)(b) CS(V) Regs

156 Reg 29 CS(V) Regs

157 Reg 9(3) CS(V) Regs

158 Reg 15B SS&CS(DA) Regs

159 Reg 15B SS&CS(DA) Regs

160 s16(6) CSA 1991

Chapter 7

Conversions

This chapter covers:
1. When 'old rules' cases convert to the 'new rules' (below)
2. The calculation and transitional phasing (p147)
3. The conversion decision (p154)
4. The linking rules (p156)
5. Revisions, supersessions and appeals (p158)
6. Conversion, benefits and collection (p163)

1. When 'old rules' cases convert to the 'new rules'

Apart from when an 'old rules' case converts to a 'new rules' case, the two systems of calculating child support operate independently. The fact that parents in the two systems are treated differently in terms of the amount of maintenance received and paid, even though their circumstances may otherwise be the same, is probably not discriminatory and does not breach human rights law.[1]

When the simplified system of calculating maintenance is introduced in 2011 (see p3), for a period of time parents will be able to choose to continue with 'old' or 'new' rules arrangements, make private arrangements or come under the new, simplified rules.[2] New applications to the simplified system will not be accepted until at least 2011. It is expected that the new simplified scheme and the two exisiting schemes will operate alongside each other between 2011 and 2013 and that the exisiting schemes will be closed during 2014. Eventually, all cases will be transferred to the new simplified scheme.[3]

As a new simplified scheme is being introduced, there is no longer any intention to convert all 'old rules' cases to the 'new rules' at a future date. The current arrangements will continue, unless there is some other reason to convert a case. An 'old rules' case may convert because there is a connection to a 'new rules' case.

If an 'old rules' case converts there may be transitional phasing to increase or decrease the old amount to the new amount due (see p148).

Where an 'old rules' assessment ceases to be in force, an application may be decided under the 'new rules' if it is made more than 13 weeks after the assessment ceases. This is not a conversion as such and, therefore, transitional phasing will not apply.

Conversions

Conversion occurs where a maintenance assessment is in force and a related decision is made.[4] The related decision may be that a maintenance calculation is made or there has been a change involving a new or existing partner who also has maintenance. A conversion will occur where:[5]

- a maintenance calculation is made in respect of a person who is a relevant person (person with care or non-resident parent) in the existing assessment, whether or not this is for a different qualifying child;
- an application is made, or treated as made (if a claim for benefit was made before 14 July 2008) that would result in a maintenance calculation but there is an assessment in force, the non-resident parent in the new application is the non-resident parent in the existing case but the person with care in the new application is different from the one in the existing case. However, if it is the non-resident parent who applies for the maintenance calculation and the person with care in the new application does not wish to co-operate, there will be no conversion of the existing case (see also p43);
- before 14 July 2008, before a maintenance calculation is made in relation to person A who is a partner to person B who has a maintenance assessment, either A or B are in receipt of income support (IS) or income-based jobseeker's allowance (JSA), and A and B are either both persons with care or both non-resident parents;
- before 14 July 2008, a maintenance assessment is in force in relation to person C and a maintenance calculation is in force in relation to person D, either C or D are in receipt of IS or income-based JSA, C and D are either both persons with care or both non-resident parents, and then C and D become partners; *or*
- before 14 July 2008, a maintenance assessment is in force in relation to person E and a maintenance calculation is in force in relation to her/his partner F. E and F are either both persons with care or both non-resident parents and then they become entitled to IS or income-based JSA as partners.

Note: from 14 July 2008, parents with care are no longer treated as applying to the Child Support Agency (CSA) when they make a claim for IS or income-based JSA.

The conversion of one case may set off a chain of conversions of other cases where the relevant person in a conversion is also a relevant person in an existing maintenance assessment.[6] The CSA calls these 'linked cases'. This may result in a lengthy sequence of interrelated decisions that need to be made. Whenever an 'old rules' case is converted, transitional phasing may apply (see p148).

Example

Celine is the parent with care of two children, Michelle and Francis. Franco is their non-resident parent in the 'old rules' assessment. After 3 March 2003 Francis goes to live with Franco and his new partner, Helen. Franco applies, as the parent with care of Francis, for maintenance from Celine, as the non-resident parent. A maintenance calculation is made. As a relevant person in the old assessment is a relevant person in the new calculation (ie, Celine is a person with care in the old and a non-resident parent in the new), the old maintenance assessment converts to the 'new rules' (transitional phasing may apply).

If Francis went to live with Franco before 3 March 2003, then both Celine and Franco would have 'old rules' assessments – ie, Celine as the person with care of Michelle in one assessment and Franco as the person with care of Francis in the other 'old rules' assessment. If Celine then moved in with a new partner, not only would her case convert to the new rules, but Franco's would as well because of the linking effect (see p156).

2. **The calculation and transitional phasing**

The new amount is worked out applying the new calculation rates, using the information that the Child Support Agency (CSA) has at the calculation date (see p145).[7] Where there are decisions outstanding on the maintenance assessment at conversion, the calculation may be carried out, and once those decisions are made, the maintenance calculation may be revised or superseded (see p158). There are additional rules for calculating the new amount at conversion where a relevant departure direction or relevant property transfer was applied to an 'old rules' case (see p151).

Where there is an interim maintenance assessment (IMA) in force when the conversion decision is being made, this may be:
- used to make the conversion decision;[8] *or*
- replaced with a default maintenance decision, if there is insufficient information to make a maintenance assessment or conversion decision.[9]

In either case, if information is subsequently provided by the non-resident parent to make a maintenance assessment, the conversion decision or default maintenance decision may be superseded.[10]

At conversion, the new rate will either be paid immediately or transitional phasing may be applied.[11] There are some situations where the new amount is always applied; in other cases, the CSA checks whether transitional phasing applies. If it does not, the new amount is paid.

When the new amount is always applied

The new amount of maintenance will be applied immediately (ie, without checking whether transitional phasing applies) if the:[12]

- 'new rules' amount is nil;
- 'old rules' amount was nil and the 'new rules' amount is the flat rate reduced to nil because of shared care (see p150);
- 'old rules' amount was more than nil but the 'new rules' amount is the flat rate (or halved flat rate where there is a partner who is a non-resident parent);
- 'old rules' amount was a Category A or D IMA;
- 'new rules' amount is a default maintenance decision.

Where none of the above apply, the CSA will check whether transitional phasing should be applied (see below). If it does not apply, the new amount will be payable.

Example

Sally is due to pay Mark maintenance at the minimum amount before conversion. After conversion she is liable for the flat rate. She pays the new amount from conversion.

Kieran pays Leah a maintenance assessment worked out under a Category A IMA. At conversion, as there is insufficient information to make a maintenance calculation, a default decision replaces the IMA and the new amount applies immediately.

If Kieran had been assessed under a Category B IMA, sufficient information would have been available to make a maintenance calculation.

Transitional phasing

Transitional phasing will apply (unless the situation is one where the new amount is always applied – see p147) where the difference between the old amount and new amount is greater than the phasing amount.[13] Where there is more than one assessment in relation to the same non-resident parent, apportionment occurs, in which case the amounts referred to are those after the apportionment has been made.[14] Where there is an application from a new person with care which triggers conversion of an existing assessment (see p146), the apportionment in the new calculation will occur as normal, then the previous assessment amount is compared with the new amount due after apportionment.[15] There are special rules in some flat-rate cases (see p150).

The phasing amount depends on the net income of the non-resident parent. This is:[16]

- £2.50, if income is £100 or less;
- £5, if income is between £100 and £400; *or*
- £10, if income is £400 or more.

Net weekly income is as worked out under the 'new rules'. (This includes where a relevant departure direction is converted and treated as a variation.) If the difference between the old and new amounts is greater than the phasing amount, the old amount is increased or decreased by the phasing amount as appropriate.[17] This increase or decrease occurs on an annual basis during the transitional period. The transitional period lasts until the new amount is reached or for up to five years, unless there is a subsequent decision which affects this.[18]

Where transitional phasing applies, the **maximum transitional amount** that the non-resident parent may pay in maintenance (to all persons with care) is 30 per cent of his net income.[19] This is worked out under the normal rules plus, if there is a relevant additional cases departure, the net income is taken to be the total of the additional income and the income from prescribed benefits (excluding those disregarded). If there is an additional cases variation this means the total income after variation.[20]

In some situations, there may be a new case being calculated, and an old case converting at the same time. If this happens, apportionment of the maintenance calculation is carried out as normal. Transitional phasing may be applied to the 'old rules' case, in which case the total amount of maintenance is checked against the 30 per cent maximum. This means adding together the apportioned amount due for the 'new rules' case and the phased amount due for the 'old rules' case. If the 30 per cent maximum is breached, the maintenance is capped at this amount. The amount for the person (or persons) with care in the new case is deducted from the maximum, and the remainder is the amount due to the person (or persons) with care in the converting 'old rules' case.[21] Rounding is to the nearest penny (amounts can be adjusted where rounding would result in inequalities over time).[22]

Example

Under her 'old rules' assessment Celine is due to get £68.40 in maintenance from Franco for Michelle and Francis. Franco lives with his new partner, Helen, and their son, Damien. Celine remains living on her own, but has a baby with a different non-resident parent. She applies for maintenance after 3 March 2003, and it is worked out under the 'new rules'. Franco's case will convert as a linked case. If Franco's net income is £360 a week at the conversion date, Celine's new amount from Franco is worked out under the basic rate.

| Basic rate | Step 1 | 15% reduction for relevant child – ie, £360 – £54 = £306 |
| | Step 2 | Maintenance is 20% x £306 = £61.20 (ie, £61 rounded to the nearest pound) |

Does transitional phasing apply?

The phasing amount is £5, as Franco's income is between £100 and £400. Since there is more than £5 difference between the old and new amounts transitional phasing applies. Celine is paid £63.40 (£68.40 – £5) in maintenance from Franco.

If Franco and Helen split up and Helen applied for maintenance for Damien after 3 March 2003, Celine's case would convert at this point, assuming this is before she has her third child. In this case there are now no relevant children living with Franco and three qualifying children.

Basic rate	**Step 1**	No reduction.
	Step 2	25% x £360 = £90
	Step 3	Apportionment between two persons with care (£90 ÷ 3 = £30)

Helen is due to receive £30.

Celine's new amount is £60.

Does transitional phasing apply?

As there is more than £5 difference between the old amount (£68.40) and the new amount (£60) phasing applies.

Year 1	£68.40 – £5 = £63.40
Year 2	£60

Therefore, the total amount of maintenance due is £93.40. This is less than the 30 per cent maximum (£108) so it does not affect maintenance.

If Celine's 'old rules' assessment was £100 a week, transitional phasing would mean:

Year 1	£100 – £5 = £95
Year 2	£95 – £5 = £90
Year 3	£90 – £5 = £85
Year 4	£85 – £5 =£80
Year 5	£60

This means Franco would pay £30 (Helen) + £95 (Celine) = £125

As this is greater than the 30 per cent maximum (£108) the calculation is adjusted. Helen still receives £30 but Celine receives £78 (£108 – £30).

Transitional amount in certain flat rate cases

If the old amount was nil and the new amount is the flat rate (because of receipt of a prescribed benefit), transitional phasing is £2.50 in the first year and then £5 in the second.[23] In cases where the non-resident parent's partner is also a non-resident parent with a maintenance calculation in force and either the non-resident parent or his partner is in receipt of income support (IS), income-based jobseeker's allowance (JSA), income-related employment and support allowance (ESA) or pension credit (PC), transitional phasing is £1.25 in the first year and £2.50 in the second.[24]

Except where the old amount was nil, if the flat rate is due but reduces to nil because of shared care, the transitional amount due will be £2.50 in the first year and £5 in the second.[25] (In cases where the flat rate is halved because a partner is a non-resident parent, the phasing amount will be £1.25.[26]) This will occur where the non-resident parent shares care with the only (or all) person(s) with care.

If the amount due reduces to nil for some, but not all, of the persons with care, transitional phasing will only apply if:[27]

- the old amount is less than the new amount and the difference is more than £2.50; *or*
- the old amount is greater than the new amount but the new amount is less than £2.50.

Apportionment of the transitional amount takes place between those persons with care for whom the amount due does not reduce to nil because of shared care.[28]

Example

Andrew has four qualifying children. Claire and Hannah are each a person with care for one qualifying child, Millie is a person with care for two. Andrew has one child living with him and also shares care with Claire. Andrew's case converts because it is a linked case.

Under the 'old rules' he was exempt from paying the minimum amount. Under the 'new rules' he is liable for the flat rate of £5. This is apportioned between the persons with care: Hannah and Claire are due £1.25 each and Millie is due £2.50.

Because of shared care, Claire's maintenance is reduced to nil. This means £3.75 is now due in maintenance. As this is greater than the old amount and there is more than a £2.50 difference between old and new amounts, phasing is applied. The £2.50 phased amount is apportioned between Hannah and Millie: Hannah receives 83p and Millie £1.67.

Relevant departure directions and property transfers

In 'old rules' cases where there is a departure direction or an allowance for a property/capital transfer in the exempt income calculation these may be taken into consideration when working out the new amount used in the conversion calculation.[29] Only a relevant departure and relevant property/capital transfer affect the calculation.

If a departure direction can be considered as a variation, it is known as a **'relevant departure direction'**. A relevant departure direction is one for:[30]

- contact costs;
- prior debts;
- illness and disability costs of a relevant child (ie, the non-resident parent or his partner receives child benefit for the child);
- a property or capital transfer;
- diversion of income;
- when lifestyle is inconsistent with stated income; *or*
- assets, where the value of the assets is greater than £65,000.

In the case of contact costs and prior debts, the £15 and £10 thresholds that apply to special expenses variations must be met for either amount or the sum of both where they apply.[31] In the case of diversion of income or an inconsistent lifestyle, the amount of income must exceed £100 in cases where the new amount would otherwise be:

- the flat rate because of receipt of a prescribed benefit (other than IS, income-based JSA, income-related ESA or PC);
- the flat rate as above, but reduced to nil because of shared care; *or*
- the nil rate (other than on income grounds).[32]

If there is a relevant departure direction, an equivalent variation will be applied to the calculation of the new amount without any separate application for a variation.[33]

> ### Example
> Joan has a maintenance assessment with a special expenses departure direction of £22 for contact costs and £18 for travel-to-work costs. When her case is converted because of a linked case, her special expenses for contact costs count as a relevant transfer but her travel-to-work costs do not.

A **'relevant property transfer'** is distinct from a property/capital departure as this is where an allowance is included at the exempt income stage (see Chapter 10) of the 'old rules' assessment formula.[34] In these cases, the amount of the relevant property transfer is deducted at conversion from the net income used to work out maintenance.[35] It may be advisable, where a relevant property transfer is applied, to seek a variation on property/capital transfer grounds.[36] If this application is successful, the conversion decision will be revised or superseded depending on when the application was made.

Adjustments to the conversion calculation

The adjustment made to the conversion calculation depends on the ground under which the departure direction has been granted – ie, special expenses, additional cases or property/capital transfer. The effect of an adjustment for departure directions and relevant property transfers (or the aggregate of those that apply) are listed below and are carried out in the following order.[37]

- **Additional cases departure direction.** The amount of the departure is added to the net income figure. Where this takes net income over the capped amount of £2,000, the net income figure used is £2,000.[38] If the non-resident parent is on benefit there is a maximum amount payable – ie, a conversion 'better-buy' (see below).
- **Special expenses departure direction.** The amount of the departure is deducted from the net weekly income.[39] Where the net income is the capped amount of £2,000, deduct the expenses from the actual net income not the capped amount. If this reduces the net income figure to below £2,000, this is

the net income figure to use in the calculation. Otherwise it is the capped amount.

- **Relevant property transfer.** The amount of the transfer is deducted from the net income of the non-resident parent. Where the net income is the capped amount of £2,000 the transfer is deducted from this capped amount.[40]
- **Property/capital transfer departure direction.** The amount of the departure is deducted from the maintenance due to the person with care.[41] This deduction can only be completed after any reduction for shared care (or part-time local authority care) has been applied.[42]

If these adjustments reduce the amount of maintenance due to below the £5 flat rate, the amount due will be the £5 flat rate. This may be apportioned between the persons with care as appropriate.[43]

Conversion better-buy

If the non-resident parent is on benefit, the maximum amount payable where there is a relevant departure on additional cases grounds is the lesser of:[44]
- the flat rate plus the appropriate rate (reduced or basic) applied to the additional income under the departure; *or*
- the amount calculated by applying the appropriate rate to the total of the additional income under the departure and the income payable under any prescribed benefits (excluding amounts that are disregarded).

The conversion calculation is carried out in the normal way. However, the conversion better-buy provision is applied and may cap the amount to be paid.

Outstanding overpayments at conversion

In 'old rules' cases, if there has been an overpayment of child support and the amount payable under the maintenance assessment has been adjusted to reflect this (see p405), the adjustment can be applied to the new amount, or the transitional amount, which applies on conversion. This will be done if the overpayment remains on the case conversion date and the CSA considers it appropriate to apply the adjustment.[45] The usual factors when considering overpayment adjustments should be taken into account (see p405).

If the conversion decision affects more than one parent with care, the adjustment of the amount payable is only applied to the apportioned amount payable to the parent with care in respect of whom the original adjusted maintenance assessment applied.

Offsetting arrears

If there are arrears of child support due in an 'old rules' case and the CSA has allocated other payments of child support against the arrears, this attribution of child support payments can be applied to the new amount, or the transitional amount, which applies on conversion.[46] This will be done if the arrears remain outstanding on the case conversion date and the CSA has used its discretion to offset the arrears against the payment of child maintenance in accordance with the regulations, as they apply to a conversion decision (see also p404).

3. **The conversion decision**

At conversion, the Child Support Agency (CSA) carries out a conversion calculation (see p147).[47]

There is no requirement to seek more up-to-date information;[48] if the information used at the calculation date is incorrect a revision can be requested. This may be particularly important in cases where there have been significant changes, which could increase or decrease the 'old rules' maintenance assessment. The policy intention is not routinely to supersede maintenance assessment decisions before conversion.

The new rate will either be paid immediately (ie, the maintenance calculation comes into force) or transitional phasing may be applied (see p148).[49] There are some situations where the new amount is always applied; in other cases, the CSA checks if transitional phasing applies and if it does not, the new amount is paid.

The effective date of the conversion decision

The effective date of the conversion decision is normally the beginning of the first maintenance period on or after the conversion date.[50] This is known as the '**case conversion date**'. If a case converts, the effective date may be the beginning of the first maintenance period on or after the effective date of the new calculation or another period depending on the circumstances.[51]

Effective date of conversion decisions

Situation	Effective date
A maintenance calculation is made in respect of a relevant person in relation to the maintenance assessment, whether or not in respect of a different qualifying child.	The beginning of the first maintenance period on or after the effective date of the new calculation.
Before 14 July 2008, a maintenance calculation is made in respect of person A who is a non-resident parent who is partner to person B who is the absent parent in relation to the maintenance assessment.[52]	The beginning of the first maintenance period on or after the effective date of the new calculation.

An application is made (or treated as made before 14 July 2008) that would result in a maintenance calculation but there is an assessment in force. The non-resident parent in the new application is the non-resident parent in the existing case but the person with care in the new application is a different one from the one in the existing case.	The beginning of the first maintenance period on or after the date of notification of the conversion decision.
Before 14 July 2008, a maintenance assessment is in force in respect of person C and a maintenance calculation is in force in relation to person D. Either C or D are in receipt of income support (IS)/income-based jobseeker's allowance (JSA). C and D are either both persons with care or both non-resident parents. C and D become partners and the benefit decision is superseded because of this.	The beginning of the first maintenance period on or after the date that the benefit supersession decision takes effect.
Before 14 July 2008, a maintenance assessment is in force in respect of person E and a maintenance calculation in force in relation to partner F. E and F are either both persons with care or both non-resident parents and they become entitled to IS/income-based JSA as partners.	The beginning of the first maintenance period on or after the date from which they become entitled to IS or income-based JSA.
All other circumstances.	The beginning of the first maintenance period on or after the conversion decision.

Note: from 14 July 2008, parents with care are no longer treated as applying to the CSA when they make a claim for IS or income-based JSA.

Notification

Once the conversion decision is made, the non-resident parent, person with care and Scottish child applicant are notified in writing.[53]
    This notification states the:
- new amount;
- transitional amount, if appropriate;
- length of the transitional period;
- date the conversion decision was made and the date from which it is effective;

- non-resident parent's net weekly income;
- number of qualifying and relevant children;
- adjustments for apportionment or shared care;
- details of departure directions or relevant property transfers taken into account;
- adjustments because of the maximum transitional amount rule.

The conversion decision is treated as a maintenance calculation decision so requests for revision, supersession, variation and appeal may be made.[54] However, when considering subsequent decisions there are additional rules to determine the amount of maintenance to be paid (see p160).

After notification of the conversion decision there may be an application for a departure direction or a variation.

When does the conversion end

Transitional phasing may be applied for up to five years from the case conversion date or until the maintenance calculation amount is reached.[55] Where there are subsequent decisions that result in the new amount being paid immediately (ie, nil rate or default rate), these may be applied. If the calculation is cancelled, conversion will end. However, in some cases where linking applies (see below), a second subsequent decision or new application may be dealt with as if the conversion decision still applied. This may affect the amount to be paid under any subsequent decision.

4. **The linking rules**

The linking rules cover a range of situations where an 'old rules' assessment or a transitional amount has been in force and there are applications and subsequent decisions made after 3 March 2003. Whether or not linking is applied depends on the timescales and circumstances. In each instance there are two key factors.

- A 13-week linking period is used.
- If there is another application in the interim that involves either the person with care or non-resident parent (but not both) there is no linking.

If linking applies, the rules on working out how much maintenance is paid are adjusted.

The linking rules and their effect

Scenario	Maintenance is worked out as if:
After 3 March 2003 there is an application, but within 13 weeks there was a maintenance assessment in force for the same parent with care, non-resident parent and qualifying child.	it is a maintenance assessment. All the 'old rules', including the formula, are applied to the case.
The conversion calculation ceases to have effect, but within 13 weeks there is an application for the same parent with care, non-resident parent and qualifying child.	the conversion calculation is still in force and subsequent decision rules are applied.
A transitional amount is being paid. There is a subsequent decision where the £5/£2.50 flat rate, nil rate for shared care or nil rate is paid. Within 13 weeks of the effective date of this, a second decision is made where none of these rates apply for the same parent with care, non-resident parent and qualifying child.	the first subsequent decision had not been made (ie, the transitional amount is still in force) and the subsequent decision rules are applied.

Applications on or after 3 March 2003

An application for a maintenance calculation made on or after 3 March 2003 can be treated as an application for a maintenance assessment if it is:[56]
- made within 13 weeks of a maintenance assessment being in force; *and*
- in relation to the same person with care, non-resident parent and qualifying child,

unless there is a new application which includes either the 'old rules' case person with care or non-resident parent (but not both) before the new application is made, in which case there is no linking and it is dealt with as a new case.[57]

Where linking applies, maintenance is worked out using the 'old rules' maintenance assessment.

Where a new application is linked to an old assessment and there is then a new application which involves the person with care or non-resident parent, the old case will be converted and a conversion calculation will be done.

If an application is made after 13 weeks of a maintenance assessment being in force, it is treated as an application under the 'new rules' and a calculation is carried out. No transitional phasing will apply. A parent with care has a right to opt out if she wishes, and to re-apply at any time, whether or not the reason for doing so is to increase her maintenance.[58]

Example

Celine is the parent with care. Franco is the non-resident parent in an 'old rules' assessment. Celine asks the Child Support Agency to stop acting (ie, she opts out). After six weeks she applies for a 'new rules' maintenance calculation. Since her 'old rules' assessment was in force within the last 13 weeks her application is treated as an application for a maintenance assessment.

If Celine opts out and waits for 14 weeks and then applies, her case will be dealt with as a 'new rules' case.

Celine opts out, but before she re-applies Franco and his partner, Helen, split up. Helen makes an application for a maintenance calculation as the parent with care, with Franco the non-resident parent, three weeks after Celine opts out. Helen is a 'new rules' case and when Celine re-applies three weeks later her case is dealt with as a new case and no linking or conversion rules apply.

If Celine opts out but, before she re-applies, Franco applies as the parent with care of Francis, Franco is a 'new rules' case. When Celine applies six weeks later, the linking rules apply and a conversion calculation will be done. Transitional phasing may apply to her maintenance.

5. **Revisions, supersessions and appeals**

At conversion there may be decisions outstanding on a maintenance assessment or departure direction. In other cases, decisions may have been made but the time limits for challenging them may not yet have expired (see below).

Once the conversion decision has been made it may be challenged in the normal way (revision, supersession, appeal and application for variation) since it is treated as if it were a maintenance calculation.[59] Adjustments of the amounts payable under the transitional phasing rules (see p148) may also be revised or superseded.[60] However, there are some conversion decisions that cannot be revised, superseded or appealed (see p159). There are also additional rules to be applied when working out how much maintenance should be paid on any subsequent decision (see p160).

Applications may also be made for a departure direction or variation that may result in decisions being revised or superseded (see p163).

Outstanding decisions and time limits at conversion

In some cases, a decision may have been made on a maintenance assessment or departure direction and the time limit for seeking a revision or making an appeal has not expired at conversion.[61] In these cases, a revision or appeal may still be sought using the 'old rules'.

Alternatively, at the conversion date there may be outstanding decisions on:[62]

- the maintenance assessment;
- a departure direction;
- a revision or supersession (including those initiated by the Child Support Agency (CSA)[63]);
- an appeal.[64]

If this is the case, a conversion decision may be made using the information held at the conversion date.[65] In the case of an outstanding maintenance assessment this may mean an interim maintenance assessment (IMA) is made and, at conversion, a default maintenance decision becomes due. The outstanding decision may be determined using the 'old rules' as if they still applied.[66] Once the outstanding decision is made or the appeal is decided, the conversion decision may be revised or superseded.[67]

Outstanding decisions on revision and supersession may themselves be appealed when they are made using the 'old rules'.[68] This means a decision not to make a departure direction may be appealed under the 'old rules'.[69] An appeal decision may be challenged on a point of law to the Upper Tribunal.

Conversion and subsequent decisions

Conversion and subsequent decisions can be revised, superseded and appealed in the same way as maintenance calculations,[70] except for the following.

- There are certain conversion decisions that may not be revised, superseded or appealed (see p160).
- When appealing against a conversion decision, the time limit for making an appeal is either from the date of notification to one month after the case conversion date, or the usual one month from the notice of the decision, whichever is the later.[71] In practice, this means that the normal time limit applies unless there is advance notification of the conversion.
- The effective date of a revision or supersession of a conversion decision is either the conversion date or the date worked out under the normal rules, whichever is the later.[72]
- Notifications contain details of the amount in any subsequent decision rather than the new amount and details of any variations taken into account.
- A conversion decision may be revised or superseded because of a revision/supersession/appeal of a maintenance assessment (including an IMA) or departure direction after the calculation date.[73]
- When further decisions are made, the linking rules may be applied (see p156) and the rules on working out the amount of maintenance due on a subsequent decision are applied.

After notification of the conversion decision there may be an application for a departure direction or a variation. If this is made after the calculation date but before the case conversion date, it may result in a series of supersession decisions.

Decisions that cannot be revised, superseded or appealed

A revision, supersession and appeal will not be allowed on the grounds:[74]
- that the CSA used the information it already had at the calculation date;
- that the CSA took into account a relevant departure direction (ie, one that counts as a variation under the 'new rules');
- that the CSA failed to take into account a departure direction (ie, where it does not count as a variation under the 'new rules');
- that the CSA applied a phasing amount;
- of the length of the transitional period;
- that the CSA took into account a relevant property transfer, except where the person with care or Scottish child applicant asks for it to be removed as it did not reflect the true value of the transfer, or a relevant person applies for a variation.

How much is paid on a further decision after conversion

There are special rules on how to work out how much is paid when there are further decisions after conversion. These are applied to conversion cases where there is transitional phasing (or there has been in cases where the linking rules apply – see p156). These are in addition to the normal rules on revisions and supersessions.

When considering a revision of the conversion decision (ie, where the effective date is the case conversion date, not the revision of a later supersession) the rules for working out an initial conversion are used.[75]

Where there is a supersession of the conversion decision, or revision of such a decision, the additional rules, explained below, are used to determine the amount of maintenance to be paid.[76]

These apply to such decisions on appeal.

The amount to be paid under a further decision could be:
- the nil rate, or £5 (£2.50) flat rate (or if it is less or reduced to nil because of shared care);
- the transitional amount (see p161);
- a new transitional amount (see p161); *or*
- the subsequent decision amount.

If the decision is the nil rate, flat rate or flat rate reduced to nil because of shared care (including where the amount due is less than £5/£2.50), this is the amount that is paid and transitional phasing ceases.[77] However, if there is a subsequent decision after this and the linking rules may apply (see p156), the rules below may be applied and transitional phasing may be revived (see the example on p162).

In all other cases, the subsequent decision amount is compared with the former assessment and the new amount due under the maintenance calculation.

Where there is more than one person with care the apportioning rules apply to the calculation (including any adjustments to the maximum transitional amount).[78] The subsequent decision amount and new amount are the amounts worked out using the maintenance calculation, including adjustments for apportionment and shared care, before any transitional phasing is applied. If linking applies (see p156), this may mean the new amount referred to is in a conversion calculation that has ceased to be in force or is in a previous decision. If, at the date of the subsequent decision, there was more than one person with care in relation to the same non-resident parent, but as a result of the subsequent decision there is only one, the new amount and the transitional amount used are the apportioned amount payable immediately before the subsequent decision to that person with care. The subsequent decision amount refers to the full amount payable under the subsequent decision.[79]

Unless the conditions in the table below are met, the amount due will be the subsequent decision amount. If this applies, transitional phasing ceases and cannot be revived for any further decisions, and only the normal supersession rules apply.

Where the original transitional phasing or a new transitional amount applies, transitional phasing then continues until the subsequent decision amount is reached or the five-year transitional period ends, whichever is earlier (see p148).

Any further decisions in the meantime will be worked out under these rules.[80] There are provisions to allow this where the subsequent decision (Decision B) replaces an earlier subsequent decision (Decision A) or one made with an incorrect effective date, so that in effect Decision A is ignored in applying the rules.[81] However, the rules do not apply in this situation if the decision before Decision A took effect from the case conversion date.

Other cases where the amount due is not the subsequent decision amount

Condition one	Condition two	Amount due
The new amount is greater than the former assessment.	Subsequent decision is greater than the new amount.	A new transitional amount is worked out, increasing the previous transitional amount by the difference between the new amount and the subsequent decision.
The new amount is greater than the former assessment.	Subsequent decision is less than or equal to the new amount and greater than the previous transitional amount.	The amount is the previous transitional amount.

| The new amount is less than the former assessment. | Subsequent decision is less than the new amount. | A new transitional amount is worked out, decreasing the previous transitional amount by the difference between the new amount and the subsequent decision. |
| The new amount is less than the former assessment. | Subsequent decision is greater than or equal to the new amount and less than the previous transitional amount. | The amount is the previous transitional amount. |

Example

Kevin is due to pay an assessment of £68. His net income is £248. When his case converts following a linked case, he is due to pay a basic rate of £50. This has transitional phasing applied, so he is due to pay £63. Four months later he gets a promotion and his ex-wife requests a supersession. As Kevin's net income has increased to £270, the 5 per cent tolerance level is breached and the CSA considers supersession. The amount he would now be due to pay is £54. The new amount of £50 was less than the assessment (Condition one) and the subsequent decision amount (£54) is greater than this and less than the previous transitional amount, £63 (Condition two). This means he continues to be due to pay the previous transitional amount of £63.

If Kevin's net income had increased to £325, the amount due would be £65. In this case he does not meet Condition two as this is greater than the previous transitional amount (£63). This means he is due to pay £65. There is no more transitional phasing. If Kevin reduces his working hours and his income decreases to £270, his maintenance due would be £54 with no transitional phasing applied.

If the situation were different, the linking rules may apply. If the case converts, but instead of a promotion Kevin is made redundant and claims contribution-based jobseeker's allowance, he is now due to pay at the flat rate of £5. Ten weeks later he gets a new job and has a net income of £210 a week. As this is within 13 weeks, the linking rules apply (see p156). The maintenance decision at the flat rate is ignored. The new amount in Condition one is, therefore, £50 and the subsequent decision amount is £42. As this is lower than the new amount a new transitional amount is worked out. The difference between the two, £8 (£50 – £42), is subtracted from the first transitional amount (£63). Kevin now has to pay £55 (£63 – £8). Unless there are further decisions, a year later transitional phasing will mean he becomes due to pay £50 (£55 – £5).

Applications for a departure direction or variation

After notification of the conversion decision a relevant person may apply for a variation, in which case the conversion decision may be revised or superseded accordingly (see p158).

Departure directions are slightly more complex. To be taken into account at conversion a departure direction must apply to the maintenance assessment used in the conversion calculation.

Where an application for a departure direction is made after the calculation date but before the case conversion date this may result in the maintenance assessment being superseded to take account of the departure direction, and then the conversion decision would be revised to reflect the change.[82] Where it is a relevant departure direction, this revision of the conversion decision will include a variation.[83] A departure direction application cannot be made after the case conversion date. However, it may be possible to seek a revision or appeal a refusal to agree a departure direction if the relevant time limits have not expired.[84] For more information on decisions and time limits outstanding at conversion, see p158.

Conversion decision made in error

If a conversion decision, or subsequent decision on a conversion, has been made and it is found that the conversion grounds did not apply (see p146), the case will be treated as if those decisions had not been made.[85] This means the maintenance assessment will be reinstated, bearing in mind any revisions, supersessions or appeals made in the meantime which would have affected that assessment.

Example

Amy's maintenance assessment is converted because of an administrative error, which is discovered two months later. When the error is discovered the maintenance assessment is reinstated. However, the non-resident parent notified changes in housing costs and travel-to-work costs that could not be taken into account under the 'new rules' but were relevant in the previous assessment. The assessment is superseded, the effective date being linked to the relevant date of notification of the changes by the non-resident parent, as there was a significant change under the 'old rules'.

6. **Conversion, benefits and collection**

All the provisions relating to 'new rules' maintenance calculations apply to old cases that convert, even though transitional phasing may apply. This section clarifies how certain issues are dealt with at conversion.

Person with care on benefit

Child maintenance bonus and child maintenance premium

Under the 'old rules' scheme, parents with care in receipt of income support or income-based jobseeker's allowance accrued a child maintenance bonus. This was replaced by the child maintenance premium in 2004. From 27 October 2008, all parents with care covered by the 'old rules' stopped accruing the child maintenance bonus. Before this date, a child maintenance bonus could be accrued until an existing maintenance assessment converted to the 'new rules'.[86]

When a child maintenance bonus was replaced by a child maintenance premium at conversion, it was sometimes possible to claim the bonus that had accrued. The time limit for claiming the bonus has now expired in the majority of cases, although there may be some rare exceptions. For more information on the child maintenance bonus, see previous editions of this *Handbook*.

Non-resident parent on benefit

A non-resident parent on benefit may be due to pay the flat rate of maintenance or a transitional amount if, under the 'old rules', he made a contribution to maintenance or was exempt. The new rules on deduction from benefit applying to conversion decisions and deductions mean that deductions may be made from benefit for maintenance and arrears (see p346). There is no appeal against deductions from benefit for flat rate maintenance or to recover arrears (see p160).

Collection and enforcement

Maintenance worked out under a conversion decision is collected and enforced in the normal way, since it is treated as a maintenance calculation.[87]

Arrears built up under the 'old rules' may be recovered using the new deduction from earnings orders or the normal enforcement action. An existing deduction from earnings order may be cancelled and a new one issued.

A payment penalty may also be imposed, but only on arrears or late payments that fall due after conversion.

Notes

1. When 'old rules' cases convert to the 'new rules'

1 In CCS/1077/2006 the commissioner stated that, even if discrimination could be shown, 'it is an objective and reasonable justification that parents are treated differently as new legislation is tested as it is brought into force.' See also R(CS) 3/07 in which the commissioner decided there was no breach of the European Convention on Human Rights, even though it is now clear that the 'new rules' scheme will not be implemented for all 'old rules' cases.
2 Sch 5 CMOPA 2008
3 C-MEC Business Plan 2009/10
4 Reg 15 CS(TP) Regs; reg 3 CSPSSA (Comm 12) O
5 Reg 15 CS(TP) Regs
6 PG, Migration and Case Conversion, Overview – CSR Case Conversion

2. The calculation and transitional phasing

7 Reg 16(1) CS(TP) Regs
8 Reg 3(1)(c) CS(TP) Regs
9 Reg 3(4) CS(TP) Regs
10 Reg 3(5) CS(TP) Regs
11 s29 CSPSSA 2000; reg 9 CS(TP) Regs
12 Reg 14 CS(TP) Regs
13 Reg 10 CS(TP) Regs
14 Reg 11(2) CS(TP) Regs
15 Reg 11(3) CS(TP) Regs
16 Reg 24 CS(TP) Regs
17 Reg 11(1) CS(TP) Regs
18 Reg 2(1) CS(TP) Regs
19 Regs 2(1) and 25(1) CS(TP) Regs
20 Reg 25(5)-(7) CS(TP) Regs
21 Reg 25(3) CS(TP) Regs
22 Reg 25(4) CS(TP) Regs
23 Reg 13(2) CS(TP) Regs
24 Reg 13(1) CS(TP) Regs
25 Reg 12(1) CS(TP) Regs
26 Reg 12(2) CS(TP) Regs
27 Reg 12(3)-(5) CS(TP) Regs
28 Reg 12(6) CS(TP) Regs
29 s29(3)(b) CSPSSA 2000
30 Reg 17 CS(TP) Regs
31 Reg 17(2) CS(TP) Regs
32 Reg 17(6) CS(TP) Regs
33 Reg 17(9) CS(TP) Regs
34 Reg 17(8) CS(TP) Regs
35 Reg 21 CS(TP) Regs
36 Reg 17(10) CS(TP) Regs
37 Regs 23 and 23A CS(TP) Regs
38 Reg 20 CS(TP) Regs
39 Reg 18 CS(TP) Regs
40 Reg 21 CS(TP) Regs
41 Reg 19 CS(TP) Regs
42 Reg 23(4) CS(TP) Regs
43 Reg 23(5) CS(TP) Regs
44 Reg 22 CS(TP) Regs
45 Reg 9A CS(TP) Regs
46 Reg 9B CS(TP) Regs

3. The conversion decision

47 Regs 3(2) and 16(1) CS(TP) Regs
48 Regs 3(2) and 16(1) CS(TP) Regs
49 s29 CSPSSA 2000
50 Reg 15(1) CS(TP) Regs
51 Reg 15(2)-(3G) CS(TP) Regs
52 Reg 7 The Child Support (Miscellaneous Amendments) (No.2) Regulations 2008
53 Reg 3(3) CS(TP) Regs
54 Reg 16(2) CS(TP) Regs
55 Reg 2 CS(TP) Regs

4. The linking rules

56 Reg 28(2) CS(TP) Regs
57 Reg 28(2A) CS(TP) Regs
58 see comments in R(CS) 1/06

5. Revisions, supersessions and appeals

59 Reg 16(2) CS(TP) Regs
60 Reg 4A CS(TP) Regs
61 Regs 14(2)(b) and (c) and 15(b) CS(D&A)(A) Regs
62 Reg 5 CS(TP) Regs
63 Reg 5A CS(TP) Regs
64 Reg 8 CS(TP) Regs
65 Regs 5(b) and 8(1) CS(TP) Regs
66 Regs 14(2) and 15(1) CS(D&A)(A) Regs
67 Regs 4(3) and 8(2) CS(TP) Regs
68 Regs 14 and 15 CS(D&A)(A) Regs
69 Reg 15(1) CS(D&A)(A) Regs
70 Reg 4(1) CS(TP) Regs
71 Reg 4(5)(b) CS(TP) Regs
72 Reg 4(4)(a) CS(TP) Regs
73 Reg 4(3) CS(TP) Regs
74 Reg 7 CS(TP) Regs

75 Reg 26 CS(TP) Regs
76 Reg 27 CS(TP) Regs
77 Reg 27(6) CS(TP) Regs
78 Reg 27(7) and (8) CS(TP) Regs
79 Reg 27(7A) and (7B) CS(TP) Regs
80 Reg 27(9) CS(TP) Regs
81 Reg 27(10) CS(TP) Regs
82 Reg 6(1)(a) and (2)(a) CS(TP) Regs
83 Reg 6(1)(b) and (2)(b) CS(TP) Regs
84 Reg 15 CS(D&A)(A) Regs
85 Reg 33 CS(TP) Regs

6. Conversion, benefits and collection

86 Art 6 CSPSSA (Comm12)O
87 Reg 16(2A) CS(TP) Regs

Part 4

Amount of maintenance: 'old rules'

Chapter 8

The 'old rules' formula

This chapter covers:
1. Introduction (below)
2. The five steps of the 'old rules' formula (p171)
3. Minimum child maintenance (p172)
4. Non-resident parents on certain benefits (p174)
5. Special cases (p175)

1. Introduction

For 'old rules' cases there is a statutory, non-discretionary formula for calculating child maintenance. An 'old rules' case is generally one where the application was made before 3 March 2003 (but some cases may be transferred to the 'new rules' – see Chapter 7). The amount of the child maintenance assessment cannot be negotiated. There is a right of appeal against the assessment, but the First-tier Tribunal is bound by the same law as the Child Support Agency (CSA), so an appeal is only likely to be successful if the CSA has made a mistake or there is room for interpretation in the law.

The amount of child maintenance payable depends largely on the circumstances and the income of both parents, but particularly the income of the non-resident parent. It may be difficult for parents and advisers to obtain all the information needed from the other parent in order to carry out an exact calculation, particularly if the other parent is the non-resident parent.

However, understanding the way in which the formula works is important for explaining the result of an assessment as well as forecasting the effect of any change of circumstances and deciding whether to seek a revision or supersession (see p351).

Deviation from the 'old rules' formula

A number of people have a duty to provide information to the CSA. If the CSA does not have sufficient information to carry out a full assessment, an interim maintenance assessment can be imposed (see p340). These are usually penalty assessments which are set a higher rate than the final assessment.

The formula is not used to calculate the contribution towards child maintenance if the non-resident parent is on income support (IS), pension credit (PC), income-related employment and support allowance or income-based jobseeker's allowance (see p174).

Non-resident parents with second families have the assessment phased in if there would be an increase in the payments of over £20 a week, compared with a pre-April 1993 maintenance agreement. The maximum phasing-in period is 18 months, so this should only apply to non-resident parents whose 'old rules' case has still not been assessed, or who still have an interim maintenance assessment (see p346).

Departure

It may be possible to request a change to the standard 'old rules' formula in certain circumstances. This is called departure. Departure is a way of taking into account a financial factor particular to that family – eg, the costs of the non-resident parent travelling to visit the children, or a partner's contribution towards housing costs. Although the decision on whether to take the factor into account (and to what extent) is discretionary, an adjusted statutory formula is then used to obtain the final assessment. See Chapter 15 for details of departure.

Weekly rates and rounding up

The child maintenance payable under the 'old rules' formula is given as a weekly rate and all stages of the calculation use weekly figures.[1] Fractions of a penny will be disregarded if less than one-half or rounded up to the next penny if equal to or more than one half-penny (except when calculating 70 per cent net income for the protected level (see p254), when any fraction of a penny is ignored).[2]

Income support rates

The formula for assessing child maintenance is based on IS components – both the personal allowances and the premiums. The 2009/10 rates are given at the front of this *Handbook*. It is important to note that although some of the rules on entitlement to allowances and premiums have changed for IS claimants, they still apply for the purpose of working out 'old rules' assessments (see Appendix 2).

The IS rates used in the calculation are those which apply on the date that the maintenance assessment comes into effect, known as the 'effective date' (see p341).[3] As the effective date is usually some time before the date on which the assessment is being made, assessments may be made in 2009/10 using a previous year's rates. Benefit rates increase in April each year. The maintenance assessment is not automatically altered at the annual April uprating of IS rates, but if a reassessment is requested after a change of circumstances, the new rates would then be relevant. CSA policy is to carry out periodic re-assessments of maintenance payable (case checks) at various intervals, but there is no legal requirement to do so (see p362).

Changes to the formula

Since the 'old rules' formula for setting assessments was introduced in April 1993, there have been several changes to it. Unless there is a specific provision, the general rule is that the calculation must be done using the regulations which applied on the effective date (see p341) of the assessment.[4] This edition of the *Handbook* covers the formula in effect during 2009/10; make sure you refer to the appropriate earlier edition for assessments with earlier effective dates.

2. **The five steps of the 'old rules' formula**

It is tempting to skip steps of the 'old rules' formula as it is long and complex, and you might think certain steps do not apply. However, you should not skip any steps without checking them unless you are very familiar with the formula.

Although only a non-resident parent is liable to pay child maintenance, the calculation involves the income of both parents. The term 'parent' applies to both the non-resident parent and the parent with care.

As elsewhere in this *Handbook*, for the sake of simplicity the parent with care is referred to as 'she' and the non-resident parent as 'he'. However, all aspects of the formula apply in the same way if the parent with care is in fact the father and the non-resident parent the mother. If the person with care is *not* the legal parent of the child, then the income of that person does not affect the amount of child maintenance payable.

Step 1: the maintenance requirement

The maintenance requirement represents the minimum day-to-day expenses of maintaining children. However, the maintenance requirement is neither the minimum nor the maximum amount of child maintenance payable. Under the formula, a non-resident parent might be assessed as liable to pay less or more than the maintenance requirement.

The main significance of this step is that a non-resident parent pays 50 per cent of his assessable income (see Chapter 11) in child maintenance until the maintenance requirement figure has been met. At this point he pays a lower percentage of any remaining assessable income.

For full details of the maintenance requirement, see Chapter 9.

Step 2: exempt income

Exempt income represents the minimum day-to-day living expenses of the parent and covers the housing costs of the family with whom s/he lives. However, it only includes amounts for living expenses of any of the parent's *own* children who are living with her/him, *not* the living expenses of a new partner or stepchildren. An allowance in recognition of property/capital settlements pre-dating April 1993 may also be included in exempt income.

Each parent is allowed to keep income equal to the exempt income before being expected to pay any child maintenance.

For full details of exempt income, see Chapter 10.

Step 3: assessable income

Assessable income is income which is available to pay child maintenance. It is the amount of the parent's income which remains after exempt income has been taken into account. If a non-resident parent has no assessable income, he may still have to pay the minimum payment.

For full details of assessable income, see Chapter 11.

Step 4: proposed maintenance

Proposed maintenance is the amount of child maintenance the non-resident parent is expected to pay as long as it does not bring his income below the protected income level (see Step 5).

A non-resident parent pays 50 per cent of his assessable income in child maintenance until he has met the maintenance requirement figure of Step 1. Once the maintenance requirement is met, he pays 15, 20 or 25 per cent of any further assessable income, depending on the number of children for whom he is being assessed to pay maintenance.

The assessable income of the parent with care can reduce the proposed maintenance.

There is an upper limit to the amount of child maintenance payable under the formula, but it may be possible for the parties to go to court to seek additional child maintenance (see p30).

For full details of proposed maintenance, see Chapter 12.

Step 5: protected income

The protected income step ensures that a non-resident parent's disposable income does not fall below a certain level as a result of paying the proposed maintenance. At this stage the whole family's expenses and income are taken into account, including those relating to a new partner and stepchildren.

In addition, a non-resident parent is not expected to pay more than 30 per cent of his own net income.

For full details of protected income, see Chapter 13.

3. **Minimum child maintenance**

There is a standard minimum of child maintenance that a non-resident parent must pay if the formula results in an amount less than this minimum.[5]

The amount of the minimum payment is currently £6.50. This is calculated by rounding 5 per cent of the income support (IS) personal allowance for someone aged 25 or over (£64.30) up to the next 5 pence and doubling it.[6]

The minimum payment must be made unless the non-resident parent falls into a category which is specifically excluded (see below). This means that a non-resident parent who has been assessed under the formula as liable to pay less than £6.50 will have to pay child maintenance of £6.50 a week unless he falls into one of the exempt categories, when he would pay nothing.

Only one minimum payment is due if the non-resident parent has qualifying children being looked after by more than one parent or person with care.[7] For example, if a non-resident parent has children with two or more women with whom he does not live, or if the qualifying children are being cared for by different people in different households, the minimum payment is divided between the persons with care in proportion to the relative maintenance requirements (see Chapter 9).

Exempt non-resident parents

A few non-resident parents do not have to pay any child maintenance at all. If a non-resident parent has been assessed under the formula as having to pay £6.50 or less, he is exempt from paying any child maintenance if he:[8]
- has the family premium (see Appendix 2) included in the calculation or estimation of his protected income level – ie, a child is a member of his family for at least two days a week;
- is a prisoner;
- receives (or would receive if he satisfied the national insurance contribution conditions or did not receive an overlapping benefit) one of the following:
  - incapacity benefit (or employment and support allowance for new claims from October 2008) or statutory sick pay;
  - maternity allowance or statutory maternity pay;
  - severe disablement allowance;
  - disability living allowance or attendance allowance;
  - an industrial disablement benefit;
  - a war disablement benefit or payment from the Armed Forces Compensation Scheme;
  - carer's allowance; or
  - payments from the Independent Living Funds;
- is under 16 years old, or under 19 and in full-time non-advanced education (ie, a child for child support purposes – see p18);
- has a net income of less than £6.50 (for details of what is net income, see Chapter 11). Trainees on approved training (eg, Entry to Employment or Skillseekers in Scotland) whose income consists solely of a training allowance/education maintenance allowance,[9] or students whose only income is a grant

or student loan,[10] have these payments ignored when calculating net income for child support purposes. This means that they are usually exempt from paying child maintenance.

4. Non-resident parents on certain benefits

If the non-resident parent is in receipt of income support (IS), pension credit (PC), income-related employment and support allowance (ESA) or income-based jobseeker's allowance (JSA), the formula is not used. Instead, the Secretary of State can make a deduction from the IS/PC/income-related ESA/income-based JSA of a non-resident parent as a contribution towards child maintenance.[11] The deduction can be made from a partner's IS/PC/income-related ESA/income-based JSA if the partner of a non-resident parent is claiming for the couple.[12]

Who cannot have the deduction made

Deductions cannot be made if the non-resident parent is exempt. In these cases a non-resident parent will pay nothing. A non-resident parent will be exempt if he:[13]

- is aged under 18; *or*
- qualifies for the family premium (see Appendix 2) and/or has day-to-day care (see p20) of any child; *or*
- receives any of the following benefits (or would receive one except for the national insurance contribution requirements or overlapping benefit rules):
  - statutory sick pay;
  - incapacity benefit (or contributory ESA for new claims from October 2008);
  - severe disablement allowance;
  - attendance allowance or disability living allowance;
  - carer's allowance;
  - maternity allowance;
  - statutory maternity pay;
  - an industrial disablement benefit;
  - a war disablement benefit or payment from the Armed Forces Compensation Scheme; *or*
  - payments from the Independent Living Funds.

Amount of the deduction

A non-resident parent on IS/PC/income-related ESA/income-based JSA who is not exempt may have an amount equal to the minimum payment (see p172) deducted from his benefit by the Department for Work and Pensions (DWP), irrespective of the age of the non-resident parent.[14] This is currently £6.50 a week. No more than one deduction of £6.50 can be made from an IS/PC/income-based JSA/income-related ESA claim at any one time.[15] In some cases, half of this amount may be deducted. Whether the deduction is actually made by the DWP, and how much is deducted, depends on the number of other deductions of higher priority being made from benefit. For more information about how deductions are made, see p403.

Only one deduction for child support can be made, even if there is more than one person with care looking after the non-resident parent's qualifying children. In this case, the minimum payment is apportioned between the persons with care in the same ratio as their respective maintenance requirements.[16]

What the deduction is for

Technically, deductions from benefit are not payments of child support maintenance, but payments in lieu of child maintenance.[17] Deductions are not the result of a maintenance assessment and the rules that apply to assessments do not apply to these contributions. In particular, liability for the contributions will not be backdated to the effective date and arrears will not accrue if the DWP is unable to make the full deduction because there are other deductions with higher priority.

No more than one deduction of £6.50 can be made from an IS/PC/income-based JSA/income-related ESA claim at any one time,[18] and because deductions can only be made where there is a non-resident parent with current liability, no amount for child maintenance arrears can ever be deducted from these benefits. Arrears of child maintenance could still be collected by other methods (see Chapter 19), but usually the arrears will just be held in abeyance until the non-resident parent comes off IS/PC/income-related ESA/income-based JSA. However, if a non-resident parent is in receipt of contribution-based JSA, an amount can be deducted from this benefit towards arrears (see p411).

Challenging decisions

CSA decisions about the liability of non-resident parents on certain benefits can be challenged in the same way as other CSA decisions[19] – ie, by seeking a revision[20] or supersession[21] (see Chapter 17) or by appealing to the First-tier Tribunal[22] (see Chapter 18). If the DWP's decision is being contested (ie, whether the non-resident parent can have £6.50 or some other amount deducted from his IS/PC/income-based JSA/income-related ESA, given other higher priority deductions), it can be challenged in a similar way (see CPAG's *Welfare Benefits and Tax Credits Handbook* for more details).

5. **Special cases**

The legislation uses the phrase 'special cases' to cover situations that are not as straightforward as where one non-resident parent has left one family and there is one person with care looking after all the children from that family.[23] However, in order to enable people to carry out calculations for all family situations, we have integrated these situations into the relevant steps of the formula – eg, where:

- both parents are non-resident (see pp180 and 242);
- more than one person with care applies for child maintenance from the same non-resident parent (see p244);
- a person cares for children of more than one non-resident parent (see pp181 and 249).

Where care of a child is being shared between different people, several modifications of the formula are necessary. Shared care under the 'old rules' is, therefore, treated separately (see Chapter 14).

Shared care is different to the situation where different children of the same family have different homes. Where the children of a family are divided between two households (eg, where one child lives with one parent and another child with the other parent), this involves two maintenance assessments. In one assessment, the first parent is the parent with care and the second parent is the non-resident parent. In the second assessment the roles are reversed. We have called this situation 'divided families' (see p248); the Child Support Agency may refer to this as 'split care'.

Notes

1. Introduction

1 Reg 33(1) CS(MAP) Regs; reg 2(1) CS(MASC) Regs
2 Reg 2(2) CS(MASC) Regs
3 Regs 3(2), 9(5) and 11(5) CS(MASC) Regs
4 Reg 2(3) CS(MASC) Regs; CCS/7312/1995

3. Minimum child maintenance

5 Sch 1 para 7 CSA 1991
6 Reg 13 CS(MASC) Regs
7 Reg 22(4) CS(MASC) Regs
8 Reg 26 and Sch 4 CS(MASC) Regs
9 Sch 2, paras 21 and 36 CS(MASC) Regs
10 Reg 7(3) CS(MASC) Regs

4. Non-resident parents on certain benefits

11 s43 and Sch 1 para 5(4) CSA 1991
12 Sch 9 para 7A(1) SS(C&P) Regs
13 Reg 28 CS(MASC) Regs
14 Reg 28(2) CS(MASC) Regs; Sch 9 para 7A(3) SS(C&P) Regs
15 Reg 28(3) and (4) CS(MASC) Regs
16 Sch 9 para 7A(2) SS(C&P) Regs
17 s43(2)(a) CSA 1991
18 Sch 9 para 7A(2) SS(C&P) Regs
19 s43(3) CSA 1991
20 Sch 4C para 1(a) CSA 1991
21 Sch 4C para 2(1)(a) CSA 1991
22 Sch 4C para 3(1)(a) CSA 1991

5. Special cases

23 Part III CS(MASC) Regs

Chapter 9

The maintenance requirement ('old rules')

This chapter covers:

1. **What is the maintenance requirement**

The maintenance requirement is intended to represent the minimum weekly cost of caring for the child(ren) for whom child maintenance is being assessed.[1] The maintenance requirement is based on income support (IS) rates. For information on the conditions of entitlement to the IS premiums, see Appendix 2. Note that some of these premiums may no longer be paid with IS (eg, because parents get child tax credit instead), but are still used in the child support formula.

Both parents' incomes affect the maintenance requirement. In the case of the parent with care, a notional contribution towards the maintenance requirement is calculated, which may reduce the amount of child maintenance a non-resident parent has to pay.

The parents may not have sufficient income to be able to pay the full maintenance requirement. If this is the case, the non-resident parent pays 50 per cent of his available income, known as 'assessable income'. Equally, the maintenance requirement is not the total amount of child maintenance that may be expected from a non-resident parent. However, once the maintenance requirement is met, the non-resident parent then pays a lower percentage of any further income (see Chapters 11 and 12).

The maintenance requirement is also used where child maintenance has to be apportioned between two persons with care. This occurs where a parent is a non-resident parent for two different maintenance assessments (see p248).

Interim maintenance assessments

When the Child Support Agency does not have sufficient information from the non-resident parent to carry out an assessment, it can make an interim maintenance assessment. Where the non-resident parent is withholding information other than information about his partner or another member of the family's income, the interim maintenance assessment is set at 1.5 times the maintenance requirement (see p340).[2]

2. **How much is the maintenance requirement**

The maintenance requirement includes an allowance for each qualifying child (see p18) being looked after by that person with care. The person who is being assessed to pay child maintenance *must* be the parent (see p15) of that qualifying child. If a person with care is looking after children of different non-resident parents, a different maintenance requirement is calculated for each of the assessments (see p181).

The maintenance requirement calculation

The maintenance requirement is calculated as follows:[3]
- for each qualifying child, the amount of the income support (IS) personal allowance for a child (£56.11); *plus*
- the amount of the IS family premium (£17.30); *plus*
- a 'parent as carer' element (see also p179):
  - where at least one qualifying child is under 11 years of age, the amount of the adult IS personal allowance at the rate for a person aged 25 years or over, irrespective of the age of the person with care (£64.30); *or*
  - where none of the qualifying children are under 11 but at least one is under 14 years of age, 75 per cent of this adult allowance (£48.23); *or*
  - where none of the children are under 14 but at least one is under 16 years of age, 50 per cent of the adult allowance (£32.15); *less*
- an amount of child benefit for the qualifying child(ren) (see below).

This is the basic maintenance requirement calculation, which is adapted in situations where more than one non-resident parent is involved (see p181).

The rates used in the calculation are the IS and child benefit rates applicable at the date on which the maintenance assessment takes effect, known as the 'effective date' (see p341).[4] The figures given above are those for 2009/10.

Deduction of child benefit

The amount of child benefit deducted is:[5]
- £20 for the only, elder or eldest child for whom child benefit is payable; *and*

- £13.20 for all other children.

The amount of child benefit deducted from the maintenance requirement may be different from that actually paid to the person with care, perhaps because she has not claimed it or because someone else (eg, the non-resident parent) is receiving it. In such cases, the person with care should consider claiming child benefit or asking the non-resident parent to make the payment of child benefit in addition to the maintenance payment (see the example on p183). Where more than one eligible person claims child benefit, the person with whom the child lives has priority. See CPAG's *Welfare Benefits and Tax Credits Handbook* for more details.

If child benefit is not payable for a child because s/he is in the care of an institution, an amount of child benefit is still deducted.[6] However, in other situations where no one is entitled to child benefit for that child (eg, because of the rules about residence in the UK) no deduction is made. For more information about child benefit, who is entitled and when it is payable, see CPAG's *Welfare Benefits and Tax Credits Handbook*.

The parent as carer element

When the 'old rules' assessment was designed, the inclusion of the adult personal allowance was intended to represent the care costs of the child. The reduction of the allowance for children over 11 years of age is based on an assumption that care needs reduce as children grow up. This means that the maintenance requirement as a whole can reduce immediately after a child's birthday.

The parent as carer element is not maintenance for a former spouse or civil partner.[7] Spousal or civil partner maintenance is completely separate from child maintenance calculated by the Child Support Agency. Any application for maintenance for the parent with care must be made to the courts (see p27).

Couples

The personal allowance for couples is never included in the maintenance requirement. This is because the non-resident parent is not responsible for maintaining a partner of the person with care.

Children with disabilities

The disabled child premium is not included in the calculation of the maintenance requirement and neither is any related carer premium. A court may be able to consider a top-up maintenance award for a child who is disabled (see p30).[8]

The maintenance requirement calculation where there is one non-resident parent and one parent with care

The most common situation in which the maintenance requirement needs to be calculated is where there is one parent with care and one non-resident parent.

Example: maintenance requirement where there is one non-resident parent and one parent with care

Anita and Bob have two children. They split up, and Anita remains in the family home with Carol (13) and David (8).

		£
Personal allowances	Anita	64.30
	Carol	56.11
	David	56.11
Family premium		17.30
Sub-total		193.82
Less child benefit		33.20
Maintenance requirement		**160.62**

Five years later, Anita remarries. David is 13; Carol is 18 and still at school.

		£
Personal allowances	Anita	48.23 (75% x 64.30)
	Carol	56.11
	David	56.11
Family premium		17.30
Sub-total		177.75
Less child benefit		33.20
Maintenance requirement		**144.55**

3. **Both parents are non-resident**

An application for maintenance can be made by a person with care who is not a parent – eg, if a child lives with her/his grandparents or another relative. Both parents of that child are then non-resident parents and liable to pay maintenance. An assessment can be carried out for each non-resident parent if an application is made in respect of her/him, and each contributes to the maintenance requirement (see p242 for the calculation of the proposed maintenance).

An application may be made for maintenance from only one of the non-resident parents. In this case, the maintenance requirement for the one non-resident parent is halved.[9] However, it is not halved when an application is made for maintenance from both non-resident parents even if an assessment cannot be made for both – eg, one parent cannot be traced or is habitually resident outside the UK.

Beverley (15) lives with her grandmother, who is a widow.

		£
Personal allowances	Grandmother	32.15 (50% x 64.30)
	Beverley	56.11
Family premium		17.30
Sub-total		105.56
Less child benefit		20.00
Maintenance requirement		**85.56**

This maintenance requirement will be halved to £42.78 if the grandmother applies for child maintenance only from her son-in-law and not her daughter.

4. **More than one non-resident parent**

A person with care may look after qualifying children who have different parents – eg, a mother is looking after her children who have different fathers, a grandmother is looking after children of two of her sons, or a lone parent is also looking after a friend's child. In these cases, if applications are made for child maintenance from each non-resident parent, a number of different assessments must be carried out, one for each non-resident parent.

The maintenance requirement for each non-resident parent includes only the child(ren) who are his own responsibility. However, the adult personal allowance and the family premium are divided among the non-resident parents[10] in proportion to the number of non-resident parents and not in proportion to the number of children who are their responsibility.[11] This apportionment should occur whether or not child maintenance is being pursued from all the non-resident parents.[12] For example, a person with care may apply for child maintenance from one father and not another, or one of the parents may be resident abroad and hence outside the Child Support Agency's jurisdiction. However, a deceased parent is not treated as a non-resident parent and there is no reduction in the maintenance requirement for living non-resident parents.[13]

The apportioned 'parent as carer' element is then further reduced if the children in the individual assessment are aged 11 or over – ie, 75 per cent of the apportioned amount is used if the youngest child is aged 11–13 and 50 per cent of the apportioned amount if s/he is 14 or 15 years old.[14]

Example: maintenance requirement where the children have different fathers
Zoe is a single parent and has three children, all of whom live with her. Wayne is the father of Yvonne (12) and Veronica (10). Terence is the father of Scott (3).

Wayne's assessment:

		£	
Personal allowances	Zoe	32.15	(50% x 64.30)
	Yvonne	56.11	
	Veronica	56.11	
Family premium		8.65	(50% x 17.30)
Sub-total		153.02	
Less child benefit		33.20	
Maintenance requirement		**119.82**	

Terence's assessment:

		£	
Personal allowances	Zoe	32.15	(50% x 64.30)
	Scott	56.11	
Family premium		8.65	(50% x 17.30)
Sub-total		96.91	
Less child benefit		13.20	
Maintenance requirement		**83.71**	

Two years later, Zoe is living with Bob and her four children. Wayne is the father of Yvonne (14) and Veronica (12). Terence is the father of Scott (5). Bob is the father of Ricky (1). However, as Bob is not a non-resident parent, the apportionment occurs between Wayne and Terence only. Terence's assessment remains as above.

Wayne's assessment:

		£	
Personal allowances	Zoe	24.11	(75% x one-half of 64.30)
	Yvonne	56.11	
	Veronica	56.11	
Family premium		8.65	(50% x 17.30)
Sub-total		144.98	
Less child benefit		33.20	
Maintenance requirement		**111.78**	

If a person with care is looking after children of different parents, but two of the non-resident parents are parents of the same child (ie, the person with care is *not* a parent of that child), those two non-resident parents will be treated as one person for the purposes of apportioning the relevant elements of the maintenance requirement.[15]

Example: maintenance requirement where there is more than one non-resident parent and both parents of one child are non-resident

Zoe's niece, Rebecca, who is aged 17 and still at school, comes to live with Zoe and Bob when her parents split up. Rebecca joining the household alters the maintenance requirement for the other children. For the four qualifying children Zoe is now looking after, there are four non-resident parents (Wayne, Terence, and both of Rebecca's parents). However, Rebecca's parents count as one unit for this purpose and therefore the amounts are divided by three.

Wayne's assessment:

		£	
Personal allowances	Zoe	16.07	(75% x one-third of 64.30)
	Yvonne	56.11	
	Veronica	56.11	
Family premium		5.77	(one-third of 17.30)
Sub-total		134.06	
Less child benefit		26.40	
Maintenance requirement		**107.66**	

Terence's assessment:

		£	
Personal allowances	Zoe	21.44	(one-third of 64.30)
	Scott (5)	56.11	
Family premium		5.77	(one-third of 17.30)
Sub-total		83.31	
Less child benefit		13.20	
Maintenance requirement		**70.11**	

Rebecca's parents' assessment:

	£	
Personal allowance for Rebecca	56.11	
Family premium	5.77	(one-third of 17.30)
Sub-total	61.88	
Less child benefit	20.00	
Maintenance requirement	**41.88**	

An assessment is carried out separately for both of Rebecca's parents, each using the maintenance requirement of £41.88. If Zoe chose to apply for child maintenance only from one of Rebecca's parents, the maintenance requirement would be halved to £20.94. **Note:** if she chose to apply for child maintenance for Rebecca on or after 3 March 2003, this would prompt conversion of the other assessments and all her child maintenance would be dealt with under the 'new rules' (see Chapter 7).

We have assumed that Zoe has claimed child benefit for Rebecca, which means that under the child benefit regulations the higher rate applies to Rebecca and the lower rate now applies to Yvonne. As the person with whom Rebecca is living, Zoe takes priority over the mother for child benefit purposes (see p274).[16]

If Rebecca's mother had continued to claim child benefit, the higher rate would be payable for Rebecca as the only child for whom her mother is claiming. At the same time, the higher rate would still be payable for Yvonne as she is the eldest child for whom Zoe is claiming child benefit.[17] If this were the case, the child benefit of £20 would be deducted for both children in the calculation, even though Zoe would not actually be receiving child benefit for Rebecca.

In this scenario, if Rebecca's mother did not give £20 each week to Zoe, whether as child maintenance or on top of the maintenance assessment, she would no longer be entitled to child benefit.[18] In this case, the maintenance requirements would be as shown above, as child benefit would not legally be payable to Rebecca's mother, even though in practice it may still be being paid. It would be to Zoe's advantage to claim the child benefit for Rebecca in this situation.

Notes

1. **What is the maintenance requirement**
   1 Sch 1 para 1(1) CSA 1991
   2 Regs 8(3)(a) and 8A(1) CS(MAP) Regs

2. **How much is the maintenance requirement**
   3 Sch 1 para 1 CSA 1991; reg 3 CS(MASC) Regs
   4 Regs 3(2) and 4 CS(MASC) Regs
   5 Reg 4 CS(MASC) Regs
   6 Sch 1 para 1(2) CSA 1991
   7 CCS/11729/1996
   8 s8(8) and (9) CSA 1991

3. **Both parents are non-resident**
   9 Reg 19(2)(d) CS(MASC) Regs

4. **More than one non-resident parent**
   10 Reg 23 CS(MASC) Regs
   11 Reg 23(3) CS(MASC) Regs
   12 Reg 23(1) CS(MASC) Regs
   13 CCS/7436/1999
   14 Reg 23(2A) CS(MASC) Regs
   15 Reg 23(3) CS(MASC) Regs
   16 Sch 10 para 2 SSCBA 1992
   17 Reg 2 CB&SS(FAR) Regs
   18 s143(1)(b) SSCBA 1992

Chapter 10

Exempt income ('old rules')

This chapter covers:
1. What is exempt income (below)
2. How much is exempt income (p186)
3. Housing costs (p188)
4. Pre-April 1993 property settlements (p196)
5. Travel-to-work costs (p200)
6. Second families (p202)

1. What is exempt income

Exempt income is income a parent can keep for her/his own essential expenses before any child maintenance is expected. The expenses are based on income support (IS) rates but also include housing costs.

When the 'old rules' assessment was designed, exempt income was intended to represent the minimum day-to-day living expenses of parents and their *own* children who are living with them. If the parent has a partner, the partner's personal expenses are *not* included in exempt income. However, the housing costs for the whole family, including any partner and stepchildren, are covered in exempt income.

'**Own child**' means a child for whom the parent is, in law, a parent – ie, the biological or adoptive parent (see p15). Exempt income does *not* include amounts for any other children in the family – eg, stepchildren. Allowances for other children are not even initially included if the child is the primary responsibility of the parent – eg, where the stepchild's other parent is dead or cannot afford to pay any child maintenance. In some cases departure from the 'old rules' assessment can be sought on these grounds (see p293).

Exempt income applies to *both* the non-resident parent and the parent with care, as both are liable to maintain their children. If the parent with care has any income available to maintain the children, this might reduce the non-resident parent's contribution (see Chapter 12). However, if the parent with care is on IS, pension credit (PC), income-related employment and support allowance (ESA), income-based jobseeker's allowance (JSA) or working tax credit (WTC), it is assumed that she has no income available for child maintenance[1] and the exempt income step is carried out for the non-resident parent only. This applies both where the parent with care is the benefit claimant and where her partner is making the claim. If the non-resident parent is on IS/PC/income-related ESA/ income-based JSA, there is no need to calculate exempt income for either parent, as the formula is not used at all in this case. Instead, the non-resident parent may have deductions made from his IS/PC/income-related ESA/income-based JSA as a contribution towards child maintenance (see p174). If the non-resident parent is on WTC, the child support calculation is still carried out unless there is also an assessment being considered or in force for a child for whom he is the parent with care (see p20).[2] If he is a parent with care in this position, he is not liable to pay any child maintenance as a non-resident parent. This does not apply if a 'new rules' calculation is being considered. If a 'new rules' calculation is carried out, the assessment as a non-resident parent will be converted and carried out as a 'new rules' calculation too. In this case, WTC is counted as income. See also Chapter 7.

If the person with care is not a parent, the exempt income step does *not* apply to her/him, as only parents have a liability to maintain their children. In this case, there will usually be two non-resident parents and a maintenance assessment (including the exempt income step) is carried out for both.

2. **How much is exempt income**

Exempt income is generally calculated in the same way for parents with care as for non-resident parents.[3] Any reference to 'parent' below applies equally to the parent with care and the non-resident parent.

The rates used in the calculation are the income support (IS) rates applicable on the date at which the maintenance assessment takes effect, known as the 'effective date' (see p341).[4] The rates given below are for 2009/10.

For the qualifying conditions of the IS premiums, see Appendix 2.

The exempt income calculation

Exempt income is calculated as follows for each parent:[5]
- the amount of the IS personal allowance for a single person aged 25 or over, irrespective of the age of the parent (£64.30); *plus*
- if there is a child – ie, the parent's own child (see above) living with the parent, the amount of the IS personal allowance for such child (£56.11);*†*plus*
- if an allowance for a child is included, the amount of the IS family premium (£17.30)*†; plus*
- if any of the children included would qualify for the IS disabled child premium, the amount of that premium for each child entitled (£51.24);*†plus*
- if any of the children included would qualify for the IS enhanced disability premium, the amount of that premium for each child entitled (£20.65);*†plus*

- if the parent would qualify for the IS disability premium if s/he is under the qualifying age for pension credit, the amount of the premium for a single person (£27.50); the disability conditions must be satisfied by the parent her/himself; *plus*
- if the parent would qualify for the IS carer premium, the amount of that premium (£29.50); *plus*
- if the parent would qualify for the IS severe disability premium, the amount of that premium (£52.85); *plus*
- if the parent would qualify for the IS enhanced disability premium, the amount of that premium (£13.40); *plus*
- housing costs (see p188); *plus*
- where applicable, an allowance for a pre-April 1993 property settlement (see p196); *plus*
- if an employee travels more than 240 kilometres a week to and from work, an amount towards travel costs (see p200).

* If the child's other parent also lives in the family and has sufficient income to help support the child, these amounts may be halved (see p202).

† These amounts will be included at a proportionate rate if the parent looks after the child(ren) for less than seven days, but at least two nights on average per week (see Chapter 14). For parents with care, this apportionment only takes place if another person also has day-to-day care of the child.[6] Special expenses can be added to exempt income after a departure direction.

Example

Bob and Anita have split up. Anita is looking after Carol and David, and remains in the family home. There is no need to calculate Anita's exempt income as she is in receipt of IS. Bob is living on his own in a bedsit, paying rent of £48 a week. He is not entitled to any housing benefit. He does not qualify for any premiums. He travels less than 240 kilometres a week to work.

Bob's exempt income is therefore:

	£
Personal allowance	64.30
Housing costs	48.00
Total exempt income	**112.30**

If Bob had moved in with his parents, his exempt income would be £64.30. If Bob was in receipt of long-term incapacity benefit and living with his parents, his exempt income would then be:

	£
Personal allowance	64.30
Disability premium	27.50
Total exempt income	**91.80**

---

3. **Housing costs**

Housing costs for the parent and any of her/his family (see p25) living with her/him are included in exempt income. If the other party believes that the parent's partner can afford to contribute to the housing costs, s/he may be able to apply for a departure direction (see p301).

To be included in exempt income, housing costs must be eligible (see p189) and payable in respect of the parent's home (see p191). Housing costs which are excessive may not be included in full (see p194).

Responsibility for housing costs

Eligible housing costs for the parent's home are included if the parent or partner is responsible for the costs and the payment is made to a person who is not a member of the same household.[7] Therefore, if a parent lives with a new partner, the housing costs are accepted, even if they are the partner's responsibility. The amount of the housing costs included in exempt income can be reduced if it is reasonable to expect the partner to contribute.[8] Otherwise the full eligible costs are covered, and not the amount paid by the parent towards the housing costs.[9]

As well as where s/he is actually liable for the costs, a parent will be treated as responsible for housing costs if:[10]

- s/he has to meet the costs in order to live in the home; *and*
- the person liable to make the payments is not doing so; *and*
- either the parent is the former partner of the liable person or is someone else whom it is reasonable to treat as liable.

If costs are shared with another person who is not a partner, only the parent's actual share of the costs is used (unless the parent is treated as liable because the other person(s) is not paying her/his share).[11] This means that where the non-resident parent continues to pay his liability of the housing costs on the former joint home in which the parent with care remains, this amount cannot be included as the parent with care's housing costs.[12] If the non-resident parent stops paying his liability, the full amount is treated as the parent with care's housing costs.[13] If three friends are joint tenants and share the rent equally, one-third of the rent is considered to be the responsibility of the parent, unless the Child Support Agency (CSA) believes that such a division would not be reasonable – eg, one of the joint occupiers is not paying her/his share (in which case the amount the parent actually pays may be used), or they have unequal shares of the accommodation.[14] However, a parent will not be treated as responsible for housing costs which a member of their family (see p25) is not paying.[15]

Before 1 December 2005, same-sex couples were not treated as partners, and so if a same-sex partner of a parent was paying or contributing to housing costs, these costs would not automatically be treated as the parent's. Eligible housing costs from 1 December 2005 should include payments made by a same-sex partner of a parent, but exempt income for periods before that date will not include such costs, unless another rule applies allowing them to be treated as the parents's costs (see below). Although a parent argued against this, it was decided that the resulting higher child support liability was not unlawful discrimination.[16]

The parent may be treated as responsible for housing costs that s/he shares with other members of the household, even if s/he makes those payments via another member of the household and not directly.[17] This applies if:

- it is reasonable for a parent to be treated as responsible for a share of the costs; *and*
- the person with responsibility is not a close relative of the parent or her/his partner (see p22); *and*
- the person with responsibility either has an equivalent responsibility for housing costs as the parent or that person is meeting the costs because the liable person is not.

However, if a parent is a non-dependent member of a household (see p258), no housing costs are included in exempt income, even if s/he is paying a contribution for housing costs to another member of the household.[18] In order for a parent to be a non-dependant, not only can there be no commercial arrangement, but s/he has to be a member of the same *household* as the person liable to make the payments (see p22).

Where a parent is living with her/his parents as a non-dependant s/he is, therefore, clearly not entitled to have her/his contribution to the housing costs included in exempt income.[19] However, where costs are shared with other people who are not close relatives and the parent is not a non-dependant, even if the parent is contributing to housing costs on a voluntary basis it might, depending on the circumstances of the case, be arguable that it is reasonable to treat the parent as responsible for a share of the costs. This is most likely to succeed in cases where the costs have previously been shared with someone else and the parent has taken over that person's share. If the parent becomes a co-owner or joint tenant, half of the housing costs will definitely be treated as the parent's responsibility. If the parent became a sub-tenant, s/he would be responsible for the costs specified in the tenancy agreement.

Eligible housing costs

Eligible housing costs are costs which have to be incurred in order to buy, rent or otherwise secure possession of the parent's home or to carry out repairs and improvements as defined below.[20] Eligible costs are:[21]

- rent (after deduction of any housing benefit (HB)[22] – see p191);
- mortgage interest payments;
- capital repayments under a mortgage;

- premiums paid under an endowment or other insurance policy, or a personal pension plan to the extent that the policy was taken out to cover the cost of the mortgage (see p191);
- interest payments on any loans for repairs and improvements to the home taken out before the maintenance application or enquiry form is sent to the parent;
- interest payments on loans for major repairs necessary to maintain the fabric of the home and for measures which improve its fitness for occupation, such as the installation of a bath, shower, wash basin or lavatory; the provision of heating, electric lighting and sockets, drainage facilities, or storage facilities for fuel and refuse; improvements to ventilation, natural lighting, insulation or structural condition; or any other improvements considered reasonable by the CSA (the previous 'unfitness' which necessitated the improvement needs to be demonstrated[23]);
- interest payments under a hire purchase agreement to buy a home;
- payments in respect of a licence or permission to occupy the home;
- payments in respect of, or as a result of, the occupation of the home. (This is intended to cover payments made by a former licensee who occupies premises unlawfully – eg, after a notice to quit has expired.[24] It does not include property and contents insurance,[25] payments in respect of the purchase of a home[26] or council tax[27]);
- payments of ground rent or feu duty;
- payments under co-ownership schemes;
- payments of service charges if such payments are a condition for occupying the home (but see p193);
- mooring charges for a houseboat;
- site rent for a caravan or mobile home;
- payments for a tent and its site;
- payments under a rental purchase scheme;
- payments in respect of croft land;
- payments in respect of a home made to an employer who provides the home;
- payments for a Crown tenancy or licence;
- payments in respect of a loan taken out to pay off (in full or in part[28]) another loan that covered eligible housing costs;
- the fees (after deduction of any HB) if a parent or a partner lives in a care home or an independent hospital, or is being provided with a care home service or independent healthcare service.[29]

Repayments of an advance of salary (see also p209) used to purchase a home cannot be housing costs.[30]

Home

For the purposes of housing costs, the parent's home is either the dwelling in which the parent normally lives or, if s/he normally lives in more than one home, her/his principal home.[31] Therefore, if a non-resident parent is paying the costs of the family home in which the parent with care remains with the child(ren), these costs cannot be included in the non-resident parent's exempt income as this is not the non-resident parent's own home.[32] Before deciding which dwelling is the principal home, the facts must show that the parent does actually live in more than one home.[33]

The test of a principal home is not simply the parent's own view nor a calculation of the time spent at each home.[34] An army officer's own home where he spends his leave could be his principal home over and above army married quarters. Expenditure on army accommodation in addition to the principal home could not in this situation also be taken into account as expenses (see p211), but army officers serving abroad may be able to have the costs of both a home in the UK and quarters overseas included in exempt income.[35]

The only other exception to the rule about only including one set of housing costs is where the parent is in a care home. The residential fees can be included as well as the costs of the parent's own home if the parent has been in the residential accommodation for less than a year or if the CSA believes that the parent intends to return home.[36]

If the payments for the property cover accommodation used for other purposes (eg, business use) the CSA has to identify the proportion of the cost attributable to housing.[37]

Housing benefit

HB is subtracted from housing costs if the parent has claimed and been awarded it.[38] In this situation, the CSA will use as housing costs the weekly amount treated as eligible rent for the purposes of HB minus the amount of HB calculated by the local authority.[39] (Because of rent restriction and local housing allowance rules in HB, eligible rent may be less than the non-resident parent's actual rent, even allowing for the deduction of ineligible charges. For more information, see CPAG's *Welfare Benefits and Tax Credits Handbook*.)

If a parent delays claiming HB until after completing the maintenance enquiry or application form, full housing costs will be included as exempt income (unless they are excessive – see p194). If a parent is awaiting a decision on an HB claim, the excessive housing costs rule does not apply, but the CSA may later seek further information about the claim.

Mortgage and other loan payments

Unlike for income support (IS), most payments connected to mortgage repayment – whether directly as capital repayments or through certain policies – are eligible housing costs for exempt income purposes.[40] However, such payments are not eligible at the protected income stage (see p258).

As well as endowment policies, other insurance policies taken out to pay off a mortgage on the home are considered to be eligible housing costs. These include premiums paid into a mortgage protection policy to cover the mortgage in the event of unemployment, sickness or disability.[41] Life assurance policies taken out with the mortgage in order to discharge the debt on death are also included.[42] However, neither building nor contents insurance is included.[43] The mortgage which any such policy is intended to discharge need not exist at the time of the assessment.[44]

Only loans for the provision of a home are eligible. A loan used to buy out a former partner's interest in a property will only be eligible if it can be shown that the loan is necessary to protect the right of occupancy.[45]

If a loan is partly for the provision of a home (see p191), only that part is an eligible housing cost.[46] If only part of the mortgage is eligible, the nature of any insurance policies should be investigated. It should not be assumed that the proportions of the premiums allowed should follow the proportion of the mortgage interest allowed.[47]

Personal pension plans taken out, at least in part, to discharge a mortgage on the parent's home are eligible housing costs.[48] If a personal pension plan has been obtained both to discharge the mortgage and to pay a pension, 25 per cent of the contributions made are included as housing costs in exempt income.[49]

If the mortgage is under £60,000, all the premiums paid to an endowment policy are eligible housing costs.[50] If the policy was also taken out to produce a lump sum and the mortgage is over £60,000, 0.0277 per cent of the mortgage is taken to be weekly housing costs, unless the CSA can ascertain what proportion of the premium is actually paid to cover the mortgage. If the parent's endowment premium is larger than this 0.0277 per cent figure, it is worth pursuing the issue of how much capital is likely to be produced, especially as many endowment policies may not produce any capital in excess of the mortgage. Any payments made in excess of those required by the mortgage agreement are not eligible housing costs.[51]

There is nothing to prevent repayments to a member of the family or friend on a loan to purchase a home being considered as housing costs, as long as a mortgage or charge has been created by depositing the title deeds or a land certificate which prevents the borrower disposing of the property without the lender's consent.[52]

Repayments made under an agreement for a loan taken out for eligible repairs and improvements (see p189) or a service charge to cover these items are included in exempt income as housing costs,[53] as are insurance policies associated with such a loan or which are taken out to pay off another loan for an eligible housing cost.[54]

Ineligible charges

Charges made for food, fuel, water or sewerage services do not count as eligible housing costs.[55] If the housing costs payments include an ineligible charge, an amount attributable to the service must be deducted.

If meals are provided, a standard weekly deduction is made:

2009/10	Aged 16 or over	For each child under 16
Full board	£22.95	£11.60
Half board	£15.25	£7.65
Breakfast only	£2.80	£2.80

If the parent provides information about the level of the fuel charge inclusive in the housing payment, this actual or estimated amount can be deducted. Otherwise standard weekly deductions are made, which for 2009/10 are: heating £21.55; hot water £2.50; cooking £2.50; and lighting £1.75. If the parent has exclusive use of only one room, the deduction for heating, hot water and/or lighting is £12.90 a week.

If the amount for water and sewerage charges is not separately identifiable, an amount will be attributed.

If other service charges are included in the rent payments, the amount deducted is any amount higher than the following, whichever is greater:[56]
- the total of eligible charges included in the rent; *or*
- 25 per cent of eligible housing costs.

If it is not clear what amount for ineligble service charges is included, the CSA attributes a reasonable amount. Ineligible services include:
- personal laundry service;
- sports and other leisure facilities, including TV rental and licence fees, but excluding children's play areas;
- cleaning, other than communal areas or where no one in the accommodation is able to do it;
- transport;
- medical or nursing services; *and*
- any other charge not connected with the provision of adequate accommodation.

Weekly amount of housing costs

The amount allowed for housing costs is usually the amount payable at the effective date (see p341), converted into a weekly amount.[57] If the costs are monthly, the amount at the effective date must be multiplied by 12 and divided by 52. Where the housing costs are paid on any basis other than weekly or calendar monthly, the CSA considers the amount and payment period of the housing costs payable on the effective date and:[58]

- divides 365 by the number of days in the payment period, rounding to the nearest whole number;
- multiplies this figure by the amount of the costs due in the payment period; *and then*
- divides this figure by 52 to give the weekly costs.

If rent is payable to a local authority or housing association on a free-week basis, the rent payable in the relevant week (see p209) is used unless that was a free week, in which case the last week which was not a free week is used.

If the housing costs are a repayment mortgage and the parent has failed to provide information on repayments and interest on the effective date but has provided a mortgage statement from the lender for a period ending less than a year before the relevant date, this statement can be used to calculate the capital repayments and, where possible, the interest payments.[59]

The calculation of housing costs should be carefully checked as this is an area where the CSA often makes mistakes.

Excessive housing costs

Excessive housing costs of a non-resident parent are not generally allowed in full. Parents are exempt from restrictions on housing costs if they:[60]

- have day-to-day care of any child;
- have claimed or been awarded HB;
- would qualify for an IS disability premium (see Appendix 2);
- remain in a home previously occupied with a former partner;
- have high housing costs because money which would otherwise be available is tied up in the former family home, which is still occupied by an ex-partner;
- have been meeting high housing costs for over 52 weeks before the application for child support, and there has been no increase in those costs other than an increase in the rate of mortgage interest or rent;
- have higher housing costs than the usual restricted amount (see below) only because of an increase in the rate of mortgage interest or rent.

Departure can be sought by the other parent if the exemption applies and the housing costs are unreasonably high (see p301).

Unless exempt, eligible housing costs are otherwise only allowed up to the greater of £80 or half of the parent's net income.[61] (See p208 for the calculation of net income.) Therefore, parents who have a net income of less than £160 are allowed to include housing costs of up to £80, while those with higher net incomes can include housing costs of up to half of the parent's income.

The excessive housing costs rule does not apply to parents with care and it is unlikely that the notional income or capital rules could be used where a parent with care takes on excessive housing costs (see p224).[62]

Example

Bob goes to live with Zoe who has three children, Yvonne (12), Veronica (10) and Scott (3). Zoe's rent on a three-bedroomed council house is £45 a week. They do not receive HB. Even though it is Zoe who is legally liable for the rent, it is still an eligible cost. Bob's exempt income is now:

	£
Personal allowance	64.30
Housing costs	45.00
Total exempt income	**109.30**

Anita is now in paid employment. As long as she is not in receipt of working tax credit, her exempt income must be calculated. She lives with her two children, Carol (13) and David (8). Her mortgage is under £60,000 and the payments, including the capital repayments, are £75 a week.

		£
Personal allowances	Anita	64.30
	Carol	56.11
	David	56.11
Family premium		17.30
Mortgage payment (total)		75.00
Total exempt income		**268.82**

Anita marries Joe and together they buy a house, taking out a mortgage of £85,000. The interest payments are £495 a month and the endowment premium £108 a month – ie, £114.23 and £24.92 a week. However, as the CSA does not have information about how much of the premium is to cover the mortgage, the endowment premium is restricted to £23.55 (0.0277% x £85,000) (see p191).

		£
Personal allowances	Anita	64.30
	Carol	56.11
	David	56.11
Family premium		17.30
Mortgage payment	(£114.23 + £23.55)	137.78
Total exempt income		**331.60**

The excessive housing costs rule does not apply because there are children in the family, but Bob could consider seeking a departure (see p301) on the grounds that Joe can afford to contribute towards the mortgage.

4. **Pre-April 1993 property settlements**

In order for an allowance to be included in 'old rules' exempt income, the property or capital transfer must satisfy certain qualifying criteria (see below).[63] Departure can be sought where the allowance in exempt income does not properly reflect the effect of the settlement (see p301).

Unlike other elements of exempt income, this allowance applies to a parent with care only if she was the non-resident parent at the time the property was transferred.[64] Where a parent with care transferred capital to the non-resident parent or the child(ren) and the non-resident parent also transferred capital, this 'compensating transfer' may be offset against that of the non-resident parent's 'qualifying transfer'.[65]

Qualifying transfer

A qualifying transfer is one which was made:[66]

- as part of a court order or written maintenance agreement made before 5 April 1993;
- when the non-resident parent and parent with care were living separately;
- between the non-resident parent and either the parent with care or a child for whom maintenance is being assessed;
- with the effect that the recipient was given the whole of the value of the transferred property (this condition can be met where the whole value of a part share in a property or asset is transferred);[67] *and*
- without its only purpose being to replace maintenance payments (either periodic or a lump sum) for the parent with care – ie, for herself as opposed to the child(ren) – and to compensate the parent with care for the loss of any right to apply for or receive such payments, or to compensate her for a reduction in such payments. 'Loss of any right' in this context should be taken to mean 'loss of any one right' rather than 'loss of all rights'.[68] This means that where a maintenance agreement for a low or nominal sum exists, it may still be the case that the only purpose of the transfer was to compensate the parent with care for this reduced maintenance and hence the transfer will not qualify.[69]

Child Support Agency (CSA) guidance gives examples of the types of evidence which might be considered in deciding whether a transfer should be excluded by the final condition listed above (a court order, written maintenance agreement, the transfer document, and/or confirmation from building society, solicitor, accountant or property valuers).[70] All evidence produced by either party should be considered, including any documents which might expressly state that the transfer was only to compensate the parent with care for the loss of some right to spousal maintenance.[71] However, although decision makers may consider other evidence beyond the transfer agreement in order to determine the purpose of the transfer, the purpose must be 'clearly and explicitly' shown by the evidence and not inferred on the balance of probabilities.[72]

Certain transfers made under Scottish law can only be for the purpose of compensating the parent with care and, therefore, cannot be qualifying transfers,[73] but transfers made under a written maintenance agreement rather than a court order may still qualify.[74]

It is possible for the non-resident parent to transfer the whole of the asset to the parent with care, but for the lender to insist that the non-resident parent's name is retained on the mortgage – eg, where the amount of the mortgage is more than the parent with care can borrow. This does not negate the fact that the whole of the asset has been transferred to the parent with care. Even where the non-resident parent retains a partial beneficial interest in the property it may still be considered a relevant transfer.[75] If a charge is placed on the property to benefit the non-resident parent, this will be deducted when calculating the allowance.[76]

Property is defined as:[77]

- cash and savings in a bank, building society or equivalent account;
- a legal estate or an equitable interest in land (or in Scotland, an interest in land);
- an endowment or other insurance policy obtained in order to discharge the mortgage or charge on a property which was also being transferred;
- a business asset, whether in the form of money, land or otherwise, which before it was transferred was being used in the course of a business in which the non-resident parent was a sole trader, a partner or a participator in a 'close' company.[78]

It does not include other assets – eg, a car or contents of the home. The value of a trust or trust fund set up betwen the non-resident parent and parent with care, or the non-resident parent and the child, can be considered.[79]

Providing evidence

Once a non-resident parent has notified the CSA that he wants a property/capital settlement taken into account, he has to supply evidence within a reasonable time.[80] If the evidence is not produced within this time, the transfer will be treated as having no value.[81]

The non-resident parent must send written evidence to the CSA of:[82]

- a court order or maintenance agreement which required the transfer of property (this evidence must be from the same time period as the court order or agreement);
- the fact of the transfer (eg, solicitors' or building society correspondence, or a copy of a Land Registry extract);

- the value of the property transferred at the date that the court order/written agreement was made (confirmed by a building society, insurance company or firm of property valuers); *and*
- the amount of any mortgage or charge outstanding at the date that the court order/written agreement was made (confirmed by a building society, bank, solicitor or accountant).

If the parent does not have this documentary evidence, it could be contained in solicitors' files, if still available. The most difficult information to obtain may be the historical value of the asset and a charge will usually be made for such a valuation.

When the non-resident parent applies for a property/capital settlement to be taken into account, the person with care is notified and asked for any relevant information.[83] Any allowance in exempt income is not calculated until 14 days after the person with care has been contacted.

Calculating the allowance

The qualifying value of a transfer of property, land or a business asset is calculated using the following formula.[84]

$$\text{Qualifying Value} = \frac{(VP\text{-}MCP)}{2} - (VAP\text{-}MCR) - (VCR)$$

Where:
- VP is the value of the property or business asset which is (wholly or in part) transferred.
- MCP is the amount of any mortgage or charge outstanding on the property immediately prior to the date of the agreement.
- VAP is the value of any interest in the property which continues to be beneficially owned by the non-resident parent (eg, if the non-resident parent transfers three-quarters of the interest in a house to the parent with care, VAP would be one-quarter of the total value).
- MCR is the amount of any mortgage or charge on the property for which the non-resident parent remains liable immediately following the transfer (this will be the same proportion of MCP as VAP is of VP).
- VCR is the value of any charge in favour of the non-resident parent on the property immediately following the transfer.

Any change in property, land or business prices since that time is irrelevant – the above figures are based on values at the agreement date. Land or property is valued on the basis that the parent with care and the child(ren) would vacate it on completion of a sale.[85] The total net value is used irrespective of whether or not the asset was previously in joint ownership.

The qualifying value in the case of a bank or building society account is half of the balance on the date of the order/agreement, and for an endowment policy, half of the surrender value at that date.[86]

Where the evidence produced shows that the whole of the transfer was made in lieu of ongoing child maintenance, the qualifying value is twice that arrived at by the above formula (in the case of property, land or business assets)[87] or (in the case of money or endowment policies) the full value transferred.[88] If there has been more than one qualifying transfer, the qualifying values of the transfers are totalled.[89]

Transfers made by the parent with care to the non-resident parent or child(ren) which satisfy the qualifying criteria (see p196), except that they are made in the reverse direction, are called compensating transfers.[90] In addition, there is provision for the whole amount of money raised by a parent with care (eg, by taking out a loan) after the date of the court order or written agreement in order that she or her child(ren) will be entitled to the whole of the property to be taken into account as a compensating transfer.[91] This applies if a non-resident parent transfers the matrimonial home to the parent with care on the condition that she buys out his interest in the property. Otherwise, compensating transfers are valued in the same way as qualifying transfers.[92]

The value of any compensatory transfer is deducted from that of the qualifying transfer to give the relevant value.[93] The allowance included in the exempt income relates to this relevant value:[94]

Relevant value	Weekly allowance
Less than £5,000	Nil
£5,000 – £9,999	£20
£10,000 – £24,999	£40
£25,000 or more	£60

Remember that this is an allowance in the exempt income and, therefore, its inclusion does not mean that the resulting maintenance assessment will be reduced by a corresponding amount.

Example: pre-April 1993 property settlement allowance

Debbie and Steve were divorced in 1991. The family home was transferred to Debbie. At the time of the court settlement, the property was worth £58,000 and the outstanding mortgage was £22,000. Almost all the contents of the house were left with Debbie, as was the car. Instead of Steve paying maintenance for Debbie, as part of the settlement, their joint savings account of £14,200 was transferred into Debbie's name. In addition, Steve gave each of the two children £3,000.

The house contents and the car do not come within the definition of property. The savings account is not a qualifying transfer as it was payment in lieu of maintenance for Debbie.

In this case, VP = £58,000 and MCP = £22,000 (see p198). VAP, MCR and VCR are nil. The qualifying value of the transfer of the house is therefore (£58,000 – £22,000) ÷ 2 = £18,000

The qualifying value of the cash to the children is the whole actual value – ie, 2 x £3,000 = £6,000

Total qualifying value = £24,000

There is no compensating value to offset.

As the relevant value is over £10,000 but less than £25,000, the allowance included in exempt income is £40.

If the savings transferred to Debbie were only £10,000 of the £14,200 and this was not for any specified purpose, this would have been another qualifying transfer valued at £5,000.

Total qualifying value = £29,000

Debbie has to pay Steve for the funds remaining in the joint account, so there is a compensating transfer with a value of £4,200 ÷ 2 = £2,100

Relevant value = £29,000 – £2,100 = £26,900

The allowance = £60

If Steve had transferred only three-quarters of the property to Debbie (retaining one-quarter interest himself), the qualifying value of the transfer of the home would be lower.

VP = £58,000, MCP = £22,000, VAP = £14,500 (25% x VP) and MCR = £5,500 (25% x MCP). VCR is nil.

The qualifying value = (£58,000 – £22,000) ÷ 2 – (£14,500 – £5,500) = £18,000 – £9,000 = £9,000

In this case, if the house were the only asset transferred, the allowance included in exempt income would be £20.

5. **Travel-to-work costs**

An allowance towards travel costs can be included in 'old rules' exempt income for parents in employment who travel long distances.[95] It does not apply to self-employed parents.

As well as buying petrol or a ticket, travel-to-work costs include contributing to the costs of someone other than the employer who pays for transport, or paying someone else to provide the transport.[96] The allowance does not apply if an employer either provides transport (including a company car) for any part of the journey between home and the workplace, or pays for any part of the travel-to-work cost.[97] If an employer has made a loan to the parent, increases the amount of pay, or makes a payment which would be taken into account as part of net income (see p209), this is not classed as an employer paying for the transport.

Calculating the allowance

The parent must supply the required information.[98] The Child Support Agency (CSA) calculates or, where this is not possible, estimates:[99]

- the straight-line distance (ie, as the crow flies), rounded to the nearest kilometre, between the parent's home and workplace;
- the number of journeys made between home and the workplace over a period of whole weeks which it thinks is representative of the parent's normal pattern of work (disregarding any two journeys made between the home and workplace within a period of two hours); *and*
- the number of journeys multiplied by the distance and divided by the number of weeks in the period used.

No allowance is included if this figure comes to less than or equal to 240 kilometres. However, where it is over this, 6 pence is included for each kilometre over 240.[100]

If the allowance does not reflect the real travel costs, either party can apply for a departure direction (see pp296 and 301).

Example: exempt income including travel costs

Steve has remarried and has a net income for child support purposes of £380 a week. He and his wife, Lisa, have a mortgage of just under £60,000 and make monthly interest and endowment premium payments totalling £416 a month. They have no children.

Steve commutes five days a week to London with a straight-line distance from home to work of 132.3km. 10 journeys x 132.3km = 1,323 km a week.

Days of annual leave or sickness are ignored.

This gives 1,083 kilometres over 240 and thus an allowance of 1,083 x 6 pence = £64.98 a week.

Steve's exempt income:	£	
Personal allowance	64.30	
Mortgage in full*	96.00	
Property settlement allowance	40.00	(from the first part of the previous example)
Travel-to-work costs	64.98	
Total exempt income	**265.28**	

*Although the housing costs are over £80, they are not considered excessive as half of Steve's net income is £190 a week (see p194).

More than one workplace

There are special rules to deal with parents who work at more than one workplace, whether for one employer or in more than one job.[101] If the pattern of work is irregular in a job, the CSA can select one of the workplaces or another location connected with the employment and assume that each day the parent travels to and from this deemed workplace.[102]

Otherwise, the CSA must calculate the straight-line distances between any of the workplaces between which the parent travels, as well as between the home and each of the workplaces.[103] The pattern of journeys is obtained over a representative period as above. Each distance is multiplied by the number of times that journey is made over the period, and the total number of kilometres is divided by the number of weeks in the period.

6. **Second families**

We use the term 'second family' loosely to describe the situation where a parent is living with a partner and children. The children may be her/his own and/or the partner's. We recognise that the word 'second' is not precise, as the family could be a parent's third or fourth family, or indeed a first family, for example, where the qualifying children are children of a relationship formed after a marriage, and the parent continues to live with her/his spouse and children of the marriage.

We have already looked at the general position of second families as regards the 'old rules' exempt income calculation. Partners and children who are not the parent's children are not considered when including personal allowances and premiums at this stage. However, a child of the parent is included and that child may have another parent who is liable to maintain her/him. If the other parent is non-resident, then the child is a qualifying child and there is the possibility of receiving child maintenance.

Alternatively, if the other parent is also living in the family, then the 'old rules' exempt income calculation can be adjusted to recognise the other parent's liability to maintain the joint child. In other words, if a parent is living with her/his own child and the child's other parent, then the partner may be able to help support the child. This will reduce the parent's responsibility for their joint child included in exempt income. If the partner has sufficient income, this will halve the amounts for the joint child in the exempt income calculation.

The partner can refuse to disclose her income, in which case it is assumed that she can afford to help support her children and their allowances are halved.

This assessment will need to be done not only where the non-resident parent has a second family, but also where a parent with care has had a child with a current partner. This is the only time in the formula that the income of the parent with care's partner is involved.

Can the partner afford to maintain a joint child?

Before including the full allowance and premiums for a joint child in the parent's exempt income, the net income of the partner must be assessed. The partner's net income is calculated in the same way as the parent's net income when working out her/his assessable income (see Chapter 11), with just one difference.[104] The income of any of the partner's own children is *not* included. This means that maintenance for any of her own qualifying children from their non-resident parent (ie, stepchildren in the second family) is ignored.

To assess whether a partner can help support a joint child(ren), compare the amount of her/his net income with the total of:[105]

- the income support (IS) personal allowance for a person aged 25 or over (£64.30); *plus*
- half the amount of the IS personal allowance for each child; *plus*
- if the child(ren) would qualify for the IS disabled child premium (see Appendix 2), half the amount of that premium for that child(ren); *plus*
- half the amount of the IS family premium, except where the family premium would be payable in respect of another child who is included in exempt income (£8.65); *plus*
- any contribution the partner is expected to make towards housing costs after a departure direction (see p301).

No personal allowances are included for any other children of the partner.

If the partner's net income is higher than the figure above, s/he can afford to contribute to their joint child's support. Therefore, the parent's exempt income will include only half the child's personal allowance, and half of any disabled child premium and (if there is no other child included in the exempt income), only half the family premium.[106]

Example: exempt income with a joint child

Bob and Zoe have a baby, Ricky. They are still living in the same house with a rent of £45 a week and Zoe's other three children (see p195).

Zoe stays at home full time. Her only income is child benefit and maintenance for Yvonne and Veronica, both of which are ignored. Therefore, Zoe cannot afford to contribute to Ricky's upkeep and Bob's exempt income will include the full allowances for Ricky.

Bob is not the father of Yvonne, Veronica and Scott, and therefore they are not included in the exempt income calculation.

Bob's exempt income:		£
Personal allowances	Bob	64.30
	Ricky	56.11
Family premium		17.30
Housing costs		45.00
Total exempt income		**182.71**

Zoe begins paid work and brings home £120 a week.
Her earnings are compared with:

Personal allowances	Zoe	64.30
	Ricky (half)	28.06
Family premium (half)		8.65
Total		**101.01**

Note: half the family premium is allowed in Zoe's means test as the family premium is only included in Bob's exempt income for Ricky. There is no other child included in exempt income.

Zoe's other three children are not taken into account.

No departure application has been made for Zoe's contribution towards housing costs.

As her earnings are higher than £101.01, Zoe is seen as being able to contribute to the maintenance of Ricky. Therefore, Bob's exempt income is adjusted.

Bob's exempt income:		£
Personal allowances	Bob	64.30
	Ricky (half)	28.06
Family premium (half)		8.65
Housing costs		45.00
Total exempt income		**146.01**

Family premium

If the only children who are included in the parent's exempt income are joint children with the current partner, whether or not the family premium is included in full or halved in the exempt income depends solely on the net income of the partner. When calculating whether the partner can afford to help support the children, half the family premium is included in the amount with which the partner's net income is compared, as in the above example.

However, if there is another child in the family who is the parent's, but not the partner's child, s/he will be included in the exempt income calculation of her/his parent. Therefore, the family premium is payable in full for this other child and the question of halving the family premium does not arise. The family premium is therefore excluded from the amount with which the partner's net income is compared when calculating whether she can support half the joint child.[107]

Example: exempt income with a joint child and a qualifying child

The situation is the same as in the above example except that Bob's daughter, Carol (15), has come to live with Bob and Zoe.

Zoe's earnings would now be compared with:

		£
Personal allowances	Zoe	64.30
	Ricky (half)	28.06
Total exempt income		**92.36**

Half of the family premium is not included as Bob is entitled to the full family premium in his exempt income for Carol, and between the two partners there cannot be more than one family premium.

As her earnings are higher than £92.36, Zoe is seen as being able to contribute to half the maintenance of Ricky. Therefore, Bob's exempt income is adjusted.

Bob's exempt income:		£
Personal allowances	Bob	64.30
	Carol	56.11
	Ricky (half)	28.06
Family premium (in full)		17.30
Housing costs		45.00
Total exempt income		**210.77**

If Carol only comes to stay some of the time, her personal allowance may be included in Bob's exempt income, but at a reduced rate, depending on how often she stays with him (see Chapter 14).

For a detailed explanation of the family premium in exempt income where there is a joint child and a shared-care child, see p276.

Notes

1. What is exempt income
1 Sch 1 para 5(4) CSA 1991; regs 10A and 10B CS(MASC) Regs
2 Sch 1 para 5(4) CSA 1991; reg 10A CS(MASC) Regs

2. How much is exempt income
3 Reg 10 CS(MASC) Regs
4 Reg 9(5) CS(MASC) Regs
5 Sch 1 para 5 CSA 1991; reg 9(1)CS(MASC) Regs
6 Reg 10(b) CS(MASC) Regs

3. Housing costs
7 Reg 14 and Sch 3 para 4(1)(b) and (c) CS(MASC) Regs
8 Reg 40(7) CSDDCA Regs
9 CCS/6741/1995; CCS/2852/1995; DMG para 5300
10 Sch 3 para 4(2)(a) CS(MASC) Regs
11 Reg 15(3) CS(MASC) Regs
12 CSCS/8/1995; CCS/8189/1995
13 CCS/13698/1996
14 DMG paras 5525-27
15 Reg 15(3) CS(MASC) Regs
16 *Secretary of State for Work and Pensions v M* [2006] UKHL 11
17 Sch 3 para 4(2)(b) CS(MASC) Regs

18 Reg 15(4) CS(MASC) Regs
19 CSCS/2/1994; CSCS/5/1995
20 Sch 3 para 4(1)(a) CS(MASC) Regs
21 Sch 3 paras 1, 2, 2A and 3 CS(MASC) Regs; CCS/12/1994 and CCS/2750/1995
22 Reg 15(2) CS(MASC) Regs
23 CSCS/3/1996
24 DMG para 5310
25 CSCS/1/1994; R(CS) 3/96
26 CCS/11252/1995
27 CSCS/13/1995
28 CCS/12897/1996
29 Regs 9(1)(h) and 11(1)(i) CS(MASC) Regs
30 CCS/11252/1995
31 Reg 1(2) CS(MASC) Regs
32 CSCS/8/1995; CCS/8189/1995
33 CCS/19/1994
34 CCS/4/1994; R(CS) 2/96
35 CCS/4305/1995
36 Regs 1(2), 9(1)(h) and 11(1)(i) CS(MASC) Regs
37 Sch 3 para 5 CS(MASC) Regs; DMG paras 5501-07
38 Reg 15(2) CS(MASC) Regs

39 Reg 15(2) CS(MASC) Regs; DMG para 5450
40 Sch 3 para 3 CS(MASC) Regs
41 Sch 3 para 3(4) CS(MASC) Regs; CCS/12598/1996
42 DMG para 5350; Sch 3 para 3 CS(MASC) Regs
43 CSCS/1/1994; DMG para 5410
44 CCS/1321/1997
45 CCS/11591/1995
46 Sch 3 para 4 CS(MASC) Regs
47 CCS/2750/1995
48 Sch 3 para 3(5A) and (5B) CS(MASC) Regs
49 Sch 3 para 3(5B) CS(MASC) Regs
50 Sch 3 para 3(5) and (5A) CS(MASC) Regs
51 Sch 3 para 3(6) CS(MASC) Regs
52 CCS/9/1995
53 Sch 3 para 3(2A) CS(MASC) Regs
54 Sch 3 para 4A CS(MASC) Regs
55 Sch 3 para 6 CS(MASC) Regs
56 Sch 3 para 6(d) CS(MASC) Regs
57 Reg 16(1) CS(MASC) Regs
58 Reg 16(2)(d) CS(MASC) Regs; DMG para 5603
59 Reg 16(2) CS(MASC) Regs
60 Reg 18(2) CS(MASC) Regs
61 Reg 18(1) CS(MASC) Regs
62 CCS/6/1995

4. Pre-April 1993 property settlements
63 Reg 9(1)(bb) and Sch 3A CS(MASC) Regs
64 Reg 10(a) CS(MASC) Regs
65 Sch 3A paras 1, 8 and 9 CS(MASC) Regs
66 Sch 3A para 1(1) CS(MASC) Regs
67 Sch 3A para 1(1)(d) CS(MASC) Regs; CCS/14368/1997; CCS/97/1997
68 CCS/97/1997
69 Sch 3A para 1(1)(d) CS(MASC) Regs
70 DMG para 3177
71 DMG para 3178
72 CCS/97/1997
73 Family Law Act (Scotland) 1985
74 CSCS/1/1998; CSCS/2/1998
75 DMG para 3168
76 DMG para 3186
77 Sch 3A para 1(1) and (2) CS(MASC) Regs
78 as defined by ss414 and 415 ICTA 1988
79 DMG para 3183
80 Sch 3A para 2(2) CS(MASC) Regs
81 Sch 3A para 2(2) CS(MASC) Regs
82 Sch 3A para 2(1) CS(MASC) Regs
83 Sch 3A para 3 CS(MASC) Regs; DMG para 3158

84 Sch 3A para 4(1) CS(MASC) Regs; DMG para 3185
85 Sch 3A para 4(2) CS(MASC) Regs
86 Sch 3A para 5 CS(MASC) Regs
87 Sch 3A para 6(a) CS(MASC) Regs
88 Sch 3A para 6(b) CS(MASC) Regs
89 Sch 3A para 7 CS(MASC) Regs
90 Sch 3A para 1 CS(MASC) Regs
91 Sch 3A para 8A CS(MASC) Regs
92 Sch 3A para 8 CS(MASC) Regs
93 Sch 3A para 9 CS(MASC) Regs
94 Sch 3A para 10 CS(MASC) Regs

5. Travel-to-work costs
95 Reg 9(1)(i) and Sch 3B CS(MASC) Regs
96 Sch 3B para 1 CS(MASC) Regs
97 Sch 3B paras 21-23 CS(MASC) Regs
98 Sch 3B para 2 CS(MASC) Regs
99 Sch 3B paras 3-6 CS(MASC) Regs
100 Sch 3B paras 7, 14 and 20 CS(MASC) Regs
101 Sch 3B paras 8-20 CS(MASC) Regs
102 Sch 3B paras 8(2) and 15(2) CS(MASC) Regs
103 Sch 3B paras 9-13 and 16-19 CS(MASC) Regs

6. Second families
104 Reg 9(2) CS(MASC) Regs
105 Reg 9(2)(c) CS(MASC) Regs
106 Reg 9(1)(f) and (g) CS(MASC) Regs
107 Reg 9(2)(c)(iv) CS(MASC) Regs

Chapter 11

. . . .

Assessable income ('old rules')

This chapter covers:
1. What is assessable income (below)
2. What is net income (p208)
3. Calculating assessable income (p226)

1. What is assessable income

Assessable income is the parent's income remaining after basic living expenses (represented by exempt income – see Chapter 10) have been accounted for. A proportion of this remaining income is used to contribute towards child maintenance payments (see Chapter 12). In the case of the parent with care, this is a notional contribution which can have the effect of reducing the maintenance payable by the non-resident parent.

Assessable income is the parent's net income minus exempt income.[1]

This step of the formula is carried out in the same way for non-resident parents and parents with care[2] and, therefore, any reference to parent in this chapter applies to both. It does not apply to a person with care who is not the parent of the qualifying child.

It is useful to calculate the non-resident parent's assessable income first because if he has no assessable income there is no need to calculate that of the parent with care (see p226).

A parent who is in receipt of income support (IS), pension credit (PC), income-related employment and support allowance (ESA) or income-based jobseeker's allowance (JSA) is treated as having *no* assessable income.[3] If only the parent with care is on IS/PC/income-related ESA/income-based JSA, the assessable income step must be done for the non-resident parent alone. If the non-resident parent is on IS/PC/income-related ESA/income-based JSA, the formula calculation is not carried out at all and instead the non-resident parent may have a deduction from his benefit (see p403). If the benefit claim of one party is thought to be fraudulent, this can be challenged by the other party (see p353).

Parents with care who are on working tax credit (WTC) are treated as having no assessable income.[4] This, as for IS/PC/income-related ESA/income-based JSA, applies whether the benefit is being paid to the parent herself or to her partner. A non-resident parent on WTC is only treated as having no assessable income if he is also a parent with care and either there is a maintenance assessment in force for his qualifying child(ren) or an application for an assessment is being considered.[5] (But if a maintenance calculation is made as a parent with care, this will convert the non-resident parent's maintenance assessment to the 'new rules', under which WTC is included as income.)

2. **What is net income**

Net income under the 'old rules' is the total income of the parent taken into account when assessing how much child maintenance the parent can afford to pay.

Net income includes earnings, benefits and other income.[6] The types of income that come within each of these categories are clearly defined in the regulations.[7] Certain types of income are ignored in full or in part.[8] The rules about income are similar, but not identical, to those for income support (IS).

The net income of a parent's partner is calculated using these rules when assessing whether s/he can afford to contribute to the support of any joint child in the exempt income calculation (see p249).[9]

These rules for calculating net income are also used when working out the family's total income at the protected income stage of the formula (see Chapter 13). However, there are a few exceptions,[10] which we explain here and in Chapter 13.

If any income which is normally received at regular intervals is not received, it can be treated as though it has been received, as long it is due to be paid and there are reasonable grounds for believing that the payment will actually be made.[11]

Capital itself is not taken into account, although any income generated from the capital does count as income (see p221).

In certain cases, a parent can be treated as having income (or capital which is a source of income) which s/he does not possess if the Child Support Agency (CSA) believes the parent deprived her/himself of it with the intention of reducing her/his assessable income (see p224).

Verification of income is expected (see p72).

Whose income is included

A partner's income is *not* included in the net income when calculating assessable income. This is commonly misunderstood (see p255 for the way in which a partner's income may affect the assessment). Where a source of income is held jointly and the proportions are not known or defined, the income available is divided equally between the people who are entitled to receive it.[12]

The income of the parent's own child living in the household can be treated as though it were the income of the parent (see p223).[13]

Relevant week

The concept of the 'relevant week'[14] is important in child support assessments, particularly when calculating income.

For the parent who is not the applicant, the relevant week is the seven days immediately before the date that the maintenance enquiry form (see p60) is sent to him. For the applicant, the relevant week is the seven days immediately before the maintenance application form (see p40) is submitted to the CSA. For the purpose of calculating earnings only, if the CSA has not been able to make an assessment (except perhaps an interim maintenance assessment – see p340), but is later supplied with the information required, the relevant week is the seven days immediately before the date on which the required information or evidence was received.[15]

If a decision is revised (or if it is superseded because of ignorance or a mistake about a material fact), the relevant week of the new decision is the same as that for the original decision. If a decision is superseded on other grounds, the relevant week is the seven days immediately prior to the application for a supersession (or the seven days prior to the date of notification if the CSA supersedes on its own initiative).[16] See Chapter 18 for more information on grounds for revision and supersession of decisions.

Earnings from employment

Earnings mean 'any remuneration or profit derived from employment' and, as well as wages, include:[17]
- any payments for overtime;
- any profit-related pay;
- any bonus or commission (including tips);
- any holiday pay (except any payable more than four weeks after the job ends);
- payment in lieu of notice;
- statutory sick pay, statutory maternity pay, statutory adoption pay and statutory paternity pay;[18]
- any payment for expenses not 'wholly, exclusively and necessarily incurred' in actually carrying out the job (these include payments made to cover travelling expenses from home to work and the care costs of any other member of the family);
- allowances paid to local councillors for local authority duties, as opposed to expenses 'wholly, exclusively and necessarily incurred';
- payment for duties as an auxiliary coastguard, part-time firefighter, or with the lifeboat services, territorial army or reserve forces relating to a period of less

than one year (such payments for a period of one year or more are disregarded);[19]
- awards of compensation for unfair dismissal;
- certain employment protection payments;
- any retaining fee;
- remuneration, but not share dividend or debenture interest (which is other income), paid to a director of a limited or unlimited registered and incorporated company (as opposed to a sole trader or partner who is self-employed – see p212).[20]

Where an employee is also a director of a company, money drawn from a director's current account or loan account could be either income or capital. If it is income, it may or may not be earnings, depending on whether it is 'derived from that employment'. A decision about this money needs to be fully explained following an investigation of the facts.[21]

The CSA should not simply adopt HM Revenue and Customs' estimate (eg, of expenses) and should carry out an independent examination of the facts, but CSA staff would have to consider carefully before taking a different position.[22] Non-taxable allowances are not automatically excluded as earnings for child support purposes.[23]

Earnings do *not* include:[24]
- occupational pension payments (these count as other income – see p218. For how payments made into a pension scheme are treated, see p212);
- payments for expenses 'wholly, exclusively and necessarily' incurred in carrying out the duties of the job (see p211);
- payments in kind;
- any advance of earnings or loan made by an employer to an employee (such a payment is also disregarded as other income,[25] and any repayments made will be included as earnings, not deducted from them[26]);
- payments made after employment ends which relate to a specific period of time, provided that a period of equal length has elapsed since the payment was received;
- earnings from a previous job where they are paid in a week or a period that earnings from a second job are received;
- payments made by an employer when an employee is on strike;
- any tax-exempt allowance paid by an employer to an employee;
- a compensation payment negotiated and made on the termination of employment[27] (with the exception of any payment in lieu of notice – see above);
- the value of free accommodation provided by an employer (although the CSA may consider the issue of notional earnings – see p224 – if the actual earnings are low in relation to the job performed).[28]

Payments made by the parent for expenses can be deducted from her/his earnings where the employer did not reimburse them,[29] but only if the expenses were incurred 'in the performance of duties'. It is possible that part of a payment (eg, towards a telephone rental or travel costs) could be 'wholly, exclusively and necessarily' incurred.[30]

A local overseas allowance paid to members of the armed forces abroad is disregarded,[31] whereas a rent or mortgage allowance paid by an employer (eg, to a police officer,[32] an army major in the UK,[33] or a civil servant[34]) would normally be taken into account as earnings, except where the housing expenses are necessarily incurred in the performance of their duties.[35] For the same reason, meals allowances are to be treated as earnings.[36]

Calculating normal weekly earnings

Average earnings are used in the child support calculation.[37] When calculating or estimating average earnings at the relevant week (see above), the CSA considers the evidence of the parent's earnings over any appropriate period, beginning no more than eight weeks before the relevant week and ending by the date of the assessment. It may also consider cumulative earnings to date in the tax year covering the relevant week.

If a parent has claimed or been paid working tax credit (WTC)/child tax credit (CTC) on any day during the eight weeks before the relevant week or up to the date the assessment is made, the CSA can use the amount of earnings taken into account in the WTC/CTC calculation even though those earnings may relate to a period outside that normally used for a child support assessment.

CSA staff are advised to give reasons for the assessment period chosen for calculating earnings and to record fully how the decision was made.[38]

If the parent is a student (see p218), earnings are averaged over 52 weeks ending with the relevant week, or as many weeks as the parent has been a student if this is shorter.[39]

If the CSA believes that the amount of weekly earnings arrived at does not accurately represent the parent's normal earnings, any other period can be used, taking into account earnings received and those due to be received.[40] The CSA must be satisfied first that the calculation of earnings at the relevant week produces a figure which is not normal,[41] and then that the period chosen reflects the parent's usual pattern of work, taking into account how aspects such as sick leave and overtime may affect normal earnings.[42] A future period can be used to ensure the usual pattern is reflected – eg, earnings from a job which has not yet begun. The CSA must also consider the expected duration and pattern of any employment. A parent may want to suggest an alternative period to the CSA, giving reasons, as the CSA cannot be expected to consider an alternative period without substantial grounds and a prompt by one of the parents.[43] The CSA must use one continuous period.[44]

If a bonus, commission or profit-related pay is paid separately from earnings or in relation to a longer period than other earnings during a year ending with the relevant week, those payments are totalled over the year and divided by 52 weeks.[45] Such a payment cannot be disregarded on the grounds that it distorts normal earnings.[46]

The CSA has to take into account any change of circumstances it is aware of between the relevant week and the effective date (see p341).[47] However, it must first calculate earnings in the usual way for the relevant week in order to determine whether there has been a material change of circumstances.[48] For changes after this date, see p325.

The calculation of earnings is one of the areas where errors are frequently made and, therefore, should be checked carefully. A commissioner held that an appeal tribunal must enquire into whether the process used to determine income was correctly carried out and whether the period used for the averaging of earnings gave an accurate picture.[49]

Calculating net earnings

Net earnings from employment are counted as net income in full. Net earnings mean gross earnings *less*:[50]

- income tax;
- Class 1 national insurance contributions;
- half of any contributions made to an occupational pension scheme; *and*
- half of any contributions made towards a personal pension scheme (unless that scheme is intended partly to pay off a mortgage on the parent's home, in which case 37.5 per cent of such contributions). Certain retirement savings plans do not come within this provision,[51] but regular contributions under a retirement annuity contract may be deducted.[52]

The amount of tax and national insurance actually paid is usually deducted.[53] However, where earnings are being estimated, the amount to be deducted as income tax is calculated using the personal allowances and the tax rates applicable at the relevant week (see p209).[54] Similarly, the amount to be deducted as Class 1 national insurance contributions will be calculated by using the appropriate percentage rate applicable in the relevant week.

Earnings from self-employment

Before 1 August 2007, self-employed earnings were based on self-assessment forms or tax calculation notices, or where these were not available or not appropriate, via gross receipts. There were also other differences, including the fact that capital allowances were not deducted. For further information, see the 2007/08 edition of this *Handbook*.

From 1 August 2007, earnings from self-employment are based on taxable profits from self-employment, as defined for income tax.[55] (This means that capital allowances can be deducted from gross profits, and balancing charges applied to them.) A parent must, on demand, supply the CSA with a copy of the HM Revenue and Customs tax calculation notice (and any revised notice).

Where the CSA is satisfied that it is not reasonably practicable for a parent to provide the tax calculation notice, earnings will be calculated using the gross receipts of self-employment, with relevant deductions (see p213).[56]

The earnings taken into account are the taxable profit from self-employment less tax, national insurance and half of pension premiums (37.5 per cent of the premium where the scheme is intended to pay off a mortgage).[57] The tax, national insurance and pension premium deductions from self-employed earnings are calculated using the rates applicable at the effective date.

If self-employed earnings are assessed as above, those profits must relate to a period of not less than six months and not more than 15 months ending within two years of the relevant week.[58] If there is more than one such period, the figure used will be the taxable profits relating to the latest period.[59]

If a parent's liability or maintenance received has changed to her/his disadvantage because of the way in which self-employed earnings are now assessed, s/he could raise the issue with her MP, or s/he may be able to complain to the CSA and ask for compensation.

Earnings from self-employment calculated from gross receipts

If the CSA is satisfied that it is not reasonably practicable for a parent to provide a tax calculation notice, earnings will be calculated on the following basis.

In these cases, earnings mean the gross receipts of the business. They include any business start-up grant which is paid in respect of the same period for which earnings are determined.[60] Payments received for providing board and lodging accommodation are counted as other income (see p218) unless they provide the largest part of the parent's income, when they are treated as earnings from self-employment.[61] If a parent is a childminder, only one-third of her gross receipts count as earnings.[62]

Net earnings to be included as net income are the gross receipts of the business *less:*[63]

- income tax (calculated using the personal allowance and the tax rates applicable on the effective date – see p341);
- national insurance contributions (Class 2 and Class 4 contributions at the rates applicable on the effective date[64]);
- half of any premium on a personal pension scheme (unless that scheme is intended partly to pay off a mortgage on the parent's home, in which case 37.5 per cent of the contributions are deducted) or on a retirement annuity contract;
- any VAT paid in excess of VAT received in the same period as that over which the earnings are assessed;
- any expenses which are reasonably incurred for the purposes of the business. If the CSA is not satisfied that the full expense was appropriate or necessary to

the business, it will allow that part considered reasonable.[65] Where an expense is part business and part private (eg, a car), the CSA has to decide on the breakdown between the two uses on the evidence available. CSA staff are given examples of how to deal with apportionment.[66] They may well follow the apportionment used by HM Revenue and Customs. CSA staff are also given guidance on what may be allowable business expenses.[67]

Business expenses include:[68]
- repayments of capital on loans used to replace or repair a business asset (but not for loans taken out for any other business purpose);
- any income used to repair a business asset;
- any payment of interest on loans taken out for business purposes (this does not include loans taken out to acquire a share of a business, nor to pay business tax liabilities).[69]

Business expenses do *not* include any capital expenditure nor any expenses incurred in providing business entertainment.[70]

There are separate rules and guidance for share fishermen, to reflect the different ways in which their expenses may be shared.[71]

If a profit and loss account is provided for a period of at least six months (but no longer than 15 months) which ended within the last two years, it can be used to calculate average weekly earnings.[72] The two years end on the date on which the assessment takes effect – ie, the effective date (see p341). The CSA may decide to wait if accounts will shortly be available and impose a Category C interim maintenance assessment in the meantime. However, it is important that accounts which include income received after the effective date are not used.[73]

The actual gross receipts relevant to the period covered by the profit and loss account will be included, whether or not they were received during that period.[74]

If there is more than one such profit and loss account covering different periods, the account covering the latest period will be used unless the CSA is satisfied that this latest account is not available for reasons beyond the parent's control.[75] Not being available includes where an accountant or another government department (eg, HM Revenue and Customs) holds them without a date set for their return, the Official Receiver has the accounts, or they have been destroyed, lost or stolen.

A trading account or balance sheet (or both) may be requested in addition to the profit and loss account, if it is appropriate to the type of self-employment.[76] The accounts do not need to be prepared by accountants or even typed. However, if they do not contain the required information, the CSA may request other evidence of gross receipts.

Where no appropriate profit and loss account is available, earnings for the self-employed will be averaged over the previous 52 weeks or, if the person has been self-employed for less than a year, over the period during which the person has been self-employed up to an including the relevant week (see p209).[77] The self-employed person is asked to provide other evidence of business receipts and expenses, such as business books, receipts of bills sent and paid, bank statements, records of wages paid, HM Revenue and Customs forms and VAT bills.[78]

If the CSA believes that either or both of the above calculations produce an amount which does not accurately represent the parent's true earnings, another period can be used.[79] This may happen where there has been a major change in trading which has resulted in higher or lower earnings or where a person who has been trading for less than a year has not established a regular pattern of trading.[80] This should not be used just because earnings fluctuate, receipts are irregular or come in a lump sum, trade is slow at times or work non-existent for a period, nor should a different period be used just because it is known that earnings will subsequently change.[81]

Self-employed parents on tax credits

If a self-employed parent has claimed or been paid WTC/CTC on any day during the eight weeks before the relevant week or up to the date the assessment is made, the CSA may use the amount of earnings taken into account in the WTC/CTC calculation even though those earnings may relate to a period different from those described on p214.[82]

Challenging self-employed earnings

There have often been delays in the self-employed parent producing all the information necessary to carry out the assessment. The CSA can impose a Category C interim maintenance assessment while awaiting the information, but this is rare. The person with care may want to request that this is done.

Many self-employed non-resident parents have, in the past, received low assessments, and some persons with care may allege that the self-employed non-resident parent, perhaps with the help of an accountant, has managed to disguise his true income. Once an assessment has been made, the person with care can seek a revision of the assessment (see p354) and ask the CSA to use an inspector (see p73) in order to obtain more detailed information. However, if the non-resident parent's accounts have been accepted by HM Revenue and Customs, it is very unlikely that the CSA would consider it worthwhile to undertake further investigations. The CSA may also refuse to revise the assessment if the person with care cannot substantiate her allegations. This refusal can be challenged if the belief that income is too low is reasonably held, as it is very difficult for one party to obtain definitive details of the other's income. The CSA is much better placed to do this.

If the person with care takes the case to the First-tier Tribunal, she will see details of the income in the appeal papers, and she may be able to argue that some of the expenses included are not reasonable or not wholly connected with the business (see p214). She should also consider the notional earnings rules (see p224) and, if relevant, suggest the First-tier Tribunal makes a finding on this. Alternatively, it can estimate net earnings based on the available evidence, including oral evidence from the person with care.[83] It can also consider data about earnings in different sectors (and in particular localities) – eg, the *New Earnings Survey*, to estimate the likely self-employed earnings in particular jobs.[84]

The person with care can apply for departure from the assessment on the grounds that a person's lifestyle is inconsistent with his level of income or that assets which do not currently produce income are capable of doing so (see p300).

Benefits

Benefits paid by the Department for Work and Pensions count as income for the purposes of net income, although some of these are disregarded in full or in part.[85] Remember that if income support (IS), income-related employment and support allowance (ESA), income-based jobseeker's allowance (JSA) or pension credit (PC) is received by the parent or her/his partner, the parent is treated as having no assessable income (see p208) and the formula is not used. See p217 for tax credits.

The amount of benefit to be taken into account is the weekly rate applying on the effective date (see p341).[86]

Whose benefit?

The income of a partner is not included when working out a parent's net income. Some non-means-tested benefits contain an extra amount for a partner, called an adult dependency increase. The amount paid in respect of that dependant is treated as the dependant's income, not the claimant's[87] – ie, if the parent is the claimant, s/he is treated as not receiving the adult dependency increase and, if the partner is the claimant, the parent is assumed to have income equal to the increase paid to the partner in respect of her/him. If a parent receives a non-means-tested benefit which includes a dependency increase for a child, this is treated as the income of the child (see p223). These rules also apply to adult and child dependency increases paid with a war disablement, war widow's, war widower's or surviving civil partner's pension.[88]

Child benefit

Child benefit is ignored when working out net income.[89] When calculating total family income for protected income purposes, child benefit is counted in full.[90]

Benefits ignored in full

The following benefits are ignored in full:
- housing benefit;[91]
- council tax benefit;[92]
- disability living allowance (or a mobility supplement);[93]
- attendance allowance (or constant attendance allowance or exceptionally severe disablement allowance paid because of industrial injury or war injury);[94]

- social fund payments;[95]
- guardian's allowance;[96] *and*
- Christmas bonus.[97]

Payments made to compensate for the loss of benefits are also disregarded.[98] Special war widows' payments granted in 1990 are likewise disregarded in full.[99]

Benefits ignored in part

A total of £10 a week of a war disablement pension, war widow's or war widower's pension, or a payment made to a parent under the Armed Forces Compensation Scheme is disregarded.[100] However, only £20 a week in total can be disregarded from a combination of war pensions, student income (see p218) and regular charitable/voluntary payments(see p221).

Other income

Unless specified below, all other income is taken into account on a weekly basis by considering the 26-week period ending in the 'relevant week' (see p209).[101] If the income has been received during each week of the period, the total received over the 26 weeks is divided by 26. In other cases, the total received is divided by the number of complete weeks for which the payment was received. However, the CSA has the discretion to use a different period if the amount produced by the above calculation does not accurately reflect actual income. Furthermore, a change occurring between the relevant week and the effective date (see p341) must be taken into account by the CSA if it is aware of the change, in the same way as for earnings (see p212).

Other income includes any payments received on a periodic basis which are not earnings, benefits or a child's income, as well as the types of payment listed below. Periodical payments drawn down from capital are not income,[102] although interest is (see p221). However, where capital is being drawn down in this way, it may indicate that the parent should be treated as having notional income (see p224). Periodical payments do not include a non-resident parent's payments towards his share of a parent with care's housing costs.[103] Some payments are taken into account in full or in part, while others are ignored completely. Payments which are ignored as earnings cannot be taken into account as other income.

Working tax credit

WTC is usually treated as the income of the parent who qualifies for the payment through her/his normal engagement in remunerative work.[104] Where a couple both meet the conditions for WTC, it is all treated as the income of the non-resident parent, provided his earnings are higher than his partner's during the period used to calculate earnings for the maintenance assessment. If the earnings are equal, half the amount of the WTC counts as the income of the non-resident parent. If the non-resident parent's earnings are less than the other person's, WTC is not counted as his income.

Child tax credit

All payments of CTC are ignored in full.[105]

Payments from occupational or personal pension schemes

These and any analogous payments are taken into account in full.[106]

Income from rent

Different provisions apply, depending on the type of income from the property.

- Payments made towards household expenses by a non-dependant (see p258) are completely ignored.[107]
- The first £20 a week of a payment from a boarder is disregarded, as is 50 per cent of any amount over £20 (as long as this is not the largest part of a parent's income when it would be treated as earnings from self-employment).[108] A boarder is someone who is liable to pay for board and lodging which includes at least one meal a day.
- Payments from a person who is liable to pay for accommodation in the parent's home (but who is not a lodger or a non-dependant) are treated as income. However, there is a disregard of £19.45 (or £4 if the payment is not inclusive of heating).[109]
- Payments for the use of a property which is not the parent's home are taken into account as other income, unless the parent is self-employed. In this case, the income is treated as part of the gross receipts of the business. If the parent is not self-employed, the amounts to cover income tax,[110] mortgage interest, interest on loans for repairs and improvements, council tax and water charges can be deducted from the amount received as rent.[111] It is not clear whether other expenses necessary to obtain the rental income (eg, servicing gas fires) may also be deducted, but there is nothing in the guidance for decision makers to suggest that they can.[112]

Student income

A student is defined as someone following a full-time course of study at an educational establishment and, if under 19 years old, the course must be advanced education – ie, above A level or Scottish Higher.[113] This can include sandwich courses. There is no definition of full time and it does not relate to the number of hours the student actually attends. The CSA attaches great weight to evidence from the educational establishment.[114] Once a course has begun, a person continues to be treated as a student until either the course ends or s/he leaves it.

Unless they have income in addition to an educational grant (including any contribution due) or student loan, students are treated as having no net income and, hence, are exempt from having to pay child maintenance.[115]

In other cases, income paid to a student as a grant, grant contribution, covenant income or student loan, is taken into account, except that which is:[116]
- intended to meet tuition fees or examination fees;
- intended to meet additional expenditure as a result of a disability;
- intended to meet expenditure connected with residential study away from the educational establishment;
- made on account of the student maintaining a home away from the educational establishment;
- intended to meet the cost of books and equipment, or, if not specified, £380 (amount for the 2008/09 academic year);
- intended to meet travel expenses.

The amount of a student's grant, covenant income and loan are apportioned equally between the weeks for which they are payable.[117] Five pounds a week can be deducted from covenant income and £10 a week from loan income, although not more than £10 a week can be deducted in total where both types of income are received.[118] Any amount disregarded under this provision counts towards the £20 disregard for war pensions (see p217) and charitable/voluntary payments (see p221).[119]

Financial assistance or awards from a local authority for courses of further education are disregarded.[120]

New Deal for 18–24-year-olds

Payments from an employer under the New Deal Employment option are treated as earnings (see p208). This also applies to payments from an employer under the Voluntary Sector and Environmental Task Force options.[121] Participants in other New Deal options, or where options include a work placement rather than actual employment, are likely to receive a training allowance. This is taken into account, but most New Deal participants will receive income-based JSA and will, therefore, not be assessed under the formula (see p173).

Training allowances

Training allowances are taken into account (but see below), except for the training premium, travelling expenses or any living away from home allowance.[122]

Work-based learning for young people

These training schemes for young people aged under 19 include apprenticeships, other work-based training and (in Scotland) Skillseekers training. Trainees who are not employees receive a training allowance or an education maintenance allowance, depending where in the UK they are training. Young people on these schemes who have no income other than their training allowance or education maintenance allowance are taken to have no net income and are exempt from paying any child maintenance (see p173).[123] Trainees who are employees have their earnings taken into account in the usual way (see p209).

Maintenance for a parent

This income is taken into account in full. There is a specific rule used to calculate the amount of maintenance to be taken into account. It is calculated by averaging the payments received in the 13 weeks preceding the assessment over the number of weeks for which a payment was due.[124] Although there is caselaw which says that payments of maintenance to a parent with care by a non-resident parent cannot be counted as the parent with care's income,[125] this approach is not reflected in guidance to CSA staff[126] and the CSA continues to regard such payments as income.

Child maintenance

Child maintenance from a non-resident parent for the qualifying child for whom the assessment is being carried out is ignored when calculating the income of the parent with care.[127]

Except at the protected income stage (see p256), the CSA treats maintenance paid to a parent for any other child as the child's income. This may still be included in net income, but there are separate rules covering when and how much of the child's income can be taken into account as the parent's income (see p223).

In the calculation of protected income, any maintenance being paid for other children under a court order is deducted from the liable person's income, as long as an application cannot be made to the CSA (see p36).[128] See p256 for further details.

Lump-sum maintenance

There is provision to disregard other maintenance payments in full, whether child support maintenance or other forms, if they are not income.[129] However, as all payments received on a periodic basis are income, this disregard appears only to apply to irregular maintenance payments. It does not apply to maintenance payments made periodically.[130]

Payments made by local authorities towards a child's living costs

Payments made by a local authority where it is looking after a child and has placed the child with a family, relative or other suitable person, including a foster parent, are ignored completely.[131] Payments made by local authorities to promote the welfare of children being looked after, or who were formerly in their care, are also ignored.[132]

Payments made as a contribution towards the maintenance of a child living with the family as a result of a residence order are ignored to the extent that they exceed the personal allowances and any disabled child premium included for the child in the exempt income calculation (see p186).[133]

Adoption allowances

A payment for an adopted child is disregarded:[134]

- to the extent that it exceeds the personal allowance and any disabled child premium for the child, if child maintenance is *not* being assessed for that particular child;
- only up to the amount of any income of the child which is included as income of the parent, if child maintenance is being assessed for that child.

Income from capital

A payment is capital and not income if it is not paid in respect of a particular period, it is paid without reference to any past payment, and it is not intended to form part of a series of payments.[135] Such capital payments are not taken into account. However, the interest, dividend or any other income produced by capital is taken into account as income and is calculated by dividing the total received over 52 weeks by 52.[136] If this gives a figure which the CSA decides is not representative of the income produced, it can use another period.

Where capital is jointly held and the shares are unknown, any income from the capital is divided equally between the joint owners.[137] If capital is divided on divorce, dissolution of a civil partnership or separation and it is intended for the purchase of a new home or furnishings, income from that capital will be ignored for one year.[138]

Although CSA staff are given examples of what may constitute capital and ownership, there is no guidance on the calculation of income from different types of capital.[139] It is the actual income received which must be taken into account, although in some cases this may be apportioned (ie, if capital is jointly owned).

Prisoners' pay

Unless they have another source of income, prisoners receiving only prisoners' pay will be assumed to have no net income and will be exempt from paying child support.[140]

Regular charitable or voluntary payments

These are disregarded in full if they are intended and used for any items *other than* food, ordinary clothing, household fuel, housing costs or council tax.[141] There has to be a mutual understanding between the donor and the recipient as to the purpose of the payment, but this does not need to be a formal agreement.[142] If the payment is for school fees, it is not counted as income at all even if part of the school fees relates to one of the specified items – eg, school meals.[143]

If the payment is for one of these specified items, the first £20 will be disregarded, although no more than £20 in total can be disregarded from the total of a student's income (see p218), a war pension (see p217) and such voluntary payments.[144] See p256 for the position if the voluntary or charitable payment is made direct to a third party.

This provision does not apply to payments made by non-resident parents which are treated as maintenance (see p220).

Other disregarded income

The following will also not be taken into account as income:

- any income tax payments;[145]
- payments in kind (except for self-employed earners);[146]
- payments made instead of Healthy Start vouchers;[147]
- all NHS health benefits, such as fares to hospital;[148]
- payments for prison visits;[149]
- payments made by a local authority to help a child take advantage of a course of study or educational facilities, including a scholarship, or an assisted place;[150]
- payments under a mortgage protection insurance policy to the extent that they exceed the interest, capital payments and any further mortgage protection premiums;[151]
- payments of expenses to unpaid voluntary workers (as long as the expenses cannot be treated as notional earnings);[152]
- payments made to assist a person with a disability to obtain or keep employment;[153]
- payments made to a person under the relevant community care provision to enable her/him to obtain community care services;[154]
- payments made by a local authority for welfare services or housing services;[155]
- payments made by a health authority, local authority or voluntary organisation for a person who is temporarily a member of the household in order to receive care;[156]
- compensation for personal injury and any payments made from a trust fund set up for that purpose[157]
- payments from the Macfarlane Trust, Independent Living (1993) Fund or Independent Living (Extension) Fund;[158]
- payments from the Family Fund;[159]
- payments (other than those for lost earnings and benefits) made to jurors and witnesses for court attendance;[160]
- certain home income annuities purchased when aged 65 or over;[161]
- charges for converting payments in another currency to sterling;[162]
- amounts payable outside the UK where transfer to the UK is prohibited;[163] *and*
- payments to a person as a result of holding the Victoria or George Cross.[164]

Children's income

If the parent has a child of her/his own living with her/him for at least 104 nights a year, the income of that child may be included in the parent's net income.[165] This does not have effect where the child is *not* a child of the parent whose income is being assessed. If a parent of the qualifying child has, for example, stepchildren or grandchildren living with her/him, the income of these children does not count in calculating net income at assessable income stage, but it is taken into account at the protected income stage.

The child's income is taken to be her/his own parent's income when calculating both net income for assessable income purposes and total family income for protected income purposes. However, the child's income is *not* included when calculating the net income of her/his parent's partner in order to find out whether the partner can help support a joint child included in the exempt income (see p249).[166]

What counts as the child's income

Child maintenance already being received for a qualifying child who is the subject of the assessment being undertaken is ignored in full.[167] Child dependency increases of any benefit received by an adult are income of the child, which is included in the parent's net income, if applicable.[168]

The following are *not* included when calculating the child's income and are, therefore, not part of a parent's net income.[169]

- a child's earnings;
- payments by a non-resident parent to the child for whom maintenance is being assessed;
- interest payable on arrears of child maintenance;
- payments from a discretionary fund which benefit the child, as long as they do not cover food, ordinary clothing/footwear, household fuel or housing costs.

How much of the child's income counts as the parent's

The first £10 a week of any income of a child is ignored.[170] In addition, once the child's income is treated as that of her/his parent, the same disregards apply as for the parent's own income.[171]

How much of the child's net income is taken into account as her/his parent's income depends on whether the child is the subject of the maintenance assessment. If the child is *not* the subject of the maintenance assessment, her/his income up to the amount of the personal allowance (and any disabled child premium) included in the exempt income calculation in respect of that child is counted as the parent's income.[172] Income above that amount is disregarded.

If the child is the subject of the maintenance assessment, the child's income counts in full if s/he is the only child for whom an assessment is being made.[173] Where there is more than one child, each child's income is counted up to the level of the child's proportion of the maximum child maintenance payment (see p240) – ie, a share of the maintenance requirement plus 1.5 times the basic rate of the family premium and the personal allowance.[174]

At the protected income stage of the formula, the rules about how much of the child's income is taken into account are different (see p256).

Notional income

Parents can be assumed to have income which they do not possess.[175] Such 'notional income' is treated in the same way as if it were actual income.[176] In practice, this provision is not used very often, and parents who are contesting the other party's income may want to remind the CSA that notional income should be considered.

Notional earnings

The issue of notional earnings arises where a person has done some work without being paid or at an insufficient rate for the job for an employer who could afford to pay full wages.[177] This cannot apply if the employer is a charity or voluntary organisation, or a member of the parent's family. The estimated forgone income is treated as earnings if the CSA decides that the principal purpose of the person doing the work without pay or for reduced pay was to reduce her/his assessable income. To estimate an appropriate level of forgone earnings the decision maker has to consider:[178]

- the nature of the service from which the employer benefits;
- the comparable rate of pay;
- the means of the employer.

If the question of notional earnings is raised, the parent should let the CSA know her/his motives for doing the work. For example, notional earnings will be an issue where a parent is paid via a personal service company at less than the market rate.[179] In such a case, if the principal purpose was for business and tax reasons, notional income cannot be included.[180]

Deprivation of income or capital

If the CSA decides that a parent has intentionally deprived her/himself of income in order to reduce her/his assessable income, an amount equal to that income will be included in her/his net income.[181]

This rule applies equally to capital which would have been a source of income – eg, where shares are given away or sold at less than their market value.[182] Lump-sum voluntary contributions towards a retirement annuity contract may count as deprivation of capital.[183] The CSA has to estimate a notional income from the notional capital, and guidance to CSA staff suggests that it may be reasonable to use rates of interest paid by high street banks and building societies.[184] When the CSA has decided that a certain sum is notional capital, that capital is reduced after

52 weeks by an amount equal to the income which would have been generated from that capital over the year.[185]

Deprivation refers both to income or capital that a person has disposed of or failed to obtain – eg, by failing to apply for a benefit. However, it does not apply to contribution-based JSA if IS is payable, nor to a payment from a discretionary trust or a trust set up with personal injury compensation.[186]Apart from social security benefits and WTC, other examples given to CSA staff of payments which could be acquired include unclaimed Premium Bond wins.[187] Where income would have been available to a parent on application, an estimated amount is included in her/his net income from the date on which it could be expected to have been paid.[188]

The CSA is most likely to identify a potential deprivation of income or capital where it finds that a source of income previously declared is no longer included.[189] The first question to be considered is whether the parent has actually disposed of the income or capital, and the onus is on the parent to prove s/he no longer has the resource.[190] CSA staff are given examples of deprivation of capital, although it is emphasised that these may not have been done for the purposes of reducing assessable income – eg, making a lump-sum payment, putting money into a trust which cannot be revoked, gambling, using capital to fund an extravagant lifestyle or purchase personal possessions.[191] Deprivation can apply to a parent who has transferred assets to a new partner or possibly to a self-employed parent who is paying his partner a reasonable salary but not drawing much himself. Once it is shown s/he no longer possesses it, the intention behind the deprivation has to be examined and on the balance of probabilities the CSA must decide whether the aim was to reduce assessable income for child support purposes.[192]

This rule is similar, but not identical, to those for means-tested benefits (see CPAG's *Welfare Benefits and Tax Credits Handbook*) and an adviser should, therefore, consider whether any social security commissioners' decisions could be cited as persuasive. Although it may be argued that the reduction of assessable income need not be the only, or even principal, motive, the CSA has to be able to show that it is satisfied that such an intention existed and that it was a significant purpose for the parent's actions. The onus of proof remains with the CSA.[193]

When deciding whether reducing assessable income was a significant factor in the disposal of the resource, CSA staff are advised to consider all the parent's reasons and the timing of the action.[194] If deprivation of capital is an issue, the CSA will consider whether the parent was aware that reducing capital would reduce the maintenance assessment.

This deprivation rule cannot be used against a parent who refuses an offer of employment,[195] but it might be applied to a non-resident parent who gave up his job.[196] It would have to be shown that by leaving the employment he had intentionally deprived himself of income, and that he did so with the intention of reducing his assessable income.

Deprivation is probably not applicable to a case where a parent has taken out a higher mortgage which reduces her/his assessable income.[197] A non-resident parent in this situation needs to consider the excessive housing costs rule (see p292). On the other hand, the use of capital as a deposit to buy a property could possibly be considered to be deprivation and motives would need to be examined.

Payments to third parties

If a payment is made on behalf of a parent or a child to a third party, it will only be treated as the parent's income if it is a payment for food, ordinary clothing or footwear, household fuel, housing costs or council tax.[198] For example, if a grandparent paid the parent's fuel bill direct to the fuel company, this would be notional income, whereas paying the telephone bill would not. Some of this notional income can be disregarded as a voluntary payment if made regularly (see p221).

A payment made by a partner to meet her/his own liability (eg, for a mortgage to a building society) is not made on behalf of the parent or child.[199] The same applies to payments made by an ex-partner for his own liability towards the former joint home in which the parent with care remains, whereas payments made by him towards her part of the mortgage count as the parent with care's income (see also p220).[200]

3. Calculating assessable income

Assessable income is the parent's total net income less her/his exempt income. For details of exempt income, see Chapter 10.

If the parent's exempt income is higher than her/his net income, assessable income is taken to be nil.[201] If his assessable income is nil, the non-resident parent may still have to make the minimum payment of child maintenance. There is, however, no need to continue with the steps of the formula in this case, as the maintenance due will either be the minimum payment of £6.50 or nil (see p172). If a non-resident parent's net income is itself less than £6.50, he is exempt from paying child maintenance.[202]

If the parent with care's assessable income is nil, the proposed maintenance step is carried out with just the non-resident parent's assessable income.

Example: assessable income of a non-resident parent
Bob is living in a bedsit on his own. His exempt income is £112.30 (see p187). His income is £154 a week in earnings after tax, national insurance and £12 weekly superannuation contribution. Only half his superannuation is taken into account when calculating Bob's net earnings for child support purposes, which are £154 + £6 = £160

Bob's net income is, therefore, his net earnings = £160

	£
Net income	160.00
Less exempt income	112.30
Assessable income	**47.70**

Bob moves in with Zoe and her three children (see p195).

	£
Net income	160.00
Less exempt income	109.30
Assessable income	**50.70**

Bob is in receipt of long-term incapacity benefit (IB) of £105.45 and lives with his parents (see p186).

	£
Net income	105.45
Less exempt income	91.80
Assessable income	**13.65**

If Bob were receiving the higher rate short-term IB of £80.15 (and was still eligible for a disability premium in his exempt income), his assessable income would be nil. He would be exempt from the minimum payment (see p172) and would receive a nil assessment. No further calculation would be required.

. . . .

Example: assessable income of a parent with care

While Anita is on income support (IS) or working tax credit (WTC), she is automatically treated as having no assessable income.

Anita receives child benefit of £33.20 (this is ignored in net income). Bob has been paying £30.50 a week in maintenance for Carol (13) and David (8). This is not taken into account as income because it is maintenance for the qualifying children – ie, the children for whom the re-assessment is being carried out.

Anita is now bringing home £265 a week (after tax, national insurance and a £15 superannuation contribution). She is entitled to child tax credit (CTC) (which is ignored as income) but not to any WTC. Only half of the superannuation payment can be taken into account (ie, £7.50) and, therefore, her net earnings for exempt income purposes are now £272.50 a week.

	£
Earnings	272.50
Total net income	272.50
Less exempt income (from p194)	268.82
Assessable income	**3.68**

Anita remarries. She brings home £195 a week after tax, national insurance and a £15 superannuation contribution. Her husband, Joe, earns £205 a week.

Net income is now £202.50. Joe's income is not taken into account.

	£
Net income	202.50
Less exempt income (from p195)	331.60
Assessable income	**Nil**

Example: Bob and Zoe have a baby

Bob is now living with Zoe, their son Ricky and three stepchildren (aged 13, 11 and 4 years old). The exempt income is £182.71 (see p202). Bob's net earnings are £260 a week. Any income of Zoe's is not taken into account, including the maintenance of £20 a week for her daughters. The couple receive £158 CTC a week, which is ignored.

	£
Earnings (Bob)	260.00
Total net income	260.00
Less exempt income	182.71
Bob's assessable income	**77.29**

Zoe begins paid work, bringing home £120 a week. The total net income remains at £260, as Zoe's earnings are not taken into account at this stage. However, her earnings have affected the exempt income (see p202), as she is now helping to support Ricky.

	£
Total net income	260.00
Less exempt income	146.01
Bob's assessable income	**113.99**

As the increase in their annual income is less than £25,000, it will not affect their final entitlement to CTC for the current tax year. In the next tax year, assuming no further changes in income, it will be taken into account and reduce their tax credits. In the meantime, the tax credit calculation will be affected by Ricky's first birthday and, if Zoe works 16 hours or more a week, by the childcare element (if they use eligible childcare). This does not affect assessable income, but it may affect the calculation at the protected income stage.

Notes

1. What is assessable income

1. Sch 1 para 5(1) and (2) CSA 1991
2. Regs 8 and 10 CS(MASC) Regs
3. Sch 1 para 5(4) CSA 1991; reg 10B CS(MASC) Regs
4. Reg 10A CS(MASC) Regs
5. Reg 10A(2) CS(MASC) Regs

2. What is net income

6. Reg 7(1) CS(MASC) Regs
7. Sch 1 CS(MASC) Regs
8. Sch 2 CS(MASC) Regs
9. Reg 9(2)(c) CS(MASC) Regs
10. Reg 11(2) CS(MASC) Regs
11. Reg 7(5) CS(MASC) Regs
12. Reg 7(4) CS(MASC) Regs
13. Sch 1 para 9(a) CSA 1991; reg 7(1)(d) CS(MASC) Regs
14. Reg 1(2) CS(MASC) Regs
15. Sch 1 para 2(3A) CS(MASC) Regs
16. Reg 1(2) CS(MASC) Regs
17. Sch 1 para 1(1) CS(MASC) Regs
18. Sch 1 para 1(1)(gg) CS(MASC) Regs
19. Sch 2 para 48B CS(MASC) Regs
20. DMG paras 4107-22
21. CCS/2287/2006; CCS/3499/2004; CCS/3671/2002
22. CCS/2750/1995; CCS/318/1995
23. CCS/11364/1995; R(CS) 2/96; CCS/4/1994; CCS/10/1994; CCS/12598/1996; CCS/1321/1997; CCS/2320/1997; CCS/2561/1998; CCS/5352/1995
24. Sch 1 para 1(2) CS(MASC) Regs
25. Sch 2 para 6 CS(MASC) Regs
26. CCS/11252/1995; CCS/5352/1995
27. CCS/3182/1995
28. DMG para 4102
29. R(CS) 2/96 (CCS/4/1994)
30. CCS/12073/1996
31. CCS/318/1995
32. CCS/10/1994; CCS/12598/1996; CCS/1321/1997; CCS/2320/1997; CCS/2561/1998
33. CCS/5352/1995
34. CCS/11242/1995
35. CCS/12769/1996
36. CCS/6807/1995
37. Sch 1 para 2(1) CS(MASC) Regs
38. DMG paras 4051-52 and 4073
39. Sch 1 para 2(3) CS(MASC) Regs
40. Sch 1 para 2(4) CS(MASC) Regs
41. CCS/16/1994; CCS/11873/1996
42. DMG paras 4069-72; CCS/6810/1995
43. CCS/511/1995
44. CCS/7312/1995; CCS/556/1995; CSCS/1/1996; CSCS/6/1996
45. Sch 1 para 2(2) CS(MASC) Regs
46. CCS/5079/1995
47. Reg 2(3) CS(MASC) Regs
48. CCS/2750/1995
49. CCS/556/1995
50. Sch 1 para 1(3) CS(MASC) Regs
51. CSCS/5/1994
52. CCS/3542/1998
53. Sch 1 para 1(3) CS(MASC) Regs
54. Reg 1(2A) CS(MASC) Regs
55. Sch 1 para 2A CS(MASC) Regs
56. Sch 1 para 2C CS(MASC) Regs
57. Sch 1 para 2A(2) CS(MASC) Regs
58. Sch 1 para 5A(1) CS(MASC) Regs
59. Sch 1 para 5A(2) CS(MASC) Regs
60. Sch 1 para 3 CS(MASC) Regs
61. Sch 1 para 3(2)(b) CS(MASC) Regs; DMG para 4601
62. Sch 1 para 4 CS(MASC) Regs
63. Sch 1 para 3(3) CS(MASC) Regs
64. Sch 1 para 3(6) CS(MASC) Regs
65. DMG para 4287
66. DMG paras 4289-91
67. DMG paras 4327-42
68. Sch 1 para 3(4)(a) CS(MASC) Regs
69. CCS/15949/1996
70. Sch 1 para 3(4)(b) CS(MASC) Regs
71. Sch 1 para 3(7) CS(MASC) Regs; DMG paras 4410-18
72. Sch 1 para 5(2) CS(MASC) Regs
73. CCS/1938/2006
74. Sch 1 para 5(2) CS(MASC) Regs; DMG paras 4281-82
75. Sch 1 para 5(2A) CS(MASC) Regs
76. DMG paras 4251-53
77. Sch 1 para 5(1) CS(MASC) Regs
78. DMG paras 4218-20
79. Sch 1 para 5(3) CS(MASC) Regs
80. DMG paras 4240-41
81. CCS/3182/1995; CCS/6145/1995
82. Sch 1 para 5(5) CS(MASC) Regs
83. CCS/7966/1995
84. CCS/13988/96; CCS/2901/02

85 Sch 1 para 6 CS(MASC) Regs; reg 10B CS(MASC) Regs
86 Sch 1 para 6(3) CS(MASC) Regs
87 Sch 1 para 7(1) CS(MASC) Regs
88 Sch 1 paras 9A and 22(1B) CS(MASC) Regs
89 Sch 2 para 16 CS(MASC) Regs
90 Reg 11(2)(a)(i) CS(MASC) Regs
91 Sch 2 para 7 CS(MASC) Regs
92 Sch 2 para 7 CS(MASC) Regs
93 Sch 2 para 8 CS(MASC) Regs
94 Sch 2 para 9 CS(MASC) Regs
95 Sch 2 para 11 CS(MASC) Regs
96 Sch 2 para 48A CS(MASC) Regs
97 Sch 2 para 10 CS(MASC) Regs
98 Sch 2 paras 8 and 12-15 CS(MASC) Regs
99 Sch 2 para 40 CS(MASC) Regs
100 Sch 2 para 18 CS(MASC) Regs
101 Sch 1 para 16 CS(MASC) Regs
102 *Chandler v Secretary of State for Work and Pensions & Another* [2007] EWCA Civ 1211
103 Sch 1 para 15 CS(MASC) Regs
104 Sch 1 para 14B CS(MASC) Regs
105 Sch 2 para 48D CS(MASC) Regs
106 Sch 1 para 9 CS(MASC) Regs
107 Sch 2 para 35 CS(MASC) Regs
108 Sch 2 para 24 CS(MASC) Regs
109 Sch 2 para 22 CS(MASC) Regs
110 Sch 2 para 2 CS(MASC) Regs
111 Sch 2 para 23 CS(MASC) Regs
112 CCS/5310/1995; CCS/3542/1998; DMG para 4669
113 Reg 1(2) CS(MASC) Regs; DMG paras 4962 and 4965
114 DMG para 4966
115 Regs 7(3)(b) and 26(1)(b)(v) CS(MASC) Regs
116 Sch 1 paras 11 and 12 CS(MASC) Regs; DMG para 4937
117 Sch 1 para 16(3) CS(MASC) Regs
118 Sch 1 para 16(4) CS(MASC) Regs
119 Sch 2 para 20 CS(MASC) Regs
120 Sch 2 paras 36 and 36A CS(MASC) Regs
121 DMG paras 4150-53
122 Sch 2 para 21 CS(MASC) Regs
123 Regs 7(3)(a) and 26(1)(b)(v) CS(MASC) Regs; DMG para 4002
124 Sch 1 paras 14 and 16(2) CS(MASC) Regs
125 CCS/13698/1996; CCS/13923/1996
126 DMG paras 4610-11
127 Sch 2 para 28 CS(MASC) Regs
128 Reg 11(2) CS(MASC) Regs
129 Schs 1 para 15 and 2 para 44 CS(MASC) Regs
130 CCS/4514/1995
131 Sch 2 para 29 CS(MASC) Regs; the payments are made under the CA 1989, the Social Work (Scotland) Act 1968 or the Boarding and Fostering Out of Children (Scotland) Regulations 1985
132 Sch 2 para 31 CS(MASC) Regs; these payments are made under the CA 1989
133 Sch 2 para 26 CS(MASC) Regs
134 Sch 2 para 25 CS(MASC) Regs
135 DMG para 4615
136 Sch 1 para 16(5) and (6) CS(MASC) Regs; DMG para 4614
137 Reg 7(4) CS(MASC) Regs
138 Sch 2 para 45 CS(MASC) Regs; CCS/4923/1995
139 DMG paras 4613-31
140 Regs 7(3) and 26(1)(b) CS(MASC) Regs
141 Sch 2 para 19 CS(MASC) Regs; DMG para 4699
142 R(SB) 53/83; CCS/15/1994
143 Sch 1 para 31 CS(MASC) Regs
144 Sch 2 paras 19 and 20 CS(MASC) Regs
145 Sch 2 para 2 CS(MASC) Regs
146 Sch 2 para 46 CS(MASC) Regs
147 Sch 2 para 17 CS(MASC) Regs
148 Sch 2 para 33 CS(MASC) Regs
149 Sch 2 para 42 CS(MASC) Regs
150 Sch 2 para 36 CS(MASC) Regs
151 Sch 2 para 27 CS(MASC) Regs
152 Sch 2 para 48 CS(MASC) Regs
153 Sch 2 para 34 CS(MASC) Regs
154 Sch 2 para 48C CS(MASC) Regs
155 Sch 2 para 48D CS(MASC) Regs
156 Sch 2 para 30 CS(MASC) Regs; this refers to payments made under s93(1) and (2) Local Government Act 2000 or s91(1) Housing (Scotland) Act 2001
157 Sch 2 para 5 CS(MASC) Regs
158 Sch 2 para 38 CS(MASC) Regs
159 Sch 2 para 47 CS(MASC) Regs
160 Sch 2 para 39 CS(MASC) Regs
161 Sch 2 para 37 CS(MASC) Regs
162 Sch 2 para 3 CS(MASC) Regs
163 Sch 2 para 4 CS(MASC) Regs
164 Sch 2 para 41 CS(MASC) Regs
165 Sch 1 Part IV CS(MASC) Regs
166 Reg 9(2)(c) CS(MASC) Regs
167 Sch 2 para 28 CS(MASC) Regs
168 Sch 1 paras 7 and 22 CS(MASC) Regs
169 Sch 1 para 23 CS(MASC) Regs
170 Sch 1 para 23 CS(MASC) Regs
171 Sch 1 para 24 CS(MASC) Regs
172 Sch 1 para 21 CS(MASC) Regs
173 Sch 1 para 19 CS(MASC) Regs
174 Sch 1 para 20 CS(MASC) Regs
175 Reg 7(1)(e) and Sch 1 Part V CS(MASC) Regs

176 Sch 1 para 32 CS(MASC) Regs
177 Sch 1 para 26 CS(MASC) Regs; DMG
     para 4831
178 DMG paras 4850-51
179 CCS/4912/1998
180 CCS/3675/2004
181 Sch 1 para 27 CS(MASC) Regs
182 CCS/4912/1998; DMG para 4875
183 CCS/3542/1998
184 DMG paras 4902-03
185 Sch 1 para 30 CS(MASC) Regs; DMG
     para 4911
186 Sch 1 para 28 CS(MASC) Regs
187 DMG para 4901
188 Sch 1 para 29 CS(MASC) Regs
189 DMG paras 4808 and 4889
190 R(SB) 38/85; DMG paras 4811
     and 4890
191 DMG para 4891
192 CCS/8172/1995; DMG paras 4885
     and 4892-94
193 R(SB) 38/85
194 DMG paras 4893-94
195 CCS/7967/1995
196 CCS/4056/2004
197 CCS/6/1995
198 Sch 1 para 31 CS(MASC) Regs; DMG
     paras 4865 and 4868
199 CCS/6/1995
200 CSCS/8/1995; CSCS/1/1996; CCS/
     8189/1995

3. Calculating assessable income
201 Sch 1 para 5(3) CSA 1991
202 Reg 26(1)(b)(v) CS(MASC) Regs

Chapter 12

· ·

Proposed maintenance ('old rules')

This chapter covers:

1. **What is proposed maintenance**

'Proposed maintenance' is not a term which is used in the legislation. We use it to describe the amount of child maintenance that, given the maintenance requirement and the assessable income of the parents, the non-resident parent would be expected to pay. There is no specific legal term for this amount; it is referred to in the legislation as 'the amount of the assessment'. However, the proposed maintenance step is not the end of the maintenance assessment. The protected income calculation still has to be done and this may reduce the amount of child maintenance payable. Therefore, a term is needed for this intermediate stage. The Child Support Agency uses the phrase 'the non-resident parent's notional assessment'.

Although the proposed maintenance figure may be reduced by the protected income calculation, it will never be increased. No non-resident parent ever pays more than the proposed maintenance figure.

There is a lot of misunderstanding about the way in which the income of a partner of the non-resident parent affects the maintenance assessment. At the protected income stage (see Chapter 13) the partner's income *is* taken into account in order to assess whether the family as a whole can afford the proposed maintenance. However, the partner's income *cannot* increase the assessment above the proposed maintenance which is arrived at using the non-resident parent's net income (see p208). The income of the partner is also used to decide whether she can help support their own children (see p202). If the partner objects to providing income details, the non-resident parent could consider the option of withholding the information and accepting a Category B interim maintenance assessment.

2. **How much is proposed maintenance**

Proposed maintenance is based on the assessable incomes of both parents. In some situations a deduction rate of 50 per cent assessable income is used and in others, a more complex calculation must be carried out. The 50 per cent calculation gives an amount of proposed maintenance which is smaller than the maintenance requirement figure (from Step 1). The additional element calculation applies where the parents have higher incomes and the maintenance requirement figure is met. The calculation for proposed maintenance becomes increasingly complex with more complex family situations.

To illustrate the principles of proposed maintenance, we first give an overview of the calculation (see below). To help readers through this step of the formula, we then identify the four situations, beginning with the most straightforward, in which the calculation of proposed maintenance varies:

- the 50 per cent calculation of proposed maintenance where the parent with care has no assessable income (see p234);
- the 50 per cent calculation of proposed maintenance where both parents have assessable income (see p235);
- the additional element calculation of proposed maintenance where the parent with care has no assessable income (see p237);
- the additional element calculation of proposed maintenance where both parents have assessable income (see p239).

These calculations are adapted if both parents are non-resident, or where there is more than one non-resident parent or more than one parent with care.

Overview of proposed maintenance
There are two alternative calculations.
– The 50 per cent calculation if the maintenance requirement is not met.
– The additional element calculation if the maintenance requirement is met.
To decide which to use, first do the 50 per cent calculation:[1]

- Add together both parents' assessable incomes (if the parent with care is on income support, income-based jobseeker's allowance, income-related employment and support allowance, pension credit or working tax credit, her assessable income is nil).
- Take 50 per cent of the joint assessable income.
- Compare the figure obtained with the maintenance requirement (from Step 1 as calculated in Chapter 9).

If 50 per cent of the joint assessable income is less than or equal to the maintenance requirement, the proposed maintenance is 50 per cent of the non-resident parent's assessable income.[2]

If 50 per cent of the joint assessable income is higher than the maintenance requirement, the additional element calculation must be done. This involves two components of proposed maintenance: a basic element and an additional element (see p237).[3] The end result is that the non-resident parent pays less than 50 per cent of his assessable income overall, but more than the maintenance requirement.

The general rule is that 50 per cent of the parents' assessable income goes towards child maintenance until the maintenance requirement is met.[4] Once the maintenance requirement is met, the non-resident parent continues to pay maintenance. However, only 15, 20 or 25 per cent of his remaining assessable income is paid as maintenance and only up to a maximum amount.[5]

Both parents are liable to maintain their child(ren) and, therefore, both their assessable incomes must be taken into account when calculating whether the maintenance requirement has been met. Although the assessable income of the parent with care may reduce the proposed maintenance, she will never end up paying child maintenance herself.

If the assessable income of the non-resident parent is nil, then the proposed maintenance is nil and the minimum payment rules must be considered (see p172). The non-resident parent either pays £6.50 or is exempt. Similarly, if the proposed maintenance is less than £6.50, the non-resident parent pays the minimum payment of £6.50 unless he is exempt. In these cases there is no need to calculate the protected income level as the proposed maintenance cannot be further reduced.

3. **The 50 per cent calculation**

Once assessable income has been calculated for both parents, the next step is to check whether the 50 per cent calculation is applicable. If the parent with care has assessable income, see p235.

The parent with care has no assessable income

In many cases the parent with care will have no assessable income – eg, because she is on income support (IS) or working tax credit (WTC).

50 per cent calculation if the parent with care has no assessable income

– Take 50 per cent of the non-resident parent's assessable income.
– Compare the figure obtained with the maintenance requirement (from Step 1 as calculated in Chapter 9).

If 50 per cent of the non-resident parent's assessable income is less than or equal to the maintenance requirement, the proposed maintenance is this figure – ie, 50 per cent of his assessable income.[6]

If 50 per cent of the non-resident parent's assessable income is higher than the maintenance requirement, the additional element calculation is used to obtain proposed maintenance (see p237).

In these cases, the proposed maintenance calculation ends at this point, and the protected income calculation must now be done (see Chapter 13).

Example: 50 per cent calculation if the parent with care has no assessable income

Anita is on IS and, therefore, has no assessable income.
The maintenance requirement is £160.62 (see p179).
Bob is living on his own and has assessable income of £47.70 (see p226). As Anita has no assessable income, the first stage is to take 50 per cent of Bob's assessable income.
50 per cent of Bob's assessable income = 50% x £47.70 = £23.85
This is less than £160.62 (the maintenance requirement) and, therefore, £23.85 is the proposed maintenance for Carol and David.

Bob is living with Zoe, three stepchildren and his baby son. His assessable income is £50.70 (see p226).
50 per cent of Bob's assessable income = 50% x £50.70 = £25.35
This is less than £160.62 (the maintenance requirement) and, therefore, £25.35 is the proposed maintenance.
Note: the maintenance payable may be reduced by the protected income step.

The parent with care has assessable income

Even when the parent with care has assessable income, this income does not necessarily affect the proposed maintenance. If, together, the parents do not have enough joint assessable income for half of it to meet the maintenance requirement, the non-resident parent pays half of his own assessable income.

This is exactly what he would have paid anyway had the parent with care had no assessable income.

---

50 per cent calculation if the parent with care has assessable income
- Add both parents' assessable incomes to give joint assessable income.
- Take 50 per cent of the joint assessable income.
- Compare the 50 per cent figure with the maintenance requirement (from Step 1 as calculated in Chapter 9).

If 50 per cent of the joint assessable income is less than or equal to the maintenance requirement, take 50 per cent of the non-resident parent's own assessable income to give proposed maintenance.

If 50 per cent of the joint assessable income is higher than the maintenance requirement, the additional element calculation must be done (see p239).

A parent with care's income does not reduce the maintenance she receives unless her notional contribution towards the maintenance requirement *plus* the non-resident parent's proposed maintenance is over the maintenance requirement. The level of the joint assessable income is the deciding factor. The higher the assessable income of a non-resident parent, the sooner the assessable income of the parent with care will reduce the maintenance payable (see p239).

Example: 50 per cent calculation if both parents have assessable income
Anita is now working full time and has assessable income of £3.68 (see p226).
Bob's assessable income = £47.70 (see p226)
Joint assessable income = £47.70 + £3.68 = £51.38
50 per cent of joint assessable income = 50% x £51.38 = £25.69
This is well below the maintenance requirement of £160.62 (see p179) and so Bob pays 50 per cent of his own assessable income (assuming the protected income calculation allows it).
Proposed maintenance = 50% x £47.70 = **£23.85** a week.
This is the same amount of proposed maintenance as when Anita had no assessable income (see p235). In this case, Anita takes home £265 a week. Although this is more than Bob, who takes home £154, her income still does not affect the level of proposed maintenance for David and Carol.

If Bob's earnings for child support were higher than £160, his assessable income would be more. For example, suppose his assessible income was £350.
Anita's assessable income = £3.68
Joint assessable income = £3.68 + £350 = £353.68
50 per cent of joint assessable income = 50% x £353.68 = **£176.84**
This is above the maintenance requirement of £160.62 and so the additional element calculation would have to be done to calculate the proposed maintenance (see p239).

Anita's assessable income, although still £3.68, would now reduce the proposed maintenance. This is because Bob's assessable income is higher and together they meet the maintenance requirement.

4. **The additional element calculation**

An alternative calculation is used to obtain the proposed maintenance if half of the parents' joint assessable income is more than the maintenance requirement.

Proposed maintenance is composed of a basic element and an additional element. Likewise, the non-resident parent's total assessable income is composed of basic assessable income and additional assessable income.

The basic assessable income contributes towards the basic element at the rate of 50 per cent. The additional assessable income contributes towards the additional element at a lower rate, up to a maximum amount. The deduction rate is 15 per cent if there is one qualifying child, 20 per cent if there are two, and 25 per cent if there are three or more qualifying children in the assessment.[7]

The assessable incomes of both parents are taken into account in calculating the basic proposed maintenance. However, to illustrate the principle of what is a complex calculation, we first address the situation where only the non-resident parent has assessable income.

The parent with care has no assessable income

If 50 per cent of the non-resident parent's assessable income is higher than the maintenance requirement, ignore the 50 per cent figure and continue as described below.

If the parent with care has no assessable income, the basic element equals the maintenance requirement.[8] As basic assessable income contributes towards the basic element at the rate of 50 per cent, the non-resident parent must (in order to meet the maintenance requirement) use up assessable income equal to twice the maintenance requirement. Additional assessable income which is not used up in meeting the maintenance requirement contributes towards the additional element at the rate of 15, 20 or 25 per cent.

The non-resident parent thus pays more than the maintenance requirement, but overall less than 50 per cent of his assessable income.

When proposed maintenance has been obtained using the additional element calculation, this figure must be compared with the maximum amount (see p240).

Additional element calculation if the parent with care has no assessable income
To calculate the proposed maintenance if only the non-resident parent has assessable income and the 50 per cent calculation has shown that it more than meets the maintenance requirement:

- Multiply the maintenance requirement (the basic element) by two to give the basic assessable income.
- Deduct the basic assessable income from the total assessable income to give the additional assessable income.
- Take:
  - 15 per cent if there is one qualifying child; *or*
  - 20 per cent if there are two qualifying children; *or*
  - 25 per cent if there are three or more qualifying children,
  of the additional assessable income to give the additional element.
- Add the basic element (the maintenance requirement) to the additional element to give the proposed maintenance.

Example: additional element calculation where the parent with care has no assessable income

Jeremy has just left his wife, Evie, who has no income of her own other than child benefit and child tax credit. They have four children, Francis (14), Georgina (12), Henry (8) and Isobel (4), who are all living with Evie.

The maintenance requirement is therefore:

		£
Personal allowances	Evie	64.30
	Francis	56.11
	Georgina	56.11
	Henry	56.11
	Isobel	56.11
Family premium		17.30
Sub-total		306.04
Less child benefit (see p178)		59.60
Maintenance requirement		**246.44**

Jeremy has an assessable income of £600 a week.

50% x £600 = £300

This is above the maintenance requirement of £246.44. Therefore, to calculate proposed maintenance, do the additional element calculation:

Basic element = £246.44 (the maintenance requirement)

Basic assessable income = 2 x £246.44 = £492.88

Additional assessable income = £600 – £492.88 = £107.12

Additional element = 25% x £107.12 = £26.78 (the 25 per cent deduction rate is applicable as there are four qualifying children)

Proposed maintenance = £246.44 + £26.78 = **£273.22**

Check whether this figure is above the maximum child maintenance payable (see example on p240).

The parent with care has assessable income

Both parents contribute towards the maintenance requirement if they can afford to do so, although in the case of a parent with care this is a notional transaction. If the parents together cannot meet the maintenance requirement, the income of the parent with care does not affect the maintenance assessment (see p235).

However, if 50 per cent of the parents' joint assessable income more than meets the maintenance requirement, the parent with care's assessable income reduces the non-resident parent's proposed maintenance. Each parent contributes towards the maintenance requirement in proportion to her/his assessable income. The parent with care's notional contribution towards the maintenance requirement reduces the amount of the non-resident parent's assessable income required to meet that maintenance requirement. Therefore, the non-resident parent begins paying at the lower deduction rate earlier than he otherwise would have done.

The additional element calculation is used to work out the proposed maintenance; the basic element does not now equal the full maintenance requirement, but only the proportion of the maintenance requirement that the non-resident parent has to contribute.[9] Once the basic element has been calculated, the rest of the calculation is the same as before.

The parent with care's assessable income can reduce the proposed maintenance below the maintenance requirement, but cannot reduce the non-resident parent's proposed maintenance to zero. The non-resident parent still pays at least some contribution towards the maintenance requirement and then a percentage of his additional assessable income.

Additional element calculation if parent with care has assessable income

To calculate proposed maintenance if the parents have joint assessable income, half of which more than meets the maintenance requirement:
– Add together both parents' assessable incomes to give their joint assessable income.
– Multiply the maintenance requirement by the non-resident parent's assessable income divided by the joint assessable income (ie, the non-resident parent's proportion of the joint assessable income) to give the basic element (ie, the non-resident parent's contribution to the maintenance requirement).
– Multiply the basic element by two to give the basic assessable income.
– Deduct the basic assessable income from the non-resident parent's total assessable income to give his additional assessable income.
– Take:
  – 15 per cent if there is one qualifying child; *or*
  – 20 per cent if there are two qualifying children; *or*
  – 25 per cent if there are three or more qualifying children,
of the additional assessable income to give the additional element.
– Add the basic element to the additional element to give the proposed maintenance.

Example: additional element calculation if both parents have assessable incomes

Evie has now taken a paid job. Her exempt income is high as it includes allowances for the four children and a significant mortgage. Although she is earning £26,000 a year, her assessable income is only £70 a week (she is not entitled to any working tax credit). Jeremy's assessable income is still £600 a week.

The maintenance requirement is still £246.44 (see p237).

Joint assessable income = £70 + £600 = £670

50 per cent of the joint assessable income is £335, which more than meets the maintenance requirement. Therefore, the additional element calculation of proposed maintenance has to be done:

Basic element (the proportion of the maintenance requirement that Jeremy has to pay) = £246.44 × (£600/£670) = £220.69

Basic assessable income = £220.69 × 2 = £441.38

Additional assessable income = £600 – £441.38 = £158.62

Additional element = £158.62 × 25% = £39.66

Proposed maintenance = £220.69 + £39.66 = **£260.35**

Check whether this figure is above the maximum child maintenance payable (see p241).

5. **Maximum child maintenance**

There is an upper limit on the amount of child maintenance payable for a child under the child support formula.[10] No further child maintenance is deducted from assessable income once the maximum is being paid.

When the maximum is being paid, the parties could go to court to seek any further maintenance. The courts can consider further weekly child maintenance in the context of any other arrangements which have been made for the children (see p27).

Like proposed maintenance, maximum child maintenance is composed of a basic element and an additional element. The basic element is the same as the basic element of proposed maintenance, whereas the additional element relates to the number and age of the qualifying children.[11]

Again, like proposed maintenance, the calculation varies slightly if the parent with care has assessable income.

The parent with care has no assessable income

When the parent with care has no assessable income, the basic element of maximum child maintenance equals the maintenance requirement. The maximum amount of child maintenance equals the maintenance requirement plus the additional element.

The additional element equals 1.5 times the total of the income support (IS) personal allowance for each child and the amount of the IS family premium for each child.[12]

> ### Example: maximum child maintenance if the person with care has no assessable income
>
> Assuming Evie has no assessable income of her own, the maximum Jeremy would have to pay for the four children, Francis (14), Georgina (12), Henry (8) and Isobel (4), is as follows:
> The maintenance requirement is £246.44.
> Additional element = 1.5 x [(4 x £56.11) + (4 x £17.30)] = 1.5 x £293.64 = £440.46
>
> | | £ |
> |---|---|
> | Basic element | 246.44 |
> | Additional element | 440.46 |
> | **Maximum child maintenance** | **686.90** |
>
> Therefore, the proposed maintenance of £273.22 is less than the maximum.
> In order to pay the maximum amount, Jeremy would have to have an assessable income of at least (£246.44 x 2) + (£440.46 x 4) = £2,254.72 a week.

The parent with care has assessable income

The non-resident parent is responsible only for paying the proportion of the maximum child maintenance which corresponds to his proportion of joint assessable income.

The basic element of the maximum child maintenance is the proportion of the maintenance requirement which the non-resident parent must contribute. It is calculated as for the additional element calculation for proposed maintenance – ie:

- *add* together both parents' assessable incomes to give their joint assessable income;
- *multiply* the maintenance requirement by the non-resident parent's assessable income divided by joint assessable income.

To calculate the additional element:

- multiply the total of the IS personal allowance for each child and the family premium for each child by 1.5; *then*
- multiply this figure by the non-resident parent's assessable income divided by the joint assessable income.

The maximum child maintenance equals the basic element plus the additional element.

Alternatively, there is a short cut for this calculation. Multiply the maximum amount (as calculated) where the parent has no assessable income by the non-resident parent's proportion of the joint assessable income.

Example: maximum child maintenance if the parent with care has assessable income

To check whether the proposed maintenance calculated in the example on p239 (£260.35) is above the maximum:

Evie's assessable income = £70

Jeremy's assessable income = £600

Joint assessable income = £670

The maintenance requirement = £246.44

Basic element = £246.44 x (£600/£670) = £220.69

Additional element =

1.5 ([4 x £56.11] + [4 x £17.30]) x (£600/£670)

= £440.46 x (£600/£670) = £394.44

Maximum child maintenance = basic element plus the additional element = £220.69 + £394.44 = **£615.31**

(Alternatively, multiply the maximum figure from the example on p240 by Jeremy's proportion of joint assessable income: £686.90 x (£600/£670) = £615.13).

Jeremy therefore pays the proposed maintenance of £260.35.

Evie's income has reduced the assessment by just £12.88.

6. **Both parents are non-resident**

If the person with care is not a parent, this usually means that there are two non-resident parents. If an application is made for maintenance from both parents, an assessment is carried out for each non-resident parent. The same maintenance requirement is used in both assessments (see p181).

When calculating the proposed maintenance for each parent, the other non-resident parent's assessable income is used where the parent with care's income would normally be taken into account – ie, to give joint assessable income.[13] In other words, the parents will together contribute towards the maintenance requirement at the rate of 50 per cent of assessable income and, once the maintenance requirement is met, each will pay a lower percentage of their own additional assessable income.

Example: proposed maintenance if both parents are non-resident

Zoe is looking after her 17-year-old niece, Rebecca, whose parents have separated. Zoe's income is not taken into account as she is not Rebecca's mother.

The maintenance requirement = £41.88 (see example on p183)

50 per cent calculation

Her mother's assessable income = £14.50

Her father's assessable income = £23.90
Joint assessable income = £38.40
50 per cent of joint assessable income = £19.20
This is less than the maintenance requirement.
Proposed maintenance from her mother = 50% x £14.50 = £7.25
Proposed maintenance from her father = 50% x £23.90 = £11.95

The additional element calculation
Her mother's assessable income = £52
Her father's assessable income = £84
Joint assessable income = £136
50 per cent of joint assessable income = £68
This is more than the maintenance requirement.
Therefore, the additional element calculation has to be done. The 15 per cent deduction rate is used as Rebecca is the only qualifying child in the assessment.

Mother's proposed maintenance:
Basic element = £41.88 x (£52/£136) = £16.01
Basic assessable income = £16.01 x 2 = £32.02
Additional assessable income = £52 – £32.02 = £19.98
Additional element = £19.98 x 15% = £3
Proposed maintenance from mother = £16.01 + £3 = £19.01

Father's proposed maintenance:
Basic element = £41.88 x (£84/£136) = £25.87
Basic assessable income = £25.87 x 2 = £51.74
Additional assessable income = £84 – £51.74 = £32.26
Additional element = £32.27 x 15% = £4.84
Proposed maintenance from father = £25.87 + £4.84 = £30.71

Note: the basic proposed maintenance from both parents is the maintenance requirement – ie, £16.01 + £25.87 = £41.88
An application is made for maintenance from the mother only. The maintenance requirement is therefore halved to £20.94.
With assessable income of £14.50, the mother still cannot meet the maintenance requirement and, therefore, she pays 50% x £14.50 = £7.25. This is the same as in the 50 per cent calculation.
With assessable income of £52, the mother can now meet the maintenance requirement on her own (50% x £52 = £26). The basic element is the maintenance requirement of £20.94.
Basic assessable income = £20.94 x 2 = £41.88
Additional assessable income = £52 – £41.88 = £10.12
Additional element = £10.12 x 15% = £1.52
Proposed maintenance = £10.12 + £1.52 = £11.64

The total proposed maintenance for a child with two non-resident parents is the same as if there were one non-resident parent (with assessable income equal to the joint assessable income of the two non-resident parents) and a parent with care with no assessable income. However, with two non-resident parents the total liability is split between the parents in proportion to their assessable incomes.

If an application is made for maintenance from both parents and the Child Support Agency (CSA) does not have the information about the other parent's income within the fortnight given to provide it (see p56), it is assumed that this second non-resident parent has no assessable income when calculating the first non-resident parent's proposed maintenance.[14] When this information is available, a fresh assessment will be carried out.[15]

The regulations do not distinguish between non-resident parents who live separately from one another and those who, although they are no longer living with their child, still live together as a couple. Therefore, in the case of a couple being assessed, two separate assessments would be carried out following the same basic rules up to this stage (ie, net income and exempt income would be calculated separately for each parent), even though between the two assessments the same housing costs would be included twice.

The person with care who is not a parent of the qualifying children may be looking after children who have different parents. For example, a grandmother may be looking after two grandchildren, one the child of her son and the other the child of her daughter. This involves two maintenance requirements. The proposed maintenance steps for the two children are completely separate and each can be carried out for both the non-resident parents of each child (see above). In theory, the grandmother could receive child maintenance from four non-resident parents.

7. **More than one person with care**

'More than one person with care' does not refer to the situation where a child is looked after for part of the time by one person and the rest of the time by another; we call that 'shared care' (see Chapter 14).

Here, we cover the situation where different children of a non-resident parent are being looked after by different people. This includes where the non-resident parent has two or more families by different women with whom he does not live and also where the children of one family are split between two carers, perhaps with one child living with the mother and the other with grandparents. The non-resident parent is equally liable to maintain all the qualifying children and must pay child maintenance to each of the persons with care who makes an application.[16]

The more than one person with care situation involves applications for maintenance for *different* children from the *same* non-resident parent.

Sharing out the proposed maintenance

If the children of a non-resident parent are in the care of two or more people and a maintenance application has been made by more than one of those persons with care, the proposed maintenance has to be shared between the persons with care.[17] This is achieved by dividing the non-resident parent's assessable income between the maintenance assessments in the same proportions as their maintenance requirements.[18] Where an allowance for a pre-April 1993 property settlement has been included in exempt income (see p196), an adjustment is made when apportioning the assessable income. The proposed maintenance step is then carried out separately for each application using the relevant portion of assessable income.

Only one protected income calculation (see Chapter 13) is carried out for the non-resident parent, using the total amount of proposed maintenance for all the assessments.[19] Where the total maintenance worked out for all the persons with care is less than £6.50 (see p172), the minimum payment is divided between the persons with care in proportion to the maintenance requirements.[20]

Example: 50 per cent calculation if there is more than one parent with care
Wayne is the father of Yvonne (12) and Veronica (10) who live with Zoe. Zoe has no assessable income. She has been receiving £20 a week child maintenance from Wayne. Zoe's maintenance requirement for Yvonne and Veronica is £119.82 (see p181).
Wayne's girlfriend, Lauren, has recently had his baby, Keith. Wayne is not living with Lauren, who is claiming income support (IS) as a single parent.

Lauren's maintenance requirement is:		£
Personal allowances	Lauren	64.30
	Keith	56.11
Family premium		17.30
Sub-total		137.71
Less child benefit		20.00
Total maintenance requirement		**117.71**

Joint maintenance requirement is £119.82 + £117.71 = £237.53

Wayne's total assessable income is £40 a week.
For calculating Zoe's child maintenance, Wayne's assessable income =
£40 x £119.82/£237.53 = £20.18
For calculating Lauren's child maintenance, Wayne's assessable income =
£40 x £117.71/£237.53 = £19.82 (or £40 − £20.18 = £19.82)
Proposed maintenance = 50 per cent assessable income
For Zoe: 50% x £20.18 = £10.09
For Lauren: 50% x £19.82 = £9.91

Subject to the protected income calculation, Wayne is paying £20 in total, but divided between the two parents with care.

When Lauren makes an application for child maintenance, Zoe's child maintenance will be reduced from £20 to £10.09 a week.

By dividing the non-resident parent's assessable income in proportion to the different maintenance requirements, persons with care responsible for a larger number of children will usually receive a greater amount of child maintenance. However, in the above example, Zoe's maintenance requirement is smaller than would usually be expected for two children. She is receiving only half of certain allowances in the maintenance requirement, as her other child, Scott, has a different non-resident father (see p181).

The division in the proposed maintenance occurs only if both of the persons with care involved actually make an application for child maintenance from the same non-resident parent.[21]

Where one assessment is already in force when the second application involving the same non-resident parent is made (eg, when his second marriage breaks down) the first assessment is reduced from the date the assessment to the second person with care takes effect (see p330).[22]

Pre-April 1993 property settlements

Before dividing the non-resident parent's assessable income between the persons with care, any allowance for a pre-April 1993 property settlement (see p196) is added on to the assessable income.[23] Once this has been apportioned, the property settlement allowance (if any) relevant to that person with care is deducted from her portion of assessable income.

Example: more than one parent with care and a property settlement allowance
The situation is as in the example on p245 except that Wayne has an allowance of £20 included in his exempt income in recognition of the capital settlement he made to Zoe at the time of their divorce in 1992.

Assessable income to be apportioned = £40 + £20 = £60

For Lauren's child maintenance, Wayne's assessable income =
£60 x £117.71/£237.53 = £29.73

Proposed maintenance for Lauren = 50% x £29.73 = £14.87

For Zoe's child maintenance, Wayne's assessable income =
(£60 x £119.82/£237.53) – £20 = £10.27

Proposed maintenance for Zoe = 50% x £10.27 = £5.14

(The minimum payment of £6.50 applies only where the total payments due from an non-resident parent to all persons with care work out at less than £6.50)

Again, Wayne continues to pay £20 a week in total, although Zoe sees her maintenance reduced from £20 to £5.13 when Lauren applies to the CSA.

The additional element calculation

The additional element calculation of proposed maintenance when there is more than one person with care is done in the same way as when there is only one person with care, except that a proportion of the non-resident parent's assessable income is substituted for his total assessable income.

Example: additional element calculation if there is more than one person with care

Jeremy has left his wife, Evie, who has no income of her own. Of their four children, Francis (14), Georgina (12), Henry (8) and Isobel (4), the three youngest are living with Evie, but Francis is living with Jeremy's brother and sister-in-law. Jeremy has an assessable income of £600 a week.

The income of Jeremy's brother is irrelevant as he is not Francis' parent. Francis now has two non-resident parents who are liable to maintain him. Evie is now a non-resident parent in respect of Francis, but as she is on IS, she has no assessable income. Because she has children living with her, she is exempt from the deductions from IS.

Jeremy must pay his brother child maintenance for Francis as well as paying Evie child maintenance for Georgina, Henry and Isobel. Both the brother and Evie have made applications for child maintenance.

Evie's maintenance requirement:

		£
Personal allowances	Evie	64.30
	Georgina	56.11
	Henry	56.11
	Isobel	56.11
Family premium		17.30
Sub-total		249.93
Less child benefit		46.40
Total maintenance requirement		**203.53**

Francis' maintenance requirement:

		£
Personal allowances	Adult (half)	32.15
	Francis	56.11
Family premium		17.30
Sub-total		105.56
Less child benefit		20.00
Total maintenance requirement		**85.56**

(The adult personal allowance is halved since Francis, the only qualifying child in the assessment, is 14 years old – see p178.)

Joint maintenance requirement = £203.53 + £85.56 = £289.09

Jeremy's £600 assessable income has to be split between the two assessments in proportion to their maintenance requirements.

Evie's child maintenance:

Jeremy's assessable income = £203.53/£289.09 x £600 = £422.42

Proposed maintenance = 50% x £422.42 = £211.21

This is above the maintenance requirement of £203.53; therefore the additional element calculation must be done (as on p237):

Basic assessable income = £203.53 x 2 = £407.06

Additional assessable income = £422.42 – £407.06 = £15.36

Additional element = £15.36 x 25% = £3.84

Proposed maintenance = £203.53 + £3.84 = £207.37

When Francis leaves home, Evie's maintenance falls from £273.22 a week (see p237) to £207.37

Note: if Evie had assessable income, then the additional element calculation would follow that on p241, using £422.42 as Jeremy's assessable income.

Child maintenance for Francis:

Jeremy's assessable income = £600 x £85.56/£289.09 = £177.58

Proposed maintenance = 50% x £177.58 = £88.79

This is above the maintenance requirement of £85.56; therefore:

Basic assessable income = £85.56 x 2 = £171.12

Additional assessable income = £177.58 – £171.12 = £6.46

Additional element = £6.46 x 15% = £0.97

Proposed maintenance = £85.56 + £0.97 = £86.53

Jeremy is paying £86.53 to his brother and £207.37 to Evie, a total of £293.90. This is £20.68 more than he paid to Evie when the four children were living together. The non-resident parent usually ends up paying more in total when there are two or more applications. This is because he is paying a larger amount of his assessable income at the 50 per cent rate, as he now has two or more maintenance requirements to meet.

8. Divided families

We use the term 'divided family' to cover the situation where some children of a family are in the care of the mother and the others in the care of the father. The

Child Support Agency may use the term 'split care'. This situation could involve two separate maintenance applications and assessments. If only one of the parents applies for maintenance, then only that application will be assessed. The calculations do not involve any variation from the basic formula.

This is not the same situation as where the care of the same child(ren) is shared between the parents ('shared care' – see Chapter 14).

Example: two proposed maintenance calculations for a divided family

Carol (now 15) does not like her stepfather, Joe, and decides that she wants to live with Bob and Zoe's family – Yvonne (14), Veronica (12), Scott (5) and Ricky (1). David (10) is still living with Anita and Joe.

Therefore, Anita is the non-resident parent for Carol, and Bob is the non-resident parent for David. Anita's net income is now £280

Maintenance requirement for Carol (15) = £85.56

Maintenance requirement for David (10) = £117.71

Although Carol is older, her maintenance requirement is lower as the carer element is halved because she is over 14.

Anita's exempt income = £275.49

(Anita's exempt income is as in the example on p195, but without the £56.11 for Carol)

Anita's assessable income = £280 (net income) – £275.49 = £4.51

Bob's exempt income = £210.76

Bob's assessable income = £260 (net income) – £210.76 = £49.24

Joint assessable income = £4.51 + £49.24 = £53.75

50 per cent of joint assessable income = £53.75 x 50% = £26.88

The 50 per cent joint assessable income figure (£26.88) is lower than the maintenance requirement for David (£117.71) and that for Carol (£85.56).

Proposed maintenance from Bob = 50% x £49.24 = £24.62

Proposed maintenance from Anita = 50% x £4.51 = £2.26

The protected income calculation (see p265) shows that both Anita and Bob can afford these amounts. Therefore, Bob in effect pays Anita: £24.62 – £2.26 = £22.36 a week.

If either or both of the maintenance requirements had been lower than 50 per cent joint assessable income, then the proposed maintenance would have been obtained using the additional element calculation (see p239).

9. **More than one non-resident parent**

A person with care may be looking after children of different non-resident parents. Here we look at the situation where the person with care is a parent of all the qualifying children. The situation where the person with care is not the parent of the qualifying child(ren) is dealt with on p242 – ie, both parents are non-resident.

If a parent with care is looking after children of different non-resident parents and applies for maintenance from more than one non-resident parent, then more than one maintenance assessment has to be done. If the parent with care has no assessable income, the two (or more) assessments will not alter from the basic formula.

Example: proposed maintenance from more than one non-resident parent where the parent with care has no assessable income

Zoe has applied for maintenance from her ex-husband, Wayne, for Yvonne (14) and Veronica (12), and from Terence for Scott (5). She is living with Bob and has no income of her own other than child benefit and child tax credit. This means that her net income is nil and, therefore, her assessable income is nil.

Child maintenance from Wayne:

Step 1: Maintenance requirement = £119.82 (see example on p181)

Step 2: Exempt income

Wayne, Zoe's ex-husband, lives on his own in a rented flat. His rent is £65 a week.

	£
Personal allowance	64.30
Housing costs	65.00
Total exempt income	**129.30**

Step 3: Assessable income

Total net income	160.00	(net earnings)
Less exempt income	129.30	
Assessable income	**30.70**	

Step 4: Proposed maintenance = 50% x £30.70 = £15.35

This is below the maintenance requirement of £119.82.

Therefore, the proposed maintenance is **£15.35**.

(You may remember that Wayne had a son with Lauren. However, she has now married Sean and moved to Eire where the CSA has no jurisdiction.)

Child maintenance from Terence:

Step 1: Maintenance requirement = £83.71 (see example on p181)

Step 2: Exempt income

Terence is married to Dipa and, although they have three children, only Rana, 17 and still at school, counts as a dependant. They have a mortgage of £34.18 a week. Dipa receives carer's allowance for looking after her mother, but this is not enough income to support half of Rana. They get working tax credit (WTC) of £27.64 and £50.54 child tax credit.

		£
Personal allowances	Terence	64.30
	Rana	56.11
Family premium		17.30
Housing costs		34.18
Total exempt income		**171.89**

Step 3: Assessable income

	190.21	(net earnings)
	27.64	WTC
Total net income	217.85	
Less exempt income	171.89	
Assessable income	**45.96**	

Step 4: Proposed maintenance = 50% x £45.96 = £22.98
This is below the maintenance requirement of £83.71.
Therefore, the proposed maintenance for Scott is **£22.98**.

The protected income calculations now have to be done to see whether Wayne and Terence can afford these amounts (see example on p260).

The parent with care has assessable income

If the parent with care has assessable income and makes an application for child maintenance from more than one non-resident father, then a proportion of her assessable income is taken into account for each of the assessments. Her assessable income is divided between the maintenance assessments in proportion to the maintenance requirements.[24] This apportioning will only happen if an application is made for maintenance from more than one non-resident parent.

Example: more than one non-resident parent and parent with care has assessable income

Jeremy left his wife, Evie, when he discovered that her youngest child, Isobel (4), was not his daughter. Evie is also looking after his three children, Francis (14), Georgina (12) and Henry (8). Evie decided to apply for child maintenance from Isobel's father, Max, as well as from Jeremy.

Maintenance requirement for Francis, Georgina and Henry:

		£	
Personal allowances	Evie	32.15	(half of 64.30)
	Francis	56.11	
	Georgina	56.11	
	Henry	56.11	
Family premium		8.65	(half of 17.30)
Sub-total		209.13	
Less child benefit		46.40	
Total maintenance requirement		**162.73**	

Maintenance requirement for Isobel:

Personal allowances	Evie	32.15	(half of 64.30)
	Isobel	56.11	
Family premium		8.65	(half of 17.30)
Sub-total		96.91	
Less child benefit		13.20	
Total maintenance requirement		**83.71**	

Joint maintenance requirements = £162.73 + £83.71 = £246.44

Evie's total assessable income is £70. This has to be shared between the two assessments in proportion to the maintenance requirements.

Proposed maintenance from Max: 50 per cent calculation

Evie's assessable income used in this assessment = £70 x £83.71/£246.44 = £23.78

Max's assessable income is £42.50

Max and Evie's joint assessable income = £23.78 + £42.50 = £66.28

50% x £66.28 = £33.14

This is less than the maintenance requirement of £83.71

Therefore, proposed maintenance is 50 per cent of Max's own assessable income: 50% x £42.50 = **£21.25**

Proposed maintenance from Jeremy: additional element calculation

Evie's total assessable income is £70

Her assessable income used in this assessment = £70 x £162.73/£246.44 = £46.22

Jeremy's assessable income is now £350

Jeremy and Evie's joint assessable income = £46.22 + £350 = £396.22

50% x £396.22 = £198.11

This is more than the maintenance requirement of £162.73 and, therefore, an additional element calculation has to be done:

Basic element = £162.73/£396.22 x £350 = £143.75

Basic assessable income = £143.75 x 2 = £287.50

Additional assessable income = £350 – £287.50 = £62.50

Additional element = £62.50 x 25% = £15.63

Proposed maintenance = £143.75 + £15.63 = **£159.38**

Subject to the protected income stage, Evie will receive £21.25 from Max and £159.38 from Jeremy.

Notes

2. **How much is proposed maintenance**
1 Sch 1 para 2(1) CSA 1991
2 Sch 1 para 2(2) CSA 1991
3 Sch 1 para 2(3) CSA 1991
4 Sch 1 para 2 CSA 1991; reg 5 CS(MASC) Regs
5 Sch 1 para 4 CSA 1991; reg 6 CS(MASC) Regs

3. **The 50 per cent calculation**
6 Sch 1 para 2(2) CSA 1991

4. **The additional element calculation**
7 Sch 1 para 4(1) CSA 1991; reg 6(1) CS(MASC) Regs
8 Sch 1 para 3 CSA 1991
9 Sch 1 para 3 CSA 1991

5. **Maximum child maintenance**
10 Sch 1 para 4(2) CSA 1991
11 Sch 1 para 4(3) CSA 1991
12 Reg 6(2) CS(MASC) Regs

6. **Both parents are non-resident**
13 Reg 19(2) CS(MASC) Regs
14 Reg 19(3) CS(MASC) Regs
15 Reg 19(4) CS(MASC) Regs

7. **More than one person with care**
16 Reg 22(5) CS(MASC) Regs
17 Reg 22(1) CS(MASC) Regs
18 Reg 22(2) CS(MASC) Regs
19 Reg 22(3) CS(MASC) Regs
20 Reg 22(4) CS(MASC) Regs
21 Reg 22(1)(a) CS(MASC) Regs
22 Reg 22(1)(b) and (2A) CS(MASC) Regs
23 Reg 22(2) CS(MASC) Regs

9. **More than one non-resident parent**
24 Reg 23(4) CS(MASC) Regs

Chapter 13

Protected income ('old rules')

This chapter covers:
1. What is protected income (below)
2. Basic protected income (p257)
3. Total protected income (p259)
4. The maintenance payable (p260)
5. Change of circumstances (p265)

---

1. **What is protected income**

Protected income is income which cannot be used for paying child maintenance.[1] At the end of the protected income calculation, the amount of maintenance payable will be known. It will either be the proposed maintenance figure or a reduced amount. The non-resident parent never ends up paying more than the proposed maintenance. This step should be carried out for all non-resident parents. The only time it does not apply is where the proposed maintenance is £6.50 or less (see p172).

There are two forms of protection for non-resident parents. One prevents them having to pay an excessive proportion of their own income as child maintenance, and the other considers the needs of the whole family.

30 per cent cap

A non-resident parent never has to pay more than 30 per cent of his net income (see p208).[2] His partner's income is ignored. If the proposed maintenance is greater than this, it will be reduced to 30 per cent of net income. In other words, 70 per cent net income is a protected level of income; all non-resident parents (except a few of those making the minimum payment) are left with at least 70 per cent of their own net income. This applies even where a non-resident parent is paying more than one Child Support Agency (CSA) assessment (see p263). Also, if a non-resident parent is paying maintenance for other children under a court order, whether inside or outside the UK, this can be deducted from net income at the protected income stage (see p256).[3]

Example

Bob is living with his parents, and is liable to pay maintenance for Carol and David. His net earnings are now £170 a week.

Step 1: Maintenance requirement = £160.62 (see p179)

Step 2: Exempt income (personal allowance) = £64.30

Step 3: Assessable income = £170 − £64.30 = £105.70

Step 4: Proposed maintenance = 50% x £105.70 = £52.85 (less than the maintenance requirement)

Step 5: Protected income = 30% x £170 = £51

The maintenance is, therefore, reduced to £51, before proceeding with the rest of the protected income step.

Two years later, Bob is living with Zoe, their son Ricky and Zoe's three other children. His net income is now £260 (see p226) and the proposed maintenance is £25.35 (see p235).

30% x £260 = £78

The proposed maintenance is less than 30 per cent net income and remains at £25.35.

Even where the proposed maintenance has been capped at 30 per cent net income, the second protected income calculation is carried out, as the maintenance payable may be further reduced. When carrying out this second calculation, substitute the capped maintenance for proposed maintenance where the latter is more than 30 per cent net income.

Total protected income

This second part of the protected income calculation is intended to prevent the non-resident parent and his family being left below the income support (IS) level as a result of paying child maintenance.[4] The 'family' is the same as that used for means-tested benefits (see p25 for a detailed definition).

What is total family income

'Total family income' includes the incomes of all members of the non-resident parent's family (see p25).[5] The CSA calls total family income 'disposable income'. We do not use this term at this stage as disposable income is also used to specify the income remaining after proposed maintenance has been paid.

Income for total family income purposes is calculated in the same way as net income (see Chapter 11) except that:[6]

- child benefit is included in full as income;
- child tax credit (CTC) is included in full as income, whether it is payable to the non-resident parent or his partner;
- part of payments under a mortgage protection insurance policy which exceed the mortgage interest repayments are disregarded; *and*
- with the exception of child maintenance, which is counted in full as the parent's income, the income of any child is included as income up to the

amount of the personal allowance for that child and any disabled child premium included in the protected income calculation. As at exempt income stage, children's earnings and the first £10 a week of other income are disregarded.

Child maintenance paid

If a non-resident parent or his partner is paying maintenance for a child under a court order where an application to the CSA cannot be made, the amount of that payment is deducted from total family income.[7] The effect is to protect the payments under the court order at the possible expense of the proposed maintenance resulting from the CSA application. This certainly applies where the person with care receiving the maintenance under the court order is not the parent of the child or where she is not receiving one of the specified benefits (see p36). Arguably, it also applies where a parent with care on benefit has refused to make an application to the CSA (eg, to preserve the court order) and the non-resident parent is now being assessed for his liability to maintain other children. It also applies where the non-resident parent or his partner is paying any child maintenance due under a court order made outside Great Britain.[8] However, no account is taken of voluntary payments, whether made in this country or abroad. In the former situation, the non-resident parent should consider making an application to the CSA as he may be better off with two CSA assessments.

Example: total family income
The proposed maintenance from Bob to Anita for Carol and David is £25.35 (see example on p235). Can he afford it?
Bob is living with Zoe and four children – Yvonne (14), Veronica (12), Scott (4) and Ricky (baby). Bob has net earnings of £260 (see p226). Zoe receives weekly maintenance of £20 for Yvonne and Veronica, CTC of £170.66 and child benefit of £59.60.

	£
Earnings (net)	160.00
Maintenance for Yvonne and Veronica	20.00
CTC	270.66
Child benefit	59.60
Total family income	**510.26**

What is total protected income

Total protected income is the level below which the non-resident parent's or second family's income must not fall. To make the calculation more manageable, we have separated the total protected income level into basic protected income (see p257) and additional protected income (see p259).

The basic protected income is based on IS rates, and it includes personal allowances, premiums, an amount towards high travel-to-work costs, housing costs for all members of the non-resident parent's family, and £30 as a margin above IS. The family is allowed additional protected income of 15 per cent of any family income over and above the basic protected level.

Maintenance payable

The total protected income level is compared with the family's income remaining were the proposed maintenance, or capped maintenance if it is lower, to be paid. If the family's income would be brought below the total protected income level by paying the proposed maintenance, the maintenance due is reduced. The child maintenance is then payable at an amount which would leave the family with disposable income equal to the protected income level.[9] However, the maintenance due cannot be reduced to less than the minimum payment[10] unless the non-resident parent is exempt (see p173).

If the family would have income remaining over the protected income level after paying the proposed maintenance, then the non-resident parent is due to pay the proposed maintenance, or the capped maintenance if that is lower. In other words, the non-resident parent pays the *lowest* of:

- 30 per cent of his net income; *or*
- the amount which would leave his family with disposable income equal to the total protected level; *or*
- the proposed maintenance from Step 4.

2. **Basic protected income**

Basic protected income includes income support (IS) personal allowances and any relevant premiums for all the members of the family, whether the family receives IS or not (including where IS is received for adults but child tax credit is received for children). See Appendix 2 for the qualifying conditions and 2009/10 rates of the premiums.

Basic protected income is:[11]

- the amount of the IS personal allowance for someone aged 25 or over (£64.30) *or* if the non-resident parent has a partner, the IS personal allowance for a couple both aged 18 or over (£100.95); *plus*
- for each child in the family, the amount of the IS personal allowance for a child (£56.11);* *plus*
- the amount of any IS premiums for which the conditions are satisfied* (note that, unlike at exempt income stage, pensioner premiums are included); *plus*
- housing costs for the whole family (see p258); *plus*
- council tax liability less any council tax benefit (CTB – see p258); *plus*
- an allowance towards high travel-to-work costs of a non-resident parent (see p259); *plus*
- a standard margin of £30.

*A proportion of the full rate of the personal allowances and any premiums will be used if a child lives in the household for between two and six nights a week.[12]

Housing costs

The rules for assessing housing costs are the same as those used at the exempt income stage (see p189),[13] except that:

- if there is a mortgage, only interest payments are allowed;[14]
- if the non-resident parent is living as a non-dependant in someone else's house, an amount is included as housing costs (see below);[15]
- excessive housing costs are the higher of £80 or half the total family income.[16] Housing costs will be restricted to this figure unless the non-resident parent is exempt from that rule – eg, because the family includes a child (see p194).

The non-resident parent is a non-dependant

A non-resident parent may be a non-dependant if he lives in a household with people who are not 'family' (see p25). He is *not* a non-dependant if he, or a partner, is:[17]

- a co-owner or joint tenant of the home;
- employed by a charitable or voluntary body as a resident carer;
- liable to make a commercial payment in order to live in the home. It will not be considered a commercial arrangement if payments are made to a close relative in the household; a close relative is a parent, son, daughter (including step-relatives and in-laws), brother and sister, and any of their partners.

The weekly amount to be included in protected income is given below.[18]

Working 16 or more hours a week and with a gross income of:	£
£382 or more	47.75
£306 to £381.99	43.50
£231 to £305.99	38.20
£178 to £230.99	23.35
£120 to £177.99	17.00
All others	7.40

When calculating gross income, disability living allowance/attendance allowance is ignored.[19]

Council tax

If the non-resident parent is the only person, other than a partner, who is liable to pay council tax in respect of the home for which housing costs are included, the weekly council tax (less any CTB) is included in basic protected income. However, if there are other people resident in the home, the amount of council tax included is either:[20]

- the weekly liability divided by the number of liable people; *or*
- the weekly amount actually paid by the non-resident parent where he is required to pay more than his share because another liable person has defaulted.

If the non-resident parent lives in Northern Ireland, liability for rates replaces council tax. Likewise, if the person with care has applied to the Child Support Agency (Northern Ireland) but the non-resident parent lives in Great Britain, council tax is used.[21]

High travel-to-work costs

This allowance applies for non-resident parents who travel more than 240 kilometres a week to and from work.[22] The allowance is calculated in exactly the same way as at exempt income stage (see p200). It does not apply to partners.

3. **Total protected income**

In order to obtain total protected income, additional protected income has to be calculated. To do this, basic protected income must be compared with total family income.

Where the total family income *exceeds* the basic protected income, an addition is made to the basic protected income.

Deduct the basic protected income from the total family income to give the excess family income. The additional protected income equals 15 per cent of this excess family income.[23] This figure is added to basic protected income to give total protected income.

Where the total family income is *below* the basic protected income, there is no additional protected income. Any payment of child maintenance will bring the family's disposable income below the protected income level. Therefore, the non-resident parent will either pay the minimum amount (£6.50) or be exempt from paying altogether (see p173).

. . . .

Example: total protected income
The situation is the same as in the example on p254, with Bob living with his parents. He is contributing towards the household but is not a co-owner of the home, nor liable to pay council tax. He travels less than 240 kilometres a week to and from work.

Basic protected income:	£
Personal allowance	64.30
Housing costs (as a non-dependant)	17.00
Margin	30.00
Basic protected income	**111.30**

Additional protected income:

Total family income	170.00
Less basic protected income	111.30
Excess family income	58.70
Additional protected income (15% x £58.70)	**8.81**

Total protected income:

Basic protected income	111.30
Plus additional protected income	8.81
Total protected income	**120.11**

Two years later, Bob lives with Zoe and the situation is the same as in the example on p256. Their rent is £45 a week and the council tax liability is £1,050.92 a year. Bob and Zoe are not entitled to housing benefit or council tax benefit.

Basic protected income:		£
Personal allowances	Couple	100.95
	Yvonne	56.11
	Veronica	56.11
	Scott	56.11
	Ricky	56.11
Family premium		17.30
Housing costs		45.00
Council tax liability		20.21
Margin		30.00
Basic protected income		**437.79**

Additional protected income:

Total family income	510.26
Less basic protected income	437.79
Excess family income	72.47
Additional protected income (15% x £72.47)	**10.87**

Total protected income:

Basic protected income	437.79
Plus additional protected income	10.87
Total protected income	**448.66**

4. **The maintenance payable**

There are two methods of calculating the maintenance payable. We cover first the full logic of the step and then a short cut.

The family's disposable income which would remain after paying child maintenance is obtained by subtracting the proposed maintenance (Step 4) from the total family income. If the proposed maintenance has been capped at 30 per cent net income (see p254), this capped amount is used instead of the proposed maintenance.

If the disposable income is *higher* than the total protected income, the parent can afford to pay the full proposed/capped maintenance. Maintenance payable is the proposed/capped maintenance figure. Where the proposed maintenance has been capped, it cannot be increased back to the originally proposed level.

If the disposable income is initially *below* the total protected income, the maintenance payable is reduced until the disposable income equals the total protected income.[24] Therefore, the maintenance payable is the total family income minus the total protected income.

The minimum payment rule still applies (see p172).[25]

The alternative way of arriving at the maintenance payable is to cut out the disposable income step and in all cases to deduct total protected income from total family income to give an alternative proposed maintenance. This is compared with proposed maintenance from Step 4 and also 30 per cent of net income; the non-resident parent pays whichever figure is smallest.

Example: maintenance payable

The proposed maintenance from Bob to Anita for Carol and David has been capped at £51 (see p254) and Bob's total protected income is £120.11 (see p259).

	£
Total family income	170.00
Less capped maintenance	51.00
Disposable income would be	**119.00**

As this is below the total protected income level, the capped maintenance is reduced. Bob can only afford to pay:

	£
Total family income	170.00
Less total protected income	120.11
Maintenance payable	**49.89**

Two years later, when Bob is living with Zoe, the proposed maintenance is £25.35 (see p254)

	£
Total family income (from p256)	510.26
Less proposed maintenance	42.58
Disposable income would be	**467.68**

This is more than the total protected income of £448.66 (see example on p259) and, therefore, the proposed maintenance is paid.

Example: protected income from start to finish

A few months later, child maintenance from Zoe's ex-husband, Wayne, for Yvonne and Veronica and from Terence for Scott is being assessed (see example on p250). The proposed maintenance from Wayne is £15.35 and from Terence £22.98. Can each of them afford it?

Wayne lives on his own in a rented flat. He earns on average £160 net a week and only travels a few kilometres to work. His rent is £65 a week and his council tax is £6 a week. He is not entitled to any council tax benefit or housing benefit. The 30 per cent cap does not reduce the proposed maintenance as: 30% x £160 = £48. Therefore, the proposed maintenance remains at £15.35.

Basic protected income:	£
Personal allowance	64.30
Housing costs	65.00
Council tax	6.00
Margin	30.00
Basic protected income	**165.30**
Total family income	160.00
Less basic protected income	165.30
Excess family income	0.00
Additional protected income (15% x £0)	**0.00**
Total protected income	**165.30**

Wayne's total family income is already slightly below his total protected income. Payment of the proposed maintenance of £15.35 would leave Wayne with a disposable income of £144.65, considerably below his total protected income. As Wayne's family income is below his total protected income there is no disposable income from which to pay maintenance. However, Wayne is not exempt from the minimum maintenance payment and, therefore, he is liable to pay £6.50 a week.

Terence is married to Dipa and they have one dependent daughter, Rana (17), who lives with them. Their mortgage is £34.18 a week, half of which is capital repayments. Their council tax is £9.32 a week. Terence is self-employed and his net earnings average £190.21 a week. Dipa receives carer's allowance of £53.10 and child benefit of £20 a week. They get £27.64 working tax credit (WTC) and child tax credit of £50.54 per week.

The 30 per cent cap does not reduce the proposed maintenance as: 30% x £217.85 (earnings plus WTC) = £65.35. Therefore, the proposed maintenance remains at £22.98.

Basic protected income:		£
Personal allowances	Couple	100.95
	Rana	56.11
Family premium		17.30
Carer premium		29.50
Housing costs (mortgage interest)		17.09
Council tax		9.32

Margin	30.00
Basic protected income	**260.27**
Total family income:	
Net earnings	190.21
Carer's allowance	53.10
Child benefit	20.00
Working tax credit	27.64
Child tax credit	50.54
Total family income	**341.49**
Less basic protected income	260.27
Excess family income	81.22
Additional protected income (15% x £81.22)	**12.18**
Total protected income	**272.45**
Total family income	341.49
Less proposed maintenance	22.98
Disposable income	**318.15**

As disposable income is above the total protected income, the maintenance payable is the proposed maintenance of £22.98.

More than one person with care

If a non-resident parent is being assessed to pay child maintenance to two or more persons with care for different qualifying children, only one protected income step is carried out on the total proposed maintenance. Both the 30 per cent cap and the total protected income check are carried out for this total.[26] If the non-resident parent cannot afford the total proposed maintenance, the amount he can afford is divided between the persons with care in proportion to their proposed maintenance.

Example: protected income step for more than one person with care

Lauren has returned to the UK. She claims income support and applies for child maintenance for Wayne's son, Keith. Wayne is also the father of Zoe's daughters. His net wages are now £174, his rent is now £50.

Step 1: Maintenance requirement

	£	
Zoe	111.78	(see p181)
Lauren	117.71	(see p245)
Total	**229.49**	

Step 2: Wayne's exempt income = £131.30

Step 3: Wayne's assessable income= £42.70
(Neither parent with care has any assessable income)

Step 4: Proposed maintenance
Zoe: (£111.78 x £42.70/£229.49) x 50% = £10.40
Lauren: (£117.51 x £42.70/£229.49) x 50% = £10.93
Total proposed maintenance = £10.40 + £10.93 = £21.33

Step 5: Protected income
Check whether the total proposed maintenance is more than 30 per cent net income:
30% x £174 = £52.20
The total proposed maintenance of £21.33 is less than this and, therefore, does not need
to be capped. Now carry out the second protected income calculation.

	£
Personal allowance	64.30
Housing costs	50.00
Council tax	6.00
Margin	30.00
Basic protected income	**150.30**
Total family income	174.00
Less basic protected income	150.30
Excess family income	23.70
Additional protected income (15% x £23.70)	3.56
Total protected income (£150.30 + £3.56)	**153.86**
Total family income	174.00
Less total proposed maintenance	21.33
Disposable income	**152.67**

This is below the total protected income (£153.86), so Wayne cannot afford to pay the
proposed maintenance.

Total family income	174.00
Less total protected income	153.86
Maintenance payable	**20.14**

The maintenance is split between Zoe and Lauren in proportion to their proposed
maintenance:
Zoe: £20.14 x £10.40/£21.33 = £9.82
Lauren: £20.14 x £10.93/£21.33 = £10.32

Note: Lauren ends up with a greater proportion of the maintenance, even though she has
one young child and Zoe has two older children. In this case, as neither of them has
assessable income, the difference is entirely due to the maintenance requirement rules.

5. **Change of circumstances**

An increase in the total family income of a second family on the protected income level can result in an increase in the maintenance payable to the first family. This arises because the total protected income level only increases by 15 per cent of any increase in family income. The net effect of a £1 a week increase in total family income is an 85 pence increase in the child maintenance payable to the first family. This begins as soon as the maintenance payable is £6.50 a week and only ceases once the maintenance due reaches the capped or proposed maintenance level.

This recycling effect is the same, irrespective of whether the income is the non-resident parent's or a partner's. There is no exception for income specifically meant for stepchildren in the second family – eg, child maintenance paid for them. The theory is that an increase in the income of the non-resident parent's partner means that she is better able to support herself and her own children. This in turn releases more of the non-resident parent's income away from supporting his partner and his stepchildren and into paying maintenance to his own children. However, this distinction may not be obvious to second families, who are likely to perceive it as unfair.

Once the proposed maintenance level is due, a £1 increase in the non-resident parent's income results in an increase of between 50 pence and 15 pence in the maintenance assessment. The partner's income then no longer increases the assessment at all (except to a limited extent in some instances where there is a joint child – see p202).

If the proposed maintenance has been capped, then increases in the partner's income do *not* increase the maintenance payable. While the maintenance remains capped, a £1 increase in the non-resident parent's own net income produces a 30 pence increase in the assessment.

Example: change in total family income

Zoe decides to take a job, earning £100 net a week. Bob is still taking home £260 a week. When their tax credit award is reassessed (Zoe's earnings will not affect their tax credits until the following tax year), they are now entitled to £170.66 a week (Ricky has had his first birthday). Zoe now receives child maintenance as assessed in the example on p260.

Step 1: Maintenance requirement = £160.62 (see p179)

Step 2: Bob's exempt income = £146

Step 3: Bob's assessable income = £113.99 (see p226)

Step 4: Proposed maintenance = 50% x £113.99 = £57

(Anita has no assessable income)

Step 5: Protected income

To check whether the proposed maintenance is less than 30 per cent net income (see p226): 30% x £260 = £78

Therefore, the proposed maintenance remains at £57.

	£
Bob's earnings	260.00
Zoe's earnings	100.00
Maintenance from Wayne	6.50
Maintenance from Terence	23.12
Child benefit	59.60
Child tax credit	170.66
Total family income	619.88
Less basic protected income (see p259)	437.79
Excess family income	182.09
Additional protected income (15% x £182.09)	**27.31**
Total protected income (£437.79 + £27.31)	**465.10**
If the proposed maintenance were paid, disposable income would be:	
Total family income	619.88
Less proposed maintenance	57.00
Disposable income	**562.88**

This is higher than the total protected income (£465.10) and, therefore, the proposed maintenance is the maintenance payable. Bob is now paying Anita £57 instead of £25.35 (see p260). Although Bob and Zoe's total family income has increased by £109.62, their disposable income after maintenance has been paid has increased by £95.20. Since the proposed maintenance is being paid, any wage increase of Zoe's will not increase Bob's maintenance assessment any further.

It would not be to Bob's advantage to ask for a supersession of the assessment on the grounds of change of circumstances (see p358).

For two reasons, not every change of circumstances will immediately affect the amount of child maintenance payable. First, the person concerned does not have to request a supersession if there is a change in her/his circumstances. It is optional. Second, if a supersession is requested and undertaken, the general rule is that the maintenance in payment will only be altered if the new assessment is at least £10 more or less than the assessment in force. However, a new assessment which is reduced by only £1 or more or increased by £5 or more from the previous assessment will always take effect if it leaves the non-resident parent's family on the protected income level (see p360). Therefore, cases which involve a non-resident parent on the protected income level will be changing more frequently than cases where the full amount of the proposed maintenance is being paid.

Example: change in family composition

Bob's daughter Carol (now 15) moves, leaving Anita, to live with Bob and Zoe. Child benefit increases to £72.80. Child tax credit increases to £210.70. Otherwise, the situation is as in the previous example.

David (10), Bob's son, still lives with Anita and her husband, Joe. Anita has net earnings of £280 and Joe has net earnings of £295. Anita's child benefit entitlement is now £20. Their mortgage interest payments are £114.23 a week, the endowment policy premium is £24.92 a week, and council tax £14.50 a week.

See the example on p248:

Proposed maintenance from Anita for Carol = £2.26
Proposed maintenance from Bob for David = £24.62

Protected income calculation for Bob

The 30 per cent cap does not reduce the proposed maintenance as:

30% x £260 = £78

Basic protected income:		£
Personal allowances	Couple	100.95
	Carol	56.11
	Yvonne	56.11
	Veronica	56.11
	Scott	56.11
	Ricky	56.11
Family premium		17.30
Housing costs		45.00
Council tax liability		20.21
Margin		30.00
Basic protected income		**494.01**

Total family income:	
£449.22 (from the previous example without former child tax credit) + £210.70 (revised child tax credit) + £13.20 (extra child benefit)	673.12
Excess family income (£673.12 – £494.01)	179.11
Additional protected income (15% x £179.11)	26.87
Total protected income (£494.01 + £26.87)	520.88
Total family income	673.12
Less proposed maintenance	24.62
Disposable income	**648.50**

This is above the total protected income of £520.88 and, therefore, Bob can afford to pay the proposed maintenance of £24.62.

Protected income calculation for Anita

Basic protected income:		£
Personal allowances	Couple	100.95
	David	56.11
Family premium		17.30
Housing costs (mortgage interest only)		114.23
Council tax liability		14.50
Margin		30.00
Basic protected income		**333.09**

Total family income:	£
Anita's earnings	280.00
Joe's earnings	295.00
Child tax credit	10.50
Child benefit	20.00
Total family income	**605.50**
Less basic protected income	333.09
Excess family income*	272.41

*At this point it is already clear that Anita will pay the proposed maintenance, but we continue with the calculation for completeness.

	£
Additional protected income (15% x £272.41)	40.86
Total protected income (£333.09 + £40.86)	373.95
Total family income	605.50
Less proposed maintenance	2.26
Disposable income	**603.24**

This is well above the total protected income of £373.95 and, therefore, Anita can afford to pay the proposed maintenance. Because this is less than the minimum amount, she will pay this (£6.50).

Note: the formula works in such a way as to leave Anita and Joe with disposable income of £603.24 when they have the care of one child, whereas Bob and Zoe are left with £648.50 when they are looking after five children.

Notes

1. What is protected income
1 Sch 1 para 6 CSA 1991
2 Regs 11(6)-(6A) and 12 CS(MASC) Regs
3 Reg 12(1)(c) CS(MASC) Regs
4 Reg 11(1)-(5) CS(MASC) Regs
5 Regs 11(1)(l) and 12(1)(a) CS(MASC) Regs
6 Reg 11(2) CS(MASC) Regs
7 Reg 11(2)(a)(ii) CS(MASC) Regs
8 Reg 11(2)(a)(v) CS(MASC) Regs
9 Reg 12(2) CS(MASC) Regs
10 Reg 12(3) CS(MASC) Regs

2. Basic protected income
11 Reg 11(1)(a)-(kk) CS(MASC) Regs
12 Reg 11(3) and (4) CS(MASC) Regs
13 Reg 11(1)(b) CS(MASC) Regs
14 Sch 3 para 3(1) CS(MASC) Regs
15 Reg 11(1)(b) CS(MASC) Regs
16 Reg 18(1)(b) CS(MASC) Regs
17 Reg 1 CS(MASC) Regs; reg 3 HB Regs or reg 3 HB(SPC) Regs
18 Reg 74(1) and (2) HB Regs or reg 55(1) and (2) HB(SPC) Regs
19 Reg 63(9) HB Regs
20 Reg 11(1)(j) CS(MASC) Regs
21 Sch 1 para 5(4) CS(NIRA) Regs
22 Reg 11(1)(kk) CS(MASC) Regs

3. Total protected income
23 Reg 11(1)(l) CS(MASC) Regs

4. The maintenance payable
24 Reg 12(2) CS(MASC) Regs
25 Reg 12(3) CS(MASC) Regs
26 Reg 22(3) CS(MASC) Regs

Chapter 14

. . . .

Shared care ('old rules')

This chapter covers:
1. What is shared care (below)
2. Care shared between separated parents (p272)
3. Care shared between a parent and another person (p281)
4. Care shared between two people who are not parents (p284)
5. Three persons with care (p285)
6. Care provided in part by the local authority (p285)
7. The maintenance requirement is met in full (p286)

1. **What is shared care**

We use the term 'shared care' to describe a situation where there is more than one person looking after a particular child and those people live in different households. If the people providing care live in the same household (see p22), this is not shared care.[1] The legislation only acknowledges shared care where more than one person has 'day-to-day care' of a child.

Day-to-day care

There is no definition of 'day-to-day care' set down for deciding whether someone is a person with care. Therefore, an everyday definition can be used (see p20). A person who is not a parent can apply to receive child maintenance only if s/he has day-to-day care of a child. Parents with care and non-resident parents can both apply for a maintenance assessment, although there are some exceptions (see p36) as well as rules governing which application takes precedence (see p43). There can be more than one person with care of a child.

However, for the purposes of shared care in the maintenance formula, a person will be treated as having day-to-day care of a child only if s/he cares for the child for at least 104 nights in the 12-month period ending with the 'relevant week'.[2] See p209 for a definition of relevant week. If 12 months have not passed since there was a shared care situation, or since the parents separated, this does not mean that there is no pattern – see p271.[3]

Another period, ending with the relevant week, may be used if that would be more representative of the current arrangement.[4] The number of nights of care in that period must be in the same ratio as 104 nights is to 12 months – ie, 52 nights in six months, 26 nights in three months, 13 nights in two months, nine nights in a month. Examples in Child Support Agency (CSA) guidance of situations where it might be appropriate to use a period other than the previous 12 months include a recent relationship breakdown, a court ruling on residence or contact, or the person now providing day-to-day care having been abroad, in prison, in hospital, away from home or otherwise unable to provide care.[5] If the arrangement has simply been renegotiated between the two parents, written acceptance of this should be provided so that the CSA knows that this is now the current arrangement and not a temporary change. A future period cannot be used. The period should generally end with the relevant week, but does not have to.[6] Therefore, if a change occurs after the relevant week, a supersession will usually have to be sought (see p358).

The parent does not have to provide continuous care throughout a period of 24 hours, but must usually be providing care during the night.[7] Where a child is a boarder at boarding school or a hospital inpatient, whoever would otherwise have day-to-care is treated as providing care. The person who is treated as having day-to-day care for such periods need not be the person who pays the school fees.[8] Parents should keep a note of the nights the child(ren) spends with them and, in case of dispute, be willing to supply further evidence – eg, a diary. The CSA – and any subsequent First-tier Tribunal appeal – must determine the amount of day-to-day care provided by each person on the basis of available evidence.[9]

Fewer than 104 nights in the year

If a non-resident parent is providing some care, but to a lesser extent than that described as day-to-day care, he is still liable to pay child maintenance and the level of care he provides is not acknowledged by the child support formula. Therefore, such a non-resident parent is expected to contribute the same amount of child maintenance as if he were not looking after the child at all. This means, for example, that fathers who have their children to stay every other weekend will pay the same level of maintenance as those who do not.

A father who looks after the child(ren) for all of the school holidays would not be accepted as a person with care if the time spent with the children was assessed over 12 months. However, the father could request a supersession during the summer holidays on the grounds that he is now a parent with care and a shorter period should then be used to calculate who has day-to-day care in order to reflect the current arrangement. It is unlikely that this would be grounds for supersession if the six-week period had already been taken into account when averaging over the year for the current assessment. However, if the arrangement for the holiday had not been known at the time, this may be successful. If not, an appeal should be considered (see p369).

If day-to-day care were to be re-assessed over this shorter period, the father would become the parent with care and the mother the non-resident parent. Indeed, the father could then apply for maintenance from the mother. **Note:** the period used to assess day-to-day care ends with the relevant week which precedes the request for a supersession – see p358. Therefore, the request should not be made right at the beginning of the summer holiday.

On the other hand, if it is held that a supersession cannot take place, such a father technically remains the non-resident parent over the holiday when he has the child(ren) full time. He would be liable to continue paying the mother the full level of maintenance even for those weeks the children spend with him. Parents in such a situation could try to come to some voluntary arrangement whereby the mother pays back some or all of the maintenance, but this may not be financially possible, especially if she is in receipt of income support.

More than one person with care

Where there are two people in different households who both have day-to-day care of a qualifying child, either can make an application for child maintenance as long as both or neither has parental responsibility (see p15) for the child.[10] If only one of them has parental responsibility, the person with that responsibility must be the applicant. This means that if the person with parental responsibility decides not to apply, the other person with care could lose out on child maintenance.

If both persons with care can, and do, make an application, only one will be accepted (see p43).[11] Which application is accepted is largely a technicality, however, as this does not change the status of the people involved nor the way in which the assessment is carried out. It does, though, affect who can cancel the assessment (see p334).

The basic formula is varied to take into account the fact that there is more than one person with care. The way in which the formula is adjusted depends on which people share the care.

---

2. Care shared between separated parents

Where it is accepted that both parents have day-to-day care (ie, there is a shared care situation), one of the parents with care still has to be treated as a non-resident parent in order to make an assessment.[12] CPAG tried to challenge this rule in the past, but a child support commissioner decided that this is the correct interpretation of the law.[13]

Where parents share care, only a parent who provides day-to-day care as defined above – ie, care of at least 104 nights out of 12 months or the equivalent (see p270) – can be deemed non-resident (see below). In almost all cases, the parents with care will both be providing care for at least 104 nights out of 12 months and, therefore, one has to be deemed non-resident. However, in some cases, although care is shared according to its everyday meaning, both parents are not providing day-to-day care according to the definition. For example, if the mother provides care during the day but the children sleep at their father's home, each cares for the children an equal number of hours a week, but because they are not providing day-to-day care, the shared care rules cannot be used to deem one of them non-resident. No maintenance assessment should be carried out. In a case like this, the Child Support Agency (CSA) may try to argue that the mother is the non-resident parent because she does not have day-to-day care; if this happens, she should appeal on the basis that the day-to-day care definition only legally has to be used in establishing whether there is shared care, not in deciding whether someone is a person with care, when a different definition can be used (see p270).

In cases where a parent with care is treated as non-resident, an assessment is carried out to find out how much child maintenance s/he has to pay to the other parent. As the remaining parent with care does not have to pay child maintenance, this can result in one parent paying child maintenance to another who has equal responsibility for the child.

Who is treated as the non-resident parent

The parent who provides day-to-day care to a 'lesser extent' is treated as the non-resident parent.[14] A **'lesser extent'** could be interpreted as meaning either for fewer *nights* per week on average or fewer *hours* per week on average. The number of nights will be considered first by the CSA, but it should be argued on the basis of hours if this would give a fairer result. Indeed, it could be said that nights involve less care than days. For example, if one parent had a school-age child from 4pm Friday to 8.30am Monday (three nights), this could be argued to be as much care as the other parent who is with the child from 4pm Monday to 8.30am Friday (four nights). It might be possible to argue that the degree of responsibility, as well as the amount of time, is relevant to determining the extent of the care – eg, who buys the child's clothes, who attends school functions or arranges visits to the dentist. These issues need not be raised if both parents agree that the number of nights of care fairly determines the question.

It is helpful if parents keep a record of the time the children spend in each household, especially if there are changes to the usual pattern of care. The extent of care is measured over the period explained on p270, usually the last year or since a change in the arrangements.

If the parents provide care for an equal amount of time, the parent who does *not* receive child benefit is treated as the non-resident parent.[15]As the right to receive child maintenance follows the receipt of child benefit, this may lead to competing claims for child benefit. If more than one person makes a claim for child benefit, an order of priority is used or, if this does not apply, HM Revenue and Customs makes a (non-appealable) decision.

For more information on the priority rules for child benefit, see CPAG's *Welfare Benefits and Tax Credits Handbook*.

If care is shared equally and neither parent receives child benefit, the CSA decides who is the principal carer.[16]

Example: shared care and a deemed non-resident parent

Marcia and Nathan are divorced. They have two children, Oscar (7) and Patrick (5). Every fortnight the children spend five nights with Nathan. The rest of the time they live with Marcia.

Marcia has the children 9 out of every 14 nights = 234 nights a year.

Nathan has the children 5 out of every 14 nights = 130 nights a year.

Do both parents have day-to-day care? Yes.

But Nathan looks after the boys to a lesser extent. Therefore, Nathan is deemed a non-resident parent and an assessment is carried out to decide how much child maintenance he should pay to Marcia.

Marcia remains a parent with care and has no liability to pay child maintenance.

There may be cases where each child of a family spends a different amount of time with the two parents – ie, the mother may be deemed the non-resident parent for one child and the father for the other. If this is the case, the situation is similar to that of a divided family in which different children live full time with different parents (also known as 'split care', see p248). Two completely separate assessments are carried out: if the mother cares for the daughter for the greater amount of time, the daughter's child maintenance will be assessed with the father as the deemed non-resident parent; child maintenance for the son, who spends more time with the father, will be assessed with the mother as the deemed non-resident parent.

Calculating child maintenance

When two parents share care, there is a remaining parent with care and a deemed non-resident parent (see p273). The five steps of the formula described in Chapters 9 to 13 are still applicable in calculating how much maintenance the deemed non-resident parent must pay. However, the standard formula is adjusted to take into account the time that the so-called non-resident parent looks after the child(ren).

Step 1: maintenance requirement

Only one maintenance requirement is calculated (see Chapter 9).

Example: maintenance requirement
The situation is as described in the above example. Marcia has remarried and looks after Oscar (7) and Patrick (5) for nine nights every fortnight.
Maintenance requirement with Marcia as parent with care:

		£
Personal allowances	Marcia	64.30
	Oscar	56.11
	Patrick	56.11
Family premium		17.30
Sub-total		193.82
Less child benefit		33.20
Maintenance requirement		**160.62**

Step 2: exempt income

When calculating the exempt income of the parents, a proportion of the personal allowance for the child (plus any disabled child premium) is included to reflect the average number of nights a week the parent has care of the child.[17] Similarly, only a proportion of the family premium is allowed unless another of the parent's children lives in the household all week (see below for the situation where there is another child).[18] See the example on p286 where the care of more than one child is shared, but the children spend a different number of nights with the parent.

For full details of exempt income, see Chapter 10.

Example: exempt income for shared care when no child lives in the household for seven nights a week
Marcia looks after Oscar and Patrick for an average of 4.5 nights a week.
Nathan looks after Oscar and Patrick for an average of 2.5 nights a week.
Marcia married Gareth recently. Their mortgage payments are £120 a week.

Marcia's exempt income:		£	
Personal allowances	Marcia	64.30	
	Oscar	36.07	(for 4.5 days)
	Patrick	36.07	(for 4.5 days)
Family premium		11.12	(for 4.5 days)
Housing costs		120.00	
Total exempt income		**267.56**	

Nathan lives on his own when the children are not with him. His privately rented flat costs £65 a week. He lives within a few kilometres of his work.

Nathan's exempt income:		£	
Personal allowances	Nathan	64.30	
	Oscar	20.04	(for 2.5 days)
	Patrick	20.04	(for 2.5 days)
Family premium		6.18	(for 2.5 days)
Housing costs		65.00	
Total exempt income		**175.56**	

See the example on p286 for the apportionment of premiums where the children spend a different number of nights with each parent.

Premiums where there is a shared-care child and another child

This section only applies if there is a child who lives in the household all week, as well as child(ren) who are there part time. If the household includes only the children whose care is shared and stepchildren, the premiums are apportioned as above. Go to Step 3.

If another child of the parent lives in the household for seven nights a week, this child can be either another qualifying child or a joint child with a new partner. The family premium is either included in full or halved.[19] It will be included in full if:

- the parent qualifies for the family premium for the shared child(ren) (ie, receives child benefit for her/him, or where no one receives child benefit, has claimed child benefit or is the person with whom the child usually lives); we call this shared-care children 'with child benefit'; *or*
- there is another qualifying child (of that parent) in the household; *or*
- a new partner cannot support the joint child (see p202).

The following outlines the various permutations.

- A lone parent with shared-care children (with or without child benefit) and another qualifying child: full family premium.
- A parent with shared-care children (with child benefit) and a joint child with a new partner: full family premium. Note that the personal allowance for the joint child is halved if the new partner can contribute to her/his support.
- A parent with shared-care children (no child benefit) and a joint child with a new partner: the family premium is halved if the new partner can contribute to the support of the joint child, but is included in full if the partner cannot (see p202).

Example: exempt income if there is shared care and a joint child

Marcia still has the qualifying children, Oscar and Patrick, 9 out of 14 nights (an average of 4.5 nights a week) and receives child benefit for them. Marcia and her husband, Gareth, now have a baby daughter, Megan. Gareth earns £450 a week. Their mortgage payments are £120 per week.

Marcia's exempt income:		£	
Personal allowances	Marcia	64.30	
	Oscar	36.07	(4.5 days)
	Patrick	36.07	(4.5 days)
	Megan (half*)	28.06	
Family premium (in full**)		17.30	
Housing costs		120.00	
Total exempt income		**301.80**	

* As Gareth earns £450 a week, he can afford to contribute to his daughter's maintenance and, therefore, only half of Megan's personal allowance is included (see p202 for details of the means test).

** Because Megan lives in the household all week, the family premium is not apportioned according to how many nights Oscar and Patrick stay. Instead, consideration has to be given to whether Marcia is entitled to the family premium as a result of looking after Oscar and Patrick. As she receives child benefit for them, she is entitled to the full rate of the premium. (If her ex-husband received the child benefit, Marcia would not be due the full family premium for them. Consideration would then be given to Megan and, since Gareth can afford to maintain half of Megan, the family premium would be halved.)

Step 3: assessable income

This step is exactly the same as for other situations (see Chapter 11).

Example: assessable income

Before the birth of her daughter, Marcia's income is net earnings of £145 a week. Her husband's earnings are not taken into account in the net income calculation and neither is any child benefit.

Marcia's assessable income:	£
Net income	145.00 (net earnings)
Less exempt income	267.56 (from example on p275)
Assessable income	**Nil**

Nathan takes home £220 a week, after £40 superannuation is deducted. Only half of the superannuation is taken into account (see p212).

Nathan's assessable income:	£
Net income	240.00 (net earnings)
Less exempt income	175.56 (from example on p275)
Assessable income	**64.44**

Step 4: proposed maintenance[20]

The proposed maintenance step is carried out in full for each parent in order to obtain the proposed maintenance from the deemed non-resident parent and a notional proposed maintenance from the remaining parent with care. When calculating the proposed maintenance from each parent, the assessable income of the other parent is taken into account in the same way as if both were non-resident parents (see the example on p242).

The amount of the deemed non-resident parent's proposed maintenance and the notional amount of proposed maintenance from the remaining parent with care are then added together to give the joint proposed maintenance. The deemed non-resident parent is taken to have already contributed a proportion of the maintenance in kind. His assumed contribution is the proportion of the joint proposed maintenance that is equivalent to the proportion of time the children spend with him. The proportion of time the parent spends with his children is given in terms of the average number of nights per week divided by seven. The average number of nights per week does not have to be a round figure; it is calculated to two decimal figures – eg, if a deemed non-resident parent has the child one week in three, the average number of nights per week is 2.33. If there is more than one child, the total average number of nights per week is divided by the number of children – eg, if a father has one child two nights a week and another child four nights a week, the average number of nights per week is three.

This contribution in kind is then subtracted from the non-resident parent's proposed maintenance to give an adjusted proposed maintenance figure. If this produces a figure less than zero, no child maintenance is payable.[21] The non-resident parent has more than contributed his proportion of the total proposed maintenance in kind by providing a certain amount of care.

The minimum payment rule (see p172) applies to an adjusted proposed maintenance figure of between £0 and £6.50.[22] Therefore, all deemed non-resident parents calculated to pay child maintenance of up to £6.50 are exempted from the payment (as they have at least part of the family premium included in their protected income calculation).

Example: proposed maintenance

As Marcia has no assessable income, the proposed maintenance is 50 per cent of Nathan's assessable income (see p277):

50% x £64.44 = £32.22

This is less than the maintenance requirement of £160.62 (see p275), so £32.22 is the proposed maintenance.

As there is no proposed maintenance from Marcia, the joint proposed maintenance is also £32.22.

Nathan contributes a proportion of the care:

2.5 + 2.5/(7 x 2) nights in the average week = 35.71%

(2 represents the number of children for whom care is shared.)

As he contributes 35.71% of the care, he is taken as contributing 35.71% of the joint proposed maintenance in kind:

$35.71\% \times £32.22 = £11.51$

Nathan is deemed to have contributed £11.51 and is, therefore, due to pay the remainder of his proposed maintenance (if protected income allows).

Adjusted proposed maintenance = £32.22 − £11.51 = £20.71

(If the caring roles were reversed and Nathan had the children for 4.5 nights a week, the proposed maintenance from Marcia, as a deemed non-resident parent, to Nathan would be nil, as Marcia has no assessable income.)

The above example gives the most straightforward shared care situation where only the deemed non-resident parent has assessable income and even then not enough to meet the maintenance requirement. See p286 for an example of the additional element calculation where both parents have assessable income.

However, any of the situations explained in Chapter 12 can apply to the assessments carried out for parents sharing care. In effect, two separate assessments are being carried out up to Step 4 to give a proposed maintenance from the deemed non-resident parent and a notional proposed maintenance from the parent with care. First, arrive at the proposed maintenance for each parent in the same way as for non-resident parents before adding together the two amounts of proposed maintenance to give the joint proposed maintenance. Only at this stage is the non-resident parent's proposed maintenance reduced in recognition of his payment in kind.

The shared care calculation is complicated, but there is a certain amount of logic to it. Both parents have a liability to maintain and, in theory, maintenance is due from each of them for the nights that the child spends with the other parent. For the child there is a notional amount of maintenance available per week. Imagine the joint proposed maintenance divided by seven to give a daily rate of maintenance. Each night of care provided is equivalent to having paid this amount of maintenance. A deemed non-resident parent has to make payments of child maintenance if the amount equivalent to the number of nights' care he contributes does not exceed his portion of the proposed maintenance.

However, the calculation can mean that the parent with a lower income who has the child for less time can end up paying maintenance to a parent with a higher income. Although this is equally true in standard cases, in cases of shared care the deemed non-resident parent may find that he does not have what he considers to be sufficient income left for those days when he is responsible for the child. In such a situation, the deemed non-resident parent on a low income will never receive any maintenance from a parent with care with a higher income. Parents may find this difficult to understand, and it may lead to competing claims for child benefit (see p273).

Step 5: protected income

Protected income is still the final stage of the calculation (see Chapter 13).[23] The deemed non-resident parent may not be able to afford the proposed adjusted maintenance. When assessing the basic protected income, the allowances for the child are adjusted as for exempt income (see p275) to represent the proportion of the average week that a child spends with the non-resident parent.[24] If there is more than one shared care child and they spend different nights with the family, the family premium is included in proportion to the average number of nights per week that at least one qualifying child is in the household.[25] However, if another child lives in the household on a full-time basis, the premium is included in full.

Example: shared care and protected income

Nathan lives on his own when his children are not with him. His rent is £65 a week and his council tax is £342 a year. He earns £240 net a week. He has Oscar and Patrick for five nights per fortnight. Can Nathan afford to pay the proposed maintenance of £20.71 (see p278)?

The 30% cap does not reduce the proposed maintenance as:

30% x £240 = £72

Therefore, the proposed maintenance remains at £20.71.

Basic protected income:		£	
Personal allowances	Nathan	64.30	
	Oscar	20.03	(for 2.5 days)
	Patrick	20.03	(for 2.5 days)
Family premium		6.18	(for 2.5 days)
Housing costs		65.00	
Council tax		6.58	
Margin		30.00	
Basic protected income		**212.12**	
Additional protected income:			
Total family income		240.00 (net earnings)	
Less basic protected income		212.12	
Excess total family income		27.88	
(15% x £27.88)		4.18	
Total protected income		**216.30**	
(£212.12 + £4.18)			
Total family income		240.00	
Less proposed maintenance		20.71	
Disposable income		**219.29**	

This disposable income is above the total protected income level of £216.30. Nathan can pay the proposed maintenance of £20.71 a week.

3. **Care shared between a parent and another person**

Once again, both the parent and the other person involved must provide day-to-day care (see p270) and live in different households. The way in which this situation is treated depends on which person with care provides day-to-day care to the lesser extent (see p273).

The parent provides care for less time

Where there are two persons with care but the one who is a parent of the child provides care for less time, the parent with care, for the purposes of the formula, is again deemed to be non-resident.[26] Therefore, there is no longer a parent with care, but a person with care and a deemed non-resident parent.

In most cases, the second parent will also be involved as a non-resident parent. For example, the grandmother has the child Monday night to Thursday night (the person with care), the mother has the child Friday to Sunday nights (deemed non-resident parent) and the father has the child for only two weeks in the summer (non-resident parent).

Both non-resident parents are liable to pay maintenance to the person with care. Therefore, two separate assessments are carried out, one for each of the liable parents as long as an effective application has been made in each case. The person with care who is actually going to receive the child maintenance cannot apply if she (eg, the grandmother) does not have parental responsibility while the deemed non-resident parent (eg, the mother) does have that responsibility (see p15).

How child maintenance is calculated

In the case of the non-resident parent who does not participate in the care of the child, the assessment is the same as it would be if there were no shared care arrangement. The fact that the care of the child is shared between two people does not affect the amount that the non-resident parent can afford to pay. However, where an application is only made against the non-resident parent, and not the parent with care, the maintenance requirement is not halved as it would be when an application is made against one of two truly non-resident parents (see p180).[27]

At the proposed maintenance step of the calculation, the assessable income of the deemed non-resident parent is added to the actual non-resident parent's assessable income to give the parents' joint assessable income, in the same way as if both parents were truly non-resident (see p242).

The deemed non-resident parent's calculation follows that described above for a deemed non-resident parent sharing care with the other parent. The only difference is that instead of adding a notional proposed maintenance for the parent with care, the actual proposed maintenance of the non-resident parent is used to obtain joint proposed maintenance.[28] Where there is no non-resident parent (eg, he has gone abroad or is deceased) or where the non-resident parent's assessable income is unknown (eg, he has not been traced) the deemed non-resident parent just pays child maintenance for those days for which she is not caring for the child(ren).[29]

Example: care shared between a parent to a lesser extent and another person to a greater extent

Gran, who is a widow, has Beverley (15) for four nights a week and her mother has her for the remaining three nights. As the mother looks after Beverley for less time than Gran, the mother is deemed to be non-resident. The mother has parental responsibility and receives child benefit.

The maintenance requirement is £85.56 (see example on p180)

The mother's assessable income is £42 a week. (When working out her exempt income, 3/7ths of the personal allowance for Beverley and 3/7ths family premium are included.)

The non-resident father's assessable income = £57

Parents' joint assessable income = £42 + £57 = £99

50% of joint assessable income = £49.50

This is below the maintenance requirement and, therefore, the 50 per cent calculation applies to each parent.

Father's proposed maintenance = 50% x £57 = £28.50

Mother's proposed maintenance = 50% x £42 = £21

Joint proposed maintenance = £28.50 + £21 = £49.50

The mother provides three out of seven nights' care = 42.86%

This is equivalent to paying 42.86% of £49.50 = £21.22 a week maintenance.

The mother's adjusted proposed maintenance: £21 – £21.22 = nil

As she is exempt from the minimum payment, she is not liable to pay any child maintenance as her contribution in kind outweighs the financial contribution.

Assuming the protected income calculation allows it, the father pays £28.50 a week to the grandmother, but nothing to the mother.

See p286 for the assessment where the parents have higher assessable incomes.

If the father emigrated or no application was made against him, the mother would pay 4/7ths of her proposed maintenance to the grandmother, assuming that the protected income calculation did not reduce this.

The mother's proposed maintenance would still be £21. She is still providing care three nights a week or 42.86% of the proposed maintenance in kind: 42.86% x £21 = £9

This leaves her with adjusted proposed maintenance of £21 − £9 = £12 a week to the grandmother. The protected income calculation has to be carried out and would include 3/7ths of Beverley's personal allowance and 3/7ths family premium.

Maintenance paid by the non-resident parent cannot be split between two persons with care where one is a deemed non-resident parent. The entire amount of child maintenance from the non-resident parent is paid to the remaining person with care. In other words, a parent with care who shares care for the lesser time can never receive child maintenance from a non-resident parent, no matter the size of the bill being paid.

This may seem illogical, particularly where the application has been made by the parent with care or where, although applications have been made by both persons with care, the application from the parent has been given priority (see p43). A parent with care who applies to the Child Support Agency (CSA) for maintenance from the non-resident parent, but ends up being deemed non-resident and paying maintenance, might therefore decide to have the assessment cancelled (see p334).

The parent provides care for greater amount of time

If a parent does a greater proportion of the caring than another person with care, she remains a parent with care for the purposes of the maintenance assessment.[30] This also applies where the parent provides care to the same extent as someone else, but the parent receives the child benefit. There is no deemed non-resident parent. Instead, there is usually a parent with care, another person with care and a non-resident parent. It can also cover the rare situation where a person cannot technically be a person with care even though s/he is providing care of at least two nights a week on average (see p20).

If only one of the persons with care has applied for a maintenance assessment, that person will receive all the child maintenance payable by the non-resident parent.[31] This also applies where both persons with care have made an application, but only one has been accepted. There is an order of priority on which applications will be accepted (see p44). It also covers cases where the second carer cannot make an application – eg, s/he does not have parental responsibility or s/he does not share a home with the child.

However, if a request is made to the CSA by *either* of the people looking after the child(ren), the child maintenance may be divided between the two of them in proportion to the day-to-day care provided.[32] The ratio of care provided does not have to be calculated on the basis of the number of nights a child spends with the carer. An alternative method could be argued for if this would give a fairer division of the maintenance (see p272).

There is no specific format needed for a request for maintenance to be divided. It is advisable to state in writing on the maintenance application form, or in a letter, that part of the maintenance should go to another person. There is no time limit for making the request.

The decision to share the child maintenance assessment between the persons with care is a discretionary decision made by the CSA on behalf of the Secretary of State for Work and Pensions. The CSA must consider the interests of the child, the current care arrangements and all representations received about the payment proposals.[33] The decision cannot be appealed.

The alternative is for the persons with care to come to a voluntary arrangement, but this may not be possible if the person who has applied is a parent with care on IS or income-based JSA.

Example: care shared between a parent to a greater extent and another person to a lesser extent

If the caring responsibilities of the grandmother and mother in the example on p281 are swapped, so that the mother has Beverley for four nights a week, the calculation is as follows.

The mother now remains the parent with care and the grandmother is still a person with care. (This also applies where care is shared equally but the mother is in receipt of child benefit.)

The father's proposed maintenance remains £28.50 a week.

However, this time the mother will receive the full amount if she makes the application for maintenance and there is no request to split the payment. If there is such a request and it is granted, then the mother will receive 4/7ths – ie, £16.29 – and the grandmother the remainder – ie, £12.21 a week.

---

4. **Care shared between two people who are not parents**

The situation may arise where two people living in different households each have day-to-day care (see p270) of a child of whom neither is the parent. The same rules apply as those where care is shared between a parent for the greater part of the time and another person for the rest of the time (see p283)[34] – ie, if a request is made by either person, the maintenance payable by each non-resident parent may be divided between the carers in proportion to the amount of care being provided. If no request is made, the full amount goes to the applicant.

In this situation, it is likely that there are two non-resident parents and, therefore, maintenance could be paid by both. If one of the persons with care chooses to apply for maintenance from only one of the non-resident parents, there is no reason why the second person with care cannot apply for child maintenance from the other non-resident parent.

5. **Three persons with care**

As a person with care has to look after the child for a minimum of two nights a week on average, there can be no more than three persons with care for any child. However, there may be a combination of parents and others providing the care as follows (in each case the first person provides the greatest amount of care and the third, the least).

- Parent, parent, other person – this situation is not covered specifically, although the intention must be to deem the second parent non-resident and for maintenance to be paid by him to the applicant.
- Parent, other person, parent – the second parent is deemed non-resident and maintenance is paid by him to the applicant.
- Other person, parent, parent – the first parent is deemed non-resident and maintenance is paid by him to the applicant, as well as by the second actual non-resident parent.
- Parent, other person, other person – the applicant receives maintenance from the non-resident parent or it may be apportioned on request.
- Other person, parent, other person – this is not explicitly covered, but we presume that the intention is that the parent would be deemed non-resident; there would, of course, be a second parent who is non-resident.
- Other person, other person, parent – the parent with care will be deemed non-resident and there would also be a second parent who is non-resident.
- Three other people – maintenance from both non-resident parents may be apportioned on request.

6. **Care provided in part by the local authority**

A local authority cannot be a person with care.[35] Therefore, if a child is in the care of the local authority for seven nights a week, no child maintenance is payable by the non-resident parents. There may be cases where a child is not being provided with care by the local authority all the time, but only for part of the time. If the local authority care provides less than day-to-day care (see p270), such a level of care can be ignored.

However, if the care provided by the local authority amounts to day-to-day care, child maintenance is not payable for any night that the child is in that local authority care.[36] Instead, the person with care who looks after the child for the remainder of the time receives reduced child maintenance from the non-resident parent. The maintenance payment is reduced to correspond to the number of nights per week that the child is in that person's care – eg, if the child is in local authority care for five nights a week, the person with care will receive two-sevenths of the amount of the maintenance assessment from the non-resident parent.

Where there is more than one qualifying child and the local authority provides some day-to-day care for at least one of the children, again the maintenance payable is reduced.[37] For example, a person with care looks after two children: one spends the whole week with the person with care, the other child spends four nights in local authority care and three nights with the person with care. To work out the maintenance payable in these circumstances, calculate the total number of nights spent with the person with care per week, and divide this by seven times the number of qualifying children. In this case 10 (7+3) out of 14 (7x2) nights are spent with the parent with care. The maintenance payable is ten-fourteenths (or 71.43 per cent) of the maintenance assessed.

7. **The maintenance requirement is met in full**

The calculations described earlier in this chapter hold true when the maintenance requirement is met in full. If 50 per cent of the parents' joint assessable income is greater than the maintenance requirement, the additional element calculation has to be done. See Chapter 12.

Example: care shared by parents

This is the same family as in the examples on pp274-280.

Oscar (now aged 9) now spends every other week with Nathan, while Patrick (6) still spends five days a fortnight with him. Marcia still receives child benefit for both boys and, therefore, Nathan is still deemed to be a non-resident parent of Oscar as well as Patrick. A calculation, therefore, has to be done to assess how much Nathan pays Marcia. However, in assessing Nathan's actual contribution, a notional contribution from Marcia has to be calculated.

Nathan's take-home earnings have risen to £450 a week and his superannuation contribution is now £50 a week.

Marcia has increased her hours and now earns £360 net a week. Her husband, Gareth, earns £450 net a week. Their mortgage payments are £120 a week. Their daughter Megan is two years old.

Step 1: the maintenance requirement = £160.62 (see p275)

Step 2: exempt income

Marcia's exempt income is as on p276 except that Oscar's personal allowance is now included for 3.5 days (£28.06) instead of 4.5 days (£36.07) so now equals £293.79

Nathan's exempt income:

		£
Personal allowances	Nathan	64.30
	Oscar	28.06 (for 3.5 days)
	Patrick	20.04 (for 2.5 days)
Family premium*		8.65 (for 3.5 days)
Housing costs		65.00
Total exempt income		**186.90**

* The family premium is included in proportion to the average number of nights a week that care is provided for a child. In this case, Patrick stays with Nathan on nights that Oscar is there – ie, care is provided for at least one child for an average of 3.5 nights a week and for the other 3.5 nights Nathan is on his own. However, if the children stayed different nights, 6/7ths of the premiums would be included.[38]

Step 3: assessable income

Marcia's assessable income:

		£
Net income	Earnings	360.00
Less exempt income		293.79
Assessable income		**66.21**

Nathan's assessable income:

Net income	Earnings*	475.00
Less exempt income		185.90
Assessable income		**289.10**

* Only half of the superannuation is taken into account.

Step 4: proposed maintenance

Joint assessable income = £66.21 + £289.10 = £355.31

50% x £355.31 = £177.66.

This is above the maintenance requirement of £160.62 and, therefore, an additional element calculation must be done (see p239).

Marcia's notional proposed maintenance:

Basic element = £160.62 x £66.21/355.31 = £29.93

Basic assessable income = £29.93 x 2 = £59.86

Additional assessable income = £66.21 – £59.86 = £6.35

Additional element = 20% x £6.35 = £1.27

Notional proposed maintenance = £29.93 + £1.27 = £31.20

Nathan's proposed maintenance to Marcia:

Basic element = £160.62 x £289.10/£355.31 = £130.69

Basic assessable income = £130.69 x 2 = £261.38

Additional assessable income = £289.10 – £261.38 = £27.72

Additional element = 20% x £27.72 = £5.54

Proposed maintenance = £130.69 + £5.54 = £136.23

Joint proposed maintenance = £31.20 + £136.23 = £167.43

Nathan contributes in kind $= \dfrac{3.5 + 2.5}{7 \times 2}$ = 42.86% of the care.

This is equivalent to £71.73 (42.86% x £167.43)

Nathan's proposed maintenance after taking into account his portion of the care = £136.23 – £71.73 = £64.50 a week.

This is below the maximum payment (see p240).

Step 5:protected income

This follows the example on p280, except that now Nathan's income has risen, and half of Oscar's personal allowance and half the family premium are included (see p280).

There could be times when there is more then one child and because the care is shared in different ways for the different children, each parent would be the person with care for one child and the deemed non-resident parent for the other. In this case, two shared care calculations would have to be carried out. This would happen in the situation described in the above example if Nathan were in receipt of the child benefit for Oscar.

Example: care shared between a parent and another person

Gran has Beverley (15) for four nights a week and her mother has her for the remaining three nights. The mother is, therefore, deemed to be a non-resident parent. When the mother's assessable income was £42 and the father's was £57, the mother's child maintenance liability was nil while the father's proposed maintenance was £28.50 (see p281).

The mother's assessable income has increased to £140

Joint assessable income = £140 + £57 = £197

50 per cent of joint assessable income = 50% x £197 = £98.50

This is above the maintenance requirement of £85.56 (see p180) and so an additional element calculation has to be done.

Father's proposed maintenance:

Basic element = £85.56 x £57/£197 = £24.76

Basic assessable income = £24.76 x 2 = £49.52

Additional assessable income = £57 – £49.52 = £7.48

Additional element = £7.48 x 15% = £1.12

Proposed maintenance = £24.76 + £1.12 = £25.88

Mother's proposed maintenance:

Basic element = £85.56 x £140/£197 = £60.80

Basic assessable income = £60.80 x 2 = £121.60

Additional assessable income = £140 – £121.60 = £18.40

Additional element = £18.40 x 15% = £2.76

Proposed maintenance = £60.80 + £2.76 = £63.56

Joint proposed maintenance = £25.88 + £63.56 = £89.44

The mother provides care three out of seven nights = 42.86% of the care. This is equivalent to paying 42.86% of £89.44 – ie, £38.33 a week maintenance. The mother's adjusted proposed maintenance = £63.56 – £38.33 = £25.23

Assuming the protected calculations allow these figures, Gran now receives £25.23 from the mother and £25.88 from the father, a total of £51.11 (instead of the £28.50 from the non-resident father).

If the non-resident father's assessable income had been £207 and the mother's £140 a week, again an additional element calculation would have been done.

Father's proposed maintenance would be £66.78

Mother's proposed maintenance would be £45.16

Joint proposed maintenance = £66.78 + £45.16 = £111.94

The mother provides care three out of seven nights = 42.86% of the care.

This is equivalent to paying 42.86% x £111.94 = £47.98 a week maintenance.

The mother, therefore, does not have to pay any maintenance as her contribution in kind (£47.98) outweighs her financial liability (£45.16). Despite the fact that her assessable income is the same, her liability has been reduced to nil as a result of the increased liability of the father.

The father still has to pay his proposed maintenance, assuming this does not bring his disposable income below the protected income level. The maintenance of £66.78 is paid to the grandmother.

Notes

1. What is shared care
1 Regs 20(1)(a) and 24(1)(a) CS(MASC) Regs
2 Reg 1(2) CS(MASC) Regs
3 CCS/2885/2005
4 Reg 1(2) CS(MASC) Regs; CCS/6/1994
5 DMG para 6022
6 CCS/128/2001
7 Regs 1(2) and 20(1) CS(MASC) Regs; CCS/449/1995
8 CCS/12686/1996
9 CCS/11728/1996
10 s5(1) CSA 1991
11 s5(2) CSA 1991

2. Care shared between separated parents
12 Reg 20(2) and (3) CS(MASC) Regs
13 CCS/13455/1996
14 Reg 20(2)(a) CS(MASC) Regs

15 Reg 20(2)(b)(i) CS(MASC) Regs
16 Reg 20(2)(b)(ii) CS(MASC) Regs
17 Reg 9(4) CS(MASC) Regs
18 Reg 9(3) CS(MASC) Regs
19 Reg 9(1)(f) and (2)(c)(iv) CS(MASC) Regs
20 Reg 20(3) and (4) CS(MASC) Regs
21 Reg 20(5) CS(MASC) Regs
22 Reg 20(6) CS(MASC) Regs
23 Reg 20(6) CS(MASC) Regs
24 Reg 11(3) and (4) CS(MASC) Regs
25 DMG paras 3201-03

3. Care shared between a parent and another person
26 Reg 20 CS(MASC) Regs
27 Reg 19(1) CS(MASC) Regs
28 Reg 20(4)(i) CS(MASC) Regs
29 Reg 20(4)(ii) CS(MASC) Regs
30 Reg 24(1) CS(MASC) Regs
31 Reg 24(2)(a) CS(MASC) Regs
32 Reg 24(2)(b) CS(MASC) Regs
33 Reg 24(2)(c) CS(MASC) Regs

4. Care shared between two people who are not parents
34 Reg 24 CS(MASC) Regs

6. Care provided in part by the local authority
35 Reg 51 CS(MAP) Regs
36 Reg 25 CS(MASC) Regs
37 Reg 25(3) CS(MASC) Regs

7. The maintenance requirement is met in full
38 Reg 9(3) and (4) CS(MASC) Regs

Chapter 15

Departures ('old rules')

This chapter covers:
1. Grounds for departure (p292)
2. Applying for departure (p302)
3. Procedure (p303)
4. Considering departure (p306)
5. The departure direction (p308)

The Child Support Agency can 'depart' from the standard formula (see Chapters 10–14) in special cases, but only once a maintenance assessment has been made (see Chapter 16). There can be no departure from a Category A or C interim maintenance assessment (IMA) (see p340).[1] A non-resident parent cannot request a departure from a Category D IMA.[2] Not all types of departure can be used with a Category D IMA where the person with care applies, or with a Category B IMA.[3]

There can be no departure if, on the date from which any departure direction would have effect (see p314):[4]

- the non-resident parent was being paid income support (IS), income-based jobseeker's allowance (JSA) or pension credit (PC), or one of those benefits was being paid for him; *or*
- the person with care was being paid IS, income-based JSA, PC or working tax credit, or one of those benefits was being paid for her. This only applies to a departure application by:
  - the person with care for special expenses (see p292); *or*
  - the non-resident parent on additional cases grounds (see p299).

A departure direction can only be made for one of the specified reasons (see p292), and only if it would be just and equitable to do so (see p306). Departure can mean changes to the amounts used in the standard formula to work out the assessment.

1. **Grounds for departure**

Grounds for departure fall into three groups.
- **Special expenses** (see below) that the standard formula does not take into account – this is mostly used by non-resident parents.
- **Additional cases** (see p299) because of the under-use of available income/assets or unreasonably high outgoings – this is mostly used by persons with care.
- **Property and capital transfers** made before April 1993 (see p301).

Special expenses

Departure is possible if the applicant has:[5]
- travel costs of contact with the child(ren) named in the assessment (see below);
- costs of supporting a stepchild and other children in the family (see p293);
- travel-to-work costs not taken into account in the assessment (see p296);
- costs of a long-term illness or disability (for himself or his dependant) (see p297);
- debts incurred before the couple separated (see p297); *or*
- pre-April 1993 financial commitments from which it would be impossible or unreasonable to withdraw (see p299).

The first £15 of the total of contact costs, travel-to-work cost, debts and pre-1993 financial commitments is disregarded.[6] Remember that there can be no departure for special expenses (or for any other reason) if the non-resident parent is on income support (IS), income-based jobseeker's allowance (JSA) or pension credit (PC), or the person with care is on IS or income-based JSA, PC or working tax credit (WTC).

Contact costs

Only the non-resident parent's costs of contact with the child(ren) named in the assessment count.[7] The contact costs of a parent with shared care who is treated as a non-resident parent (see p273) are not treated as special expenses, and a departure would not be granted for such costs.[8]

Only travel costs count, not the cost of treats or overnight stays. Travel costs can be for the non-resident parent travelling to see the children, or the children travelling to see him. Costs incurred for the purpose of maintaining contact may include costs of some travel once the non-resident parent and child(ren) are together – eg, taking the child from the person with care's home to the non-resident parent's home. However, the cost of travel to the cinema from the person with care's home will not normally be considered.

Only the following count as travel costs:[9]
- the cost of a ticket by public transport (eg, train, coach, boat or plane);
- the cost of fuel by private vehicle – there is no allowance for repairs;

- the cost of taxi fares, but only for a non-resident parent whose disability or illness makes it impracticable for him to use another form of available transport.[10] Any financial assistance he receives towards contact costs is offset from the fare.[11]

Minor incidental costs also count. These may include bridge tolls, parking and ticket reservation fees.[12]

The costs are based on an established pattern of visits if one exists.[13] If there is no established pattern, the non-resident parent and person with care must have agreed a pattern of future contact. This will be used.[14]

The Child Support Agency (CSA) can decide that contact costs are unreasonably high or unreasonably incurred – eg, because the method of travel is too expensive, and may substitute lower amounts than those provided.

Where visits are frequent, the CSA may only allow travel costs of some of them. The CSA must allow enough costs for visits specified in a court order, as long as those visits are being made.[15] Non-resident parents who visit more often than the court order states may wish to change the order to reflect the true position.

Changes in contact may mean changes in any departure direction. If contact stops, even through no fault of the non-resident parent, the departure direction will be cancelled.[16]

The first £15 of these costs (or the total of these and other costs) is disregarded.

Costs of supporting a stepchild

If a non-resident parent or person with care supports a child who is part of her/his household (see p22), but of whom s/he is not the parent (see p15), an amount for those costs may be allowed.[17] This amount is set by a formula (see below). This ground cannot be used by a departure applicant subject to a Category B interim maintenance assessment (IMA).[18]

A 'stepchild' is one who:[19]
- counts as a member of the applicant's family. This is limited to children of:
  - the applicant's current partner; *and*
  - the applicant's former partner who live in the applicant's household every night of the week; *and*
- was part of the applicant's family and household before 5 April 1993; *and*
- remained part of that family and household from 5 April 1993 continuously to the effective date of the proposed departure direction (see p314).[20]

The expenses allowed depend upon the support for the stepchild from her/his non-resident parent and, if the applicant's partner is the child's parent, from that partner. The **cost** of the stepchild is based on the amount excluded from exempt income and is the:[21]
- IS personal allowance for a child of that age; *plus*

- IS family premium if the family contains no children of whom the applicant is the parent. Where special expenses are sought for more than one stepchild, the family premium is divided equally between them;[22] *plus*
- IS disabled child premium if the stepchild would qualify.

If the care of the stepchild is shared between the applicant's current partner and the stepchild's other parent, the cost is reduced by the proportion of time the child spends away from the applicant's household.[23]

No expenses are allowed if maintenance payable to or for the stepchild by her/his non-resident parent is more than the cost, whether the maintenance is a deduction from his IS/income-based JSA (see p174) *or* is under an order or written agreement for maintenance or a maintenance assessment.[24] The CSA can ignore maintenance payable (but not deductions due) if, for example, the stepchild's non-resident parent cannot be found.[25]

If maintenance is less than the cost, the **allowable amount** is the cost less any maintenance payable (unless ignored) or deductions.[26]

If the applicant's partner is *not* the stepchild's parent, the maximum special expenses allowed is the allowable amount.[27]

Where special expenses are sought for stepchildren of different parents, a separate allowable amount is worked out for each child (or group of children who have the same parents), and the allowable amount is the total of those amounts.[28]

If the applicant's partner is the stepchild's parent, her ability to support the child is taken into account in a similar way to the joint child calculation for exempt income (see p202). Her **net income** is worked out as if it were a non-resident parent's assessable income (see Chapter 11) plus child benefit for the stepchildren and any income of her children (except earnings) above £10.[29] Her **outgoings** are:[30]

- the IS personal allowance for a person aged 25 or over (regardless of the partner's actual age); *plus*
- any partner's contribution for joint child(ren) assumed under the standard formula (see p202); *plus*
- the allowable amount (see above); *plus*
- any partner's contribution to housing costs assumed under an existing departure direction (see p301).

If the partner's net income is more than her outgoings, no costs are allowed.[31] If it is less, maximum special expenses are the allowable amount.[32]

Example

Bob has been assessed to pay £25.35 for Carol and David (p260). He lives with his partner, Zoe, their child, Ricky, and three stepchildren so departure is possible if the stepfamily was formed before April 1993. Zoe receives maintenance of £20 a week for Yvonne (14) and Veronica (12), but nothing for Scott (5).

The **allowable amount** is worked out for each non-resident parent.

Wayne's children:		£
Personal allowances (no	Yvonne	56.11
family premium applies as there	Veronica	56.11
is a joint child, Ricky)		
Total		112.22
Less maintenance due		20.00
Allowable amount		92.22

Terence's child:		
Personal allowance (no family	Scott	56.11
premium applies as there is a		
joint child, Ricky)		
No maintenance due		
Allowable amount		**56.11**
Total allowable amount		**148.33**
(£92.22 + £56.11)		
Zoe's **net income** is child benefit		59.60
Personal allowance		64.30
Total allowable amount		148.33
Outgoings		**212.63**

Zoe's income is less than her outgoings so the maximum special expenses is the total allowable amount of £148.33 (WTC counts as Bob's income and not Zoe's because he is the partner in employment). A departure direction for a special expense of £148.33 can, therefore, be made (but see p308). However, if Zoe had refused to accept maintenance for Scott, the departure decision maker may decide that departure would not be fair.

Zoe had recently applied for a CSA assessment: the departure decision maker may not make a decision until that application is decided.

Some months later the CSA issues assessments of £6.50 from Wayne and £22.98 from Terence. Also, Zoe is now working and when Bob's liability is reassessed it rises to £57. The new allowable amount is:

Wayne's children:	£
Personal allowances	112.22
Less child support due	6.50
Allowable amount	**105.72**

Terence's child:	56.11
Personal allowance	
Less child support due	23.12
Allowable amount	**32.99**

		£
Total allowable amount (£105.72 + £32.99)		**138.71**

Zoe's maintenance has increased from £20 to £29.48, and the total allowable amount has gone down by £9.62. Zoe's **net income** is now:

	£
Child benefit	59.60
Earnings	100.00
Net income	**159.60**

WTC is still not treated as her income because it is paid to the partner who works at least 16 hours a week – ie, Bob. Because Zoe is now treated as able to support the joint child (see example on p202) her **outgoings** are considered to be higher.

		£
Personal allowances	Zoe	64.30
	Ricky (half)	28.06
Family premium (half)		8.65
Allowable amount		138.71
Partner's contribution to housing costs		Nil
Total		**239.72**

Zoe's net income is lower than this, so a departure direction for the reduced allowable expenses of £138.71 can be made. However, had Zoe's income been higher it would have failed.

Travel-to-work costs

If the travel-to-work costs of a non-resident parent or person with care are not adequately covered by the broad-brush allowance in the formula (see p200), a departure can be made. As the formula allowance works on straight-line distances, those who travel around estuaries or mountains, or are in rural areas may benefit. Those whose reasonable public transport costs are more than 6 pence per straight line kilometre may also benefit. Self-employed people can benefit for travel costs which are not tax-deductible.[33]

Travel costs allowable are the same as for contact costs (see p292), except that taxi fares are allowable regardless of disability, but only where the journey is unavoidably taken at a time when no other reasonable type of transport is available.[34] Minor incidental costs count. Costs can be reduced or refused where they are considered high or unreasonably incurred.[35]

The travel cost special expenses allowance replaces the formula allowance (see p200). There is a £15 disregard on the total of travel-to-work costs and certain other special expenses (see p292). Disabled people's parking costs should be claimed as costs of a long-term disability, rather than travel-to-work costs (see p292), in order to avoid the disregard.

Example
Steve (see p200) has an allowance of £64.98 included in his exempt income for travel to
work. However, Steve's season ticket to London is £5,100 a year, or £98 a week. Even with
the first £15 disregarded, this is greater than the allowance. The departure decision maker
has decided that a direction is reasonable because Steve lives in Leicestershire in order to
be near his two children and he has not been able to find an equivalent job nearer to home.
The special expense of £83 replaces the broad-brush allowance of £64.98. See p308 for
the re-calculated assessment.

Costs of a long-term illness or disability

Special expenses include costs of a long-term illness or disability of the non-
resident parent or person with care and/or his/her dependant(s).[36] Long-term
illness is one that is current at the date of the departure application and which is
likely to last for a further 52 weeks or to be terminal.[37] Dependant means:[38]
- the departure applicant's partner (see p25);
- a child (see p18) of the applicant or partner, living with the applicant, except a
child named in the assessment to which the departure application applies (see
also p30 for additional maintenance).

Costs allowable are the reasonable costs of:[39]
- personal care, attendance and communication needs;
- mobility;
- domestic help;
- medical aids which cannot be provided under the NHS;[40]
- heating, clothing and laundry;
- food essential for a diet recommended by a medical practitioner;
- adaptations to the applicant's home; *and*
- day care, respite care and rehabilitation.

Any financial help towards these costs from any source is deducted.[41] This
includes disability living allowance (DLA) and attendance allowance (AA). If a
DLA/AA claim has been made, the CSA will wait for that decision before deciding
on departure.[42] If no claim has been made, but the CSA considers that the disabled
person may be entitled, the CSA will notify the applicant, who has six weeks in
which to claim. If no claim is made, the CSA deducts the highest rate of the
appropriate component(s) of DLA (or AA if appropriate) from the costs.[43] The CSA
has a discretion to ignore DLA/AA awarded to a dependant.[44]

Debts of the relationship

A non-resident parent or person with care may be repaying debts incurred *before*
the non-resident parent became a non-resident parent (see p21) of the child
named in the assessment (whether before or after April 1993). Repayment can

count as special expenses, but only if the debt was incurred when the departure applicant and ex-partner were a couple (see p25) and was for the benefit of:[45]
- the departure applicant and an ex-partner, jointly;
- the ex-partner alone, if the applicant is liable for the repayments;
- a child (see p18) of the applicant and/or ex-partner, who lived with the applicant and ex-partner at the time the debt arose; *and/or*
- a child named in the assessment to which the departure application applies.

Ex-partner includes any ex-partner of the non-resident parent (not just the parent with care), but, if the person with care applies for departure only the non-resident parent counts as an ex-partner.[46]

Loans only count if they are from a bank, building society or other registered lender, or from the departure applicant's current or former employer.[47] The following do *not* count as debts:
- debts incurred to buy something that the applicant kept after the relationship ended;[48]
- a debt for which the applicant took responsibility under a financial settlement with the ex-partner or a court order;[49]
- secured mortgage repayments; *and*
- endowment/insurance premiums,[50] except for mortgage/insurance incurred to buy or repair/improve (see p189)[51] the home of the parent with care and child named in the assessment.

The following also do *not* count as debts:[52]
- debts of a business or trade;
- gambling debts;
- legal costs of the separation, divorce or dissolution of a civil partnership;
- credit card repayments;
- overdrafts, unless taken out for a specified amount repayable over a specified period;
- fines imposed on the applicant;
- any debt incurred to pay off one of these (except for business/trade debts); *or*
- any other debt the CSA considers it reasonable to exclude.

Debts incurred to pay off a debt which would have counted also count.[53] However, any direction is based upon the repayment period and rate of the original debt.[54]

The first £15 of the total of allowable debts of the relationship and certain other special expenses is disregarded (see p292).

Any departure direction is for the debt repayment period.[55] If the applicant cannot meet the repayments, the direction can be extended, but only if the creditor agreed to extend time for repayment because of:[56]
- the applicant's unemployment or incapacity for work; *or*
- a substantial fall in the applicant's income.

Pre-April 1993 financial commitments

Special expenses can include other financial commitments of the non-resident parent – eg, hire purchase or school fees. Commitments like those on p297 do not count. The only commitments that count are those:[57]

- made before 5 April 1993;
- from which it would be impossible or unreasonable to withdraw; *and*
- where an order or written agreement for maintenance was made before 5 April 1993 for all the non-resident parent's children (see p18) (including at least one child named in the assessment) *and* that order/agreement was in force on both the date the commitment was made and on 5 April 1993.[58] There can be more than one order/agreement for different children.

Additional cases

This can be used by a person with care who is not a parent. However, for convenience, we refer to 'parent'.

Grounds for departure are if:[59]

- a parent's lifestyle is inconsistent with the level of her/his income;
- a parent's assets could produce some or more income;
- a parent has diverted her/his income so it is not taken into account in the formula;
- the housing costs used in the formula are unreasonably high;
- it is reasonable for a parent's partner to contribute towards the couple's housing costs;
- travel-to-work costs used in the formula are unreasonably high; *or*
- travel-to-work costs should be disregarded completely.

There can be no departure on additional cases grounds if the non-resident parent is on IS or income-based JSA *or* if he is the departure applicant and the person with care is on IS, income-based JSA or WTC (see p291). However, it is possible that information about undeclared income will be passed to Jobcentre Plus (see p76) and/or the case referred to the CSA to consider whether there is notional income (see p224).

Example

A non-resident parent has a large well-furnished house in a stockbroker belt, with several cars in the drive and a lifestyle which suggests wealth. He is a director of his own company and pays a modest salary to himself and to his new partner. His declared income is only a few pounds above the mortgage so the assessment is nil. He is not subject to the excessive housing cost rule (see p194) nor to the minimum payment (see p172) as the couple have a child. The person with care could seek a departure on the grounds that:

– the non-resident parent's lifestyle is incompatible with his declared income;
– the non-resident parent's partner should contribute to housing costs; *and*

– the housing costs are unreasonably high.

If the new partner does not do much work for the business, the non-resident parent's income may have been unreasonably diverted to her.

Lifestyle inconsistent with income

Departure is possible where a parent's overall lifestyle requires substantially higher income than the amount of her/his income on which the maintenance assessment is based.[60] This cannot be done if the lifestyle is paid for:[61]

- from the parent's capital; *or*
- by her/his partner, unless the parent can influence the amount of the partner's income (eg, as employer). If s/he cannot, the CSA can consider whether the partner could contribute to housing costs (see p301).[62]

The CSA is unlikely to investigate a parent's lifestyle. If there appear to be grounds for investigation, it may refer the case to the First-tier Tribunal, which could direct the parties to provide evidence (see Chapter 18).

If departure is directed, notional extra income will be set (see p313).

Under-use of assets

A parent may be under-using her/his money or property. Departure can only happen if the total value of the assets found to be under-used (less any mortgage or charge) is £10,000 or more.[63] This can apply if s/he is the beneficiary of, or can control:[64]

- an asset which does not produce income but could do so;
- an investment producing less income than is reasonable;
- a claim to money (eg, a debt or legal action) which it is reasonable to enforce; *and/or*
- an asset which it would be reasonable to sell.

This also applies to any trust funds of which the parent is a beneficiary.[65]

The CSA can ignore assets which are to be used for a reasonable purpose.[66] The parent's home would not normally be treated as an asset for the purpose of this ground, but any second or holiday home could be considered.

If an under-used asset exists, any departure direction will set the notional extra income which the asset could produce. The asset is assumed to produce income at the judgment rate: currently 8 per cent.[67] Any actual income from the asset is deducted from that notional income.

Diversion of income

Departure is possible where a parent can control her/his income *and* has unreasonably reduced her/his income (as worked out for the standard formula) by diverting it to other people or other purposes.[68] For example, a non-resident parent's company pays him no salary but pays his partner an inflated one.

Unreasonable housing costs

If a parent's housing costs are more than the amount normally allowed under the formula but s/he is exempt from that restriction (see p194), departure is possible if those costs are unreasonably high.[69] Departure only removes the exemption, so weekly housing costs still cannot be set at less than £80 or half the parent's net income, whichever is greater.[70]

Partner's contribution towards housing costs

Departure is possible if a parent has a partner who occupies the home and it is reasonable for that partner to contribute towards housing costs.[71] The CSA will decide what proportion the partner should pay, considering the parent's income and the partner's income.[72] This can be 100 per cent, especially if a Category B IMA is in force and/or the parent is withholding information about her/his partner's income.[73]

Unreasonable travel-to-work costs/allowance

Departure is possible where travel costs allowed under the formula (see p200):
* are unreasonably high – eg, the parent shares a car;[74] *or*
* ought not to be allowed because the parent can pay maintenance assessed without an allowance for part or all of those costs.[75]

Property and capital transfers

The broad-brush formula allowance for pre-1993 property transfers (see p196) may not result in a proper reflection of the effect of that transfer in the amount of child support maintenance. Also, some parents cannot use that allowance – eg, because of lack of evidence. Departure allows for a more flexible approach. Property is not defined (as it is for the broad-brush allowance – see p196) so it includes things such as household items and shares. It is not a ground for departure, however, from a Category D IMA.[76]

Departure is possible if:[77]
* before 5 April 1993 a court order or written agreement was in force between the non-resident parent and the person with care and/or the child(ren) named in the assessment; *and*
* in connection with that order/agreement, property which the non-resident parent owned (or had the benefit of) was transferred to that person with care or that child, or to a trust for payment of the normal day-to-day living expenses of that child; *and either:*
  – that transfer reduced the non-resident parent's maintenance liability (not child support) *and* the effect of that transfer is not properly reflected in the current maintenance assessment; *or*
  – that transfer did *not* reduce the non-resident parent's maintenance liability (not child support) *but* the current maintenance assessment is reduced

because of that transfer *and* that reduction is inappropriate because of the purpose of the transfer – eg, it was for spousal maintenance.

No departure can be made if:
- the change in maintenance would be less than £1;[78] *or*
- the transfer was temporary and ends before the effective date of the direction.[79]

To see if the broad-brush property allowance fairly reflects the child maintenance forgone, the CSA first works out the value of the transfer, ignoring any part which was not in lieu of child maintenance. Unless there is evidence to show otherwise, the CSA assumes that:[80]
- the property covered by the order/agreement was held in equal shares by the non-resident parent and person with care;
- if those parties had been married, half of the value of the transfer was for the person with care's benefit, and not for the child(ren);
- if those parties were *never* married, *none* of the value of the transfer was for the person with care's benefit.

The equivalent weekly value is then worked out. The number of years of liability is deemed to begin on the date of the order/agreement and to end on the date it sets for maintenance to end (for the youngest child if there is more than one), or, if no date is given, when the youngest child reaches 18.[81] Using that figure and the interest rate on judgment debts at the date of the order/agreement, a multiplier is given by a table.[82] That gives an equivalent weekly value which replaces the broad-brush allowance (see p196). If that would lead to a departed assessment of less than the child maintenance payable under the order/agreement, a lower weekly value can be set. The weekly value of a transfer of less than £5,000 is nil.[83]

The result is difficult to predict (see p311). The assessment may be increased or reduced, irrespective of who applied for departure.

2. **Applying for departure**

Once an assessment has been made, a person with care, non-resident parent or child applicant in Scotland may apply for a departure direction.[84] This applies to any assessment – whether made on initial application or after a revision or supersession – but not to all categories of interim maintenance assessment (see p291). Information about departure is provided with an assessment.

The Child Support Agency (CSA) can provide an application form on request, or a letter can be accepted if it has all the information required by the form.[85] The applicant should fill in the form as fully as possible. The date of the application is the date it is received by the CSA, unless there was unavoidable delay.[86] The date of the application affects the effective date of any direction (see p314).

If the application is not accepted because it is not properly made, the CSA can send it back (or send a form) to the applicant. If it is properly made within 14 days of the day the CSA sends it back, it counts as made when the defective application was made.[87]

An application cannot be made before the assessment is made.[88] Even if the reason for departure is in the maintenance application form or maintenance enquiry form, a separate application must still be made.

A departure applicant can be represented by any other person.[89]

A departure application can be withdrawn or amended by the applicant at any time before it is decided.[90] S/he may want to do this after seeing the other party's information. However, a person considering applying may want to try to work out what any departure would be *before* applying. This is because a departure may work against the applicant.

3. **Procedure**

Departure applications on several grounds or by both parties will be considered together to ensure that the outcome is just and equitable (see p306). Each party may have a departure direction granted (on multiple grounds) and applied to the assessment.

Preliminary consideration

The decision maker will carry out a preliminary consideration of each application before asking the other party for information.[91] If the application has no chance of success, it will be refused.[92]

The Child Support Agency (CSA) may ask the applicant for further information, which must be provided within one month (longer may be allowed if the CSA is satisfied that this is reasonable).[93] If it is not, and the decision maker is satisfied on the available evidence that a departure direction should not be given, the application may be refused without the other party being asked for information.[94]

Because the decision maker wants the assessment to be correct *before* departure is considered, s/he may pass the case to other CSA staff for revision or supersession before completing the preliminary consideration (see p315).

There is a right of appeal against refusal on preliminary consideration (see p317).

If the case passes the preliminary consideration, but the decision maker considers that a direction is unlikely to be given, s/he can decide the application without asking the other party for information.[95] However, if the decision maker then considers a direction should be made, s/he must ask for that information before making a decision (see below).[96]

Information

If the application passes the preliminary consideration, the CSA must (unless a direction is unlikely to be made) write to the other party (or parties if the maintenance application was by a Scottish child):[97]
- notifying her/him that the departure application has been made;
- sending details of the grounds for the application and any relevant information the applicant has given (but see below); *and*
- asking for representations about the application to be made within 14 days.[98]

If representations are sent, the CSA may send them to the applicant asking for comments.[99] However, this is only likely to happen where the evidence provided by the parent contradicts that supplied by the applicant, and the CSA cannot make a decision based on the evidence available. The contradictory evidence may then be copied to the other party for comments.[100] Any party can send further information to the CSA at any time. If a response cannot be made within 14 days, the information available should be sent with a request for more time to provide the rest. The CSA is unlikely to make its own enquiries so each party must make their own case. On appeal, the First-tier Tribunal can require information to be provided (see Chapter 18).

Where one party does not know the whereabouts of another party or a child named in the maintenance assessment and that party has not agreed to disclosure, then that address and any information which could reasonably be expected to lead to them being located will not be disclosed unless:[101]
- that address/information is necessary to decide the departure application; *and*
- there is no risk of harm or undue distress to that party/child if disclosure were made.

Undisclosed medical evidence will not be sent to a person if it would harm her/his health.[102]

Regular payments condition

If a non-resident parent applies for departure, the CSA can impose a regular payments condition (RPC).[103] This will only normally be done where the non-resident parent has persistently failed to pay maintenance due and only once the application has passed a preliminary consideration (see p303). A person with care who knows a departure application has been made can ask the CSA to make an RPC.

Decisions about an RPC may be initiated by the CSA debt management section, but the decision maker decides whether to impose the RPC and the rate at which it should be paid. An RPC will usually be set at the rate of the current assessment.[104] The exception is where the departure application is for special expenses for travel costs, contact costs or illness/disability.[105] If this applies, the RPC will be set for a lower amount on the assumption that a departure direction has been made for those expenses, unless the non-resident parent has exaggerated or claimed unreasonable expenses.[106]

The CSA notifies the non-resident parent and person with care of any RPC and the effect of failing to comply.[107] If the non-resident parent fails to comply, he will usually be contacted and the RPC may be re-negotiated.

If this does not work, the CSA can decide that the non-resident parent has failed to comply with the RPC. Written notice of this is sent to the non-resident parent and person with care. If the CSA decides that the non-resident parent has failed to comply with the RPC within 28 days of the notice, the departure application lapses.[108]

An RPC does not affect the amount of maintenance the non-resident parent is *liable* to pay. Even if he complies with the RPC, if this is less than the amount of the current assessment, there will be arrears if the departure application fails (see p407).

The RPC will end once the departure decision has been made.

Revision or supersession of the assessment

A departure application can be made even if a revision or supersession of the existing assessment has been applied for.[109] An assessment can also be revised or superseded while a departure application is being considered. In a case where a fresh assessment is made on a revision or supersession the decision maker may direct that the departure application lapse, unless the applicant asks for it to stand.[110] See Chapter 17 for revisions and supersessions.

If the application shows a ground for changing the assessment (eg, a mistake or a change of circumstances), the case will be considered for revision or supersession.

Where an assessment is revised or superseded (see p315), the departure decision maker treats that fresh assessment as the current assessment when considering departure.

Decision on the application

If the decision maker decides the application (rather than referring it to a tribunal) s/he must notify the parties of that decision and the reasons for it.[111] If the decision is to make a direction, the notification must state the way in which maintenance is to be worked out as a result of the direction. The CSA will then make a new assessment, taking into account the instructions in the departure direction (see p308). The decision on the departure direction and the maintenance assessment after the departure is taken into account can both be appealed. It is, therefore, important to be clear which decision is being appealed to the First-tier Tribunal. For more information on appeals, see Chapter 18.

Referral to the First-tier Tribunal

Once a departure application has passed the preliminary consideration and the parties' representations have been sought, a decision maker can refer it to the First-tier Tribunal instead of deciding it her/himself.[112] Many departure cases will be complex or difficult, but these should normally be decided by a decision maker. A referral might be made if, for example:

- the case raises new points – ie, ones which have never arisen in a departure case before; *or*
- the case is very contentious – eg, both parties have solicitors and the evidence is completely contradictory; *or*
- only the First-tier Tribunal will be able to obtain the necessary evidence.

The First-tier Tribunal is subject to the rules which apply to a decision maker and will either give a direction or refuse to give one.[113] However, the procedure will be similar to an appeal and the Tribunal's decision can be appealed on a point of law (see Chapter 18).

4. Considering departure

A departure direction can only be made if it would change the amount of the assessment by £1 or more.[114] The possible effect of 'old rules' phasing-in (see p329) is ignored.[115]

Discretion to make a direction

When considering whether and how to make a direction, the departure decision maker must:[116]

- treat parents as responsible for maintaining their children when they can afford to do so;
- treat parents as responsible for maintaining all their children equally;
- ignore the fact that all, or part, of the income of the person with care (or her partner) includes (or would, on departure, include) income support, income-based jobseeker's allowance, working tax credit, housing benefit or council tax benefit, or that child maintenance might be taken into account for benefit entitlement.

Just and equitable

Even though the grounds for departure are met and the assessment would change by £1 or more, a direction will only be made if it would be just and equitable to do so – ie, fair to all concerned.[117] The decision maker will first work out what direction would be appropriate and how it would affect the assessment. When considering whether it would be fair to make that direction, the decision maker must consider:[118]

- the financial circumstances of the non-resident parent, including any liability to pay maintenance before the assessment's effective date;
- the financial circumstances of the person with care (but ignore her receipt of certain benefits);
- whether a direction would lead to the non-resident parent or person with care giving up employment;[119]
- where the application is for special expenses, whether the applicant could have made financial arrangements to cover those expenses, or could pay for them from money s/he is spending on non-essentials.

This may mean taking into account circumstances for which either party could have sought a direction, even if s/he did not. For example, since contact costs have an effect on the financial circumstances of the non-resident parent, it may be just and equitable to take these into account when deciding on departure, even if the departure application was about something else (and may have been made by the person with care).[120] However, if such circumstances are taken into account, it must be made clear to all parties on what basis the departure has been decided.

The decision maker must *not* take into account:

- the circumstances of the child's conception;
- the reasons for the breakdown of the relationship;
- the fact that either party is now involved in a new relationship;
- any contact arrangements;
- the failure of the non-resident parent to pay maintenance under the CSA assessment or any previous arrangement; *nor*
- any representations made by a person other than the person with care, the non-resident parent or a Scottish child applicant.

Discretion should only rarely be used to refuse a departure direction outright. However, it may well be used to reduce the amount of the direction. Both parties are seen as responsible for organising their lives so as to support their children. If parties have unreasonably taken on new responsibilities (eg, a second family), failed to reduce outgoings (eg, re-schedule debts) or failed to increase their income (eg, through work), the CSA may decide that it is not just and equitable for a departure direction to be made.

5. **The departure direction**

A direction is not a new assessment. It is a direction to reassess child maintenance on a different basis.[121] The Child Support Agency (CSA) must comply as soon as reasonably practicable.[122]

The direction cannot take maintenance above the formula maximum (see p240) or below the £6.50 weekly minimum (see p172).[123] A non-resident parent cannot fall below the protected income level (see Chapter 13), though the direction may change that level.[124]

Phased assessments

If the assessment is being phased in (see p329), special rules apply. If the effective date of the departure direction (see p314) is the *same* as that of the assessment, the direction is applied to the formula assessment.[125] The CSA then applies any phasing to that departed assessment.

If the effective date of the departure direction is *later* than that of the assessment, the direction is applied to the formula assessment. This proposed departed assessment is then compared with both the formula assessment and the phased assessment. If the proposed departed assessment is:[126]

- higher than the formula assessment, the difference between them is added to the phased assessment to give the actual departed assessment;
- less than the formula assessment but more than the phased assessment, then departure has no effect and the phased assessment is used; *or*
- less than the phased assessment, the proposed departed assessment is used.

Special expenses directions

The direction states an amount for special expenses. The CSA includes this in the applicant's exempt income and any protected income.[127] Expenses for a stepchild do not change protected income because they are already included (see p263).[128] If the direction is for travel-to-work costs (see p296), any amount for those already included in exempt income or protected income is replaced by the amount stated in the direction.[129]

If the direction reduces the non-resident parent's assessable income, the departed assessment is *the lowest of*:[130]

- the assessment current on the direction's effective date (see p314);
- 50 per cent of his assessable income after departure (see Chapter 11); *and*
- protected income level (see Chapter 13). This applies regardless of the maintenance requirement or the number of children.

If the direction would also change the figures to be used because of over-generous provision (see p299), the same calculation is done assuming those changes have taken effect.[131] For the rules if a direction for property/capital transfer is also made, see p311.

If a non-resident parent is liable to more than one person with care (see p244), his total liability is set by these rules.[132] The amount of each departed assessment will be the same proportion of total liability as it would be if liability were based on the maintenance requirements.[133]

Example: special expenses – debts and travel costs

Steve has been assessed to pay £59.26 a week to Debbie as maintenance for Paul (17), Grace (15) and Lewis (10). In July 2008, Steve applies for departure on the grounds of travel-to-work costs, debts of the relationship and pre-April 1993 commitments. He does not apply on the ground of the property settlement (see p199) as he wants first to ask his solicitor whether it would be to his advantage.

Steve is awarded special expenses of £83 travel-to-work costs (see p296). He divorced in 1991 and has already cleared some debts, but there remains one debt of the relationship and another commitment pre-dating the divorce. The total repayments amount to £34.60 a week: there is no £15 disregard as this has already been applied to the travel costs.

Debbie has net earnings of £300 and assessable income of £64.98. These were taken into account under the formula but, on departure, Steve simply pays 50 per cent of his own assessable income (as long as this is below the current assessment).

Steve's exempt income:	£
Personal allowance	64.30
Mortgage (in full – see p200)	96.00
Property settlement allowance	40.00
Travel-to-work costs	83.00
Debt repayments	34.60
Total	**317.90**
Steve's net income for child support purposes	380.00
Steve's assessable income	**62.10**
(£380 – £317.90)	
Proposed maintenance	**31.05**
(50% x £62.10)	
Protected income:	
Personal allowance Couple	100.95
Mortgage (interest only)	78.46
Council tax	15.00
Travel-to-work costs	83.00
Debt repayments	34.60
Standard margin	30.00
Basic protected income	**342.01**

Total family income: Steve's new wife, Lisa, has net earnings of £280, so total family income = £380 + £280 = £660. This is far above protected income so Steve can afford the proposed maintenance of £31.05.

The departure direction has, therefore, reduced the assessment from £59.26 to £31.05.

Because the 50 per cent taper applies right up the income range, there comes a point where a non-resident parent's income is too high to benefit from departure (see example on p308).

Example: the well-off and special expenses

Jeremy has been assessed to pay £273.22 a week for his four children (see p238). He applies for departure for contact costs. The children stay with Jeremy every other weekend. He collects and returns them in his car. This is cheaper than four return train fares: the petrol used is £112 a weekend. As this is £56 a week, the £15 disregard leaves a special expense of £41.

Jeremy's exempt income is increased by £41.

His assessable income would be now £559 (instead of £600).

The proposed maintenance after the departure would be: 50% x £559 = £279.50. As this is higher the current maintenance assessment of £273.22, no departure direction is given.

If, instead, Jeremy had net income of £800 a week and assessable income of £500 a week, the current assessment would be:

Basic element = maintenance requirement = £246.44 (see p238)

Basic assessable income = 2 x £246.44 = £492.88

Additional assessable income = £500 – £492.88 = £7.12

Additional element = £7.12 x 25% = £1.78

Proposed maintenance = £246.44 + £1.78 = £248.22

The 30% protected income (£240) is less, so the assessment is capped at £240 (total protected income does not affect the assessment).

If Jeremy were awarded special expenses of £41, his assessable income would be £500 – £41 = £459.

Proposed maintenance = 50% x £459 = £229.50, which is less than the previous assessment of £240.

The protected income needs checking again as special expenses are now included:

	£
Personal allowance	64.30
Mortgage (interest only)	123.08
Council tax	21.00
Travel-to-contact costs	52.00
Standard margin	30.00
Basic protected income	**290.38**

His total family income = £800 net earnings

Excess income = £800 – £290.38 = £509.62

15% x £509.62 = £76.44

Total protected income = £290.38 + £76.44 = £366.82

Jeremy can, therefore, afford to pay the £229.50 assessment without his disposable income falling below £366.82 a week.

Even if Evie applies for departure for excessive housing costs, none can be made because these are less than half Jeremy's net income.

Property/capital transfer directions

The direction states the weekly value of the transfer (see p301). Any property settlement allowance in exempt income (see p196) is removed, even if the weekly value is nil.[134] Proposed maintenance (see Chapter 12) is then reduced by the amount of any transfer value and the protected income level worked out again.[135] Maintenance payable cannot be below the £6 minimum (see p172).[136]

If a special expenses direction is also made, any property settlement allowance is removed from assessable income and the special expenses calculation is then carried out (see p308).[137] The result is then reduced by the transfer value (if any).[138]

If a non-resident parent is liable to more than one person with care (see p244) the transfer value is deducted from the assessment for the person with care or for the child for whom the transfer was made.[139]

The removal of the allowance from exempt income continues after the direction ends because it has compensated for the transfer.[140]

Where the transfer was to trustees and the weekly value is more than nil, any child maintenance from that trust is disregarded from the parent with care's assessable income.[141]

Example: property transfer direction

Hamish and Kirsty divorced in February 1993, when their only child, Angus, now age 17, was two. The house, then worth £31,000, was transferred to Kirsty with a mortgage of about £9,000. From April 1995, Kirsty's assessment was reduced when Hamish was given an allowance of £40 in his exempt income. Kirsty has remarried, has a baby and has no net income of her own. Hamish is single.

The current assessment is:

	£
Maintenance requirement	53.41
Hamish's exempt income:	
Personal allowance	64.30
Housing costs	45.00
Property settlement allowance	40.00
Total	**149.30**

Hamish's net income = £205 a week net earnings

Assessable income = £205 − £149.30 = £55.70

Proposed maintenance = £55.70 x 50% = **£27.85** (less than the maintenance requirement).

Protected income shows that Hamish can afford this.

The purpose of the capital transfer was unspecified. Kirsty believes it was in lieu of spousal maintenance forgone and to provide a home for Angus. Hamish also had to pay £15 a week under a court order as maintenance for Angus. The departure decision maker decides that the property transfer in lieu of child maintenance was £6,000. Given that Angus was to be dependent for at least another 14 years from the date of the order, a transfer of £6,000 does not amount to £20 a week child maintenance in advance as implied by the £40 allowance.

No date was set in the order for maintenance payment to end, so it is deemed to end when Angus turns 18. The number of years of liability is, therefore, 16. The interest rate for judgment debt was 14 per cent at the time of the order, so the table gives a multiplier of 0.00320: £6,000 x 0.00320 = £19.20. This is, therefore, the equivalent weekly value.

Hamish's exempt income = £64.30 + £45.00 = £109.30

Hamish's net income = £205 a week net earnings

Assessable income = £205 – £109.30 = £95.70

Proposed maintenance = (£95.70 x 50%) = £47.85 (less than the maintenance requirement of £53.41)

Therefore, proposed maintenance is £47.85

Protected income shows that Hamish can afford this.

The amount under the departure direction is then deducted: £47.85 – £19.20 = £28.65

If Hamish's net income is £315, but exempt income the same (£149.30), the current assessment would be:

Assessable income = £315 – £149.30 = £165.70

£165.70 x 50% = £82.85 (more than maintenance requirement of £53.41).

Therefore proposed maintenance =

£53.41 + 15% x (£165.70 – (£53.41 x 2)) = £53.41 + £8.83 = £62.24

Protected income shows that Hamish can afford this.

With a property transfer direction of £19.20 (where the £40 allowance in exempt income does not apply).

Assessable income = £315 – £109.30 = £205.70

Proposed maintenance = £53.41 + 15% x (£205.70 – (£53.41 x 2)) = £53.41 + £14.83 = £68.24

The amount under the departure direction is deducted:

£68.24 – £19.20 = £49.04

The departure has in fact ended up reducing the assessment by £13.20

Additional cases directions

If departure is on the grounds of *lifestyle inconsistent with income, under-use of assets* or *diversion of income*, the direction states a figure of notional income to be added to net income (see p185) and so is also included in protected income (see p257).[142]

If *housing costs are unreasonably high*, the direction states the costs that are considered reasonable, and this replaces actual housing costs for exempt income (see p188) and protected income (see p258).[143] The limit of half income/£80 still applies.

If the *partner is to contribute to housing costs*, the direction states the proportion of costs by which housing costs are to be reduced (which may be 100 per cent).[144] Housing costs are reduced by that proportion for exempt income, but not for protected income (see p258). If the direction also states that housing costs are unreasonably high, housing costs used in exempt income are reasonable costs reduced by the stated proportion. The limit of half income/£80 still applies.

If *travel-to-work costs are unreasonably high or should be disregarded*, the direction states the amount of costs allowed (which may be nil). This replaces any travel costs included in exempt income or protected income.[145]

If a direction for special expenses has been given and one for over-generous provision is then sought (or *vice versa*), the case is reconsidered as if a single application were made on both grounds (see p299).[146]

Example: housing costs relating to the partner

A departure direction (see p308) reduced Steve's assessment from £59.26 to £31.05 a week. Debbie, his ex-wife, then applies for departure on the ground that Steve's second wife, Lisa, can contribute towards the couple's housing costs.

Lisa has net earnings of £280 compared with Steve's net earnings of £380. However, once Steve's travelling expenses of £83 a week are taken from his earnings, both partners have roughly the same amount to contribute towards the joint mortgage. Therefore, the departure decision maker decides Lisa can afford to contribute half the mortgage payments.

Therefore, Steve's exempt income is now:

	£
Personal allowance	64.30
Mortgage (half of £96)	48.00
Property settlement allowance	40.00
Travel-to-work costs	83.00
Debt repayments	34.60
Total	**269.90**

Steve's assessable income = £380 − £269.90 = £110.10
Proposed maintenance = 50% x £110.10 = £55.05

The protected income calculation remains as on p308 and, therefore, Steve can afford £55.05 (which is still slightly below the original assessment).

Note: the 50 per cent calculation is used because of the special expenses departure; if only the housing costs departure had been made, proposed maintenance would have been calculated in the usual way (see Chapter 12).

Effective date of the direction

Normally, the effective date of a departure direction is:[147]

- the maintenance assessment's effective date, if the departure application is made within one month of the notification of the current assessment (see p328). If there was unavoidable delay the CSA can treat the application as received in time;[148] *otherwise*
- the first day of the maintenance period in which the departure application was received.

However, if the reason for departure is a change of circumstances after the assessment's effective date, the effective date of the direction is:

- the first day of the maintenance period after the change of circumstances, if the departure application is made within one month of the notification of the assessment (see p328);[149] *otherwise*
- the first day of the maintenance period in which the departure application was received.[150]

If the direction is for contact costs and there was no established pattern of visits at the date of the application (see p302), the effective date is the first day of the first maintenance period after *either* the date the parents have agreed that pattern is to start *or*, if there is no agreed date, the date of the direction.[151]

Normally, a direction can only be made for the current assessment when the departure application was made. However, in some cases an application cannot be made while the assessment is current because notification was not sent until after the period covered by the assessment – eg, because it is made for a past period. The departure decision maker can still make a direction for that assessment, as if it were the current one, if:[152]

- a departure direction is given for the current maintenance assessment; *and*
- s/he considers that a direction would have been made for the assessment for the earlier period if an application had been made.

Duration of the direction

The direction may last for a specified period (eg, a 30-week repayment period) or until a specified event (eg, a child leaves school).[153] A direction may require the CSA to make a fresh assessment on a later change of circumstances and specify how that assessment is to be made.[154]

Changing the direction

The rules on changing a decision on departure are similar to those on changing a decision on the assessment itself (see Chapter 17). Any decision of the CSA (or one referred to the First-tier Tribunal) regarding departure can be revised[155] or superseded.[156] This would appear to include a decision that regular payments conditions have not been complied with. Where it is considered that an application for departure is defective, there is no formal notified decision and this may only be challenged by judicial review. Refusal and rejection of applications may be revised. The 'test case' rules (see p392) also apply to revisions and supersessions of departure decisions.[157]

The rules on who can initiate a revision/supersession, on what grounds and when are summarised below.

Change of decision	Grounds	Initiated by	Time limit
Revision	Any	CSA/Any party*	1 month
Revision	Official error	CSA	No limit
Revision	Misrepresentation	CSA	No limit
Supersession	Change of circumstances	CSA/Any party*	No limit
Supersession	Erroneous in point of law	CSA/Any party*	No limit
Supersession	Ignorance/Mistake as to fact	CSA/Any party*	No limit

*'Any party' includes any parent with care, non-resident parent or Scottish child applicant of the assessment to which the departure relates.

Disputing decisions

Any party to an assessment can apply to have a departure direction decision revised. This includes decisions made on referral to the First-tier Tribunal (see p306). The CSA can also act to revise a decision on any grounds within one month of notification of the original decision.[158] In addition, the CSA can also act to revise a decision at any time where that decision was made as a result of official error (see p356)[159] or where the original decision was wrong because a person misrepresented or failed to disclose a material fact (see p356) and the decision was, therefore, more advantageous to that person.[160] Revision cannot occur if a material change of circumstances has occurred (or is expected to occur) since the original decision.[161] In this case supersession may be possible. Revision is not possible where the original decision is being appealed to an appeal tribunal and the revised decision (if made) would be less advantageous to the person making the appeal.[162]

An application for revision must normally be made within one month of notification of the decision.[163] Where an application for revision is made and the CSA informs the applicant that the revision will not be made because there is insufficient evidence or information, the applicant has one month from the date of this notification to re-apply with the required information.[164] The one-month time limit may be extended where the CSA accepts that it is reasonable to grant an extension. The application for the decision to be revised must have merit and there must have been special circumstances which meant that it was not practicable for the application to have been made within the one-month limit.[165] The longer the extension requested, the more compelling the relevant special circumstances would need to be.[166] An application for an extension must be made within 13 months of notification of the original decision.[167] When deciding whether to grant an extension the CSA will take no account of an applicant's ignorance or misunderstanding of the law relating to her/his case, nor will account be taken of a commissioner's or court's new interpretation of the relevant law (see p355).[168] Applications for extension which are refused cannot be renewed.[169]

The revised decision normally takes effect on the same date as the original decision.[170] If the effective date from which the original decision takes effect is wrong, the revised decision takes effect from the correct date.[171] If, on revision of the decision, the CSA decides that a departure direction should not have been given, the direction will be cancelled.[172]

Supersession of a decision on departure

A decision relating to departure may be superseded if there has been a material change of circumstances since the original decision was made. Any party to the assessment can apply for a supersession on this ground or, where the CSA becomes aware of a relevant change of circumstances, it can act on its own initiative.[173] A party to the assessment can also apply for a supersession if s/he expects that a material change of circumstances is going to occur.[174] No supersession on a change of circumstances will be made if the amount of child maintenance payable would be changed by less than £1.[175] Decisions may also be superseded (either on application by a party or on the initiative of the CSA) where the original decision was made in ignorance of (or based on a mistake as to) a material fact[176] or (apart from decisions given on appeal) where the original decision was wrong in point of law.[177] Decisions to refuse or reject an application for departure and decisions to cancel a departure direction cannot be superseded,[178] nor can any decision which can be revised (see p315).[179]

A superseding decision normally takes effect on the first day of the maintenance period (see p333) in which the application for supersession is made.[180] This also applies where the CSA supersedes a decision on its own initiative on the basis of information or evidence contained in an unsuccessful application for revision or supersession.[181] If an application is made because of an anticipated change of circumstances, the new decision takes effect from the first day of the maintenance period immediately after the maintenance period in which the change of circumstances is expected to occur.[182] If the CSA supersedes a decision on its own initiative because it becomes aware of a change of circumstances following a revision or supersession of a social security decision, the superseding decision takes effect from the first day of the maintenance period in which the social security decision maker became aware of the change of circumstances.[183]

If, on supersession, the CSA decides that a departure direction should no longer have effect, the direction will be cancelled.[184]

Correction of accidental errors

A minor accidental error can be corrected by the departure decision maker at any time, without making a fresh direction. The parties must be notified and the normal time for appealing starts to run again (see Chapter 18).[185]

Change to the assessment

If the assessment is changed on revision or supersession, the direction normally applies to any fresh assessment. This may not mean there is a decision on departure that may be appealed at this stage. It has been recommended that the Secretary of State should always give a departure decision when making a new assessment to allow the party appeal rights.[186] Where this does not occur and an appeal relates in part to the continuation of the departure direction, the tribunal does not have jurisdiction to deal with the departure issue and should refer the case to the CSA as a request for supersession of the departure, which would lead to a decision that carried appeal rights.

In some cases, the CSA may replace the existing assessment with an interim maintenance assessment (IMA) (see p340). If the direction could not have been made for that IMA (see p291), the direction is suspended.[187] The suspension continues until the IMA is replaced by an assessment for which the direction could have been made.

If an assessment is cancelled or ceases to have effect (see p345), the direction normally ceases to have effect and does not apply to any later assessment.[188] However, if the cancellation is because of the CSA ceasing to have jurisdiction, and the CSA later gets jurisdiction again for the same parties and at least one of the same children, a property transfer direction has effect again from the effective date of any new assessment.[189] This only applies where a party moves away from the UK and then returns or where the parents reconcile but later split up again.

Appealing the decision

Decisions on departure can be appealed to the First-tier Tribunal.[190] Any party to the assessment can appeal. The time limit and procedures for appealing are the same as for other appeals (see p372).[191] Any decision with respect to a departure application can be appealed.[192] This includes a decision to refuse an application and one to make a direction. A decision that an application is defective can only be challenged via judicial review. Where more than one departure direction is appealed and those departure directions relate to the same maintenance assessment, the First-tier Tribunal can consider both appeals at the same time.[193]

When making an appeal it is important to distinguish whether the appeal is against the direction and/or any fresh maintenance assessment. See Chapter 18 for further details of appeals.

Notes

1 Reg 10(1)(a) CSDDCA Regs
2 Reg 10(1)(c) CSDDCA Regs
3 Reg 10(1)(b) and (c) CSDDCA Regs
4 Reg 9 CSDDCA Regs

1. Grounds for departure
5 Sch 4B para 2 CSA 1991
6 Reg 19 CSDDCA Regs
7 Reg 14(1) CSDDCA Regs
8 Reg 14(4) CSDDCA Regs
9 Reg 14(1) CSDDCA Regs
10 Reg 14(1)(c) and (6) CSDDCA Regs
11 Reg 14(5) CSDDCA Regs
12 Reg 14(1) CSDDCA Regs
13 Reg 14(1) CSDDCA Regs
14 Reg 14(7) CSDDCA Regs
15 Reg 14(3) CSDDCA Regs
16 Reg 32F(b) CSDDCA Regs
17 Reg 18 CSDDCA Regs
18 Reg 10(1)(b) CSDDCA Regs
19 Sch 4B para 2(6) CSA 1991; reg 18(8)(a) CSDDCA Regs
20 Reg 18(1) and (2)(a) CSDDCA Regs
21 Reg 18(4) CSDDCA Regs
22 Reg 18(4B) CSDDCA Regs
23 Reg 18(4A) CSDDCA Regs
24 Reg 18(2)(b) CSDDCA Regs
25 Reg 18(7) CSDDCA Regs
26 Reg 18(3) CSDDCA Regs
27 Reg 18(3) CSDDCA Regs
28 Reg 18(7A) CSDDCA Regs
29 Reg 18(5) CSDDCA Regs
30 Reg 18(6) CSDDCA Regs
31 Reg 18(2)(c) CSDDCA Regs
32 Reg 18(3) CSDDCA Regs
33 Reg 13(3) CSDDCA Regs
34 Reg 13(1) CSDDCA Regs
35 Reg 13(2) CSDDCA Regs
36 Reg 15(1) and (6)(a) and (b) CSDDCA Regs
37 Reg 15(6)(b) CSDDCA Regs
38 Reg 15(5) CSDDCA Regs

39 Reg 15(1) and (2) CSDDCA Regs
40 Reg 15(6)(c) CSDDCA Regs
41 Reg 15(3) CSDDCA Regs
42 Reg 15(4)(a) CSDDCA Regs
43 Reg 15(3)(b) and (4)(b) CSDDCA Regs; see also reg 32(6) CSDDCA Regs
44 Reg 15(4A) CSDDCA Regs
45 Reg 16(1) CSDDCA Regs
46 Reg 16(5)(b) CSDDCA Regs
47 Reg 16(2)(k) and (5)(c) CSDDCA Regs; s376(4) ICTA 1988
48 Reg 16(2)(a) CSDDCA Regs
49 Reg 16(3) CSDDCA Regs
50 Reg 16(2)(h) and (i) CSDDCA Regs
51 Reg 16(5)(d) CSDDCA Regs
52 Reg 16(2)(a)-(g), (j) and (m) CSDDCA Regs
53 Reg 16(4) CSDDCA Regs
54 Reg 37(4) CSDDCA Regs
55 Regs 16(2)(l) and 37(3) CSDDCA Regs
56 Reg 37(3) CSDDCA Regs
57 Reg 17 CSDDCA Regs
58 Reg 17(1)(a) CSDDCA Regs
59 Sch 4B para 5 CSA 1991; regs 23-29 CSDDCA Regs
60 Reg 25 CSDDCA Regs
61 Reg 25(2) CSDDCA Regs
62 Reg 25(3) CSDDCA Regs
63 Reg 23(2)(a) CSDDCA Regs
64 Reg 23(1)(a) CSDDCA Regs
65 Reg 23(1)(b) and (c) CSDDCA Regs
66 Reg 23(2)(b) CSDDCA Regs
67 Reg 40(2) and (3) CSDDCA Regs
68 Reg 24 CSDDCA Regs
69 Reg 26 CSDDCA Regs
70 Reg 40(6) CSDDCA Regs
71 Reg 27 CSDDCA Regs
72 Reg 40(7) CSDDCA Regs
73 Reg 40(9) CSDDCA Regs
74 Reg 28 CSDDCA Regs
75 Reg 29 CSDDCA Regs
76 Reg 10(1)(c) CSDDCA Regs

77 Sch 4B paras 3(1) and 4(1) CSA
1991; regs 21(1) and (2) and 22(4)
CSDDCA Regs
78 Reg 21(5)(a) CSDDCA Regs
79 Reg 21(5)(b) CSDDCA Regs
80 Reg 22(2) CSDDCA Regs
81 Sch para 1(3)(b) CSDDCA Regs
82 Reg 22(3) and Sch CSDDCA Regs
83 Sch para 3 CSDDCA Regs

2. Applying for departure
84 s28A(1) CSA 1991
85 s28A(2) and (3) CSA 1991; reg 4(1)
CSDDCA Regs
86 Reg 2 CSDDCA Regs
87 Reg 4(4)-(8) CSDDCA Regs
88 s28A(1) CSA 1991
89 Reg 4(9) and (10) CSDDCA Regs
90 Reg 5 CSDDCA Regs

3. Procedure
91 s28B CSA 1991
92 s28B(2) CSA 1991; reg 7 CSDDCA Regs
93 Reg 6 CSDDCA Regs
94 Reg 8(4) CSDDCA Regs
95 Reg 8(1) CSDDCA Regs
96 Reg 8(4A) CSDDCA Regs
97 Reg 8(1) and (3) CSDDCA Regs
98 Reg 8(5) CSDDCA Regs
99 Reg 8(6) CSDDCA Regs
100 Reg 8(7) CSDDCA Regs
101 Reg 8(2)(b) CSDDCA Regs
102 Reg 8(2)(a) CSDDCA Regs
103 s28C(1) CSA 1991
104 s28C(2)(a) CSA 1991
105 Reg 45 CSDDCA Regs
106 Reg 45(1)-(3) CSDDCA Regs
107 s28C(3) CSA 1991
108 s28C(6)(b) CSA 1991; reg 45(4)
CSDDCA Regs
109 s28A(4) CSA 1991
110 s28B(6) CSA 1991
111 s28F(8) CSA 1991; reg 8(9)(a) and
(10)(a) CSDDCA Regs
112 s28D(1)(b) CSA 1991
113 s28D(3) CSA 1991

4. Considering departure
114 s28F(4)-(5) CSA 1991; reg 7 CSDDCA
Regs
115 Reg 44(4) CSDDCA Regs
116 s28E(2) and (4) CSA 1991; reg 12
CSDDCA Regs
117 s28F(1)(b) CSA 1991
118 s28F(2) and (3) CSA 1991; reg 30
CSDDCA Regs
119 Reg 1 CSDDCA Regs
120 CCS/1131/2005

5. The departure direction
121 s28F(6) CSA 1991
122 s28G(1) CSA 1991
123 Sch 1 paras 4(2) and (3) and 7 CSA
1991. A direction does not change the
way these work.
124 Sch 4B para 6(6) CSA 1991
125 Reg 44(1) and (2) CSDDCA Regs
126 Reg 44(1) and (3) CSDDCA Regs
127 Reg 37(1) CSDDCA Regs
128 Reg 38(2) CSDDCA Regs
129 Regs 37(2) and 38(3) CSDDCA Regs
130 Reg 41(1)-(5) CSDDCA Regs
131 Reg 42A(1)-(6) CSDDCA Regs
132 Reg 43(1) CSDDCA Regs
133 Reg 43(2) CSDDCA Regs
134 Reg 39(1)(a) and (c) and (6) CSDDCA
Regs
135 Reg 39(1)(b) CSDDCA Regs
136 Reg 39(2) CSDDCA Regs
137 Reg 42(1) and (2) CSDDCA Regs
138 Reg 42(3) CSDDCA Regs
139 Reg 43(3) CSDDCA Regs
140 Reg 39(5) CSDDCA Regs
141 Reg 39(3) CSDDCA Regs
142 Reg 40(2)-(5) CSDDCA Regs
143 Reg 40(6) CSDDCA Regs
144 Reg 40(7) CSDDCA Regs
145 Reg 40(10) CSDDCA Regs
146 Reg 42A(7) and (8) CSDDCA Regs
147 Reg 32(1)(a) and (2)(a) CSDDCA Regs.
Different rules apply for assessments in
force on 2 December 1996 if the
application was made before 2
December 1997 – see 1997/98 edition
of this *Handbook*.
148 Reg 32(2)(b) CSDDCA Regs
149 Reg 32(1)(b) CSDDCA Regs
150 Reg 32(4) CSDDCA Regs
151 Reg 32(3A) CSDDCA Regs
152 Reg 46 CSDDCA Regs
153 s28G(2) CSA 1991
154 Sch 4A para 5 CSA 1991
155 Reg 32A CSDDCA Regs
156 Reg 32D CSDDCA Regs
157 s28ZA and Sch 4C para 1(a)(i) CSA 1991
158 Reg 32A(1)(f) CSDDCA Regs
159 Reg 32A(1)(c) CSDDCA Regs
160 Reg 32A(1)(d) CSDDCA Regs
161 Reg 32A(2)(a) CSDDCA Regs
162 Reg 32A(2)(b) CSDDCA Regs
163 Reg 32A(1)(a) CSDDCA Regs
164 Reg 32A(1)(b) CSDDCA Regs
165 Reg 32B(4) CSDDCA Regs
166 Reg 32B(5) CSDDCA Regs
167 Reg 32B(3)(a) CSDDCA Regs
168 Reg 32B(6) CSDDCA Regs
169 Reg 32B(7) CSDDCA Regs

170 s16(3) CSA 1991
171 Reg 32C CSDDCA Regs
172 Reg 32F(a) CSDDCA Regs
173 Reg 32D(2)(a) and (3)(a)(i) CSDDCA Regs
174 Reg 32D(3)(a)(ii) CSDDCA Regs
175 Reg 32D(6) CSDDCA Regs
176 Reg 32D(2)(b) and (4) CSDDCA Regs
177 Reg 32D(5) CSDDCA Regs
178 Reg 32D(10) CSDDCA Regs
179 Reg 32D(9) CSDDCA Regs
180 s17(4) CSA 1991; reg 32E(2) CSDDCA Regs
181 Reg 32E(5) CSDDCA Regs
182 Reg 32E(4) CSDDCA Regs
183 Reg 32E(3) CSDDCA Regs
184 Reg 32F(b) CSDDCA Regs
185 Reg 34A CSDDCA Regs. This does not say the error must be minor, but its terms suggest it does not cover major errors.
186 CCS/1641/2001
187 Reg 35(4) CSDDCA Regs
188 Reg 35(1) CSDDCA Regs
189 Reg 35(2) CSDDCA Regs
190 Sch 4C para 3(4) CSA 1991
191 Regs 31, 32 and 33 SS&CS(DA) Regs
192 Sch 4C para 3(1)(a) CSA 1991
193 Reg 45 SS&CS(DA) Regs

Part 5

Decisions, enforcement and challenges

Chapter 16

....

Maintenance decisions

This chapter covers:
1. Making the initial maintenance decision (below)
2. Default maintenance decisions (p326)
3. Notification of decisions (p328)
4. Court order phasing of calculations (p329)
5. When the first maintenance calculation begins (p330)
6. When a maintenance calculation ends (p334)
7. How a maintenance calculation affects means-tested benefits (p336)
8. Taxation of child maintenance (p339)
9. Existing 'old rules' cases (p340)

....

This chapter does not contain information on the conversion of 'old rules' maintenance assessments to the new rules. For information on conversion decisions, see Chapter 7. For information on revision and supersession decisions, see Chapter 17.

Where there are multiple applications under the 'old' and 'new' rules, the Child Support Agency (CSA) decides which application to proceed with. For more information on how the CSA decides applications, see Chapter 3.

....

1. Making the initial maintenance decision

Once an effective maintenance application has been made and the Child Support Agency (CSA) has obtained, or tried to obtain, the necessary information, it can:[1]
- make a maintenance calculation;
- make a default maintenance decision (see p340); *or*
- refuse to make a maintenance calculation (p326).

Details of the case are entered onto the CSA computer and maintenance is calculated automatically.

Relationship with Child Support Agency Northern Ireland

For child support cases, there are two territories: Great Britain and Northern Ireland (see p8). If the person with care, non-resident parent and qualifying child do not all reside in the same territory, the application is dealt with by the CSA of the territory where the person with care lives.[2] If more than one application names the same non-resident parent, those applications are dealt with by the CSA of the territory where the person with care named in the first application received by the CSA lives.[3] Where a case has been allocated to a CSA by these rules and the person with care applies again, naming a further non-resident parent, that application is dealt with by the CSA already dealing with the earlier case(s).[4]

These rules do not apply if an application is made by a child in Scotland (see p36). Instead, that application and any others naming the same non-resident parent are dealt with by the CSA for the territory where the person with care of the child applicant lives.[5]

Any calculation made under these rules must take into account the rules of the other territory.[6] Because the rules for the two territories are very similar, this should not make any difference.

Waiting for the calculation decision

If the person with care can provide contact details for the non-resident parent, the CSA aims to make an accurate decision within 12 weeks of an application, but some cases may take 26 weeks.[7] If the CSA has to trace the non-resident parent, it is likely to take longer before it can make a decision.

Delays in dealing with applications

Even though it is intended that much of the contact with parents to collect and check information needed to make a maintenance calculation and collect payments is done by phone, there may still be a delay between the application and a decision.

Applicants are contacted at certain stages during the progress of the case – eg, to let them know about negotiations with the non-resident parent about collection or where the applicant has made a complaint. The CSA has also said that it will do more to let its clients know about progress on a case, and it is reviewing and revising letters sent to clients so that they 'have a better understanding of what is happening with their case'.[8] However, you should continue to contact the CSA regularly for progress reports.

Delay after the non-resident parent is contacted about the application does not normally put off the starting date of any calculation (see p330), but the date of the decision on maintenance may be delayed. Liability under an order or agreement continues and these remain enforceable. Other non-resident parents should consider putting money aside or making voluntary payments (see p408). Parents who are already contributing voluntarily should check whether such payments might be used to offset initial arrears (see p405).

If the non-resident parent is not co-operating, the CSA should make a default maintenance decision (see p326) and may impose a criminal sanction. If the person with care is told by the CSA that the non-resident parent is causing the delay by failing to provide information and the CSA has not made a default maintenance decision, the person with care should write to the CSA requesting that one be made. If this does not happen, a complaint should be made (see p439).

Withdrawing the application

If an application is withdrawn or treated as withdrawn (see p42), the CSA cannot make a calculation. If a calculation *is* made after withdrawal, it can be challenged (see Chapter 18).

The application cannot be withdrawn after a decision has been made, but the applicant can ask the CSA to cease acting, in which case the calculation can be cancelled (see p334). In other cases, the decision may be revised or superseded (see Chapter 18).

Change of circumstances

Unlike under social security law, there is no general requirement to notify the CSA of changes. However, both the person with care and the non-resident parent are required to notify the CSA of some changes (see p74). Since September 2008, it is an offence for a non-resident parent not to notify the CSA of a change of address.[9] In addition, the non-resident parent must inform the CSA of changes when a deduction from earnings order is in force (see p418).

In practice, any party may want to tell the CSA of changes or new information about the case – eg, the parent with care may have discovered that the non-resident parent has a second job which she believes has not been disclosed to the CSA.

If the CSA is told about a change or given new information that relates to *before* the effective date (see p341), it has discretion on whether to take this information into account. This can be done in the initial calculation or by making two or more calculations for the different periods.[10]

If the date or period normally used is before the effective date (eg, for earnings) and the CSA knows about a relevant change which happened after that date or period but before the effective date, it must take that change into account.[11] If the change is after the normal 'relevant week' (see p209), the relevant week for each later calculation is the week before the date the CSA was notified of the relevant change.[12]

Any information about a change *after* the effective date but before the maintenance calculation can lead to a series of calculations.[13] The effective date of each such maintenance calculation will be the beginning of the maintenance period in which the change occurred or is expected to occur.[14]

Once a calculation is made, the person with care has a duty to notify the CSA of certain changes that happen after that (see p74). These may result in a revision or supersession, depending on when the change is notified and its significance (see Chapter 17).

Refusal to make a calculation

The CSA *must* refuse to make a calculation if:

- the application was made by a person who is *not* a non-resident parent, a person with care or, in Scotland, a qualifying child aged 12 or over (see p36);
- it is a voluntary application and there is a pre-3 March 2003 court order (registered agreement in Scotland) or written agreement;
- it is a voluntary application and there is a post-3 March 2003 court order (registered maintenance agreement in Scotland) that has been in force for less than one year;
- not all the parties are habitually resident in the UK (see p26);
- there is no non-resident parent, either because both parents live in the same household as the child (see p22) or because the CSA does not accept that the person named is a parent of the child (see p15); *or*
- there is no qualifying child (see p18).

The CSA can also refuse to make a calculation pending the outcome of a test case (see p392). Otherwise, the CSA must make a calculation.

If there is a change of circumstances so that one of these situations applies for a period beginning after the effective date (see p341), the CSA makes a calculation that ends on the date of the change.

If the only child (or all the children) dies before the calculation is made, the CSA can treat the application as if it had not been made.[15] The CSA cannot refuse to make a calculation just because it has insufficient information or because it may affect the welfare of a child.[16] The CSA may make a default maintenance decision (see below). If the CSA refuses to make a calculation, the applicant (and, if the applicant is a child in Scotland, any person with care or non-resident parent who had been notified of the application) must be notified in writing of the decision, the right of appeal (see Chapter 18) and how to seek a revision and supersession (see Chapter 17).[17]

A fresh application may be made after the refusal – eg, if there is a change of circumstances such as the non-resident parent returning to live in the UK.

2. Default maintenance decisions

If the Child Support Agency (CSA) does not have enough information to make a maintenance calculation, or to revise or supersede a decision, it may make a default maintenance decision.[18] A default maintenance decision can also be made at conversion (see p147). (In 'old rules' cases prior to conversion, where there is not enough information to make a full assessment, an interim maintenance assessment may be made, see p340.)

The amount of the default maintenance decision is based on the number of qualifying children applied for:[19]
- £30 if there is one qualifying child;
- £40 if there are two qualifying children; *or*
- £50 if there are three or more qualifying children.

This amount may be apportioned if there is more than one person with care. (Any relevant non-resident children are ignored.[20])

Court order phasing may be applied to a default maintenance decision (see p329).

The effective date of a default maintenance decision is the same as it would have been for a maintenance calculation decision (see p341).

Notification of a default maintenance decision must state the effective date, the default rate, the number of qualifying children, details of any apportionment, revision/supersession/appeal rights and the information needed to make a maintenance calculation.[21]

When a default maintenance decision ends

A default maintenance decision may be revised at any time – eg, when it is replaced by a maintenance calculation.[22] If the default decision is replaced with a maintenance calculation, the date from which this revision takes effect depends on the circumstances.[23]
- If the total amount of maintenance for the relevant period is greater than the default maintenance decision, the date the revision takes effect is the date of the default maintenance decision.
- If the total amount of maintenance for the relevant period is less than the default maintenance decision, the date the revision takes effect is the first day of the maintenance period in which the information needed to make the calculation was provided.

Example

Paul was contacted on 7 April 2004 about Cassandra's application for maintenance for his two daughters, Hannah and Ella. He refused to provide information to calculate maintenance.

A default maintenance decision was made for £40 with an effective date of 7 April 2004. Paul took advice from an advice agency and he provided information on 29 April 2004 which enabled the CSA to calculate maintenance.

If Paul's maintenance is based on net income of £190, he is due to pay £37 a week at the reduced rate. As this is less than the default maintenance decision, he is due to pay £40 a week for the period 7 April to 27 April and £37 a week from 28 April when the default maintenance decision is revised by the maintenance calculation.

16

> If Paul's maintenance is based on net income of £220, he is due to pay £44 a week at the
> basic rate. As this is greater than the default maintenance decision, it is revised and the
> maintenance calculation of £44 takes effect from 7 April 2004.

If the CSA is satisfied that the failure to provide information is not the parent's
fault and that s/he tried her/his best to provide it, the date the revision takes effect
is the date of the default maintenance decision.[24]

> If Paul had been in hospital and did not return the child maintenance enquiry form sent to
> him on 7 April 2004, a default maintenance decision of £40 would be applied from 7 April
> 2004. If, on leaving hopsital on 16 May 2004, Paul contacted the CSA and the CSA
> accepted that the failure to provide information was not his fault, then based on his net
> income being £190, the maintenance calculation of £37 would revise the default decision
> with effect from 7 April 2004.

'Relevant period' means the period for which the default maintenance decision
applied.[25]

In other circumstances – eg, the person with care stops being the person with
care, normal revision and supersession rules apply (see Chapter 17).

3. **Notification of decisions**

The Child Support Agency must notify the person with care, non-resident parent
and Scottish child applicant once a maintenance calculation or interim
maintenance decision has been made.[26] This also includes default maintenance
decisions (but see p329). There are similar rules regarding notification of revision
and supersession decisions (see Chapter 17).

The notification of the maintenance calculation or interim maintenance
decision *must* include information on:[27]

- the effective date (see p341);
- the net weekly income of the non-resident parent;
- the number of qualifying children;
- the number of relevant other children;
- the weekly rate;
- any variations;
- any adjustments for apportionment, shared care by the non-resident parent or
  part-time local authority care, or maintenance to another relevant non-
  resident child; *and*
- revision, supersession and appeal.

Notification of a default maintenance decision must state the effective date, the default date, the number of qualifying children, details of any apportionment, revision/supersession/appeal rights and the information needed to make a maintenance calculation.[28]

Unless there is written permission, the notification should not contain:[29]

- the address of anyone else other than the recipient or information that could lead to her/him being located; *or*
- information on anyone other than persons with care, non-resident parents or qualifying children.

If there are errors or someone disagrees with the decision, s/he may seek a revision (see p354) or appeal (see Chapter 18).

If there is a court order for maintenance, the court is notified of the calculation (see p30). In addition, where court order phasing applies the amount due may be replaced by a transitional amount (see p330).

4. **Court order phasing of calculations**

If weekly liability under the calculation is higher than under an existing court order or agreement, the calculation can be introduced in up to three stages.

A calculation may *only* be phased in if:[30]

- a court order or maintenance agreement (see below) in relation to one or more qualifying children was in force on 4 April 1993 and remained in force until the date the calculation was made;
- the calculation exceeds that due under the old order/agreement; *and*
- either the non-resident parent is a member of a family or there is a reduction for shared care to the basic or reduced rate.

Any payments in kind or to third parties are ignored when determining the old amount. Arrears are also ignored – it is the weekly liability that counts.[31]

Maintenance agreements which count for phasing must have been:[32]

- made in writing (see p37); *or*
- evidenced in writing,

and must meet all the other requirements of a maintenance agreement (see p37).

Court orders which count for phasing must have been made under:[33]

- one of the provisions listed in Appendix 3 for court maintenance orders;
- section 151 of the Army Act 1955;
- section 151A of the Air Force Act 1955;
- articles 1(b) or 3 of the Naval and Marine Pay and Pension (Deductions for Maintenance) Order 1959.

The Child Support Agency will seek verification of the order or written maintenance agreement, which could be an original document or a copy.[34] In some instances, confirmation may be obtained by Jobcentre Plus.

Where court order phasing applies, instead of the calculation amount a transitional amount is paid.[35] The transitional amount is:[36]

- for the first 26 weeks, the old amount *plus* the greater of £20 and a quarter of the difference between the calculation and the old amount;
- for the next 26 weeks, the old amount *plus* the greater of £40 and half of the difference between the calculation and the old amount; *and*
- for the last 26 weeks of the phasing-in period, the old amount *plus* the greater of £60 and three-quarters of the difference between the calculation and the old amount.

The maintenance payable becomes the calculation amount if the transitional amount would be larger than that.[37] Therefore, it is only where the difference between the old amount and the calculation amount is more than £60 a week that the phasing-in period lasts the full 18 months.

Revision and supersession where there is phasing

Where phasing applies and there is a subsequent decision, the following amount is payable:[38]

- if the subsequent decision is less than the calculation amount and less than or equal to the transitional amount, the subsequent decision;
- if the subsequent decision is less than the previous calculation but more than the transitional amount, the transitional amount;
- if the subsequent decision is higher than the previous calculation, the transitional amount is increased by the same amount as the increase between the calculation and the subsequent decision.

5. **When the first maintenance calculation begins**

The date a maintenance calculation takes effect is called the **'effective date'** (see below).[39] There are different rules for effective dates after a supersession (see Chapter 17), for calculations replacing default maintenance decisions (see p326) and where there is conversion of an 'old rules' case (see p333). For effective dates in 'old rules' cases prior to conversion, see p341.

The effective date

Unless there is a maintenance order in force in relation to all the qualifying children (see p354), the effective date of the calculation depends on who made the application. However, where there is, or has been, a maintenance calculation (or 'old rules' maintenance assessment) in force, special rules may apply (see p332).

If the application is made before 3 March 2003 but the effective date under the 'old rules' is after 3 March 2003 the case is dealt with as a 'new rules' case (unless the linking rules apply). However, the effective date remains that worked out under the 'old rules'.[40]

If the application was made by the person with care, a Scottish child applicant or, before 14 July 2008, treated as made by a parent with care on benefit, the effective date is:[41]

- the date the non-resident parent is notified of the application; *or*
- if the non-resident parent has intentionally avoided notification, the date on which notification would have been given but for the avoidance.

The non-resident parent is normally notified of the application by phone. In some cases, a maintenance enquiry form may be issued (see p50). In this case, notification is treated as given or sent on the day it is given or posted.[42] Notification is treated as occurring if the maintenance enquiry form is sent to the non-resident parent at his last known or last notified address. A commissioner's decision has stated that it is for the Child Support Agency (CSA) to decide whether an address is sufficiently reliable to send a maintenance enquiry form; it does not have to be beyond reasonable doubt that it is the non-resident parent's current address.[43]

The non-resident parent cannot delay the effective date of a calculation by disputing paternity. The CSA does not make a calculation until the issue of paternity is resolved (see p18) but, if it later decides that the alleged non-resident parent is the father, the calculation is then backdated to the effective date.

If the **non-resident parent** made the application, the effective date of the first calculation is the date of the effective application (see p341).[44]

If there are multiple applications for child maintenance and these are treated as a single application (see p43), the effective date is set by the earlier or earliest application.[45]

Court orders

The following rules apply where there is, or has been, a maintenance order in force for all of the qualifying children named in the calculation.[46] This means that where the order covers one but not all of the qualifying children, the normal rules regarding the effective date apply to those qualifying children.

The following rules apply in relation to court orders regardless of whether a maintenance calculation or default maintenance decision is being made.[47]

If the application is treated as made by a parent with care on benefit and the order is in force on the date the calculation is made, the effective date is two days after that.[48]

If the decision is in response to a voluntary application and an order made on or after 3 March 2003 has been in force for one year, the effective date is two months and two days after the application is made.[49]

In either case, if the order ceases to have effect after the application is made, the effective date is the day after the order ceased to have effect.[50]

Liability for maintenance continues until the order stops being in force, so the non-resident parent should continue making payments while awaiting the calculation. If a calculation is made following a voluntary application, an order made on or after 3 March 2003 has been in force for at least a year, and the non-resident parent makes payments due under the order but after the effective date of the maintenance calculation (and so will have been making them retrospectively after the order ceased to have effect), these will be treated as payments of child support maintenance (see also p408).[51] For collection and enforcement of arrears, see Chapter 19.

Effective dates in special cases

The effective date may be set earlier or later than under the normal rules in certain circumstances where there is, or has been, a maintenance calculation in force.

Condition	Effective date
A maintenance calculation is in force, the non-resident parent in the new application is the non-resident parent in the current calculation and the application is in respect of a different person with care and qualifying child.	The beginning of the maintenance period in the existing case which is not more than seven days after the non-resident parent is notified of the new calculation.[52]
A maintenance calculation is in force and the person with care in the new application is the non-resident parent in the current calculation.	The beginning of the maintenance period in the existing case which is not more than seven days after the non-resident parent in the new application is notified of that application.[53]
A maintenance calculation was in force within eight weeks of the application in relation to the same non-resident parent and qualifying child(ren) but a different person with care.	The date on which the previous maintenance calculation ceased to have effect.[54]

A maintenance calculation is in force, a new application is made in respect of the same non-resident parent but a different parent with care and the previous maintenance calculation ceases to have effect before a decision is made on the new application.	If the non-resident parent has been notified before the previous calculation ceases to have effect, the day after it ceases to have effect. If the non-resident parent is not notified until after the previous calculation ceases to have effect, the date of notification.[55]
A maintenance calculation was in force within the eight weeks preceding the application and the parent with care and non-resident parent have swapped roles in relation to all the qualifying child(ren) concerned – ie, the person with care in the old calculation is the non-resident parent in the new application.	The date on which the previous maintenance calculation ceased to have effect.[56]

If there is, or has been, an 'old rules' maintenance assessment in force

If an 'old rules' maintenance assessment is, or has been, in force, the case may be dealt with under the 'old rules' or 'new rules' depending on who is involved and when the application is made.

Applications for a maintenance calculation after 3 March 2003 but within 13 weeks of an assessment being in force involving the same person with care, non-resident parent and qualifying child(ren) may be treated as an application for a maintenance assessment.[57] In these circumstances, the effective date is set in relation to the 'old rules'.

Otherwise, the effective date of the new maintenance calculation is dealt with under the:

- normal effective date rules; *or*
- special cases rules explained above, as if references to the calculation were to the assessment.[58]

However, if there is a maintenance assessment in force that converts to the 'new rules' early (eg, because of an application from another person with care), there are special rules for working out the effective date of the conversion decision for that existing assessment (see Chapter 7).

Maintenance periods

Child maintenance is calculated on a weekly basis, although it is not always paid weekly (see p401). It is payable in respect of successive seven-day periods with the first period beginning on the effective date.[59]

The only exception is where, when the calculation is made, there is already a calculation in force for the same non-resident parent but for a different child and person with care. In that case, the maintenance periods of the new calculation begin on the same day of the week as the existing calculation.[60]

After a supersession, any fresh calculation comes into effect on the first day of the maintenance period (see p363).

6. **When a maintenance calculation ends**

A maintenance calculation continues until the Child Support Agency (CSA):
- cancels it following a request (see below);
- supersedes it because it has ceased to have effect (see below); *or*
- revises it (see p354);
- supersedes it for another reason (see p358).

In some cases the calculation is replaced by another, while in others no further calculation is made. Any arrears remaining after a calculation ends may still be collected (see Chapter 19). Also, if an application is made for children of the non-resident parent who are not named in the existing calculation, the new calculation replaces the old one.

Request to cancel a calculation

A maintenance calculation must be cancelled when the applicant requests that the CSA ceases acting.[61]

The request may be made verbally or in writing. If the request is made, the CSA must stop all action, including collection and enforcement of arrears, though the person may, if s/he wishes, specifically ask for action in relation to arrears to continue.

Living together

When the request is made, reasons need not be given. However, if the reason is because the parent with care and non-resident parent are living together the CSA should be told. This is because once all the parties share a household, the non-resident parent is no longer non-resident (see p21), so the child is no longer a qualifying child and the calculation ceases to have effect (see below).[62] Both parents should inform the CSA, though the CSA will seek other verification.[63]

The calculation ceases to have effect

Some changes of circumstances lead to a cancellation, whether or not a request is made. The CSA may be aware of a change from, for example, a request or a notification by the parent with care under her duty to do so (see p74) or from the Department for Work and Pensions. The CSA *must* supersede the decision and

cancel a calculation (including a default decision) if the calculation ceases to have effect. The calculation will cease to have effect if:[64]
- the non-resident parent or person with care dies;
- the only, or all, qualifying child(ren) is no longer a qualifying child(ren); *or*
- the non-resident parent ceases to be a parent of the only, or all, qualifying child(ren).

This means cancellation occurs, for example, when:
- a child aged 16 or over leaves school or becomes too old to count as a child;
- the qualifying child, non-resident parent and parent with care start living together;
- the qualifying child goes to live with someone else and as a result the person with care no longer counts as a person with care;
- the qualifying child is adopted, in which case the non-resident parent is no longer a parent; *or*
- the non-resident parent is no longer considered a parent because of the results of a DNA test or a declaration of parentage.

Where the maintenance calculation has been made from an application by a child in Scotland and that child is no longer a child, the CSA must notify the person with care, non-resident parent and other children over 12.[65]

Other cancellations

The CSA must cancel the calculation if the person with care, non-resident parent or qualifying child is no longer habitually resident in the UK (see p26).[66]

A non-resident parent who has successfully contested paternity will have any maintenance calculation cancelled and, if he has paid maintenance, may obtain a refund.

If an applicant fails to provide the CSA with enough information to make a revision or supersession decision, the CSA *may* cancel the calculation.

Date cancellation has effect

If the calculation is cancelled because it ceases to have effect or because of another relevant change, the cancellation takes effect from the first day in the maintenance period in which the change occurred. This includes where:
- the person with care is no longer the person with care for the child(ren) named in the calculation;[67] *or*
- a party is no longer habitually resident in the UK;[68] *or*
- the person with care, non-resident parent or qualifying child dies;[69] *or*
- the non-resident parent ceases to be a parent.[70]

If the cancellation is because the non-resident parent is not considered to be the parent because of a DNA test or declarator of parentage, the effective date is the date of the original maintenance calculation.[71]

Cancellation following a request

A calculation is cancelled with effect from the first day of the maintenance period in which the request was received *or* a different date depending on the reason for the cancellation.[72] A later date may be appropriate if an applicant has requested that the calculation ends on a later date.

If a calculation is cancelled because the non-resident parent and parent with care are living together, and both request the cancellation, it takes effect from the first day of the maintenance period in which the later request to cancel the calculation is made.[73]

Notification of the cancellation decision

When the CSA cancels a calculation or refuses to cancel one, it must notify the non-resident parent, person with care and Scottish child applicant of that decision, and must also provide information on the right of appeal and on revisions and supersessions.[74]

If the maintenance calculation has been made following an application from a child in Scotland and that child is no longer a qualifying child, the CSA must notify the person with care, non-resident parent and other children over 12 who are potential child applicants.[75]

7. How a maintenance calculation affects means-tested benefits

This section covers the effect of receiving child support maintenance on:
- income support (IS);
- income-based jobseeker's allowance (JSA);
- income-related employment and support allowance (ESA).

Other social security benefits, including pension credit (PC) and tax credits are not affected. From 27 October 2008, all child maintenance is also disregarded as income for persons with care when calculating housing benefit and council tax benefit.

Child maintenance paid by a non-resident parent is not taken into account when calculating his, or his partner's, means-tested benefits. However, deductions for flat rate maintenance or arrears may be taken from a non-resident parent's benefits when the Child Support Agency (CSA) requests this to be done.[76] For full details of how means-tested benefits are calculated, including the effect of maintenance other than child support, see CPAG's *Welfare Benefits and Tax Credits Handbook*.

Housing costs

Full mortgage interest is not usually included in the calculation for the first 13 weeks of any IS/income-basedJSA/income-related ESA award. Nevertheless, the benefit calculation includes 100 per cent of eligible mortgage interest if:[77]

- a person with care stops being entitled to IS/income-based JSA/income-related ESA as a result of receiving child maintenance; *and*
- when that happened, she was receiving IS/income-based JSA/income-related ESA including 100 per cent eligible mortgage interest; *and*
- her maintenance calculation is later reduced or ended because:
  - the child support regulations are changed; *or*
  - the calculation is an interim maintenance assessment (IMA) under the 'old rules' and it is ended and not replaced or is replaced by another IMA/default decision or by a full assessment/calculation; *and*
- she then claims IS/income-based JSA/income-related ESA within 26 weeks of the date she stopped being entitled to either benefit.[78]

Child maintenance premium

Before 27 October 2008, a person with care on IS/income-based JSA who was paid child maintenance under the 'new rules' had a child maintenance premium (effectively, an amount of maintenance ignored in the calculation of benefit) applied when working out her/his benefit.[79] When an 'old rules' case converts to the 'new rules' the child maintenance premium may replace a child maintenance bonus (see p348). The premium also applies if maintenance is first paid on or after 3 March 2003 under an agreement or court order,[80] or paid from 16 February 2004.[81]

Just because the parent was paid, or was due to be paid, maintenance for a different child or under an earlier agreement/order, this does not preclude the premium from being applied.

From 27 October 2008, a person with care on IS/income-based JSA/income-related ESA who is paid child maintenance will have up to £20 a week ignored when working out her benefit entitlement.[82] This means that if maintenance paid is £6.50, only £6.50 will be ignored. The maintenance may be made in respect of one child or more, but the amounts are aggregated and only up to £20 is ignored. The child maintenance premium applies whether maintenance is paid directly to the parent with care or via the CSA. Payments can be made under a CSA calculation, maintenance order, written maintenance agreement or voluntarily.[83] This includes where the CSA makes a payment in lieu of maintenance and the non-resident parent is on the flat rate of maintenance.[84]

Changes from April 2010

From April 2010, child maintenance will be fully disregarded when calculating entitlement to IS/income-based JSA/income-related ESA. This means that the parent with care can keep 100 per cent of her benefit and all of the maintenance she receives.[85]

Payment direct to the person with care

The parent with care may ask that payments of maintenance are not made via the CSA but direct from the non-resident parent. For how to request a change to the collection service, see p400. Payments of child maintenance, including lump sums, are treated as income and are taken into account when assessing entitlement to IS/income-based JSA/income-related ESA on a weekly basis.[86] Payments are treated as income in the week they are received by the parent with care, except that child maintenance due before the benefit award is always treated as paid in the week it was due – ie, before the award began.[87]

Payments made regularly are converted into a weekly amount to work out IS/income-based JSA/income-related ESA – eg, where payments are made monthly, multiply by 12 and divide by 52.[88] Where payments are made at irregular intervals, each payment is divided over the weeks since the previous payment.[89]

If the child maintenance premium applies, up to £20 of the maintenance is ignored. The remainder counts in full as income and benefit is, therefore, reduced by this amount.

Jobcentre Plus should not assume that child maintenance is paid as soon as the CSA sends notification of the calculation. Benefit should not be reduced until payments begin. Since October 2008, all child maintenance that is recieved is paid directly to the person with care by the CSA. It is the responsibility of the person with care to ensure that Jobcentre Plus know about any maintenance they are receiving.

Once a person with care's benefit has been reduced because of maintenance payments, if a payment due direct from the non-resident parent is missed, she should ask the Jobcentre Plus for extra benefit to be paid for that period. The Jobcentre Plus should do this without waiting for the CSA to enforce payment of maintenance. The person with care can contact the CSA to chase missing payments and to have payments made to the CSA (see Chapter 19).

Payment of arrears

Non-resident parents are encouraged by the CSA to pay arrears direct to the CSA, which then keeps the arrears up to the amount of IS/income-based JSA/income-related ESA paid because the maintenance was not paid on the due date.[90] Any balance is passed to the person with care.

If the non-resident parent pays arrears direct to the person with care, the full amount of overpaid benefit for the period when that maintenance was due can be recovered from her by the Jobcentre Plus.[91]

Arrears of child support should usually be treated as income for IS/income-based JSA/income-related ESA, but there may be difficulty in working out the period covered by the arrears and this treatment may be open to argument.[92]

Loss of benefit

Persons with care lose IS/income-based JSA/income-related ESA when the child maintenance paid (after the child maintenance premium) increases their income over the benefit applicable amount. If the person with care is only a few pounds over the benefit level, she may find herself worse off because of the loss of passported benefits – eg, free school meals, full health service benefits (see below) and access to the social fund.

A person with care can ask for the calculation to be cancelled (see p334). She could then be deemed to have notional income for IS/income-based JSA/income-related ESA (see CPAG's *Welfare Benefits and Tax Credits Handbook*) but, in practice, it would be difficult for Jobcentre Plus to work out the level of notional income as it would not have the necessary information.

However, this problem should be resolved in April 2010, when child maintenance will be fully disregarded for IS/income-based JSA/income-related ESA. Parents with care who have previously not been entitled to these benefits because of the amount of child maintenance paid should be advised to apply to Jobcentre Plus again in April.

Health service benefits

People on IS/income-based JSA/income-related ESA or the guarantee credit of PC are automatically exempt from all NHS charges. Others may be entitled to full or partial reductions of charges on low-income grounds. This covers prescriptions, dental treatment, sight tests, glasses, wigs, fabric support and fares to hospital.

For these purposes, where child maintenance payments are made:

- regularly, income is the weekly equivalent of payments; *or*
- not regularly, income is the total payments in the 13 weeks before the claim, divided by 13.

There is no disregard. For full details, see CPAG's *Welfare Benefits and Tax Credits Handbook*.

8. Taxation of child maintenance

Person with care

Child support maintenance is not taxable income.

Non-resident parent

From 6 April 2000 maintenance, including child support maintenance, no longer qualifies for tax relief.

9. **Existing 'old rules' cases**

Existing cases continue to be dealt with under the legislation prior to reform, except for some provision for parents with care on benefit – eg, they can ask the Child Support Agency (CSA) to cease acting in both 'new' or 'old' cases. For full details of the 'old rules', see Chapter 14 in the 2002/03 edition of this *Handbook*.

This section outlines the areas where there are differences between the 'new rules' and 'old rules' on maintenance decisions and provides an overview of the relevant provisions.

The following are minor differences between the 'old' and 'new' rules.

- Notifications under the 'old rules' are treated as given or sent by the CSA two days after posting, apart from the issue of a maintenance enquiry form, which is treated as given or sent on the day that it is posted.
- Cancellations are now possible by 'old rules' parents with care on income support (IS)/income-based jobseeker's allowance (JSA)/income-related employment and support allowance (ESA) – ie, they can opt out. There are several other differences for parents with care on benefit (see p336).

Some provisions are completely different.

- Interim maintenance assessments (IMA – see p340) are made under the 'old rules' where there is insufficient information to make an assessment. Default maintenance decisions apply to 'new rules' cases only. At conversion, an IMA may convert to a maintenance calculation or default maintenance decision (see p326).
- The effective dates of a maintenance assessment or IMA have different rules (see p341).
- A person with care on benefit may accrue up to £5 a week child maintenance bonus (see p348). The child maintenance premium does not apply to 'old rules' cases. When a case converts, the premium may apply, but any bonus may be claimed if the conditions are met.

Interim maintenance assessments

If the CSA does not have sufficient information to make a full assessment using the formula, or to decide whether to revise or supersede a decision, it may make an IMA rather than a full assessment.[93] The decision to make an IMA is discretionary, so the CSA must take into account the welfare of any child(ren) affected by the decision (see p24).

There are four types of IMA.[94] For IMA commencement see p344, for cancellation see p345, and for revisions and supersessions see Chapter 17.

Interim maintenance assessments

Category	When it is applied	How it is worked out
A	A non-resident parent has failed to provide information about his own circumstances (not any new partner).	One-and-a-half times the maintenance requirement.
B	Either the person with care or non-resident parent has failed to provide information about the income of their new partner, or about other members of their family.	Calculated as a full assessment except that in exempt income it is assumed a new partner can help maintain a joint child and there is no protected income calculation, although the 30 per cent cap may apply.
C	The non-resident parent is self-employed and is unable to provide information about earnings.	Normally £30, but may be less.
D	A Category A IMA is in force but on the information available it appears that a full assessment would be higher.	Calculated as a full assessment, except: – there is no protected income, nor a 30 per cent cap; – no housing costs are allowed; – exempt income is the adult personal allowance only; *and* – when working out income, there is no disregard of payments to personal or occupational pension schemes or to pension schemes intended to provide capital sums to discharge a mortgage.

For full information, see the 2002/03 edition of this *Handbook*.

The effective date of an assessment

Under the 'old rules' there are different rules on setting the effective date of assessments, IMAs and maintenance assessments replacing IMAs. In some cases the CSA may set an interim effective date.

Effective date of assessments

Circumstances	Effective date
Application by person with care or qualifying child in Scotland.[95]	Eight weeks from the date on which the maintenance enquiry form (MEF) is given or sent to a non-resident parent as long as, within four weeks of being sent the MEF, he returns it with his name, address and written confirmation that he is the parent of the child(ren) named in the maintenance application form (MAF). *Otherwise,* the date the non-resident parent was actually given or sent the MEF.
Application by non-resident parent.[96]	Eight weeks from the date on which the application was received by the CSA as long as the non-resident parent provides his name, address and written confirmation that he is the parent of the child(ren) named in the MAF as part of the MAF or provides these details within four weeks of the date of the application. *Otherwise,* the date an effective MAF (see p41) is received.
In either case where there is a court order in force for at least one of the qualifying children on the date the assessment is made.[97]	Two days after the date the assessment is made. The order for maintenance ceases to have effect from the effective date (see p29).[98]
The court order ceases (not because of an IMA) before the assessment is made and after the MEF/MAF is received, depending on the applicant.[99]	The day after the order ceased to be in force.
Another assessment is already in force and an application by a different person with care is then made.[100]	The CSA may treat the new application as received up to eight weeks earlier than the date it was actually received, but no earlier than the date on which the previous assessment ended.[101]

An assessment made following an application from a qualifying child in Scotland has been cancelled at the child's request or because s/he is no longer a child and an application for children who were qualifying children under the previous assessment has been made.[102]	The CSA may treat the new application as received up to eight weeks earlier than the date it was actually received, but no earlier than the date on which the previous assessment ended.[103]
An assessment is in force for a non-resident parent and a different person with care then applies for child maintenance.	The first day of the first maintenance period (see p333) not more than seven days after the parties are notified of the second assessment.[104] If this would make the effective date fall within the eight-week period and the non-resident parent meets the rules for that period (see p341), the effective date is the first day of the first maintenance period after the eight-week period.[105]
There is a previous maintenance calculation in relation to the same non-resident parent, which is no longer in force.	The effective date of a maintenance calculation can be aligned with the first day of the maintenance period of a maintenance calculation or assessment that has previously been, but has ceased to be in force in relation to the non-resident parent. The previous maintenance assessment does not have to be in relation to the same person with care. In this situation, the effective date will be within six days of the new assessment and on the same day of the week on which the previous maintenance assessment began.[106] This provision applies to both 'old' and 'new 'rules cases.[107]

If there are multiple applications for child maintenance and these are treated as a single application, the effective date is set by the earlier or earliest application.[108]

Effective date of interim maintenance assessments

Circumstances	Effective date
Category A or C unless there is a court order in force.	The first day after it is made which falls on the same day of the week as the day the MEF was actually given or sent to the non-resident parent or, where the non-resident parent is the applicant, the day the MAF was received by the CSA (but see the exception below).[109]
Category B unless there is a court order in force.	The date the MEF was actually given or sent to the non-resident parent or, where the non-resident parent is the applicant, the day the MAF was received by the CSA (but see the exception below).[110]
There is a court order in force.	See normal effective date rules.
Superseding IMA with another Category A, C or D IMA.	The first day of the maintenance period in which the CSA decides to make the new IMA.[111]
Superseding IMA is a Category B IMA.	Where the cancelled IMA (or the first cancelled IMA, if there is more than one) had caused a court order to cease to have effect, the effective date of that (or that first) IMA.[112] *Otherwise,* the day the MEF was actually given or sent to the non-resident parent or, where the non-resident parent is the applicant, the day the MAF was received by the CSA.[113]

The exception to these rules is that, if the effective date set by them would fall within the eight-week period and the non-resident parent meets the rules for that period for a full assessment (see p330), the effective date is set by those rules.[114]

Effective date of a maintenance assessment replacing an interim maintenance assessment

If the CSA:

- has sufficient information to make a full assessment for the *whole of the period* beginning with the usual effective date (see p341), the IMA ceases to have effect on the first day of the maintenance period (see p333) in which the CSA received the information.[115] The CSA revises (see p354) the IMA decision.[116] The amount payable under the IMA becomes that of the full assessment;[117] *or*
- has sufficient information to make a full assessment for *only part of that period*, the IMA ceases to have effect on the first day of the maintenance period in which the CSA received the information.[118] The CSA supersedes the IMA decision.[119] The effective date of the full assessment is also that date.[120] The amount payable under the IMA remains that of the IMA.[121]

If the information which enables the CSA to make a full assessment is that IS/income-based JSA/income-related ESA has been awarded, the CSA is treated as receiving that information on the day benefit became payable.[122]

Interim effective date

If the CSA does not have sufficient information to make a full assessment from the usual effective date (see p341), but has enough to make one running from a later date, it can make a full assessment from that later date.[123] The interim effective date is the first day of the maintenance period (see p344) in which the CSA received the information.[124]

If the CSA later receives sufficient information to make a full assessment from the usual effective date, the assessment already made for the later period then has effect from the usual effective date instead.[125]

Cancelling assessments

The information on ending assessments is the same as that under the 'new rules' except for the following.

- From 3 March 2003, any applicant (including a parent with care on benefits) under the 'old rules' may ask the CSA to stop acting. The calculation will be cancelled, although until 14 July 2008 a parent with care on IS or income-based JSA may have had a reduced benefit decision made.
- Under the 'old rules', if a Scottish child applicant is no longer habitually resident in Scotland the assessment is cancelled.[126] This takes effect from the first day in the maintenance period in which the change occurred.
- Under the 'old rules', the CSA had discretion, in some cases, on when to set the effective date of the cancellation – eg, if the person with care and non-resident parent are living together.[127] Guidance indicates that effective dates are now set in the same way under both 'old' and 'new' rules.

- Before cancelling a calculation, the CSA must, if possible, give written notice to the person with care, non-resident parent and any Scottish child applicant of intention to cancel the calculation, and allow 14 days from the date the notice is sent before cancelling.[128]
- The full amount of the assessment is due for the maintenance period in which the cancellation date falls,[129] except if a Category A or D IMA is cancelled, when it is only due to the cancellation date.[130]
- An IMA must be cancelled when the CSA has enough information to make a full assessment. Otherwise the only provision for cancellation is when the CSA accepts that the non-resident parent was unavoidably delayed in providing the information. The effective date of the maintenance assessment is as under the normal rules. However, where the new decision is another category of IMA, the date is:[131]
  - for a Category A or D IMA, the first day of the maintenance period in which the CSA decides to make the new IMA; *or*
  - for a Category B IMA, the day the MEF was given or sent to the non-resident parent or if the non-resident parent is the applicant, the day the MAF was received by the CSA.

Court order phasing of assessments

The definition of maintenance agreement and court order are the same as in court order phasing for 'new rules' cases, but the legislative references are slightly different.[132] Evidence of the order must be provided.

In the regulations there are two similar types of phasing, which we call 'original phasing' and '1994 phasing'. As phasing can last for a maximum of 18 months, it should only apply to 'old rules' cases which have had considerable delays in assessment, or for which there is still an IMA.

For full information on court order phasing and supersession of decisions where court order phasing applies, see the 2002/03 edition of this *Handbook*.

Original phasing

This has existed since April 1993 and the reduced amount payable is known as the **'modified amount'**.[133] It does not apply to a Category A IMA.[134] It applies where:[135]

- the old maintenance order/agreement covered all the children named in the assessment; *and*
- the non-resident parent is responsible for maintaining a child (see p18) living with him who is not named in the assessment; *and*
- the assessment is £60 or less.

The weekly modified amount is the weekly amount due under the old order/agreement *plus* £20.[136] This continues for a year, but ends before that if one of the above conditions is no longer met.

1994 phasing

This was introduced on 7 February 1994 and the reduced amount payable is known as the **'transitional amount'**.[137] It does not apply to a Category A or D IMA.[138] It applies where:[139]

- the old maintenance order/agreement covered at least one child named in the assessment; *and*
- the non-resident parent was a member of a family (see p25) which included at least one child on the effective date (see p341) and is still a member of a family with a child; *and*
- original phasing does not apply;[140] *and*
- the assessment does not replace a Category A or D IMA made after 22 January 1996.[141]

If the assessment is £60 or less, the transitional amount is the amount under the old order/agreement *plus* £20.[142] This lasts for 52 weeks.

If the assessment is more than £60 a week, the transitional amount is:[143]

- for the first 26 weeks, the old amount *plus* the greater of £20 and a quarter of the difference between the assessment and the old amount;
- for the next 26 weeks, the old amount *plus* the greater of £40 and half of the difference between the assessment and the old amount; *and*
- for the last 26 weeks of the phasing-in period, the old amount *plus* the greater of £60 and three-quarters of the difference between the assessment and the old amount.

The maintenance payable becomes the assessment amount if the transitional amount would be larger than that. Therefore, it is only where the difference between the old amount and the assessment amount is more than £60 a week that the phasing-in period lasts the full 18 months.

Which type of phasing applies

CSA guidance covers only 1994 phasing, implying that original phasing cannot be applied. However, the provisions remain in force.[144] This is only likely to matter if a Category D IMA is made or replaced, because only original and not 1994 phasing can apply to a Category D IMA. If the wrong (or no) phasing is applied, an appeal can be made (see Chapter 18).

Revisions and supersessions

Where original phasing applies and the assessment decision is revised (see p354) or superseded (see p358) and the conditions for phasing are still met, phasing continues until the 52-week period ends.[145]

Where 1994 phasing applies (or where original phasing applies and there is a change of circumstances), then the following amount is payable:[146]

- if the fresh assessment is less than the modified/transitional amount, the fresh assessment;
- if the fresh assessment is less than the previous assessment but more than the modified/transitional amount, the modified/transitional amount;
- if the fresh assessment is higher than the previous assessment, the modified/transitional amount is increased by the same amount as the increase between the two formula assessments.

Child maintenance bonus

The child maintenance bonus has now been abolished for all cases. From 27 October 2008, all parents with care who claimed IS/income-based JSA and had 'old rules' child maintenance assessments stopped accruing the child maintenance bonus and started to receive the child maintenance premium instead (see p337).

For information on the child maintenance bonus, see previous editions of this *Handbook*.

Notes

1. Making the initial maintenance decision
1 s11 CSA 1991
2 Sch 1 Art 5(5) CS(NIRA) Regs
3 Sch 1 Art 5(1) CS(NIRA) Regs
4 Sch 1 Art 5(3) CS(NIRA) Regs
5 Sch 1 Art 5(2) and (6) CS(NIRA) Regs
6 Sch 1 Art 5(4) and (7) CS(NIRA) Regs
7 CSA Business Plan 2008/09
8 CSA Operational Improvement Plan 2006-2009
9 s36 CMOPA 2008
10 Sch 1 para 15 CSA 1991
11 Reg 2(4) CS(MCSC) Regs; CCS/2750/1995
12 Reg 1(2)(c) CS(MCSC) Regs
13 PG, Calculation and Decision Types, Taking Account of Changes That Happen at Different Times
14 Reg 25(5) CS(MCP) Regs
15 Reg 6 CS(MCP) Regs
16 R(CS) 2/98
17 Reg 10(1) and (4) CS(MAP) Regs

2. Default maintenance decisions
18 s12(1) CSA 1991
19 Reg 7 CS(MCP) Regs
20 PG, Calculation and Decision Types, Calculate a DMD
21 Reg 23(2) CS(MCP) Regs
22 s16(1B)CSA 1991; reg 3A(5) SS&CS(DA) Regs
23 Reg 5A(2) SS&CS(DA) Regs
24 Reg 8A(2)(a) SS&CS(DA) Regs
25 Reg 5A(3) SS&CS(DA) Regs

3. Notification of decisions
26 Reg 23 CS(MCP) Regs
27 Reg 23(1) CS(MCP) Regs
28 Reg 23(2) CS(MCP) Regs
29 Reg 23(3) CS(MCP) Regs

4. Court order phasing of calculations
30 Reg 30 CS(TP) Regs
31 Reg 30 CS(TP) Regs
32 Reg 30(a)(iii) CS(TP) Regs
33 Reg 30(a)(i) and (ii) CS(TP) Regs
34 PG, Gather Information and Evidence, Court Order Details Dialog; Court Order and WMA Verification Levels

35 Reg 31 CS(TP) Regs
36 Reg 31(2) CS(TP) Regs
37 Reg 31(3) CS(TP) Regs
38 Reg 32 CS(TP) Regs

5. **When the first maintenance calculation begins**
39 Reg 1(2) CS(MCP) Regs
40 Reg 31(2) CS(MCP) Regs
41 Regs 1(2) and 25(3) and (4) CS(MCP) Regs
42 Reg 2 CS(MCP) Regs
43 CCS/2288/2005
44 Reg 26(2) CS(MCP) Regs
45 Reg 4(3) CS(MCP) Regs
46 Regs 26 and 27 CS(MCP) Regs
47 PG, Calculation and Decision Types, Effective Date of a New Rules Calculation
48 Reg 27 CS(MCP) Regs
49 Reg 26 CS(MCP) Regs
50 Reg 28 CS(MCP) Regs
51 Reg 8A CS(MAJ) Regs
52 Reg 7B(21) SS&CS(DA) Regs
53 Reg 29(1)(b) CS(MCP) Regs
54 Reg 29(1)(a) CS(MCP) Regs
55 Reg 29(1)(d) CS(MCP) Regs
56 Reg 29(1)(c) CS(MCP) Regs
57 Reg 28(1) CS(TP) Regs
58 Reg 31(1) CS(MCP) Regs
59 s4A CSA 1991
60 Reg 7B(21) SS&CS(DA) Regs

6. **When a maintenance calculation ends**
61 ss4(5), 6(5) and 7(6) CSA 1991
62 PG, Withdraw/Cancel Application and Close Case, User Initiated – Reason and Effective Date for Withdrawal/ Cancellation
63 PG, Withdraw/Cancel Application and Close Case, Non-resident Parent and Parent with Care Living Together Verification Levels
64 Sch 1 para 16 CSA 1991
65 Reg 24 CS(MCP) Regs
66 s44(1) CSA 1991
67 Reg 7B(17A) SS&CS(DA) Regs
68 Reg 7B (18) SS&CS(DA) Regs
69 Reg 7B(17) SS&CS(DA) Regs
70 Sch 1 para 16(1)(c) CSA 1991
71 s16(3) CSA 1991
72 s17(4) CSA 1991
73 Reg 7B(20) SS&CS(DA) Regs
74 Reg 15C(5) SS&CS(DA) Regs
75 Reg 24 CS(MCP) Regs; reg 15C(5)(b) SS&CS(DA) Regs

7. **How a maintenance calculation affects means-tested benefits**
76 s43 CSA 1991; Sch 9B SS(C&P) Regs
77 Sch 3 para 14(2) IS Regs; Sch 2 para 13(2) JSA Regs
78 Reg 32 IS Regs; Sch 2 para 18(1)(c) JSA Regs
79 Art 6 CSPSSA (Comm 12)O
80 Reg 1 SS(CMPMA) Regs 2000
81 Reg 1 SS(CMP)A Regs
82 Sch 9 para 73 IS Regs as substituted by reg 2 SS(CMP)A Regs; Sch 7 para 70 JSA Regs as substituted by reg 3 SS(CMP)A Regs
83 Sch 9 para 73(4) IS Regs as substituted by reg 2 SS(CMP)A Regs; Sch7 para 70 JSA Regs as substituted by reg 3 SS(CMP)A Regs
84 Reg 60A IS Regs; reg 125 JSA Regs
85 The Social Security (Miscellaneous Amendments) (No.4) Regulations 2009
86 Reg 60B IS Regs; reg 126 JSA Regs
87 Reg 60D IS Regs; reg 129 JSA Regs
88 Reg 60C(2) and (3) IS Regs; reg 128(2) and (3) JSA Regs
89 Reg 60C(4) IS Regs; reg 128(4) JSA Regs
90 Reg 8 CS(AIAMA) Regs
91 s74(1) SSAA 1992; reg 7(1)(b) SS(PAOR) Regs
92 *Secretary of State for Work and Pensions v Menary-Smith* [2006] EWCA Civ 1689

9. **Existing 'old rules' cases**
93 s12(1) CSA 1991
94 Reg 8 CS(MAP) Regs
95 Reg 30(2)(a) CS(MAP) Regs
96 Reg 30(2)(b) CS(MAP) Regs
97 Reg 3(5) CS(MAJ) Regs
98 Reg 3(6) CS(MAJ) Regs
99 Reg 3(8) CS(MAJ) Regs
100 Reg 3(1) CS(MAP) Regs
101 Reg 3(3) CS(MAP) Regs
102 Reg 3(2) CS(MAP) Regs
103 Reg 3(3) CS(MAP) Regs
104 Reg 33(6) and (7) CS(MAP) Regs
105 Reg 33(9) CS(MAP) Regs
106 Reg 4(3) CS(MAP) Regs
107 Reg 4(8) and (9) The Child Support (Miscellaneous Amendments) (No.2) Regulations 2008
108 Reg 5 The Child Support (Miscellaneous Amendments) (No.2) Regulations 2008
109 Reg 8C(1)(a) CS(MAP) Regs
110 Reg 8C(1)(b) CS(MAP) Regs
111 Regs 9(4) and 23(13) CS(MAP) Regs
112 Reg 9(5) and (6) CS(MAP) Regs
113 Reg 9(3) CS(MAP) Regs
114 Reg 8C(1)(d) CS(MAP) Regs

115 Reg 8D(5) CS(MAP) Regs
116 Reg 17(3)(a) CS(MAP) Regs
117 Reg 30A(2) CS(MAP) Regs
118 Reg 8D(6) CS(MAP) Regs
119 Reg 20(6) CS(MAP) Regs
120 Reg 30A(1) CS(MAP) Regs
121 Reg 8D(2) CS(MAP) Regs
122 Reg 8D(8) CS(MAP) Regs
123 Reg 30A(4) CS(MAP) Regs
124 Reg 30A(3) CS(MAP) Regs
125 Reg 30A(6) CS(MAP) Regs
126 Sch 1 para 16(5) CSA 1991; reg 7(1)
     CS(MAJ) Regs; reg 32A(1) CS(MAP)
     Regs
127 Sch 1 para 16(7) CSA 1991
128 Reg 32B CS(MAP) Regs
129 Reg 33(5) CS(MAP) Regs
130 Reg 8D(4) CS(MAP) Regs
131 Reg 9(1) CS(MAP) Regs
132 Sch para 7(1)(a)(iii) CSA(Comm3)O; reg
     7(1)(a) CS(MATP) Regs
133 Sch para 6 CSA(Comm3)O
134 Sch para 7(2) CSA(Comm3)O
135 Sch para 7(1) CSA(Comm3)O
136 Sch paras 6 and 8 CSA(Comm3)O
137 Reg 6(1) CS(MATP) Regs
138 Reg 7(2)(a) CS(MATP) Regs
139 Reg 7(1) CS(MATP) Regs
140 Reg 7(2)(b) CS(MATP) Regs
141 Reg 7(2)(c) CS(MATP) Regs
142 Reg 8(2)(a) CS(MATP) Regs
143 Reg 8(2) CS(MATP) Regs
144 Reg 7(2)(b) CS(MATP) Regs
145 Sch para 8 CSA(Comm3)O
146 Sch para 12 CSA(Comm3)O; reg 11
     CS(MATP) Regs

Chapter 17

Revisions and supersessions

This chapter covers:
1. Changing decisions (below)
2. Revisions (p354)
3. Supersessions (p358)

Note: this chapter does not include information on revisions and supersessions outstanding at conversion. These are covered in Chapter 7. Conversion decisions themselves may be revised or superseded as described in this chapter.[1] However, the amount of any maintenance to be paid (eg, transitional amount) will be worked out using the rules described in Chapter 7.

---

1. Changing decisions

Most decisions can be changed or challenged by revision or supersession. However, there are some decisions that cannot (see p352).

A supersession or revision is a decision which changes an earlier decision. As with all decisions, they are made by 'decision makers' who work for the Child Support Agency (CSA) and who make decisions in the name of the Child Maintenance and Enforcement Commission (C-MEC). A revision or supersession normally happens because the decision maker is told that something is wrong or has changed since the initial decision was made. A decision maker may also initiate a revision or supersession her/himself.

The table on p352 is a quick guide to when decisions are revised and superseded. Put simply, the main difference between a revision and supersession is that:

- a revision means the decision which is wrong or has been challenged is itself changed;
- a supersession means that a new decision is made with effect from a later date.

If a decision is challenged within one month, it may be revised. Outside this time period a decision can only be revised in special circumstances – eg, if there has been official error (see p356). If these special circumstances are not met, the decision may be superseded instead.

* *

Quick guide to revisions and supersessions

Why is the decision being challenged?	When?	What can be done?
The decision is wrong for any reason.	Within a month of being told the decision.	The decision can be revised.
The CSA made a mistake ('official error'), was misled or did not know about something that would have affected the decision.	At any time.	The decision can be revised. If the CSA did not know something or was misled, the decision can only be revised in certain circumstances (see p354). If these do not apply, the decision can be superseded.
The decision is wrong for any reason (except someone not being a parent of a child to whom a calculation relates).	Later than one month after being told the decision.	The decision may be superseded, but the person can make a late application for a revision to be considered (see p355).
Something that affects the decision has changed.	At any time.	The decision can be superseded.
The CSA has not properly dealt with the case.	At any time.	The person may make a complaint (see p352).

Variations are an element of the calculation. This means that any change relating to a variation element can give rise to a revision or supersession of the maintenance calculation.

For changing decisions on deductions of maintenance from income support (IS), income-based jobseeker's allowance (JSA), income-related employment and support allowance (ESA) and pension credit (PC), see CPAG's *Welfare Benefits and Tax Credits Handbook*.

Decisions of the First-tier Tribunal and the Upper Tribunal (see Chapter 18) can also be superseded or revised, but only in certain circumstances (see pp354 and 359).

If a non-resident parent thinks the revision/supersession may reduce the amount of his calculation, he may try to negotiate lower payments pending the decision, although this is usually difficult (see p410).

Challenging decisions that cannot be revised or superseded

Decisions that cannot be revised or superseded are mainly in the areas of information gathering, collection and enforcement. Deduction from earnings orders can be appealed to a court (see p416). Judicial review may also be possible (see below).

Further information can be given to the CSA and the decision maker can be asked to reconsider. If the decision maker refuses to change the decision, a complaint can be made. There may be other occasions that do not involve a decision, but where the behaviour of CSA staff or others acting for C-MEC is unsatisfactory – eg, intimidating or unnecessarily intrusive questioning, or unwarranted demands for evidence and documentation. In these cases, a complaint can be made.

Complaints should initially be made through the CSA's own complaints system before being taken further if necessary – eg, to the Independent Case Examiner (see Chapter 20).

Judicial review

A person affected by a decision or action of a public body or one of its officers can ask the High Court to carry out a judicial review of the decision or action. The court can 'set aside' the decision and also order the decision maker to consider it again in a lawful way. Judicial review cannot usually be brought if there is a right to raise the issue in an appeal to the First-tier Tribunal, Upper Tribunal or court. Otherwise, judicial review may be sought of a decision of the CSA (eg, on enforcement). Legal advice *must* be taken as soon as possible after the decision is made. Legal aid may be available.

Judicial review can succeed if:[2]

- the decision maker makes an error in law (illegality) – eg, does something s/he has no power to do; *or*
- a decision maker fails to have regard to a relevant matter or has regard to an irrelevant matter, or where a decision is 'so outrageous in its defiance of logic or of accepted moral standards that no sensible person who had applied his mind to the question could have arrived at it' (irrationality); *or*
- there has been procedural unfairness.

Challenging decisions about benefit entitlement

Some CSA decisions depend on a decision of the Jobcentre Plus or the Pension Service. For example, a non-resident parent in receipt of IS, income-related ESA, income-based JSA or the guarantee credit of PC will pay the minimum rate (see p172) or the flat rate (see p85) of child support. As long as Jobcentre Plus or the Pension Service pay one of these benefits, even if the non-resident parent has other income, there can be no application for a variation on additional income grounds (see p124). A parent who believes that the other parent should not be allowed to claim a benefit (eg, because s/he is working full time) cannot directly challenge a Jobcentre Plus/the Pension Service decision to award it. However, s/he can raise the issue with the CSA, which will contact Jobcentre Plus or the

Pension Service, which then investigates. Jobcentre Plus/the Pension Service reports the result to the CSA, but not to the person who made the allegation. The person cannot appeal to the First-tier Tribunal against the Jobcentre Plus/ Pension Service decision,[3] although judicial review could be sought.

2. **Revisions**

The decision maker can revise a decision if a person applies within one month (or longer if special circumstances exist – see p355), applies for a variation within one month (provided the grounds for variation existed from the date of the decision under revision) or if the decision maker her/himself initiates the revision within one month of the original decision. A revised decision normally takes effect from the date the original decision had effect.

Decisions that can be revised

Most child maintenance decisions can be revised, including:[4]
- a decision to make or refuse to make a maintenance calculation, including interim and default maintenance decisions (see p340), except where a decision has been made not to make a determination on the application – eg, if an application from a parent with care is cancelled because she is found not to be the principal provider of day-to-day care;
- a decision of the First-tier Tribunal to make or refuse to agree a variation to a maintenance calculation. However, a decision to make or to refuse to make a variation made by an appeal tribunal before 3 November 2008 (when appeal tribunals were replaced by the First-tier Tribunal) cannot be revised;
- a decision to adjust maintenance payable or to cancel an adjustment (see p405);[5]
- any decision made on supersession (see p358).[6]

When a decision can be revised

The decision maker can revise a decision if, within a month of notification of the decision:[7]
- s/he starts action leading to a revision;
- a person (person with care, non-resident parent or Scottish child applicant) applies for a revision; *or*
- a person applies for a variation.

Outside this one-month time period the decision maker can revise a decision if:
- an appeal is made in time (or within the time allowed for late appeals if the application meets those conditions and the appeal has not yet been determined (see p355);[8]

- there has been 'official error' (see p356);[9]
- the decision is wrong because of a misrepresentation or failure to disclose a material fact (see p356) and, because of this, the decision is more advantageous to the person who misrepresented or failed to disclose than it would otherwise have been;[10]
- a late application is accepted;[11]
- it was made pending a test case decision, which has now been given (see p392);[12]
- the person applied for a revision within a month of the decision but it was refused because there was insufficient information or evidence to carry out a revision and the person has provided the further information within a month (or such longer period as is reasonable in the circumstances) of being notified of the refusal;[13] *or*
- the decision is wrong because a person with respect to whom the maintenance calculation has been made was not, at the time the calculation was made, a parent of a child to whom the calculation relates.[14]

If an appeal is lodged, the decision maker checks to see whether the decision should be revised (see p354).

A decision *cannot* be revised because of a change in circumstances after the date the decision was made, or because of an expected change.[15] Instead, the decision may be superseded (see p358).

For revisions of default maintenance decisions, see p327.

Under the test case rules (see p392), the decision maker may refuse to follow the law as decided by the Upper Tribunal or the courts, or even suspend a decision on revision while an appeal is being brought in another case.

Late applications

Because a supersession (see p358) cannot usually lead to a decision being backdated to the original effective date, a late application for a revision (which can) may need to be made. However, in case it should not be accepted, an application for a supersession can be made at the same time, if appropriate. For example, a decision may be based on the wrong mortgage payment details. If the person concerned missed the deadline for applying for a revision, s/he can make a late application (giving special reasons – see below) and also apply for a supersession on the grounds that there has been a mistake of fact (see p359). S/he should also file a late notice of appeal (see p372). This is because the circumstances in which a late appeal can be accepted are wider than those for revisions.

The decision maker can extend the one-month period for applying for a revision if s/he considers that:[16]

- it was not practicable to apply within one month because of 'special circumstances' (see p356);
- the application for revision has merit; *and*
- it is reasonable to grant the application.

'**Special circumstances**' are not defined, but they are not the same as the special circumstances needed for bringing a late appeal (see p372). However, ignorance of, or a mistake about, the law, including time limits, or a new interpretation of the law by the Upper Tribunal or court are *not* special circumstances and must be ignored when considering the application.[17] The person applying for a revision must apply for an extension within 13 months of the notification.[18] However, if s/he has asked for written reasons for the decision s/he is seeking to revise, the 13 months can be extended. If the statement of reasons is provided within one month of notification of the decision, the 13-month period is extended by 14 days. If the statement of reasons is provided after one month, the 13 months plus 14 days runs from the date it is provided.[19] The longer the delay in applying for a revision, the more compelling the special circumstances must be.[20]

An application for an extension must identify the decision that it is sought to revise and explain why an extension should be granted.[21] An application that is refused may not be renewed,[22] although the decision maker may have power to reconsider a refusal to extend.[23] It is for this reason that if a person is within the time limit to appeal a decision s/he should file a late appeal as well as asking for a late revision. Judicial review of a refusal to extend the time limit for making a revision may be possible (see p353).

Official error

'**Official error**' is a mistake made by an officer of the Child Support Agency (CSA), Child Maintenance Enforcement Commission (C-MEC), Department for Work and Pensions, HM Revenue and Customs, or a designated authority, which was not caused or contributed to by anyone outside one of these bodies.[24] This includes mistakes of law (see p361), except those only shown as an error by the Upper Tribunal or court, as well as mistakes of fact, such as:

- a mistake of arithmetic;
- a wrong assumption about a person's circumstances where there was no evidence for it;
- a mistake made because CSA or C-MEC staff did not pass information or evidence to the officer who made the decision, when they should have done.

Misrepresentation and failure to disclose

A '**misrepresentation**' is a written or spoken statement of fact which is untrue.[25] This applies to an untrue statement, even if the person making it believes it to be true ('innocent misrepresentation').[26]

There is only a '**failure to disclose**' a fact if there is a legal duty to report that fact to the CSA or C-MEC.[27] Therefore, a person who is asked to give information but does not has failed to disclose that information. However, if the person is not asked for the information, there can be no failure to disclose unless it is one of the facts a parent with care must always report (see p74). There is no general duty to report changes of circumstances to the CSA (see p74).

The decision that the decision maker wishes to revise must have been wrong because of a fact that was misrepresented or not disclosed and the decision was more advantageous to the person who misrepresented or failed to disclose.[28] Therefore, if a decision maker ignored that fact or if that fact made no difference, the decision maker cannot base a revision on misrepresentation or failure to disclose.

Example

When Amy applied for maintenance she also applied for a variation on the ground that Shaun had assets over £65,000. However, the variation was not agreed and her maintenance calculation was made without this element, based on the information Shaun provided. A few months later Amy discovers that Shaun inherited a property from his aunt a few weeks before her application for maintenance. She informs the CSA, it investigates and confirms that he failed to disclose this when he was asked to provide information for the variation element. Because he failed to disclose the inheritance, his maintenance calculation is less than it would have been with the variation element. Since there was failure to disclose that resulted in a decision that was more advantageous to him, the decision maker revises the original maintenance calculation.

However, had Shaun only inherited the property some time after he was asked for information in relation to the variation application the decision maker could not decide that he had failed to disclose information. In this case, the maintenance calculation cannot be revised, but it may be superseded if Amy asks for a variation to be considered.

Procedure for revising

A notification of a decision sets out how to ask the decision maker to revise that decision.[29] The revision request may be made by telephone. However, unless the issue is straightforward, it is best to follow up any telephone call with a letter to the CSA confirming the reason for the request.

There is no general requirement for the decision maker to notify the parties that s/he is considering a revision or to inform one party that the other has applied for a revision. However, if an application for variation has passed preliminary consideration[30] or there is a request for a revision of a calculation with a previously agreed variation,[31] the other parties may be contacted and asked for their representations.

The rules about disclosure apply to the information given in any notification (see p75).

If a revision has been requested, the burden of proof is on the applicant.[32] In cases where the applicant fails to provide sufficient information to make a decision, the decision maker may ask her/him to provide further information within an agreed time limit. In this situation, the decision maker may decide to:

- close the case; *or*

- make a default maintenance decision; *or*
- refuse to revise the decision.

If a default decision would be less than the current maintenance calculation the decision maker may refuse to revise rather than make a default maintenance decision. For further information on default maintenance decisions, see p326.

If a revision is considered because an appeal has been lodged, unless the revised decision would be worse for the appellant, the revision is carried out and the appeal lapses.[33] The appellant could then decide to appeal against the revised decision, within the usual time limits. If the revised decision does not benefit the appellant, it is still carried out but the appellant is asked whether s/he wishes the appeal to go ahead against the revised decision and, if so, whether s/he wants to make further representations.

The revised decision

The revised decision normally has the same effective date as the decision it replaces.[34] However, if the effective date of that decision was wrong, the revised decision has the effective date that the replaced decision should have had.[35]

Notification

If the decision is revised, whether or not this results in a fresh or new maintenance calculation (including a default maintenance decision), the parties must be notified of the decision and given the usual details (see p328).[36] If there is more than one person with care in relation to a non-resident parent, this means all must be notified. The normal rules on information disclosure apply.[37]

If the request for revision is refused, only the applicant will be informed, unless the other parties have been contacted – eg, where there has been a request for a variation. Notification of the decision includes reasons for refusal and details of appeal rights.[38]

The time limit for appealing against a decision that has been revised runs from the date of the notice of the revised decision. If the request for a revision is refused, the time limit for appealing runs from the date on which this refusal is notified only if the request was made within a month of the original decision being notified or a late application for revision was accepted.[39]

3. **Supersessions**

The decision maker can supersede a decision at any time if certain rules are met, with or without an application. Usually a decision is superseded because of a change in circumstances. A superseded decision normally takes effect from the date of the application for a supersession. Unlike social security cases, there is no duty to tell the Child Support Agency (CSA) of all changes of circumstances (see p74 for changes that must be notified). An application for a variation to the maintenance calculation may be treated as a request for a supersession (see p305).

> *Future changes*
>
> When the new system of calculating child maintenance starts in 2011, the amount will usually be fixed for a year. There are likely to be regulations to restrict the situations in which a supersession can be made – eg, whether a particular change in circumstances can result in a supersession during the year.[40]

Decisions that can be superseded

Most child support decisions (whether made by the CSA, the First-tier Tribunal or the Upper Tribunal) can be superseded. However, a decision made before 3 November 2008 (when the new tribunal system was introduced) by an appeal tribunal or the child support commissioners cannot now be superseded. Decisions that can be superseded include:[41]

- a decision to make a maintenance calculation, including default and interim maintenance decisions (see p328);
- a decision of a First-tier Tribunal on a CSA referral of a variation application (see p306);
- a decision to make, or refuse to make, a departure direction;[42]
- any decisions made on revision (see p354).

It may also be possible to supersede other CSA decisions, depending on how the CSA (and the First-tier Tribunal and Upper Tribunal) interprets the rules. For decisions which may be possible to revise, see p354.

When a decision can be superseded

The decision maker can *normally* supersede a decision if:[43]

- it is a decision of the CSA, the First-tier Tribunal or the Upper Tribunal and there has been a relevant change of circumstances since the decision had effect or it is expected that there will be such a change and there would be a significant change in the amount of the calculation;
- it is a decision of the CSA, the First-tier Tribunal or the Upper Tribunal and the decision was made in ignorance of, or was based on a mistake about, a material fact;
- it is a decision of the CSA, the First-tier Tribunal or the Upper Tribunal and there is an application for a variation to the calculation; *or*
- the decision was made by the CSA and it is wrong in law (see p361).

Any information or evidence on which a superseding decision is to be based must be known to the CSA and not be based on supposition.[44] If a change of circumstances has taken place or is expected, this must be based on fact and not on probability.

However, the decision maker cannot supersede a decision:

- which can be revised instead (see p354);[45]
- refusing to make or cancelling a maintenance calculation.[46] A further application for a maintenance calculation should be made instead.

Note: the CSA carries out periodic case checks. In some cases, a notified change of circumstances can be treated as a periodic case check instead of a request for a supersession (see p362).

Under the test case rules, the decision maker may refuse to follow the law as decided by the Upper Tribunal or courts, or even suspend a decision on supersession, while an appeal is being brought in another case. See p392 for details.

When a decision cannot be superseded

A decision cannot be superseded on the basis that there has been, or it is anticipated that there will be, a change of circumstances unless there is a change of 5 per cent or more in the non-resident parent's net income used in the calculation.[47] The CSA refers to this as the 'tolerance level'. However, this does not apply if the superseding decision:[48]

- is on the outcome of a variation application;
- affects a variation ground in a maintenance calculation, or a revised/ superseded decision on this;
- is made on an interim maintenance decision, or on the revised/superseded decision;
- is made by the decision maker acting on her/his own initiative on the basis of information or evidence which was also the basis of a decision of the Department for Work and Pensions on a claim for benefit or a revision or supersession of a decision on a claim or an award of benefit;[49]
- is made following an application on more than one ground, and the grounds which do not relate to the net income of the non-resident parent lead to a superseding decision. The change in income can also be taken into account.[50]

Some of these exceptions to the tolerance rule do not apply in 'old rules' cases. For further information, see the 2002/03 edition of this *Handbook*.

The tolerance rule is not applied to other changes of circumstances – eg:[51]

- relevant children joining or leaving the household;
- applications for other qualifying children;
- changes in shared care arrangements;
- changes notified by a third party (eg, Jobcentre Plus);

- the person with care, non-resident parent or qualifying child are no longer habitually resident in the UK;[52] *or*
- the person with care and non-resident parent start living together.[53]

If an application for a supersession is made to which the tolerance rule would apply and a further application is then made on a ground(s) that does not relate to the net income of the non-resident parent, a superseding decision can be made as if the two applications had been made at the same time (ie, so that the change in income can be taken into account).[54]

Wrong in law

A decision is 'erroneous in point of law' if:[55]

- when making the decision, the CSA misinterpreted or overlooked part or all of an Act of Parliament, a regulation or relevant caselaw;
- there is no evidence to support the decision;
- the facts are such that no reasonable person applying the law could have come to such a conclusion;
- there is a breach of natural justice – ie, the procedure used led to unfairness or the officer who took the decision appeared to be biased;[56]
- the CSA has not given sufficient reasons for the decision;
- when exercising a discretion, the CSA took into account something irrelevant or ignored something relevant – eg, the welfare of the child (see p24).[57]

A decision is wrong in law if the regulation under which it is made was not made lawfully. Such a regulation is said to be *ultra vires* (outside the powers). The courts and tribunals can decide that a regulation is *ultra vires*,[58] and the First-tier and Upper Tribunals have done so in benefit cases.

A decision is also wrong in law if it is contrary to European law (European Union (EU) law and the European Convention on Human Rights (ECHR)). EU law will rarely be relevant to child support issues. Commissioners have decided that European law on the equal treatment of men and women in social security matters do not apply to child support.[59]

ECHR law is more likely to be relevant. The CSA, courts and the First-tier and Upper Tribunals are required to interpret Acts of Parliament consistently with the ECHR as far as it is possible to do so.[60] They cannot use the ECHR to overrule an Act of Parliament, but the courts can issue a declaration of incompatability.[61] However, courts and the Tribunals can use the ECHR to override regulations which are incompatible with the provisions of the ECHR. It is unlawful for the CSA, courts or the Tribunals to act in a way which is incompatible with an ECHR right.[62] In practice, few challenges using these principles have succeeded.

Otherwise, the CSA, Jobcentre Plus, First-tier and Upper Tribunals cannot override or ignore the Acts or regulations.

Procedure for superseding

A party to the calculation can apply for a supersession at any time. There are no time limits,but any superseding decision usually runs from the date of the application (see p363). If an application is made, the decision maker must consider it and supersede if the conditions set out above are met.

The decision maker can initiate a supersession her/himself. S/he must take into account the welfare of the child (see p24) when considering whether or not to do so. The decision maker learns of some changes automatically from the Jobcentre Plus or may do so from a third party.

If the decision maker is considering a supersession on her/his own initiative in a 'new rules' case, s/he must give 28 days' notice to the relevant parties – ie, person with care, non-resident parent and/or Scottish child applicant.[63] The decision maker can give notice of the intention to supersede orally (eg, by telephone) or in writing.[64] If more than one method of notification is used, the earliest date is treated as the date of notification. If the parties are notified on different dates, the latest is counted as the date of notifrcation.[65]

In an 'old rules' case, the decision maker must notify parties who 'could be materially affected' if s/he is proposing to supersede a decision.[66] A request for information may be sufficient notice that the decision maker is proposing to supersede in an 'old rules' case, although both parties should still be notified. Notification may be oral or written, and the date of written notification is the date it is handed or sent to a person.[67]

If the supersession is in relation to an application for a variation that has passed preliminary consideration,[68] or a supersession of a previously agreed variation,[69] the other relevant parties may be contacted. Otherwise, the other party may not be notified of the application for a supersession. The normal rules about disclosure apply to the information given in any notification (see p75).[70]

The decision maker does not have to check all the facts again so can (and usually will) limit her/his consideration to the issues raised in the application.[71] Information provided may need to be verified in the normal way (see Chapter 4). If the 'tolerance rule' (see p360) is breached, or there are other relevant changes, a decision to supersede will be made.

Periodic case checks

The CSA carries out periodic case checks on every calculation. The 'normal' period within which a check should be carried out is every two years. However, a longer or shorter period can be used.[72] The 'tolerance rule' (see p360) does not apply to periodic case checks.[73]

A periodic case check may be requested by any party, but the CSA may decide not to conduct one – eg, because the non-resident parent remains on income support (IS)/income-based jobseeker's allowance (JSA)/income-related employment and support allowance (ESA) or pension credit (PC). A case check is not a supersession, but if the information gathered shows there are grounds for a supersession the CSA will start the procedure for a supersession. A change of circumstances which occurs within 26 weeks of a later periodic case check may be treated as part of the case check rather than a grounds for a separate supersession.

When a periodic case check is due or the decision maker decides to conduct one, each party should be given 28 days' notice of any resulting supersession.[74] This notification may be oral or in writing, with the date of notification being the earliest if more than one method is used. If the parties are notified on different dates, the notification is counted from the latest. The parties are invited to tell the decision maker about any changes within 14 days. If the parties do not respond, or no relevant changes are notified, no further action is taken. If changes are reported, these may need to be verified.

If the information does not show there are grounds for supersession, the decision maker does not make a new decision, so no notification need be issued. However, where there is a supersession decision, notification continues in the normal way (see p366).

The effective date of any supersession depends on how the periodic case check was initiated.

- If it was initiated by the decision maker, the effective date is the first day of the maintenance period that contains the 28th day from the date of notification of the periodic check.[75]
- If a change of circumstances was treated as a periodic case check, the effective date is the first day of the week in the maintenance period on, or prior to, the date the change of circumstances was notified.[76]

The superseding decision

The decision maker may decide that:
- there are no grounds for supersession and so refuse to supersede;
- there are grounds for supersession but the maintenance calculation remains unchanged;
- there are grounds for supersession and the maintenance calculation is changed; *or*
- the maintenance calculation should be cancelled.

Effective date of the superseding decision

The general rule is that a supersession takes effect from the first day in the maintenance period in which the decision is made or the application for the supersession/variation was made.[77] However, the effective date may be from a different date in certain circumstances, as shown in the table on p364. There are special rules for supersession decisions relating to periodic case checks (see p362) and cancellations.

Circumstances	Effective date
An application for an anticipated change in circumstances.	The first day in the maintenance period in which the change is expected to occur.[78]
The relevant circumstance is that a variation ground is expected to occur.	The first day in the maintenance period in which the ground is expected to occur.[79]
A qualifiying child dies or ceases to be a qualifying child.	The first day in the maintenance period in which the change occurred.[80]
The person with care ceases to be a person with care in relation to a qualifying child.	The first day in the maintenance period in which the change occurred.[81]
The person with care, non-resident parent or a qualifying child ceases to be habitually resident in the UK.	The first day in the maintenance period in which the change occurred.[82]
The non-resident parent begins to be liable or stops being liable to pay for half of the flat rate – ie, the following set of circumstances start to apply or stop applying to the non-resident parent: – his partner is also a non-resident parent; – there is a maintenance application in force in respect of the partner; *and* – either he or his partner receive IS, income-based JSA, income-related ESA or PC;	The first day in the maintenance period in which the change occurred.[83]
The decision maker has acted on her/his own initiative.	If the decision maker acts on information or evidence which also led the Jobcentre/Pension Service to make a decision on a claim for or an award of benefit, the effective date is the first day in the maintenance period in which the CSA became aware of the information or evidence.[84] In all other cases, the decision takes effect from the first day of the maintenance period which includes the date 28 days after the date on which notice that s/he is proposing to supersede is given to the relevant persons.[85]

There is a further qualifying child in relation to the same non-resident parent and person with care.	If this is brought to the attention of the CSA by the non-resident parent, the first day of the maintenance period in which the CSA are told about the child.[86] If this is brought to the attention of the CSA by the person with care, the first day of the maintenance period in which the non-resident parent is given notification of the application for that child.[87]
A non-resident parent has another qualifying child with a different parent with care and an application for maintenance is made by either the non-resident parent or the new parent with care.	The beginning of the maintenance period in which notification of the calculation is given to the non-resident parent.[88]
A non-resident parent or person with care applies for a supersession and the decision maker decides when superseding that different amounts of child maintenance need to be calculated in respect of different specified periods.	The beginning of the maintenance period in which the change of circumstances to which the calculation relates occurred or is expected to occur, unless that change occurred before the date of the application for supersession and was notified after that date. In which case, the effective date is the date of application for supersession.[89]
The decision maker is superseding a decision of the First-tier Tribunal or the Upper Tribunal given following the decision maker having served notice that a test case which could have affected that decision was pending before the Upper Tribunal or a court.	The beginning of the maintenance period following the date on which the decision of the First-tier Tribunal or Upper Tribunal would have taken effect had it been decided in accordance with the decision in the test case.[90]
The decision maker is superseding a decision of the First-tier Tribunal or the Upper Tribunal on the ground that it is wrong because of a misrepresentation about or a failure to disclose a material fact and the decision is more advantageous to the person who misrepresented or failed to disclose than it would otherwise have been but for that error.	The date on which the First-tier Tribunal or Upper Tribunal decision took or was to take effect.[91]

A decision of a decision maker is superseded because it is shown to have been wrong as a result of an Upper Tribunal or court decision in which the CSA lost.	The date of the relevant Upper Tribunal or court decision.[92]

Notification

If the decision results in a supersession, whether or not a new maintenance calculation is made (including an interim maintenance decision or default maintenance decision), the parties must be notified of the decision and given the usual details (see p328).[93] The notice must also state how to seek a revision, supersession and appeal.[94]

If the decision is to refuse to supersede, notification will be given including the reasons for refusal and appeal rights.[95]

If the CSA intends to cancel the case it may notify each party and, where the reason for cancellation is a child applicant in Scotland ceasing to be a qualifying child, inform other potential child applicants.[96]

Whether to request supersession

Before requesting a supersession because of a change of circumstances, you should try to work out whether a fresh calculation would be higher or lower. You only need tell the CSA about the changes in your favour. If the change only relates to one party, the CSA may not tell the other person, but if it does, that party might tell the CSA about other changes. These may cancel out the effect of the changes which led you to ask for a supersession.

If you believe the other person's circumstances have changed (eg, a non-resident parent no longer has children living with him) you can ask for a supersession and for the CSA to investigate (see Chapter 4). The CSA does not have to, but any changes it is aware of must be taken into account when it decides whether or not to supersede.

Notes

1 Reg 4(1)(a) CS(TP) Regs

1. Changing decisions

2 *Council of Civil Service Unions v Minister for the Civil Service* [1984] 1 WLR 1174, [1984] 3 All ER 935

3 s12(2)(b) SSA 1998; reg 25 SS&CS(DA) Regs

2. Revisions

4 s16 CSA 1991
5 Reg 3A(6) SS&CS(DA) Regs
6 s16 1A(a) CSA 1991
7 Reg 3A(1)(a) and (d) SS&CS(DA) Regs
8 Reg 3A(1)(cc) SS&CS(DA) Regs
9 Reg 3A(1)(e) SS&CS(DA) Regs
10 Reg 3A(1)(c) SS&CS(DA) Regs
11 Regs 3(A)(1) and 4 SS&CS(DA) Regs
12 Reg 3A(5A) SS&CS(DA) Regs
13 Reg 3A(1)(b) SS&CS(DA) Regs
14 Reg 3A(1)(f) SS&CS(DA) Regs
15 Reg 3A(2) SS&CS(DA) Regs
16 Reg 4(4) SS&CS(DA) Regs
17 Reg 4(6) SS&CS(DA) Regs
18 Reg 4(3)(b) SS&CS(DA) Regs
19 Reg 4(3)(b) SS&CS(DA) Regs
20 Reg 4(5) SS&CS(DA) Regs
21 Reg 4(3)(a) SS&CS(DA) Regs
22 Reg 4(7) SS&CS(DA) Regs
23 See CIS/93/1992
24 Reg 1(2) SS&CS(DA) Regs
25 R(SB) 9/85
26 R(SB) 2/92 (*Page and Davis v CAO*); PG, Calculation and Decision Types, Misrepresentation or Failure to Disclose Information
27 CCS/15846/1996
28 Reg 3A(c) SS&CS(DA) Regs
29 Reg 23(4) CS(MCP) Regs
30 Reg 9 CS(V) Regs
31 Reg 15B SS&CS(DA) Regs
32 PG, Calculation and Decision Types, Burden of Proof
33 s16(6) CSA 1991; reg 30(1) and (2)(f) SS&CS(DA) Regs
34 s16(3) CSA 1991
35 Reg 5A SS&CS(DA) Regs
36 Reg 15C SS&CS(DA) Regs
37 Reg 15C(3) SS&CS(DA) Regs
38 Reg 15C(9)-(11) SS&CS(DA) Regs
39 r23(1) and Sch 1 TP(FT) Rules

3. Supersessions

40 s17 CMOPA 2008
41 s17(1) CSA 1991
42 s28H and Sch 4C para 1(a) CSA 1991
43 Reg 6A(2)-(6) SS&CS(DA) Regs
44 CCS/162/2006
45 Reg 6A(5) SS&CS(DA) Regs
46 Reg 6A(6) SS&CS(DA) Regs
47 Reg 6B(1) SS&CS(DA) Regs
48 Reg 6B(4) SS&CS(DA) Regs
49 Regs 6B(4)(e)and Sch 3D para 4 SS&CS(DA) Regs
50 Reg 6B(3) SS&CS(DA) Regs
51 PG, Calculation and Decision Types, When Tolerance is Applied – New Rules Cases
52 Regs 6B(4)(e) and 7B(18) SS&CS(DA) Regs
53 Regs 6B(4)(e) and 7B(20) SS&CS(DA) Regs
54 Reg 6B(5) SS&CS(DA) Regs
55 R(A) 1/72; R(SB) 11/83
56 *R v Gough* [1993] AC 646, [1993] 2 WLR 883, [1993] 2 All ER 724
57 *Wednesbury Corporation v Ministry of Housing and Local Government (No.2)* [1965] 3 WLR 956, [1965] 3 All ER 571
58 *CAO v Foster* [1993] AC 754, [1993] 2 WLR 292, [1993] 1 All ER 705
59 R(CS) 3/96; R(CS) 2/95; CCS/17/1994. These concerned the application of Art 141 of the EC treaty (formerly Art 119), and Council Directives 75/117 and 79/7. The Sex Discrimination Act 1975 also has no effect. CCS/6/1995
60 s3 HRA 1998
61 s4 HRA 1998
62 s6 HRA 1998
63 Reg 7B(7) SS&CS(DA) Regs
64 Reg 7B(8)(b) SS&CS(DA) Regs
65 Reg 7B(8)(a) SS&CS(DA) Regs
66 Reg 24 CS(MAP) Regs
67 Reg 23(8) CS(MAP) Regs
68 Reg 9 CS(V) Regs
69 Reg 15B SS&CS(DA) Regs
70 Reg 15B SS&CS(DA) Regs
71 s17(2) CSA 1991
72 PG, Calculation and Decision Types, Periodic Case Checks

Chapter 18

Appeals

This chapter covers:
1. Decisions that can be appealed (below)
2. Appealing to the First-tier Tribunal (p371)
3. The appeal procedure (p374)
4. Preparing a case (p381)
5. Hearings (p382)
6. Decisions (p385)
7. Changing a First-tier Tribunal decision (p387)
8. Appealing to the Upper Tribunal (p388)
9. Test case rules (p392)

Note: this chapter does not include information on appeals outstanding at conversion (see Chapter 7). However, conversion decisions themselves can be appealed as described in this chapter.[1]

Most child maintenance decisions made by a decision maker in the Child Support Agency (CSA) or Child Maintenance Enforcement Commission (C-MEC) can be appealed to an independent appeal tribunal: the First-tier Tribunal (Social Entitlement Chamber). An application for a variation can also be referred to the First-tier Tribunal by the decision maker.[2] The First-tier Tribunal looks at all the evidence in the case and gives a new decision. This decision replaces the decision of the decision maker. A First-tier Tribunal decision can be appealed on a question of law to the Upper Tribunal (Administrative Appeals Chamber).

Both the First-tier Tribunal and the Upper Tribunal are administered by the Tribunals Service.

The new tribunal system from 3 November 2008

The rules described in this chapter relate to the tribunal system introduced from 3 November 2008. For details about the rules that applied before this date, see previous editions of this *Handbook*. If an appeal was made before 3 November 2008 and is still ongoing, the First-tier Tribunal or Upper Tribunal can apply the old procedural rules if this would be fair.[3]

Except for appeals about a refusal to make a calculation, each party to the calculation has the right of appeal.

Otherwise, regardless of who appealed, all parties have the same rights, except that only the appellant can ask to withdraw the appeal. Because an appeal can be withdrawn without the consent of any other party (see p380), it is best for each party who wishes to challenge the decision to bring her/his own appeal. The appeals can be heard together.

1. Decisions that can be appealed

Usually, any relevant person (ie, person with care, non-resident parent or Scottish child applicant) has the right to appeal.[4] However, there are some exceptions to this.

Decisions that can be appealed	Who can appeal
A decision (including default and interim maintenance decisions) about whether maintenance is payable and, if so, how much or, in 'new rules' cases, a decision to supersede a calculation.	Any relevant person.
A refusal to make a maintenance calculation (including default and interim maintenance decisions) or, in 'new rules' cases, a refusal to supersede.	Any relevant person.
In 'old rules' cases, a decision to cancel or to refuse to cancel a maintenance assessment or interim maintenance assessment, and a decision to make, or refuse to make, a departure direction.	In these cases, only the person who requests the cancellation or departure direction can appeal the refusal to cancel the assessment or make a departure direction. Any relevant person can appeal against other 'old rules' decisions.
A decision to impose penalty payments or payment of fees.	In these cases, only the parent required to pay the penalty or person required to pay the fees can appeal.
An adjustment, or cancellation of an adjustment, of the amount paid because of an overpayment of maintenance or voluntary payments.	Any relevant person.

A supersession decision, whether as originally made or as revised. Conversion decisions can therefore be appealed, since these are supersession decisions.

Any relevant person.

The Child Support Agency (CSA) may also refer a variation application to the First-tier Tribunal in certain cases. The First-tier Tribunal can also consider departures in 'old rules' cases.

Decisions that cannot be appealed

Only decisions and, in some cases, refusals to make decisions, can be appealed. It is not possible to appeal if no decision has been made – eg, because of a delay. Instead, a complaint (see Chapter 20) or application for judicial review could be considered. Similarly, decisions about the method of collection or the enforcement of payment cannot be appealed.

Parentage disputes

If the appellant denies s/he is the parent of a child named in the maintenance application, the appeal is not dealt with by the First-tier Tribunal, but by a court.[5] If there are other grounds for appeal apart from the dispute about parentage, the First-tier Tribunal will deal with those issues and the parentage issue will be dealt with at court. An appeal involving a dispute about parentage is made in exactly the same way as any other appeal.[6] If the appeal is sent by the CSA to the First-tier Tribunal and it involves a denial of parentage, the First-tier Tribunal should transfer that issue to the court.[7] For parentage disputes that arise before the appeal stage is reached see p18 and p62.

2. Appealing to the First-tier Tribunal

When the decision maker makes a decision, each person must get a notice of that decision and information on the right of appeal.[8]

An appeal is started by the person with a right of appeal sending a 'notice of appeal' to the Child Support Agency (CSA) office that issued the decision. There is a CSA form that can be used. The notice of appeal must include:
- the name and address of the person making the appeal;
- the name and address of that person's representative (if s/he has one);
- an address to which documents about the appeal may be sent or delivered to the person making the appeal;
- details of the decision being appealed;
- the grounds of the appeal.

There are strict time limits for making an appeal (see below), which can only be extended in certain circumstances (see below). If the notice of appeal does not include sufficient information or is not made on the approved form, see p373.

Time limits

An appeal must be received at the relevant CSA office within one month of the notice of the decision being sent to the appellant.[9]

If the appellant is appealing against a refusal to revise a decision following a late application for a revision (see p355) where time was not extended, this one-month time limit runs from the date of the original decision being notified, not the date on which the CSA notified her/him of its refusal to revise. However, if the CSA refused to revise a decision following an application for a revision that was made within the time limit (see p354) or the extended time limit, the one-month time limit runs from the date on which the notice of refusal to revise was issued. Similarly, if a decision is revised, the time for appealing runs from the date on which the revised decision is sent to the appellant.[10]

A notice counts as having been sent to the person on the day it is issued by the CSA.[11]

Late appeals

In certain situations, the above time limits can be extended. However, the period in which an appeal must be made can never be extended by more than 12 months from the time limit that applied.[12]

If a notice of appeal is submitted outside the time limit, in addition to the information listed above, it must also include the reasons why it is late.[13]

A decision maker can extend the time limit for appealing, but only if s/he is satisfied that it is in the interest of justice.[14] It will be in the interests of justice to extend the time for appealing if it was not practicable to make the application in time because of special circumstances – ie:[15]

- the applicant, her/his partner or dependant has died or has a serious illness;
- the applicant is not resident in the UK;
- normal postal services were disrupted; *or*
- other wholly exceptional special circumstances.

The later the appeal, the more compelling the special circumstances must be.[16] When considering whether there are special circumstances, the decision maker must not take into account any mistake made by the applicant (or her/his representative) about the law, a time limit or an interpretation of the law by the Upper Tribunal, a commissioner or a court, which is different from the way the CSA had understood and applied the law.[17]

If the decision maker does not think it is in the interests of justice for the appeal to be admitted, s/he should still send the appeal to the First-tier Tribunal. The First-tier Tribunal can decide to admit the appeal simply on the basis that it believes it is fair and just to do so – ie, it does not have to be satisfied that there are special reasons.[18] If the decision maker objects to the First-tier Tribunal admitting the appeal or believes the appeal is outside the maximum extension of 12 months, s/he should refer the case immediately to the First-tier Tribunal, indicating that s/he objects to its admission.[19] If the decision maker does not object, the First-tier Tribunal must admit the appeal unless it is made outside the maximum 12-month extension period.[20]

If the First-tier Tribunal does not admit the late appeal, it may be possible to appeal against this decision to the Upper Tribunal (see p388). If this is not possible, an application for judicial review could be made.

The appeal form or letter has insufficient information

The CSA can forward to the First-tier Tribunal a written appeal which is not on the appeal form (or which is, but is not fully completed) if it contains sufficient information for the appeal to proceed.[21] However, if the form is not used or is not properly completed, the CSA may return it to the appellant for completion or ask for further information.[22] If the appellant returns the completed form/information within 14 days of the CSA request (or a longer period if the CSA accepts), the appeal is treated as made on time.[23] If the appellant does not do this, the CSA refers the appeal form/letter (with any relevant documents or evidence) to the First-tier Tribunal for it to decide if it meets the rules.[24] Any information received by the CSA after the referral is made but before the First-tier Tribunal's decision must be referred to the First-tier Tribunal, which must take it into account.[25]

After the appeal is made

The decision maker should prepare a 'response' to the appeal. This should be sent to the First-tier Tribunal and to the parties to the appeal as soon as reasonably practical after receiving the notice of appeal. The response should state:
* the name and address of the decision maker;
* the name and address of the decision maker's representative (if any). These are known as 'presenting officers';
* an address where documents for the decision maker can be sent or delivered;
* the name and addresses of any other respondents and their representatives (if any).

The response should explain (or have attached documents which explain) what parts of the grounds put forward for the appeal the decision maker disagrees with, and why.

The response may also indicate whether the decision maker thinks the case requires a hearing or could be decided by just considering the papers.

The response should have attached to it:
* a copy of any written record of the decision being appealed;

- copies of all documents relevant to the case that the CSA has;
- a copy of the notice of appeal, together with any documents submitted by the appellant.

If a parent with care or non-resident parent has told the CSA that s/he would like her/his address to be kept confidential, the decision maker should take steps to ensure that this is not revealed to the other party(ies).[26]

3. **The appeal procedure**

Once an appeal has been made, the First-tier Tribunal deals with the case. The First-tier Tribunal will not be aware of the case until it receives the response from the decision maker. Both the First-tier and Upper Tribunal have procedural rules, setting out their powers and how they should deal with cases. There are also Practice Directions and Practice Statements, which set out how they should conduct themselves in various situations. The rules are similar for both the First-tier and Upper Tribunal and so this section applies to both (and explains where there are differences). The rules about hearings and decisions are also part of the procedural rules, but are dealt with on pp382 and 385. See p387 for challenging and p388 for appealing against a First-tier Tribunal decision.

The overriding objective: fair and just

The overriding objective of the rules is to enable the Tribunal to deal with cases 'fairly and justly'.[27] Whenever the Tribunal exercises a power under the rules (eg, to admit or not admit a late appeal, or to strike out an appeal), it must have regard to whether it would be fair and just. Similarly, when the Tribunal interprets what the rules mean or what the Practice Directions say, it must try to come to the interpretation which meets the overriding objective – ie, to enable a case to be dealt with in a way which is fair and just.[28]

It is therefore important to bear in mind the overriding objective in any dealings with the Tribunal about the conduct of the proceedings – eg, directions that should be given, witnesses to be summoned, a child giving evidence, asking for an adjournment, asking for more time to give submissions or get evidence, and objecting to the decision maker being given more time to get evidence. It may be worthwhile explaining to the Tribunal why doing what you want would be fair and just.

The rules set out some of the things that must be taken into account when deciding whether a particular interpretation of the rules is fair and just or in deciding whether it would be fair and just to exercise a power conferred by the rules in a particular way.[29] The Tribunal should:

- deal with the case in a way which is proportionate to its importance, the complexity of the issues, the anticipated costs and the resources of the parties;

- avoid unnecessary formality and be flexible in the proceedings;
- ensure, so far as practicable, that the parties are able to participate fully in the proceedings;
- use any special expertise of the Tribunal effectively; *and*
- avoid delay, so far as it is compatible with the proper consideration of the issues.

Note: the above is just a list of what dealing with a case fairly and justly includes. Matters that are not listed can still be taken into account when considering what is fair and just in a particular case.

The parties to an appeal have a duty to assist the Tribunal in dealing with cases fairly and justly.

Applying for directions

Tribunals can give a wide range of directions in order to manage cases. When doing so the Tribunal must ensure that its action is consistent with the overriding objective (see p374).

A direction can be given at any time, either on the initiative of the Tribunal or following an application by a party to the proceedings.[30]

An application for a direction can be made either orally at a hearing or by writing to the Tribunal. The application must include the reason for seeking the direction.

The Tribunal must, unless it considers there is a good reason not to do so, send a written notice of the direction to every party and to anyone else affected by it.

If a party is unhappy with a particular direction, s/he can use this same procedure to apply for another direction which amends, suspends or sets aside the earlier direction.

If a party fails to comply with a direction, the case could be struck out (see p378) or the party barred from the hearing (see p378).

General case management powers

In particular, the Tribunal can give directions to:
- extend or shorten the time for complying with any rule, Practice Direction or direction. This is the only rule there is on extending time. It is relevant to any late application (eg, to appeal, for a statement of reasons or to set aside). Importantly, it does not contain any upper limit (although there is an upper limit of a 12-month extension for late appeals);
- consolidate or hear together two or more sets of proceedings (or parts of proceedings) raising common issues, or treat a case as a lead case;
- permit or require a party to amend a document;

permit or require a party or another person to provide documents, information, evidence or submissions to the Upper Tribunal or a party. There are more specific powers to obtain evidence (see below);

- deal with an issue in the proceedings as a preliminary issue – eg, to decide precisely what decision is under appeal or whether the Tribunal has jurisdiction;
- hold a hearing to consider any matter, including a case management issue. This could include, for example, a preliminary hearing to decide what further evidence is needed and who should provide it, how much time the final hearing needs or whether the appeal should be struck out because of a failure to comply with a direction;
- decide the form of any hearing – eg, the order in which parties speak or give evidence and who questions the appellant. If the Tribunal consists of more than one member, this is decided by the presiding member (see p383);[31]
- adjourn or postpone a hearing;
- require a party to produce a 'bundle' (an indexed set of documents and legal authorities relating to the case) for a hearing. Because the Tribunal must take into account the resources of the parties when issuing a direction and the fact that there is a disparity of resources between a typical parent with care/non-resident parent and the Child Support Agency (CSA), it will be rare for anyone but the CSA to be required to produce a bundle;
- 'stay' (or, in Scotland, 'sist') proceedings. This allows the Tribunal to put the case on hold pending the outcome of another case in which it is expected legal issues will be decided which are relevant to the outcome to be given in the stayed case;
- transfer proceeding to another court or tribunal if that has jurisdiction in relation to the proceedings. This will happen if there has been a change of circumstance since the proceedings were started and the Tribunal no longer has jurisdiction – eg, because the non-resident parent has denied parentage, or if the Tribunal considers the other court or tribunal to be more appropriate to determine the case;
- suspend the effect of its own decision pending the determination of an application for permission to appeal against, and any appeal or review of, that decision.

Evidence

The Tribunal can give directions about:[32]
- issues on which it requires evidence or submissions;
- the nature of the evidence or submissions it requires;
- whether the parties are permitted or required to provide expert evidence;
- any limit on the number of witnesses whose evidence a party may put forward, whether in relation to a particular issue or generally;
- the manner in which any evidence or submissions are to be provided;

- the time at which any evidence or submissions are to be provided.

The Tribunal can exclude evidence if:
- it was not provided within a time limit in a direction or Practice Direction;
- it does not comply with a direction or a Practice Direction in some other way;
- it would be unfair to admit the evidence.

Harmful evidence

If a parent with care or non-resident parent has told the CSA that s/he would like her/his address to be kept confidential, the decision maker should take steps to ensure that the address is not revealed to the other party(ies).[33] In addition, the Tribunal can order that documents or information relating to the proceedings are not to be disclosed or that any matter which could allow members of the public to identify the people involved should not be disclosed.[34]

The Tribunal can also direct that a particular person does not get a document or information if:[35]
- disclosure would be likely to cause her/him or some other person serious harm; *and*
- weighing up that potential harm against the interests of justice, it is proportionate not to disclose the information.

If a party thinks the Tribunal should direct that a particular document or piece of information should be withheld from another party, s/he must not give the document or information to that party. Instead, s/he must write to the Tribunal with a copy of the document or information and explain why it should not be disclosed.[36]

The Tribunal can, however, disclose the document or information to the party's representative if it is satisfied that s/he will not disclose the document to another person without the consent of the Tribunal and that such disclosure is in the interests of justice.[37]

Witnesses

The Tribunal has a power to summons (in Scotland, cite) witnesses and to order other documents to be produced.[38] The Tribunal may require any person (this extends to all people and not just to one of the parties to the appeal, including companies) to:
- attend as a witness at a hearing at the time and place specified in the summons (citation in Scotland);
- to answer any questions which relate to the proceedings;
- to provide any documents in their possession or control which relate to the proceedings.

The Tribunal must give the person summoned at least 14 days' notice of the hearing (or a shorter period if the Tribunal directs this). If the person summoned is not a party to the proceedings, her/his expenses will be paid.

If the person has not already had an opportunity to object to being summonsed or ordered, the summons/order should state that s/he can apply to the Tribunal to vary or set aside the summons/order. The summons must state the consequences of failing to comply. The First-tier Tribunal can refer the person to the Upper Tribunal if s/he fails to comply (see p388).[39]

Note: the Tribunal cannot summons a child if this would be detrimental to her/his welfare.

Costs

Neither the First-tier Tribunal nor the Upper Tribunal when hearing an appeal (other than in a judicial review) can award costs.[40]

Failure to comply with rules

If there has been a failure to comply with the rules, a Practice Direction or a direction, the Tribunal may take any action which it considers just, including:

- waiving the requirement;
- requiring the failure to be remedied;
- striking out the appeal (see below);
- referring the matter to the Upper Tribunal (see below);
- restricting a party's participation in the proceedings;
- fining or committing someone to prison (Upper Tribunal only – see below).

The Upper Tribunal has the same powers as the High Court concerning the attendance and examination of witnesses and the production and inspection of documents.[41] It can therefore commit (imprison) a person who does not comply with its rules (eg, if she does not obey a summons) or impose a fine.

The First-tier Tribunal does not have this power, but can refer a person to the Upper Tribunal in order for the Upper Tribunal to deal with her/him under its own powers as if s/he had failed to comply with one of its own rules or directions.[42] The First-tier Tribunal can only refer someone if s/he has failed to:

- attend at any place to give evidence;
- otherwise make her/himself available to give evidence;
- swear an oath in connection with giving evidence;
- produce a document;
- facilitate the inspection of a document or any other thing (including premises).

Striking out an appeal and barring

In certain circumstances, the Tribunal can 'strike out' (ie, dismiss without considering the decision under appeal) the appeal, or part of the appeal.

The Tribunal **must** strike out the appeal, or part of the appeal, if:

- the appellant has failed to comply with a direction which stated that the appeal, or that part of the appeal, *would* be struck out for failure to comply;[43] *or*
- it does not have jurisdiction to decide the appeal (or that part of it) and it has not transferred the appeal (or part of the appeal) to another tribunal or court.[44]

The Tribunal **may** strike out the appeal, or part of the appeal, if:
- the appellant has failed to comply with a direction which stated that the appeal, or that part of the appeal, *could* be struck out for failure to comply; *or*
- the appellant has failed to co-operate with the Tribunal to such an extent that the Tribunal cannot deal with the proceedings fairly and justly;[45] *or*
- it considers that the appeal has no reasonable prospects of success.[46]

The Tribunal must give a written notice of its decision to strike out the appeal, or part of it. A party to the appeal can ask for a written statement of reasons for the decision and can seek permission to appeal against the striking-out decision to the Upper Tribunal.[47]

If the appeal, or part of the appeal, is struck out because the appellant has failed to comply with a direction, s/he may apply in writing for the appeal, or that part of it, to be reinstated.[48] This should be received by the Tribunal within one month of the Tribunal sending the appellant notice of the striking out.[49] This one-month time limit can be extended if the Tribunal considers it is fair and just to do so.[50]

It is not possible for an appeal, or part of it, to be reinstated if it is struck out for a reason other than a failure to comply with a direction. However, the Tribunal cannot strike out an appeal for one of these reasons unless it has first invited the appellant to make representations about whether or not it should do so.[51]

The rules for striking out an appeal apply to the CSA in exactly the same way that they apply to the appellant, except that references to 'striking out' are to 'barring'. When the Tribunal 'bars' the respondent it need not consider any response or other submission made by that respondent.

Sending and receiving documents

Anything that has to be done by a particular day must be done by 5pm on that day.[52]

If the final day of any time limit for doing something is not a working day (ie, Saturday, Sunday, Christmas Day, Good Friday or a Bank Holiday), the act will be treated as in time if it is done on the next working day.[53]

Where there is a time limit for a party to provide a document, this starts to run from when the Tribunal sends the request. The time limit is met when the Tribunal receives the response.

Documents can be sent to the Tribunal by pre-paid post (or fax) to the address (or number) specified for the proceedings. The Tribunal may give directions permitting documents to be sent by other methods.[54]

If a party provides a fax, email address or other method for receiving documents electronically, s/he must accept delivery of documents by that method unless s/he has explicitly stated that this is not acceptable.[55]

If a document is sent electronically, the recipient can request a hard copy and the sender must supply it (this also applies to appellants and their representatives). The request for a hard copy should be made as soon as reasonably practicable after receiving the document electronically.[56]

Each party should assume that the address provided by another party remains valid unless s/he has received written notice to the contrary.[57]

Representatives

A party has a right to appoint a representative (whether legally qualified or not) to represent her/him in the proceedings. Once appointed, a representative can do anything permitted or required to be done by the party (except sign a witness statement).[58] It is possible, therefore, that a authorised representative can sign the notice of appeal. However, until this is positively decided by the Upper Tribunal or a court, it is advisable for the person who wants to appeal to sign her/himself.

The Tribunal should notify all other parties when a representative has been appointed. When a person (including the Tribunal itself) receives the notice of the appointment of a representative, s/he must provide her/him with any documents required to be issued to the represented party and need not send the documents to that party.[59]

It should be assumed that the representative continues to act unless notice to the contrary from either the representative or the represented party is received.

Even if a party has not appointed a representative, s/he can still be accompanied at the hearing. Her/his companion may, with the permission of the Tribunal, act as a representative or otherwise assist in presenting the case at the hearing.

Withdrawing an appeal

A party can withdraw all of part of her/his case.[60]

In the First-tier Tribunal, a case may be withdrawn either by writing to the Tribunal before the hearing, or orally at a hearing. If a party waits until a hearing to withdraw, s/he can only do so with the Tribunal's consent.[61] In the Upper Tribunal, consent is always needed to withdraw an appeal (even if the request is made in writing), unless the case is still at the stage awaiting permission to appeal.[62]

Once a case has been withdrawn, it can be reinstated if the party writes to the Tribunal requesting this within one month of the notice of withdrawal being received by the Tribunal, or within a month of the date of the hearing at which the case was withdrawn.

When a case is withdrawn the Tribunal must notify each party.

If the appellant or her/his representative wishes to stop an appeal proceeding before it has been referred to the First-tier Tribunal, s/he can simply write to the CSA, which discontinues the action.[63]

4. **Preparing a case**

The First-tier Tribunal may be the first chance for an independent evaluation of the decision under appeal. It may also be the last chance because there can only be an appeal to the Upper Tribunal on a point of law. Therefore, each party should make sure that the First-tier Tribunal knows the facts and arguments about the case.

Considering the facts and law

Each party should:
- read the response from the Child Support Agency (CSA) and any other documents to see whether the decision maker now accepts some of the arguments previously rejected or ignored. However, just because the decision maker accepts part of a person's case does not mean that the Tribunal will, especially if the other party disputes it;
- check the law using this *Handbook* and other sources (see Appendix 5). If the CSA quotes a decision of the commissioners or the Upper Tribunal, consider getting a copy. The Tribunals Service does not have copies of unreported decisions. If an unreported decision is to be relied on by the decision maker, a copy should be supplied to the parties and to the First-tier Tribunal. If a party wishes to quote an unreported decision, s/he should supply copies to everyone, preferably by sending a copy to the Tribunal clerk in advance of the hearing. A party can quote the CSA's internal procedural guidance, but it is not legally binding;
- check the documents attached to the response. If anything relevant is missing, write to the First-tier Tribunal asking it to direct the decision maker to provide it.

If the CSA delays producing its response to the appeal, the appellant can write directly to the First-tier Tribunal and ask for a direction that the appeal be heard. This may mean that the First-tier Tribunal will not have all the evidence the decision maker has. However, a party can ask the First-tier Tribunal to direct the CSA (see p375) to provide copies of all the papers, explaining why those papers are needed.

Further evidence

Each party should consider:
- whether s/he has (or can get) any further relevant written evidence. This can be sent to the First-tier Tribunal at any stage, but it is best to do this soon after the response is sent out so papers can be copied to the other parties. If evidence or unreported commissioners'/Upper Tribunal decisions are produced at the

hearing or sent in shortly before, this may cause a postponement or an adjournment;
- how to tell the First-tier Tribunal about the facts and law at the hearing. A party can 'give evidence' – ie, say what s/he has seen and heard. For example: 'I look after the child from Friday night to Monday night' may be the best evidence of those facts;
- whether to call any witnesses at the hearing (see p377).

From 1 October 2007, information relating to court proceedings concerning children heard in private or ancillary relief proceedings (ie, dealing with money and property) can be disclosed to the First-tier Tribunal by any party to the proceedings without permission being sought, as long as the court does not direct otherwise.[64] This means that one parent can supply information about the finances of the other parent, to which s/he admitted in the course of divorce proceedings.

Obtaining information and evidence

A party may want another person to provide further information or documents. The party can write to the First-tier Tribunal requesting that the other person be directed to provide these. It is best for the party to send a prepared list to the Tribunals Service which is as precise as possible and explains why the documents are needed. For example, the parent with care may believe the non-resident parent has received a pay increase; she decides to ask for 'pay-slips from February to May 2009 (inclusive)'. A person who is not a party (eg, an employer) cannot be directed to provide evidence, but can be ordered to attend as a witness and produce documents (see p377). This should be done before the full hearing so the parties can consider that evidence.

If a person fails to comply without a good explanation, the First-tier Tribunal may decide that s/he has something to hide and so may disbelieve that person's evidence. If the person is the appellant, the appeal can be struck out (see p378).

5. Hearings

This section applies to both the First-tier and Upper Tribunal.

'Hearing' means an oral hearing (including one conducted by video link, telephone or other instant two-way electronic communication).[65]

When must a hearing be held

The rules about when a hearing must be held are different for the First-tier and Upper Tribunal.

The **First-tier Tribunal** must hold a hearing before making a final decision in a case unless:[66]

- it is exercising its powers to strike out the proceedings;
- each party has consented to, or has not objected to, the matter being decided without a hearing and it considers it is able to decide the matter without a hearing;
- it is deciding whether to admit an application for permission to appeal, set aside a decision or correct a decision;
- it is disposing of the proceedings through a consent order.

The **Upper Tribunal** may decide any case without a hearing, but must consider any views expressed by a party when making a decision on whether or to hold a hearing.[67]

Notice

The Tribunal must give reasonable notice of the time and place of the hearing and of any changes to the arrangements.[68] This period of notice must be at least 14 days, although shorter notice can be given with the parties' consent or in urgent or exceptional circumstances (if shorter notice is given it must still be reasonable).[69]

Attending a hearing

Generally, all hearings must be held in public and a party has a right to attend. There are limited exceptions to these general principles: the Tribunal may direct that a hearing, or part of it, is to be held in private and may determine who is allowed to attend.

Even in a public hearing, the Tribunal may exclude from all or part of it:[70]
- anyone whose conduct is disrupting, or is likely to disrupt, the hearing;
- anyone whose presence is likely to prevent another person from giving evidence or making submissions freely;
- anyone who should be excluded in order to prevent her/him hearing information that is likely to cause harm;
- anyone whose attendance would defeat the purpose of the hearing;
- a witness in the proceedings, s/he is called to give evidence.

If a party fails to attend a hearing and the Tribunal is satisfied that s/he has been notified or that reasonable steps to notify her/him have been taken, it may proceed with the hearing if it is in the interests of justice.[71]

Composition of the Tribunal

When the First-tier Tribunal deals with a case involving a child support decision it will usually consist of a single member called a 'tribunal judge'.[72] The judge is a person qualified as a lawyer.[73] If the appeal raises difficult issues about financial accounts, the First-tier Tribunal can include a financially qualified member (a 'tribunal member') – ie, a chartered or certified accountant.[74] Formally, the President of the Social Entitlement Chamber of the First-tier Tribunal decides who is on the panel and who hears each appeal, but in practice this is delegated to the more senior tribunal judge.[75] If a First-tier Tribunal is composed of other members in addition to the tribunal judge, the judge is the 'presiding member', can regulate the proceedings and has the casting vote if there are an even number of members.[76]

The Upper Tribunal almost always consists of a single judge, who is legally qualified. If the case is of particular difficulty or there is conflicting caselaw, there may be a three-judge panel.

The venue

The Tribunals Service intends that every hearing venue to have separate waiting rooms for the non-resident parent, parent with care and presenting officer. If another party or witness may be violent, the Tribunal clerk should be told as soon as possible and asked what steps will be taken.

The hearing is usually held in the appellant's area. Expenses, including travel expenses, subsistence and some compensation for loss of earnings, are paid to those who attend as a party, witness or unpaid representative. The clerk pays travel and subsistence on the day, unless these are high. Travel expenses can be paid in advance.

A party for whom it is difficult to attend the hearing (eg, because of disability) should inform the clerk. An alternative venue may be possible, but convenience to the other parties to the appeal will also have to be considered.

Conduct of the hearing

The First-tier Tribunal attempts to be informal. Its member(s) usually sit on one side of a table. The clerk to the Tribunal (who does not take any part in making the decision) shows the parties into the room and they usually sit on the other side of the table, with the presenting officer between them. The judge introduces everyone and explains the Tribunal's role. If anyone's role is unclear, the judge should be asked for clarification.

Every party has the right to address the Tribunal, give evidence, call witnesses and put questions to any other party, the presenting officer or witnesses. The order in which the parties present their cases is up to the judge. The Child Support Agency (CSA) is there to explain the decision, not to argue for the CSA. The presenting officer has a role, for example, to inform the Tribunal about CSA procedures. It is rare for the presenting officer to call any witnesses. The Tribunal may require any witness, including a party, to take an oath or affirm.

It is Tribunals Service policy to arrange an interpreter, if requested, in good time; this should be requested on the pre-hearing enquiry form. The Tribunal should not place itself in the position of being seen to assist one of the parties make her/his case.[77]

The First-tier Tribunal can adjourn a hearing at any point – eg, if more documents are needed. If evidence has been taken, a new panel hearing the case must be made up of either exactly the same, or entirely different, members. Hearings can take one hour or longer.

6. **Decisions**

After the hearing, the First-tier Tribunal considers the case and makes its decision. If the appeal is allowed, the decision of the First-tier Tribunal replaces that of the Child Support Agency (CSA). If the appeal is dismissed, the decision of the CSA remains in force. Similarly, the Upper Tribunal may replace the decision of the First-tier Tribunal (or can direct that the case be reconsidered by a new First-tier Tribunal).

Decisions of the First-tier Tribunal

In making its decision, the First-tier Tribunal looks afresh at the issues raised as was the situation up to the date of the CSA decision under appeal.[78] It cannot consider any circumstances which exist only in relation to a period after that date. It can consider any evidence and arguments, including those rejected or overlooked by the decision maker and those which have not been used before.[79] The First-tier Tribunal has no duty to consider any issue not raised in the appeal.[80] However, it is 'inquisitorial', which means it can consider legal arguments and factual questions on its own initiative, if appropriate.[81] The First-tier Tribunal must decide what it believes are the relevant facts by evaluating all the relevant available evidence. It must then decide what decision the legislation (interpreted by caselaw) specifies must be given in the light of those facts.

If the First-tier Tribunal reaches a different conclusion from that of the decision maker, it allows the appeal. **Note:** it may make a decision that is less advantageous to the appellant than the decision which has been appealed.[82]

If the appeal is against a refusal to revise/supersede, the First-tier Tribunal must decide whether a revision/supersession can be carried out. When considering this, it looks at the facts as they were when the decision maker refused to supersede, or at the date of the original decision in the case of a refusal to revise, even if the decision maker did not know those facts.[83] Unless there was a basis for a revision/supersession at that time, a later change of circumstances is irrelevant.[84] A request for a supersession on the basis of the later change should be made instead.

When deciding the appeal, the First-tier Tribunal cannot take into account any change of circumstances that occurred after the date of the decision under appeal[85] If it decides to allow the appeal because the decision was wrong on the facts at the time it was made, it cannot go on to direct how the decision maker should deal with a later change of circumstances. Supersession could be sought instead.

Decision notices

Usually, at the First-tier Tribunal the parties are invited to wait outside the hearing room and then asked to come back in to get the result. A First-tier Tribunal is also obliged to give a decision notice to the parties (unless it decided to withhold harmful information) as soon as reasonably practicable, stating:[86]

- its decision;
- where it exists, the right to apply for reasons for the decision;
- where it exists, the right of appeal against the decision together with information about the time and manner in which such an appeal must be made.

The First-tier Tribunal can decide to issue the full reasons for its decision.[87] If it does not do this, a party can apply for the reasons in writing, provided this is received by the Tribunal within a month of being given or sent the decision notice.[88]

If a party has applied for reasons (subject to the rules about withholding harmful information), the Tribunal must, unless the decision was a consent order, send them within one month of receiving the application, or as soon as reasonably practicable after that. The one-month limit, although not absolute, provides a useful guideline on how long to expect to wait for a statement of reasons.

Decisions of the Upper Tribunal

The Upper Tribunal may announce its final decision orally at a hearing (although this is far less common than in the First-tier Tribunal) and must then (subject to the harmful information rule) provide the parties with a notice stating its decision and details of any onward rights of review and appeal. The Upper Tribunal must always give reasons for its decision unless the decision was made with the consent of the parties or the parties have consented to a decision being given without reasons.[89]

Record of proceedings

The presiding member of the First-tier Tribunal must keep a record of proceedings. This should include any evidence taken, submissions made and any procedural issues – eg, if a party asked for an adjournment.[90]

The record can be in any form determined by the presiding member and must be kept by the Tribunals Service for at least six months from either the date of the decision, the date the reasons for the decision were given, the date the decision was corrected, the date a refusal to set aside was made or the date of the determination of an application for permission to appeal (unless the documents are sent to the Upper Tribunal before the six months expire), whichever is the later. A party can apply to the First-tier Tribunal within this six-month period for a copy of the record of proceedings and it must be sent to her/him.

In the Upper Tribunal, if the proceedings are recorded, this should be kept for six months. A party can apply for a transcript, but will have to pay for it unless s/he intends to or has challenged the decision of the Upper Tribunal, the transcript is necessary in order to bring that challenge and the Upper Tribunal is satisfied that s/he cannot afford to pay.

Consent orders

The parties can request that the First-tier Tribunal makes an order disposing of the proceedings by their consent. It is not bound to do so and will only make a consent order if it considers it is appropriate.

7. **Changing a First-tier Tribunal decision**

A First-tier Tribunal decision can be changed by:[91]
- correcting an accidental error (see below);
- setting aside the decision (see below);
- reviewing the decision (see p388);
- allowing an appeal to the Upper Tribunal (see p388).

Note: an application for any of the first three options can be treated by the First-tier Tribunal as an application for either of the other two options.

Correcting an error

The First-tier Tribunal can, at any time, correct a clerical mistake or accidental slip or omission in a decision, direction or any document it produces by sending notice of the amended decision or direction to all parties.[92]

Setting aside the decision

A decision, or part of a final decision, can be set aside by the First-tier Tribunal if it considers it is in the interests of justice to do so and:[93]
- a document relating to the proceedings was not sent to or received by, the First-tier Tribunal, a party or representative at an appropriate time; *or*
- a party or representative was not present at the hearing; *or*
- there has been some other procedural irregularity.

An application for a set-aside must be received within one month of being sent the decision by the First-tier Tribunal. However, it appears that the Tribunal may exercise this power without receiving an application (ie, of its own volition).

The rules state that the First-tier Tribunal, on setting aside a decision, can then 're-make' the decision (ie, give a new final decision). Presumably, if the ground for a set-aside was that a party was not present, this would require the First-tier Tribunal to hold a hearing to avoid perpetuating the problem. Furthermore, presumably it would not be right to re-make a decision where new documentary evidence or submissions were now put before the First-tier Tribunal, unless the parties had been given an opportunity to comment on the significance of the new documents.

In addition, if following an application for permission to appeal, all parties agree the decision is in error of law, it will be set aside.

Reviewing a decision

The power of the First-tier Tribunal to 'review' a decision is a new one.[94] Broadly speaking, it combines the previous power to set aside a decision on the grounds that there had been an error of law[95] with a new power to then go on and re-make the decision. Strictly speaking, within the rules no application for a review of a final decision can be made. However, the First-tier Tribunal is required to consider whether to review its own decision prior to any consideration of whether to grant permission to appeal and so, in practice, every application for permission to appeal is *de facto* an application for a review.

The First-tier Tribunal may only review a decision if an application for permission to appeal has been made and it considers that there is an error of law in the decision. However, given that an application for a correction of an accidental error or set-aside can be treated as an application for permission to appeal, there is some scope for the power to be exercised in a slightly wider way.

The First-tier Tribunal is required to notify the parties of the outcome of any review and of any right of appeal against it. **Note:** a decision which has been reviewed can still be appealed to the Upper Tribunal.

8. **Appealing to the Upper Tribunal**

Any party (including the decision maker) can appeal to the Upper Tribunal against a final decision of the First-tier Tribunal. An appeal will only succeed if there is an error of law in the First-tier Tribunal decision. See CPAG's *Welfare Benefits and Tax Credits Handbook* for information about when a decision contains an error of law. It is not an error of law for the First-tier Tribunal to have simply disbelieved what one of the parties said, provided that decision is one which a reasonable tribunal could have arrived at, is properly explained and is based on all the evidence.

The Upper Tribunal can give the decision it thinks the First-tier Tribunal should have given. Alternatively (particularly if it thinks the First-tier Tribunal did not find all the relevant facts or consider the evidence properly), it may refer the case back to the First-tier Tribunal for a new decision to be made.

Before the appeal can be dealt with by the Upper Tribunal, permission to make the appeal needs to be obtained. This permission must first be sought from the First-tier Tribunal. If permission is refused, an application for permission can be made directly to the Upper Tribunal. Permission should only be granted if it is arguable that there is an error of law in the First-tier Tribunal decision.

The procedural rules set out above also apply in the Upper Tribunal (except where stated).

Applying for permission to appeal from the First-tier Tribunal

An application for permission to appeal against a final decision of the First-tier Tribunal must be in writing and be received by the Tribunal within one month of being sent the following, whichever is the latest:[96]

- written reasons for the decision;
- notification of the amended reasons for, or correction of, the decision following a review;
- notification that an in-time (either within the month or such longer period as was allowed) application for a set-aside was refused.

The application must state:

- the decision of the First-tier Tribunal to which it relates;
- the alleged errors of law in the decision;
- the result the party making the application is seeking.

If the application is made late, it must also include a request for an extension of time and explain why it was not made in time. The First-tier Tribunal cannot consider a late application unless it has extended the time for applying.

Usually, it is necessary to have obtained the full statement of reasons for a decision before seeking permission to appeal. However, if this has not been done, the First-tier Tribunal must treat the application as an application for reasons for the decision (unless they have already been refused). The First-tier Tribunal cannot treat such an application as one for permission unless the request for reasons is, or has been, refused. In these circumstances it can only grant permission to appeal if it is in the interests of justice to do so.

When considering an application, the First-tier Tribunal must consider whether to review its decision (see above). If it has not changed the decision (or part of it) on review, it must consider whether to grant permission to appeal in respect of its decision, or the unchanged part of it.

The First-tier Tribunal must send a record of its decision on the application for permission to appeal to the parties. It must include the reasons for refusal of permission to appeal against all or part of the decision. It must also include notice of the right to apply directly to the Upper Tribunal for permission to appeal, the time within which this must be done and the method for making such an application.

It is possible for the First-tier Tribunal to grant permission to appeal in respect of part of a decision. A party may then wish to file that appeal with the Upper Tribunal and also to seek permission to appeal directly from the Upper Tribunal in respect of the parts of the decision where permission has not been granted by the First-tier Tribunal.

Applying for permission to appeal from the Upper Tribunal

If permission to appeal (in whole or in part) has been refused by the First-tier Tribunal, an application can be made to the Upper Tribunal. An application can only be made to the Upper Tribunal if the First-tier Tribunal has refused permission to appeal or has refused to admit an application.[97]

The application to the Upper Tribunal must be made in writing and within one month of being sent the refusal of permission. If made late, the application must include an explanation for why it is late and it will not be considered unless the time limit is extended by the Upper Tribunal. If the earlier application for a written statement of reasons to the First-tier Tribunal or the application for permission to appeal to the First-tier Tribunal was made late, an explanation must also be given and can only be considered if the Upper Tribunal considers it in the interests of justice to do so.

The application must include details of:
- the name and address of the appellant;
- the name and address of the representative (if any);
- an address for sending/delivery of documents;
- details (including a full reference) of the decision challenged;
- the grounds on which the appellant is relying;
- whether the appellant wants a hearing of the application.

The application must include copies of:
- the written record of the decision challenged;
- the written statement of reasons for the decision (where it exists);
- the First-tier Tribunal's notice of refusal of permission to appeal or refusal to admit the application.

Using Form UT1, *Application for Permission to Appeal and Notice of Appeal from First-tier Tribunal (Social Entitlement Chamber)*, available online should ensure that applications are correctly made.

The Upper Tribunal must send the appellant (but not the respondent) reasons for refusing an application.[98] There is no right of appeal against a decision of the Upper Tribunal to refuse permission to appeal.[99]

The Upper Tribunal must send notice of permission to appeal to all the parties.[100] If this happens, generally the application for permission will be treated as the notice of appeal.[101] If the parties agree, the Upper Tribunal can determine the appeal without a need for any further response from them.[102]

Notice of appeal

If the First-tier Tribunal grants permission to appeal, the appellant should send a notice of appeal to the Upper Tribunal. If the appellant has received permission to appeal directly from the Upper Tribunal, this will be treated as the notice of appeal.[103]

Where needed, the notice of appeal must be received by the Upper Tribunal within one month of the party being sent the notice of permission to appeal by the First-tier Tribunal.[104]

The same information and documents must be included with the notice of appeal as for an application for permission to appeal (except that the appellant will be sending the notice of grant and not of refusal of permission).[105]

Late notices of appeal must include a request for an extension of time and the reasons why the notice was not provided in time, and cannot be admitted unless time is extended.[106]

The Upper Tribunal must send a copy of the notice of appeal and accompanying documents to each respondent.[107]

Responses and replies

A response to the appeal can be provided by the other party but does not have to be unless the Upper Tribunal so directs.[108]

A response must be in writing and received by the Upper Tribunal within one month of being sent the notice of appeal (or the notice of a grant of permission to appeal where that is treated as the notice of appeal). Late responses must include an application for an extension of this time limit and an explanation for why they are late.[109]

The response must state:[110]
- the name and address of the respondent;
- the name and address of her/his representative (if any);
- an address for sending/delivery of documents;
- whether the respondent opposes the appeal;
- the grounds on which the respondent intends to rely in the appeal;
- whether the respondent wants a hearing.

The Upper Tribunal must provide a copy of the response to the appellant and the other parties (if there are any).[111]

The appellant may then, unless directed that s/he must, reply to the response. The reply must be received within one month of being sent the response and is then copied to each other party by the Upper Tribunal.[112]

Challenging decisions of the Upper Tribunal

Note: legal advice should always be sought when considering whether to challenge an Upper Tribunal decision.

Upper Tribunal decisions can be changed by:
- correcting an accidental error (see p387);[113]
- setting aside the decision (see p387);[114]
- appealing to the Court of Appeal, for which permission is needed.[115] This is similar to the procedure for applying for permission from the First-tier Tribunal, except the time limit is three months, not one month. The Upper Tribunal must also consider a review (see below) before deciding whether to grant permission. Permission can only be granted if the Upper Tribunal considers the appeal would raise an important point of principle or practice, or there is some other compelling reason to grant it.[116] If the Upper Tribunal refuses permission, the request can be put before the Court of Appeal;
- reviewing the decision (see p388). The procedure is as for the First-tier Tribunal except that the Upper Tribunal can only exercise this power if, when making its decision, it overlooked a legislative decision or binding authority which could have affected the decision or, since giving its decision, a court has made a decision which could have affected its decision.[117]

9. Test case rules

Special rules apply if a court or Upper Tribunal decision on a 'test case' is pending or an Upper Tribunal or court decision on a test case has been made. A 'test case' is one in which a person is challenging the Child Support Agency's (CSA's) interpretation of the law, even if it is the CSA's own appeal and even if the person does not consider the case to be a test case.

These rules apply to maintenance calculation decisions, revision and supersession decisions and appeals in relation to a different matter by the Upper Tribunal or courts.

Test case pending

If a test case is decided against the CSA, normally the CSA has to follow the law as decided in that case in all other cases. However, if an appeal is pending before the Upper Tribunal or a court, then, in any case which might be affected by the decision to be given in that appeal, the CSA can:[118]

- suspend a decision on the application, revision or supersession until the test case appeal has been decided; *or*
- make a decision on the assumption that the test case appeal has already been decided and has been decided against the person who applied for the decision (ie, the calculation, revision or supersession), but only if:[119]
  - the CSA would otherwise have to make a calculation (including one on revision or supersession) leading to the parent with care becoming entitled to income support (IS) or a higher rate of IS; *or*
  - the non-resident parent is employed or self-employed.[120]

An appeal is 'pending' before a court if:[121]
- an appeal (including a judicial review) about child support has been made to the High Court, Court of Session, Court of Appeal or House of Lords, but has not been determined;
- an application for permission to make such an appeal (or judicial review) has been made, but has not been determined;
- the CSA has certified in writing that it is considering making such an appeal or application and the time for appealing/applying has not expired and the CSA considers that the appeal might result in the non-resident parent having no, or less, liability for child maintenance.[122]

An appeal also counts as pending if a court (but not the Upper Tribunal) has referred a question to the European Court of Justice (ECJ) for a preliminary ruling.

If the CSA does not make an application/appeal in time, it can no longer suspend making a decision. The time limits for making applications/appeals are as follows.
- Applying the Upper Tribunal for permission to appeal to the Court of Appeal/ Court of Session: three months from the date the Upper Tribunal decision is issued).[123]
- Applying to the Court of Appeal/Court of Session for permission to appeal from the Upper Tribunal to it (or appealing to one of those courts with permission of the Upper Tribunal): six weeks from the date the Upper Tribunal decision is issued.
- Applying to the Court of Appeal/Court of Session for permission to appeal to the Supreme Court: this is usually done at the end of the hearing in which the court gives its judgment.
- Applying to the Supreme Court for permission to appeal to it: 28 days from the date the order of the court below.[124]
- Appealing to the Supreme Court with permission of the Court of Appeal/Court of Session: 42 days from the date on which permission is given.[125]
- Applying to the High Court/Court of Session for permission to apply for judicial review: three months from the date of the decision for High Court

challenges. There is no time limit to apply to the Court of Session, but an application should be made as soon as possible.

A decision to suspend or make a decision on the assumption that the CSA will win the test case is a discretionary one. The CSA must, therefore, have regard to the welfare of the child when making it.

Test case decisions

If the Upper Tribunal or court interprets child support law, the CSA normally has to apply that interpretation of the law in the period before that decision was given. This would usually require the CSA to supersede all decisions which are affected.

However, if the Upper Tribunal/court rejected the CSA's interpretation of the law, that test case decision only has effect from the date it is given by the Upper Tribunal/court.[126] For the period before that date, the CSA (and either Tribunal) assumes that it was right in its interpretation of the law when making the original decision which led to the appeal.[127] This includes cases where the test case appeal began with a First-tier Tribunal decision on a referral of an application for a variation to the maintenance calculation. This rule applies:

- to maintenance calculations and reduced benefit decisions;[128]
- even if the application for a revision or supersession was made before the test case decision was given and regardless of whether the person applying raised that issue of law;[129]
- even if the Upper Tribunal/court decides that a regulation is *ultra vires*.[130] If this decision is made because the regulation is inconsistent with the European Convention on Human Rights, this rule may also breach that Convention;[131]
- even to decisions of the ECJ.[132] This rule is unlawful under European Community law, except in a case where the ECJ has itself decided that its decision only has effect from the date it is given.[133]

This rule does not apply to:

- an application for maintenance made before 1 June 1999 or a reduced benefit decision;[134]
- a revision of any decision made before 1 June 1999;[135]
- a supersession of any decision made before 1 June 1999;[136]
- a decision in a case where the CSA had suspended a decision under the test case pending rules (see p392);[137]
- a revision or supersession decision in a case where the CSA had required the First-tier or Upper Tribunal to refer the case to the CSA, or deal with it on the assumption that the test case had already been decided against the appellant (see p395).[138]

Test case rules affecting appeals

If a test case pending before a court may affect a similar case awaiting a decision from the First-tier Tribunal or Upper Tribunal, or there is a possibility that the CSA may appeal, the CSA may:[139]

- direct the Tribunal to refer the similar case to the CSA. The CSA makes no decision until the test case is decided. It then revises the CSA decision under appeal or supersedes the Tribunal decision under appeal; *or*
- direct the Tribunal to deal with the case itself. The Tribunal must then either:
- 'stay' the appeal (ie, postpone its decision) until the test case is decided; *or*
- decide the appeal on the assumption that the test case appeal has already been decided and has been decided against the person who appealed in the similar case. If the test case is later decided in that person's favour, the CSA supersedes the Tribunal decision in the similar case.

Notes

1 Reg 4(1)(b) CS(TP) Regs
2 s28D(1)(b) CSA 1991
3 Sch 3 para 4 TTFO
4 Reg 1(3) SS&CS(DA) Regs

1. Decisions that can be appealed
5 **EW** Arts 3 and 4 CSA(JC)O 2002
  S Arts 2, 3 and 4 CSA(JC)(S)O 2003
6 **EW** Art 5 CSA(JC)O 2002
  S Art 5 CSA(JC)(S)O 2003
7 r5(3)(k) TP(FT) Rules

2. Appealing to the First-tier Tribunal
8 s20(3) CSA 1991; reg 23 CS(MCP) Regs; reg 15C SS&CS(DA) Regs
9 r23(2) and Sch 1 TP(FT) Rules
10 s16(5) CSA 1991
11 Reg 2(b) SS&CS(DA) Regs
12 r23(5) and (8) TP(FT) Rules
13 r23(3) TP(FT) Rules
14 Reg 32(2) SS&CS(DA) Regs
15 Reg 32(5) and (6) SS&CS(DA) Regs
16 Reg 32(7) SS&CS(DA) Regs
17 Reg 32(8) SS&CS(DA) Regs
18 rs2(1), (2) and (3)(a) and 5(3)(a) TP(FT) Rules
19 r23(7) TP(FT) Rules
20 r23(4) and (5) TP(FT) Rules

21 Reg 33(4) and (5) SS&CS(DA) Regs
22 Reg 33(3) SS&CS(DA) Regs
23 Reg 33(7) SS&CS(DA) Regs
24 Reg 33(8) SS&CS(DA) Regs
25 Reg 33(9) SS&CS(DA) Regs
26 r19(3) TP(FT) Rules

3. The appeal procedure
27 r2 TP(FT) Rules; r2 TP(UT) Rules
28 r2(3) TP(FT) Rules; r2(3) TP(UT) Rules
29 r2(2) TP(FT) Rules; r2(2) TP(UT) Rules
30 r6(1) TP(FT) Rules; r6(1) TP(UT) Rules
31 Para 12 Practice Statement: Composition of Tribunals in Social Security and Child Support Cases in the Social Entitlement Chamber on or after 3 November 2008. Para 8 Practice Statement: Composition of Tribunals in Relation to Matters that Fall to be Decided by the Administrative Appeals Chamber of the Upper Tribunal on or after 3 November 2008.
32 r15 TP(FT) Rules; r15 TP(UT) Rules
33 r19(3) TP(FT) Rules
34 r14(1) TP(FT) Rules; r14(1) TP(UT) Rules
35 r14(2) TP(FT) Rules; r14(2) TP(UT) Rules
36 r14(3) TP(FT) Rules; r14(3) TP(UT) Rules

37　r14(5) and (6) TP(FT) Rules; r14(5) and (6) TP(UT) Rules
38　r17 TP(FT) Rules; r17 TP(UT) Rules
39　r7(3) TP(FT) Rules
40　r10 TP(FT) Rules; r10 TP(UT) Rules
41　r25 TP(UT) Rules
42　r7(3) and (4) TP(UT) Rules
43　r8(1) TP(FT) Rules
44　r8(2) TP(FT) Rules
45　r8(3)(b) TP(FT) Rules
46　r8(3)(c) TP(FT) Rules
47　*Synergy Child Services Ltd v Ofsted* [2009] UKUT 125 (AAC)
48　r8(5) TP(FT) Rules
49　r8(6) TP(FT) Rules
50　rs2(1) and (3)(a) and 5(3)(a) TP(FT) Rules
51　r8(4) TP(FT) Rules
52　r12(1) TP(FT) Rules; r12(1) TP(UT) Rules
53　r12(2) and (3) TP(FT) Rules; r12(2) and (3) TP(UT) Rules
54　r13(1) TP(FT) Rules; r13(1) TP(UT) Rules
55　r13(2) and (3) TP(FT) Rules; r13(2) and (3) TP(UT) Rules
56　r13(4) TP(FT) Rules; r13(4) TP(UT) Rules
57　r13(5) TP(FT) Rules; r13(5) TP(UT) Rules
58　r11(5) TP(FT) Rules; r11(3) TP(UT) Rules
59　r11(6) TP(FT) Rules; r11(4) TP(UT) Rules
60　r17 TP(FT) Rules; r17 TP(UT) Rules
61　r17(1)(b), (2) and (3)(b) TP(FT) Rules
62　r17(1) and (2) TP(UT) Rules
63　Reg 33(10) SS&CS(DA) Regs

4. Preparing a case
64　r5 Family Proceedings Courts (CSA 1991) Rules; r10.21A Family Proceedings Rules

5. Hearings
65　r1(3) TP(FT) Rules; r1(3) TP(UT) Rules
66　r27 TP(FT) Rules
67　r34 TP(UT) Rules
68　r29(1) TP(FT) Rules; r36(1) TP(UT) Rules
69　r29(2) TP(FT) Rules; r36(2)(b) TP(UT) Rules. The only other exception to this is when the Upper Tribunal is conducting a hearing of an application for permission to bring judicial review in which at least two working days' notice must be given. Such proceedings are outside the scope of this *Handbook*.
70　r30 TP(FT) Rules; r37 TP(UT) Rules
71　r31 TP(FT) Rules; r38 TP(UT) Rules
72　Art 2 FT&UT(CT)O and para 6 Practice Statement: Composition of Tribunals in Social Security and Child Support Cases in the Social Entitlement Chamber on or after 3 November 2008

73　Sch 2 para 1(2) TCEA 2007
74　Para 7 Practice Statement: Composition of Tribunals in Social Security and Child Support Cases in the Social Entitlement Chamber on or after 3 November 2008
75　Para 9 Practice Statement: Composition of Tribunals in Social Security and Child Support Cases in the Social Entitlement Chamber on or after 3 November 2008
76　Para 12 Practice Statement: Composition of Tribunals in Social Security and Child Support Cases in the Social Entitlement Chamber on or after 3 November 2008; Art 8 FT&UT(CT) Order
77　CSCS/16/07

6. Decisions
78　s20(7) CSA 1991
79　CCS/16351/1996
80　S20(7)(a) CSA 1991
81　R(IB)2/04
82　R(IB)2/04
83　CSCS/2/1994; CSCS/3/1994
84　CCS/511/1995
85　s20(7)(b) CSA 1991
86　r33 TP(FT) Rules
87　r34(2)(b) TP(FT) Rules
88　r34(3) and (4) TP(FT) Rules
89　r40 TP(UT) Rules
90　Practice Statement: Record of Proceedings in Social Security and Child Support Cases in the Social Entitlement Chamber on or after 3 November 2008

7. Changing a decision on appeal
91　Not including judicial review of non-appealable decisions.
92　r42 TP(FT) Rules
93　r43 TP(FT) Rules
94　Introduced by s9 TCEA 2007; see also r46 TP(FT) Rules
95　Under s13 SSA 1998

8. Appealing to the Upper Tribunal
96　r44 TP(UT) Rules
97　r21(2) TP(UT) Rules
98　r22(1) TP(UT) Rules
99　*Court and Others R (on the application of) v The Upper Tribunal & Others* [2009] EWHC 3052 (Admin) (1 December 2009)
100　r22(2)(a) TP(UT) Rules
101　r22(2)(b) TP(UT) Rules

102 r22(2)(c) TP(UT) Rules
103 r23(1) TP(UT) Rules
104 r23(2) TP(UT) Rules
105 r23(3) and (4) TP(UT) Rules
106 r23(5) TP(UT) Rules
107 r23(6) TP(UT) Rules
108 r24(1) TP(UT) Rules
109 r24(2) and (4) TP(UT) Rules
110 r24(3) TP(UT) Rules
111 r24(5) TP(UT) Rules
112 r25 TP(UT) Rules
113 r42 TP(UT) Rules
114 r43 TP(UT) Rules
115 rs44 and 45 TP(UT) Rules
116 Art 2 AUTCA
117 r46 TP(UT) Rules

9. Test case rules
118 s28ZA(1) and (2) CSA 1991
119 Reg 23(3) and (5) SS&CS(DA) Regs
120 As defined in s2(1) SSCBA 1992
121 s28ZA(4) and (5) CSA 1991
122 s28ZA(4)(c) CSA 1991; reg 23(4)
     SS&CS(DA) Regs
123 Reg 30(1) CSC(P) Regs
124 r11(1) SCR
125 r19(2) SCR
126 s28ZC(1) and (3) CSA 1991; reg 7B(10)
     SS&CS(DA) Regs
127 s28ZC(1) and (6) CSA 1991
128 s28ZC(3) CSA 1991
129 s28ZC(5) CSA 1991
130 s28ZC(4) CSA 1991
131 Art 13 ECHR requires an effective
     remedy for violations
132 s28ZC(6) CSA 1991
133 C-35/97 *Commission v France* [1998]
     ECR I-5325
134 s28ZC(1)(b)(i) CSA 1991
135 s28ZC(1)(b)(ii) CSA 1991
136 s28ZC(1)(b)(iii) CSA 1991
137 s28ZC(2)(a) CSA 1991
138 s28ZC(2)(b) CSA 1991
139 s28ZB CSA 1991

Chapter 19

Collection and enforcement

This chapter covers:
1. Payment of child maintenance (p399)
2. Collection of other payments (p406)
3. Arrears (p407)
4. Enforcement (p416)
5. Existing 'old rules' and conversion cases (p432)

The legal power to collect and enforce the payment of child maintenance now rests with the Child Maintenance and Enforcement Commission (C-MEC). In particular, new enforcement powers (such as lump-sum and regular deduction orders) were granted directly to C-MEC. However, at the time of writing, C-MEC's powers are operated via the Child Support Agency (CSA) and it is the CSA with which most parents will have contact. We therefore continue to refer to the CSA, rather than C-MEC, in this chapter.

The CSA can arrange the collection and enforcement of child support maintenance[1] and certain other maintenance payments (see p406).[2] This service has been free to all CSA clients since April 1995.[3] However, fees may be introduced by C-MEC sometime in the future (see Chapter 1).

Once the calculation has been made, a collection schedule is set up. If the payment schedule breaks down and arrears accrue, debt management procedures may be put in place, or the CSA may decide to take enforcment action.

Within the limits of the regulations, decisions about how payment is enforced are discretionary, so there is scope for negotiation between CSA staff and the individuals involved. If there are instructions or practices for dealing with a type of case in a certain way, it may be helpful to remind the CSA of these. If guidance is not helpful, the CSA can be reminded that it is not binding, and the individual officer dealing with the case may apply discretion. As the decisions are discretionary, the welfare of any child likely to be affected must be taken into account by the CSA (see p24).

The amount of maintenance calculated cannot be altered except by revision, supersession, appeal or variation (departure under the 'old rules'). The CSA does not suspend current collection just because the non-resident parent states that he cannot afford to pay. However, the CSA may agree to lower payments if a revision, supersession, appeal or variation/departure is pending (see p410).

There is no right of appeal to the First-tier Tribunal about a decision concerning collection and enforcement (see p370 for which CSA decisions can be appealed). A deduction from earnings order can, in limited circumstances, be appealed to a magistrates' court (see p416) and judicial review may be possible for other decisions (see p353). The Independent Case Examiner (see p443) can consider complaints about the CSA's exercise of discretion once the CSA's internal complaints procedure has been followed (see Chapter 20). For regular payment conditions imposed because a departure application has been made, see p304.

1. **Payment of child maintenance**

If a maintenance calculation has been made and the Child Support Agency (CSA) is collecting and enforcing the maintenance, it has discretion to decide:
- the method by which the non-resident parent pays;[4]
- the person to whom it is paid;[5]
- if payments are made through the CSA or someone else, the method by which payment is made to the person with care;[6]
- the timing of payments;[7] *and*
- the amount of payments towards arrears.[8]

Before making these decisions, the CSA must, as far as is possible, give the non-resident parent and the person with care an opportunity to make representations and must take these into account.[9] In every case, the CSA must notify the non-resident parent in writing of the amounts and timing of payments due, to whom he must make payment, how he must pay and details of any amount that is overdue and remains outstanding.[10] This notice is sent as soon as possible after the calculation is made and again after any change in the details in the notice.[11] A copy is sent to the person with care. If the payments are to be made directly between the two parties, the CSA takes no further action regarding collection unless the person with care notifies the CSA that the non-resident parent has failed to comply as directed. Therefore, the parties can agree between them to use another method or frequency of payment.

If there are arrears and the CSA has imposed a penalty payment, see p413.

Who is paid

The CSA can require the non-resident parent to pay child maintenance:[12]
- directly to the person with care;
- directly to a Scottish child applicant;
- to, or via, the CSA (this cannot be required in all cases); *or*
- to, or via, another person.

The CSA prefers the non-resident parent to make payments directly to the person with care.[13] This is known as 'maintenance direct'. Once the CSA has calculated the amount of maintenance owed, the parents make their own payment arrangements. Letters are sent by the CSA telling each parent the amount of arrears and the date regular payments should start. These direct payments are not monitored by the CSA. If the payment arrangement breaks down, the parent with care can ask to use the collection service (see below).

Although some non-resident parents and, indeed, some persons with care, may want to have payments made to a third party (eg, their mortgage lender) the CSA does not usually accept these as being child maintenance payments. However, any such payments made between the effective date and the date of calculation may be considered as voluntary payments to offset any initial arrears.

The collection service

When child maintenance payments are to be made to or via the CSA, this is referred to as the collection service. Any party to a case can request that payment be via the CSA.[14] The CSA normally provides the collection service if an applicant requests it, even where the other party does not.

The CSA can only provide the collection service on the request of one of the parties to the calculation.[15]

If the non-resident parent is on benefit the person with care may use the collection service to secure direct deductions from his benefit. This is particularly useful if a voluntary arrangement cannot be reached with the non-resident parent.

The collection service can be requested at a later date – eg, if payments become irregular. The request can be made verbally or in writing. The CSA has the discretion to collect arrears already due when the request is made.[16]

Where payments are made to the CSA, only payments actually received by the CSA can be passed on. The CSA aims to make the first payment to the person with care within six weeks of making initial payment arrangements with the non-resident parent. Once maintenance is received from the non-resident parent, the CSA 'will make maintenance payments to parents with care within a week'.[17]

The collection service has a number of advantages.

- It removes the need for direct contact between the non-resident parent and person with care.
- If the person with care is not on IS/income-based JSA/income-related ESA, the collection service is supposed to ensure regular payments by starting enforcement action (see p416) as soon as payments are missed, although this does not always happen.

The following are disadvantages.

- A payment statement is only issued periodically or on request (see p404) and these are often considered to be inaccurate. The parties should, therefore, always keep their own records and evidence of payments. The majority of accounts are in arrears and many persons with care and some non-resident parents are unhappy with the level of service from the CSA.
- The CSA negotiates collection and arrears schedules with the parents and may agree to an arrears arrangement, notwithstanding objections from the person with care.

Person with care on benefits

Arrears of child support maintenance collected by the CSA may be retained if the person with care or her/his partner is (or was during the relevant period) in receipt of IS/income-based JSA/income-related ESA (see p338).[18] The amount retained is equal to the difference between the amount of benefit paid to the person with care and the amount that would have been paid if the non-resident parent had kept to the maintenance arrangement during the relevant period.

Previously, if payments were made via the CSA, the person with care used to receive one credit transfer from Jobcentre Plus that included both IS/income-based JSA and child maintenance. If the non-resident parent did not make a payment to the CSA, the person with care's benefit was still paid, but there was no maintenance element. From the 27 October 2008, the CSA now pays all maintenance collected directly to the person with care. This is paid into the same account as that into which benefits are paid, unless the CSA is notified otherwise. It is the responsibility of the person with care to notify Jobcentre Plus of any maintenance received. If Jobcentre Plus is not notified promptly, the person with care could be accused of benefit fraud. Presumably, this requirement will become obsolete once maintenance is fully disregarded for IS/income-based JSA/income-related ESA, expected in April 2010.

For when arrears of child maintenance are paid later, see p338.

For the effect of child maintenance on IS/income-based JSA/income-related ESA, see p336.

Method of payment

The non-resident parent can make payments by standing order, direct debit, automated credit transfer, credit card, debit card, cheque, postal order, voluntary deductions from earnings arrangements, or cash.[19] A debit card means one that can be used as a substitute for a cheque – ie, where the non-resident parent's bank account is debited instantly, such as with a Switch card.[20] If the collection service is being used, the CSA prefers payment by direct debit.[21] The CSA can direct a non-resident parent to take all reasonable steps to open a bank or building society account.[22] However, there is no penalty if he fails to do so. Some non-resident parents pay by deductions from benefit (see p174).

When deciding the method of payment, the CSA must take into account any representations from the parties.[23]

The CSA can accept payment by cheque, bankers draft, postal order, cash and foreign currency, but it does not encourage the use of these methods.[24] Non-resident parents who wish to pay in one of these ways should insist on doing so. So long as payments are made when due, no deduction from earnings order should be made.

Where payment is made via the CSA, the person with care is paid by automated credit transfer wherever possible, and if not, by cheque (although in theory cash is also possible, it is not used).[25] The person with care is asked to provide details of a bank, building society or Post Office account. If she does not have an account, or experiences difficulty opening one, she should contact the CSA national helpline on 08457 133133.

Deductions from benefit: new rules

If a non-resident parent on benefit is required to pay child maintenance at the flat rate (see Chapter 5), the CSA may request Jobcentre Plus to make a deduction for maintenance.[26] Deductions can be made from:[27]

- IS;
- income-based JSA;
- contribution-based JSA;
- maternity allowance;
- bereavement benefits;
- widows' benefits;
- retirement pension;
- incapacity benefit (IB);
- ESA;
- carer's allowance;
- severe disablement allowance (SDA);
- industrial injuries schemes benefits;
- war disablement pension;
- pension credit (PC).

If someone should pay at the flat rate but a variation has been made which results in the reduced or basic rate being payable, deductions can be made towards the new amount of maintenance calculated.

If both the non-resident parent and his partner are:[28]

- on IS, income-related ESA or income-based JSA; *and*
- each is a non-resident parent,

the £5 flat rate deduction will be split between them so that each contributes £2.50 to their respective persons with care.[29] (In polygamous relationships where there is more than one new partner who is also a non-resident parent the £5 is apportioned between all the non-resident parents.[30])

The CSA requests the deduction and Jobcentre Plus must make it in full wherever possible. The parent must be left with at least 10 pence a week.[31] Partial deductions will not be made. In addition, priority debt rules do not apply to deductions for child support maintenance under the 'new rules'. This means the deduction for child support is always made, whatever other deductions are due.

Both the person with care and non-resident parent are notified that deductions are to be made.

If there are arrears of maintenance, a £1 deduction towards arrears may be made from the benefits listed on p402, except IS, income-based JSA, income-related ESA or PC (see p411).

Deductions from benefit: old rules

When an application is received by the CSA and it is found that the non-resident parent is on IS/income-based JSA/income-related ESA/PC, both parties will be notified as to whether or not deductions from benefit are a possibility. If the non-resident parent is not exempt from deductions, the Department for Work and Pensions (DWP) will be sent notification requesting that a deduction is made. This is binding on the DWP, unless there are other deductions being made from the benefit which take precedence.[32]

Direct deductions for contributions of child maintenance cannot be made from any benefit other than IS/income-based JSA/income-related ESA/PC, unless contribution-based JSA, IB, SDA or retirement pension are paid together with IS/income-based JSA/income-related ESA/PC.[33] After the deductions are made, the claimant must be left with at least 10 pence a week.[34]

There is a maximum amount which can be deducted from IS/income-based JSA/income-related ESA/PC for various payments.[35] The contribution for child maintenance has a lower priority than any of the other possible deductions.[36] Therefore, in some cases where non-resident parents have other deductions, it will not be possible to deduct the full £6.50 for the contribution to child maintenance. The DWP can deduct half of the £6.50 contribution.[37] For more information about deductions from benefit, see CPAG's *Welfare Benefits and Tax Credits Handbook*.

If full deductions from IS/income-based JSA/income-related ESA/PC are not possible, arrears of child maintenance contributions do *not* accrue.

The DWP will tell the CSA whether deductions are possible. The CSA, in turn, notifies the non-resident parent and the person with care if deductions are going to begin. The £6.50 is paid to the person with care via the CSA.[38] The CSA notifies her of the way in which the payments will be made.

If there are arrears of maintenance, these can be deducted from contribution-based JSA or contributory ESA only (see p411).

Timing of payments

The CSA decides the day and frequency of payments,[39] but asks for the person's preference. When deciding the day and the interval for payment by the non-resident parent, the CSA must take into account:[40]

- the day on which, and the interval at which, the non-resident parent receives his income;
- any other relevant circumstances of the non-resident parent;
- time for cheques to clear, if applicable, and for payments to be transferred to the person with care; *and*
- any representations of the parties, in particular the preference of the non-resident parent.[41]

Unless undue hardship would be caused to the non-resident parent or the person with care, the frequency of payments to the person with care will be the same as the frequency set for the non-resident parent's payments (but see p418 for deduction from earnings orders).[42]

Unless payments are to be by direct debit or standing order, the non-resident parent is advised to make each payment three to four days before the due date in order to ensure that payments are received on time and avoid arrears. Clearance times are allowed for each method of payment, but the CSA aims to make payments to the person with care within a week of receiving them from the non-resident parent.[43] If a delay in payments is caused by maladministration on the part of the CSA, the person with care may be entitled to compensation. She will need to make a complaint first. See Chapter 20 for more information.[44]

Payment statements

Statements of the CSA account can be supplied when a request is made by a person with care, non-resident parent or child in Scotland.[45] Statements can be important when contesting the level of arrears. However, both parties should keep records and evidence of payments made and received, given the high level of errors on CSA accounts.

Overpayments

An overpayment can arise either because the amount of the maintenance due for a past period has been reduced, there has been a CSA error or the non-resident parent has paid more than the regular payment due. The CSA has a discretion about allocating the overpayment,[46] including setting it against any arrears of child maintenance resulting from a previous calculation.[47]

If there is a surplus remaining after current maintenance, arrears and other liabilities have been met, the non-resident parent may have the amount he pays adjusted or a refund made. An adjustment is the preferred option.

If the CSA receives an unexpected payment from the non-resident parent, it should check to determine the reason for this – eg, it could be for an overdue collection to offset arrears or an amount towards a future collection. Following this investigation, the amount may be allocated to reduce arrears arising under a previous calculation or, if there are no arrears, it can be used to reduce the amount payable under the current calculation. If the current calculation is to be reduced, the CSA should consider the amount by which it is appropriate to reduce a current calculation given the circumstances of both the parent with care and the non-resident parent (see below).[48]

Refunds are only usually made if there are no overdue collections or arrears on the case.

The CSA should refund overpayments made because of CSA error – eg, if a person was told to pay more than the calculation required. In such cases, the non-resident parent may also wish to complain and seek compensation (see Chapter 20).

Adjustments

If an overpayment remains after offsetting against regular maintenance, arrears and other liability, the CSA can reduce the amount payable to compensate the non-resident parent for the overpayment.[49] Adjustments may also be made where there are overpayments of voluntary payments in the initial payment period.[50] When making this discretionary decision, the CSA must consider, in particular:

- the circumstances of the non-resident parent and person with care;
- the welfare of any children (see p24);
- the amount of the overpayment in relation to the amount of the current calculation; *and*
- the period over which it would be reasonable to recoup it.

An adjustment of the amount payable in relation to the current maintenance calculation may reduce the amount to nil.[51]

If the amount of an adjusted calculation changes because of a revision, supersession or variation, the adjustment applies to the fresh calculation unless the CSA considers that this would be inappropriate, in which case it can either change the amount of the adjustment or cancel it.[52]

The non-resident parent, person with care and any Scottish child applicant must be notified of an adjustment or cancellation of an adjustment.[53] The decision to make or cancel an adjustment can be revised or superseded by the CSA (see Chapter 17) or appealed to the First-tier Tribunal (see Chapter 18).[54]

Recovery of overpayments from the person with care

If the CSA reimburses an overpayment to a non-resident parent, it can recover from the person with care any maintenance overpaid to her.[55] This does not include overpaid voluntary payments.[56] The CSA cannot enforce recovery of overpayments because of CSA administrative error but the person with care will be asked if she is prepared to repay.

Recovery of overpayments is a discretionary decision, so the welfare of any children likely to be affected by reimbursement must be taken into account (see p24). The CSA cannot recover the overpayment if:[57]

- the person with care was on IS, income-based JSA or income-related ESA at any time during the period she was overpaid; *or*
- the person with care was on IS/income-based JSA/income-related ESA on any of the dates reimbursement to the non-resident parent was made; *or*
- either of the above apply, if the non-resident parent made voluntary payments.

The overpayment is, therefore, collected from any current maintenance; where there is no ongoing maintenance, other collection arrangements can be made.[58]

2. Collection of other payments

The Child Support Agency (CSA) can collect and enforce other forms of maintenance where child support maintenance is being collected.[59]

The power to collect other maintenance is discretionary. However, the CSA may agree to requests to collect other types of maintenance for parents with care. The CSA can only collect other maintenance that falls due after the CSA gives the non-resident parent written notice that the other maintenance will be collected.[60]

The following payments under a court order (see p30) can be collected by the CSA:[61]

- additional child maintenance in excess of the CSA maximum;
- maintenance for a child's education or training;
- maintenance paid to meet the expenses of a child with a disability;
- maintenance paid for a stepchild – ie, a child living with the person with care who used to live with the non-resident parent and was accepted by him as a member of his family;
- spousal or civil partner maintenance for a person with care of a child for whom child support maintenance is being collected.

The methods used by the CSA for collecting and enforcing other types of maintenance are the same as for child support maintenance.[62] Where a non-resident parent is paying more than one type of maintenance and pays less than the total amount required, he should stipulate how the amounts are to be allocated. The CSA will allocate as requested, except that where arrears of child support maintenance are specified, current child support maintenance will be paid before arrears. If the non-resident parent does not stipulate, the CSA will allocate according to the following order of priority:[63]

- current child support maintenance liability;
- regular child maintenance;
- arrears of child support maintenance to the person with care;
- arrears of other child maintenance to the CSA; *and*
- other liabilities, with the oldest first.

Where arrears of child support maintenance are due to the CSA and others are due to the person with care, the priorities are the same as for overpayments caused by a change in the amount of the calculation (see p404).

If there is more than one person with care, the CSA will apportion the payment between them.[64] This means that the non-resident parent cannot choose to pay one parent but not the other.

Collection of court costs and penalty payments

Fees have not been charged for CSA services since April 1995 (see p398). From 5 August 2008, the requirement to pay any outstanding fees from years before 1995 has also been removed.[65]

If the CSA applies to the court for a decision on whether a person is a parent and the court decides that he is, the court can order him to pay the CSA's costs in bringing the case, including the cost of any DNA tests which have been carried out (see p70). Also, a non-resident parent may have agreed to pay DNA test fees to the CSA without a court order (see p66).

The CSA may also have imposed a penalty payment on the non-resident parent for failure to pay.

The CSA will negotiate with the liable person about payment of these other liabilities.[66] It will initially request the full amount due, but payments by instalment may be agreed.

Fees and costs can only be enforced through court action. The rules for enforcement of maintenance (see p416) do not apply. The court is the sheriff court in Scotland and the county court in England and Wales. If the case is contested, a hearing is arranged in the court with jurisdiction for the area in which the parent lives. A money judgment can be enforced by the usual debt enforcement procedures.

3. Arrears

The Child Support Agency (CSA) acts on arrears only if the collection service (see p400) is being used. If a person with care has not requested the collection service, she should consider doing so if a payment is missed. The CSA should then pursue all outstanding arrears.

Initial arrears

As the first calculation is usually made after its effective date, there are usually always initial arrears. If a court order made on, or after, 3 March 2003 has been in force for more than a year and there is an application to the CSA, the effective date is two months and two days from the date of the application. If the non-resident parent has continued to make payments due under the order beyond the effective date, these payments will be treated as payments of child support.[67] This helps to avoid additional liability for child support where, for whatever reason, it takes the CSA longer than two months and two days to make the maintenance calculation, so that when it is made, its effective date (and, therefore, the date the court order ceases to have effect) is in the past. If the payments made under the court order are at a higher rate than those due under the calculation, this will be treated as an overpayment of child support and the maintenance calculation can be adjusted accordingly.

The CSA prefers to notify the non-resident parent about the collection schedule, including initial arrears, by telephone.[68] The parent can request and negotiate changes to the schedule. Written confirmation of the collection schedule is issued once the non-resident parent has agreed to it. Where telephone contact is not possible, the CSA will write to the non-resident parent.

The written notification states:[69]

- the amount due and to whom it is to be paid;
- how it is to be paid – ie, method, day and interval between payments;
- any amounts that are overdue and outstanding.

The CSA requests payment of the initial arrears as a lump sum.[70] If a non-resident parent cannot pay this all at once, he may negotiate an agreement to pay in instalments or a collection schedule to cover both the initial payment and ongoing liability (see p409).

A parent who fails to make payment of the outstanding arrears within seven days of written notification of the amount due may face financial penalties and further enforcement action.

A parent who thinks the calculation is wrong may be able to seek a revision or make an appeal. If he objects to the way the CSA is dealing with collections he may make a complaint (see Chapter 20).

Voluntary payments made in the initial period

Voluntary payments made by the non-resident parent through the CSA (or, where the CSA agrees, to the person with care or a third party) after the effective date but before the calculation is made and notified may be offset against arrears of child maintenance.[71]

Only the following types of payment can be offset:[72]
- in lieu of child support maintenance;
- in respect of a mortgage or loan on the child's home, or for repairs or improvements to the property;
- rent on the child's home;
- mains gas, water or electricity at the child's home;
- council tax payable at the child's home;
- repairs to the heating system at the child's home; *or*
- repairs to the child's home.

Payments can be made by cash, standing order, cheque, postal order, debit card or other method/arrangement from an account of the non-resident parent or on his behalf (eg, credit card).[73]

If the payments are made to the CSA they will be passed on to the person with care. Once the calculation has been made, the voluntary payments will be offset against the initial arrears.

If the payments are made direct to the person with care or a third party, the CSA will check with the person with care whether payments have been made.[74] This is normally done by phone. If the person with care confirms the payments were made, this is usually accepted without any further need for proof. If there is a dispute about whether a payment has been made, the CSA will ask the non-resident parent to provide proof. Payment can be verified by bank statements, duplicates of cashed cheques, receipts, paid bills/invoices, or written or oral statement from the person with care.[75] It is in the interest of both parties to ensure payments are recorded, and the CSA should explain to the non-resident parent the importance of keeping a record and provide a form on which to do so.

If either party disagrees with a decision about offsetting, a complaint can be made (see Chapter 20).

If offsetting means that there is an overpayment, the calculation may be adjusted to compensate the non-resident parent or a refund may be made (see p405).

Negotiating an arrears agreement

If the non-resident parent is in arrears, the CSA will seek an arrears agreement.[76]

Negotiations with the CSA may begin on notification of the collection schedule or at a later date if the non-resident parent has difficulty making ongoing payments. However, the CSA does not normally agree to defer payment of current liability, though it may do so if a revision, supersession or appeal is pending.

Limitations on the level of payments or how quickly the arrears must be cleared are not specified in child support law. Although CSA staff always begin by requesting full payment of the outstanding arrears, an arrears agreement may be reached to pay the amount in instalments.

In making this discretionary decision the CSA should consider the:

- needs of the non-resident parent or any new family;
- representations of the non-resident parent about hardship; *or*
- needs of the person with care and the qualifying child.

If a non-resident parent has other priorities (eg, fuel) or other large debts, he should seek independent money advice. Preparing a financial statement and sending it to the CSA may assist in reaching an agreement. However, existing arrangements with other creditors may have to be renegotiated to take into account the CSA calculation. However, it is important to keep the CSA informed so that it does not assume that the non-resident parent is refusing to come to an agreement.

The CSA can use other methods of recovery, such as a deduction from earnings order (see p416). Therefore, CSA staff are unlikely to agree to a non-resident parent making low payments over a very long period. It is in his interests to come to an agreement if he wishes to avoid further payment penalties and enforcement action. If he has children living with him, the welfare of those children must be taken into account.

At the time of writing, it is understood that the CSA aims to collect arrears within two years, at a rate of up to 40 per cent of a non-resident parent's income.[77] CSA staff can use their discretion and take into account the non-resident parent's particular circumstances, where appropriate to do so.[78]

A plan to pay arrears by instalments that lasts more than two years may be accepted, but the CSA is likely to obtain a liability order if there will be more than £1,000 outstanding at the end of two years. A liability order gives the CSA discretion to use other methods to enforce payment, should the plan not be completed.

Repayments spread over several years may help non-resident parents who are in financial hardship but it is very late payment to the person with care. She may want to make representations to the CSA. No interest will be paid to the person with care in respect of arrears, even though the arrears may have accrued because of CSA delay and error, and/or the non-compliance of the non-resident parent.

The parent with care and qualifying children are not consulted about the level at which arrears are collected, but will be informed when the decision has been made. This practice may be contrary to the European Convention on Human Rights' protection of private property,[79] but there has been no reported caselaw on this point (see also p415 on the fact that a person with care cannot directly enforce the payment of child support).

Revision, supersession or appeal pending

The CSA can suspend collection of arrears if a revision, supersession, variation or appeal is pending. If the calculation is likely to be reduced, the CSA may agree to suspend collection of some of the ongoing payments. However, this does not often happen; the CSA prefers to speed up its consideration of the case.

A non-resident parent who requests a revision, supersession or appeal and is having problems paying the current maintenance or any arrears should make representations to the CSA for lower regular payments.

Payment of arrears

Arrears do not have to be paid by the same method as continuing child maintenance payments. For example, arrears could be collected via the CSA, while ongoing payments are made to the person with care. However, in practice the CSA prefers to use the same method of payment for both.

If the CSA collects arrears and income support (IS) or income-based jobseeker's allowance (JSA) is paid to or for the person with care, the CSA can keep the part of the arrears payments that would not have been passed to the parent with care had it been made when due.[80] That is, the CSA can retain an amount equal to the difference between the amount of IS/income-based JSA that was paid to the parent with care and the amount that would have been paid had the non-resident parent not been in arrears.[81] Payments of arrears are allocated between the CSA and person with care in the same way as overpayments (see p404).

Collection of arrears from a non-resident parent on benefit

In 'new rules' cases, if the non-resident parent is in receipt of one of the following contribution-based benefits a deduction of £1 may be made towards arrears. This is in addition to a deduction for flat-rate maintenance. These deductions are separate to other deductions made from benefit and are not affected by priority rules on which deductions should be made first. The £1 deduction can be made from the following benefits, except where IS, income-based JSA, income-related employment and support allowance (ESA) or pension credit (PC) are also being paid to the non-resident parent or his partner:[82]

- contribution-based JSA;
- maternity allowance;
- bereavement allowance;
- widowed parent's allowance;
- war widow's pension;
- widow's pension;
- widowed mother's allowance;
- reduced earnings allowance;
- industrial death benefit and retirement allowance;
- retirement pension;
- incapacity benefit;
- contributory ESA;
- carer's allowance;
- severe disablement allowance;
- industrial injuries benefits;
- war disablement pension.

This means that arrears action in 'new rules' cases will be suspended against non-resident parents on IS/income-based JSA/income-related ESA/PC. If a person with care believes that the arrears action should be pursued in some other way, she should contact the CSA and explain her reasons. If the CSA is unwilling to take action, a complaint may be made (see Chapter 20).

In 'old rules' cases, a deduction for arrears can only be made from contribution-based JSA, at a maximum of one-third of the age-related amount payable (eg, £21.43 a week for a non-resident parent aged 25 or over in 2009/10).[83] In 'old rules' cases, the priority rules on deductions from benefit do apply and therefore the deduction may not be made where certain other deductions take priority (eg, for arrears of council tax). For more information on the priority rules on deductions from benefit, see CPAG's *Welfare Benefits and Tax Credits Handbook*.

Starting recovery action

The CSA may begin to consider recovery action when:
- a payment from the non-resident parent to the CSA is not received;
- the person with care notifies the CSA that a payment due has not been received; *or*
- the person with care requests an increase in IS/income-based JSA/income-related ESA because child maintenance has not been paid.

The CSA contacts the non-resident parent to investigate the situation. Contact is normally initially by telephone and followed up in writing if no response is received. The non-resident parent may request an appointment at a local office if he wishes to discuss payment face to face with CSA staff.

If the non-resident parent intends to pay the amount, the CSA may:
- accept a delayed payment, setting a time limit by when payment must be received; *or*
- reschedule the amount to include it within the arrears.

If the non-resident parent indicates that a change of circumstances is causing difficulty in making the payments, the CSA may collect information to check whether or not there should be a supersession.

If the non-resident parent refuses to pay, the CSA will inform him of its powers to collect and enforce maintenance. The CSA may discuss imposing a payment penalty to encourage the non-resident parent to pay the maintenance due. A non-resident parent can also be fined up to £1,000 for failing to provide required information or providing false information.[84]

To avoid payment penalties and other methods of recovery, the non-resident parent should come to an agreement (see p409) as soon as possible and comply with that agreement. The CSA has discretion over the agreements reached with non-resident parents about debt recovery. However, where a parent fails to come to a voluntary agreement or breaks it, the CSA may then impose payment penalties. The CSA may enforce a deduction from earnings order (DEO) at up to 40 per cent of net income and/or take further enforcement action.

Arrears notice

If the non-resident parent has missed one or more child maintenance payments, the CSA must send him an arrears notice itemising the amounts owed. The notice also explains the regulations about arrears and requests payment of the outstanding amount.[85] The CSA will then contact the non-resident parent to discuss the issue.

The non-resident parent should check that the amount owed is correct and tell the CSA of any mistakes. There have been high levels of mistakes on accounts in the past. Therefore, if there is a concern that the balance is incorrect, the non-resident parent should ask for a payment statement (see p404) and compare this with his own record. While doing this, it is important that he keeps the CSA informed so that a penalty payment and a DEO are not imposed in the meantime.

The non-resident parent can contact the CSA to negotiate payment by instalments (see p409). Once an arrears notice has been served, another does not have to be sent if arrears remain uncleared, unless the non-resident parent has paid all arranged payments for a 12-week period.[86]

When the non-resident parent defaults

If the non-resident parent fails to keep to an arrears agreement:

- a penalty payment may be imposed; *and*
- a DEO (see p416) or other method of enforcement may be considered (see p416).

In all cases, a non-resident parent who wants to co-operate should try to renegotiate an agreement in good time before a change in his circumstances – eg, redundancy. If the non-resident parent has paid regularly and the change would produce a reduction in the amount due, the CSA may accept a lower amount. The non-resident parent could also try to negotiate a suspension in payments if his personal circumstances make it difficult or insensitive to enforce recovery – eg, he is unemployed, sick or in prison.

Penalty payments

In 'new rules' cases, the power exists to impose a penalty payment on a non-resident parent who is in arrears with his child maintenance payments.[87] In practice, this power does not seem to be used, although it is possible that it could be if the CSA changes its policy. All references to late payment penalties have been removed from CSA leaflets and letters to its clients.[88]

Delays in collection and enforcement

Despite CSA steps to avoid debts building up, many cases may accumulate arrears. The intention under the new scheme is for the CSA to take action more quickly to respond to failure to pay and impose financial penalties to encourage payment or establish arrears agreements. The Operational Improvement Plan that ran from 2006 to 2009 stated that the CSA would take 'quicker and firmer action' where non-resident parents default. This included increasing the use of DEOs and the number of non-resident parents brought to court,[89] which has had some success in increased collection rates. The CSA's 2008/09 Business Plan pledges improvements to its computer system to aid debt and legal enforcement activities, the outcome of which is yet to be seen.[90]

Persons with care who are concerned at the speed of pursuit and who want quicker action should contact the CSA by phone, letter or in person. A person with care may want to explain any effect the lack of arrears action has on the welfare of the child(ren). In particular, a person with care may want to request that a DEO be issued and, if there is undue delay, make a complaint (see Chapter 20). If a DEO or another form of enforcement is refused, the person with care should be given the reasons for this. As well as making a complaint, it is possible that judicial review (see p353) could also be considered.

If there are arrears of over £100 that have built up because of CSA maladministration, the person with care may be eligible for an advance payment (see below). This may be in addition to any payment of compensation (see p434).

There are persons with care who, as a result of the payment of child maintenance, are no longer on IS/income-based JSA/income-related ESA/PC because their income, including child maintenance, is now too high. If child maintenance is not paid, a fresh benefit claim should be made. This requirement will cease in April 2010, when child maintenance will be disregarded for all work-replacement benefits.

Advance payments

An advance payment of maintenance is not compensation. The payment is to ensure the person with care is not worse off as a result of maladministration by the CSA.[91] Essentially, it is advance payment of arrears that the CSA is collecting from the non-resident parent. The decision on whether or not to make an advance payment is discretionary. It can only be considered where the:

- arrears of maintenance because of CSA maladministration are £100 or more;
- non-resident parent is making regular maintenance payments;
- non-resident parent has made, and is paying, an arrears agreement and it would take more than 26 weeks to pay these arrears;
- CSA is satisfied that the non-resident parent would have complied with the calculation but for the maladministration; *and*
- person with care has shown an interest in progressing the case during the period of delay.

There must be clear evidence that there has been maladministration by the CSA for an advance payment to be considered. Maladministration may include:[92]

- rudeness;
- delay;
- refusal to answer reasonable questions;
- knowingly giving advice which is misleading or inadequate;
- incompetence;
- bias because of, for example, gender or ethnicity; *or*
- disregard of guidance that should be followed.

The CSA may consider payment on its own initiative or at the request of the person with care. If an advance payment is to be made, the amount is the arrears of maintenance due as a result of the maladministration. Allowances are made for normal processing time so only that time over and above the normal processing time is considered. Payment is usually in the form of a lump sum, paid either directly into the person's bank account or by cheque.[93] The person with care must sign a declaration agreeing that the CSA retains child support payments subsequently made in respect of the period of arrears and to refund any relevant direct payments.

If a decision is made not to make a payment, there is no right of appeal. The person with care may provide further information to support her case, complain (see Chapter 20), contact her MP or possibly seek judicial review (see p353).

Enforcement by the person with care

While there is no provision in child support legislation for the parent with care to bring her own court action against the non-resident parent for the child support maintenance due, it may be possible for the parent to raise an action to recover the amount owed to her. In practice, however, such action may be difficult. The House of Lords has decided that the lack of direct access to the courts by a person with care to enforce child support payments from a non-resident parent does not breach the right to a fair hearing under the European Convention of Human Rights (although it is understood that this decision is being challenged in the European Court of Human Rights).[94]

If the person with care has lost out because of CSA delay or maladministration, it may be possible to sue the CSA for negligence. Anyone considering doing either of the above should seek legal advice. Using the complaints procedure is more likely to be an effective means of obtaining redress within a reasonable timescale (see Chapter 20).

Interest

Interest is no longer added to child maintenance arrears. In addition, since August 2008, interest is no longer collected for outstanding liabilities accrued before 17 April 1995.[95]

4. **Enforcement**

A case should usually considered for enforcement action as soon as it is clear that:[97]

- the non-resident parent has missed payments and there is no acceptable explanation of this; *or*
- a deduction from earnings order (DEO) cannot be implemented or has proved ineffective (see below).

For many enforcement actions, the CSA must obtain a **liability order**. The CSA cannot get an injunction (inhibition in Scotland) to prevent the non-resident parent from disposing of assets or removing them out of the jurisdiction before a liability order is made.[98] When making any discretionary decision about enforcement, the CSA must consider the welfare of any children likely to be affected (see p24).

From 12 July 2006, a liability order can be sought no matter how old the debt, except for amounts that became due on or before 12 July 2000.[99]

Debts that are older than six years on 12 July 2006 cannot be enforced and will be recovered by other methods, such as a DEO. The six years do not begin to run until the non-resident parent is notified of the assessment or calculation. Although an assessment can be backdated, liability does not exist until the assessment is made.[100]

Deduction from earnings orders

The CSA may make a DEO. This is an order to the non-resident parent's employer to make deductions from his earnings and pay them to the CSA.[101] The CSA does not need to go to court to make a DEO. A DEO is the principle enforcement tool where a non-resident parent is in arrears and chooses not to co-operate[102] – eg, does not respond to enquiries, refuses to make an arrears agreement or persistently defaults on an agreement.

A non-resident parent can choose a voluntary DEO, even if he is not in arrears (see p401).

Persons with care have complained in the past that the CSA is slow to make DEOs. However, as part of the Operational Improvement Plan, the CSA planned to increase the use and effectiveness of DEOs, using this method earlier and more frequently, for either non-resident parents who default or those who 'indicate that they are unlikely to pay'.[103] A DEO will therefore usually be made as a matter of course, unless there is a good reason not to.[104]

The best way for a non-resident parent to avoid a DEO is to negotiate an arrears agreement (see p409) and keep to it wherever possible. However, making ongoing liability payments in full may be enough to prevent a DEO being made. A non-resident parent's objection to a DEO is likely to be outweighed if it is unlikely that regular payments would be made using a different method.

The decision to make a DEO is discretionary and the welfare of any children must be considered (see p24).[105] If warned of a DEO, the non-resident parent should tell the CSA, preferably in writing, how any child(ren) would be affected. If a DEO is made, the non-resident parent can appeal to the magistrates' court in England and Wales, or sheriff's court in Scotland (see below).

A DEO can be made while the non-resident parent is waiting for a revision, supersession or appeal. Staff should consider the grounds of the revision, supersession or appeal before making a DEO. They may check the likelihood and timing of any change in the calculation, and arrange for that consideration to be 'fast-tracked'. A non-resident parent can also make representations about the amount and method of payments (see pp401 and 407). The CSA may accept lower payments, but this will not remove its right to impose a DEO.

A DEO cannot be made if the employer is based outside the UK and has no place of business in the UK,[106] but a DEO can be made in Great Britain against an employer in Northern Ireland and *vice versa*.[107]

A DEO cannot be made if the non-resident parent is in the armed forces. Instead, the CSA can request the armed forces to make deductions for child maintenance under armed forces law, known as a DER, which sets limits on the amounts which can be deducted.[108]

If the full amount requested by the CSA cannot be deducted from earnings, the CSA uses other methods to collect and enforce the remainder.

If a deduction from earnings order is made

A DEO is an instruction to the employer of a non-resident parent to make deductions from his earnings.[109] A copy of the DEO must be served on the employer and the non-resident parent.[110] The employer has to comply with the

DEO within seven days of receiving it.[111] An employer can be fined up to £1,000 if it provides false or misleading information, or deliberately withholds information from the CSA.[112]

The DEO must state:[113]

- the name and address of the non-resident parent;
- the name of the employer;
- the non-resident parent's place of work, the nature of his work, his employee number and national insurance number (if known by the CSA);
- the normal deduction rate(s) (see p433) and the date on which each takes effect;
- the protected earnings proportion;
- the address to which the deductions are to be sent.

The CSA national helpline (see Appendix 1) provides further information for employers. The CSA leaflets *What is My Role in Helping My Employees Pay Child Maintenance?* (CSL313) and *Advice for Employers* (CSA2002) also provide guidance to employers on deductions. If an employer is implementing a DEO incorrectly and the non-resident parent is disputing this, the non-resident parent should ask the CSA to intervene.

Date of payment

The employer must pay the CSA monthly by the 19th of the month following the month in which the deduction is made.[114] This means that there is always a delay before the person with care receives the first payment from the CSA. Because the employer makes monthly payments, the person with care receives monthly payments, even if the non-resident parent is having weekly deductions. These monthly payments may not always be for the same amount (see p421 and p434).

The payment by the employer may be made by credit transfer, cheque or any other method to which the CSA agrees.[115] The DEO reference number must be given so that the CSA can identify the person with care.

The employer commits a criminal offence punishable by a fine of up to £500 if s/he fails to take all reasonable steps to pay the CSA on time.[116]

Providing information

In each of the following cases, any notice that is sent from the CSA will be treated as though it was given or sent on the day that it was posted.[117]

Failure to take all reasonable steps to comply with any of the following requirements to provide information to the CSA is an offence punishable by a fine.[118]

The non-resident parent

The non-resident parent must provide the name and address of his employer, the amount of earnings and anticipated earnings, place of work, nature of work and any works number within seven days of being asked to do so in writing by the

CSA.[119] Once a DEO is in force, a non-resident parent must inform the CSA within seven days of leaving employment or becoming employed or re-employed.[120] The CSA can take court action to fine a non-resident parent for failing to provide required information.[121]

The employer

An employer must inform the CSA in writing within 10 days of being served with a DEO if s/he does not, in fact, employ the non-resident parent.[122] If a non-resident parent who is subject to a DEO leaves his job, the employer must notify the CSA within 10 days of his leaving.[123] If an employer finds out that a DEO is in force against an employee (eg, on becoming his employer), s/he must notify the CSA within seven days of becoming aware of this information.[124]

The employer must inform the non-resident parent in writing of the amount of each deduction no later than the date of the deduction or, if not practicable, by the following payday.[125] Although child support law imposes no penalty on an employer who fails to do this, employment protection law requires the employer to give the non-resident parent a written statement of deductions on or before the payday.[126] Where the deduction will always be the same amount, this can be done by a standing statement given at least annually.[127] If the employer does not give notice of the deduction, the non-resident parent may complain to an employment tribunal, which can order the employer to pay the non-resident parent a fine up to the total amount of the unnotified deductions, even if paid to the CSA.[128] This fine would not affect deductions already paid to the CSA.

For other duties about providing information, see p53.

Earnings

Earnings include wages, salary, fees, bonus, commission, overtime pay, occupational pension or statutory sick pay, any other payment made under an employment contract and a regular payment made in compensation for loss of wages.[129] Earnings do not include a payment by a foreign government or the government of Northern Ireland,[130] or a payment to a special member of a British reserved armed force.[131] Net earnings means, in this context, the amount remaining after tax, national insurance and contributions towards a pension scheme have been deducted.[132]

How much is deducted

The DEO states a **normal deduction rate** and a **protected earnings proportion**.[133] These rates should usually correspond to the pay periods of the non-resident parent – ie, at a weekly rate if paid weekly and a monthly rate if paid monthly.[134] More than one normal deduction rate can be set, each applying to a different period.[135]

Normal deduction rate

The normal deduction rate is the amount that will be deducted each payday as long as net earnings are not brought below the protected earnings proportion. The normal deduction rate can include not only current maintenance liability but also an amount for any arrears, penalty payments and fees due. There are no special rules on how quickly the CSA should seek to clear the liability. It is normally negotiated and CSA guidance sets limits for payments towards arrears (see p409).

Protected earnings proportion

The protected earnings proportion is the level below which earnings must not be reduced by the deductions. The protected earnings proportion is 60 per cent of net earnings.[136]

Administering a deduction from earnings order

The employer can deduct a charge for administrative costs each time a deduction is made under the DEO.[137] This means that employees paid weekly can be charged more for administrative costs. The additional amount must not exceed £1 per deduction and can be made even where this would bring earnings below the protected earnings proportion.

Each payday the employer should make a deduction from net earnings at the normal deduction rate plus any administration charge, unless deducting the normal deduction rate would reduce net earnings below the protected earnings proportion. If this would be the case, the amount of the deduction is the excess of net earnings over the protected earnings proportion. In addition, an administration charge may be deducted.[138]

If the employer fails to make a deduction, or the deduction is less than the normal deduction rate, arrears build up and are deducted at the next payday in addition to the normal deduction, applying the same rules for protected earnings.[139]

If, on a payday, the non-resident parent is paid for a period longer than that for which the normal deduction rate is set, the deduction is increased in proportion to the length of the pay period.[140]

Such fluctuations in deductions may mean that the person with care receives irregular payments.

Example

The non-resident parent is due to pay child maintenance of £48 a week and his net earnings are £240 a week. When a DEO is considered, there are arrears of £432 and penalty payments of £26.40. The DEO shows a normal deduction rate of £60 (maintenance due + 5 per cent net income) and a protected earnings proportion of £144. His employer can deduct £1 administrative costs for weeks in which a deduction is made.

Payday	Net pay	Child support due	Deduction	Pay	DEO unpaid
	£	£	£	£	£
5/7	240	60	61	179	
12/7	250	60	61	189	
19/7	160	60	17	143	44
26/7	160	104	17	143	88
2/8	240	148	97	143	52
9/8	250	112	107	143	6
16/8	250	66	67	183	
23/8	240	60	61	179	
30/8	120	60	Nil	120	60
6/9	240	120	97	143	24
13/9	240	84	85	155	
20/9	250	60	61	189	
27/9	240	60	61	179	

In the week 19/7 the full deduction cannot be made, as this would take income below the protected earnings proportion. A deduction is made of £16 plus a £1 administration fee. The amount of the DEO outstanding is added to the next amount due on 26/7. As earnings are again low, the full deduction cannot be taken and is carried forward.

In the week 30/8, earnings are too low for a deduction to be made, and, therefore there is no deduction and no administrative charge.

Payment to the person with care

The employer has to pass the month's payments to the CSA by the 19th of the following month. When this has reached the CSA's account, the payment should be passed on to the person with care within 10 days – unless it is retained because the person with care is on IS/income-related ESA/income-basedJSA (see p401). When the person with care comes off IS/income-related ESA/income-based JSA, the current liability will be due to her, but some (or all) of the arrears may be retained in lieu of IS paid for an earlier period.

Example
Following on from the previous example, the parent with care would receive the following payments.

Month	Payment to CSA by the 19th of the month	Current liability paid (£48 a week due)	Arrears paid (assigned to oldest debt)
	£	£	£
July		Nil	Nil
August	156	156	Nil
September	328	192	136
October	300	192	108

> By the time the parent gets her first payment from the DEO in August she is owed £624 (£432 + £192 (July)), but because of the fluctuating earnings of the non-resident parent she will receive less than the maintenance due. It is only in September that she begins to obtain arrears of maintenance, even though the DEO was put into place in July.

Priority of orders

A DEO takes priority over an attachment of earnings order for a judgment or administration debt (non-priority debts), and any arrestment of earnings under Scottish law.[141] In England and Wales, when a DEO is served on an employee who is already subject to an attachment of earnings order for a priority debt (eg, council tax or fine), the earliest order has priority.[142]

Any deductions under a lower priority order are taken from the net earnings left after deductions under the first order have been made.[143]

Reviews, cancellations and lapsed orders

The CSA must **review** a DEO if there is a change in the amount of the calculation or if any arrears, penalty payments (interest in some cases – see p415) and fees included have been paid off.[144] This does not apply where a normal deduction rate that takes into account the change has already been specified (see p433). A DEO can be changed on this review.[145] The employer must comply with the change within seven days of a copy of the new DEO being served on her/him.[146] The usual penalties for failure to comply apply.

The CSA can **cancel** the DEO if:[147]

- no further payments are due under it;
- the DEO is ineffective or there appears to be a more effective way of collecting the payments;
- the DEO is defective (see p423) or does not comply with some other procedural provision in the legislation;
- the CSA did not have, or has ceased to have, jurisdiction to make a DEO; *or*
- a DEO being used to enforce a default maintenance decision or interim maintenance decision is no longer appropriate given the compliance or attempted compliance of the non-resident parent.

The CSA must send written notice of cancellation to the non-resident parent and employer.[148]

A DEO **lapses** when a non-resident parent leaves the employment.[149] The CSA can revive it if he finds a new job with the same or a different employer.[150] If it is revived, copies of the notice must be served on the non-resident parent and new employer.[151] Any shortfall under the DEO prior to the revival cannot be carried over to the revived DEO.[152]

Appeals

A non-resident parent can appeal against a DEO to the magistrates' court in England and Wales or sheriff's court in Scotland.[153] The appeal must be made within 28 days (56 days if the non-resident parent is not resident in the UK).[154] An appeal can only be made on the grounds that the order is defective (see below), or that the payments made to the non-resident parent are not earnings (see p419),[155] or that there is not a 'good reason' to use a DEO.[156] At the time of writing, what consitutes 'good reason' for not imposing a DEO is not yet clear and no caselaw is available. A freedom of information request could be used to establish the current guidance being used by CSA staff.

If the CSA has not properly exercised its discretion in making a DEO, judicial review can be sought (see p353) and/or a complaint made first to the CSA and then, if not resolved, to the Independent Case Examiner (see Chapter 20).

A DEO is **defective** if it is impracticable for the employer to comply with it because it does not include the correct information required.[157] Many DEOs have included incorrect information (such as errors in names, addresses and dates) but an appeal will not succeed on this basis if the employer can still comply with the DEO. Although some early appeals were upheld because the DEO was unsigned, there is no requirement in the regulations for a signature.

In Scotland, the form of the application is laid out in the child support rules.[158] In England and Wales, a complaint is made against the Secretary of State for Work and Pensions (who acts through the CSA). As there is no specific form given, we suggest that the Scottish wording is followed as an example, but including, 'This complaint is made under section 32(5) of the Child Support Act 1991 and regulation 22 of the Child Support (Collection and Enforcement) Regulations 1992.'

Once the complaint or application is made, the court notifies the CSA. The CSA checks the DEO and contacts the employer to check the earnings. If the DEO is based on the wrong amounts, the CSA varies and reissues it. If the case does get as far as a court hearing, the magistrates/sheriff may quash the DEO or specify which payments, if any, constitute earnings.[159] The court cannot question the maintenance calculation itself.[160]

Even if the court quashes the DEO, it cannot order the CSA to repay deductions to the non-resident parent.[161] Because of this, where deductions are being made from payments that are not earnings, or on the basis of an incorrect normal deduction rate or protected earnings proportion, it may be better to challenge the DEO by judicial review.

Either party can be represented by a lawyer. The CSA can (and does) instead appoint its own staff to conduct DEO appeals and appear at related hearings before magistrates in England and Wales or a sheriff in Scotland.[162] The non-resident parent can also be represented by a lay person, if the sheriff accepts s/he is suitable. An authorised lay representative does not have the full rights of a legal representative, but may be entitled to expenses.

Obtaining a liability order

If a DEO is inappropriate (eg, because the non-resident parent is not employed) or one has been made but proved ineffective, the CSA may apply to the magistrates' court in England and Wales, or sheriff's court in Scotland, for a liability order.[163] A liability order provides the CSA with legal recognition of the debt, and allows the CSA to take further enforcement measures.

If the court decides that the payments are due but have not been made, it must make the order.[164] The court cannot question the maintenance calculation itself.[165] The great majority of liability orders have been against self-employed non-resident parents.[166]

An order (including one made in Northern Ireland) can be enforced anywhere in the UK.[167]

Either party can be represented by a lawyer. The CSA can (and does) instead appoint its own staff to apply for liability orders and appear at related hearings before magistrates in England and Wales or a sheriff in Scotland.[168] The non-resident parent can also be represented by a lay person, if the sheriff accepts s/he is suitable. An authorised lay representative does not have the full rights of a legal representative, but may be entitled to expenses.

If the court makes the order, it can (and usually will) order the non-resident parent to pay the CSA's legal expenses.

England and Wales

The CSA must give the non-resident parent seven days' notice of its intention to seek a liability order (28 days if the non-resident parent is not resident in the UK).[169] The notice must state the amount of maintenance outstanding, including any penalty payments. If the non-resident parent makes an arrangement to pay, the action may be stopped, but where there is a history of broken agreements the CSA may pursue a liability order.[170] There is no time limit for applying for a liability order, except that applications cannot be made for amounts that became due to be paid on or or before 12 July 2000.[171]

The non-resident parent will be sent a summons giving 14 days' notice of the hearing. The magistrates decide whether or not to issue the liability order, but cannot consider whether the non-resident parent is liable or the assessment/calculation has been properly made.[172] If an appeal against the CSA is pending, however, the magistrates' court might decide to adjourn.

The magistrates may decide not to issue an order if the non-resident parent appears to be co-operating. However, the CSA will still ask for the order to be granted on the understanding that it will not be enforced if the non-resident parent continues to co-operate.[173] If the non-resident parent does not attend, the CSA may still obtain the order unless it is defective. If the non-resident parent attends, the magistrate may adjourn to allow more time.

The form of the court order in England and Wales is set out in the regulations. The order must specify the outstanding amounts of child support maintenance, penalty payments, fees (interest in some cases – see p415) and other forms of maintenance.[174]

Scotland

A CSA litigation officer can sign the liability order application instead of a solicitor.[175] Court officials serve notice of the application on the non-resident parent.[176] The non-resident parent has 21 days to object to the liability order being made. This should be done in writing by returning the notice stating the grounds of the objection and enclosing evidence. If objections are received, a hearing is held. Even if the non-resident parent does not attend, the sheriff must still consider his objections.[177] As in England and Wales, the sheriff court cannot consider whether the non-resident parent is liable, nor whether liablity has been correctly calculated. An extract of the liability order may be issued 14 days after the order is actually made. All the forms used in this procedure are included in the child support rules.[178]

Enforcing a liability order in England and Wales

The CSA can decide to levy distress or take action in the county court. The Operational Improvement Plan stated that the CSA would utilise the full range of sanctions available, including driving licence removal, imprisonment or seizure of assets, where appropriate.[179]

Distress

If a liability order has been made, the amount specified on the order can be enforced in England and Wales by distress (ie, seizure) and sale of goods.[180] The bailiff levying distress must either carry written authority to hand to the non-resident parent, or leave at the address where distress is to be levied a copy of the relevant regulations and a memorandum setting out the amount to be levied.[181] If payment is made in full, the levy of the goods or the subsequent sale will not take place.[182]

Certain items cannot be seized. These are:[183]
- tools, books, vehicles and other items necessary for work; *and*
- clothing, bedding, furniture, household equipment and provisions necessary to meet the basic domestic needs of the non-resident parent and any member of his family who lives with him; *and*
- any money, promissory notes, bond or other securities for money belonging to the non-resident parent.

Charges can be made at each of the stages involved in distress proceedings.[184]

Any person aggrieved by the levy, or by an attempt to levy distress, can appeal to the magistrates' court by making a complaint to the court.[185] If the court is satisfied that the levy was irregular, it may order the goods to be returned if they have been seized, and order compensation in respect of any goods sold.

County court action

Once a liability order has been made, the CSA can arrange for the county court to record the order as if it were a judgment debt.[186] This record is publicly available and damages the non-resident parent's credit rating. The CSA can also use the county court to recover any amount that remains unpaid.[187] This means applying for a charging order or using third party debt proceedings.

A **charging order** allows a debt to be registered against certain assets, such as land, stocks, shares and any interest the non-resident parent may have in a trust. If a charge is registered and the assets are sold, the debt due under the liability order can be recovered from the proceeds of the sale. In some cases it may not be possible to register a charge, in which case a caution against dealings may be obtained to prevent the property from being sold without the CSA's knowledge. Once a charge or caution has been registered the CSA can consider applying to the courts for an order of sale.

A **third-party debt order** can be obtained by the CSA if it is aware that the non-resident parent has a bank account or is owed money by a third party. The order freezes funds in the account and requires that person to release funds to the CSA up to the amount of the liability order.

Enforcing a liability order in Scotland

In Scotland, a liability order can be enforced by diligence.[188] The form of the demand for payment sent by the sheriff's court is given in the child support rules.[189] It states the sum owed, including court charges, and specifies that further action will be taken if payment is not made within 14 days (28 days if the non-resident parent is outside the UK). Otherwise, there are no procedures specific to child maintenance. The procedures are the same as for any other debt enforced in Scotland following the granting of a liability order.[190]

The liability order may be enforced by inhibition of sale of property and arrestment of bank accounts.[191]

Deduction orders

Since 3 August 2009, the CSA has had the power to make deductions from bank or savings accounts without the consent of the non-resident parent. To exercise this power, the CSA does not need to apply to court, or obtain a liability order. The deductions can be either regular or made as a lump-sum payment.[192] Technically, as soon as a non-resident parent is in arrears, a deduction order becomes possible as a method of enforcement.

If a non-resident parent has failed to pay child maintenance, the CSA can make an order requiring a deposit taker (usually a bank or building society) with which the non-resident parent has an account to make deductions from that account and pay the CSA. The CSA has discretion to choose the most suitable account from which to make deductions. Generally, regular deduction orders will be directed at current accounts and lump-sum deduction orders at savings accounts.

A lump-sum or regular deduction order cannot be made in respect of an account which is used wholly or partly for business purposes. This does not apply if a regular deduction order is made in respect of an account that relates to a non-resident parent who is a sole trader.[193]

The deposit taker is able to take an amount from the non-resident parent's account to cover the administrative costs of setting up and paying a deduction order. The maximum amounts that can be charged are:
- £10, in the case of a regular deduction order;
- £55, in the case of a lump-sum deduction order.[194]

Regular deduction orders

A regular deduction order can be used to collect both arrears and ongoing maintenance payments that will become due under the calculation that is in place.[195]

When a regular deduction order is made, a copy is served on both the deposit taker and the non-resident parent. The order must specify the amount of the regular deduction and the dates on which regular deductions are due to be made.[196]

If there is a current maintenance calculation, or arrears are being collected for a maintenance arrangement which is no longer in force, the maximum that can be deducted is 40 per cent of the non-resident parent's net weekly income. If a default maintenance decision has been made, the maximum that can be deducted is £80 a week.[197]

Before a regular deduction can be made from a joint account, each of the account holders should be given an opportunity to make representations on the making of the order and the amounts to be deducted.[198]

A deduction cannot be made if the amount of credit in the relevant account is below a certain level on the date a deduction is due to be made. The minimum amounts are:
- £40, if deductions are made monthly;
- £10, if deductions are made weekly;
- if deductions are made for any other period, £10 for each whole week in that period plus £1 for each additional day in that period.

In addition to these amounts, there must be sufficient funds in the account to pay the administrative costs charged the deposit taker.[199]

If the non-resident parent's account is subject to other deduction orders, such as third-party debt orders and garnishee orders, these will generally be paid first before a regular deduction order is dealt with. The exception to this is where a third-party debt order or garnishee order is served on the deposit taker after the regular deduction order but on or before the date a payment is due to be made under the deduction order. In this case, the deduction order will be paid first on that occasion, unless the deposit taker has already taken steps to process the other orders. For future payments, it is assumed that the third-party debt order or garnishee order will take priority.[200]

It is an offence for a person not to comply with the requirements of a regular deduction order and failure to do so can lead to a fine of up to £500. However, there is a defence if the person can show that all reasonable steps were taken to comply with the order or regulation.[201]

Reviews and variations of regular deduction orders

A non-resident parent or a deposit taker can apply to the CSA for a review of a regular deduction order if:

- the CSA is satisfied that the non-resident parent does not have a beneficial interest in some or all of the amount of money in the account that is subject to the order; *or*
- there has been a change in the amount of the maintenance calculation in question; *or*
- any amounts payable under the order have been paid; *or*
- there has been a change in the non-resident parent's net weekly income; *or*
- due to an official error, an incorrect amount has been specified in the order.[202]

A regular deduction order can be varied to change the amount that is deducted if:

- the CSA accepts that the non-resident parent has made a payment of child support and no alternative method of payment of child support maintenance is in place; *or*
- there has been a successful appeal against a maintenance calculation; *or*
- the order has been changed following a successful review.[203]

Lump-sum deduction orders

If it is established that the non-resident parent owes child maintenance arrears, the CSA will consider whether a lump-sum deduction order is the most appropriate method of recovering them.

Once the CSA has decided to make a lump-sum deduction order, it serves an interim order on the deposit taker (the non-resident parent's bank or building society, or other third party). The interim order acts as an instruction to the deposit taker to secure funds up to the amount of the order in a specified account until further notice. The deposit maker is expected to prevent the funds from being moved or reduced below the amount that is ordered or, if funds are already below this amount, not to allow them to decrease further.

Once funds have been secured, a copy of the order will be served on the non-resident parent. Both the deposit maker and the non-resident parent have 14 days from the date the order was served in which to make representations to the CSA. The order is treated as having been served on the non-resident parent at the end of the day on which the copy is posted to his last known address.[204]

When issuing the order and instructing the deposit taker to secure funds, the CSA should have regard to:

- any hardship that may be caused to the non-resident parent's partner or a relevant child;
- any written, contractual obligations regarding the money that were made prior to the lump-sum deduction order being made;
- any other circumstances that the CSA considers appropriate in the particular case.[205]

The CSA should also ensure that the amount deducted from a joint account does not exceed an amount that is fair, given all the circumstances, especially the amounts contributed to the account by each of the account holders.[206]

In addition to this 14-day period, it should be possible for the non-resident parent or the deposit taker to make an application to the CSA to vary the order in certain circumstances. These include if:

- the CSA accepts the non-resident parent's agreement to make a payment;
- there has been a successful appeal against the maintenance calculation that is the subject of the order;
- the CSA agrees that hardship may be caused to the non-resident parent's partner or a relevant child;
- the non-resident parent is under a written contractual obligation, made before the lump-sum deduction order was made.[207]

Priority of payments

In England and Wales, if there is a final lump-sum deduction order and other interim third-party debt orders or garnishee orders *nisi*, the deposit taker must comply with them in the order in which they were served on the deposit taker. If an interim lump-sum deduction order is served after an interim third-party debt order or garnishee order *nisi*, the final versions of these other orders will take priority.[208]

In Scotland, the deposit taker must give priority to the lump-sum deduction order and any other orders, according to the order in which they were served on the deposit taker.[209]

Minimum amounts

A deduction should not be made if the amount of credit in the relevant bank account is below a minimum level. The current minimum level is £55 plus the amount of administrative costs charged by the deposit taker. The administrative costs must not be more than £55 for a lump-sum deduction order.

Appeals

The non-resident parent has a right to appeal against a lump-sum deduction order or a regular deduction order and related decisions made by the CSA. The appeal is made to the county court in England and Wales, or the sheriff's court in Scotland.

The non-resident parent can appeal against:

- the making of a regular deduction order;
- any decision by the CSA in relation to a request to review a regular deduction order;
- a refusal to consent to the waiving of the requirement to freeze or protect funds which are the subject of an interim lump-sum deduction order;
- the making of a final lump-sum deduction order.[210]

There is a time limit of 21 days from the date the final lump-sum deduction order is received in which to appeal against it being made. The non-resident parent is considered to have received the final lump-sum deduction order two days after it was posted. If, after 21 days has expired, no appeals have been made, the CSA will instruct the deposit taker to pay the funds to the CSA.

Disqualification from driving or imprisonment

The CSA may take action to disqualify the non-resident parent from driving or for imprisonment if all other methods of recovery have failed.[211]

Before taking action every attempt must be made to contact the non-resident parent. If no phone contact has been successful during the enforcement action, a face-to-face visit may be appropriate.

When considering whether to take this action the CSA should consider:[212]

- the welfare of any child(ren) affected;
- whether all the appropriate procedures have been followed;
- any serious ill health of the non-resident parent or member of his family;
- whether the action could affect future regular maintenance;
- whether the CSA could be considered insensitive in pursuing action;
- whether the non-resident parent has sufficient funds to pay the debt;
- whether the non-resident parent is under 18 and would count as a child for child support purposes (commitment to prison will not be an option here, but disqualification from driving can still be considered); *or*
- whether the non-resident parent is on benefit.

If it is decided not to pursue the action, the person with care should be informed.[213] The case will be reviewed in three months time to consider further enforcement action.

Action for committal or disqualification from driving

In England and Wales, if distress and/or county court proceedings have been tried or, in Scotland, diligence via arrestments or inhibitions on sale, but an amount is still due under the liability order, the CSA can apply to the court to issue either a warrant committing the non-resident parent to prison or an order disqualifying him from driving.[214] The hearing must take place in the presence of the non-resident parent.[215] The court can summon him to appear in court and produce his driving licence.[216] If he does not appear, the court may issue a warrant (citation in Scotland) for his arrest.[217] The CSA can make representations to the court on whether to issue a warrant or order disqualification.[218] The non-resident parent may reply to these.

The court must enquire into the non-resident parent's means, whether he needs a driving licence to make a living and whether there has been 'wilful refusal or culpable neglect' on his part.[219] Only if there has been, can the court commit the non-resident parent to prison or disqualify him from driving;[220] the decision whether to do so is at the discretion of the court. A non-resident parent should seek advice in preparing a statement of his income and outgoings.[221] A written statement from an employer will be accepted as proof of earnings.[222] The CSA can appoint its own staff to apply for committal and appear at related hearings before magistrates in England and Wales or a sheriff in Scotland.[223]

Imprisonment

If the court decides that there has been wilful refusal or culpable neglect and committal is appropriate, a warrant for imprisonment will be issued.[224] A warrant for imprisonment cannot be issued against a non-resident parent who is under 18.[225]

Instead of immediate committal, the court usually fixes a term of imprisonment and postpones it on conditions, usually of regular payments.[226] A warrant of commitment is issued stating the total amount outstanding, including child maintenance, penalty payments, fees (interest in some cases – see p415), court costs and any other charges.[227] If the amount is paid in full, the non-resident parent will not be imprisoned.

The maximum period of imprisonment is six weeks.[228] If, after the warrant has been issued, part-payment is made, the period of imprisonment is reduced by the same proportion as that by which the debt has been reduced.[229]

The court cannot write off the arrears, so if full payment is not made, arrears will still exist following the period of imprisonment. In this case, the CSA will look at the circumstances again to check whether any earlier enforcement options would be appropriate, and should consider applying for a further liability order.[230] If a warrant is not issued or the court does not fix a term of imprisonment, the CSA can renew the application at a later date on the grounds that the non-resident parent's circumstances have changed.[231]

Disqualification from driving

If the court decides that there has been wilful refusal or culpable neglect and disqualification from driving is appropriate, an order will be issued.[232] The order may be issued but its implementation suspended on conditions – eg, regular payments. The order will state the amount outstanding, including child maintenance, interest, court costs and any other charges.[233] If the amount is paid in full, the order is revoked.

The maximum period of disqualification is two years.[234] If, after the order has been issued, part-payment is made, the period of disqualification is reduced.[235] If the amount is paid in full, the order is revoked. If at the end of the period of disqualification the arrears have not been paid in full, the CSA may apply again for imprisonment or disqualification.[236]

Bankruptcy

The CSA does not pursue bankruptcy (sequestration in Scotland), but a non-resident parent may have child support maintenance arrears when he is made bankrupt.[237]

In England and Wales, the CSA can take action to obtain a liability order including amounts due before the date of the bankruptcy.

In Scotland, a liability order can only recover amounts due after the date of the sequestration.

In either case, the CSA may decide not to enforce the order because it may not be practical – eg, a charging order/inhibition of sale may not be effective, as any property may already have been sold to pay off creditors. The CSA may secure a liability order to remind the non-resident parent that he cannot avoid his maintenance responsibility.

Bankruptcy/sequestration may not prevent the CSA considering action for committal to prison or disqualification from driving – eg, the non-resident parent may have a steady income and it would be up to him to show in court that he cannot afford to meet his child support liability.

---

5. **Existing 'old rules' and conversion cases**

Existing 'old rules' maintenance assessments are collected and enforced in much the same way as 'new rules' maintenance calculations – involving negotiations, deduction from earnings orders, liability orders and action for committal or disqualification from driving. Some differences are indicated in the rest of this chapter – eg, how deductions from benefit can be made. However, there are some other important differences, which we outline here.

The legislation applied to existing 'old rules' is that prior to its reform by the Child Support, Pensions and Social Security Act 2000 and associated regulations. On conversion the case comes under the reformed legislation.

Penalty payments do not apply to 'old rules' cases; once the case converts, the 'new rules' penalty payments may be applied. This means that penalty payments can only be made in respect of missed or late payments after the date of conversion.

Voluntary payments under the 'new rules' are governed by statute – ie, there is law which stipulates how they are dealt with. In 'old rules' case the Child Support Agency (CSA) exercises discretion in how it treats such payments. A complaint may be possible if a parent is not happy with the way in which they are treated (see Chapter 20).

Deduction from earnings orders (DEOs) are calculated and applied in a slightly different way. At conversion, any old arrears uncollected under the previous order may be included in a new one issued under the 'new rules'.

Certain non-resident parents with a maintenance assessment may make a deferred debt agreement under the **temporary compensation scheme**. This agreement may continue in force after conversion. If it is discharged, the person with care may be eligible for a **deferred debt compensation payment** (see p434).

Deduction from earnings orders

Deductions made are based on the **normal deduction rate** and the **protected earnings rate**.

Normal deduction rate

The normal deduction rate is the amount that will be deducted each payday as long as net earnings are not brought below the protected earnings rate. The normal deduction rate can include current maintenance liability and amounts for arrears and interest due. No arrears or interest can be included if they would have brought the non-resident parent's disposable income, on the date the current assessment was made, below the protected income level (not the protected earnings rate) *minus* the minimum payment (see p172).[238] This does not apply if the current assessment is an interim maintenance assessment (IMA – see p340). See Chapter 13 for protected income level and disposable income.

Protected earnings rate

The protected earnings rate is the level below which earnings must not be reduced by the deductions. Unless a Category A or D IMA is in force, it is set at the exempt income level (see Chapter 10).[239] Where a Category A or D IMA is in force, the protected earnings rate is either:[240]

- if the CSA knows something of the non-resident parent's circumstances:
  - the income support (IS) single or couple personal allowance;
  - the IS personal allowance for any children under 16 living with him;
  - any relevant IS premiums (see Appendix 2); *plus*
  - £30; *or*
- otherwise, the IS adult personal allowance plus £30.

Where there is no assessment in force, the protected earnings rate is the exempt income level for the last assessment. If the non-resident parent satisfies the CSA that his circumstances have since changed, the protected earnings rate is the exempt income level he would have if his assessment were superseded.[241] If the last assessment was a Category A or C IMA, the protected earnings rate is still worked out as for IMAs.

Where the non-resident parent has more than one employer and a deduction order is made in respect of more than one of them, the protected earnings rate for each order is divided proportionally between the non-resident parent's earnings with each employer.[242]

Administering a deduction from earnings order

The rules are almost identical to those described in this chapter – ie, each payday the employer:

- should make a deduction from net earnings at the normal deduction rate. If this reduces earnings below the protected earnings rate, the deduction is adjusted and the unpaid amount is carried forward to the next payday;[243]
- may deduct up to £1 as an administrative charge. This can be made even if this would bring earnings below the protected earnings rate.[244]

However, in addition to these rules, if on any payday net earnings are below the protected earnings rate, no deduction or charge can be made. When this occurs, the difference between net earnings and protected earnings is carried over and treated as additional protected earnings on the next payday.[245] For an illustration of how this operates in practice, see Example 18.1 in the 2001/02 edition of this *Handbook*.

If two or more DEOs have been issued, the employer should deal with the earliest first.[246]

Temporary compensation payment scheme (deferred debt)

From 31 January 2001 a temporary compensation payment scheme was introduced to allow the CSA to reduce the arrears liability of a non-resident parent in certain circumstances.[247] In CSA terminology this means that the arrears were classed as a deferred debt. The scheme only applied to parents with assessments made before certain dates (the latest being 1 April 2005), and who had at least six months' arrrears, at least half of which were caused because of unreasonable delay by the CSA.

If a non-resident parent entered and kept to an agreement to pay regular maintenance and repay the arrears, the CSA could reduce the amount of arrears to be repaid.[248] Throughout the period of the agreement the parent was still liable for the full amount, which could be enforced immediately if he defaulted, unless the default was outside his control or due to exceptional circumstances. For more information about what happened if a non-resident parent defaulted, see the

2006/07 edition of this *Handbook*. Agreements could only be made before 1 April 2005 and all had to expire before 1 April 2006.[249]

The CSA could make a deferred debt compensatory payment to the person with care, in respect of all or some of the arrears which were not to be collected if the non-resident parent kept to the agreement. This was a discretionary decision. For more information about deferred debt compensation payments, see the 2006/07 edition of this *Handbook*. While technically the deferred debt was not written off, it would not be enforced by the CSA if the non-resident parent kept to the agreement for the full period.

Notes

1 s29(1) CSA 1991
2 s30(1) CSA 1991
3 Reg 3(3A) CSF Regs as revoked by reg 4 CS(CEMA) Regs

1. **Payment of child maintenance**
4 Reg 3 CS(C&E) Regs
5 Reg 2 CS(C&E) Regs
6 Reg 5 CS(C&E) Regs
7 Reg 4 CS(C&E) Regs
8 Reg 5 CS(AIAMA) Regs
9 Reg 6 CS(C&E) Regs
10 Reg 7(1) CS(C&E) Regs
11 Reg 7(2) CS(C&E) Regs
12 s29 CSA 1991; reg 2 CS(C&E) Regs
13 www.csa.gov.uk/en/case/child-maintenance-changing.asp
14 PG, Collections, Non-maintenance Direct
15 s29(1)(b) CSA 1991
16 PG, Collections, Failure of Maintenance Direct Reported by the PWC
17 CSA Business Plan 2008/09
18 Reg 8 CS(AIAMA) Regs
19 Reg 3(1) CS(C&E) Regs
20 Reg 3(1A) CS(C&E) Regs
21 PG, Collections, Non-maintenance Direct
22 Reg 3(2) CS(C&E) Regs
23 Reg 6 CS(C&E) Regs
24 PG, Collections, Non-maintenance Direct
25 Reg 5(1) CS(C&E) Regs; PG, Payments
26 s43 CSA 1991

27 s43 CSA 1991; Sch 9B SS(C&P.) Regs
28 Sch 4 para 4(2) CSA 1991; reg 4(2) CS(MCSC) Regs
29 Reg 4(3)(a) CS(MCSC) Regs
30 Reg 4(3)(b) CS(MCSC) Regs
31 Reg 35(l) SS(C&P) Regs; Sch 9B SS(C&P) Regs
32 Sch 9 para 7A(1) SS(C&P) Regs
33 Sch 9 paras 1 and 2(1)(f) SS(C&P) Regs
34 Sch 9 para 2(2) SS(C&P) Regs
35 Sch 9 para 8 SS(C&P) Regs
36 Sch 9 para 9 SS(C&P) Regs
37 Sch 9 para 7A(4) SS(C&P) Regs
38 Sch 5 para 9 CS(MASC) Regs
39 Reg 4(1) CS(C&E) Regs
40 Reg 4(2) CS(C&E) Regs
41 Reg 6 CS(C&E) Regs
42 Reg 5(3) CS(C&E) Regs
43 CSA Business Plan 2008/09
44 *How Do I Complain About the Service I Get From the Child Support Agency?* October 2009
45 PG, Services of the CSA, Post April 2002
46 Reg 9 CS(AIAMA) Regs
47 Reg 10(1)(a) CS(AIAMA) Regs
48 Reg 10(3)(a) and (b) and (4) CS(AIAMA) Regs
49 Reg 10(1)(b) CS(AIAMA) Regs
50 Reg 10(3A)(b) CS(AIAMA) Regs
51 Reg 9(3) The Child Support (Management of Payments and Arrears) Regulations 2009
52 Reg 10(2) and (3) CS(AIAMA) Regs; regs 3A(6) and 15D SS&CS(D&A) Regs

53 Reg 11 CS(AIAMA) Regs; reg 15C(6)
   SS&CS(DA) Regs
54 Regs 12, 13, 14, 15 and 16 CS(AIAMA)
   Regs; regs 3A(6), 6A(9) and 30A
   SS&CS(DA) Regs
55 s41B CSA 1991
56 s23 CSA 1995
57 Regs 10A(1) and 10B CS(AIAMA) Regs
58 s41B(6) CSA 1991; reg 10A(2)
   CS(AIAMA) Regs

2. Collection of other payments
59 s30 CSA 1991; CS(CEOFM) Regs
60 Reg 5 CS(CEOFM) Regs
61 Reg 2 CS(CEOFM) Regs
62 Regs 3 and 4 CS(CEOFM) Regs
63 s30(3) CSA 1991; PG, Receipt
   Assignments and Allocation,
   Allocation Rules
64 PG, Receipt Assignments and Allocation,
   Receipt Received for Multiple Cases
65 s43 CMOPA 2008
66 PG, Collections, Negotiating other
   Liabilities

3. Arrears
67 Reg 8A CS(MAJ) Regs 1992
68 PG, Collections, Notifying the NRP of
   the Collection Schedule
69 Reg 7 CS(C&E) Regs
70 PG, Arrears Management, Arrears
   Amount
71 s28J CSA 1991 as inserted by s20
   CSPSSA 2000
72 Reg 3(b) CS(VP) Regs
73 Reg 3(a) CS(VP) Regs
74 Regs 2(2) and 4(b) CS(VP) Regs
75 Reg 4(a) CS(VP) Regs
76 Reg 5(10) CS(AIAMA) Regs
77 Independent Case Examiner's Annual
   Report 2008/09
78 Independent Case Examiner's Annual
   Report 2008/09
79 First protocol, Art 1 ECHR
80 s41(2) and (2A) CSA 1991; reg 8
   CS(AIAMA) Regs
81 Reg 8 CS(AIAMA) Regs
82 s43 CSA 1991; Sch 9B SS(C&P) Regs
83 Sch 9 para 7B SS(C&P) Regs
84 *What Action Can the CSA Take if Parents
   Don't Pay?* August 2009
85 Reg 2 CS(AIAMA) Regs
86 Reg 2(4) CS(AIAMA) Regs
87 s41A CSA 1991
88 Independent Case Examiner's Annual
   Report 2006/07
89 CSA Operational Improvement Plan
   2006-2009

90 CSA Business Plan 2008/09
91 PG, Payments, Advance Payment of
   Maintenance
92 PG, Payments, Maladministration
93 PG, Payments, Making the Advance
   Payment Amount to the PWC
94 *R v Secretary of State for Work and
   Pensions ex parte Kehoe* [2005] UKHL 48
   (1 July 2005); the case concerned Art
   6(1) ECHR
95 s43 CMOPA 2008

4. Enforcement
96 s51 Welfare Reform Act 2009
97 PG, Enforcement, Deciding if Debt
   Enforcement Action is Suitable
98 *DSS v Butler* [1995] 1 WLR 1528, [1995]
   4 All ER 193
99 Reg 28(2) and (2a) CS(C&E) Regs
100 *R Sutherland (on the application of) v
   Secretary of State for Work and Pensions*
   [2004] EWHC 800 (Admin), 25 March
   2004
101 s31 CSA 1991
102 PG Arrears Management,
   Considerations Before Imposing a DEO
103 CSA Operational Improvement Plan
   2006-2009
104 Reg 22 Child Support (Collection and
   Enforcement) Regs 1992, as amended
   by reg 2(4) Child Support
   (Miscellaneous Amendments) (No.2)
   Regulations 2008
105 *R v Secretary of State for Social Security ex
   parte Biggin* [1995] 2 FCR 595, [1995] 1
   FLR 851
106 PG, Arrears Management, DEO/DER,
   Employer Outside CSA Jurisdiction
107 Sch 1 para 10 CS(NIRA) Regs
108 CSA(CA)O; Army Act 1955; Air Force Act
   1955; Naval Forces Act 1947; Merchant
   Shipping Act 1970
109 s31(5) CSA 1991
110 s31(6) CSA 1991
111 s31(7) CSA 1991
112 *CSA Advice to Employers,* October 2009
113 Reg 9 CS(C&E) Regs
114 Reg 14(1) CS(C&E) Regs; see also *Advice
   to Employers,* 2002
115 Reg 14(2) CS(C&E) Regs
116 s32(8) and (11) CSA 1991; reg 25(aa)
   CS(C&E) Regs
117 Reg 1(3)(b) CS(C&E) Regs
118 s32(8) and (11) CSA 1991; reg 25(ab)
   and (b) CS(C&E) Regs
119 Reg 3 CS(MA) Regs 2008
120 Reg 15(2) CS(C&E) Regs

121 *What Action Can the CSA Take if Parents Don't Pay?,* August 2009
122 Reg 16(1) CS(C&E) Regs
123 Reg 16(2) CS(C&E) Regs
124 Reg 16(3) CS(C&E) Regs
125 Reg 13 CS(C&E) Regs
126 s8(2)(b) ERA 1996
127 s9 ERA 1996
128 s12(3)-(5) ERA 1996
129 Reg 8(3) and (4) CS(C&E) Regs
130 Reg 8(4)(a) CS(C&E) Regs
131 Reg 8(4)(b) CS(C&E) Regs
132 Reg 8(5) CS(C&E) Regs
133 Reg 9 CS(C&E) Regs
134 Regs 10(1) and 11(1) CS(C&E) Regs
135 Reg 9(d) CS(C&E) Regs
136 Reg 11(2) CS(C&E) Regs
137 Reg 12(6) CS(C&E) Regs
138 Reg 12(20) CS(C&E) Regs
139 Reg 12(4) CS(C&E) Regs
140 Reg 12(3A) CS(C&E) Regs
141 Reg 24(2)(a) CS(C&E) Regs
142 Reg 24(2)(b) CS(C&E) Regs
143 Reg 24(2)(a) and (3) CS(C&E) Regs
144 Reg 17 CS(C&E) Regs
145 Reg 18 CS(C&E) Regs
146 Reg 19 CS(C&E) Regs
147 Reg 20(1) CS(C&E) Regs
148 Reg 20(2) CS(C&E) Regs
149 Reg 21(1) CS(C&E) Regs
150 Reg 21(4) CS(C&E) Regs
151 Reg 21(5) CS(C&E) Regs
152 Reg 21(6) CS(C&E) Regs
153 Reg 22(1) CS(C&E) Regs
154 Reg 22(2) CS(C&E) Regs
155 Reg 22(3) CS(C&E) Regs
156 Reg 22(3A) CS (C&E) Regs
157 Reg 8(1) CS(C&E) Regs
158 r5 and form 6 AS(CSR)
159 Reg 22(4) CS(C&E) Regs
160 s32(6) CSA 1991
161 *Secretary of State for Social Security v Shotton* [1996] 2 FLR 241
162 ss48 and 49 CSA 1991; r6 AS(CSR)
163 s33 CSA 1991
164 s33(3) CSA 1991
165 s33(4) CSA 1991
166 HC *Hansard,* 2 February 1996, col990
167 Reg 29 CS(C&E) Regs; r3 AS(CSR)
168 ss48 and 49 CSA 1991; r6 AS(CSR)
169 Reg 27 CS(C&E) Regs
170 PG, NRP Responds to the Warning Letter
171 Reg 28(2) and (2A) CS(C&E) Regs
172 *Farley v CSA and another* [2006] UKHL 31 (28 June 2006)
173 PG, Enforcement, NRP Responds to the Warning Letter
174 Reg 29(1) and Sch 1 CS(C&E) Regs

175 *Secretary of State for Social Security v Love* [1996] SLT 78
176 r2 AS(CSR)
177 *Secretary of State for Social Security v Nicol* [1996] SLT 34
178 Forms 1-4 AS(CSR)
179 CSA Operational Improvement Plan 2006-2009
180 s35 CSA 1991
181 Reg 30(2) CS(C&E) Regs
182 Reg 30(4) and (5) CS(C&E) Regs
183 s35(3) and (4) CSA 1991
184 Reg 32 and Sch 2 CS(C&E) Regs
185 Reg 31 CS(C&E) Regs
186 s33(5) CSA 1991
187 s36 CSA 1991
188 ss38(1)(a) and 58(9) CSA 1991
189 r4 and form 5 AS(CSR)
190 under Part II Debtors (Scotland) Act 1987
191 s38(1)(b) CSA 1991
192 CS(C&E)(DO)(A) Regs
193 Reg 25X CS(C&E)(DO)(A) Regs
194 Reg 25Z CS(C&E)(DO)(A) Regs
195 s32A(2) CMOPA 2008
196 Reg 25B(1) CS(C&E)(DO)(A) Regs
197 Reg 25C CS(C&E)(DO)(A) Regs
198 s32B CMOPA 2008
199 Reg 25D CS(C&E)(DO)(A) Regs
200 Reg 25H CS(C&E)(DO)(A) Regs
201 s32D CMOPA 2008
202 Reg 25G CS(C&E)(DO)(A) Regs
203 Reg 25I CS(C&E)(DO)(A) Regs
204 Reg 25A(3)(b) CS(C&E)(DO)(A) Regs
205 Reg 25N(1) CS(C&E)(DO)(A) Regs
206 s32F(3)(b) and (4) CMOPA 2008
207 Regs 25R and 25N CS(C&E)(DO)(A) Regs
208 Reg 25P(1) and (2) CS(C&E)(DO)(A) Regs
209 Reg 25P(6) CS(C&E)(DO)(A) Regs
210 Reg 25AB CS(C&E)(DO)(A) Regs
211 s39A CSA 1991
212 PG, Enforcement, Is Commitment to Prison or Disqualification from Driving Appropriate
213 PG, Enforcement, Deciding Not to Apply for Commitment to Prison/ Driving Licence Action
214 ss39A(2) and 40(1)-(11) CSA 1991
215 s39A(3) CSA 1991
216 Reg 35(1) CS(C&E) Regs
217 s40(11) CSA 1991
218 s39A(4) CSA 1991
219 s39A(3) CSA 1991; PG, Enforcement, Court Hearing
220 s40A(1) CSA 1991
221 ss40(5) and 40A(3) CSA 1991

19

222 ss40(11) and 40A(8) CSA 1991; reg
35(2) CS(C&E) Regs
223 ss48 and 49 CSA 1991
224 ss40 and 40B CSA 1991
225 ss40(5) and 40A(3) CSA 1991
226 ss40(3) and 40B(1) CSA 1991
227 Sch 3 CS(C&E) Regs
228 ss40(7) and 40A(5) CSA 1991
229 Reg 34(5) and (6) CS(C&E) Regs
230 Enforcement Guide, Chapter 7, If
Commitment to Prison/
Disqualification Proceedings
Unsuccessful
231 Reg 33(3) CS(C&E) Regs
232 s40B CSA 1991
233 Reg 35(4)-(5) and Sch 4 CS(C&E) Regs
234 s40B(1) CSA 1991
235 s40B(5) CSA 1991
236 s40B(7) CSA 1991
237 PG, Enforcement, NRP
Bankrupt (England and Wales);
Sequestration (Scotland)

5. Existing 'old rules' and conversion cases

238 Reg 10 CS(C&E) Regs
239 Reg 11(2) CS(C&E) Regs
240 Reg 11(3) CS(C&E) Regs
241 Reg 11(4) CS(C&E) Regs
242 Reg 11(6) CS(C&E) Regs, as amended
by The Child Support (Miscellaneous
Amendments) (No.2) Regulations 2008
243 Reg 12(4) CS(C&E) Regs
244 Reg 12(2) CS(C&E) Regs
245 Reg 12(5) CS(C&E) Regs
246 Reg 24(1) CS(C&E) Regs
247 Reg 2(2) CSPSSA(Comm 13)O
248 s27(3) CSPSSA 2000
249 s27(5) CSPSSA 2000 as modified by reg
2 CS(TCPS)(MA) Regs

Chapter 20

Complaints

This chapter covers:
1. Complaining to the Child Support Agency (p440)
2. Complaining to Child Maintenance Options (p442)
3. Complaining to Jobcentre Plus (p443)
4. Complaining to the Independent Case Examiner (p443)
5. Using an MP (p445)
6. Complaining to the Ombudsman (p445)

There are many reasons why people using the Child Support Agency (CSA) may wish to complain. Complaints are obviously appropriate in situations where there has been rudeness, discrimination, poor administration (eg, lost papers) and delays. They may also be appropriate in situations where the CSA (or Jobcentre Plus) has a discretion about how to act – eg, where enforcement action is not taken.

A complaint is a separate process to an appeal or revision and does not necessarily lead to a decision being changed. However, it may be appropriate where the decision is one with no right of appeal. In some of these cases, judicial review may also be possible (instead of, or as well as, making a complaint). Legal advice should be sought if a judicial review is being considered (see also p353). In some cases, an appeal may be appropriate as well as a complaint – eg, if a parent thinks a maintenance calculation has been wrongly calculated and appeals against the decision but also wishes to complain about the delay in making the calculation.

It is important to be clear which organisation has caused the problem. In most cases this will be the CSA. However, problems concerning the deduction of payments from benefits may be caused by Jobcentre Plus. Complaints about any Jobcentre Plus function should be directed at Jobcentre Plus. If a parent (or qualifying child in Scotland) has appealed, and there are delays or poor administration on the part of the Tribunals Service, the complaint should be directed to the Tribunals Service. For information about making complaints to the Tribunals Service, see CPAG *Welfare Benefits and Tax Credits Handbook*.

1. **Complaining to the Child Support Agency**

Most complaints involving child support will be made to the Child Support Agency (CSA). Complaints are likely to fall into two groups:

- complaints about standards of service, including delays, staff communications, poor administration and lost papers;
- complaints about how discretionary decisions are made – eg, failure to follow guidance, following it too strictly or failing to take all the relevant circumstances into account. It may be appropriate to seek advice on whether judicial review is also appropriate.

A parent (or qualifying child in Scotland) should begin her/his complaint by contacting the person who has been dealing with her/his case, or her/his manager. This information should be on letters sent by the CSA. The complaint can be made either by telephone or in writing, but records of all communications should be kept in case it is necessary to take the complaint further.

If the CSA officer concerned or her/his manager cannot resolve the complaint, the complainant can take things further by contacting the complaints resolution team at the office handling the case. All contact details of Child Support Agency Centres (CSACs) are in Appendix 1, or on the CSA website. Contact details should also be given on any letters which have been sent.

If a parent is not satisfied with the outcome of the complaints resolution team or if there has been an unreasonable delay, s/he can ask for a review. The complaints review team can check to see if the complaint was dealt with properly and if anything else can be done. Contact details for the complaints review team should be given on the letter recieved from the complaints resolution team.

More detailed information about the complaints procedure is given in the leaflet *How Do I Complain About the Service I Get From the Child Support Agency?* (CSL 308).

If, after going through this procedure, a complainant is not satisfied that the complaint has been resolved, s/he can contact the Independent Case Examiner (see p443). A complainant can only do this if:

- s/he has received a final reply from or on behalf of the Chief Executive of the CSA; *and*
- no more than six months have passed since s/he received that final reply. Usually, this reply will be from a senior CSA manager.

When complaining to the CSA, it may be useful to quote its standards of service. These may also be useful when considering whether, or at what point, to make a complaint.

Standards of service

It is useful to refer to the CSA's standards of service when making a complaint or considering whether to make one. A summary of standards of service used to be found in the CSA's Client Charter, which was last updated in 2007.[1] However, since the introduction of the Child Maintenance and Enforcement Commission, this has not been replaced and it is no longer in use. Some of the service standards can still be found in the CSA's Business Plan.[2]

Many of the standards are mentioned elsewhere in this *Handbook* and include the following. This is not an exhaustive list.

- The CSA aims to start gathering information from the non-resident parent within four weeks of a maintenance application, if it has contact details.
- The CSA aims to make an accurate decision on an application within 12 weeks (but in some cases a decision may take up to 26 weeks).
- Where the collection service is being used, the CSA aims to make payments to the person with care within a week of receiving the money from the non-resident parent.
- The CSA aims to answer telephone calls within one minute.
- The CSA aims to respond to letters, and either resolve complaints or agree on the next course of action, within three weeks of receiving them.

At the time of writing, the 2009/10 Business Plan was not available. Check the CSA website for the latest version.

Compensation

If a parent (or qualifying child in Scotland) has lost out because of CSA error, delay or standard of service, it may be appropriate to request compensation or a consolatory payment when making a complaint. *Ex-gratia* payments can be made where someone has suffered an actual financial loss, significant delay or has been caused severe distress or inconvenience.

A complainant has no legal right to these payments, but it can sometimes be useful to make it clear that financial compensation would help to resolve the complaint. A Court of Appeal judgment concluded that no duty of care can be imposed on the CSA in order to recover damages in negligence and that the complaints system (together with the ability to seek judicial review where the CSA acts (or does not act) unreasonably), offers sufficient redress.[3]

Where a complainant is not offered compensation and believes that it should have been offered, s/he can consider taking the complaint further – ie, to the Independent Case Examiner or the Ombudsman.

Compensation payments may be appropriate where there has been:

- significant delay in issuing forms, making calculations or reviewing liability. It is useful to refer to the service standards when assessing how severe the delay has been;
- delays or errors in enforcement;
- delays in passing maintenance to the person with care;
- wrong identification of non-resident parents;
- financial loss because of CSA error – eg, in bank, postal or telephone charges;
- other examples of gross inconvenience, embarrassment, breach of confidentiality or severe distress.

Consolatory payments are smaller payments that can be made where actions by the CSA have caused serious inconvenience because the same mistakes were made more than once, or they caused severe embarrassment or humiliation. Evidence of a parent's health being affected as a result may also be considered.[4]

The publication *Financial Redress AdministrationGuide* applies to the CSA as it does to other parts of the Department for Work and Pensions (DWP). It is available from the DWP website (see Appendix 1) and should also be provided in CSACs. It gives guidance on circumstances in which financial compensation should be paid, and how much is appropriate.

2. Complaining to Child Maintenance Options

The complaints process for the Child Maintenance Options service is similar to that for the Child Support Agency (see p440). A complaint should be started by talking to the person dealing with the enquiry, or to her/his manager. If the matter cannot be resolved in this way, a complaint should be made to the complaints resolution team. A complaint can be made over the phone, in writing or by email via the website www.cmoptions.org.

If a complainant is not satisfied after following this procedure, s/he can ask for a review. The complaints review team should look at the complaint again to see if there is more that can be done. The review team aims to resolve complaints within 15 days.[5]

Further details of the complaints process can be found in the publication *How Can I Complain About the Child Maintenance Options Service?*, which is available from the above website or by telephoning 0800 988 0988.

If a complainant has gone through every stage of the Child Maintenance Options complaints procedure and is still not satisfied, s/he can complain to the Independent Case Examiner (see p443), or, via her/his MP, to the Parliamentary Ombudsman.

3. **Complaining to Jobcentre Plus**

It is important to remember that some decisions about benefits carry the right of appeal and a parent can request a revision or appeal against them. It may be necessary to do this as well as, or instead of, complaining. For example, a parent with care can appeal against a decision made by Jobcentre Plus if she is not receiving the amount of maintenance Jobcentre Plus assumes.

As part of the Department for Work and Pensions, Jobcentre Plus has a similar complaints procedure to the Child Support Agency (CSA). Non-resident parents may want to complain about the way in which their maintenance payments have (or have not) been deducted from their benefit. However, a non-resident parent receiving benefits who disagrees with the rate of maintenance he should be paying (and therefore with the deduction being made from his benefit) should appeal to the CSA about the maintenance decision, not to Jobcentre Plus. A complaint to Jobcentre Plus could be made if it were about the administration of the deductions.

Note: the CSA may not automatically know if a non-resident parent or a parent with care is in receipt of benefits. Caselaw has established that, although the Secretary of State for Work and Pensions is ultimately responsible for administering both Jobcentre Plus and the CSA, knowledge gained by her/him in one role should not be attributed to her/his other area of responsibility.[6]

The Jobcentre Plus complaints procedure is described in the leaflet *Tell Us What You Think*. A complainant should begin by speaking to the person s/he has been dealing with, or the manager of that person. If this does not resolve matters, the district manager or delivery manager for the office concerned should be contacted. The third stage of the process, if the complaint is still not resolved, is to write to the Chief Executive of Jobcentre Plus. The Chief Executive should ensure that the complaint is fully considered by an appropriate senior officer.

Like the CSA, Jobcentre Plus can make compensatory payments if these are seen as appropriate. More information about compensation payments is provided in CPAG's *Welfare Benefits and Tax Credits Handbook*.

If a complainant has gone through every stage of the Jobcentre Plus complaints procedure and is still not satisfied, s/he can complain to the Independent Case Examiner (see below), or, via her/his MP, to the Parliamentary Ombudsman.

4. **Complaining to the Independent Case Examiner**

The Independent Case Examiner's (ICE) office is a body set up to help resolve the situation where people feel that certain government agencies have not dealt with them fairly or resolved complaints to their satisfaction. ICE is an independent referee, completely separate from the Child Support Agency (CSA), the Child Maintenance Options service or any other government department. ICE was set up to deal with complaints about the CSA but, since April 2007, it has also dealt with complaints about several other government agencies and businesses, including Jobcentre Plus and the Northern Ireland Social Security Agency.

A complainant can only go through ICE after using the CSA's (or other agency's) complaints procedure in full. A final response from the agency is normally a reply from the Chief Executive or on her/his behalf (eg, from a senior manager). The complaint to ICE should be made within six months of the CSA's final response. ICE cannot look at complaints made after this date.

ICE cannot consider a complaint which is being investigated, or which has been investigated, by the Parliamentary Ombudsman (see p445). A complainant may have the choice of complaining directly to the Ombudsman via an MP, but the Ombudsman's office will usually encourage people to use ICE first.

Complaints can be made in writing or by telephone on 0845 606 0777. A complaint form can be found on the ICE website. It can be printed, or completed online. Hard copies of the complaint form can be obtained from the helpline number above. The complainant should include all relevant facts, including the CSA office s/he is complaining about, details of the complaint and the CSA's response. ICE can give complainants further advice on making their complaint, or appoint a representative to act on their behalf, if required.

ICE will investigate and decide whether or not it can accept the complaint. If it can, the first attempt will be to settle the complaint by suggesting ways in which the CSA (or other agency) and the complainant can come to an agreement. If this fails, ICE prepares a formal report setting out how the complaint arose and how it believes it should be settled. If it makes a recommendation of action to the agency, this is almost always followed. ICE aims to clear 55 per cent of cases within six months and 85 per cent within 12 months.[7] Other details of its standards of service are available in the leaflet *Our Standards of Service* or at www.ind-case-exam.org.uk.

---

5. **Using an MP**

It may be appropriate for a parent (or qualifying child in Scotland) to consult her/his MP at any stage of the complaints process. An MP may be able to provide advocacy or other support to get the matter resolved more quickly. However, consulting an MP is particularly important if the complainant has been through the complaints process of the Child Support Agency (or Child Maintenance Options or Jobcentre Plus) without a satisfactory resolution, and even more so if s/he has used the Independent Case Examiner but still wants to take matters further.

An MP may be able to advise on whether taking the complaint further is worthwhile. It may be that the complainant is unhappy about an aspect of child support law, in which case a complaint is not appropriate. Whether the issue concerns law or procedure, an MP may be willing to take matters further to try and get legislation changed or practice improved. The MP may also (or in addition) refer the complaint to the Parliamentary Ombudsman (see below).

A parent can find out who her/his MP is by using a constituency locator on the internet, or by ringing the House of Commons information service on 020 7219 4272. Most MPs have surgeries held locally where they meet constituents. Alternatively, the complaint can be passed to the MP in writing.

6. **Complaining to the Ombudsman**

The Parliamentary and Health Service Ombudsman investigates complaints about a range of government departments and other public bodies. The complainant should first give the organisation a full chance to respond to the complaint and put things right. For complaints about the Child Support Agency, Child Maintenance Options and Jobcentre Plus, a complainant has the option of first using the Independent Case Examiner (ICE) (see p443). This avoids the need to contact her/his MP. The Ombudsman's office will encourage people to use ICE first.

The first stage of using the Ombudsman is to send the complaint to the relevant MP, who will decide whether or not to pass it on to the Ombudsman. Normally, the Ombudsman will not investigate if the complaint is passed to an MP more than 12 months after the complainant became aware that s/he had a good reason to complain – ie, that there was a need to take the complaint further.

If the complaint is investigated, the MP will be sent a full report. The Ombudsman may recommend an apology and possibly compensation. Ombudsman reports can also lead to changed practices and procedures in the agencies under investigation.

More information about the Ombudsman is available at www.ombudsman.org.uk, or from the helpline on 0345 015 4033.

Notes

1. **Complaining to the Child Support Agency**
   1 CSA Client Charter 2007
   2 CSA Business Plan 2008/09
   3 *Rowley and Others v Secretary of State for Department of Work and Pensions* [2007] EWCA Civ 598 (19 June 2007)
   4 *How Do I Complain About the Service I Get From the Chlld Supprot Agency?* October 2009

2. **Complaining to Child Maintenance Options**
   5 *How Can I Complain About the Child Maintenance Options Service?* October 2008

3. **Complaining to Jobcentre Plus**
   6 *R(Rew) v Secretary of State for Work and Pensions* [2008] EWHC 2120 (Admin) (13 June 2008)

4. **Complaining to the Independent Case Examiner**
   7 *Our Standards of Service*, Independent Case Examiner, 2009

Appendices

Appendix 1

Useful addresses

Department for Work and Pensions

www.dwp.gov.uk

Child Maintenance and Enforcement Commission

www.childmaintenance.org

Child Maintenance Options Service

www.cmoptions.org

Child Support Agency

Chief Executive
Stephen Geraghty
PO Box 55
Brierley Hill
Dudley
West Midlands DY5 1YL
Tel: 0845 7133133
www.csa.gov.uk

Child Support Agency Centres

(including for first stage complaints)

Hastings CSAC
  South East Business Unit
  Ashdown House
  Sedlescombe Road North
  St Leonards on Sea
  East Sussex TN37 7NL

Offices covered:
Acton, Brixton, Lewisham,
Tunbridge Wells, London Highgate,
Croydon, Bloomsbury, Bromley,
Ilford, Canterbury, Colchester,
Basildon, Wandsworth, Woolwich

Plymouth CSAC
  South West Business Unit
  Clearbrook House
  Towerfield Drive
  Bickleigh Down Business Park
  Plymouth
  Devon PL6 7TN

Offices covered:
Bristol, Crownhill (Plymouth),
Exeter, Gloucester, Guildford,
Hounslow, Isle of Wight, Poole,
Portsmouth, Southampton,
Swindon, Taunton, Truro,
Weymouth, Worthing

Dudley CSAC
  Midlands Business Unit
  Postal address:
  2 Weston Road
  Crewe CW98 1BD

Offices covered:
Birmingham, Chester, Hanley,
Lichfield, Stockport, Banbury, Milton
Keynes, Shrewsbury, Telford

Birkenhead CSAC

Wales and North West Business Unit

Postal address:
2 Weston Road
Crewe CW98 1BD

Offices covered:
North West: Barrow-in-Furness, Blackpool North, Bury, Carlisle, Huyton (Liverpool), Kendal, Lancaster, Penrith, Salford, Skelmersdale, St Helens, Wirral, Workington

Wales: Aberystwyth, Anglesey, Caernarfon, Cardiff, Haverfordwest, Holyhead, Newport, Pontypridd, Rhyl, Swansea, Wrexham

Belfast CSAC (GB)

Eastern Business Unit
Great Northern Tower
17 Great Victoria Street
Belfast
Northern Ireland BT2 7AD
The Northern Ireland Agency has the same address.

Offices covered:
Ipswich, Cambridge, Peterborough, Great Yarmouth, King's Lynn, Norwich, St Albans, Northampton, Leicester, Nottingham, Lincoln, Sutton-in-Ashfield, Doncaster, Huddersfield, Bradford, Hull, Scarborough, Pontefract, Grimsby

Falkirk CSAC

Scotland and North East England Business Unit
Parklands
Callendar Business Park
Callendar Road
Falkirk FK1 1XT

Offices covered:
Aberdeen, Campbeltown, Darlington, Dundee, Edinburgh, Falkirk, Galashiels, Inverness, Irvine, Leeds, Middlesborough, Mosspark, Newcastle upon Tyne, Northshields, Oban, Sunderland, Wick

Local rate telephone lines

National enquiry line (for general enquires)   08457 133 133

Hastings CSAC:
  'old rules'   08457 134 000
  'new rules'   08456 090 052
Plymouth CSAC:
  'old rules'   08457 137 000
  'new rules'   08456 090 072
Dudley CSAC:
  'old rules'   08457 131 000
  'new rules'   08456 090 062
Birkenhead CSAC:
  'old rules'   08457 138 000
  'new rules'   08456 090 082
Belfast (GB) CSAC:
  'old rules'   08457 132 000
  'new rules'   08456 090 092
Belfast
Northern Ireland CSA:
  'old rules'   08457 139 896
  'new rules'   08456 080 022
Falkirk CSAC:
  'old rules'   08457 136 000
  'new rules'   08456 090 042
Welsh language
enquiry line   08457 138 091

The Tribunals Service

The President
Social Security and Child Support Appeals
Fox Court
14 Grays Inn Road

London WC1X 8HN
Tel: 020 7712 2600

Tribunals Service regional offices (for child support and social security appeals)

Leeds
York House
York Place
Leeds LS1 2ED
Tel: 0113 251 9500

Liverpool
36 Dale Street
Liverpool L2 5UZ
Tel: 0151 243 1400

Newcastle
Manor View House
Kings Manor
Newcastle upon Tyne NE1 6PA
Tel: 0191 201 2300

Sutton
Copthall House
9 The Pavement
Grove Road
Sutton
Surrey SM1 1DA
Tel: 0208 652 2300

Birmingham
Administrative Support Centre
PO BOX 14620
Birmingham B16 6FR
Tel: 0845 408 3500

Nottingham
The Pearson Building
57 Upper Parliament Street
Nottingham NG1 6AZ
Tel: 0115 909 3600

Cardiff
Eastgate House
Newport Road
Cardiff CF24 0YP
Tel: 02920 662180

Glasgow
Wellington House
134-136 Wellington Street
Glasgow G2 2XL
Tel: 0141 354 8400

Offices of the Social Security and Child Support Commissioners

England and Wales
3rd Floor
Procession House
55 Ludgate Hill
London EC4M 7JW
Tel: 020 7029 9850
www.osscsc.gov.uk

Scotland
George House
126 George Street
Edinburgh EH2 4HH
Tel: 0131 271 4310
www.ossc-scotland.gov.uk

Northern Ireland
Headline Building
10 –14 Victoria Street
Belfast BT1 3GG
Tel: 028 9033 2344

Independent Case Examiner
PO Box 155
Chester CH99 9SA
Tel: 0845 606 0777
Minicom: 0151 801 8888
www.ind-case-exam.org.uk

Office of the Parliamentary Commissioner for Administration
Millbank Tower
Millbank
London SW1P 4RP
Tel: 0845 015 4033
www.ombudsman.org.uk

Appendix 2

Income support premiums

Premiums are added to income support (IS) personal allowances and are intended to help with the extra expenses associated with age, disability or children. The premiums are used in the child support formula irrespective of whether the parent is in receipt of IS, although not all apply at each stage. **Note:** although some of the rules below no longer apply to all IS claimants, they are still relevant for working out 'old rules' assessments.

Family premium	£17.30
Disabled child premium	£51.24
Carer premium (per carer)	£29.50
Disability premium	
Single	£27.50
Couple	£39.15
Severe disability premium	
One qualifies	£52.85
Two qualify	£105.70
Enhanced disability premium	
Single	£13.40
Couple	£19.30
Child	£20.65
Pensioner premium	
Single	£65.70
Couple	£97.50

*These amounts are only ever used at the protected income stage.

Family premium

A person is entitled to family premium if her/his family includes a child, even if s/he is not the child's parent. It does not matter how much capital a child has. For child support purposes, a child is taken to be a member of the household if the adult has 'day-to-day care' of that child. If a child does not live in the household full time, a proportion of the family premium can be included in exempt income and protected income (see Chapter 14). Only one family premium is payable regardless of the number of children a person has.

If a child who is in the care of or being looked after by a local authority, or who is in custody, comes home for part of a week, a proportion of the premium is payable, according to the number of days the child is at home.

Disabled child premium

A person is entitled to a disabled child premium for each child who gets disability living allowance (DLA) or who is blind. A child is treated as blind if s/he is registered as blind and for the first 28 weeks after s/he has been taken off the register on regaining her/his sight. For how to qualify for DLA, see CPAG's *Welfare Benefits and Tax Credits Handbook*.

If DLA has stopped because the child is in hospital, this premium continues as long as the child continues to be treated as a member of your family. See CPAG's *Welfare Benefits and Tax Credits Handbook* for more details. If the child does not live in the household full time, a proportion of the premium is included in exempt income and in protected income (see Chapter 14).

If a child has over £3,000 capital, there is no entitlement to this premium.

Carer premium

A person qualifies for this if s/he or her/his partner is getting carer's allowance (CA), or would get it but for the overlapping benefit rules – ie, because s/he is receiving another 'earnings replacement' benefit paid at a higher rate. For example, a woman getting CA who at 60 is awarded retirement pension at a higher rate than CA continues to qualify for the premium as long as the person being cared for continues to get the higher or middle rate care component of DLA or attendance allowance (AA).

A double premium is awarded where both the person concerned and her/his partner satisfy the conditions for it.

See CPAG's *Welfare Benefits and Tax Credits Handbook* for more details on the premium and conditions of entitlement for CA.

Disability premium

A person can get a disability premium if s/he is under the qualifying age for pension credit (note that in the exempt income step of the child support formula, the age rule does not apply) and:

- s/he (or her/his partner) is getting a qualifying benefit. These are DLA (or an equivalent benefit paid to meet attendance needs because of an injury at work or a war injury), disability or severe disability element of working tax credit, war pensioner's mobility supplement, incapacity benefit (IB) paid at the long-term rate or when terminally ill, or severe disablement allowance (SDA). A person or her/his partner must be getting the benefit for her/himself, not on behalf of someone else – eg, as a parent or an appointee. In some situations, entitlement to the premium continues after the person stops receiving the qualifying benefit – see CPAG's *Welfare Benefits and Tax Credits Handbook*;

- s/he (or her/his partner) is registered as blind with a local authority (England and Wales) or regional or islands council (Scotland); if sight is regained, s/he will still qualify for 28 weeks after s/he is taken off the register;
- s/he (or her/his partner) has an NHS invalid trike or private car allowance because of disability;
- s/he is 'incapable of work' (or exempt from the 'all-work test') and either entitled to statutory sick pay or has been incapable for at least:
  - 196 days if certified as 'terminally ill' – ie, it can reasonably be expected that s/he will die within six months due to a progressive disease;
  - 364 days in all other cases, provided s/he has claimed IB (it is not necessary to send in medical certificates).

  Breaks in incapacity/entitlement of up to 56 days (104 weeks if a 'welfare to work beneficiary') are included in these periods. For more on incapacity for work, see CPAG's *Welfare Benefits and Tax Credits Handbook.*

Entitlement to the disabilty premium stops when someone has been in hospital for more than 52 weeks.

At the protected income stage of the child support calculation, couples will get the disability premium at the couple rate provided either of them qualifies under one of the first three of the above rules. But they will only get the premium under the last condition if the person who qualifies is the parent being assessed for child maintenance.

Severe disability premium

A person can get this premium if:
- s/he is receiving AA (or the equivalent war pension or industrial injury benefit), or the higher or middle rate care component of DLA (or extra-statutory payments to compensate for not receiving any of these). If s/he is part of a couple, they must both be getting one of these benefits or the partner who does not get AA/DLA must be registered or treated as blind; *and*
- no non-dependant aged 18 or over is living with her/him (see below); *and*
- no one is getting CA for looking after her/him.

A couple who are both severely disabled only get the single rate if someone is getting CA in respect of one of them or one of them qualifies only because s/he is registered or treated as blind.

Non-dependants aged 18 or over

The following people living with a person do not count:
- a partner (but s/he must be getting AA/DLA or be blind);
- anyone aged under 18;
- anyone staying in a person's home who normally lives elsewhere;

- a person (who may be her/his partner) employed by a charitable or voluntary body as a resident carer for a person or her/his partner if s/he pays for that service (even if the charge is only nominal);
- a person receiving AA or the higher or middle rate care component of DLA;
- a person who is registered blind or treated as blind;
- a person, or her/his partner, who jointly occupies her/his home and is either a co-owner with the person or her/his partner, or jointly liable with them to make payments to a landlord in respect of occupying it;
- a person, or any member of her/his household, who is liable to pay on a commercial basis for occupying the dwelling (eg, tenant or licensee), unless s/he is a close relative;
- a person, or any member of her/his household, to whom a person or her/his partner is liable to make such payments on a commercial basis, unless s/he is a close relative.

If someone (other than those listed above) comes to live with a person in order to look after her/him or her/his partner, her/his severe disability premium will only remain in payment for the first 12 weeks.

For more detail of these rules, see CPAG's *Welfare Benefits and Tax Credits Handbook*.

Enhanced disability premium

The enhanced disability premium applies if the person or a member of her/his family receives the highest rate of the DLA care component and is aged under 60.

The following people cannot qualify:
- children or young people with more than £3,000 in capital;
- a claimant who has been a hospital inpatient for more than 52 weeks; *or*
- a claimant whose partner has been a hospital inpatient for more than 52 weeks.

Pensioner premium

There are three pensioner premiums, all paid at the same rate:
- pensioner premium if a person or her/his partner is aged 60–74 inclusive;
- pensioner premium (also known as an enhanced pensioner premium) if a person or her/his partner is 75–79 inclusive;
- higher pensioner premium if a person or her/his partner is aged over 80 or satifies other conditions detailed below.

Each of these can be paid at a couple rate if one partner fulfils the age condition. If a person or her/his partner is sick or disabled, check to see if the higher pensioner premium described below applies.

Higher pensioner premium

A person can get this if:

- s/he or her/his partner is 80 or over; *or*
- s/he was getting a disability premium as part of her/his IS at some time during the eight weeks (104 weeks for 'welfare to work beneficiaries') before s/he was 60 and has continued to get IS since the age of 60 (breaks of up to eight (or 104) weeks are ignored). Couples can qualify under this rule regardless of which partner meets the condition; *or*
- s/he or her/his partner is aged 60–79 *and* either of them receives a qualifying benefit (as for the disability premium but including AA), is registered blind, or has an NHS trike or private car allowance. If a person stops getting IB or SDA to change to retirement pension, the higher pensioner premium still applies if there is a continuous entitlement (apart from breaks of eight weeks (104 weeks for 'welfare to work beneficiaries') or less) to IS.

Entitlement to the higher pension premium stops if someone has been a hospital inpatient for more than 52 weeks.

For more details on the premium and who is a 'welfare to work beneficiary', see CPAG's *Welfare Benefits and Tax Credits Handbook*.

Appendix 3
Statutes

A man is assumed to be the father of a child for child support purposes if he is found to be the father by a court in England or Wales in proceedings under the following.

s42 National Assistance Act 1948
Affiliation Proceedings Act 1957
s6 Family Law Reform Act 1969
Guardianship of Minors Act 1971
Children Act 1975
Child Care Act 1980
Children Act 1989
s26 Social Security Act 1986
s4 Family Law Reform Act 1987
s105 Social Security Administration Act 1992

A maintenance order only prevents a s4 or s7 application to the Child Support Agency if it was made in proceedings under the following. In addition, a variation for property/capital transfers can only be made if the transfer was made under the following.

Conjugal Rights (Scotland) Amendment Act 1861
Court of Session Act 1868
Sheriff Courts (Scotland) Act 1907
Guardianship of Infants Act 1925
Illegitimate Children (Scotland) Act 1930
Children and Young Persons (Scotland) Act 1932
Children and Young Persons (Scotland) Act 1937
Custody of Children (Scotland) Act 1939
National Assistance Act 1948
Affiliation Orders Act 1952
Affiliation Proceedings Act 1957
Guardianship of Minors Act 1971
Part II Matrimonial Causes Act 1973

Guardianship Act 1973
Children Act 1975
Supplementary Benefits Act 1976
Domestic Proceedings and Magistrates' Courts Act 178
Part II Matrimonial and Family Proceedings Act 1984
Family Law (Scotland) Act 1985
Schedule 1 Children Act 1989
Social Security Act 1986
Social Security Administration Act 1992
Schedule 5, 6 or 7 Civil Partnership Act 2004

The court order usually states the legal provisions under which it was made.

Appendix 4
Information and advice

It is often difficult for unsupported individuals to get a positive response from the Child Support Agency. You may be more successful if you have taken advice about your rights or have an adviser assisting you. The following agencies may be able to help.

- Citizens Advice Bureaux (CABx) and other local advice centres provide information and may be able to represent you. You can find your nearest CAB from www.citizensadvice.org.uk.
- Law centres can help with advice and representation, but may not cover child support problems and may limit their help to people who live and work in certain areas. You can check if you are near a law centre from www.lawcentres.org.uk
- Solicitors can give free legal advice to people on low incomes under the 'legal help' scheme (advice and assistance scheme in Scotland). This does not cover the cost of representation at an appeal hearing, but can cover the cost of preparing written submissions and obtaining evidence such as medical reports. However, solicitors do not always have a good working knowledge of the child support rules and you may need to shop around until you find one who does.
- www.communitylegaladvice.org.uk (0845 345 4345) can be used to find high quality legal advisers in England and Wales, including advice agencies and solicitors.
- Local authority welfare rights workers provide an advice and representation service for benefit claimants in many areas.
- Lone-parent organisations may offer help and advice about child support, or it may help to talk to other parents about their experiences. For details of your local group and for helpline advice contact: Single Parent Action Network (0117 951 4231); Gingerbread (single parent helpline 0808 802 0925); One Parent Families Scotland (helpline 0808 801 0323).
- There are some groups supporting parents who may be able to provide advice. These include National Association for Child Support Action, PO Box 4454, Dudley, West Midlands DY1 9AN. You can write or email enquiries@nacsa.co.uk.
- Many trade unions provide advice to members on child support.
- Local organisations for particular groups may offer help – eg, unemployed centres, claimants' unions, centres for people with disabilities.

Representation at the First-tier Trbunal

Some parents may find it difficult to obtain representation at appeal hearings. Although many parents, especially with the help of Chapter 18, will be perfectly able to present their own cases, it can be invaluable to obtain objective independent advice which draws on the legislation. An advice centre which has a copy of the legislation (see Appendix 5) and experience of representing at tribunals in other sorts of cases (eg, social security) may be able to provide a representative for a child support appeal.

Child Poverty Action Group

Unfortunately, CPAG is unable to deal with enquiries, either from advisers or members of the public, on child support issues.

Appendix 5

Useful publications

Stationery Office books are available from Stationery Office bookshops or can be ordered from The Stationery Office, Post Cash Department, PO Box 29, Norwich NR3 1GN (tel: 0870 600 5522; fax: 0870 600 5533; email: customer.services@tso.co.uk; web: www.tso.co.uk). Many publications listed are available from CPAG. See below for order details, or order from www.cpag.org.uk/publications/.

1. Caselaw and legislation

Social Security Case Law – Digest of Commissioners' Decisions
D Neligan (Stationery Office, looseleaf in two volumes).

CPAG's Welfare Benefits and Tax Credits Law Online
(CPAG) Includes all social security and tax credits legislation, updated and consolidated throughout the year; decisions of the courts, commissioners and the Upper Tribunal, many with commentary; the *Welfare Benefits and Tax Credits Handbook* updated throughout the year with links to the relevant legislation, decisions and caselaw. £53 + VAT per concurrent user (bulk discounts available). More information and free seven-day trial at http://onlineservices.cpag.org.uk

CPAG's Child Support Law Online
(CPAG) Includes all child support legislation, updated and consolidated throughout the year;

expert commentary on the legislation (from early 2010); the *Child Support Handbook* updated once a year in line with the print edition, with links to the relevant legislation, decisions and caselaw. £65 + VAT per concurrent user (bulk discounts available). More information at http://onlineservices.cpag.org.uk

CPAG's Housing Benefit and Council Tax Benefit Law Online
(CPAG) Includes complete housing benefit and council tax benefit legislation, updated and consolidated throughout the year; commentary from *CPAG's Housing Benefit & Council Tax Benefit Legislation* (Findlay), updated twice a year in line with the print edition, with links to decisions, of the courts, commissioners and the Upper Tribunal, and other relevant material. £110 + VAT per user (bulk discounts available). More information at http://onlineservices.cpag.org.uk

The Law Relating to Social Security
(Stationery Office, looseleaf, 12
volumes) All the legislation but
without any comment. Known as the
'Blue Book'. Also available at
www.dwp.gov.uk/advisers.

The Law Relating to Child Support
Consolidated legislation without any
commentary. Shows the law as it
applies both before and after the
'new rules' changes come into force
for a particular case. Also known as
the 'Orange Volumes'. Available at
www.dwp.gov.uk/advisers.

Social Security Legislation, Volume I:
Non-Means-Tested Benefits
D Bonner, I Hooker and R White
(Sweet & Maxwell) Legislation with
commentary. 2009/10 edition
(October 2009): £89 for the main
volume.

Social Security Legislation, Volume II:
Income Support, Jobseeker's Allowance,
State Pension Credit and the Social Fund
J Mesher, P Wood, R Poynter, N
Wikeley and D Bonner (Sweet &
Maxwell) Legislation with
commentary. 2009/10 edition
(October 2009): £89 for the main
volume.

Social Security Legislation, Volume III:
Administration, Adjudication and the
European Dimension
M Rowland and R White (Sweet &
Maxwell) Legislation with
commentary. 2009/10 edition
(October 2009): £89 for the main
volume.

Social Security Legislation, Volume IV:
Tax Credits, Child Trust Funds and
Employer-Paid Social Security Benefits
N Wikeley and D Williams (Sweet &
Maxwell) Legislation with
commentary. 2009/10 edition
(October 2009): £89 for the main
volume.

Social Security Legislation – updating
supplement to Volumes I, II, III & IV
(Sweet & Maxwell) The spring 2010
update to the 2009/10 main
volumes: £55.

CPAG's Housing Benefit and Council
Tax Benefit Legislation
L Findlay, R Poynter, S Wright and C
George (CPAG) Legislation with
detailed commentary. 2008/09 (21st)
edition (November 2008): £97
including Supplement. Also
available as part of *CPAG's Housing*
Benefit and Council Tax Law Online.

Child Support: The Legislation
E Jacobs (CPAG) 9th edition main
volume (January 2010): £87. 9th
edition supplement (autumn 2010)
£49.

2. Periodicals
Welfare Rights Bulletin
(CPAG, bimonthly). Covers
developments in social security law,
including decisions of the courts and
the Upper Tribunal, and updates
CPAG's *Welfare Benefits and Tax*
Credits Handbook. The annual
subscription is £33 but it is sent
automatically to certain categories of
CPAG member (contact CPAG for
details).

Articles on social security can also be found in *Legal Action* (Legal Action Group, monthly magazine), *The Adviser* (Citizens Advice, bi-monthly magazine) and the *Journal of Social Security Law* (Sweet & Maxwell, quarterly).

3. Child Support
Agency publications
For guidance issued to CSA staff, see Appendix 6.

A full list of CSA leaflets is available on the CSA website. Leaflets and most other CSA publications can be obtained from the national enquiry line: 08457 133 133. Many leaflets and other publications are also available at www.csa.gov.uk. The following is only a selection of the publications available. Some of the leaflets listed have 'old rules' equivalents with different titles and numbers.

Child Support: your child maintenance interview (CSL100)

What Happens if Someone Denies They are the Parent of a Child? (CSL304)

How Do I Complain About the Service I Get From the Child Support Agency? (CSL308)

What is My Role in Helping My Employees Pay Child Maintenance? (CSL313)

Child Support Agency Client Charter 2007 (CSA2047)

Child Support Agency Operational Improvement Plan 2006-2009

Child Support Agency Business Plan 2007/8 (CSA2091)

4. Other publications: child support
This section lists other publications on child support, including some relevant leaflets, but only includes the most recent research, reports and commentary. For earlier research and reports on child support, please see previous editions of this *Handbook*.

Our Services and Standards: Independent Case Examiner for the Child Support Agency (ICE SAS) (available from www.csa.gov.uk or www.ind-case-exam.org.uk)

Independent Case Examiner's Annual Report 2006/07 (available from www.ind-case-exam.org.uk)

House of Commons Select Committee for Work and Pensions, Fourth Report of 2006/07, *Child Support Reform*, 7 March 2007 (available from www.parliament.uk)

N Wikeley, *Child Support Law and Policy*, Hart Publishing, 2006

5. Other publications: general
Tell Us What You Think (TELLUSA5JP)(available from Jobcentre Plus offices and www.jobcentreplus.gov.uk)

Department for Work and Pensions Business Plan 2007/08 (available from www.dwp.gov.uk)

Welfare Benefits and Tax Credits Handbook
£39/£9 for claimants (2009/10, April 2009). Also available as part of CPAG's Welfare Benefits and Tax Credits Law Online.

Personal Finance Handbook
£16.50 (3rd edition, November 2009)

Paying for Care Handbook
£19.50 (6th edition, March 2009)

Student Support and Benefits Handbook: England, Wales and Northern Ireland
£13.00 (7th edition, December 2009)

Benefits for Students in Scotland Handbook
£13.00 (7th edition, September 2009)
Available free online at www.scottishhandbooks.cpag.org.uk, funded by the Scottish Government.

Council Tax Handbook
£17 (8th edition, November 2009)

Debt Advice Handbook
£20 (8th edition, December 2008)

Fuel Rights Handbook
£19 (15th edition, summer 2010)

Benefits for Migrants Handbook
£23 (5th edition, spring 2010)

Children's Handbook Scotland: a benefits guide for children living away from their parents
£12.50 (2nd edition, October 2009)

Tribunal Practice and Procedure
£40 (1st edition, October 2009)
Published by Legal Action Group.

Guide to Housing Benefit and Council Tax Benefit
£25.00 (June 2009) Published by Shelter/CIoH.

Disability Rights Handbook
£25 (May 2009) Published by Disability Alliance/ERA.

The Young Persons Handbook
£15.95 (4th edition, December 2009) Published by the Centre for Economic and Social Inclusion.

For CPAG publications and most of those in Sections 1 and 5 contact:
CPAG, 94 White Lion Street, London N1 9PF, tel: 020 7837 7979, fax: 020 7837 6414. Order forms are available at www.cpag.org.uk/publications. Postage and packing: free for orders up to £10 in value; for order value £10.01–£100 add a flat rate charge of £3.99; for order value £100.01–£400 add £5.99; for order value £400+ add £9.99.

Appendix 6
Abbreviations used in the notes

AC	Appeal Cases	FLR	Family Law Reports
All ER	All England Reports	HC	High Court
App	Appendix	HL	House of Lords
Art(s)	Article(s)	para(s)	Paragraph(s)
CA	Court of Appeal	QB	Queen's Bench Reports
CCR	County Court Rules	r(s)	Rule(s)
Ch	Chapter	Reg(s)	Regulation(s)
col	Column	s(s)	Section(s)
DC	Divisional Court	SCLR	Scottish Civil Law Reports
ECJ	European Court of Justice	Sch(s)	Schedule(s)
ECR	European court Reports	SLT	Scots Law Times
FamD	Family Division	Vol	Volume
FCR	Family Court Reports	WLR	Weekly Law Reports

1. The legislation

Acts of Parliament

Unless information in this *Handbook* specifically relates to 'old rules' cases, legislative references are for 'new rules' cases only. Provisions for 'old rules' cases are as the law stood before the Child Support, Pensions and Social Security Act 2000 came into force. Full legislative referencing for 'old rules' cases can be found in the 2001/02 and 2002/03 editions of this *Handbook*.

A&CA 2002	Adoption and Children Act 2002
A&C(S)A 2007	Adoption and Children (Scotland) Act 2007
CA 1989	Children Act 1989
CPA 2004	Civil Partnership Act 2004
CMOPA 2008	Child Maintenance and Other Payments Act 2008
CSA 1991	Child Support Act 1991

C(S)A 1995	Children (Scotland) Act 1995
CSPSSA 2000	Child Support, Pensions and Social Security Act 2000
DPMCA 1978	Domestic Proceedings and Magistrates' Courts Act 1978
ERA 1996	Employment Rights Act 1996
FL(S)A 1958	Family Law (Scotland) Act 1958
FLRA 1969	Family Law Reform Act 1969
HF&EA 1990	Human Fertilisation and Embryology Act 1990
HRA 1998	Human Rights Act 1998
ICTA 1988	Income and Corporation Taxes Act 1988
LR(PC)(S)A 1986	Law Reform (Parent and Child) (Scotland) Act 1986
MCA 1973	Matrimonial Causes Act 1973
MO(RE)A 1992	Maintenance Orders (Reciprocal Enforcement) Act 1992
SSA 1998	Social Security Act 1998
SSAA 1992	Social Security Administration Act 1992
SSCBA 1992	Social Security Contributions and Benefits Act 1992
TCA 2002	Tax Credits Act 2002
TCEA 2007	Tribunals, Courts and Enforcement Act 2007

Regulations and other statutory instruments

Unless information specifically relates to 'old rules' cases, legislative references in this *Handbook* are correct for 'new rules' cases only. Most 'new rules' statutory instruments have 'old rules' equivalents. For example, the CS(MAP) Regs are the 'old rules' equivalent of the CS(MCP) Regs. Full legislative referencing for 'old rules' cases can be found in the 2001/02 and 2002/03 editions of this *Handbook*. If you are unsure of the correct 'old rules' legislative reference, seek advice.

AS(CSA)(AOCSCR)	The Act of Sederunt (Child Support Act 1991) (Amendment of Ordinary Cause and Summary Cause Rules) 1993 No.919
AS(CSR)	The Act of Sederunt (Child Support Rules) 1993 No.920
AUTCAO	The Appeals from the Upper Tribunal to the Court of Appeal Order 2008 No.2834
C(AP)O	The Children (Allocation of Proceedings) Order 1991 No.1677
CB&SS(FAR) Regs	The Child Benefit and Social Security (Fixing and Adjustment of Rates) Regulations 1976 No.1267
CP(PSS&CS)(CP)O	The Civil Partnership (Pensions, Social Security and Child Support)(Consequential, etc. Provisions) Order 2005 No.2877
CPA 2004(RACP)O	The Civil Partnership Act 2004 (Relationships Arising Through Civil Partnership) Order 2005 No.3137

CS(AIAMA) Regs	The Child Support (Arrears, Interest and Adjustment of Maintenance Assessments) Regulations 1992 No.1816
CS(APD)	The Child Support (Applications: Prescribed Dates) Regulations 2003 No.194
CS(MA) Regs	The Child Support (Miscellaneous Amendments) Regulations 2008 No. 536
CS(MA)(No.2) Regs	The Child Support (Miscellaneous Amendment)(No.2) Regulations 2008 No.1042
CS(C&E) Regs	The Child Support (Collection and Enforcement) Regulations 1992 No.1989
CS(C&E)(DO)(A) Regs	The Child Support Collection and Enforcement (Deduction Orders) Amendment Regulations 2009 No.1815
CS(CEMA) Regs	Child Support (Collection and Enforcement and Miscellaneous Amendments) Regulations 2000 No.2001/162
CS(CEOFM) Regs	The Child Support (Collection and Enforcement of Other Forms of Maintenance) Regulations 1992 No.2643
CS(D&A)(A) Regs	The Child Support (Decisions and Appeals) (Amendment) Regulations 2000 No.3185
CS(IED) Regs	The Child Support (Information, Evidence and Disclosure) Regulations 1992 No.1812
CS(IEDMAJ)(A) Regs	Child Support (Information, Evidence and Disclosure and Maintenance Arrangements and Jurisdiction) (Amendment) Regulations 2000 No.2001/161
CS(MAJ) Regs	The Child Support (Maintenance Arrangements and Jurisdiction) Regulations 1992 No.2645
CS(MAP) Regs	The Child Support (Maintenance Assessment Procedure) Regulations 1992 No.1813
CS(MASC) Regs	The Child Support (Maintenance Assessments and Special Cases) Regulations 1992 No.1815
CS(MATP) Regs	The Child Support (Miscellaneous Amendments and Transitional Provisions) Regulations 1994 No.1227
CS(MCP) Regs	The Child Support (Maintenance Calculation Procedure) Regulations 2000 No.2001/157
CS(MCSC) Regs	The Child Support (Maintenance Calculation and Special Cases) Regulations 2000 No.2001/155
CS(NIRA) Regs	The Child Support (Northern Ireland Reciprocal Arrangements) Regulations 1993 No.584

CS(TCPS)(MA) Regs	The Child Support (Temporary Compensation Payment Scheme) (Modification and Amendment) Regulations 2002 No.1854
CS(TP) Regs	The Child Support (Transitional Provisions) Regulations 2000 No.3186
CS(V) Regs	The Child Support (Variations) Regulations 2000 No.2001/156
CS(V)(MSP) Regs	The Child Support (Variations)(Modification of Statutory Provisions) Regulations 2000 No.3173
CS(VP) Regs	The Child Support (Voluntary Payments) Regulations 2000 No.3177
CSA(CA)O	The Child Support Act 1991 (Consequential Amendments) Order 1993 No.785
CSA(JC)O	The Child Support Appeals (Jurisdiction of Courts) Order 1993 No.961 (L.12)
CSA(JCO 2002	The Child Support Appeals (Jurisdiction of Courts) Order 2002 No.1915
CSA(JC)(S)O 2003	The Child Support Appeals (Jurisdiction of Courts) (Scotland) Order 2003 No.96
CSC(P) Regs	The Child Support Commissioners (Procedure) Regulations 1999 No.1305
CSDDCA Regs	The Child Support Departure Directions and Consequential Amendments Regulations 1996 No.2907
CSF Regs	The Child Support Fees Regulations 1992 No.3094
CSMA Regs	The Child Support Miscellaneous Amendments 2007 No.1979
CSPSSA(Comm3)O	The Child Support, Pensions and Social Security Act 2000 (Commencement No.3) Order 2000 No.2994
CSPSSA(Comm12)O	The Child Support, Pensions and Social Security Act 2003 (Commencement No.12) Order 2003 No.192
CSPSSA(Comm13)O	The Child Support, Pensions and Social Security Act 2000 (Commencement No.13) Order 2003 No.346
CTB Regs	The Council Tax Benefit (General) Regulations 2006 No.215
CTB(SPC) Regs	The Council Tax Benefit (Persons who have Attained the Qualifying Age for State Pension Credit) Regulations 2006 No.216

FT&UT(CT)O	The First-tier Tribunal and Upper Tribunal (Composition of Tribunal) Order 2008 No.2835
HB Regs	The Housing Benefit (General) Regulations 2006 No.213
HB(SPC) Regs	The Housing Benefit (Persons who have Attained the Qualifying Age for State Pension Credit) Regulations 2006 No.214
HB&CTB(D&A) Regs	The Housing Benefit and Council Tax Benefit (Decisions and Appeals) Regulations 2001 No.1002
IS Regs	The Income Support (General) Regulations 1987 No.1967
JSA Regs	The Jobseeker's Allowance Regulations 1996 No.207
SCR	The Supreme Court Rules 2009 No.3
SS(C&P) Regs	The Social Security (Claims and Payments) Regulations 1987 No.1968
SS(CMB) Regs	The Social Security (Child Maintenance Bonus) Regulations 1996 No.3195
SS(CMP)A Regs	The Social Security (Child Maintenance Premium) Amendment Regulations 2004 No.98
SS(CMPMA) Regs	The Social Security (Child Maintenance Premium and Miscellaneous Amendments) Regulations 2000 No.3176
SS(PAOR) Regs	The Social Security (Payments on Account, Overpayments and Recovery) Regulations 1988 No.664
SS&CS(DA) Regs	The Social Security and Child Support (Decisions and Appeals) Regulations 1999 No.991
TP(FT) Rules	The Tribunal Procedure (First-tier Tribunal)(Social Entitlement Chamber) Rules 2008 No.2685
TP(UT) Rules	The Tribunal Procedure (Upper Tribunal) Rules 2008 No.2698
TTF Order	The Transfer of Tribunal Functions Order 2008 No. 2833

2. **Guidance**

References to guidance are given either with the relevant paragraph numbers, or with volume titles and nearest heading.

Guidance for Child Support Agency staff

CSG	*Child Support Guide*
DMG	*Decision Makers Guide for Child Support*
DDMG	*Departures Decision Makers Guide*
EFIG	*Effective Full Maintenance Assessments and Interim Maintenance Assessments Guide*
EG	*Enforcement Guide* (Note: there are two separate guides, one for England and Wales and one for Scotland)
PatG	*Paternity Guide*
PG	*Procedures Guide*
RCG	*Requirement to Co-operate Guide*
TG	*Trace Guide*

Child Support Agency guidance can be obtained following a Freedom of Information request to the Child Support Agency.

Guidance for Jobcentre Plus staff

ISGAP	*Income Support Guidance and Procedure* manuals are a series of volumes produced by the DWP. Volume 10 covers CSA-related action. There is an equivalent set for jobseeker's allowance, but for ease of reference we refer to income support guidance only.

The Jobcentre Plus guidance can be obtained following a Freedom of Information request to Jobcentre Plus.

Index

Gingerbread

Single parents, equal families

Gingerbread Single Parent Helpline
Freephone 0808 802 0925
Open 9am to 5pm Mondays to Fridays
with extended opening to 8pm on Wednesdays
Expert telephone information and advice
for single parents

Gingerbread Single Parent Information Online
www.gingerbread.org.uk/information
Dedicated online information and advice
for single parents

Gingerbread Membership
www.gingerbread.org.uk/membership
Share experiences, hear about discounts and
get involved with Gingerbread's work

Gingerbread Development and Skills
www.gingerbread.org.uk/skills
Training, employability and confidence-building programmes
for single parents, advisers and practitioners

Gingerbread Policy and Campaigning
www.gingerbread.org.uk/policy
Building on over 90 years of campaigning expertise to deliver
change for single parent families

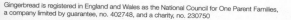

Child Support: The Legislation

9th edition

This volume contains the primary and secondary legislation relating to all three child support schemes under the Child Support Act 1991, the Child Support, Pensions and Social Security Act 2000 and the Child Maintenance and Other Payments Act 2008.

It also has expert commentary and guidance, including the effect of the transfer of responsibility from the Child Support Agency to the Child Maintenance and Enforcement Commission.

The author provides authoritative analysis of decisions made by the courts, the Child Support Commissioners and the Upper Tribunal to show how the law governing each scheme has been interpreted and applied. This book will enable tribunal judges and members, parents and their representatives to deal with cases under all versions of the child support legislation.

Price £87.00   February 2010   ISBN: 978-1-906076-25-2

Child Support: The Legislation: Supplement

9th edition

This supplement to *Child Support: The Legislation* updates the previous main volume, and covers all important changes to legislation, and new court and Upper Tribunal decisions. (NB main volume and supplement are published in alternate years so the next main volume will not be until 2011/12.).

Price £49.00   Autumn 2010   ISBN: 978-1-906076-48-1

Published by Child Poverty Action Group, 94 White Lion St, London N1 9PF
Tel: 020 7837 7979
Email: bookorders@cpag.org.uk
Website: www.cpag.org.uk/publications

Child Support Law Online

This online service is a one-stop resource for anyone working with the child support scheme. Contents include:

- the full text of the *Child Support Handbook*, updated annually in line with the print version, with links from the text to child support legislation, regulations etc.

- all child support legislation, together with expert commentary, updated throughout the year

- commissioners' and Upper Tribunal decisions, reported and unreported, with CPAG commentary where available

- relevant court cases, taken from CPAG's *Welfare Rights Bulletin*

Annual subscription £65 + VAT per user (discounts available for bulk subscriptions of 10+ users)

For more information about this and other online services from CPAG, visit the website **http://onlineservices.cpag.org.uk**

Published by Child Poverty Action Group, 94 White Lion St, London N1 9PF
Tel: 020 7837 7979
Email: bookorders@cpag.org.uk
Website: www.cpag.org.uk/publications

Welfare Benefits and Tax Credits Handbook

2010/2011

The **Welfare Benefits and Tax Credits Handbook** is the definitive comprehensive guide for claimants and their advisers. It explains:

- who can claim benefits and tax credits
- disability and incapacity benefits, and the work capability assessment for employment and support allowance
- how housing benefit and council tax benefit are calculated
- jobseeker's allowance and benefit sanctions
- how to claim from the social fund
- which benefits can be claimed if you are unemployed, a parent or carer, a student, retired or widowed, pregnant, entering the UK, or sick or disabled
- challenging decisions, backdating, overpayments, income and capital, and national insurance contributions.

It is fully indexed and cross-referenced to law and regulations.

The best value in publishing ... All legal aid firms must have this book.
Solicitors Journal

The one thing that can be relied on in this ever changing world of welfare ... the adviser's bible. **The Adviser (Citizens Advice)**

Price £39.00   April 2010   ISBN: 978-1-906076-39-9

Published by Child Poverty Action Group, 94 White Lion St, London N1 9PF
Tel: 020 7837 7979
Email: bookorders@cpag.org.uk
Website: www.cpag.org.uk/publications

Training at CPAG

CPAG courses provide comprehensive rights training for advisers and detailed coverage of up-to-the minute legislative changes. Our tutors are expert in their areas of work and draw on the extensive training experience of CPAG's own welfare rights specialists. Courses include:

- Child support: liability and enforcement
- An introduction to welfare rights
- Benefit take-up campaigns
- AA/DLA – revisions, supersessions and appeals
- Immigration law and social security
- Tax credit overpayments
- Employment and support allowance.

For full course information and online booking please see our website (details below). Our courses can also be tailored to meet the needs of specific groups, including those not normally concerned with welfare rights. To assess your training needs, we are happy to discuss your requirements for 'in-house' training to meet the internal needs of your organisation.

CPAG's London-based courses are Law Society and Bar Council accredited and carry continuing education points. They are also approved by The Institute of Legal Executives and the UK College of Family Mediators. Courses in Scotland have Law Society Scotland accreditation.

Contacts for further information:

London   Judy Allen, Training Co-ordinator,
tel: 020 7812 5228   email: jallen@cpag.org.uk
website: www.cpag.org.uk/training

Scotland   Pauline Chalmers, Training Administrator
Tel: 0141 552 3420   email: pchalmers@cpagscotland.org.uk
website: www.cpag.org.uk/scotland/training